Donald Clarke

The Rise and Fall of Popular Music

St. Martin's Press
New York

Library of Congress Cataloging-in-Publication Data available on request

ISBN 0–312–11573–3

First published in Great Britain by Viking, 1995

First U.S. edition: January 1995
10 9 8 7 6 5 4 3 3 2 1

In memory of

MARTHA JEAN CHATTERTON

A beautiful girl who loved to dance,
she married Dad even though he couldn't.

Contents

Preface

During the 1980s, while I was working for five years on *The Penguin Encyclopedia of Popular Music*, my friends and acquaintances assumed, according to what they knew about music or about me, that I was working on a book either about pop music or about jazz. The word 'popular' had long since been appropriated by the post-Beatles industry that separates adolescents from their pocket money; the first time I heard the term 'pop music' was from the lips of the wonderful Welsh headmistress of a high school in south London in early 1974, and her pronunciation of the phrase left no doubt about what she thought of it.

Opera houses and symphony orchestras are subsidized, and very few classical composers ever make a living solely from their music. But there are no subsidies in popular music; if you want to play jazz piano, rock drums or country guitar, or write hit songs or sing on Broadway or form a pop group, you do not give up your day job until you can make a living at it. Popular music includes all the genres; we could also call it commercial music.

Popular music as a commercial enterprise got under way in Britain in the eighteenth century, when for the first time music publishers sprang up who published nothing but new songs, hoping that people who had heard the songs in the pleasure gardens or music halls would then buy the sheet music. It is now an international business worth many billions of dollars a year, and the number of carriers, from 'personal stereos' and piped-in music in restaurants to booming rock in shops that sell jeans, is such that the stuff is inescapable. Yet there is growing evidence that most of it could disappear overnight and nobody would miss it.

Listening to music on the radio was fun in the 1940s in the USA;

by 1953 it was not much fun any more; in the late 1950s for a while it seemed to be fun again, but nowadays serious music fans – the kind who buy records regularly and hang on to them for decades, building up large collections – no longer bother to listen to the radio much. This is because what most people think of as popular music is dominated by technology and chosen for us by lawyers and accountants who seem to be tone-deaf. The music business has always chased fads and has always been dominated by greed, but nowadays, like the US government, it is out of control and would appear to be heading for the wall. This downward spiral is assisted by the media. The reporting of the rest of the news, including most of the arts news, may seem to have some connection with the real world, but when it comes to popular music, even the so-called quality newspapers devote pages to meaningless fads that follow one another with dizzying speed. Take grunge, for example: grunge is pop-rock played by groups in Seattle, Washington, who dress in rags, hence the name; young people have been enjoying dressing in what look like rags and old bedspreads for decades, yet grunge is all the rage as this is being written. By the time this book is published grunge will probably be forgotten, but a fashion parade has taken the place of musical values.

I have written a survey of the history of popular music because music has always been the most important thing in the world to me; and because the time seemed right for such a survey. Most popular music has always been second-rate or worse, but I listen to recordings of it that have been made over a period of nearly seventy years, made for commercial reasons, speculatively, just like that eighteenth-century English sheet music. It will always be true that the best stuff lasts, but it does seem as though the music industry of today cranks out a higher percentage of inferior product than ever before.

Each nation has popular music of its own; I make no apology for concentrating here on the English-speaking world, and especially the USA, because that is where the economic power of the music business has been developed, until it now sells us an ocean of factory-made music that sounds cheap, yet has to sell in the millions before it breaks even. Today's multi-national record labels are so desperate that they will soon be trying to sell you their latest boondoggles whether you live in Australia, Argentina or Azerbaydzhanskaya.

The British pop music press insists that each new pop/rock act is going to sweep the world and become the new Beatles. From 1984 to 1993, to name just the ones who were cursed with the endorsement of Morrissey, formerly of The Smiths, there were James, The Woodentops, Shop Assistants, Easterhouse, Raymonde, Bradford, The Sundays, Phranc, Suede and Gallon Drunk. None have stayed the course. I don't run out and buy any of this stuff because I know that if the music is any good it will find me, rather than me having to risk my money on something that will almost certainly disappoint.

On the other hand, there may be cause for hope: this book has been underway in fits and jerks since 1987, and the music business is always restless, as though something good has to happen sooner or later. The latest news from the USA in 1994 was that there has been a demographic upturn; the number of young people is apparently growing again, and if this baby-boom will probably not equal that of the 1950s, at least the customers will be there, and maybe some of them will have some taste. And speaking of grunge, just when the fuss over it seemed to be on the wane, the startling international wave of grief at Kurt Cobain's suicide last spring revealed that some people admired his lyrics as much as his dress sense. This is a good sign, and my spies in the USA tell me that some of the acts coming along there are putting across some interesting things in the lyrical line. I will not name any of the up-and-comers I am mildly curious about, for fear that my imprimatur will be a curse; but I am going to keep listening.

The first people I have to thank are the authors of all the books on my shelves in which I have gleefully wallowed, in some cases for decades; they have guided and informed me. (There is a bibliography at the back of this book which will be useful as a guide to further reading.)

Chris Parker first commissioned the present volume, when he was editor of the music book list at another publisher; then Jon Riley at Viking took it on. Clare Alexander, Judith Flanders, Andrew Cameron and many others at Viking have been extraordinarily helpful and supportive, as always. Cal Morgan at St Martin's Press in New York liked the concept of the book so much that at first he wanted it to be *longer*, which was impossible. Chris, Jon and Cal made valuable suggestions and criticisms; then when it came to obtaining permissions to print the song lyrics, Jerry Leiber and Mike Stoller did the same. (None of the other publishers cared what we said, as long as we paid them.) David Duguid read the manuscript for Viking and did his usual wonderful job of querying this and that. Meanwhile, Max Harrison, one of the best writers and most rigorous critics of jazz and classical music I know of, had agreed to read the first draft of the manuscript, even though he doesn't really agree with one of its premises, that jazz has been, for most of its history, commercial music. Max gave that first draft a line-by-line going over; and with all this help, a publishable book seems to have resulted.

A reader at a certain publisher in New York also read the manuscript, and pronounced me an amateur, a nobody, a bad writer, an anti-Semite and a gay-basher, and complained that I loathed Elvis Presley. I was buying Presley records before he was born, but I am grateful to him, too, for reminding me that whether you like the book or not, I alone am responsible.

September 1994
Norfolk, England

Acknowledgements

The publishers would like to express their thanks to the music publishers who have given their permission to reprint the following lyrics:

'Some of These Days' (Brooks): by permission of Francis Day and Hunter Ltd, London WC2H 0EA, and J. Albert & Son Pty Ltd. Copyright © 1910, Will Rossiter Pub. Co., USA.

'After You've Gone' (Layton and Creamer): by permission of Francis Day and Hunter Ltd, London WC2H 0EA, and Hal Leonard Corporation. Copyright © 1918 (renewed) Edwin Morris & Company, a division of MPL Communications, Inc. All rights reserved.

'I Get a Kick Out of You' (Porter), 'I Wish I Were In Love Again' (Hart), 'Settin' the Woods on Fire' (Rose), 'Stormy Monday Blues' (Walker), 'Blue Monday' (Domino and Bartholomew), 'Desperadoes Waiting for a Train' (Clark), 'Express Yourself' (Wright): by permission of International Music Publications Limited. Copyright © Warner Chappell Music Ltd, London W1Y 3FA.

'Cool Drink of Water Blues' (Johnson): by permission of Peermusic (UK) Ltd, London WC1. Copyright © 1929 Peer International Corporation, USA.

'I Won't be Home No More' (Hank Williams, Sr): copyright © 1952 (renewed) Hiriam Music & Acuff-Rose Music, Inc. All rights on behalf of Hiriam Music administered by Rightsong Music, Inc. All rights reserved. Used by permission.

'Low Down Blues' (Hank Williams, Sr): by permission of Acuff-Rose Music, Inc. Copyright © 1954, renewed 1982. All rights reserved.

'It Wasn't God Who Made Honky Tonk Angels' (Miller): by permission of Peermusic (UK) Ltd, London WC1. Copyright © 1952 Peer International Corporation, USA.

'Well, You Needn't' (Monk): by permission of Mautoglade Music Ltd. Copyright © 1961 Regent Music Corporation.

'Long Tall Sally' (Johnson, Blackwell and Penniman): by permission of Peermusic (UK) Ltd, London WC1. Copyright © 1956 Venice Music Inc., USA.

'Tutti Frutti' (Penniman, La Bostrie and Lubin): by permission of Music Sales Ltd. Copyright © 1955 Venice Music Inc., USA. ATV Music for the UK, Eire, British Commonwealth (excluding Canada and Australasia) and the Continent of Europe. All rights reserved. International copyright secured.

'Summertime Blues' (Capehart and Cochran): by permission of Campbell Connelly & Co. Ltd and International Music Publications Ltd.

'Shake, Rattle and Roll' (Calhoun): by permission of Campbell Connelly & Co. Ltd and International Music Publications Ltd. Copyright © Warner Chappell Music Ltd, London W1Y 3FA.

'Movie Magg' (Perkins), 'Blue Suede Shoes' (Perkins), 'Honey Don't' (Perkins): by kind permission of Carlin Music Corporation, UK administrator.

'Yakety Yak' (Jerry Leiber and Mike Stoller): by kind permission of Carlin Music Corporation, UK administrator, and Warner Chappell Music, Inc. Copyright © 1958 (renewed) Jerry Leiber Music, Mike Stoller Music, and Chappell & Co. All rights reserved. Used by permission.

'Too Much Monkey Business' (Berry): by permission of Mautoglade Music Ltd. Copyright © 1956 Arc Music Corp.

'Firewater' (Hancock): copyright © 1991 Rainlight Music (ASCAP)/administered by Bug Music. All rights reserved. Used by permission.

'Senor *Aka* Tales of Yankee Power' (Dylan): copyright © 1978 by Special Rider Music (ASCAP). Used by permission.

Untitled (2 Live Crew): by permission of MCA Music Limited.

Every effort has been made to contact all copyright holders. The publishers will be pleased to make good in future editions any errors or omissions brought to our attention.

1

The Origins of Popular Music

Once upon a time there were only two kinds of music in Europe: religious music and secular music.

The earliest polyphonic music, from around 900 AD, was probably inspired by the music of Byzantium and the Middle East. Polyphonic folk-singing survives today in eastern Europe, but the music of the church was of great importance, for it encouraged technical development: in the early sixteenth century two organs were installed in the two apses of St Mark's Cathedral in Venice, which led to the use of separate choruses of singers, and increasing harmonic experimentation by the composers. As well as music for the Mass, written by some of the greatest composers in history, we have less formal music such as carols, mostly written for religious festivals. The word comes from the medieval French *carole*, a round dance; many early Christmas carols are still familiar to us today.

In the Middle Ages much secular music was dance music, which was played at court and in the halls of the aristocracy. The best tunes were also popular in the street; a good tune would soon have words fitted to it, and a clever rhyme or broadside would find a tune. A common store of tunes and ideas crossed back and forth across class barriers, and there was little distinction between 'popular' and 'serious' music.

In all times and places there was also folksong, invented and performed by the less privileged classes: lullabies, love songs, work songs, story songs and so on. By the fourteenth century the ballad (from the Latin *ballare*, 'to dance') had become a narrative solo song, often of unknown origin. The minstrel was originally an itinerant singer of such songs. They were usually story songs, but some were written in praise of powerful patrons, a practice carried on today in African music.

For over four hundred years, until the introduction in the mid nineteenth century of penny newspapers and affordable books, the English-speaking masses received much of their education and entertainment from street literature. One of the earliest surviving broadsides, from 1423, was about St Christopher and was illustrated by a woodcut. The broadside was so called because it consisted of a broad piece of paper printed on one side only, often with a combination of verse, prose and an illustration. (The broadsheet was a large piece of paper printed on both sides, which could be folded several times to make a pamphlet; hence today's 'broadsheet' newspaper.)

An uncut and unstitched pamphlet was known as a chapbook, or cheap book (perhaps from the Anglo-Saxon *ceap*, meaning 'trade'), and was sold by pedlars of needles, buttons and other household goods. The pamphlets preserved the romantic and traditional stories which were ignored by publishing in the days when books were only for the rich. A properly finished pamphlet, far too expensive for the common people, became one of the main forums for political discussion, especially in the eighteenth century.

News of royal proclamations, grisly crimes and gossip were circulated by the broadside; those who could not read could hear others read them, and the pedlars who sold them would cry them aloud in the streets. The battle of Flodden in 1513, when a Scottish king was killed, was described by John Skelton in a broadside, which included a woodcut; a fragment of this was discovered in the late nineteenth century in the binding of a book which had been sent to London generations before for repair. It is the earliest-known example of English journalism. Street literature was of enormous importance because of the influence it had on the masses, but it is usually ignored by historians in favour of the legitimate press. What concerns us here, however, is the broadside ballad.

Broadside verses were not printed with music; the pedlars would sing the songs as they hawked them, and it was assumed that the customer in the street would know a tune that would fit, or make one up. If notation was included, it was a meaningless decoration intended to impress the customer, who could not read music anyway. All broadsides were supposed to be registered with the authorities; about three thousand ballads were so recorded between 1557 and

1709, but several times that number were probably printed illegally. The broadside ballads recycled folksongs which were already well known, and carried on the minstrel tradition. But the genre was also a kind of musical journalism, for it contained social and political satire, well disguised in the days when one could lose one's head for offending the powerful.

Familiar nursery rhymes began in this way. Zealots wrote and rewrote verses for political and religious reasons, so that none of the historical sources can be pinned down conclusively. Jack Sprat and his wife may have been Charles I and his French queen Henrietta: she was fond of the spoils of war (the fat), while Charles dissolved Parliament because it would not grant supplies for his Spanish war, thus 'licking the platter clean'. In a rhyme from the seventeenth century 'Mary, Mary, quite contrary' has 'silver bells and cockle shells and pretty maids all in a row' in her garden. This is said to be either about Ann, Lady Roos, an heiress who taunted her husband with 'cuckolds all in a row', or about Mary, Queen of Scots, a brave and headstrong woman whose four ladies-in-waiting, all also called Mary, were the pretty maids. Both Protestants and Catholics claim it as a lament for their respective religions at the time of 'Bloody Mary', eldest daughter of Henry VIII, who caused much blood to be shed in the name of God.

'Hey Diddle Diddle' is said to have been a jolly description of the court of Elizabeth I, Henry's other daughter: the cat who loved to dance to the fiddle was the 'Virgin Queen' herself; the plate was the young man who brought Elizabeth her dinner, and the spoon the girl who tasted it, in case it was poisoned; the cow jumping over the moon referred to the entertainments that were organized at court; and the lap-dog who found it all so funny was one of the Queen's would-be suitors. But the rhyme is also said to be about Catherine of Aragon ('Catherine la Fidèle'), Henry's long-suffering first wife and Mary's mother.

Best of all is the story of Little Jack Horner. The name Jack was commonly used of a knave or a rogue, and there were already stories about finding things in pies. In 1539 Richard Whiting was abbot of Glastonbury Cathedral, a wealthy establishment, and to keep the peace he allegedly sent Henry VIII a pie containing the deeds to several manor houses. On the way to London, Whiting's steward, called Horner, pulled out a plum – the deed to the manor of Mells. Whatever the details, Horner testified against Whiting at a trial, helping Henry to grab all the property, and the Horners still lived at Mells four hundred years later. The manor may also be 'The House That Jack Built'.

The printers and pedlars of broadsides had a thriving industry, but a modern English-language music business waited until the language itself was established. English had been made up of Angle, Saxon, German and other elements; its development was both sidetracked and influenced by the Norman victory of William the Conqueror in 1066, after which the affairs of the government were conducted in French, while Latin remained the language of international business. Then an English composer became one of the greatest of his time, a profound influence on Renaissance music: Italians wrote of the 'new art which originated with the English under the leadership of Dunstable'. Among other things, John Dunstable introduced the declamatory motet, in which the rhythm of the music is determined by the rhythm of the words. Unfortunately, much of his music was lost in the wars of the period.

The earliest English song extant is the round 'Summer is icumen in' (*c.* 1280). Not until 1363 was Parliament opened with a speech in the vernacular, and not until 1530 was a book of songs in English published, *Twenty Songs*. It included compositions by William Cornyshe, who had been master of the boys in the Chapel Royal of Henry VIII, and John Taverner. Henry's dissolution of the Catholic Church in England encouraged religious music in English; it was very different from the broadside ballads of the people, but the strands of English music then began slowly to come together.

Nearly all of Shakespeare's plays used music and dancing; Elizabethan England was a place where musical instruments were available in shops, in case a passing customer wanted to strike up a tune; and the 'Virgin Queen' herself enjoyed secular music. From 1592 to 1594, when the theatres were closed because of the plague, the players took the plays to the Continent, songs and all. The music of William Byrd and John Dowland was popular in the most complete sense of the word. Dowland, in particular, also a great lutenist in an age that loved the lute, was famous in many countries. His tunes were played by people who had never heard of him and assumed they were folksongs. In 1602 a German visitor to Blackfriars wrote about the excellent music that was played for an hour before a play began, and impresario John Banister produced public concerts in London a hundred years before they became common in Vienna.

As the sophistication of the musical craft developed through the Renaissance, the secular dance rhythms were used in instrumental suites, and opera came into being, eventually becoming opulent entertainment for the upper classes. The early operas were modelled after what Greek theatrical music was thought to have been, and included dances. Monteverdi's *Orfeo*, first performed in 1607 at Mantua, is considered to be the first fully developed opera, astonishing with its fulsome and varied sound (a full choir of trombones, for example), but it was still tied to the conventions of court entertainment; his *L'incoronazione di Poppea* (Venice, 1642) was on a much larger scale, and may have been designed for people who bought tickets.

Instrumental suites and opera overtures evolved until in the eighteenth century symphonies and string quartets were written, while the technique of the virtuoso soloist was celebrated in the concerto. When these forms emerged during the glorious flowering of Viennese music, they were based on sonata form, the rules governing their composition corresponding to what was regarded as the logical orderliness of philosophy and the arts in classical Greece: hence 'classical' music. The masterpieces created for the concert hall and the opera house were great in number and are still loved around the world, but popular music in the sense of the term as we use it today then had to be invented, at least for English-speaking people. Other nations stayed closer in many ways to their musical traditions: in Italy the best tunes from the operas were whistled by barrow boys in the street, while German composers never hesitated to use folk tunes in their compositions, or wrote tunes which sounded as though they had always existed. The great nineteenth-century *Lieder* of Schubert, Schumann, Brahms, Mahler, Wolf and others carried more 'cultural' value than art song in English-speaking countries: they were much more accessible and more widely popular.

It was no doubt England's already highly developed class-consciousness that led to a greater gulf between serious and popular music. England was called 'the land without music', which seems absurd; yet it is true that the greatest 'English' composers of the eighteenth century were German immigrants, George Frideric Handel and Johann Christian Bach, and the audience for their music became more and more upper class. The English had beheaded Charles I in 1649, which shocked the world; they told themselves that they did it in order to restore the historical purity of their politics, but they were slowly finding political freedom. As they were unwilling to allow Italian popes and French kings to tell them what to do, so their composers did not seem to care much for strict Continental rules governing composition. When the rules began to be broken in the twentieth century, English composers of formal music again attracted worldwide attention; but in the eighteenth and nineteenth centuries English-speaking upper-class audiences listened to foreign music, while increasing economic freedom allowed the lower orders to do as they wished. The emerging middle classes conquered India, for example, by accident, beginning with a few trading posts; and they invented popular music.

The popular song may be defined as a song written for a single voice or a small vocal group, accompanied by a single chord-playing instrument or a small ensemble, usually first performed in some sort of public entertainment and afterwards published in the form of sheet music (or mechanically reproduced in the twentieth century); it is written for profit, for amateur listeners and performers. What we call popular music (or commercial music) began in the eighteenth century in the pleasure gardens in what are now the suburbs of London. But the seeds of it can certainly be found earlier, and one nominee for first popular songwriter is Henry Purcell.

Any country that could produce a Purcell was most emphatically not a 'land without music', but in his short life he wrote only one full-blown operatic masterpiece, *Dido and Aeneas* (1689). Its songs were sold in sheet music in the theatre between the acts. Most of his theatrical work was incidental music, ideally suited to commercial exploitation in the form of excerpts. For example, 'What Shall I Do to Show' was written (with words by Thomas Betterton) for the 'semi-opera' *The History of Dioclesian* (1690):

> What shall I do to show how much I love her?
> How many millions of sighs will suffice?
> That which wins others' hearts never can move her,
> Those common methods of love she'll despise.

It has a memorable and wistful tune, it is singable and its subject is still the songwriters' favourite: love, preferably unrequited. It would be surprising if this song had not been sung in many a drawing room to simple accompaniment, and perhaps by frustrated swains in their baths. It is as good a candidate as any for the title of first popular song.

Not that songwriters made any money from the sale of their music. Publishing of all kinds had been state monopolies, granted to favourite individuals, since the earliest printing in England, partly for reasons of censorship. Early publishers began as printers, and copyright law evolved as courts had to adjudicate between them. They squabbled among themselves for the right to exploit the authors, who usually received nothing at all, except perhaps a flat fee for the first sale of their work. Composers of hit songs depended upon this success to generate more work; producers of musical entertainments had occasional benefit nights, so that the composers could feed their families, and most of them died poor, no matter how successful their music. The most popular composers were the most frequently robbed. The publishers John May and John Hedgebutt blithely explained to Henry Purcell, when they published the complete music and libretto of *The Indian Queen* (1695):

Indeed we well know your innate modesty to be such, as not to be easily prevail'd upon to set anything in print, much less to Patronise your own works . . . But in regard that any one might print an imperfect copy of these admirable songs, or publish them in the nature of a Common Ballad, we were so much the more emboldened to make this attempt, even without acquainting you of our Design.

In other words, we will steal from you more elegantly than the others. This was not against the law, and there was nothing composers could do about it.

Music publishing had begun in Venice in 1501. One of the first modern English music publishers was John Playford, born in Norwich in 1623, son of a bookseller. Norwich had always been an important centre of English music; it was home of one of the oldest guilds of professional musicians, and Playford was probably also influenced by the music at Norwich Cathedral. He was apprenticed to a bookseller in London, and got into trouble with the Puritans for publishing a pamphlet on the death of Charles I. But he soon concentrated on music, and his collections of old tunes were best-sellers. *The English Dancing Master, or Plain and Easy Rules for the Dancing of Country Dances, with the Tune to Each Dance* was initially aimed at the social pretensions of Playford's customers, but went through eighteen editions between 1649 and 1728. Having expanded to a collection of nine hundred tunes in three volumes, it was known as *The Dancing Master* and was used in the American colonies, where the dancing would have been influenced by the fiddle and banjo playing of black slaves: thus Playford must have had a more or less direct effect on American music.

Playford's son sold the business in the early years of the eighteenth century, at the very time when there was a rising demand for sheet music of the latest theatre songs to be printed overnight. Music publishing was ready for the pleasure gardens, where the commercial possibilities of popular music were first fully exploited. In the seventeenth century Londoners such as Samuel Pepys and John Evelyn wrote in their diaries that they enjoyed admission to privately owned gardens; these gardens increased in number and in size, many of them beginning as spas. London had numerous springs, where the water was said to be good for this or that ailment or condition, and entertainment sprang up to keep the customers happy. Sadler's Wells, which became one of the most famous small opera houses in the world, began as a spa; a pub called the London Spa only a few hundred yards away marks the site of another.

It is curious that England thinks of itself as a law-abiding country: it has been so only for relatively short periods in the present century. Getting to and from the pleasure gardens could be dangerous, for foot-pads and thugs were common, and only the rich had carriages. On one occasion in 1757 the management of Sadler's Wells advertised that a horse patrol would be provided by Mr Fielding (a blind magistrate and relative of the novelist Henry Fielding) to protect the gentry; the next year armed patrols were stationed between Grosvenor Square and the Wells. Link-boys were employed to light the way home for revellers on foot, and the theatre management often announced at the foot of their playbills whether or not there would be moonlight on the night, allowing visitors to get home more safely.

Nevertheless, the spas and gardens were enormously popular. There were spas at Islington, Clerkenwell, Tunbridge Wells and many other places, and music was offered as early as 1697 in Lambeth and 1701 in Hampstead. John Evelyn had written about the 'pretty contrived plantation' of the New Spring Gardens at Vauxhall, near Lambeth Palace, in 1661. Vauxhall's spring was not of much account; it became the most important of the pleasure gardens because it was one of the biggest, and also the boskiest.

In most of the gardens promenades and pathways were arranged on a simple grid pattern. The grid at Ranelagh in Chelsea was merely a setting for a rotunda or 'Amphitheatrical Building' by the architect William Jones, where the fashionable walked endlessly around in a circle: 'Nobody goes anywhere else,' wrote Horace Walpole in 1742, and Mozart performed there as a child in 1764. But Vauxhall also had thickly wooded areas with larks and nightingales ('feathered minstrels'), where the illusion of Arcadia could be complete, and where no doubt many pairs of lovers sported over the decades. There was then only one bridge over the Thames, and a rehearsal of Handel's *Music for the Royal Fireworks* at Vauxhall in 1749 caused a massive traffic jam.

Jonathan Tyers had leased Vauxhall in 1728. He was only twenty-one years old; not much is known of his background, but he had money to invest. When he reopened the garden in 1732, it had a concert hall, an organ and a famous statue of Handel by Louis François Roubiliac (which is remarkably informal for the period and is now in London's Victoria and Albert Museum). William Hogarth is thought to have persuaded Tyers to decorate the supper-boxes around the Grove with large paintings by members of his academy;

this was priceless publicity, and provided a captive audience for Hogarth and his followers.

In 1758 Tyers purchased the gardens outright, and built an 'orchestra' (hall) in the Gothic style. The orchestra was the last substantial addition to the gardens, though Robert Adam wrote that Tyers had talked about commissioning a Temple of Venus. Tyers had already enlarged his orchestra (that is, the band), and hired Thomas Augustine Arne to write music for it.

While the Purcell song quoted above is not especially florid, in general the ornate Italian model strongly influenced songwriting, until Arne. A talented musical journeyman, he wrote 'Rule, Britannia' to words by James Thomson for the finale of a masque called *Alfred* (1740); his London-style instrumental pieces are still found in compilations of baroque music, and are full of good tunes. His songs were particularly innovative. Anyone who could pay the price of admission could get in at Vauxhall, and Arne had to write songs for a classless audience; they had to make their impression on the musically sophisticated and the ignorant alike at the first hearing. Often drawing on rural imagery of stylized shepherds importuning resistant maidens, the songs were tonal and diatonic, and relied mostly on common chords; they were strophic in structure, so that listeners heard recurring melodic fragments. (In other words, they were repetitious.) The excellent seventh edition of *Baker's Biographical Dictionary of Musicians* (edited by Nicolas Slonimsky) does not mention Arne's tenure at Vauxhall. Modern critics of classical music may not think much of Arne's songs, but in the function he was performing he was a predecessor of Irving Berlin.

Arne's wife Cecilia was one of many popular London singers of the day to perform at Vauxhall. According to Charles Dibdin, in his five-volume *A Complete History of the London Stage* (1800), 'Mrs Arne was deliciously captivating. She knew nothing in singing or in nature but sweetness and simplicity.' Another popular vocalist was Joe Vernon, who 'had no voice . . . It is impossible to imagine that he could have arrived to any degree of reputation had he not been favoured by nature with strong conception, quick sensibility, and a correct taste.' That is still a good description of a pop singer.

Dibdin would have known what he was talking about: in his long career as actor, vocalist, playwright and impresario he worked on the Continent and even in the Orient as well as England, and wrote about nine hundred songs, of which as many as two hundred were known all over the English-speaking world. (The most successful were about the hard lot of the sailor, such as 'Poor Jack'.) Since there were no composer's royalties, if it had not been for a benefit dinner in 1810 and later a government pension, Dibdin might have starved to death. Yet thousands of popular songs were published in the second half of the eighteenth century, and sheet music sales supported several publishers. (Bookseller George Walker opened a music shop in London in the 1790s, advertising 'half-price' sheet music: he used tinted paper, claimed higher production costs and printed a price on the music which was twice the half-price.)

Also important were songs from ballad and comic operas, which bore little resemblance to opera of the Italian kind. The earliest and best example is *The Beggar's Opera*, with libretto by John Gay and music by Johann Christoph Pepusch (born in Berlin), first performed in 1728. This dispensed with recitative and used spoken dialogue, for which the beggar apologizes at the outset: 'I hope I may be forgiven, that I have not made my Opera throughout unnatural, like those in vogue.' Pepusch's music borrowed some of the tunes from already familiar street ballads, and also included Purcell's 'What Shall I Do', quoted above. The characters were not the usual operatic noblemen and pretty peasant girls, but pickpockets, prostitutes and lawyers, no doubt resembling some members of the audiences in the pleasure gardens. *The Beggar's Opera* spawned many imitations and was a spectacular success in all the principal towns in England. Dibdin quotes Jonathan Swift's praise: it had 'not wit, nor humour, but something better than either'.

At Vauxhall, along with the promenading and the enjoyment of the fresh air, there were daily concerts which started in the afternoon and continued until nine o'clock. Another important venue was Marylebone Gardens, which offered music from 1732; the garden began with the bowling green of the Rose Tavern, then a popular gambling spot. (Macheath, the thug in *The Begger's Opera*, said of the Rose: 'There will be deep play to-night and consequently money may be picked up on the road. Meet me there and I'll give you the hint who's worth setting.') James Hook, a young organist, began playing at Marylebone in 1769.

Like Playford, Hook was born in Norwich; a child prodigy, he earned his living as a musician from the age of eleven. He was lured away from Marylebone to become music director at Vauxhall in 1774. Hook's songs were similar to Arne's, but assimilated even more successfully all the elements that made up the London style: influences from the Italian through Purcell and Handel to the various ballad styles of the day resulted in graceful and technically admirable melodies; furthermore, the characters in the songs often resembled real people, as opposed to the stock shepherds. 'The Tear', one of Hook's biggest hits, was about a woman whose loved one had gone away to war.

Hook played an organ concerto every evening, and a strolling wind band perambulated after the main concert. At a celebration of the birthday of the Prince of Wales in 1799, 20,000 lanterns were lit and 1,200 chickens and 1,680 bottles of port were consumed. But soon times were changing: the entertainment at Vauxhall in 1816 included a tightrope act, and Hook retired in 1820, having written perhaps 2,000 songs, as well as much other music. Complete comic operas were presented at Vauxhall from 1830 to 1832, but the management lowered the admission price in 1833, and attracted 27,000 people on the first night.

Vauxhall remained the most important of the pleasure gardens as long as they lasted, but finally closed in 1859. It has long since disappeared into the sprawl of Greater London, and is now only a name on a railway station. (When the first station was built there, it became one of the most famous in the world, so that a word for railway station in Russian is a cognate of 'vauxhall'.) Lesser gardens survived into the 1880s, by which time the music was moving indoors, to the music halls. The pleasure gardens presented music for nearly 200 years altogether, and without a single amplifier.

In the American colonies the trial of John Peter Zenger in New York in 1735 was concerned with ballads. Zenger, who printed one of the city's two newspapers, published ballads about the election of opposition candidates, which were enjoyed in the local taverns, and the city government had him thrown into jail for libel. The court contended that it should decide on the libel, restricting the jury to the fact of publication, but Zenger's lawyer, Andrew Hamilton, successfully argued that the jury should determine whether or not the ballads were libellous. It decided they were not, and the principle of freedom of the press was established in America.

Of the forty most popular songs printed in the USA in the 1790s (the list, compiled by Charles Hamm, appears in his *Yesterdays: Popular Song in America*), no fewer than ten were written by James Hook.

The infant United States of America was a frontier in more senses than one. America's taste in music, drama and literature initially reflected the divisive War of Independence the new nation had gone through, the hardships endured and the homesickness of a people who were nearly all immigrants. Of that early top forty, only five songs were written by composers living in the USA. A difference was apparent between the most successful imports and the rest of an English composer's output: English songs covered the gamut of styles – humorous, sentimental, salacious and so on – but those most popular in America were the tear-jerkers. At the top was 'The Galley Slave' by William Reeve; the one anonymous song on the list was 'Since Then I'm Doomed'; Hook's 'The Tear' made the list (as did 'A Prey to Tender Anguish' by Haydn, whose chamber music was popular in colonial America).

A popular subject of early American musical entertainment on the stage was the Swiss patriot William Tell. *The Patriot, or Liberty Asserted* (1794) and its successor, *The Archers* (1796), were written by William Dunlap, who was born in New Jersey. The music for *The Archers* was by Benjamin Carr, an English immigrant; his 'The Little Sailor Boy' (another song about loss) was a success in the 1790s. Carr also played 'Yankee Doodle' in a concert in New York in 1794, the year it was first printed in America. This was a traditional tune with different verses in several languages; among the contributors to the American words was a British Army surgeon stationed near Albany, New York, in 1758.

American music was inevitably dominated for some time by composers and musicians who had emigrated from England. They were all necessarily versatile, playing several instruments and being able to turn a hand to any type of entertainment; they were also mostly second-rate, otherwise they would not have left the musical capital of the English-speaking world to try their luck on a frontier. But Francis Hopkinson was born in Philadelphia. A lawyer and a judge, a signer of the Declaration of Independence and the first Secretary of the Navy, he was the first American to write secular songs for voice and harpsichord. His 'My Days Have Been So Wondrous Free', often cited as the first American secular song, was one of his earliest but was discovered only after his death; he had not included it in his first printed book of songs, published in 1788. He also wrote what is described as the first American grand opera, *America Independent, or The Temple of Minerva* (1781), a pastiche of tunes from the London stage, with his own words.

The importance of the colonial music master cannot be overestimated. One famous full-time professional, William Billings, had only one eye, a short leg and was deformed by a broken shoulder, but he had a fine voice and thought everyone should sing for the joy of it. His *The New England Psalm-singer* (1770) was the first book of songs by a native-born American. Billings wrote in a joyous style, believing his work to be 'twenty times more powerful than the old slow tunes'. One of his best known was 'Chester (Let Tyrants Shake Their Iron Rods)' (1788), a marching song. He never made much money, however, for his songs were pirated, and he spent much of his time convincing people that he was the author of his own work. Oliver Shaw, who went blind after a series of accidents, was born in Massachusetts. He wrote 'Mary's Tears' (1812) and 'There's Nothing True But Heaven' (1829), both of which were enormously popular. Shaw was more typical than Billings of early American composers, being convinced that good music could be written only in emulation of the great European composers of the period.

John Hill Hewitt, the son of James Hewitt, wrote one of the first songs to be generally regarded as truly American, 'The Minstrel's Return'd from the War' (1825). It resembled his father's 'The Wounded Hussar' (on the top forty in 1800), and was the biggest American hit until the songs of Stephen Foster. The song is about a soldier who returns from battle, pledging to his sweetheart that the bugle will not part them again; but it does, and he dies on the batttle-

field. The piano accompaniment suggests a march and trumpet fan-
fares in its introduction. There were still five editions in print in 1870.

Many of Hewitt's other songs were successful; he was among the
earliest professional American songwriters in the modern sense, in
that he wrote skilfully simple songs which followed trends, specifically
for the American market. In the early 1830s his songs reflected the
contemporary popularity of Italian opera (Rossini's *Barber of Seville*
was first performed in New York in 1825). Later in the decade,
singing families from Austria and Switzerland toured the USA, and
Hewitt wrote mountain songs; 'The Alpine Horn' (1843) included a
yodel. 'Mary, Now the Sea Divides Us' (1840), written to words by
J. T. S. Sullivan, was described as a 'Southern refrain'; according to
Hamm, 'its pentatonic character' suggests 'that it may have been
adapted from a tune in the Scotch-Irish-English oral tradition',
already well established in the USA and the most important strain in
what would become country music in the next century. Hewitt wrote
'answer' songs: 'The Fallen Oak' (1841) was inspired by Henry
Russell's 'Woodman, Spare That Tree', and 'I Would Not Die at All'
parodied Foster's 'I Would Not Die in Spring Time'.

Henry Russell was born and died in England, but had much of his
success as a songwriter and performer in America. He had a pleasant
voice, and Hewitt admired the way he made the most of a limited
range; most of his songs used only five notes or so. They were a
great influence on parlour singing, often appealing to nostalgia and
using the word 'old', as in 'The Old Arm Chair' (1840). Like Dibdin
at the height of his fame, Russell was a solo recital artist; 'Woodman,
Spare That Tree' (1837) was his first and biggest hit. A setting of a
poem by George Pope Morris, it was inspired by a true story: Morris
and Russell were visiting in upstate New York and saw a giant oak
being saved by a present to the woodcutter of a $10 gold piece. In
later years Russell's favourite anecdote told of a 'snowy-bearded
gentleman' who, after a performance of the song, leapt up from his
seat to demand, 'Mr Russell, in the name of Heaven, tell me, was the
tree spared?' Receiving an answer in the affirmative, the old fellow
sat down in relief, saying, 'Thank God! Thank God! I breathe again!'

Irish emigration to the USA had an important impact long before
the potato famine. Of around thirty thousand settlers in 1817,

two-thirds were from the British Isles, and most of these were Irish. Their songs were already popular, and had been sung in America before 1790. Ten volumes of *Irish Melodies* published in Dublin between 1808 and 1834 included some of the most popular songs of the entire century, adapted with new texts by Thomas Moore (1779–1852); they owed much to an earlier collection of wordless tunes from the same publisher. Some of Moore's poems and his adaptations, which he sang himself in public, are still sung today: two of the best known are '('Tis) the Last Rose of Summer' (using a tune called 'The Groves of Blarney', also heard in Friedrich von Flotow's opera *Martha*, and set for piano by Beethoven and Mendelssohn), and 'Believe Me, If All These Endearing Young Charms' (sung to the tune of 'My Lodging is on the Cold Ground'). They appeared in a more modern hit parade: they were hits on Victor records, by Elizabeth Wheeler in 1909 and John McCormack in 1911.

'Yankee Doodle' had been meant by the British at the time of the War of Independence and earlier to satirize the supposedly rough and credulous colonials, who cheerfully turned the tables and adopted it as their own first patriotic song. During the War of 1812 theatre managers and song publishers were quick to capitalize on a new surge of nationalism. 'To Anacreon in Heaven' was an old drinking song, the tune of which had been used dozens of times, for example for 'Adams and Liberty' in 1798, one of the earliest native American hits. A Baltimore lawyer and poet, Francis Scott Key, adopted the tune in 1805 for verses about the struggle against the Barbary pirates, in which he first used the phrase 'star-spangled banner'. He made use of the tune and the phrase again in 1814, during the British bombardment of Baltimore's defences, creating what became the American national anthem.

The Anacreontic Society of London was a drinking club, and the original lyrics of the song urged the members to 'entwine the myrtle of Venus with Bacchus's vine'. Perhaps the tune had long been a popular drinking song because of the comic effect created by drunks trying to sing the unsingable. Key's setting is a poor piece of lyric writing, for the stresses of the music fall on the wrong syllables, making it even harder to sing; all the same, it was chosen as America's national anthem in 1931 over 'America the Beautiful'. This is a poem by Katherine Lee Bates written at Pike's Peak in Colorado in 1893, set to a hymn tune by Samuel Augustus Ward: it is singable, it celebrates beauty and it proposes love of country without hatred of somebody else's. When the Americans chose a British drinking song with words that don't fit, the British got the last laugh after all.

The War of 1812, as Americans called it, was only a sideshow of the Napoleonic Wars in Europe, and its last battle was fought in New Orleans on 8 January 1815: the news of the Treaty of Ghent of 24 December 1814 could not reach the USA in only two weeks. Two thousand Kentucky riflemen, in response to a call from Andrew Jackson, arrived in New Orleans a few days before the battle and soundly defeated some fifteen thousand of the best-trained troops in the world. A fiddle tune, 'Eighth of January', celebrated the victory; with words collected by folklorist Jimmy Driftwood, this became 'The Battle of New Orleans', a huge hit in 1959. 'My Country, 'tis of Thee' was written by Samuel Francis Smith, a Harvard-trained clergyman, in 1831; he used the tune of the British anthem 'God Save the Queen', though he is said to have been unaware of that.

A rude patriotism continued to play a large part in the nature of American entertainment and in the treatment of visiting performers: theatre audiences would often demand to hear 'Yankee Doodle', especially if the visitors were British. This combination of chauvinism and anti-élitism led to the Astor Place Riot in 1849 in New York, in which twenty-two people were killed. The conflict was between the supporters of an American and a British Shakespearian actor (the British thespian was seen to represent an aristocratic élitism), but the riot was a turning point in more ways than one. Public entertainment began to separate into several genres, each with its own audience, moving away from the pastiches of songs and melodrama which had been common until then; and art in America began to develop into highbrow and lowbrow, absurd terms from nineteenth-century anthropology. This anti-élitism has had a more ominous cultural effect in more recent times.

Yet there still was not the gulf between classical and popular music that there is today. The French-born conductor Louis Jullien was promoted by P. T. Barnum in America; a showman, he used a baton 6 feet long, wore white gloves and kept a plush chair on the podium, into which he sank, exhausted, at the end of his labours. But he was a thoughtful musician, who wrote an opera as well as dance music, and conducted both music by contemporary American composers and movements from Beethoven's symphonies.

Americans have often held contradictory attitudes. While foreigners were despised for patronizing America, foreign music was seen as somehow superior, a result of the attitude towards class inherited from Britain. Americans learned their music from their own singing masters, and American hymnals began to take on a native flavour in the late seventeenth century. But neither churches nor publishers would have admitted it, and publishers continued to look down on popular songs as the 'trash' of the 'common people'. This high regard for foreign material, however, did not extend to paying royalties on it. During the nineteenth century performing rights societies were formed in Europe, but American publishers refused to entertain such notions. They helped themselves to European music, which was therefore cheaper, and for much of the nineteenth century got away with charging twice as much for it because it was perceived to be better. This did nothing to inspire American composers of formal music. More to the point, it was an early indication of the myopia of which the musical establishment has always been capable: today's record companies and broadcasters, stumbling over themselves to milk last year's fashions, are merely an echo of their ancestors.

The operas of Rossini, Bellini and other Italian composers were immensely popular all over the world. Lorenzo Da Ponte, who had written the librettos for several of Mozart's operas, was a celebrated resident of New York City in his old age. It was thanks partly to his influence that Rossini's *Barber of Seville* was mounted there in 1825, only seven years after its Italian première, at a time when most of Beethoven's music had not been heard in America. The orchestra of twenty-four musicians was said to be the largest yet to have appeared in an American theatre. But English-speaking people still resisted opera in a foreign language, turning to English-language versions and substituting dialogue for recitative. The tunes were pirated for completely new songs, such as 'I'll Pray for Thee' (from Donizetti's *Lucia di Lammermoor*) and 'Over the Summer Sea' ('La donna è mobile' from Verdi's *Rigoletto*). Not all the Italian operas were written by Italians: *The Bohemian Girl*, by the Irishman Michael William Balfe with a libretto by Alfred Bunn, was premièred in 1843 in London, and in New York the next year, and became the most successful production on the English-speaking musical stage until the operettas of Gilbert and Sullivan. It included 'I Dreamt That I Dwelt in Marble Halls' and 'Then You'll Remember Me', two huge hits. Opera became an upper-class preserve, but not before it had had its influence: the Italian trick of holding back the accompaniment on a climactic vocal note is still heard in pop today.

The biggest success of the century was 'Home, Sweet Home', written by the Englishman Henry Bishop, with words by the American John Howard Payne, which was first performed in the opera *Clari, or The Maid of Milan* in London in 1823. It was the favourite song of both sides during the American Civil War, and there were six hit records of it between 1891 and 1915. Critics never liked it, but of its type it was a perfect marriage of words and music, so that many people have thought it was written by Stephen Foster, the first great American songwriter, and an important contributor to the first fully American genre: minstrelsy.

2

Minstrelsy, and the War between the States

Americans of African descent began making their mark very early in the nation's cultural history. There was a black playhouse in New York City in the 1820s: the African Grove Theatre presented its own versions of hit shows, such as Pierce Egan's *Tom and Jerry, or Life in London* (1823), establishing the comic convention of the city slicker and his visiting country cousin. *The Drama of King Shotaway* was probably the first play by a black playwright to be mounted in America. The theatre's director, Henry Brown, may have based the drama of a slave insurrection in the island of St Vincent on personal experience: he had emigrated from there.

The idea was to present entertainment for blacks who wished to join the white mainstream of society, but audiences of the time were unruly anyway, and white hoodlums liked to go to the Grove to disrupt proceedings. The theatre also became a tourist attraction. Its stars included James Hewlett and Ira Aldridge, both of whom toured as far as England. Aldridge played Othello to Edmund Kean's Iago; he performed Shakespeare in Russia, and died in 1864 while on tour in Poland. Regarded as one of the great actors of his day, he had also performed the first American 'slave song' that we know of: 'Opossum up a Gum Tree'.

Free blacks such as the bugle player and bandleader Francis (Frank) Johnson, born in the West Indies, made much history. Johnson was the first American black to publish music (1818), to give formal band concerts, to tour the USA and to appear in integrated concerts with white musicians. In 1824, when the French General Lafayette toured the USA to wild acclaim, Johnson was engaged for the Lafayette Ball in Philadelphia and played his 'Lafayette March', which obtained its share of publicity. He seems to have been the first American musician of any race to tour abroad, taking a band to London in 1837, the year Victoria came to the throne; she gave him a silver trumpet. On his return he introduced the promenade concert to the USA.

There were many other black bandleaders, who were often popular with the upper classes for parties and dances, and indeed talented black musicians in every category. Yet most of these were pursuing success in the American musical world by playing the styles and genres that were already popular in that world. Despite (or perhaps because of) the severe handicap of slavery, it was the music of the slaves that made the first of many profoundly important black contributions to the American mainstream.

The tradition of 'blacking up' goes back at least as far as Ben Jonson's masque for James I's Danish queen, who expressed a desire to wear black make-up with a dazzling white costume. Set-pieces requiring the performer to black up with burnt cork became a staple in America: the *New York Journal* referred to a 'Negro dance, in character' seen on stage in 1767. But the minstrel show suddenly appeared in the 1840s, and was the first entirely American musical form to become internationally popular.

Minstrelsy saw the introduction of patterns still extant in American culture. First, minstrelsy was essentially black music, while the most successful acts were white, so that songs and dances of black origin were imitated by white performers and then taken up by black performers, who thus to some extent ended up imitating themselves. Secondly, more than a few people wondered how a nation could be free which allowed the institution of slavery; but as the nation became more wealthy, it also became more powerful. As the trauma of the Revolutionary War receded, as the young nation won the War of 1812 against the British (but were soundly beaten by the Canadians when they attempted to 'liberate' that country) and as the slaughter of the American aboriginal tribes provided yet another manifestation of racism, Americans established a pattern of resisting the loss of their innocence. The affectionate, patronizing vision of plantation life conveyed by minstrelsy was similar to the simplistic and idealized depiction of family life in the television sitcoms of a hundred years later.

The phenomenon of black culture was widely and often sympathetically discussed. Blacks sang the watered-down songs of minstrelsy, as well as their own, and critics noticed the difference: there was a flavour of sadness in their own songs that was absent from the 'Ethiopian' songs that were all the rage. There is a famous quotation from *Knickerbocker Magazine* (1845) on the subject of Negro poets:

Let one of them, in the swamps of Carolina, compose a new song, and it no sooner reaches the ear of a white amateur, than it is written down, amended (that is, almost spoilt), printed, and then put upon a course of rapid dissemination, to cease only with the utmost bounds of Anglo-Saxondom, perhaps with the world. Meanwhile, the poor author digs away with his hoe, utterly ignorant of his greatness.

There were a few black minstrels, even in the early years, especially in New Orleans, where Signor Cornmeali (Mr Cornmeal, real name unknown) began as a street trader singing 'Ethiopian' songs, went on the stage and influenced white performers. William Henry Lane, known as Master Juba, was probably the only black to tour with early white companies; in England in 1849 he was praised by Charles Dickens. He was born in Rhode Island, but began entertaining in New York City, playing the banjo and the tambourine as well as dancing; he had learned some of his jigs from his desperately poor Irish neighbours, who lived on pennies they earned dancing in pubs, but then made them his own. Both blacks and whites copied his dancing. He won a grand contest (promoted by P. T. Barnum) in 1844, and historians of dance consider him to be the virtual inventor of black dancing, including tap-dancing, as we have known it ever since. He died in England; none of his fame extended to allowing numbers of blacks to make a good living with their own talent. The majority of minstrels were always white.

Much of minstrelsy's material was copied from the songs and dances of slavery and many minstrels visited plantations in search of ideas. In 1829 Thomas Dartmouth 'Daddy' Rice struck it rich with his 'Jim Crow' song and dance, copied from a crippled stable-hand named Jim who worked for a white Crow family. He 'jumped' his

'Jim Crow' between the acts of whatever shows he could get billed on, but the jump was mostly a shuffle, and the tune was borrowed from an Irish jig. 'Jim Crow' later became the stock plantation slave, while 'Zip Coon', first a song by George Washington Dixon, became the city dandy: the 'Tom and Jerry' routine reduced to racist farce.

The earliest full-length minstrel shows were organized by quartets. The Virginia Minstrels first met to rehearse in a rooming house in New York early in 1843, during an economic depression which resulted in one of the worst seasons in theatrical history. Daniel Emmett Decatur was a printer who played banjo and fiddle, working with a circus during the summer, and then began writing songs: 'Old Dan Tucker', 'Turkey in the Straw' (which used part of 'Zip Coon') and 'I Wish I Was in Dixie's Land', written for Bryant's Minstrels in 1859, were all his (but like many songwriters, he died poor). Billy Whitlock, also a printer, had learned to play banjo from Jim Sweeney, a virtuoso who is credited with adding the fifth 'thumb' string to the instrument. Dick Pelham and Frank Brower were both dancers and singers; Brower also played the bones, a set of 12-inch-long dried horse bones which were clacked together to make a rhythm instrument. Brower became one of the best vocalists in minstrelsy.

Black-face performers had been known as 'Ethiopian delineators'. The word 'minstrel' had applied to any professional entertainer since the twelfth century in Europe, but the Virginia Minstrels, who toured for only a few months before breaking up, tied the word for ever to black-face. Immediately successful, they played at record-breaking engagements in New York and Boston, and sailed for England in April. The English already loved black-face entertainment; Sweeney was touring Britain playing the banjo, and the Virginia Minstrels were a hit, but box office receipts mysteriously evaporated, so they could not support themselves and broke up.

The equally famous Christy Minstrels were formed in 1844 by Edwin P. Christy, who wrote 'Goodnight Ladies' and other songs. Born in Philadelphia, he studied black rhythms in Congo Square in New Orleans, where he was a factory foreman. First he toured as one of many imitators of Daddy Rice; he formed a group in Buffalo, New York, and borrowed the name of the Virginia Minstrels for a while, but he always billed his group as the 'oldest' and the 'first'. When he was ready, he booked a theatre in New York in 1846, and developed a family show which ran for over 2,700 performances; he also toured England. He committed suicide by jumping out of a hotel window in New York City, depressed by the outbreak of the Civil War.

The first minstrel companies made history and permanently changed show business by inventing 'black' entertainment for families, and by creating a show rather than just a series of comic turns and dances. The shows were in three parts. For the songs and jokes in the first part the performers stood in a semicircle; the comic end-men 'Tambo' and 'Bones' were distinguished by their tambourine and bone clackers, with which they would register noisy approval of a joke. (This was a signal that the audience too was supposed to laugh, a precursor of canned laughter on radio and television.) An interlocutor or master of ceremonies presided in the centre and represented the boss, so that when Tambo or Bones made a joke at his expense, there was an extra dimension to the glee. Another principal was a singer of sentimental ballads. The similar but less formal second part was made up of a string of speciality acts and novelties, called the olio. This term was already in use in white show business and survived in later vaudeville; it is probably from the Spanish *olla*, meaning 'pot-pourri'. Last came a walk-around finale, with dances, which became more and more of a spectacle.

The 'Ethiopian' dances (for example, breakdowns, double-shuffles and heel-and-toe) and instrumentation (especially the banjo) were more or less authentic, and profoundly influential. The ancestors of the banjo are thought to have been the stringed instruments of the Wolof, of what are now Senegal and Gambia in west Africa, and may be as ancient as Mesopotamia. Minstrel banjo players included Sweeney, Tom Briggs (who joined Christy's Minstrels and published *Briggs' Banjo Instructor*) and Frank Converse, who preserved the first piece he had heard played by a black musician. All of them freely admitted that they had learned from blacks, and the music they played included accents and additive rhythms that came partly from the playing style and were not obvious from the notation, like African drumming in the past and ragtime in the future.

A later element in the show was the cakewalk, in which members of the audience were invited to invent the most ridiculous strutting march, for which the prize was a cake. Interestingly, Master Juba reversed the procedure, in that some of his dances are said to have resembled Irish jigs. But minstrelsy was laden with ironies: the supposed ability of the blacks to invent outlandish dances (though it was whites who were doing most of the dancing) turned the word 'jig' into an offensive euphemism.

As the spectacle in the last act became more elaborate, playlets were mounted that included lampoons of current events and spoofs of popular plays. In one version of *Uncle Tom's Cabin* Uncle Tom was not sold down the river, Simon Legree did not appear and the author's subtitle 'Life among the Lowly' became a song called 'Life among the Happy'.

Some of minstrelsy's songs were sympathetic, such as 'The Negro Boy' ('I Sold a Guiltless Negro Boy') and 'A Negro Song' (or 'The Negro's Humanity'); the latter's words were adapted from an African song which had been transcribed by trader Mungo Park in the eighteenth century. But in general the genre had little room for abolitionist sentiment, and became more overtly racist after the Civil War: the image of the 'darky' as a comic buffoon insulated whites from the reality of free black Americans, and survived in films and television until well into the 1950s. (The 'blaxploitation' films of the 1960s, such as *Shaft*, were a profitable novelty only until blacks tired of constantly seeing themselves portrayed as violent gangsters and pimps in flashy clothes.) Minstrelsy's jokes seem to have been among the oldest in show business, some with double meanings: 'Why am I like a young widow?' a white comedian in burnt cork would ask. 'Because I do not stay long in black.'

Many 'Negro' songs were published. One of the best was 'Yellow Rose of Texas', about a 'darky' longing for his girlfriend. First published in 1858, it became a Civil War campfire song and remained popular for decades. But after the Civil War it was no longer possible to pretend that everything was all right down on the plantation. Charles A. White, whose minstrel songs were his most famous, had a big hit in 1874 with 'The Old Home Ain't What It Used To Be', known to have been sung in the North by black minstrels.

The first successful black songwriter in America was James Bland, whose father found a government job in Washington, DC, just after the war, when the capital was full of ex-slaves. Bland's songs reflect the pentatonic scales of black folk music. His best known are 'Oh Dem Golden Slippers' and 'Carry Me Back to Old Virginny' (and he is still the only black to have written a State Song). Among his more than seven hundred songs are celebrations of the end of slavery: 'De Slavery Chains am Broke at Last', 'Keep Dem Golden Gates Wide Open', 'In the Morning by the Bright Light'. He went to England in 1880 with the Haverly Colored Minstrels and organized his own troupe there; he performed for the British royal family, and also became very popular in Germany.

For decades minstrelsy was a staple of white show business, a simple format for entertainment in the days when all entertainment was necessarily live, and audiences may have been easier to please. In Philadelphia, Carncross and Dixey's Minstrels enjoyed the unique feat of prospering for forty years as a permanent organization in its own theatre. The interlocutor was J. L. Carncross, whose light tenor voice was at its best in plaintive ballads, while E. F. Dixey was the bone man, on the right-hand end of the semi-circle. He played solos on his clackers – his big finale was an imitation of a horse race – and he was also a singer. Hughey Dougherty, with the tambourine at the other end, rasped and cackled his way through comic songs, and had one of the biggest personal followings of anyone in minstrelsy.

In the same town, another famous Tambo was Lew Simmons, who owned a baseball team. (There was little money in sandlot baseball, so he sold it to Cornelius McGillicudy, who changed his name to Connie Mack and made millions with the Philadelphia Athletics.) Simmons was killed by a beer truck, which might have amused him; he himself liked a drink, and was said to be able to see the humour in almost any situation. Billy Sweatnum was the interlocutor and a man named Slocum the bone end in Simmons and Slocum's Minstrels. Charlie Reynolds was a comic who could not sing or dance and was in fact tone-deaf; he would bring down the house by making a shambles of his own act. Jimmy Mackin and Francis Wilson were a touring song and dance team who had a 'rivals' act, both after the same girl. Wilson helped found Actor's Equity in 1919.

During the long decline of minstrelsy, as with the decline of many genres, it slowly exploded into the grandiose: some of the troupes had more than a hundred members. Female impersonations and ever fancier spectacles were included in the shows; among the stock characters were uppity blacks and northern carpet-baggers. Soon minstrelsy and ragtime combined in the 'coon songs' and 'coon shouting' of early vaudeville, and by the early 1880s a minstrel show was becoming effectively a black-face variety show. Lew Dockstader's Minstrels still performed, and George M. Cohan was a partner in a minstrel show, as late as 1908. A white blacked-up minstrel show was popular on British television until well into the 1960s.

To add to all the ironies, black as well as white performers were required to 'black up'. Minstrel shows were popular among ordinary blacks, though conditions were terrible for black performers and a full-time first-class black minstrel troupe, Brooker and Clayton's Georgia Minstrels, was not organized until 1865. Furthermore, the black companies that were formed were mostly owned and managed by white businessmen. But minstrelsy established a demand for black performers, and the origins of black as well as white vaudeville are to be found in it.

We may see black-face minstrelsy as racist nowadays, but America's insistence on its innocence has often been convincing, at least in cultural terms. Of the songs to come out of minstrelsy, those of Stephen Foster survived the crude crucible of racist comedy and made him easily the most successful nineteenth-century composer of popular songs.

Stephen Collins Foster was born in Pittsburgh on the Fourth of July in 1826, the fiftieth anniversary of the signing of the Declaration of Independence. He managed to die an alcoholic and in poverty in 1864, having sold the rights to some of his most popular songs, but he was one of the first American songwriters to sign contracts for royalties and to support himself as a full-time songwriter (others were also publishers, performers or teachers). Above all, he was the first indubitably American composer whose songs are still sung more than a century after his death.

Foster was of Irish descent, and was steeped in music from childhood. He was educated in good private schools and then worked in his brother's mercantile business, but he never strayed far from music. His first published song was 'Open Thy Lattice, Love' (1844);

his early songs were simple, romantic and mediocre, based on the models of Arne and the later example of Bishop, whose songs (except for 'Home, Sweet Home') were already being forgotten.

Foster must have been familiar with slave music from childhood, but it was not until around 1845, through singing and playing them with friends, that he wrote some minstrel songs. 'Lou'siana Belle' was published in 1847, 'Away Down South', 'Uncle Ned' and 'Oh! Susanna' in 1848. The last especially was sung by minstrel companies all over the country, and became a favourite during the California gold rush, but Foster had sold it outright; only in 1849 did he sign contracts with two publishers and become a full-time songwriter. Eight more minstrel songs were published in 1850, including 'Gwine to Run All Night' (also known as 'Camptown Racetrack'); fifteen more in 1852 show him at his peak, among them 'Old Folks At Home' (or 'Way Down Upon the Swanee River'), 'My Old Kentucky Home', 'Massa's in the Cold Ground' and 'Old Dog Tray'.

He wrote a few more minstrel songs, and other fine period songs based on Italian, German and Irish models. His most famous later songs are 'Jeanie With the Light Brown Hair' (1854), which could not have been written without the influence of Thomas Moore, yet is immediately and convincingly Foster, and 'Beautiful Dreamer', which has a fine Italianate melody and was written in the last months of his life. He had a streak of melancholy, and his songs are often nostalgic for a remembered past that is happier than the flawed present. But the minstrel songs written around 1850 made him famous.

It is not true, as nineteenth-century biographers claimed, that Foster had visited 'negro camp meetings' or that he imitated 'the melodic forms and tonal characteristics of the songs of the colored slaves'. He did not need to steal his material, having a natural sympathy for it, and his best songs can stand on their own considerable merits. The melodies have proved to be deathless. More interestingly, every one of the minstrel songs has a chorus, to be sung in three- and four-part harmony, making them more complete and satisfying compositions, while none of his earlier songs have choruses at all. 'Oh! Susanna' is simply a delightful nonsense song, and is not obviously a 'Plantation Melody', as some of the later songs were called. Although many of these were written in dialect, which was later rejected for reasons of taste, they were a considerable advance on the songs of the period.

Nostalgia for a half-remembered past was not just a propensity of Foster's, but the most popular sentiment of the time; homesickness is another familiar emotion. 'Massa's in the Cold Ground' may seem to be a clear attempt to sentimentalize slavery, but many slaves must have loved their masters, on whom they depended for everything. 'Uncle Ned' emerges through the dialect as a kindly human being who was loved; in 'Nelly Was a Lady' (1850) the black man mourns the death of his own wife. The slaves experience, in all these songs, ordinary human feelings; they are people as real as the characters in Shakespeare. And because they were good songs, they must have had a consciousness-raising effect, intended or not.

Slavery made a mockery of the Declaration of Independence, and the issue came to centre on the right of individual states to practise slavery as opposed to the right of the federal government to contain it. Finally it had to be settled. Before 1860 the typical American popular song was a sentimental ballad, expressing the virtues of homeliness, fidelity and so forth. This type of song made a big comeback in the 1880s, but in the meantime, the Civil War of 1861–5, or the War between the States, brought about the end of the nation's adolescence, and should have ended its innocence. Americans were not – could not be – as free as they thought they were; questions sometimes arise which have to be resolved. So it was with the contradiction of states' rights versus federalism in the USA. Brother fought brother in one of the bloodiest wars in history; more than 630,000 died, more Americans than were killed in all other wars from the French and Indian to the Korean.

The Civil War produced a greater number of songs than any other war in American history. Many soldiers carried songbooks; one early book contained songs that were already popular, such as Foster's songs, 'Yankee Doodle', 'Annie Laurie' (from Moore's collection) and 'Pop Goes the Weasel' (a traditional English tune with words from 1858 about a London hatter pawning, or 'popping', his weasel, the tool of his trade). Both sides sang many of the same songs, since both included semi-literate recruits from the same tradition. On the evening before the Battle of Murfreesboro rival army bands, camped within earshot, took turns playing their patriotic songs, then joined together to play 'Home, Sweet Home'. The next day they slaughtered each other.

A camp-meeting song called 'Brother, Will You Meet Us?', to a tune believed to be by William Steffe of North Carolina, had new words bestowed on it by soldiers who sang it as they marched to the front in 1861: 'John Brown's body lies a-mouldering in the grave / but his soul goes marching on' honoured a radical who had been hanged in 1859 after an unsuccessful raid on the government arsenal at Harper's Ferry, intended to arm a slave revolt. Julia Ward Howe heard it and wrote new words: 'Mine eyes have seen the glory of the coming of the Lord / And His truth goes marching on ...' 'The Battle Hymn of the Republic', published in 1862, is as well known to Americans as their national anthem. 'Tenting on the Old Camp Ground', by Walter Kittredge, was almost as popular.

Songs by George Frederick Root included 'Battle Cry of Freedom'; it was later said of Root that he ought to have been made a general. John Hill Hewitt wrote new patriotic words to his own big hit 'The Minstrel's Return'd from the War'. Among his many other songs were 'The Picket Guard', a setting of a poem that had been published in *Harper's Weekly* and told of the night a picket had been shot; since he was only an enlisted man, the official report was 'All quiet along the Potomac tonight'. James Sloane Gibbons wrote a poem called 'We are Coming, Father Abra'am' in response to Lincoln's call for volunteers. This was set to music by Luther O. Emerson and was a great commercial success, but more people sang it than volunteered: Lincoln resorted to the nation's first conscription in 1863, and riots ensued in many cities.

Dan Emmett's 'Dixie' was first sung in the South in 1860, and became wildly popular, with somewhat more bellicose words than the original; one southern commentator wrote that 'we shall be fortunate if it does not impose its very name on our country'. There was a legend of a kindly slave-owner called Dixey, and Dixey's Land was heaven for a slave; surveyors named Mason and Dixon had settled a boundary dispute between Maryland and Pennsylvania, and the 'Mason-Dixon line' thus separated the slave states from the North. But there had also been a ten-dollar note printed by a New

Orleans bank with the word 'dix' on it – French for 'ten' – which may have been the origin of Dixie-land.

The South's favourite songs included 'Aura Lee or The Maid with the Golden Hair', by W. W. Fosdick and George R. Poulton, which later became (with different words) 'Army Blue', a traditional West Point song. 'Maryland! My Maryland!' had words by James Ryder Randall and was sung to the tune of the German 'O Tannenbaum, O Tannenbaum'; it was to become a favourite of dixieland jazz bands. The Confederacy's unofficial national anthem was 'Bonnie Blue Flag', written by Harry B. Macarthy to a traditional tune, 'The Irish Jaunting Car'. Macarthy was an Englishman who left the South when the tide of battle turned.

Many tunes were borrowed more than once. 'Bonnie Blue Flag' was used by Septimus Winner for the satirical 'He's Gone to the Arms of Abraham', while the Irish tune 'The Wearing of the Green' was used for another setting of the poem 'We are Coming, Father Abra'am', and also for 'Wearing of the Gray!' in the South. 'Lorena', a song about parted lovers that was written by brothers called Webster and first published in 1857 in Chicago, was a huge hit in the South. As the slaughter dragged on with no end in sight, southern songs became ever more sentimental and tragic. Music published in the South used cheap inks and poor paper; the weak industrial base that defeated the South encompassed publishing and paper-making.

In the end the federal republic survived, at the expense of a purer political freedom which, paradoxically, had meant enslavement for many: of nearly 4.5 million Americans of African descent in 1860, fewer than 0.5 million had been free. The great southern families with their enormous plantations were the closest thing America had to an aristocracy, and the War between the States destroyed their way of life. Some said that the Civil War was an unnecessary tragedy, because slavery was becoming an economic anachronism and could not have survived much longer anyway, but that notion has been refuted by today's economists. Not only was slavery profitable, but it was cheap labour that had made the comfort of the southern aristocracy possible. That aristocracy would never have given up its primacy easily, and the aftermath of the war was very badly handled.

Americans had slaughtered each other to get rid of slavery, but clung to their innocence; they did not want to admit that slavery had been a mistake in the first place.

3

The Rise of Vaudeville and Tin Pan Alley

In order to preserve the Union, Abraham Lincoln said, he might have freed some of the slaves, or none of them; he ended by freeing them all. While the Russians had freed their serfs first, Americans were much quicker at killing their emancipator, their greatest president, whom they now needed more than ever. As with a later assassination of a lesser president, the nation was a very long time in recovering from it. The worst legacy of the war was the institutionalization of racism in its hopelessly unsuccessful aftermath.

The slave-owners had not argued that some people are born to serve others; that would have been too obvious a contradiction of the American idea. Very suddenly, as cotton became a vital crop in the 1830s, the South had taken the position that blacks were subhuman, capable only of being owned. During the reconstruction period following the Civil War much of this naked racism might have been attenuated – at first there were black congressmen from southern states – but a corrupt Congress soon sold the South to carpet-baggers, crooked politicians whose allegiance was so portable that it would fit into a holdall made of a piece of carpet, and later to the South's self-interested factions, whose cynicism became typical of the rest of the country. Poor whites were pitted against poor blacks, so that a new aristocracy of dishonesty could stay in control. And the result of Lincoln's Emancipation Proclamation was a *de facto* slavery of 'free' citizens who had no rights, while Washington became the centre of an orgy of corruption which has not been exceeded since.

Many of the popular tavern ditties of the period could not be printed in Douglas Gilbert's *Lost Chords: The Diverting Story of*

American Popular Music in 1942, yet, as Gilbert pointed out, none of them approaches the scurrility of the political songs. During the presidential race of 1868 a campaign song for Seymour, who was running against General Ulysses S. Grant, contained the paean 'Here's to the man that pulled the trigger / That killed the old cuss that freed the nigger.'

Singer Pauline Markham, a burlesque queen, took a more direct role in the profligacy of the period. She was hired by people with financial and political interests to sleep with the Hon. Robert K. Scott of Ohio, who signed a great many spurious convertible bonds, his reward being (apart from Markham) the carpet-bag governorship of South Carolina.

Among the era's larger-than-life citizens was Jim Fisk, a sort of Robin Hood who supplied coal, food and rent money to the needy, and who sent a trainload of supplies when the Chicago fire of 1871 made thousands homeless. He was also a famous crook: with Jay Gould he created a gold panic which ruined hundreds of people in 1869. For a time he led President Grant (not a crook, but not too bright either) by the nose. Fisk was murdered by a pimp who had tried and failed to blackmail him, with the cooperation of Fisk's brassy mistress, Josie Mansfield, using letters Fisk had written to her. Fisk left the courtroom in tears at the sound of Mansfield's perjury, he so loved the faithless hussy. Ed Stokes shot him a few hours later, and the letters, it turned out, were so innocent they could have been read to a child. Fisk was buried in Brattleboro, Vermont, whose citizens gave $25,000 for a monument of Italian marble.

Henry Ward Beecher was the most famous preacher and pseudo-moralist of the age, yet he also had an eye for the ladies. In 1875 he was sued by a parishioner, Theodore Tilton, accused of adultery with Tilton's wife. The jury could not agree, but Beecher was probably guilty, and none of it would have come to light except for the hypocrisy of the principals. Beecher and his sister Harriet Beecher Stowe, who wrote *Uncle Tom's Cabin*, condemned leading feminists of the period as flaming harlots. One of them, Victoria Woodhull, took no nonsense from anyone; she began by hinting in *The New York Times* that she knew of prominent people who preached against free love, but practised it in private. When they did not ameliorate their attacks on her, Woodhull blew the whistle on the lot of them, and Tilton had to bring suit.

Songs were sung about all these people, such as 'Jim Fisk, or He Never Went Back on the Poor'. Beecher never lived down the comedy; a song of thirty-two lines took a swipe at Woodhull ('sour grapes') and ended:

> They say he is nearly sixty-five
> By the time he is ninety, he'll contrive
> To set our country all alive
> With little sons of Beecher'os.

The public scandals and relaxed moral atmosphere that followed the Civil War led to a new frankness, along with the cynicism. Large taverns with music and prostitutes, called 'free-and-easies', often appeared on the outskirts of market towns to catch the farmers on their way home with money in their pockets. Among drinking songs, 'Little Brown Jug' was popular in the 1860s:

> My wife and I live all alone
> In a little log hut we call our own
> She loves gin and I love rum
> I tell you what we've lots of fun!

> If I had a cow that gave such milk
> I'd dress her in the finest silk.
> Feed her on the choicest hay
> And milk her forty times a day.

Story songs were sung, many of them salacious. The mother-in-law became fair game, and was combined with a political gibe in the chorus 'I'd rather be sent off to jail or to Congress / Than live all my life with my mother-in-law'. 'Captain Jinks of the Horse Marines' was written in 1868 by William Horace Lingard (words by T. Maclagan) for the British Lingard Comedy Company at a theatre in New York; it was sung by a chorus of girls in military costume (and generations later by children in primary schools, who adored it). Another song was a parody of it, describing what the marine's wife got up to when he was not at home. Still another song sent up 'Home, Sweet Home':

When relations come to visit you,
    There's no place like home.
They bring all their trunks and they stick like glue,
    There's no place like home.
When you've got to give up the best room you've got
And go and sleep on a rough old cot
With your brother-in-law who is always half-shot –
    There's no place like home.

The 1860s and 1870s were marked by the attitude of the free-and-easies: the crooks and the politicians were getting theirs, so everyone else might as well have a good time. No major songwriting talent of Stephen Foster's stature emerged until the 1890s, but the American music business went from strength to strength as trends developed which would become the business we know in more modern times.

The post-war music business was confused, to say the least. The industry believed that the enormous amount of sheet music sold during the war in both North and South had been a patriotic fluke, and that sheet music was for 'the rich and aristocratic', as in Europe, where it was twice as expensive. (This argument, incidentally, was used against any proposal to improve copyright law.) Cheap paperback songbooks were sold, like dime novels, which contained the words to songs but not the music; it was widely believed that the best vernacular music was borrowed from older and 'better' composers. In fact, music teachers all over the USA were doing a good job, and standards were going up. More and more pianos were being bought, and in 1872–3 Steinway paid the great Russian virtuoso Anton Rubinstein $40,000 to do a nationwide tour, not only promoting Steinway pianos, but showing Americans what piano music could sound like. Educated songwriters were emerging to write vernacular songs, the very individuals who, the musical snobs thought, would write high-class art songs. 'When You and I Were Young, Maggie' was written in 1866 by James Austin Butterfield, setting a poem by George W. Johnson, a teacher, for his sweetheart (who died the year they were married). It was just one of the many songs that sold in the same sort of numbers as the wartime hits (and good enough to be revived in a musical film in 1944). The mainstream music publishers failed to take advantage of songs that struck a common chord in millions of people, leaving them to new independent firms.

While 'Home, Sweet Home' and other songs of the earlier nineteenth century may sound old-fashioned to our ears, after the Civil War more songs began to be written which survive today. The American popular song (as opposed to story songs or novelties) had developed a formula. By the 1870s a piece of sheet music usually had a piano introduction of four or eight bars; this was followed by two to four verses, sung to a melody of sixteen bars, which was divided into four phrases of four bars each and conformed to a pattern such as AABC, ABAC or AABA. The chorus or refrain was most often arranged for four voices and was derived from parts of the verse, acting as a commentary or emphasis on it. In its simplicity and directness it will be seen that this form is directly descended from the repeated strophes of the English songs of the eighteenth century.

Septimus Winner was one of the most successful of the era and three of his songs (each very different) are still familiar: 'Listen to the Mockingbird', 'Whispering Hope' and 'Where, Oh Where Has My Little Dog Gone', the last foreshadowing a flood of songs in 3/4 time at the turn of the century. He had also been one of the first to arrange traditional black melodies, such as 'Heaven's a Long Way Off'.

'I'll Take You Home Again, Kathleen' was written in 1875 by Thomas Paine Westendorf, who worked as a teacher in schools for juvenile offenders. It was purchased outright by the John Church Company, and at first printed in their house journal. It made its own great reputation at a time when the marketing of songs was not highly developed, and the company paid Westendorf a mere $50 a month for years. Thomas Edison loved it so much that he requested it be sung at his funeral and sent Westendorf a cheque for $250 in appreciation. Westendorf wrote more songs, but 'Kathleen' was the only one on which the copyright was worth renewing when the time came.

Perhaps the only song from the period that was nearly as successful was 'Silver Threads Among the Gold' (1872) by Hart Pease Danks, who, unlike Westendorf, made a living from his songs; the words were by Eben Rexford, who had published them in a farm magazine.

Danks's other songs included 'Roses Underneath the Snow' and 'Don't Be Angry with Me, Darling'. 'Darling' was his wife, who left him; and Danks died a lonely and angry man. But 'Silver Threads Among the Gold' had sold two million copies by 1900, and another million in 1907, when it was revived. There were several hit recordings of it, among them one in 1904 by Richard Jose, who had first made it popular by singing it in minstrel shows, and another in 1912 by John McCormack.

Alongside all the scurrility and sentimentality of the years after the Civil War white gospel music grew in strength, and had an importance which is almost forgotten today. The respectable Protestant churches – for example, the Methodist and Congregationalist – printed their own hymnals (with words but without music, for most of the nineteenth century), and the churches had tried to control music publishing, especially religious music, since early colonial times, excluding popular 'trash'. But from earliest times singing masters had also combined secular and religious values, knowing that ordinary people loved to sing.

Shape-note music, also called fa-sol-la, was a simplified method of notation which made it possible to teach part-singing to large groups of people: each part was on a single line, and notes of various shapes were used to denote pitch, rather than a five-line stave. It was also called brush arbour music, from the practice of clearing a small area and building an arbour for an outdoor religious meeting, or 'Sacred Harp' music, from the most famous songbook in the style, compiled in 1844. Another book, *Harmonia Sacra* (1851), had been inspired by a similar simplified notation, and was called 'Hominy Soaker' by the less reverent.

The evangelical movement had got under way near a settlement on the Green River in Logan County, Kentucky, called Rogues Harbor, a haven for runaway slaves, thieves and border settlers. A self-educated minister named James McGready won over souls with his fervent brand of Calvinist Presbyterianism, urging a 'new birth' to escape the wrath of Jehovah. By 1800 McGready's followers were so numerous that they held huge outdoor meetings that went on for days, and 'camp meeting' was an accurate description. Fundamentalist evangelism became a growing phenomenon, and whenever there was an economic recession, the evangelists' business improved: before the days of the welfare state and the Social Security Act, the helpless working class would turn to religion in despair. After gold was discovered in California in 1848, more than $800 million was added to the nation's wealth, leading to speculation and then the failure of nearly thirteen thousand businesses in 1857–8: the twelfth business depression since 1790 started yet another religious revival.

Lowell Mason was musically precocious as a child, and compiled a book of psalm tunes which he reharmonized himself: *The Boston Handel and Haydn Society Collection of Church Music* (1822) was the beginning of a family publishing empire which eventually became part of Oliver Ditson in Boston. Mason had a particular interest in teaching music to children, instinctively understanding that it is easier to learn in childhood, which was then a revolutionary notion. Among Mason's over eighty collections were more than a thousand original tunes and nearly five hundred reharmonizations and arrangements, including 'From Greenland's Icy Mountains', 'Nearer, My God, to Thee', 'Joy to the World', 'Blest Be the Tie That Binds' and 'When I Survey the Wondrous Cross'.

Dwight Moody came from poverty to be a great evangelist and a good businessman. Working in a shoe store in Chicago, he saved $7,000 in five years, partly by lending money out at interest rates of up to 17 per cent a day; he also earned a handsome income by collecting overdue accounts after the depression of 1857. He was never ordained and was known as 'Crazy' Moody because of his gospel fervour, but he dressed and behaved like a businessman, which made it easier to save souls as well as bodies. He formed a non-denominational fundamentalist church for slum dwellers and a Sunday school for their children, which might have been the only school some of them ever saw; he was also president of the YMCA, and when the Chicago fire of 1871 destroyed it all, he raised the money to rebuild it. Moody had also erected prayer tents and nursed the wounded behind the lines during the Civil War; later he toured and preached in England. He returned to the USA in 1875, when the corruption at the highest levels of President Grant's administration had become public knowledge. Businessmen like J. P. Morgan and Cornelius Vanderbilt in New York, John Wanamaker in Philadelphia and Cyrus McCormick and George Armour in Chicago were only too happy to help save souls, to demonstrate the Christian side of American business.

Moody had taken vocalist Ira David Sankey with him to England, and their partnership lasted until Moody retired in 1892. Sankey also trained enormous choirs for Moody's huge new tabernacles. Moody had written: 'If you have singing that will reach the heart, it will fill the church every time.' In Brooklyn, New York, extra trolley-car tracks had to be laid to transport all the people who wanted to hear Sankey sing songs like 'Sweet Bye and Bye', 'Go Tell It to Jesus', 'Hold the Fort' and 'Where is My Wandering Boy Tonight?' He was a genuinely popular vocalist, and those who came to hear him stayed to hear Moody preach.

Fanny Crosby, who was called the Queen of Gospel Music, wrote 'Saved By Grace' and many others. Adam Geibel, like Crosby, had been blinded in childhood; he wrote 'Gathering Sea Shells from the Sea Shore' in ten minutes, and it became widely popular. (Geibel also wrote pop hits, such as the coon song 'Kentucky Babe'.) Will Lamartine also wrote both pop and gospel; Moody told W. L. Thompson that he would rather have written 'Softly and Tenderly Jesus is Calling' than have done all the good works in his life. Some of these songs were as popular in the 1890s as any secular hit.

William Ashley Sunday played baseball for the Chicago Whitestockings, later known as the White Sox. As Billy Sunday he became the most famous evangelist of all, named in 1914 as one of America's top ten favourite great men. His musical associate for twenty years was Homer Alvan 'Rody' Rodeheaver, a trombone-playing choir-leader, composer and publisher. Sunday and many others, such as Sam Jones (who was a leading figure in the Lake Chautauqua evangelist movement in western New York state, and whose favourite song was the comic plantation song 'De Brewer's Big Hosses Cain't Run Over Me'), were leaders of the temperance movement, which led to the Prohibition amendment to the Constitution in 1919, one of the biggest disasters Americans ever perpetrated on themselves: it promoted alcohol abuse rather than preventing it, and created a permanent second government of organized crime.

Rodeheaver was the first gospel artist to go into the recording studio, and formed Rainbow Records, the first label of its kind. He lived until 1955; his privately owned publishing empire was estimated to have sold more than a million copies of gospel sheet music and hymnals that year. But about seventy years earlier, when costs were lower and profits higher, Biglow and Main had sold eighteen million copies in one year. Popular-style gospel music had influenced the more mainstream churches, and all this had given birth to a thriving publishing industry that made many fortunes, and also had a deep effect on American music: its joyous, optimistic songs in the vernacular style had been the most important musical experience of many Americans. In the twentieth century, vaudeville, records and radio have made music of all kinds accessible to everyone; white gospel music is still a thriving genre, but despite fine songs such as Stuart Hamblen's 'It is No Secret', and singers such as the popular bass-baritone George Beverley Shea, it has long since ceased to have musical influence.

Black gospel, however, is another story. For the purposes of this chapter it is only necessary to mention the black college students at Fisk University in Nashville (just one of whom had not been a slave), who were trained by the school's treasurer, a young white man named George White. Fisk had been founded by the American Missionary Association in 1866. A collection of black spirituals, *Slave Songs of the United States*, was first published in 1867, but it remained obscure and was not recognized as a landmark until 1929; White was probably unaware of it. The school was in financial trouble, so White took his students on the road. Younger students replaced older ones as they left the group; they sang pop songs, such as those by Foster, and also spirituals which they remembered from their own experience. Their name was changed to the Jubilee Singers, and they performed at Henry Ward Beecher's Plymouth Church in New York City (where the press, which hated Beecher, called them 'Beecher's Nigger Minstrels').

The public didn't know what to make of them at first. For one thing, many northerners outside big cities were used to black-face entertainers, and had hardly seen real black people. (Minstrelsy had had a similar problem: sheet music was often published with pictures of composers and performers without the burnt cork, so that the public would know that they were not really black.) Enter bandleader and cornettist Patrick Gilmore, who had started a series of International Peace Festivals in Boston after the Civil War; in a new venue that could hold fifty thousand people he directed an orchestra of a thousand and a chorus of ten thousand. In 1872 the eighteen-day festival had to be underwritten by the publisher Oliver Ditson; the support of President Grant led to visits from some of the best military bands in the world, and Johann Strauss came to conduct his 'Blue Danube' waltz. The Jubilee Singers were a tremendous hit, and *Jubilee Songs as Sung by the Jubilee Singers* was published by Biglow and Main. Over a hundred of the songs, among them 'Swing Low, Sweet Chariot', 'Go Down, Moses' and 'Steal Away to Jesus', were transcribed and arranged by T. F. Seward, who also became the group's music director. On European tours they earned $175,000 for their school in six years, and the 'slave songs' entered the world's musical vocabulary for good. In the next century the passionate style of the black pentecostal churches would have an even greater impact.

In the secular world of the 1880s the post-war binge of permissiveness turned into a hangover. The decade was anything but dull. The West was being won, native Americans effectively exterminated and the railways built, while settlers still found cheap homestead land; the Brooklyn Bridge was opened and the building of the Statue of Liberty began. New immigrants were mostly Scandinavians and Germans, who did not immediately contribute to popular song, and Jews, who would make their spectacular mark in the second generation. Perhaps the Civil War was far enough in the past for regret to have crept into the lingering hatred between North and South; whatever the reason, there was a rebirth of nostalgia, which spilled over into the maudlin. Songs like 'The Old Slave's Dream' – evidence of nostalgia for slavery – were sung in white parlours.

At a time when childbirth was far more risky than it is today, many unbearably sentimental songs created a genre that W. S. Gilbert called 'shabby genteel'. One Harry Kennedy published 'A Flower from My Angel Mother's Grave', 'A Little Faded Rosebud in Our Bible' and 'Cradle's Empty, Baby's Gone', among others. Temperance songs were common: 'Father, Come Home' was written in 1864 by Henry Clay Work, but became popular much later. Work's Civil War songs had included 'Kingdom's Coming', an anti-slavery song, and 'Marching Through Georgia'; his other best-known song is 'Grandfather's Clock' (1875), in which the music in the accompaniment pauses on an abrupt quaver as the clock stops at the moment of the old man's death.

'Ten Nights in a Barroom', by Timothy Arthur, is a tear-jerker about a little girl who is sent to the tavern to bring Father home to see his dying little boy, whose last words are 'I want to kiss Papa goodnight'. Kennedy's 'Cradle's Empty, Baby's Gone' was parodied as 'Bottle's Empty, Daddy's Tight'. It is to be wondered if temperance people knew a parody when they heard one; some of these songs might be amusing in retrospect, except that they eventually encouraged the disaster of Prohibition. 'The Old Man's Drunk Again' began 'You've no doubt heard the song / Called Father dear come home', and included the lines 'How the old man used to smile / And cause his family pain'. (To 'smile' was a period euphemism for having a taste.)

Not all the songs were dreary. 'Fizz, Fizz, Glorious Fizz' was intended to be funny and there were many 'girly' songs celebrating permissiveness, which after all could never recede entirely: 'My Gal in Kalamazoo', 'Up at Jones' Wood', 'The Dance at Battery Park' were about the good times boys and girls could have. 'Flirting on Our Block' made great use of the word 'it', as in 'all the girls will "do it"', when flirting on our block'. 'It' soon became one of the most suggestive words in the language.

And some songs celebrated America's polyglot population: 'Finnegan's Wake' was already popular, and there were numerous Irish songs, others in German dialect, still others about the Jews. Harry Thompson's 'Let Us Go to the Sheeny Wedding', far from casting a slur, took note of the Jews' ability to have a good time. Frank Bush was a Yiddish comedian who sang his own songs, such as 'Sheenies in the Sand', a parody of Harrigan and Hart's 'Babies on Our Block', about Jews relaxing on Coney Island.

A traditional English tune called 'Willikens and His Dinah', well known in New England in the 1840s, had become 'Sweet Betsy from Pike' when it was sung by miners in the California gold rush, and was first published in 1853. (Stephen Foster used the tune for 'The Great Baby Show, or The Abolition Show' during the 1856 presidential campaign; and the miners also sang a parody of 'Camptown Racetrack' called 'Sacramento'.) One of the biggest hits of the 1880s, as the decade started to recover from its binge of self-pity, was '(Oh My Darling) Clementine', by Percy Montrose, with which America began to celebrate its own past: 'Clementine', a humorous song about a 'miner 49-er' and his daughter, became a huge hit, and in future years it was forgotten that the song had been written thirty years after the gold rush.

In the decades preceding the 'gay nineties', among the most popular acts in the country was Harrigan and Hart in New York City. Edward 'Ned' Harrigan was born in a neighbourhood which included, census records showed, nearly 1,500 people, of whom only 10 were native-born Americans. He wandered, worked on the West Coast waterfront and made his way east on the stage: in 1870 he played an Irishman to Sam Rickey's coon in a comedy duo that was a success in Chicago. Rickey's swelled head took him off on his own, but Harrigan had met Tony Hart (Anthony J. Cannon, born in an Irish slum in Massachusetts) while singing in a minstrel show in Chicago, and they later dominated the New York stage. Harrigan wrote the material, and the music director of the Theatre Comique variety house, David Braham (born in London), wrote the music. The sketches, with songs and ethnic characters, eventually stretched to an evening's entertainment: *The Mulligan Guard's Ball* in 1879 ran for one hundred performances. The sketches were about urban life; the ethnic identities were stereotyped, but affectionate, about basically good people. A collection of nearly a hundred of their songs was published in 1883. Harrigan and Braham wrote together for a decade after Hart left in 1885, though their work always had less appeal outside New York.

Minstrel troupes were still going strong, most of them touring, but minstrelsy as a genre was running out of steam in the 1880s, becoming a black-face variety show. With the taverns and local 'opera houses' available as venues for touring talent, and with the railways making it possible for the talent to go anywhere, a variety show circuit began to develop all over the USA. *Chanson du vau de Vire* originated in a valley in Calvados, France, which was famous for its satirical songs in the fifteenth century, and the corruption 'vau de ville' was used of any light entertainment; the American music hall tradition came to be called vaudeville. There was a Vaudeville Theatre in San Antonio, Texas, in 1882; John W. Ransone, whose speciality was the Dutch comic in dialect, is thought to have been the first to use the word generically.

Tony Pastor (born Antonio Pastore) preferred the term 'variety'. He had worked in minstrelsy, and became one of the fathers of vaudeville, opening his Opera House in the Bowery in 1865. He hired the country's most popular entertainers, but also kept an eye out for talented newcomers (not only the stars of the future, but cheaper). At first he offered prizes – a half-barrel of flour, half a ton of coal, dress patterns – to get respectable women to come to the variety theatre, which then had something of the reputation of the free-and-easies; he insisted that his acts keep their material wholesome, so that families could come without fear of being offended. Pastor opened his second theatre in 1875, as variety was replacing minstrelsy as the most important American format for entertainment. A former free-and-easy was converted by women's haberdashers Koster and Bial into a glorified concert salon, and suddenly after 1887 New York was full of variety theatres. In early 1893 F. F. Proctor put on continuous vaudeville (that is, without intervals or starting times) in a converted church, using the slogan 'After breakfast go to Proctor's; after Proctor's go to bed'. Pastor resisted all-day programming for years, but they were all overtaken by a pair of New Englanders.

B. F. (Benjamin Franklin) Keith, like Pastor, was a censor, keeping the acts suitable for families with the help of his wife. Performers were not allowed to use such phrases as 'by heck' or 'son of a gun'. He began in the circus, but during the seasonal lull one year he operated a dime-show featuring freaks, and business was so good he never went back to the tents. He opened a theatre in Boston and hired a seventeen-year-old circus animal keeper as a boy of all work. E. F. (Edward Franklin) Albee soon proposed a pirated production of *The Mikado*; a huge success, it went on the road and paid for Boston's Bijou Theatre, a 'Temple of the Arts' and first of about seven hundred Keith–Albee theatres. In 1885 they were the first to offer continuous vaudeville from ten in the morning until almost midnight.

Keith died in 1914, several years after handing over operations to Albee, who had begun by stealing Gilbert and Sullivan and never stopped stealing. The restrictive practices and blacklisting he perfected included a covert agreement with Martin Beck's Orpheum circuit, from Chicago to the Pacific, and made him the most hated man in show business. Beck had moved his Orpheum headquarters to New York in 1905; he built the Palace Theatre there, with Albee's permission, and it became the one place every vaudevillian wanted to play. But Albee secretly bought up 51 per cent of the Orpheum circuit and forced Beck to hand over the Palace, whereupon Albee made it a 'cut house': anyone working in the one place where everybody wanted to perform had to take a 25 per cent cut. During a recession there would be several times as many vaudevillians out of work as there were treading the boards, but Albee would not give up his stranglehold on national variety. The only time he was ever investigated by the federal government he lied his head off and got away with it. The pride and joy of this greedy hypocrite, who was worth $25 million when he died, was the traditional $1,000 death benefit paid by the National Vaudeville Artists union. The corpse had usually paid in twice what it got out.

The established theatrical traditional of burlesque came to accommodate the more racy fare, and eventually included strippers. A town's burlesque house might be in a seedier neighbourhood, but while the vaudeville palace put on a more respectable face, it was still regarded with a jaundiced eye by respectable citizens, and the local law kept an eye on it all.

Despite the success of all-black musical shows on Broadway, black artists were restricted to the bottom of the vaudeville hierarchy. The Theatre Owners Booking Association (TOBA), in the South and the Midwest, was formed in 1920 with an investment of $300 from each theatre operator (black or white). The circuit of thirty to forty-five theatres paid $1,200 a week for a black vaudeville troupe, so that after deductions an average weekly pay was about $20 a person. TOBA was also known as Tough On Black Asses.

The most dazzling vaudeville shows were produced by Florenz Ziegfeld, Jr. After making a start at the Chicago World's Fair in 1893, he realized that his French-born showgirl wife, Anna Held, and in particular her legs, were an instant public attraction. She was famous for bathing in milk, and sometimes receiving the press while doing so; her songs, such as 'Won't You Come and Play Wiz Me?', were meant to suggest Continental naughtiness. By 1906 Ziegfeld was 'glorifying the American girl', using costumes and lighting to give the impression of lots of flesh. The quality of it all was high, though, and from 1907 the annual *Ziegfeld Follies* set the standard and broke box office records. It comprised a succession of skits, dancing and songs, often topical; in 1907 Salome's 'Dance of the Seven Veils' was parodied, when singer Mary Garden was titillating audiences with it in Richard Strauss's version at the Metropolitan Opera House.

The New York run of each edition of the *Follies* was followed by a tour; then, after a summer vacation in Paris, Ziegfeld and Held returned to New York with new songs and skits. Ziegfeld deserves to be remembered for the stars and songs he presented: Eddie Cantor, Fanny Brice, Bert Williams, Ruth Etting, Helen Morgan, Marilyn Miller and many more of the best of the era. Ziegfeld was paid the compliment of having quality imitators, such as *George White's Scandals* and *Earl Carroll's Vanities*. He also produced other shows, among them Jerome Kern's *Show Boat*. After his death the Shubert brothers bought the name and produced some more *Follies*, the last in 1940, but the era was over. (The three-hour-long film *The Great Ziegfeld*, of 1936, was described by Graham Greene as 'This huge inflated gas-blown object . . .')

For decades vaudeville presented everything from singing and dancing to juggling and trained dogs. In each town touring performers had their favourite boarding houses that took in theatrical folk; many a child working in a family hotel eventually trod the boards, having first learned a few turns from the show business fraternity. Sophie Tucker's autobiography *Some of These Days* (1945) is excellent on the tribulations of the artist. She was responsible for her own transport, lodging, costumes, songs, arrangements and so forth; she collected her wages from the theatre manager, who decided where on the bill she would appear, and she paid a commission to her booking agent. (Under certain circumstances Albee could require an extra stagehand to travel with the star, who had to pay his wages.) It was sheer talent rather than hype or television exposure that got a performer to the top. The ultimate goal was the 'legitimate' theatre, on Broadway, where there were few jugglers to be seen.

The biggest stars of vaudeville included Norah Bayes, whose real name was Dora Goldberg. With the second of five husbands she wrote 'Shine On Harvest Moon', which they performed together in Ziegfeld's *Follies of 1908* and later that year in a Ziegfeld show called *Miss Innocence*. A plump and not very pretty black-face singer was stealing the show every night with 'Moving Day in Jungle Town', so Bayes had her fired, and that was the end of Sophie Tucker's first Broadway appearance (though she outlasted them all). Eva Tanguay, known as the 'I Don't Care' girl after her hit song of 1905, was a top performer for many years. But the first and greatest female singing star of vaudeville was Lillian Russell, discovered and named by Pastor (her real name was Helen Louise Leonard). She began singing concert ballads and became a comic opera star; according to the *New York Mirror*, she looked like 'Venus after her bath'. During her long career she played the dairymaid in Gilbert and Sullivan's *Patience*, and wore the snug-fitting clothes of young boys or sailors on stage; her speciality was spectacular hats. In later years, as her weight increased, she won a court case versus a producer when she refused to appear in tights.

The lingering prejudice against British performers was finally overcome, partly by the excellent music hall songs they brought with them. Felix McGlennon's hits included 'And Her Golden Hair Was Hanging Down Her Back' (which he had written, but Monroe Rosenfeld copyrighted in the USA), as well as 'Tell Me, Pretty Maiden' and the rest of the score of the long-running show *Florodora*. Vesta Tilley made an international hit of McGlennon's 'Daughters'. A male impersonator, Tilley was also famous for 'Birmingham Bertie' and others; in the USA her cross-dressing was considered daring. The legendary Marie Lloyd and her sister Alice Lloyd did well in the USA, but Alice was hampered by the risqué nature of some of her material. Albert Chevalier, a singing Cockney comedian in pearly costume, wrote his own songs, including 'The Old Kent Road' and 'My Old Dutch', about his wife. Chevalier was one of the highest-paid Britons to work in the USA, but Harry Lauder, the Scottish dialect singer, was among the biggest vaudeville stars of all, making $4,000 a week.

The most popular radio and screen comedy acts of the twentieth century, such as the Three Stooges, Jack Benny, W. C. Fields (who began as a juggler), Abbott and Costello, George Burns and Gracie Allen, served their time on the vaudeville stage; Phil Silvers (TV's Sergeant Bilko), Ed Wynne and many more came from the burlesque end of the spectrum. In the late 1920s vaudeville began to succumb to the competition of radio and films, and was finished off by the Depression; it was said to have died at the Palace in 1932 (though the Keith circuit was briefly revived in the early 1950s for nostalgia buffs). In 1928 there were just four theatres in the country that still presented live variety only (no films). The avaricious Albee did not even see the end coming, and was bamboozled out of his empire by a coalition, one of whose members was Joseph P. Kennedy, a financial genius, father of a future president and just as greedy as Albee. Kennedy made several million dollars out of the deal, which included RCA Photophone – an acknowledgement that talking pictures were coming – and swallowed the original Keith–Albee circuit into a merger that became RKO Pictures. Variety survived, of course, on television: Ed Sullivan's show, presented on Sunday evenings in the 1950s and 1960s by a Broadway columnist, was nothing more than weekly vaudeville, complete with the occasional dog act.

Songwriters and music publishers kept an eye on up-and-coming talent in vaudeville. It soon became apparent that the best way to make a song a hit was to get someone good to sing it. The apotheosis of this was Al Jolson, the greatest star of vaudeville's golden age, neither the first nor the last artist to be offered a songwriting credit (and hence part of the royalties) if he would sing the song. He was listed as co-writer of 'The Anniversary Song', 'Avalon', 'Back in Your Own Back Yard', 'Me and My Shadow', 'There's a Rainbow 'Round My Shoulder' and many more, but may not have written anything at all.

New York has been described as the capital of a country that does not exist. Certainly if you are not from New York, you might be from Kenosha, from Oz or from Mars, but to a New Yorker you are from out of town. During its golden age New York was the melting-pot, bubbling with all the energy and emerging talent that that implies. Music publishing was centred in New York from the 1890s; songwriting had become almost a factory process, and soon the factory had a home: the songwriting of our century began in Tin Pan Alley.

Frank Harding was one of the first song publishers to commercialize the industry. He inherited a small printing firm in the theatre district from his father, who had worked in minstrelsy; he played poker with songwriters, from whom he bought songs, sometimes getting six for $25. In the 1880s, instead of paying performers to sing his songs, he charged them for the privilege of having their pictures printed on the sheet music, and gave them free copies that they could hand out; the back covers were filled with advertising by tradesmen. One of the songs was 'December and May', with words by E. B. Marks, a travelling salesman who learned the business from Harding and sold the sheet music as a sideline on his travels. Marks became a giant of Tin Pan Alley, eventually buying out Harding.

In 1881 the music publishing company of T. B. Harms opened in New York, and in 1906 it was taken over by employees Max Dreyfus and the young composer Jerome Kern when Harms died. Kern had begun with Harms as a song plugger, and Dreyfus had one of the best noses for talent ever seen: he published Paul Dresser's 'On the Banks of the Wabash', Lawlor and Blake's 'The Sidewalks of New York', George Evans's 'In the Good Old Summer Time' and Hughie Cannon's 'Bill Bailey, Won't You Please Come Home', and over the years he discovered Rudolf Friml, George Gershwin, Vincent Youmans and Richard Rodgers.

Willis Woodward began in 1884, soon luring Dresser from Harms. M. Witmark and Sons opened in 1886: teenaged Julius Witmark, a performer in minstrelsy, had accepted credit for a song called 'Always Take Mother's Advice' from Woodward, on condition that he perform it regularly, but then never collected much in the way of royalties. With his brothers, using their father's name because they were all under age, he started a music publishing company that eventually put Woodward out of business. The Witmarks became the most powerful publishers of all, and turned out to be no different from the others: Charles K. Harris formed his own company in 1892 because he had received a royalty cheque for 85 cents from the Witmarks. Julius offered Harris $10,000 for outright ownership of another Harris song, but Harris turned publisher himself, and was soon making $25,000 a month from 'After the Ball'. Leo Feist was provided with his first hit in 1884 by Monroe Rosenfeld, when he lifted the English hit 'And Her Golden Hair Was Hanging Down Her Back'. Feist was one of the industry's best self-publicists: 'You can't go wrong with any Leo Feist song.' He was among the first to go over to full-colour covers on popular songs, and was later particularly good at choosing songs to sell in chain stores, such as Woolworth's.

Chicago, Cincinnati, Baltimore and Philadelphia had been centres of music publishing. Oliver Ditson in Boston, for example, had long been a highly respected house, formed in 1835, and had one of the biggest catalogues. But Ditson published all kinds of music, as well as thousands of popular songs, and did not risk any money on anything untried. The new New York firms (like the eighteenth-century publishers in London) published nothing but popular songs, and were willing to gamble on hunches at a time when the only place most Americans heard new songs was on the vaudeville stage.

Furthermore, in the 1890s a more modern American national consciousness was being created: the nation threw its weight about, taking over the former Spanish colonies of Cuba and the Philippines. There was a serious economic recession and there was labour strife, but in 1901 the government decreed an eight-hour working day for federal employees. Most Americans felt that everything was all right, and were optimistic about the future. Songs, along with other cultural phenomena, were becoming of national rather than regional interest. The nation had been knit together by railways and the telegraph, and the national postal service was so good that anybody could buy any song: indeed, Gottschalk's piano pieces, mentioned in the next chapter, had sold all over the country for 25 cents plus a penny postage in the 1850s. Baseball's annual World Series began in 1903, and the first American cinema was opened in McKeesport, Pennsylvania, in 1905, when two entrepreneurs remodelled a disused shop to resemble a theatre and showed a continuous twenty-minute programme all day long; they called it a Nickelodeon because it cost a nickel (5 cents) to get in. In two years there were five thousand of them all over the country.

Music publishers (and, later, record companies) have always been good at shooting themselves in the foot, but in the 1890s even they had to acknowledge that there was big money to be made in the songs of the 'common people'. Between 1890 and 1909 the wholesale value of sheet music printed in the USA (and reported to the government) more than tripled. By 1900 New York was the centre of vaudeville, with the most famous theatres and the most powerful booking agents; soon it was almost impossible for a song to become a hit unless it was published in New York first. Harris's 'After the Ball', one of the era's earliest and greatest successes, was also one of the last to be first published outside New York, and when Harris formed his own publishing company, he moved it to the Big Apple.

The publishers were located mainly in the heart of the theatre district, around Union Square on 14th Street, and then they followed the theatres uptown. Witmark led the move to 28th Street between Broadway and Sixth Avenue, which soon became a warren of small rooms, each with a piano. During the summer the windows were open, cacophony spilling out, and by 1900 the street was allegedly dubbed Tin Pan Alley by Rosenfeld.

Monroe Rosenfeld was a colourful hack with taste, a magpie when it came to tunes, a gambler, womanizer, columnist and editor; he published an article praising Scott Joplin's music in 1903. He had worked for the *New York Herald* in the 1880s, when it published pop songs as a circulation gimmick. His forte was sentimental ballads, such as 'With All Her Faults I Love Her Still' (1888). An example of what Marks called Rosenfeld's 'melodic kleptomania' was his hit 'Johnny Get Your Gun' (1886), itself later quoted by George M. Cohan in 'Over There'. One story is that after hearing Harry Von Tilzer's prepared piano (with paper strips woven through the wires), Rosenfeld titled the article on which he was working 'Tin Pan Alley'.

Charles K. Harris was more successful as a publisher than a songwriter, though his 'After the Ball' was so popular that it inaugurated the era. Nobody liked it at first, but he bribed a variety artist in Milwaukee to sing it and published it there. Most of his songs were based on events he overheard or read about: 'After the Ball' tells of a man at a dance who sees his sweetheart kissing another man; he walks out, but never gets over it, and finds out years later that the other man was her brother. His other biggest hit, 'Hello Central, Give Me Heaven' (1901), began with a news item about a child whose mother had died and who tried to phone her.

Among the other successes of the era were Albert Von Tilzer (born Albert Gumm), who wrote 'Take Me Out to the Ball Game', 'Put Your Arms Around Me, Honey' and 'I'll Be With You in Apple Blossom Time', and his brother Harry, who wrote 'Wait Till the Sun Shines, Nellie', 'A Bird in a Gilded Cage', 'I Want a Girl Just Like the Girl That Married Dear Old Dad'. (They took their mother's maiden name of Tilzer and added the 'Von'.) Kerry Mills wrote 'At a Georgia Camp Meeting', 'Red Wing (an Indian Fantasy)', 'Meet Me in St Louis, Louis'. Paul Dresser had begun as a black-face end-man; his many songs included 'My Gal Sal' and 'On the Banks of the Wabash', for which his brother, novelist Theodore Dreiser, wrote the words to the chorus.

It will be immediately obvious that we have entered a new era of popular songwriting. Plenty of sentiment and nostalgia is distributed among these titles, but the craft of writing a song with staying power had reached a new peak. We will look at the effect of the invention of sound recording in a later chapter, but meanwhile it is worth noting that there were no fewer than thirty-nine hit recordings between 1893 and 1943 of the twelve Tin Pan Alley songs mentioned above since 'After the Ball'. 'At a Georgia Camp Meeting' became a dixieland jazz favourite (at least seven recordings of it were listed in the British Music Master record catalogue in 1988); there was an instrumental Swing Era recording of 'Red Wing', a fine tune and a modern one, in the sense that it is superbly adaptable. In fact, these songs and others like them have been used throughout the twentieth century, in films, cartoons, plays and so on, to evoke what we like to think of as a happier time, when everyone believed in progress and race riots and world wars had not yet happened.

The overtly maudlin song was still around: Dresser's earlier efforts had included 'The Letter That Never Came' and 'The Pardon Came Too Late', while 'My Gal Sal' and 'In the Shade of the Old Apple Tree' (by Harry H. Williams and Egbert Van Alstyne, 1905) were about graves. But most of the songs that have survived from the period are of more general appeal and usually good-time songs. 'Down By the Old Mill Stream' and 'Sweet Adeline' became the quintessential barber-shop harmony songs. Among the many songs in 3/4 time were 'In the Good Old Summer Time', 'I Wonder Who's Kissing Her Now', 'The Band Played On', 'You Tell Me Your Dream' and 'When You Were Sweet Sixteen'; 'Meet Me Tonight in Dreamland' and 'Let Me Call You Sweetheart' (1909–10), both by Leo Friedman and Beth Slater Whitson, sold millions of copies of sheet music. Songs specifically about New York included Percy Gaunt's 'The Bowery', already a hit in 1892, and 'Sidewalks of New York' (1894), which commemorates a time when children could play in the side-streets of the world's biggest cities.

Harry Dacre was an English songwriter and performer who came to New York in the 1890s, bringing his bicycle. To his surprise, the customs people exacted a toll on it. 'Lucky for you it wasn't built for two,' a friend remarked. And the result was 'Daisy Bell', also known as 'Daisy, Daisy' or 'Bicycle Built for Two'. No publisher in America wanted the song, so Dacre gave it to Kate Lawrence, a British music hall artist on her way back to London; from there it swept the world.

Another song with a similar history is 'Ta-ra-ra-boom-de-ay'. Nobody knew where it came from – it was apparently heard in Babe Conners's brothel in St Louis in the late 1880s, where Mama Lou played the piano and sang. With cleaned-up (but not very good) lyrics, it was a flop when published in New York in 1891 by Henry J. Sayers, who admitted that he had not written it. Then Lottie Collins sang it in London. In 1892 the *New York Herald* correspondent wrote that the refrain had become 'a hideous nightmare' and had even been blurted out by an actor on stage in Oscar Wilde's *Lady Windermere's Fan*, convulsing the audience. The song shows how words, phrases and tunes from this era entered the common consciousness: sixty years later an English newspaper article about top people having to rent jewellery for Elizabeth II's coronation carried the headline 'Tiara Boom Today'.

Semi-art songs, aimed at the parlours of the genteel, included 'Oh Promise Me' (1889) by Reginald De Koven, a darling of Chicago's musical snobs; all his other attempts at high-class parlour art were failures. 'Mother Machree' (1910) and 'When Irish Eyes are Smiling' (1913) can still reduce the sort of Irish-American who has never set foot in Ireland to sentimental blubber; they were written by Ernest R. Ball, who was born in Cleveland, Ohio. This genre produced almost the only big hits of the period not published in New York: Carrie Jacobs Bond set up in Chicago when Tin Pan Alley rejected her. To support herself and her child after her husband died, she designed and hand-painted the covers of her sheet music and plugged her songs in recitals. 'Just a-Wearyin' for You' (1901), 'I Love You Truly' (1906) and 'A Perfect Day' (1910) were her best known.

Sheet music sales achieved an all-time high in 1910, led by 'Let Me Call You Sweetheart' and 'Down By the Old Mill Stream', at a time when every respectable parlour in the country had a piano. We regard these songs as corny now; we know some of the choruses, but many of them were story songs and are not complete without introductions and verses. On recent recordings of some of them William Bolcom plays a vigorously sympathetic piano accompaniment, while the talent of his wife, mezzo-soprano Joan Morris, would have made her a worldwide star in the golden afternoon of the Edwardian era. The worth of the songs is clear: they were written for an audience that had more time to listen, an audience whose ears had not been dulled by constant Muzak. They are the peak of the songwriting that began in the English pleasure gardens, artless art songs for the English-speaking masses. That we have lost the ability to appreciate the songs our ancestors loved suggests we may have lost even more.

But already hits of a new type were arriving. They came from the second American genre, after minstrelsy, to be created largely by black Americans and to become internationally popular: ragtime.

4

The Ragtime Era and the Coon Shouters

The history of modern popular music may be seen as the repeated rescuing of a moribund scene by the music of African-Americans. Stephen Foster's songs were a brilliant oasis in a desert in the mid nineteenth century. Not only were his minstrel songs sympathetic, but they had some of the feeling of the Negro church in them. He died after emancipation but before the end of the Civil War, and the black influence in mainstream songwriting temporarily disappeared with him.

When British art critic Giles Auty visited the Soviet Union in 1988, a Russian painter said to him, 'We are told that we have this thing called freedom now, but nobody knows what it is.' Auty pointed out that the rapid re-establishment of a genuine Russian identity in art would have a welcome effect on stale western criticism and the sale-room mentality, but also that it would take many years of *perestroika* before the artists found out what they wanted to do. The newly freed American slaves were in the same position after 1865, which is partly why popular music in the second half of the nineteenth century was dominated by good-time jingles and maudlin songs like 'Cradle's Empty, Baby's Gone'.

In the almost thirty years between 1885 and the First World War the modern American popular song began to emerge. The rhythms of minstrelsy continued to percolate into the mainstream; the cake-walk demanded something that the waltzes, polkas and marches of European music simply could not supply. The trauma of the Civil War was slowly left behind as the South was ignored and the North became richer and more powerful. A new American identity generated songs which could not have been written anywhere else. Many of the ex-slaves and their families drifted across the country, establishing themselves in their own neighbourhoods in most northern towns of any size. Coon songs came out of minstrelsy, and were already established in vaudeville, when all this culminated in ragtime.

Ragtime used a march-type (oompah) bass line, but set syncopated melodies against it. It swept the world between 1897 and 1920. In retrospect, ragtime is widely regarded as a solo piano music, but that was only its most highly developed and most enduring manifestation. Ragtime songs, music for small groups and brass bands and ragtime waltzes were all important, as was banjo music: ragtime may have begun with attempts to imitate the banjo on the keyboard.

The concert pianist and composer Louis Moreau Gottschalk was born in New Orleans. He studied music privately in Europe, and was praised by Berlioz and Liszt; he could be described as America's Liszt, for ladies swooned at his recitals. Like Edwin Christy, he was influenced by the dancing at Congo Square. Instead of playing florid keyboard imitations of Wagnerian operas, he used Creole and Afro-Hispanic idioms. His piano pieces, such as 'Bamboula', 'The Banjo' and 'La Bananier', and his more ambitious works might have made him America's Glinka (the great Russian nationalist) had he not died (of either yellow fever or peritonitis) while on tour in Rio de Janeiro, where a trunkful of his music, probably including operas, was lost.

He had left San Francisco suddenly on a night boat in 1865. He had taken two young ladies for a late-night carriage ride, one of whom happened to be from a prominent family. The incident was exaggerated by an enemy, who was also angry because Gottschalk preferred the Chickering piano (competition between Steinway and Chickering was intense). Gottschalk was a sensualist, and also capable of sentimentality. His biggest hit, 'The Last Hope', was written in 1850 for a Cuban fan who claimed she would expire if he did not do something about her passion; along with 'The Dying Poet', it was later a staple of cinema pianists accompanying death scenes. ('The Last Hope' also became a Protestant hymn called 'Mercy'.)

As well as Gottschalk's 'The Banjo', there was a piano piece called 'Imitation of the Banjo' (1854), by one W. K. Batchelder, which was dedicated to Christy's banjoist Thomas Briggs. If the 'banjar' is thought to have come directly from Africa, African music also features the additive rhythms that became a principal feature of ragtime. While European music has often been polyrhythmic as well as polyphonic (as for example in Italian and English madrigals), it divides its rhythms by means of bar lines. The African was unrestricted by sheet music, and loved to add rhythms in a different way. Western musicologists discovered that a chorus of several percussion instruments in an African piece, if notated in the style of western orchestral music, would have bar lines that do not coincide vertically, as they would in a European manuscript. In their dancing, in minstrelsy and then in ragtime, black Americans were insisting on setting European-style music free by refusing to be restricted to a ground beat. The dancing in Congo Square was described as in 'ragged' time in 1886; in 1888 a banjo player in Nebraska wrote to a music magazine requesting music in 'broken time' like the 'ear-players' played, but none had been printed yet.

The Chicago World's Fair of 1893, also called the World's Columbian Exposition, was a watershed in national American culture. Chicago then had more railways going in and out of it than any other city in the country, and the fair attracted tourists from all over the world; every American performer wanted to play there. One of the stars of the show was John Hutchinson, of the Hutchinson Family, thirteen brothers and sisters who had known national fame since beginning as a quartet in the 1840s. Their harmony was so close and accurate that the individual voices could not be heard. They sang in England in 1846, and in the White House for Lincoln in 1862. They hated slavery, and preferred smaller venues where they might find sympathetic audiences for abolitionist songs. During the Civil War they sang Root's 'Battle Cry of Freedom' and Kittredge's 'Tenting on the Old Camp Ground'; later they sang the spirituals of Fisk's Jubilee Singers, taking them to white audiences who might not otherwise have heard them. By 1893 the Hutchinsons' stardom was over, having spawned uncounted imitators, but John was one of the grand old men of American popular music.

Florenz Ziegfeld, a prominent local music teacher, was music director at the 1893 Fair, and sent his son to Europe to hire exciting talent. Florenz Ziegfeld, Jr, did not do that very well, but made some money by exhibiting the World's Strongest Man in Chicago (with flesh-coloured tights) and never looked back. The Fair attracted itinerant pianists, who were already playing ragtime.

Ragtime seemed to emerge in the Midwest, chiefly in Chicago, St Louis and Louisville, Kentucky; but, like jazz later, it probably grew up in many places at once, and certainly spread rapidly. The first compositions that were labelled as ragtime were published in 1896: songs called 'My Coal Black Lady', by W. H. Krell, and 'All Coons Look Alike to Me', by Ernest Hogan; the latter included optional 'Negro "Rag" Accompaniment'. In 1897 the first tunes calling themselves rags, Krell's 'Mississippi Rag' and Tom Turpin's 'Harlem Rag', appeared, the first recordings were made, on the banjo by Vess L. Ossman, who became an international celebrity, and by the Metropolitan Band, and pianist-composer Ben Harney published his *Rag-time Instructor*.

Between two and three thousand instrumental rags and a similar number of ragtime songs were published, as well as about one hundred ragtime waltzes. Most of the songs are forgotten now, but the instrumental rags remain the essence of ragtime today, and the best-known composer of these was Scott Joplin.

Born in Texarkana, Arkansas, as a young man Joplin played cornet in the Queen City Negro Band of Sedalia, Missouri, in the 1890s; he probably played at the Chicago World's Fair. He sold his first compositions ('Please Say You Will' and 'Picture of Her Face') in 1895 and his first rags in 1899. 'Original Rags' was sold outright to a publisher in Kansas City, but 'Maple Leaf Rag' was published in Sedalia by John Stark, with whom Joplin made a royalty agreement. It was the biggest ragtime hit of all: on the strength of it Stark moved his business to St Louis and then to New York. By 1915 Stark had published an orchestral folio, *Standard High-class Rags*, which became known as the 'Red Back Book' because of its binding.

Joplin wrote about fifty piano rags of his own, as well as collaborations (such as 'Sunflower Slow Drag', with Scott Hayden). He wrote the best ragtime waltzes, for example, 'Bethena' and 'Pleasant Moments'. Joplin and Stark tried to establish the classic rag in the face of a national obsession with ragtime as 'rinky-tink' party music; it became the fashion in Joplin's lifetime to play rags at breakneck speed, partly because of coin-operated player pianos in penny arcades, which were speeded up to make money faster, like some jukeboxes in more modern times. This was despite the fact that some of Joplin's pieces were printed with the admonition 'Ragtime should never be played fast'.

Joplin knew minstrelsy and vaudeville, having worked in both; he was exposed to opera by the conductor of the St Louis Choral Symphony Society, who played some of Wagner's *Tannhäuser* for him; he may have heard the great piano virtuoso Ignacy Paderewski and he probably met Harry Lawrence Freeman, the first black American to compose operas. In Joplin's time educational opportunities for blacks were few, and there were not many who had the chance to study music formally. The diminished-seventh chords which Joplin often used are found in abundance in barber-shop-quartet singing, and there is a considerable body of evidence to suggest that that style was also developed by black Americans: the well-known vaudevillian Billy McClain recalled that in the 1880s 'about every four dark faces you met was a quartet'.

Joplin aimed to create a body of serious American music in the ragtime style, but even if the form could have borne the weight of Joplin's ambition for it, he was doomed to disappointment. He worked on ballets and operas, but had little success; he died in a mental hospital in 1917. His opera *Treemonisha* was produced in Atlanta, Georgia, in 1973, and a recording was made; it received a special Pulitzer Prize in 1976. That the Pulitzer committee gave this bouncy pastiche a prize it would not give to Duke Ellington while he was alive is unfortunate, but Joplin's picture on a US postage stamp in 1983 was appropriate: his rags will live for ever.

Other rag composers whose work is often considered equal and sometimes superior to Joplin's include Tom Turpin, James Scott, Eubie Blake and Luckey Roberts, all of whom were black, and white composers Joseph Lamb (a close friend of Joplin, for whom he played part of *Treemonisha* in 1908), George Botsford, Charles L. Johnson and Percy Wenrich. Artie Matthews wrote fine rags, worked for Stark as an arranger and was later one of the first to publish songs with the word 'blues' in the title; his 'Weary Blues' became a jazz classic. Women also wrote fine rags, the most prolific being May Aufderheide and Irene Giblin, both white. Prominent banjo players apart from Ossman included Fred Van Eps, father of jazz guitarist George Van Eps.

When Douglas Gilbert published *Lost Chords*, a history of American popular music, in 1942, he thought that Ben Harney was the greatest of ragtime artists, and possibly the inventor of the genre. In fact, it was Harney who brought ragtime to New York, where he was billed at Tony Pastor's theatre as the 'Inventor of Ragtime', in the same year he published his instruction book. He wrote the hit songs 'You've Been a Good Old Wagon but You've Done Broke Down' and 'Mr Johnson, Turn Me Loose' (1895–6). The former especially has survived, possibly in variants: the Bessie Smith song of that title (recorded in 1925) is credited to John Henry, a pseudonym of Perry Bradford, and its ownership has changed hands since then. (At the turn of the century 'Mr Johnson' was black argot for a policeman.) It is not clear from most books on the subject whether or not Harney was black; Eubie Blake stated most definitely that he was. In any case, we cannot tell from the sheet music how he played his own songs: it was edited by somebody else, and the notation is old-fashioned.

It was not so much the rhythmic pattern of ragtime in each bar which distinguished it from other musics, but the fact that it was tied across to the next bar, and that the next note of the melody (in the treble clef) was not supposed to be struck on the first beat of the second bar: this is what made the melody syncopated. By this definition, as far as popular songs were concerned, a great many ragtime songs (including Harney's) were not ragtime at all, but, as with 'jazz' and 'rock' in the future, the term 'ragtime' was widely appropriated. Classical instrumental and operatic pieces were 'ragged' (played in a syncopated way). It seemed that almost any uptempo song could be called ragtime: so Irving Berlin became the most famous ragtime composer of all, thanks to 'Alexander's Ragtime Band' (1911), though Berlin is said to have confessed that he did not know what ragtime was.

Mama Lou (mentioned in the last chapter) was playing and singing 'There'll Be a Hot Time in the Old Town Tonight' and 'Who Stole the Lock on the Henhouse Door', as well as 'Ta-ra-ra-boom-de-ay', in St Louis. (The first of these, with cleaned-up lyrics, became a marching song in the Spanish-American War.) Two enormously popular songs forever described as ragtime, despite their lack of technical qualifications, are 'Hello! Ma Baby' (1899), by Joseph E. Howard, and 'Bill Bailey, Won't You Please Come Home' (1902), by Hughie Cannon. These and many others, however, were also coon songs, the black-face vaudeville genre which was already established when ragtime came along. It was the combination of ragtime and coon songs (probably the same thing to the public of the 1890s) that led to the mainstream pop songs of the next century.

One of the first coon hits was 'New Coon in Town' (1883) by J. S. Putnam. The singers were called coon shouters, and included May Irwin, who was famous for the 'Bully Song' and Harney's 'Mr Johnson, Turn Me Loose'. The biggest coon hit was Ernest Hogan's 'All Coons Look Alike to Me' (1896), about a woman rejecting her lover for another man with more money. While a great many writers of coon songs and other hits of the era were Irish, Hogan was black. His real name was Reuben Crowder, and he began his show business career as a child in *Uncle Tom's Cabin* in 1876. (The play was first staged in 1852, before the book was published, but it was well over twenty years before a producer had enough nerve to use 'real Negroes'.)

Not only did 'coon' soon become an obnoxious epithet, but Hogan's title became an obnoxious catch-phrase; Hogan is said to have regretted his greatest success. In the original version of the 'Bully Song' Mama Lou herself sang 'I'm a Tennessee nigger and I don't allow / No red-eyed river roustabout with me to raise a row'. Ethnic stereotypes of all kinds were taken for granted by a polyglot nation that still attracted millions of immigrants each year, and the institutionalization of racism was less complete in the North than in the South. Later in the twentieth century ethnic humour would be one of the casualties of racism.

Other performers who were described as ragtime singers or coon shouters were Dolly Connolly, Billy Murray, Bert Williams, Sophie Tucker and Al Jolson, all very different. Connolly was married to rag composer Percy Wenrich; her hit records in 1911–12 included 'Waiting for the Robert E. Lee' (by Lewis F. Muir). The southern or 'Dixie-land' flavour of such songs helped them into the ragtime category. Billy Murray was one of the best-known stars in the history of recording; his 'The Grand Old Rag' (1906, by George M. Cohan, and soon retitled 'You're a Grand Old Flag') was said to be the biggest hit in Victor's first decade.

Bert Williams was born in the West Indies and became the first and most successful black performer in vaudeville and then on Broadway, with his partner George Walker; in 1903 they were the stars of the first full-length musical show to be written and performed by blacks on Broadway, *In Dahomey*. Williams had a streak of melancholy; W. C. Fields described him as 'the funniest man I ever saw, and the saddest man I ever knew'. In his personal life he had middle-class tastes and aspirations, but he had to wear black-face during his entire career as a singer, dancer and comedian. Later, when he became a star of the *Ziegfeld Follies*, he had to be defended against the racism of fellow performers by the producer. On one occasion, when Williams and his wife went to visit the Ziegfelds at home, a doorman refused to admit them until Ziegfeld threatened to move out of the building. Williams made two short silent films, which had to be withdrawn; racist reaction was violent when they were shown, though he was an accepted star on the stage. His most famous number was 'Nobody', a sort of half-sung, half-spoken bit of pathos which he recorded twice (reworked by Ry Cooder on his *Jazz* album in 1978). He made dozens of hit recordings from 1902, and was immortalized by Duke Ellington in 'A Portrait of Bert Williams' in 1940.

Sophie Tucker was billed as a coon shouter early in her long career, but made no black-face appearances after 1911, by which time she was a top performer. She sang 'I'm the Last of the Red Hot Mamas' in a film in 1929, and that became her billing. Always plump and not very pretty, she astonished audiences with her costumes and her powerful stage presence, and a repertory much of which could not be broadcast. Born in 1884 somewhere between Russia and Poland, where her family escaped from tsarist pogroms, she later played the wife of the American ambassador to the Soviet Union in a Broadway musical. At her first Royal Command Performance in London in 1934 she greeted King George V with 'Hiya, King!' She was still performing three years before she died in 1966. Her best-known songs were 'Some of These Days' written by Shelton Brooks, who also wrote 'Darktown Strutters' Ball', about Chicago's State Street when the black culture scene was located near the Loop, and 'My Yiddishe Mama', by Jack Yellen and Lew Pollack, who also wrote 'Cheatin' on Me', later a hit for Jimmie Lunceford. (Yellen co-wrote 'Ain't She Sweet?' and 'Happy Days Are Here Again'.) 'My Yiddishe Mama' was recorded in 1928, in English on one side and Yiddish on the other, and sold a million copies.

Al Jolson billed himself as 'The World's Greatest Entertainer', not without justification: he was the biggest star vaudeville ever had. Born Asa Yoelson in Russia in 1886, he was an inspiration to many later artists, such as Bing Crosby, not for his style (he milked black-face for sentimentality decades after everyone else had dropped it), but for his professionalism and dedication to pleasing his audience. His catch-phrase, 'You ain't heard nothin' yet!', was first used when he followed Caruso at a benefit in 1918.

We have already seen that Jolson was the best example of a successful artist who was given co-writing credit from Tin Pan Alley in return for singing a song. Tucker was first to sing 'When the Red Red Robin Goes Bob Bob Bobbin' Along', but it was identified with Jolson. He made the first talking film, *The Jazz Singer*, in 1927. (He was no jazz singer, and the film, though a sensation, was only partly a 'talkie'.) He sang George Gershwin's 'Swanee', 'My Mammy', by Sam Lewis, Joe Young and Walter Donaldson, and 'Sonny Boy' in black-face and white gloves, and typically on one knee. 'Sonny Boy' was written by one of the most successful songwriting teams of all time, DeSylva, Brown and Henderson, as a joke. When they sent it to Jolson, to their astonishment he liked it, and sang it along with 'There's a Rainbow 'Round My Shoulder' in the 1928 film *The Singing Fool*.

Of Jolson's eighty-five hit records between 1912 and 1930, twenty-three are calculated to have been the equivalent of number one hits (most of them in the acoustic era, long before pop charts). Many were probably considered ragtime songs, such as 'California, Here I Come', 'Swanee' and 'Toot Toot Tootsie (Goo'bye)', as well as 'You Made Me Love You (I Didn't Want to Do It)' and 'April Showers'.

'Hello Central, Give Me No Man's Land' was a First World War success in 1918; Jolson sang it in the show *Sinbad*, which made him Broadway's biggest star, along with 'Rock-a-bye Your Baby With a Dixie Melody'. The next year, after the war, Irving Berlin's 'I've Got My Captain Working for Me Now' was topical. 'My Mammy' was introduced in vaudeville by William Frawley (who became famous decades later as Fred Mertz in *I Love Lucy* on television); Jolson added it to *Sinbad* after the show's New York opening.

Jolson turned producer in 1944, and sang on the soundtrack of *The Jolson Story* (1946) and *Jolson Sings Again* (1949). Since handsome Larry Parks played him on screen, teenaged girls bought Jolson's records. Jolson entertained troops in Japan and Korea a month before he died in 1950.

Ragtime also led to novelty piano music: Felix Arndt's 'Nola' and Gus Chandler's 'Canadian Capers' were hits in 1915; 'Kitten on the Keys' and 'Nickel in the Slot' were played by composer Zez Confrey at the same concert as Gershwin's *Rhapsody in Blue* in 1924. Novelty piano pieces, based on ragtime but exploiting the idiomatic possibilities of the keyboard, became a minor industry. Confrey's 'Stumbling' used rhythmic patterns of three over a basic beat of four, foreshadowing Gershwin's 'Fascinatin' Rhythm', while Gershwin himself wrote 'Rialto Ripples' in 1917. Rube Bloom's piano pieces were a prelude to his first-class popular songs, such as 'Fools Rush In' and 'Day In, Day Out'; Nacio Herb Brown's 'The Doll Dance' has never been out of print; his 'When Buddha Smiles' was a hit during the Swing Era, and he also went on to be a successful songwriter. The novelty genre died with the 1920s, but not before having its influence.

The overall effect of ragtime on popular music was permanent, and classic ragtime has never really gone away for long. It was part of the revival of early jazz which began in the late 1930s, and in 1947 bands led by Bunk Johnson and Mutt Carey recorded selections from Stark's 'Red Back Book'. *They All Played Ragtime* by Rudi Blesh and Harriet Janis was seminal in 1950, though it has since been superseded by better books. Ragtime was kept alive in the 1950s by studio musicians Dick Hyman (as Knuckles O'Toole) and Lou Busch (as Joe 'Fingers' Carr), and the novelty aspect was milked by Fritz Schulz-Reichel in Germany ('Crazy Otto') and in the USA by

Johnny Maddox (a staff musician at Dot Records, whose recording of a 'Crazy Otto' medley was a huge pop hit in 1955). Whereas many of the players of ragtime had cause to complain about the state of the piano in the average tavern, in the 1950s it was sometimes deliberately made to sound tinny, often by sticking thumbtacks on the hammers. Winifred Atwell in the UK made 'the other piano' part of her act.

Max Morath, William Bolcom, Joshua Rifkin, Gunther Schuller and André Previn have all played ragtime properly in recent decades. Rifkin's three Nonesuch albums made the USA pop album chart in 1974, after the soundtrack of the film *The Sting* (1973) gave ragtime its biggest boost in fifty years. It was Schuller who conducted the 1973 performance of *Treemonisha* and made an album of arrangements from the 'Red Back Book'.

The fact that a ragtimer's left hand rarely indulged in syncopation is perhaps less important than the fact that it sometimes did, as in the third strain of Joplin's 'The Cascades'. Ragtime pianists, like the banjo players in minstrelsy, played things that were not on the page. They took part in 'cutting' contests (where they tried to outplay each other), ranging from tavern entertainments to spectacular events, for example at Tammany Hall in New York in 1900 (sponsored by *Police Gazette* magazine) and at the St Louis World's Fair in 1904. Some of the contestants in these affairs must have been presented with unfamiliar music to play, and many of them must have been capable of faking it, or improvising. Edward A. Berlin thinks that virtually every ragtime pianist was expected to improvise. There are also 'variation' rags, such as Tom Turpin's 'Harlem Rag' (the first rag by a black musician to be published, in 1897), and 'Lion Tamer Rag' (1913), by the mysterious Mark Janza, of whom nothing is known. We have to wonder whether these were written-down improvisations.

Some of the rag composers did not approve of improvisation. Artie Matthews wrote 'Don't Fake' on some of his, and Joplin was explicit: '"Joplin ragtime" is destroyed by careless or imperfect rendering . . . [It is] harmonized with the supposition that each note will be played as it is written, as it takes this and also the proper time divisions to complete the sense intended.'

But the valuable tension with European rules was well advanced in

American black music. Controversial in its day, and seen as a racial threat by some, ragtime encouraged the posing of questions about what American music was and could be. It had made another contribution even as the first rags were being published: ragtime was one of the final ingredients in jazz. Many early jazzmen thought of themselves as ragtimers, and equated the term with improvisation.

While popular musics since the eighteenth century had been written down, with jazz the role of performer as composer was rediscovered. But it would not have developed in the way it did without another invention, already decades old when jazz began: recorded sound.

Thomas A. Edison invented his phonograph in 1877, and before 1900 there was a thriving worldwide record industry. (The greed and constant litigation characteristic of the industry were also present from the beginning.) The 'phonograph parlour' was the beginning of the penny arcade, and the ancestor of today's amusement parlours with their computerized games, while many of the songs mentioned in this chapter and in the last one made million-selling hit records during the acoustic era. Then the invention of electric recording in 1925, along with broadcasting, changed everything again: singers like Bing Crosby and Louis Armstrong did not have to be shouters, like the singers of the coon-song era, but could use the microphone to sing apparently to each individual in the audience or listening at home; this in turn influenced the way composers wrote their songs.

The performing styles of earlier times can only be approximately re-created; thanks to recording, we are more influenced musically by our immediate ancestors than ever before. Yet paradoxically, the worldwide availability of the latest trends also means that the pace of change has been accelerated. The access of African-Americans, hillbillies and other minorities to the recording studio means that never again can the music of the 'common people' be ignored. To use an appropriately modern metaphor, sound recording meant that popular music became a whole new ball game.

5

The Early Years of Jazz

Jazz has been described as the first American art form. It is character-ized by self-expression; the performer is both composer and trouba-dour. Jazz belonged to its performers, and could be developed as their abilities and needs demanded.

The word was also spelled 'jass'. Some think it came from the French *jaser* (to converse, perhaps indiscreetly); attempts to trace the word back to Africa have been inconclusive. It was used in print as early as 1909 in reference to dancing, and in 1913 about US Army musicians who were 'trained on ragtime and "jazz"' (*Oxford English Dictionary*). Clarence Williams claimed to be first to use the word on sheet music around 1915, when he described 'Brown Skin, Who You For?' as 'Jazz Song': 'I don't exactly remember where the words came from, but I heard a lady say it to me when we were playin' some music. "Oh, jazz me, baby," she said.' It certainly had sexual connotations: American slang for the male seminal emission is 'jism' or 'jizz'. Song titles such as 'Jazz Me Blues', 'Jazzin' Babies Blues' were common. The word has been used of any jazz-influenced popular music, from the time of Paul Whiteman, 'King of Jazz', to the 'jazz rock' or 'jazz funk' of recent times, and today has so many connotations that many young musicians will not use it.

The purest origins of jazz are lost in ancient history, but more scholarship is now being done than ever before. We are too much the prisoners of our received knowledge; we are taught that Columbus discovered America, and we get the impression that he discovered that the world is round. But some people believe that the Irish visited North America even before the Vikings, and many educated people knew that the world was round before 1492. There was trade between Africans and South-east Asia as early as 1000 AD, which is thought to be how xylophone-like instruments got to Africa. We are taught that polyphonic music was invented in Europe, but the musical development that took place then was inspired by musics from other places. The moresca, an African fertility dance performed with small bells on the costumes, spread to Europe, where its rhythm is found in Monteverdi's *Orfeo*. Shakespeare referred to 'a Morris for May Day' in *As You Like It*, and the morris dance was revived in England around 1900, probably because the English thought they invented it. Similarly, jazz was not a discovery, but a rediscovery of musical values which in some parts of the world had never been lost.

Samuel A. Floyd, Jr, editor of Chicago's *Black Music Research Journal*, has defined black music as 'that which reflects and expresses essentials of the Afro-American experience in the United States'. To a great extent the mainstream music business had co-opted minstrelsy and ragtime, making fads of these musics with no respect for their black input. But in the case of jazz, helped by recordings and broadcasting, the beauty, honesty and joy in the music belonged to its creators. Airchecks (off-the-air recordings) from the 1930s and 1940s are always of interest since we can hear jazz musicians trying and sometimes failing to get their message across; even the classic Benny Goodman band of the late 1930s, a precise and well-drilled outfit, sounded somehow more exciting on the bandstand than it did in the studio, because it was communicating to a human audience rather than recording a commercial product. And the jam sessions and cutting contests, which have now disappeared, were never as successful as money-spinning enterprises as they were in their original late-night informal atmosphere, where the competition and invention were untrammelled. It is thanks to this aspect of direct communication between musicians and their listeners that jazz conquered the world, and remains at the root of twentieth-century popular music.

Jazz has evolved, as any art form must, encountering resistance at every step of the way. But it is not true that it was not taken seriously in the USA; perceptive writing on the subject began there in the 1920s. Conspiracy theories about the suppression of jazz were once spread by the American far left, which tried to co-opt jazz (as it did folk music) as a music of the oppressed for political reasons, following a decision by the Communist Internationale to define jazz

as a proletarian music in 1928. It was already too late for that
nonsense, and in any case the so-called socialist countries then
disapproved of jazz for decades on the grounds that it was an
example of western decadence. Great black jazz men and women did
not receive the recognition or the money they deserved because of
racism, but by the time the music reached Chicago white businessmen
were recording the musicians and singers and hiring them to perform
for enthusiastic white audiences. The Melrose brothers, Walter and
Lester, ran a music store in Chicago and were involved in jazz and
blues in that city at an early stage; they became powerful music
publishers as a result, and copyrighted many of the early compositions. The Lincoln Gardens, where King Oliver's Creole Jazz Band
played in the early 1920s, was visited by the best white dance band
musicians, who knew where the good music was, while white kids
(Chicago jazzmen of the next generation) sat on the kerb outside
because they were too young to get in. When we were growing up,
we Americans were taught that Europeans appreciated our music
more than we did, while we took it for granted; Europeans were first
to compile discographies. We could take it for granted because it was
so popular in America.

It is true that the white entrepreneurs often tried to water down
the music, yet it survived and remained honest, becoming popular
and influential around the world. But it is also true that most
Americans hear little or no jazz today, because broadcasting and
major record labels in the USA have been turned over entirely to
accountants, who are interested only in easy money.

There have been countless fine white jazz musicians, but the great
innovators (advancing the music's stylistic frontier) were almost all
black, a situation that may now be becoming an historical one: jazz,
or 'improvised music', or just 'the music', now has so many streams
that it has become a repertory music and a viable international genre.
Yet for me at least, in the 1990s the essence of it still comes from
African-Americans.

Jazz quickly spread all over America, but New Orleans was the
most important incubator because of its location. Ragtime and the
call-and-response pattern of work songs were vital ingredients.
African-Americans had retained an astonishing amount of their Afri-

can heritage for generations, mainly because slaves had not been allowed to take part in American culture. But Louisiana slave-owners, who were French-speaking Catholics rather than Anglo-Saxon Protestants, did not try to forbid slaves to play music and dance as strictly as owners in other areas did. New Orleans was a seaport, so that influences came in from the Caribbean, and it had an easier racial atmosphere than the rest of the South, at least until the First World War. And while every town in the USA had a brass band, New Orleans had them in every neighbourhood.

It has long since become a cliché that jazz bands played hymns for funerals on the way to the graveyard, and on the way back celebrated the life of the departed, with tunes such as 'Oh, Didn't He Ramble' and 'When the Saints Go Marching In'. Just as important was the New Orleans 'second line'. The mourners were joined by anybody who happened to be nearby; they followed the band down the road, marching and dancing along and enjoying the music. The second line is still important in New Orleans clubs today, as the dancers and ringside fans have been important in the whole history of the music: the communication extends beyond mere entertainment.

The blues (like the other American rural music, now called country music) began as a folk music, but jazz was never folk music. From the beginning there was a formal content. New Orleans clarinettist Paul 'Polo' Barnes said to British journalist Max Jones in 1973, 'You see, in ragtime music they had books and . . . you just had to read that music, and when you read it you were reading another man's idea . . . We played ragtime, but we couldn't read. And we played a different ragtime from those reading musicians who actually played it. We put our own version in there.' But Barnes also said that Buddy Bolden, one of the first jazzmen, played 'the way he feel the music go. So traditional jazz is really that: you play your feelings.' There was also a difference between the better-off Creoles and the 'uptown' blacks who had recently been slaves. Clarinettist Albert Nicholas was a Creole, from a musical family, and there were musical instruments at home; he knew Louis Armstrong when they were children, but Louis came from a much harder background. The Creole and uptown players 'all played together in the brass bands . . . Those were mixed bands, Creole and uptown. In a brass band they were solid.' But the

Creoles also had their own dance bands, 'and your uptown . . . sounded a little different, more gut-bucket'. The musical influence was two-way: the self-taught musician wanted to learn to play 'straight', while musicians in marching and concert bands were proud of their ability to read and to play either straight or 'ragtime', using crying tones, slurred notes and so forth. The early jazz standard 'Fidgety Feet' was a syncopated march.

Alderman Joseph Story set aside a neighbourhood for brothels and gambling in 1897, known as the District, or Storyville; but at the beginning of the First World War Storyville was closed by order of the US Navy. While pianists found their work in bars and brothels, and bands played mostly at picnics, funerals and in the street, musicians also worked in dance halls and on riverboats. The closure of Storyville accelerated travel to the West Coast and especially up the Mississippi to Chicago, and thence to New York City. There is nothing intrinsically wrong with the 'up the river from New Orleans' version of jazz history, as long as it is understood that jazz was being played all over the country. New Orleans was where many of the best musicians came from, and they followed the work.

The most famous riverboat bandleader was Fate Marable, born in Kentucky. He played piano and calliope, and first worked on a boat at the age of seventeen with a white violinist (Emil Flindt, who wrote 'The Waltz You Saved for Me'). Marable, who was not a jazzman, formed his own band in 1917 and worked for the Streckfus line out of St Louis until 1940. He made only one recording, in 1924, which is said to be terrible. But no leader ever hired more talent: the list of sidemen who played with Marable begins with Henry 'Red' Allen, Louis Armstrong, Jimmy Blanton and Earl Bostic and continues through the alphabet. Young people who heard the music up and down the river were impressed; pianist Jess Stacy remembered hearing a Marable band with Armstrong, Baby Dodds and Johnny Dodds.

Pianist and vocalist Tony Jackson, who wrote 'Pretty Baby', and cornettist and bandleader Charles 'Buddy' Bolden probably formed links between ragtime and jazz; neither ever recorded. Bolden was renowned for his tone and his strength – it was said he could be heard clear across Lake Pontchartrain – but he was committed to a hospital in 1907 and never emerged again. Cornettist Freddie Keppard took his Original Creole Orchestra to California in 1914 and caused a sensation, playing a new ragtime music called 'jass', a 'white-tie, all-musical act, with neither blackface minstrel clowning, nor even verbal comedy', according to Rudi Blesh. Keppard's band appeared in Chicago in 1915, as did Tom Brown's Band from Dixieland, called a jazz band at a time when any new, lively dance music was already known as jazz. There is a story that the local musicians' union, which resented the competition of out-of-town outfits like Brown's, spread the word that it was nothing but a 'jazz' band, and that this backfired and helped Brown's business. Keppard was allegedly offered a chance to record for Victor late in 1916, but turned it down, afraid that other people would steal his material; he recorded only once as a leader, in Chicago in 1926. The excellent trumpeter Doc Cheatham said Keppard sounded like 'a military trumpeter playing jazz'.

Early jazz history was confused by the fact that the first jazz recordings were made by the Original Dixieland Jazz Band, a white band from New Orleans that won great acclaim at Reisenweber's Restaurant in New York. Cornettist Nick LaRocca, clarinettist Larry Shields, trombonist Eddie Edwards, drummer Tony Sbarbaro and pianist Henry Ragas recorded Keppard's 'Livery Stable Blues' early in 1917 for Victor; they also recorded for Columbia and made obsolescent vertical-cut records for Aeolian Vocalion the same year, but most of their recordings were for Victor. They later caused the same sensation in London, with a slightly different personnel. The recordings were regarded as novelties, and did much to establish the public's view of jazz as a noisy party music. LaRocca copyrighted 'Tiger Rag' (their biggest hit), 'Fidgety Feet' and other New Orleans classics, and in an interview with Leonard Feather in 1936 claimed that white musicians had invented jazz and taught it to the blacks. By then the whole world knew better than that.

Spikes' Seven Pods of Pepper, with Edward 'Kid' Ory on trombone and cornet player Thomas 'Papa Mutt' Carey, recorded in Los Angeles in 1922, but the New Orleans style was best captured by King Oliver's Creole Jazz Band in 1923. More than two dozen sides were made in Chicago and Richmond, Indiana, on the Gennett, Paramount, Okeh and Columbia labels by a New Orleans line-up.

The front line of the band included Oliver on lead cornet, Louis

Armstrong on second cornet, Johnny Dodds on clarinet and Honoré Dutrey on trombone; Lillian Hardin played piano, Bill Johnson, Arthur 'Bud' Scott or Johnny St Cyr banjo and Warren 'Baby' Dodds drums. Stump Evans on C-melody saxophone or Charlie Jackson on bass saxophone were added on some tracks. The cornets carried the melody, the clarinet added a filigree commentary on it and the trombone played a bass line or 'tailgate' style (so called because in New Orleans the trombonist sat on the tailgate of the wagon so as not to knock anyone's hat off with his slide). In fact, this was collective improvisation, with everybody listening to everybody else: an improvised counterpoint. The acoustic recording process restricted Baby Dodds to using woodblocks instead of his drum kit, but the records still sound surprisingly good, and they preserved the style in the nick of time. The band swings madly or lopes easily, sometimes seeming to do both at once.

'Dipper Mouth Blues' and 'High Society Rag' sold well enough to have been national hits, had charts existed at the time. Oliver would allow only a bucket of sugared water on the bandstand for refreshment, hence 'Dipper Mouth Blues' (which became 'Sugar Foot Stomp' a few years later). In 'High Society Rag' the harmony between Johnny Dodds's clarinet and the leader's cornet is exquisitely beautiful, harmony in jazz always being coloured by the personal sound of each musician; and Dodds gives us the famous solo on this tune that was originated by Alphonse Picou. In performance and on record Oliver and Armstrong astonished everyone by playing breaks together in harmony that were apparently improvised; years later Armstrong revealed that Oliver would show him the fingering secretly just before each break.

The concatenation of historical events often poses mysteries. Why did recorded sound come along just in time to capture a great American musician like Oliver, one of the fathers of popular music? Or perhaps there is an illusion here, created by recorded sound itself. We will never know what Frank Johnson's music sounded like (mentioned in chapter 2), because he lived before the phonograph; but, according to contemporary newspaper accounts, his bugle, in a piece called 'Philadelphia Fireman's Quadrille' of around 1840, could be heard to cry 'Fire! Fire!' Joe 'King' Oliver succeeded Bolden as the leading cornettist in New Orleans, and the vocal-like colour that emerged from his horn was one of the things that made it so deeply moving. His playing was marked by subtlety, unlike that of the 'ragtimers' or of contemporary white musicians, and its dignified melancholy reminds us of the importance of the blues in jazz. Oliver was the principal influence on Louis Armstrong, and the way he growled through his cornet was immediately influential: trumpeter Bill Coleman heard a musician called Nassau doing it in Cincinnati in 1923; Bubber Miley did it in the Duke Ellington band a few years later, and it became an element in that band's sound, and hence in all of jazz.

Oliver played in Chicago and on the West Coast, and then returned to Chicago, where he led the band at the Lincoln Gardens that made the classic recordings. He recorded two duets with Jelly Roll Morton in 1924, which are not considered very successful; from 1926 to 1928 he recorded around forty sides (including alternative takes) with the Dixie Syncopators, a band whose personnel often changed. The line-up included Ory on trombone, Buster Bailey, Omer Simeon and Albert Nicholas on reeds, Luis Russell on piano and Lawson Buford on tuba. By now the original style was already mutating: more of the music was arranged and there was more solo space and less counterpoint. In my opinion Dixie Syncopator recordings such as 'Farewell Blues', 'Every Tub', 'Willie the Weeper' and 'Someday Sweetheart' are among the most heartbreakingly beautiful ever made, in any genre, by anybody.

In 1927 Oliver moved to New York, and his career began to decline. His music was already being regarded as old-fashioned; he made many fine recordings for Victor from 1929 to 1931, but could not play on them all because his teeth were going bad. His nephew Dave Nelson played trumpet on some of them, and many other good sidemen were included. Oliver later ran a fruit stall and worked in a pool room, while collectors were already paying good prices for second-hand copies of his records; if he had lived a little longer he would have been lionized by the revivalists who re-created the New Orleans style just before the Second World War.

The Red Onion Jazz Babies, a pick-up group put together for recordings only, recorded in 1924. It included reedmen Bailey and

Sidney Bechet, and vocals by Alberta Hunter; the recordings are probably the best example we have of how the bands played in the bars and dance halls of New Orleans. In 1923 Clarence Williams's Blue Five made similar classics with his wife Eva Taylor singing, Armstrong, Bechet, Charlie Irvis on trombone and Williams instead of Lil Hardin on piano.

Clarence Williams was part Creole Negro and part Choctaw Indian; he grew up in a hotel in Louisiana and ran away from home to join a minstrel show. Inspired by Tony Jackson, he ran a cabaret in New Orleans in 1913, began writing songs and formed a publishing company. He went to Chicago and then New York, where he was the first New Orleans musician to influence others there, and the first publisher to help black musicians. He organized and participated in countless recording sessions, helping the careers of scores of black jazzmen and blues singers. He wrote words and/or music for 'Baby Won't You Please Come Home', 'Royal Garden Blues' and other jazz classics.

As Ben Harney claimed to have invented ragtime for commercial reasons, so Jelly Roll Morton claimed to have invented jazz in 1902 (he gave various dates), but with somewhat more justification: a comparison of his recording of Joplin's 'Original Rags' (made in 1939) with Joplin's sheet music provides a good illustration of the difference between the genres. Anybody can practise for years and learn to play Scott Joplin well, but nobody else sounded like Jelly Roll. He must have been one of the first to play the new style.

He was born Ferdinand Joseph Lemott in New Orleans in 1890, but he always gave a birthdate of 1885 to add weight to his claim to have invented jazz. His Creole family (of Haitian descent) had never been slaves; his godmother disowned him when she discovered he was playing piano in brothels. One of the most flamboyant characters in the history of jazz (not to say big-mouthed – the urbane Duke Ellington despised him), he got by as an entertainer, a pimp, a gambler and a pool shark. He recorded piano solos and with small bands during the acoustic era; his several sides with the white New Orleans Rhythm Kings in Chicago in 1923 were probably made at the first interracial recording session. The piano solos include the first recording of 'King Porter Stomp', still a hit twenty years later in the Swing Era. Tracks such as 'New Orleans Joys' (also known as 'New Orleans Blues'), 'Tia Juana' and 'Mamanita' are the first to show what he called his 'Spanish tinge': a habanera rhythm, which is ingrained in New Orleans music, and played over a rock-steady beat results in a tension still to be heard in New Orleans rhythm and blues decades later.

From 1926 to 1930 Morton made nearly ninety sides (including alternative takes) with a studio group of varying personnel, called Jelly Roll Morton and his Red Hot Peppers. He was not only a fine pianist but an incomparable composer and arranger in his neo-New Orleans style; as well as occasional corny humour, virtually all of these recordings present much finely judged and beautiful music. 'Black Bottom Stomp', 'Original Jelly Roll Blues' and 'Grandpa's Spells' are all from 1927 and all with Ory; 'Wolverine Blues' was made the next year with Johnny Dodds. One high point was a 1928 session that produced 'Boogaboo', 'Georgia Swing' and others, including a trio 'Shreveport Stomp', with Simeon's beautiful, liquid clarinet and Tommy Benford on drums, and a quartet 'Mournful Serenade', with Simeon, Benford and Geechie Fields on trombone. During the Peppers period Morton, like Oliver, moved to New York and began to decline. He recorded again in 1939: a dozen fine piano solos including his version of Joplin's 'Original Rags'. Among his best-known recordings are those made for Alan Lomax at the Library of Congress; his playing, singing and talking are a priceless source of information about early jazz.

Sidney Bechet was a New Orleans clarinettist of unsurpassed lyricism, and had a famous wide vibrato. His recording career was peripatetic – he had a volatile temperament and never stayed long in one place – but he was nevertheless influential. He played with Freddie Keppard as a child and later with Clarence Williams, plugging songs. He went to New York, where in 1919 he joined the Southern Syncopated Orchestra, led by Will Marion Cook, and travelled with it to Europe. Swiss conductor Ernest Ansermet heard this band and wrote: 'I wish to declaim the name of this artist of genius, because for my part, I will never forget it: it is Sidney Bechet ... who is so happy that you like what he does, but does not know how to speak of his art, save to say that he is following his "own way" ... perhaps

the great road that the whole world will be swept along tomorrow.'
Bechet bought a straight soprano saxophone in London and thence-
forth concentrated on that difficult instrument, the only jazzman to
do so until Steve Lacy and John Coltrane, decades later; he continued
to play clarinet, especially on recordings.

Bechet performed with Williams in 1923, Armstrong in 1924 and
briefly with Duke Ellington in 1925 in New York; he gave lessons to
young Johnny Hodges, and played with Oliver in 1926. He led the
New Orleans Feetwarmers with trumpeter Tommy Ladnier and
recorded for Victor in 1932, but times were so bad that he and
Ladnier ran a tailor's shop. He recorded with various small groups
for Victor until 1941 and for Blue Note in 1939; the Port of Harlem
Jazzmen session included 'Summertime' and 'Blues for Tommy'. He
moved to France in 1949, where he became a national hero. His most
famous tunes were 'Les Oignons', recorded in France in 1949 with
bandleader and clarinettist Claude Luter, and 'Petite Fleur', which
was an international pop hit for a British trad band in 1959.

The musician who set the music world on its ear as the first and
greatest soloist in recorded jazz, later becoming one of the best-
known and best-loved entertainers in the world, was Louis Armstrong
(known as Dippermouth, then Satchelmouth, then Satchmo, but
always Pops). He came from utter poverty in New Orleans. Early in
1913 Armstrong was sent to the Home for Colored Waifs after firing
a pistol in the air on the previous Fourth of July; there he learned to
play the cornet. He played in Marable's riverboat band, and back
in New Orleans replaced Oliver in Kid Ory's band. Oliver sent for
him and in mid-1922 he went to Chicago to play second cornet in
Oliver's band.

Louis gave different versions of his arrival in Chicago: there was
no one to meet him, and he took a cab to the Lincoln Gardens,
where Oliver was playing; or Oliver had tipped off a porter, who
took Louis to the right place. It seems to be agreed that he was a
'hick' when he got off the train, and looked it. Having been a
hungry child, he loved to eat; he was overweight and all his clothes
were too small. Furthermore, he was in awe of Oliver, and lacked
self-confidence; but he was always a first-rate musician. Oliver's band
did not need two cornets. The music it played was beautiful, but

stylized, and Louis stayed in the background because that is what the music demanded. When he can be heard on the recordings of the Creole Jazz Band, it is clear that he is already doing something that the others are not: he is swinging more freely. The earliest jazz musicians were still ragtimers, inventing a style that came out of the brass band tradition, while the three most important and influential of the New Orleans natives, Morton, Bechet and Armstrong, were deeply familiar with the blues, and with the music of the brothels and dance halls. They took jazz to its first peak of creative freedom.

Lil Hardin, the band's pianist, became Armstrong's second wife. She was a formally trained musician from Memphis, Tennessee, and urged Louis to think of himself as a soloist. He left Oliver in 1924, and was hired to play third trumpet by Fletcher Henderson, who remembered him from a 1922 tour to New Orleans with Ethel Waters. Henderson's orchestra was then becoming a hot dance band in New York, and Louis set it alight. He was still a hick, wearing high-button shoes, and he reported later that the drummer Kaiser Marshall said to him at a rehearsal, 'Man, you come up here with them policeman shoes on?' On one occasion when he played something too loud, he had his own opportunity to make the band laugh: upon being reminded that the marking in the music was 'pp', he is supposed to have said, 'Oh, I thought that meant "pound plenty"!' But nobody laughed at his solos, which were revelatory: music in New York was transformed. Henderson's men drank too much, and sometimes played sloppily, Louis later said. After a year he left.

He returned to Chicago and worked with Lil in her band, but in November 1925 he began making his famous Hot Five and Hot Seven recordings with studio groups, using the new electrical process. It is hard for us now to imagine how these records must have astonished musicians hearing them for the first time.

The Hot Five included Ory, Johnny Dodds, Johnny St Cyr on banjo and Lil on piano. They made thirty-three sides in about two years. Maturing as an artist and leaving behind the collective improvisation of the New Orleans style, Louis began doing it all himself: with complete mastery he demonstrated all the self-expression possible in jazz at the time. His tone was clear, accurate and beautiful; he was the first to improvise freely in the lower registers of the instrument;

his technical skill allowed him to place notes as he wished, bending a note or placing emphasis within it, and playing around the beat. Swing was part of the essence of jazz from the beginning, but Louis fully understood the importance of playing free from the ground beat. He could swing the entire group himself. As an improvising melodist, he went further than anyone in recomposing a song. He did not invent the stop-time chorus (in which the band just marks the time each one or two bars, leaving the soloist to do as he wishes), but he was the first to take complete advantage of that freedom. His solos were perfectly constructed, yet obviously improvised in their ebullience. He sang the same way: he seemed to have invented scat singing (wordless, improvised, swinging nonsense syllables) since he did that too with such abandon. Among the Hot Five's best recordings were 'Cornet Chop Suey' (whose roots lay in the virtuoso solos that were always a part of brass band music), 'Heebie Jeebies' (for the scat singing) and 'Hotter Than That' (for a fine series of solo choruses).

During the Hot Five series he changed permanently from cornet to the brighter trumpet. For the Hot Seven recordings Pete Briggs (tuba) and Baby Dodds (drums) were added and John Thomas replaced Ory on trombone. 'Wild Man Blues', 'Gully Low Blues' and 'Potato Head Blues' are mostly solos, the last famous for its stop-time chorus. The members of the Hot Seven were drawn from Carroll Dickerson's Savoyagers, who recorded 'Savoyagers' Stomp'; 'Chicago Breakdown' was made by Louis Armstrong and his Stompers, a group that worked in a Chicago café: these ten- or eleven-piece bands included Earl Hines on piano.

The Savoy Ballroom Five made eighteen sides in 1928, with no New Orleans players, except Louis and Zutty Singleton on drums, but with Hines, one of the few musicians Armstrong ever worked with who was his equal. Recording director Tommy Rockwell had learned how to use electrical recording, holding Singleton's snare drum above the microphone as he played brushes on the opening bars of 'Muggles'. 'West End Blues' is famous for its perfect architecture and contains the basic elements which would identify some of the best popular music for decades: a well-known introduction, in the nature of an announcement (actually based on phrases Louis had invented while accompanying blues singers), followed by the statement of the theme by the leader and a series of solos, backed harmonically by other members of the band, among them Louis's heartfelt scat singing, seemingly improvised. A classic duet with Hines, 'Weather Bird', shows two very great musicians near their peak.

From 1928 Armstrong fronted larger bands, directed by others, at first the excellent Luis Russell. In his prime at the end of the silent film era he was a top cabaret and theatre entertainer, singing as much as playing and seen as a star by audiences who often cared little about jazz itself. Armstrong frequently played more than a hundred consecutive high notes at the end of hackneyed show-stoppers such as 'Shine' or 'Tiger Rag'; but he always made beautiful recordings. An early example of Lionel Hampton's vibraphone may be heard on 'Memories of You' (1930); in 1931 the hits included a classic version of 'Stardust', as well as 'All of Me', and 'The Peanut Vendor'. 'Body and Soul' (1932) shows Armstrong's beautiful muted trumpet to advantage, while 'Rockin' Chair' was a vocal duet with the song's composer, Hoagy Carmichael. All these were made for Okeh and then Columbia, and are thus the property of Sony today; among his recordings for Victor in late 1932 and 1933 are medleys on an early attempt at a long-playing record. In 1935 he signed with Jack Kapp's new Decca label, with which he stayed for twenty years. On Decca he recorded with the Mills Brothers, Bing Crosby and Ella Fitzgerald; towards the end of that period he was often accompanied by Gordon Jenkins and his studio orchestra.

Armstrong always suffered from insecurity due to racism and the extreme poverty of his youth. He was managed at first by Rockwell, and then by Johnny Collins, a small-time gangster. Sometimes booked 365 nights a year, and never having acquired a proper embouchure, he developed a chronic lip problem. In 1933 he went to Europe, where he was idolized and had a rest. Not content with stealing from Armstrong, Collins abandoned him in London without his passport. Louis had not forgotten Oliver's advice, to find himself a white man who would put his hand on his shoulder and say, 'This is my nigger.' He put his affairs in the hands of Joe Glaser, a playboy who then became a successful booking agent. Glaser was a ruthless businessman, but he understood the value of the property he controlled, and even travelled with the band in the early years. Armstrong began appearing in better films, for example, *Pennies from Heaven* (1936); he made more than fifty altogether, and finally had financial security.

Armstrong's big bands were sometimes not very good, for their only purpose was to back him, and there is some evidence that he did not want to compete with musicians who might be his equal. Jazz fans were disappointed by his emphasis on entertainment, but Louis was grateful to his public and always gave full measure. In a famous remark he said that his favourite band was Guy Lombardo's, his point being that Lombardo's 'sweet' band was reliable and musically impeccable. Armstrong's pop records are charming. As a soloist he continued to innovate long after 1930, too good a musician to stop creating; a 1938 broadcast aircheck with Fats Waller, Bud Freeman, Al Casey, Jack Teagarden and Willmore 'Slick' Jones (Waller's drummer at the time) is priceless for Louis's singing of the introduction to 'Jeepers Creepers' alone.

At the end of the Swing Era in the late 1940s Armstrong gave up the big band and thereafter toured with a small group. We will come back to Louis later, but it is worth noting here that many Americans, on reading his obituaries in 1971, were surprised to discover that he had been one of the most influential musicians of the twentieth century.

Swing can be said to begin with Armstrong. None had such complete mastery as he of the manipulation of time in performance, according to the performer's skill, personality and mood, and the nature of the song or tune. Many other factors might enter the equation, such as how long it had been since the last square meal, or the last fight with the spouse. By the time the Swing or Big Band Era began in 1935 the word 'swing' was in common use; earlier musicians had spoken of 'getting off' or 'taking a Boston', and a swinging ensemble was 'in the groove'. Sometimes it happened, sometimes not: the band had to be in the mood. There are stories about Armstrong or Waller being asked what swing was, and replying, 'If you don't know what it is, don't mess with it', or 'If you gotta ask, you'll never know.' A medium tempo that is easy to dance to is best for swinging, *pace* the popular conception of loud, fast 'killer dillers'.

Blacks were said to have 'natural rhythm', but the truth is more interesting than such racial stereotyping might suggest. To begin with, as we have seen, African-Americans had maintained the aspect of music as a means of social intercourse as well as of self-expression from Africa, aspects that had been played down in European music. Mozart, Beethoven and Chopin were great improvisers, unlike today's concert pianists. Classical music can swing, if everybody is in the groove, but nothing has put more people off classical music than second-rate performances, and a great performance is a matter of genius interpreting the written notes: nowadays there is often not much spontaneity.

Secondly, blacks in America had less to lose from self-expression, while hundreds of years of European Protestantism on top of three thousand years of Aristotelian consciousness had left whites somewhat restrained. Slaves in America were often not allowed to learn to read; dependent upon the spoken word for communication, they were forced to live in the present, which is where you have to be to manipulate time, while whites, on the other hand, felt guilty about the past or anxious about the future. Finally, as we have seen, rhythm is at the centre of African music (and not melody, as in European music). The performer who is swinging is commenting on the beat, which is somewhere else; swing is thus a polyrhythmic phenomenon. One way to describe jazz is to say that in the performer's improvisations the rhythmic element works additional magic on the melodic and the harmonic.

Soon enough, arrangers and composers would learn to write music that would swing, if the right people were playing it and everybody was in the mood. A good comparison is provided by Fletcher Henderson's two recordings of the Fats Waller tune 'Stealin' Apples'. The first, delightful version was made in March 1936, at a session when 'Blue Lou', 'Christopher Columbus' and 'Grand Terrace Swing' were also recorded. The second, eighteen months later, was made by a band with almost completely different personnel, and in a series of sessions that included mostly pop ballads (among them a version of Joyce Kilmer's sentimental poem 'Trees'). The second version is workmanlike, but the band's heart is not in it, and Henderson's piano introduction is unusually stiff even for him.

A more modern example is found in two recordings of Thelonious Monk's 'Hackensack', made in London in 1971. In the second Monk re-enters in the wrong place after Art Blakey's drum solo, intentionally or not, and stays there. The result is recognizably Monk's tune, but sounds like something that could have been invented by a cocktail pianist.

White musicians learned quickly. Jews and Italians were especially prominent among white jazz musicians of the 1920s, while in Britain a considerable number of jazz musicians have been Scottish. Benny Carter, whose European band of the 1930s included Scots, said it was because 'wherever they are, there's happiness'. Before long many white musicians were influencing blacks, and combining technical skill, good tone and harmonic adventurousness. Many years later cornettist Rex Stewart spoke in an interview about the first time he heard Bix Beiderbecke.

Bix, for Pete's sake. You know, I worshipped Louis at that time, tried to walk like him, talk like him, even dress like him. He was God to me, and to all the other cats too. Then, all of a sudden, comes this white boy from out west, playin' stuff all his own. Didn't sound like Louis or anybody else. But just so pretty. And all that *tone* he got. Knocked us all out.

Doc Cheatham put it this way: 'All trumpet players had been playing alike when Bix came along and opened the gate.' Leon Bix Beiderbecke became a distorted legend after his death from alcoholism; a book and a film were loosely based on the life of the 'young man with a horn'. Born in Davenport, Iowa, he began learning piano at the age of three. His brother brought home records such as the Original Dixieland Jazz Band's 'Tiger Rag'; Bix slowed down the turntable so that he could pick out the cornet part on the piano, and soon took up the cornet. He performed in Chicago and on Lake Michigan excursion boats as a teenager, and joined a band called the Wolverines in 1923. He made his first recordings the following year and became the earliest white jazz musician to have a considerable influence on everybody else.

He continued studying piano, and was the first important jazzman to be inspired by contemporary classical music. But in later life he hated to perform as a pianist in public. In the modern harmonies of impressionist composers he heard the same freedom as in jazz, but he would have needed more formal training and more personal discipline than he possessed to develop this. Yet what he did was miraculous. It was with Bix's solos, and the more fully realized composition of Duke Ellington, that jazz began to absorb other influences and put them to work in the late 1920s.

Bix's technique was unorthodox and he never learned to read music well, but his intonation was perfect. He had a faultness ear, a gorgeous tone and so perfect an attack that contemporaries said each note sounded like a chime struck by a mallet. Although he knew little about the blues, he was a lyrical, linear soloist. Unlike Armstrong, he avoided bravura; he experimented harmonically from the start, but, like Armstrong, was a natural melodist. He was among the first to play solo for thirty-two bars using logically compatible phrases, recomposing as he went along rather than improvising close to the melody, and building on phrases he had just invented in a previous bar. James Lincoln Collier described 'a humility in his playing, a humbleness toward his art. Always he is saying, I do not wish to intrude, but let me show you this marvel. And marvels they were.'

The Wolverines were not a great band and their recordings were acoustic; Bix's sound has been likened to piercing a curtain of fudge. Yet in good modern transfers the records are not all that bad. On Hoagy Carmichael's recommendation the band played at Indiana University, and it became a sensation on campuses. Bix was hired by bandleader Jean Goldkette, and spent the peak of his career with Paul Whiteman; these were the best white bands of the period. Whiteman was one of the biggest recording stars of the century and his band was admired by everybody in show business, yet even there Bix's marvels stood out.

The story that Bix was frustrated by his position in that band is not true. He was at the top of his trade and knew it, and Whiteman kept a chair open for him until the end. Bix's problem was his alcoholism (he had his first breakdown with delirium tremens in 1929), together with his German Protestant background. He sent copies of his records to his family, but they did not even open the parcels. (The same thing happened decades later to Ornette Coleman.)

Bix earned the respect and admiration of his peers, and increasingly of the public, but he never had confidence in himself or in the value of his work.

Beiderbecke's best recordings were made with small groups from 1927, led by reedman Frankie Trumbauer, which often included Eddie Lang, Jimmy Dorsey and Adrian Rollini on bass saxophone. The most famous are 'I'm Comin' Virginia' and 'Singin' the Blues'; the latter especially was memorized and played by white and black bands. Bix's impressionistic compositions include 'In the Dark', 'Candlelight', 'Flashes' and 'In a Mist', the last of which he recorded as a piano solo.

His admiration of Armstrong was mutual. Louis allegedly lent Bix his horn so that he could sit in, a thing he rarely, if ever, did for anyone else. Bix influenced Red Nichols and Bobby Hackett, who influenced Roy Eldridge and Miles Davis respectively; Eldridge was in turn the greatest influence on Dizzy Gillespie. There are links between Bix's advanced harmonic thinking and that of Charlie Parker, but the beauty of his tone and his phrasing can stand alone. Carmichael's songs 'Stardust' and 'Skylark' may have been based on Bix's solos; Carmichael carried Bix's mouthpiece in his pocket for the rest of his life.

Other young white players, particularly in Chicago, imitated their black heroes: Oliver, Armstrong and clarinettists Baby Dodds and Jimmie Noone. The late show at the Lincoln Gardens would be attended by the musicians whose own gigs had finished; the teenagers sat on the pavement outside. Bud Freeman wrote many years later that the bouncer at the door would say, 'Well, it looks like the little white boys is out here to get their music lessons.' The white boys soon invented a free-wheeling small-group Chicago style, with solos between orchestral, ragtime-like ensemble passages; there was usually an 'explosion' of sound at a climax just before the repetition of the melody, and a 'clambake' ride-out at the end. With a band of soloists, collective improvisation as it had been practised in New Orleans receded into the past.

The Chicagoans include the Austin High Gang, so called because some attended Austin High School: Frank Teschemacher on reeds, guitarist Dick McPartland, trumpeter Jimmy McPartland and Bud

Freeman on tenor saxophone. Other Chicagoans were singer and kazoo player Red McKenzie, pianist Joe Sullivan, banjoist and guitarist Eddie Condon, Gene Krupa and Benny Goodman. The style may be heard on recordings as early as 1927 by McKenzie and Condon's Chicagoans. Also usually counted as Chicagoans are clarinettist Pee Wee Russell, trumpeters Wingy Manone and Muggsy Spanier and a third Melrose brother, Frank, a pianist who recorded with Manone and Freeman, among others.

The Friar's Society Orchestra became the New Orleans Rhythm Kings and began recording in 1922. This white group included cornet player Paul Mares, clarinettist Leon Roppolo (whose name is often wrongly spelled Rappolo), reedman Eddie Miller (later with Bob Crosby's band), trombonist George Brunis and drummer Ben Pollack (later an important bandleader).

Pee Wee Russell and Bud Freeman were as innovative on their instruments as Beiderbecke on his, playing pretty, thoughtful and original solos while eschewing bravura. Freeman was the first tenor saxophonist to take a fundamentally different direction from Coleman Hawkins, while Russell was an original to the end of his life. Their 'sweet' jazz may have stemmed from the use of the microphone in that they did not have to play loud to be heard in their small groups; their ability to construct solos was always underrated. Freeman's recording sessions with his Summa Cum Laude Orchestra (an octet, with Russell, Max Kaminsky and Eddie Condon) in 1939 probably represent the high point of the Chicago style, especially Freeman's *tour de force* in 'The Eel'. Muggsy Spanier's Ragtime Band (also an octet, one of whose members was George Brunis, not a great trombonist but a fine accompanist in this style) made sixteen sides the same year, playing with integrity the tunes they had all loved in their youth, including 'Livery Stable Blues', and Spanier's 'Relaxin' at the Touro', a souvenir of his stay in a New Orleans hospital. But that was the end of the era. In later years many of these musicians were submerged by their dixieland identities, making a living playing for middle-aged businessmen in cocktail lounges. Even when record companies in the LP era occasionally wanted them, it was only to re-record the dixieland chestnuts.

In the mid-1920s on the East Coast cornettist Red Nichols and trombonist Miff Mole came from Paul Whiteman's band to play in each other's small groups, under such names as the Charleston Stompers, Red and Miff's Stompers, Miff Mole and his Molers, Red Nichols and his Five Pennies and so on. Their playing was less rowdy than the Chicagoans, and has been described as a New York style. Nichols was inspired by Beiderbecke, but was thought by some to play and compose in an innovative open-chord way of his own. Mole was one of the first to liberate the trombone from the New Orleans tailgate style. Nichols and Mole split up in 1928 and Nichols's influence was short-lived; in later years he was popular with tourists visiting Las Vegas.

Eddie Lang was born Salvatore Massaro, the son of a banjo- and guitar-maker in south Philadelphia. He invented jazz guitar playing, playing rhythm and solos in an advanced style: he played four-to-the-bar rhythm, often with a newly created chord on each stroke. His solo work sparkled with innovation, and he acquired a deep and genuine feeling for the blues. On some of his duets with black guitarist Lonnie Johnson he was billed as Blind Willie Dunn. He was Bing Crosby's favourite accompanist, and his unexpected early death (from an embolism while having his tonsils out) was as great a loss as that of Bix.

Jack Teagarden came from Texas. He began learning trombone as a child, and developed a method of playing all the notes without the long positions, using his lips rather than the slide. He had perfect pitch and read music well from an early age. He could play as fast as a valve-trombone player, and made the difficult sound easy; he combined his technical proficiency with a deep southern understanding of the blues, so that his rapid execution did not contradict the impression he gave of being completely relaxed. He sang the same way, in a warm baritone drawl. When he reached New York in 1927, he was fully-fledged and caused a sensation. He ended Mole's brief dominance of eastern trombone playing and quickly became close friends with Coleman Hawkins and trombonist Jimmy Harrison, both of whom were in Henderson's band. It is interesting to speculate how different Teagarden's career would have been if he had not been white: would he have joined Henderson? He played on more than a hundred recordings in 1929, but none at all in 1932. In

1933 he signed a five-year contract with Paul Whiteman, and his talent was largely hidden, except in his freelance work. He led a big band in 1938–9 but went broke, and the rest of his recording career was peripatetic. He never played or sang a note that was not instantly recognizable.

Meanwhile, on the East Coast, Eubie Blake, Luckey Roberts, Willie 'the Lion' Smith, James P. Johnson and others had been playing stride piano, a two-fisted style built on ragtime that emphasized a strong beat with tenths in the bass. Territory bands played all over the country, and larger dance bands were learning to swing. The Swing Era itself was not far off.

6

Broadway and the Golden Age of Songwriting

If the great songs of the first Tin Pan Alley period (*c.* 1900–10) represent the peak of the popular songwriting that began in the English pleasure gardens of the eighteenth century, they also represent the end of it. These were parlour songs, to be played and sung at home as well as in public music halls. They consisted of any number of verses that told a story, and a chorus that summed up the story, or commented on it, and with which everybody was supposed to sing along.

Typical of these songs was 'Waltz Me Around Again, Willie' (1906), by Will Cobb and Ren Shields:

> Willie Fitzgibbons who used to sell ribbons,
> And stood up all day on his feet,
> Grew very spooney on Madeline Mooney,
> Who'd rather be dancing than eat.
> Each evening she'd tag him, to some dance hall drag him,
> And when the band started to play,
> She'd up like a silly and grab tired Willie,
> Steer him on the floor and she'd say:
>
> > 'Waltz me around again, Willie,
> > Around, around, around;
> > The music is dreamy, it's peaches and creamy,
> > Oh! don't let my feet touch the ground.
> > I feel just like a ship on an ocean of joy,
> > I just want to holler out loud "Ship Ahoy!"
> > Oh! waltz me around again, Willie,
> > Around, around, around.'

In another verse we learn that Willie De Vere is a dry-goods cashier who sits all day; his doctor tells him to get more exercise, so Willie Fitzgibbons hands him over to Madeline. This story-song construction survives in children's songs, campfire songs and folksongs; but the coon song, inspired by minstrelsy and ragtime, began to demonstrate its rhythmic freedom in its construction, adopting the rhythms as well as the words of the idiomatic slang of the street.

Shelton Brooks's 'Some of These Days', like 'Waltz Me Around Again, Willie', is from 1906, but it is deeply influenced by the earlier coon songs. It has rather ordinary verses, about two sweethearts in a country town who, 'the neighbors say, lived happily the whole day long, until one day he told her he must go away'; later it has a happy ending. But the verse has been ignored (as in Jimmy Rushing's driving recording from the mid-1950s, backed by a Buck Clayton big band), because in the meantime the chorus became an anthem of the new century:

> Some of these days, you'll miss me honey,
> Some of these days, you'll feel so lonely.
> You'll miss my hugging, you'll miss my kissing,
> You'll miss me honey, when you're away . . .

The words look a bit flat on the page, but this is a new kind of combination of words and melody. Although it is still about disappointed love, it is a warning, not a lament, conveying the sort of bravery that people have to find in their everyday lives, and a pride that is dented but not daunted.

Another, later pop song (from 1918) is 'After You've Gone', by the black songwriters Turner Layton and Henry Creamer:

> Now listen honey while I say
> How can you tell me that you're going away?
> Don't say that we must part,
> Don't break my achin' heart.
>
> You know I love you true for many years,
> Love you night and day,
> How can you leave me? Can't you see my tears?
> So listen while I say:

> After you've gone and left me cryin',
> After you've gone – there's no denyin' –
> You'll feel blue, you'll feel sad,
> You'll miss the dearest pal you ever had.
> There'll come a time, now don't forget it,
> There'll come a time when you'll regret it,
> Some day when you grow lonely
> Your heart will break like mine
> And you'll want me only,
> After you've gone, after you've gone away.

Creamer and Layton also wrote songs for musical shows. Layton teamed up with Clarence Johnstone when they both worked for W. C. Handy in 1923, and the following year worked in London. As Layton and Johnstone, with just a piano and a repertory of over a thousand songs, they were one of the most successful acts in British variety until 1935, when Johnstone was named co-respondent in a scandalous divorce suit. Creamer, from Virginia, also co-wrote 'Dear Old Southland', 'Way Down Yonder in New Orleans' and 'If I Could Be With You One Hour Tonight', more songs which move further away from the barroom atmosphere of the coon song, but are filled with American demotic speech, and certainly have nothing of the parlour sweetness of the 'Sweet Sixteen' genre.

Creamer and Layton's 'After You've Gone' is an advance on 'Some of These Days', and an even better example of the new age of songwriting. The verse is more powerful and sophisticated, and less sentimental, but again it was the chorus that became famous. In 1937 Lionel Hampton skipped the verse and sang an affecting straight version of the chorus (backed by Art Rollini's tenor saxophone) before jazzing up the tune at double time, as if to say, 'Take that, baby!' But it is Bessie Smith's 1927 recording that is truly outstanding. In the chorus it seems that 'Some day when you grow lonely' is not going to fit, but she phrases it across the bar lines, and by contrast makes the single syllables in the next phrase, 'Your heart will break like mine', land like hammer blows. She also sings the verse, and her treatment of words like 'heart' and 'tears' is one of the keys to the interpretation of twentieth-century songs. Paradoxically, it was the ordinariness of powerfully rhyming phrases, married to a memorable tune, that lent the song to imaginative interpretation.

Although there may be several verses or stanzas in a modern song, it is all of a piece. An individual song may be technically divisible into sections such as introduction, verse, chorus, release or bridge and so forth, but modern songs are more integrated. Perhaps partly because of the explosion of a national entertainment business, a nationwide audience now had songs that referred more directly to the emotions, rather than telling a story. A new phenomenon was the frequency with which a song came to be identified with a certain artist (as 'Some of These Days' with Sophie Tucker), so that the interpretation could be almost as important as the song itself.

An increasingly sophisticated audience for these new songs was not foreseen, but as happens again and again in popular music, that part of the audience that delights in something new can drag along the rest. On the other hand, the new popular song was partly a triumph of the masses over the 'Sunday-school circuit', as Keith and Albee's national network was called. The success of variety in the late 1880s depended upon keeping it respectable, but the stars of the early twentieth century were such big attractions that they could give the audience a slice of real life. Instead of complaining that she was 'Only a Bird in a Gilded Cage', Eva Tanguay assured fans that 'It's All been Done Before, But Not the Way I Do It'. When Tucker sang 'You're gonna miss me, honey', what the errant male was 'gonna miss' was not the sight of her looking sweet upon the seat of a bicycle built for two.

A song tended to have a short introduction which was certainly sung on stage, but was later frequently dropped as gramophone records (with their limited playing time) took over from sheet music. From the ordinary listener's point of view, this was a vestigial verse, setting the scene for the chorus, which now has several stanzas and tells the story, but the introduction was often musically important. Everybody knows the tune of 'Love Me or Leave Me' (1928), by Gus Kahn and Walter Donaldson; the hit recording by Ruth Etting includes the introduction, making the subsequent drop of nearly an octave between the words 'or' and 'leave' far more dramatic, as well as lending it musical sense. Billie Holiday in her 1941 recording also sings the introduction, but then ignores the drop in the first line of the chorus, improvises across it and restores it in the next line, 'You won't believe me': it is even more dramatic because we've had to wait for it.

Rodgers and Hammerstein's 'Hello Young Lovers' (from *The King and I*, 1951) needs its lovely introduction to justify its syrupy quality (and is a good example of a true show song, which doesn't work so well outside its intended context). Hoagy Carmichael's 'Stardust' has a beautiful introduction, which was omitted on all those smoochy dance band versions that were hits around 1940 (especially those of Glenn Miller and Artie Shaw). When Nat 'King' Cole restored it on an album track in 1957, the delightful shock took a 45 EP high in the *Billboard* singles chart, while Frank Sinatra is said to have recorded a version using just the introduction.

In *American Popular Song: The Great Innovators 1900–1950* Alec Wilder states that the introduction to 'Stardust' was added only when the words were written by Mitchell Parish, but I don't know if that is true. The song was published in 1929; the first big hit recording, by Isham Jones with no words, was in 1930, but the uptempo instrumental recording made by the Chocolate Dandies, led by Don Redman, already used the introduction in 1928. But of course many songs have been written with no introduction at all: 'I Concentrate on You', 'Begin the Beguine', 'In the Still of the Night' and 'I've Got You Under My Skin', all by Cole Porter, are such consummate syntheses of words and music that they need no preface.

The terminology of songwriting is sometimes used confusingly by the authorities themselves. Although thousands of the new songs were in a thirty-two-bar AABA format, they were freely constructed in many ways, according to the genius of the songwriter, who, after all, was combining words and music in a way that had not been done by earlier craftsmen. A song may or may not be divisible into these parts. For dramatic purposes a song often requires a bridge or release, separating the statement of the drama (corresponding to the old verse) from its resolution or commentary (the chorus). The bridge sometimes presents the composer or the arranger, and sometimes the singer, with an interesting problem; and a classic treatment of a bridge may become part of the song as we know it.

The verse came to be called the introduction to the chorus; and to make things thoroughly complicated, the labels on old 78s often carried the legend 'With Vocal Chorus' or 'Vocal Refrain'. (In poetry and in medieval and Renaissance music a refrain was a short chorus of one or two lines at the end of a verse or a stanza, so familiar that the audience was presumed to know it.) Jazz musicians use the word 'chorus' to mean a complete statement of the tune (without the introduction, typically thirty-two bars), as in 'Take another chorus.'

Songwriting in its golden age (*c.* 1914–50) provided an astonishing variety of masterpieces that are popular around the world. They are often sorted into categories of theatre, film and pop. The work of some of the composers for the musical stage is consistently ranked among the greatest songwriting of all, and inspired the best of the rest, setting a standard to aim at.

It is sometimes said that the reason for this is the greater pressure involved in writing a song that fits into a plot, but the plots of Broadway musicals were often little more than fluff, and too many fine songs have long outlasted their original settings. A more likely reason is that composers for the stage were literate and thoughtful artists, working in a genre with a long and honourable history, and were willing to have their tunes compared with those of Puccini or Verdi. Jerome Kern, perhaps the most important innovator of all, was influenced by operetta (born as he was in 1885), yet invented something new.

As with the invention of the popular song in the eighteenth century, however, modern writing for the musical stage happened the way it did and where it did, among the English-speaking peoples, because it had to fill a gap. Opera was big business in New York and Chicago in the nineteenth century, and a great many provincial towns had their local 'opera' houses (actually the local vaudeville palace). Once again foreign music became the preserve of the upper classes, while the *hoi polloi* was left to amuse itself. However tuneful (and indeed popular) the works of the great opera composers might be, America needed its own genre of musical drama.

The first performance on the American musical stage may have been in 1732, in Charleston, South Carolina. A masque by Francis Hopkinson called *The Temple of Minerva* was performed as part of a

concert in Philadelphia in 1781, presented by the French minister in
honour of George Washington. There may have been an opera called
The Blockheads, or The Fortunate Contractor, published in 1782, said to
be a burlesque of *The Blockade of Boston*, which had been written and
mounted by the British General Burgoyne himself while he occupied
that city. But little survives of these early productions.

By the 1820s and 1830s comedies and operettas (usually with
foreign settings) were contributing to a slowly simmering stew, but
these were pastiches, and the music often had nothing to do with the
action. The genre did not discover any native composers or a style of
its own until the next century.

To the various strands of ballad opera and light *opéra bouffe*
(such as Lingard presented) was added *The Black Crook* in 1866,
which was a step forward principally because it made so much money
(though not for Thomas Baker, who wrote original music for it – the
Copyright Act of 1856 had secured performing rights in copyrighted
drama for the owners, but not for authors). The phenomenon was an
accident: several theatres had burned down in New York, with the
result that an imported French ballet company had no stage, so they
joined a heavily written melodrama based on Carl Maria von Weber's
romantic opera *Der Freischütz* (1821), creating a musical show full of
grand spectacle. The theatre chosen was owned by British-born
actress Laura Keene, the first woman theatrical manager in the
USA. Her first success as star and producer was *Our American
Cousin*, in which she was playing the night Abraham Lincoln was
shot.

The Black Crook was another pastiche; the songs were changed
regularly throughout the show's run, and none was a big hit. But the
girls were good dancers. They were tall, and their costumes were
padded in appropriate places to cater for the tastes of the time; they
wore pink tights, but word spread (not discouraged by the management) that they were showing a great deal more flesh than was usual,
and *The Black Crook* was supposed to be a saucy evening. The one
song that remained as long as the show lasted was 'You Naughty,
Naughty Men', which was not Baker's, but imported from England.
It listed many of the faults of the male sex, only to conclude: 'But
with all your faults we clearly / Love you wicked fellows dearly . . .'

The show's combination of girls, costumes, dancing and expensive sets led to a run of 475 performances, outstanding for the time. One of the succeeding 'burlettas' was *Lydia Thompson's British Blondes*, starring Pauline Markham (mentioned in chapter 3); but for many years, nothing much happened on the American musical stage of other than historical interest. Blondes and 'leg shows' became a staple, and the idea was to throw some songs and dances together and have a good time. *The Black Crook* was such a legend that it was revived a dozen times, until it was well and truly out of date.

The songs of Arthur Sullivan had some popularity in the USA, and the English operettas of Gilbert and Sullivan soon followed. Composer Sir Arthur Seymour Sullivan and journalist Sir William Schwenck Gilbert collaborated on thirteen brilliant comic operettas which are still performed today, and both became very rich. Sullivan felt guilty about not pursuing more 'serious' composition; no one set English lyrics better than he did, but no less an authority than Queen Victoria told him he was wasting his time.

The first American performance of *HMS Pinafore* took place in Boston in November 1878, and in January it swept New York; by May it had played in twelve houses (up to three at once), sometimes with all-black and all-children casts. The absurd story sent up the Admiralty, as in Sir Joseph's patter song 'When I Was a Boy', as well as the romantic fiction that a well-born lady could fall in love with a simple sailor (who in the end turns out to be a runaway aristocrat). So loose were the copyright laws of the time, so successful the show and so terrible some of the American productions that in one edition Buttercup was played by a 7-foot tall female impersonator. Gilbert and Sullivan went across the Atlantic to produce *Pirates of Penzance* themselves at the end of the same year. 'With Cat-like Tread', the song of its delightful stage policemen, was a success all over America, with new lyrics, as 'Hail, Hail, the Gang's All Here'. Major-General Stanley's patter song was 'I am the very model / Of a modern Major-General.' Perhaps their best-known work is *The Mikado* (1885), which has a pseudo-Japanese setting and sends up bureaucracy; Poo-Bah resembles a certain type of British civil servant as much as a Japanese one (the portrait still rings true a century later), while 'A Wandering Minstrel', 'The Flowers That Bloom in the Spring' and 'Willow,

Tit-willow' are still familiar, even to people who do not know where they came from.

These shows had plots, set-pieces, comedy and exotic settings in foreign places and earlier times, with sets and costumes to match; Sullivan's orchestrations were as good as his tunes, and all these parts added up to a whole that was like an opera rather than a pastiche, yet they were written in English, intended to be amusing and not too demanding for a middle-class audience. They helped establish an appetite for operetta in the USA. Franz Lehár was born in what was then Hungary; *The Merry Widow* was first produced in Vienna in 1905. Some of his shows were not produced in the USA at all, and he remained an operetta composer, famous for his waltzes. Others such as Victor Herbert, Rudolf Friml and Sigmund Romberg composed songs that transcended the genre to become American standards. The operetta form was stilted by later standards, but a model which could be modernized.

Born in Dublin, Herbert was an accomplished cellist and composer. He wrote about forty musical shows, of which the best known are *Babes in Toyland* (1903; filmed in 1934 with Laurel and Hardy); *Mlle Modiste* (1906; filmed in 1930), including 'Kiss Me Again'; *Naughty Marietta* (1910; the 1935 film made stars of the romantic duo Nelson Eddy and Jeanette MacDonald), with 'Ah! Sweet Mystery of Life'; and *Orange Blossoms* (1922), with 'A Kiss in the Dark'.

Friml was born in Prague. Among his biggest hits were *Rose Marie* (1924), whose book and lyrics were written by Otto Harbach and Oscar Hammerstein II; its enduring tunes are the title song and 'Indian Love Call'. It was filmed in 1936 with Allan Jones and also starred Eddy and MacDonald, as did the film of *The Firefly* in 1937. *The Vagabond King* was filmed as late as 1956, with Kathryn Grayson.

Romberg was born in Hungary. His *Maytime* was a hit in 1917, but the Shubert brothers apparently refused to take him seriously for a long time. (Sam, Lee and J. J., or Jake, Shubert were all born in the 1870s, sons of a pedlar who had fled tsarist pogroms; from 1900 they were the most influential theatre-owners in New York. Sam was killed in a train crash in 1905; Lee remained the best-known Shubert, but Jake's love for operetta was important.) Romberg's songs were dropped into various shows over the years, and *Blossom Time* did well in 1921, but it was *The Student Prince* (1924; filmed in 1954 with Mario Lanza) and *The Desert Song* (1926; filmed three times, in 1929, 1943 and 1953) which established Romberg. He wrote about fifty shows, and songs that became standards include 'Lover, Come Back to Me', 'Softly, as in a Morning Sunrise', 'When I Grow Too Old to Dream' and 'Close as Pages in a Book'.

No survey would be complete without George M. Cohan, a huge figure on Broadway but a unique one, who does not fit into any category. An all-round talent who came from a vaudeville family to be a singer, dancer, actor, composer, lyricist, director and producer, he had written 150 sketches by the time he was twenty-one. He wrote the most successful of all American First World War songs, 'Over There', for which he received the Congressional Medal of Honor, and was associated with about thirty-five plays, musicals and straight drama, as writer or producer. His shows always had strong story lines and his dialogue contained plenty of demotic speech, making his characters credible; some of the same critics who complained that most Broadway productions were stilted and unbelievable also did not like Cohan's use of slang. *Little Johnny Jones* (1904) included 'Yankee Doodle Boy' ('I'm a Yankee Doodle Dandy . . .') and 'Give My Regards to Broadway'. Several of his songs were big hits, among them 'Mary's a Grand Old Name', 'You're a Grand Old Flag' and 'Harrigan'. (Cohan had attended a funeral at which a folded flag was stroked sentimentally by a Civil War veteran, saying, 'You're a grand old rag.' Cohan changed the title of the song at the request of veterans' groups.) He was seen as the first to break away from the operetta style, but his dynamic, tub-thumping Americanism had no sequel. Cohan's *Little Nellie Kelly* (1922) was revived in 1940 as a film for Judy Garland. James Cagney won an Oscar portraying Cohan in the film biography *Yankee Doodle Dandy* in 1942, and Joel Grey played him in the 1968 Broadway musical *George M!* (*Little Johnny Jones* was revived in 1984, starring Donny Osmond, but closed after one performance.)

While Cohan was in his prime, black Americans were already making a contribution to the stage that was to be far more influential in the end. By 1900 Harlem was already becoming the biggest black city on earth. It had been a middle-class self-contained community, in which tenement blocks were built to attract commuters from downtown; when the speculating builders were in danger of going out of business, racial prejudice did not keep them from renting to blacks. Before long the concentration of talent was so great that it exploded into the Harlem Renaissance of poetry and literature, an African-American influence in all the arts.

James Reese Europe was a bandleader and organizer of concerts and musical clubs. Born in Alabama, he went to New York in 1905 and formed an association with the dance team of Vernon and Irene Castle, who were all the rage on the Broadway stage just before the First World War. During the war he led a US Army band and in 1918 took Paris by storm. His music was called jazz, which it was not; but he encouraged techniques of brass playing, for example, which he thought were racial characteristics, and then found that he had to rehearse his men to keep them from adding more to the music than he wanted. Widely admired in the black community, he would have had an even greater influence had he not been stabbed to death by a crazy musician in Boston.

Will Marion Cook was a formally trained composer, conductor and violinist who had studied with Antonín Dvořák. His musical shows included *Clorindy or The Origin of the Cakewalk* (1898), *In Dahomey* (1903), starring Bert Williams and George Walker, and *In Darkeydom* (1914), which used Europe's band and the lyrics of the black poet Paul Lawrence Dunbar. *In Dahomey*, about the 'back to Africa' movement, was the first black show to open on Broadway itself; its long run in London was followed by a national American tour. It was the first part of a trilogy in which blacks commented on their own condition as Americans; the other two shows were *Abyssinia* (1907) and *Bandana Land* (1909), which also starred Williams and Walker. Cook's best-known composition is 'I'm Coming Virginia'. Will Vodery led a band at a theatre roof garden in 1915, worked as an arranger for the Ziegfeld Follies for twenty years and was the first black to work as a music director for a film company (Fox, in the early 1930s). Cook and Vodery gave informal advice on harmony and composition to Duke Ellington.

The first black musical to be a big hit was *Shuffle Along*, in 1921.

Two black vaudeville teams met in Philadelphia and created a libretto; they hired Eubie Blake and Noble Sissle to write the music, which was arranged by Vodery. The show featured Hall Johnson, who played violin in Europe's band and formed the Hall Johnson Choir in 1925; dancer Josephine Baker, who later went to Paris and became a European superstar; and Florence Mills, Harlem's biggest star. Mills's early sudden death was marked by a huge funeral, and she was immortalized in Duke Ellington's composition 'Black Beauty', as well as in the English composer Constant Lambert's 'Elegiac Blues'. It was Mills who sang the show's biggest hit, 'I'm Just Wild About Harry'; other songs included 'Love Will Find a Way' and 'Bandana Days'. Launched on a shoestring, tried out in one-night stands in Philadelphia and New Jersey and using costumes left over from a flop of 1919, *Shuffle Along* ran for more than five hundred perform-ances, and visited a theatre in Chicago's Loop. Blake and Sissle's later shows, among them *Chocolate Dandies* (1924), were less well received, but both had long careers. Blake also wrote 'Memories of You' and 'You Were Meant for Me'. Sissle, who had worked for Europe, became a successful bandleader.

James P. Johnson's music for *Runnin' Wild* (1923) included 'Charleston', which launched one of the most famous dance fads of the century. *Blackbirds of 1928* had an all-white score by Jimmy McHugh and Dorothy Fields, and starred Adelaide Hall and Bill 'Bojangles' Robinson. Among its songs were 'I Can't Give You Anything But Love' and the hot rhythmic numbers 'Diga Diga Doo', 'Bandana Babies' and 'Doin' the New Low-down', all recorded by Duke Ellington on Victor; Don Redman made two recordings of 'Doin' the New Low-down', on one of which Robinson's tap-dancing may be heard. Harlem's greatest dancer, Robinson later taught Shirley Temple and danced with her on screen, and was commemorated in another Duke Ellington composition, 'Bojangles (A Portrait of Bill Robinson)'.

Hot Chocolates (1929) had begun as a floor show at Connie's Inn, written by Andy Razaf and Fats Waller, who had contributed to the less popular *Keep Shufflin'* the year before. On Broadway Louis Armstrong played in the pit band and came on stage for a solo. 'Ain't Misbehavin'' became one of Armstrong's and Waller's biggest hits, and the show ran for six months.

We will come back to some of these names. There were a score of other black shows in the 1920s, for example, *Plantation Review*, which included Mills, Vodery and Shelton Brooks. Elements of racism were evident in two kinds of reviews: white critics often compared black shows not with white shows, but with their own patronizing view of what a black show should be like; blacks sometimes criticized the shows for being too white. But the music and the dancing in all of them brought the flavour of jazz to Broadway: the tap-dancing, soft shoe, buck-and-wing and other routines put paid to the cakewalk once and for all, and were immediately influential on the part of Broadway that was further downtown. Florenz Ziegfeld knew a good thing when he saw it, and bought 'Ballin' the Jack' from a Harlem show to use in his own *Follies* in 1913; the next year there was a hit recording of it, and the tune was revived many times.

By then, the second generation of Tin Pan Alley songwriters was creating an American musical theatre. It was a phenomenon second in importance only to jazz itself in establishing the commercial dominance of American popular music in the twentieth century. Jerome Kern, Irving Berlin, George Gershwin, Vincent Youmans, Cole Porter, Richard Rodgers and others broke the mould of operetta and turned the 'musical comedy' into something as American as baseball. Hundreds of the songs have been so popular for so long that they gave rise to the genre of 'the standard'. Those named above are the most important creators of the American musical stage. Of these Berlin and Porter were the only ones who wrote both words and music, and Porter was the only one who was not born poor, and almost the only one who was not Jewish.

The nineteenth-century persecution of the Jews in eastern Europe was a turning point in world history in more ways than one. The plight of the Jews in the Russian Empire was so severe that the era saw the beginning of much modern history, including Zionism; but for our purposes the important thing was the emigration. The natural increase of the Jewish population was lost to Europe when large numbers of Jews settled in America: in the period of 1881–92 19,000 Jews a year went to the USA; in 1892–1903 the average number rose to 37,000 a year, and in 1903–14 to 76,000. The newcomers were huddled and crowded into poor neighbourhoods and sweatshops, but not for long. They organized themselves within a couple of generations, and New York became the largest Jewish city on earth. Apart from all their other accomplishments, succeeding generations of these new Americans yielded a considerable number of great entertainers (we have already met Al Jolson, Sophie Tucker and the Shuberts), and perhaps most of the best songwriters in the history of American songs.

Oscar Hammerstein II and others have recalled the occasion when Jerome Kern was thinking of writing a musical version of a popular novel by Donn Byrne, *Messer Marco Polo*. It was a book by an Irishman set in China about an Italian. 'What kind of music are you going to write?' someone asked. 'Don't worry,' said Kern. 'It'll be good Jewish music.'

Jerome David Kern was born and died in New York City. *Clorindy, or The Origin of the Cakewalk* (1898) had been 'the first Negro operetta in the new syncopated style'; six years later its white producer, Edward Everett Rice, gave Kern his first theatrical assignment: writing additional songs for a show called *Mr Wix of Wickham*. The teenage Kern was a song plugger in Wanamaker's department store and wanted to move. Ernest Ball advised him to go not to Witmark, Ball's publisher at the time, but to T. B. Harms, on the grounds that Witmark was a large house, where a young composer would get lost in the shuffle, whereas Harms was not doing too well.

Perhaps Ball had spotted the great Max Dreyfus, at Harms, as the giant he would become. It was Dreyfus who sent Kern to work in London in 1905. In early 1906, at the age of twenty-one, Kern had twelve songs performed in five theatres, his patrons including some of the most powerful producers in the business, such as Charles Frohman. Kern's first hit, 'How'd You Like To Spoon With Me?', was turned down by Frohman's New York manager in 1905, but was accepted by the Shuberts, and later by Frohman himself in London. Frohman was an American whose interest in British hit shows was entirely practical: it was in London at this time that some of the most innovative work was being done in turning the operetta into the modern musical show.

In November 1899 *Florodora*, with music mostly by Leslie Stuart and lyrics by Stuart and three other writers, had opened in London, where it had 455 performances; it opened in November 1900 in New York and, unusually for the time, ran even longer in the USA, for over 500 performances, thanks to its hit song 'Tell Me Pretty Maiden', which was performed by pairs of parasol-twirling girls and straw-hatted boys. It was the first musical show to be recorded by its original cast, on 7-inch Berliner 78s in England in 1900; an American recording of 'Maiden' by the 'Florodora Girls' was a huge hit in 1901. Clearly inspired by minstrelsy in its rhythms and its near-jazz tunes, it was itself profoundly influential on American composers. It is no coincidence that *In Dahomey* was a hit in London in 1903; without the complicated feelings of the Americans towards blacks, British showgoers may have been able to embrace it more wholeheartedly. In the exciting English musical atmosphere, Kern's collaborating lyricists included George Grossmith (performer, author and later a renowned producer, whose father had been a famous leading man in Gilbert and Sullivan shows) and P. G. Wodehouse (one of the great humorists, and prose stylists, of the century).

Kern married an English girl and returned to New York in 1910. Dreyfus continued to find him writing assignments: about a hundred Kern songs were interpolated into various Broadway shows, while Wodehouse continued to be one of his collaborators; Kern's own first show was *The Red Petticoat* in 1912. He wrote several songs for a show imported from England, *The Girl from Utah* (1914), among them 'They Didn't Believe Me' (lyrics by Herbert Reynolds), generally considered to be his first masterpiece. However successful the songs of Victor Herbert or George M. Cohan, they soon became period pieces, but 'They Didn't Believe Me' was different: having no clichéd elements, but a key change and other innovations in construction, it was naturally shapely and made most Tin Pan Alley hits sound like jingles. It was like an art song, yet singable and memorable, the aim of the popular songwriter since the time of Thomas Arne.

Kern was a craftsman, trying to write something of which he could be proud, as well as making money. He was also the first great genius of the genre, and popular music could never be the same again. He wrote or substantially contributed to thirty-seven Broadway shows, for example *Sally* (1920), whose lyrics by Buddy DeSylva included 'Look for the Silver Lining', a distinctive song with a hymn-like quality, and *Sunny* (1925), with Harbach and Hammerstein. One of its songs, 'Who?', is unusual in that the first note is held for two and a quarter bars ('Who . . . stole my heart away?'); it was used in several films, and recorded by Tommy Dorsey (1937), among others.

In 1927, though, Kern made yet another advance on the Broadway musical. The songs had been the main element, closely followed by the dancing and the sets, while the plots were usually insignificant. *Show Boat*, however, was based on a novel by Edna Ferber, with a believable plot and characters. It contained such songs (with lyrics by Hammerstein) as 'Bill', 'Make Believe', 'Why Do I Love You?', 'Ol' Man River' and 'Can't Help Lovin' Dat Man'. It was the first great American musical show; it was filmed in 1929 and 1936, and a new full-length recording of it in 1988 restored the original orchestration by Robert Russell Bennett. (Bennett deserves to be better known. A composer hired by Dreyfus and put in charge of arranging the firm's theatre music, he worked on so many hit shows that he helped shape the very sound of Broadway, from *Show Boat* and the biggest hits of Rodgers and Hammerstein to Lerner and Loewe's *My Fair Lady*.)

What Kern wrote in *Show Boat* was perhaps the best of all operettas; his finest songs were still to come. *Roberta* (1933), with lyrics by Harbach, did not get good reviews; one critic wrote: 'There's no tune you can whistle when you leave the theatre.' This was the show that contained 'Smoke Gets in Your Eyes', 'The Touch of Your Hand' and 'Yesterdays'. Kern's writing had moved well beyond the simplicity required in the English pleasure gardens, but the public is often underestimated. Like many composers for the stage, Kern tried to insist on the restriction of his music from broadcasting for six months, but he changed his mind when the plugging of 'Smoke Gets in Your Eyes' made a hit out of the show. The film version in 1935 added 'Lovely to Look At' and 'I Won't Dance'; it was filmed again in 1952 as *Lovely to Look At*.

Kern wrote songs for several original films, among them *Swing Time* (1936), with Fred Astaire and Ginger Rogers, which included 'The Way You Look Tonight', 'Pick Yourself Up' and 'A Fine Romance' (lyrics by Dorothy Fields), as well as the instrumental 'Waltz in Swingtime'. Other Kern film songs are 'The Last Time I

Saw Paris' (lyrics by Hammerstein) for *Lady Be Good* (1941, adapted from the 1924 Gershwin show) and 'Long Ago and Far Away' for *Cover Girl* (1944, lyrics by Ira Gershwin).

New harmonic devices and suggestions of additional harmonic resources led to the adoption of the modern Broadway show song as a vehicle for the interpretation of jazz musicians. Kern's 'The Way You Look Tonight' and 'A Fine Romance' were among Billie Holiday's most beautiful recordings, and Charles Mingus interpolated 'All the Things You Are' with a Rachmaninov prelude to make the dramatic 'All the Things You C Sharp' in 1955. Indeed, such outstanding songwriters as Johnny Green ('Body and Soul'), Arthur Schwartz ('Dancing in the Dark', 'You and the Night and the Music') and Harry Warren (film hits without number) considered 'All the Things You Are', from the show *Very Warm for May* (1939), to be one of the greatest songs ever written. Not only does it change key, but its unexpected notes suggest more key changes all the way through. Even Kern was afraid that its construction would be too much for the public, but it was one of his biggest hits.

Kern's work appeared to reflect the times he lived in, yet turned out to be timeless: 'All in Fun' (also from *Very Warm for May*) seemed to hark back to the more happy-go-lucky songs Kern was writing around the time of the First World War, but the bitter-sweet harmony made it sound more modern. And this was years after George Gershwin claimed to be imitating Kern, and the schoolboy Richard Rodgers had spent all his pocket money at matinées, seeing Kern shows over and over again.

Kern died suddenly, in the street in 1945, without any identification in his pockets; it was some hours before the world knew what it had lost. He left no autobiography and no revealing interviews, deepening the mystery of where such mastery of craft came from.

George Gershwin, still one of the world's most popular composers more than fifty years after his death, was an excellent pianist. Influenced by jazz, he was one of the few great songwriters who sought out black entertainers and musicians to listen to for pleasure. He was taking American music into unexplored areas when he died because of a brain tumour in 1937.

The family acquired a piano when George was twelve; having

shown little interest in music, he surprised everyone by quickly becoming proficient. His first hit song was an untypical potboiler: 'Swanee', as we have seen, was picked up by Al Jolson in 1919; it sold a million copies of sheet music and two million records by various artists. Gershwin wrote for *George White's Scandals* for several years, collaborating with DeSylva and others, but more and more with his brother Ira (who, until he proved himself, worked under the name Arthur Francis). Ira became one of the finest American lyricists. Their first show together was *Lady Be Good* (1924), with Fred and Adele Astaire, which offered 'Fascinatin' Rhythm', the title song 'Oh, Lady Be Good!' and, originally, 'The Man I Love' (which, dropped from three shows, still became a standard).

Songs for other shows included 'That Certain Feeling', 'Someone to Watch Over Me', 'How Long Has This Been Going On?', ''S Wonderful', and 'Liza'. *Girl Crazy* (1930) was very rich: 'Bidin' My Time', 'But Not For Me', 'Embraceable You' and 'I Got Rhythm', from the chords of which more jazz tunes have been derived than perhaps any other. *Strike Up the Band* in 1927 failed in its Philadelphia try-out, despite the title song and 'I've Got a Crush On You'. It had an excellent book by George S. Kaufman, one of Broadway's most acerbic wits, but its anti-war, anti-government message was too strong. It was watered down in 1930 on Broadway and had a six-month run.

Gershwin's film work included two Fred Astaire pictures: *A Damsel in Distress* and *Shall We Dance?* (both 1937), which yielded 'A Foggy Day', 'Nice Work If You Can Get It', 'Shall We Dance?', 'They Can't Take That Away From Me' and 'Let's Call the Whole Thing Off'. The film *Goldwyn Follies* in 1938 contained 'Love Walked In' and 'Love is Here to Stay'.

His more ambitious compositions had begun in 1924. Already famous, he was commissioned by Paul Whiteman to write *Rhapsody in Blue* for piano and jazz band, for a concert at the Aeolian Hall to celebrate American music. The concert began with 'Livery Stable Blues', introduced apologetically by Whiteman 'as an example of the depraved past from which modern jazz has risen', according to Olin Downes in *The New York Times*. He added: 'The apology is herewith indignantly rejected, for this is a gorgeous piece of impudence, much

better . . . than other and more polite compositions that came later.'
Downes was not a jazz critic, but he was sensibly unimpressed by
what he had heard of its co-option.

The concert continued with piano novelties by Zez Confrey, taken
for jazz by the audience, and a large helping of Whiteman's dance
band music. The second half opened with Herbert's specially commissioned *Suite of Serenades*, hastily put together from the scraps that any
composer has in his trunk. It was followed by Edward MacDowell's
'To a Wild Rose' (1896), Friml's 'Chansonette' (later popular as
'Donkey Serenade') and more; members of the audience were looking
at their watches as the penultimate piece on the programme began.

Herbert had helped Gershwin with the piece, advising a longer
piano introduction to the main themes to add to its drama. *Rhapsody
in Blue* caused a sensation. It was apparently Ross Gorman's idea to
play the clarinet introduction as a glissando, instead of seventeen
separately tongued notes, and this was enough to stop the audience
leaving. At the end they must have left feeling as though they had
heard an entire evening of the best in modern American music
(despite the concert's closing piece, one of Elgar's *Pomp and Circum-
stance* marches). The *Rhapsody* is still one of the most popular of
American compositions; it seemed to have come from nowhere, but
it had been preceded by Gershwin's own 'Blue Monday' / '135th
Street' (1922) to say nothing of Milhaud's ballet *Le boeuf sur le toit*
(1919). Yet *Rhapsody in Blue* was and is problematical. There is such a
thing as a jazz composer, but a jazz composer is a jazz musician first,
and Gershwin was not. The piece is diffuse and structurally weak,
and too much of a piano showcase. Nevertheless, it has some
unforgettable melodies, and one would like to have heard that first
performance, with Gershwin's improvisation (the piano part was not
fully written out) and Gorman's free, mocking interpretation of the
clarinet part. Various arrangements were made, all by Whiteman's
arranger, Ferde Grofé; the one that is usually heard is the grandest,
but Grofé's original, played in 1924, is among the best.

Gershwin's piano roll recordings include an arrangement for solo
piano of the *Rhapsody*. Whiteman's band at the Aeolian Hall (in
Grofé's first arrangement) had twenty-two players, but *Rhapsody in
Blue* is usually played by a symphony orchestra. One of the more

interesting recordings of the *Rhapsody* was made by RCA's artists and repertoire (A&R) executive Hugo Winterhalter in the early 1950s, with the excellent Byron Janis at the piano, a performance which tried to get away from the symphonic feeling and to make the piece swing. Critics such as Max Harrison in England campaigned for years for a more sensible treatment; finally Michael Tilson Thomas recorded the original version, using Gershwin's suitably edited piano roll, and was followed by Simon Rattle and others.

Gershwin continued to compose piano preludes and pieces for orchestra, as well as the great songs. He orchestrated the Concerto in F for piano and orchestra himself in 1925; it is better realized in its structure than the *Rhapsody*, and it too contains good tunes, especially in the bluesy slow movement. The delightful *An American in Paris* was recorded in 1928 by Nat Shilkret, with the original French taxi horns and Gershwin playing celesta, and was used in a film of the same title in 1951. (The film spoiled the music: Gershwin may not have pandered to the public, but Hollywood almost always did.)

It was Gershwin's masterpiece, *Porgy and Bess*, which suffered most from tampering, so that it did not emerge as the first successful American opera until the 1970s. DuBose Heyward's novel, inspired by a crippled beggar called Samuel Smalls, or 'Goat Sammy', had been successfully dramatized by his wife, Dorothy, who changed the completely downbeat ending to one offering an open-ended sort of hope, as Porgy sets off for New York in his goat-cart to look for Bess; the new ending was used in Gershwin's version. Gershwin spent some time with Heyward in Charleston's Cabbage Row slum and on Folly Beach off the Carolina coast, resting and relaxing as well as soaking up the Gullah dialect of the local black population. Heyward and Gershwin worked together by post, and brought Ira in to help with the lyrics. It was an unusually harmonious collaboration for a musical show.

The first run of the piece lost money in 1935–6, partly because of the public's confusion over what it expected from Gershwin. In 1918 Otto Kahn, then chairman of the Metropolitan Opera, had proposed the idea of an American opera to Jerome Kern, Irving Berlin and Gershwin; Berlin knew he was not qualified, while Kern hinted that Gershwin was a likely candidate. But when Gershwin got around to it, the Metropolitan Opera was not interested, the USA had no equivalent of European comic opera or folk opera venues and Broadway was not ready to have its horizons extended.

John W. 'Bubbles' Sublett (of the black vaudeville team Buck and Bubbles) played Sportin' Life, a flashy drug pedlar, in the first production; he was troublesome in rehearsal, but brilliant on stage. A revised version in 1942 ran longer than any revival had up to then. Sportin' Life had allegedly been written with Cab Calloway in mind, who played it in performances in the 1950s; a film was made in 1959 with Sammy Davis, Jr, as Sportin' Life. The songs, including 'Summertime', 'I Loves You, Porgy', 'I Got Plenty o' Nuttin'' and 'Bess, You is My Woman Now', had long since become standards by the time the original score was restored, as orchestrated by Gershwin and with recitatives instead of spoken dialogue. A concert version conducted by Lorin Maazel in 1975 and a production conducted by John DeMain in Houston, Texas, in 1976 were recorded; Edward Greenfield, writing in *Gramophone* magazine, compared *Porgy* to Alban Berg's *Wozzeck* and Benjamin Britten's *Peter Grimes* as a great modern portrait of human nature. The Glyndebourne Festival's production in England in 1986 was a triumph; it was recorded in 1989, conducted by Simon Rattle, with Willard White and Cynthia Haymon in the title roles and Damon Evans as Sportin' Life.

'The rest of us were songwriters,' said Irving Berlin. 'George was a composer.' If the greatest twentieth-century songs have not only been memorable and singable, but have also lent themselves to interpretation by the greatest of jazzmen, then Gershwin's songs alone would have earned him immortality; but *Porgy and Bess* has revealed him as a great 'serious' composer as well. This late recognition is better than none: he was not yet thirty-nine when he died, and his is among the greatest unfinished careers in music.

Vincent Youmans was another composer who had a relatively short career. He was a poor businessman and hopeless as his own producer; he changed lyricists for each of his twelve shows, some of which were failures; he published only ninety-three songs, yet a handful of them are standards. *No, No, Nannette* (1925) was a smash hit, perhaps the quintessential 1920s show; Irving Caesar and Otto Harbach wrote the lyrics of 'Tea for Two' and 'I Want to be Happy'.

Oh, Please (1926) was a flop though it included 'I Know That You Know', with Harbach. *Hit the Deck* (1927), another success, contained 'Sometimes I'm Happy' and 'Hallelujah' (written as a march while Youmans was in the navy), with lyrics by Caesar. *Great Day!* (1929) was again a disaster, but yielded 'Without a Song' and 'More Than You Know', with lyrics by Billy Rose. *Smiles* (1930) offered 'Time on My Hands', with Harold Adamson and Mack Gordon, but lost money in spite of being produced by Ziegfeld. Youmans went to Hollywood, where his only successful picture was *Flying Down to Rio* in 1933, the first film to team Astaire with Ginger Rogers; it included the title song, 'The Carioca' and 'Orchids in the Moonlight'. He went bankrupt and fell ill with tuberculosis. 'Tea for Two' is one of *Variety*'s top hundred Tin Pan Alley songs, and it rivals Gershwin's 'I Got Rhythm' as the tune that most inspired the era's jazz musicians; Fats Waller may have found 'Honeysuckle Rose' in it.

Another mysterious talent, an enigma in every way, is the songwriter whom every other composer in the business has admired: Irving Berlin. He was born Israel Baline in Russia, and his family settled in New York in the 1890s. He worked as a singing waiter and then a song plugger. His name was changed by a printer's error on his first published song, 'Marie from Sunny Italy'.

Many of the great songwriters of the golden age of Broadway and Tin Pan Alley had studied music formally and were familiar with classical music. They were influenced by ragtime, then jazz; they influenced jazzmen in turn, writing songs which were worthwhile vehicles for new interpretations and improvisation. Most of them could read music and play the piano well. (Kern and Friml, also a good pianist, were sometimes mildly annoyed when not asked to play at a party, because Gershwin, the best pianist, was willing to play all evening.) Irving Berlin did not have any of these qualifications; he is unique. He had no formal studies and never learned to read or write music well, but hired an arranger to write down his songs and to harmonize them. He did not like jazz or 'swing bands', and he had a piano built with a lever to shift the keyboard so that he could play in more than one key. A devoted family man who valued his privacy, he did not go to many parties.

Berlin should have been a hack; his only object was to have a hit, and his measure of a song's quality was whether it made money. Another unusual thing about Berlin's songs is that they leave no fingerprints. It is possible – we think – to tell a Kern song or a Gershwin song, but each Berlin song seems to have come out of nowhere. Yet Berlin not only wrote good songs, he did so in every category. There could be said to be broadly three types of songs from this era – show songs, film songs and pop hits – but Berlin was actually a master of four types, for he began with a knack for writing unusually catchy, cheerful Tin Pan Alley songs which were hits well before the First World War, and when Tin Pan Alley became more sophisticated, his skill became more than a knack. Berlin favoured sentimentality, and his lyrics are not as witty as Lorenz Hart's or Cole Porter's, and never cynical at all; he wrote some that are almost corny, and a few tub-thumpers. Yet he somehow held it all in check, rarely going over the top, creating a great many unpretentious songs which are still memorable.

Furthermore, the arranging and harmonizing of his songs for publication, under his close supervision, never failed to impress other composers. Although he could not do it himself, he seemed to know more about harmony instinctively than others did after years of study. If the harmony that he hired displeased him, he would pester his assistant until he got what he wanted, and his taste was invariably impeccable. His work had such variety in it and was of such high quality that he was regarded by his peers as representing American popular music all by himself.

Berlin sang his own songs on Broadway in 1910, and was already world-famous before the First World War for 'Alexander's Ragtime Band'. In 1909 he had gone to work as a song plugger and lyric writer for Ted Snyder. When 'Alexander' had sold two million copies of sheet music by the end of 1911, Snyder's manager, Henry Waterson, formed the firm of Waterson, Berlin and Snyder, which provided Berlin with his transposing piano. His first helper was Max Winslow, who offered tips as Berlin picked out his tunes. Winslow was also a superb vocal coach, and helped many female variety artists develop their musical personalities, as well as make hits of Berlin's songs; he became known as 'the man who discovered Irving Berlin', and his girl singers were known as 'Winslow's singles'. When Berlin complained about the royalties Waterson paid, Winslow suggested they start their own firm, whereupon Berlin's royalties tripled.

When he was drafted, the newspaper headline was 'Army Takes Berlin'. He organized a soldier revue in 1918, *Yip Yip Yaphank*, which included the hit 'Oh! How I Hate to Get Up in the Morning' and another song that even he thought was over the top: he put it aside, but gave it to Kate Smith in 1938, and 'God Bless America' became a second national anthem. Smith was a popular soprano on radio, and later on television; her recording of 'God Bless America' was a hit in 1939, and again in 1940 and 1942. 'God Bless America' was written by an immigrant who came from utter poverty and who had much reason to love America; he gave away all the royalties.

Among Berlin's other early hits were 'Everybody's Doing It (Now)' (1911), sung by Eddie Cantor (another singing waiter who became one of America's most popular entertainers), 'When the Midnight Choo Choo Leaves for Alabam', 'I Want to Go Back to Michigan', 'Play a Simple Melody' (which contains its own counter-melody) and many other charmers which ought to be revived more often. In 1912 Berlin had married Dorothy Goetz (sister of songwriter-producer Ray Goetz, who wrote 'For Me and My Gal'). After she died of typhus a few months later, he wrote 'When I Lost You', his first tender, sentimental ballad.

Berlin had initially used collaborators, but soon wrote his own words. 'A Pretty Girl is Like a Melody' came in 1919, 'All Alone' in 1924. He began buying back the rights to his earlier work and eventually owned virtually all his own songs. He built his own theatre, the Music Box, and presented revues there in the 1920s. Berlin married Ellin MacKay, against the wishes of her wealthy Catholic father, and during the difficult courtship he wrote 'What'll I Do?' He gave her the royalties to 'Always' (1925) as a wedding present. The press chased the couple across the Atlantic and back. MacKay later lost money in the stock market, and found that his son-in-law was richer than he was.

Berlin's songs were not usually natural material for jazzmen, but some were so good they could not be left out: 'Blue Skies' (1927) was later recorded by Benny Goodman in a Fletcher Henderson arrangement; 'Marie' (1929) became one of the biggest hits of the Swing Era for Tommy Dorsey; in 1949 Count Basie made a delightful recording of 'Cheek to Cheek' (1935), probably arranged by Don Redman. 'How Deep Is the Ocean?', a ballad, was later recorded by Coleman Hawkins, Erroll Garner, Charlie Parker and many other jazzmen, and 'Say It Isn't So' was almost as successful.

On the other hand, Berlin's 'Easter Parade' was instantly old-fashioned, yet an unforgettable hit, a perfect example of how he could celebrate the American appetite for nostalgia and sentimentality. The tune sounds as though it has always existed, and its marriage of words and melody keeps it on the safe side of pure corn. It was first heard in *As Thousands Cheer* in 1933, then in 1948 was the title song of a film with Berlin's music starring Fred Astaire and Judy Garland.

Berlin's other film work included two other Astaire pictures, *Top Hat* (1935), with 'Cheek to Cheek' and 'Top Hat, White Tie and Tails' and *Follow the Fleet* (1936), with 'Let's Face the Music and Dance'. *On the Avenue*, starring Dick Powell (1937), included 'You're Laughing at Me' and 'I've Got My Love to Keep Me Warm'; Fats Waller had a hilarious hit with the former, and the latter, in an instrumental recording of 1948 by Les Brown, was regarded as the last number one hit of the Swing Era. *Holiday Inn* (1942) contained 'Happy Holiday', 'Be Careful, It's My Heart' and 'White Christmas', which was voted best film song at the Academy Awards that year; Berlin presented his Oscar to himself, saying, 'This goes to a nice guy; I've known him all my life.' (Crosby's record of 'White Christmas' sold millions every year for decades, and the various recordings of it were said to have sold more than 225 million by 1976.)

Jerome Kern had been hired to write a show to be put on in 1946; when he died, producers Rodgers and Hammerstein hired Berlin instead. The show, *Annie Get Your Gun*, had more hits than any other in history, and presents almost a cross-section of Berlin's work: 'They Say It's Wonderful' and 'I Got the Sun in the Morning' would have been quite suitable for the pop charts at that time; 'Doin' What Comes Natur'ly' is an attempt at a hillbilly feeling; 'The Girl That I Marry' is a sentimental song in 3/4 time, harking back to the turn of the century; and 'There's No Business Like Show Business', which has belonged ever since to Ethel Merman, the show's star, is a tub-thumper like Cohan's 'Give My Regards to Broadway'.

All these represent only the highlights of Berlin's accomplishment. He controlled his own material, to the extent that he would not allow Alec Wilder to quote from it in his *American Popular Song*, and he always refused permission for a dramatized biography on stage or screen. He died, over one hundred years old, as this book was being written, our last link with Tin Pan Alley before the First World War.

Cole Porter was a late starter, and his well-to-do family did not approve of his chosen vocation even after he reached the top of it. He studied law, but dabbled in music; he went to France and served in the French army during the First World War. In 1919 he married a wealthy woman and settled in Paris, where he was at the centre of one of the richest club scenes the world has ever seen. He became a close friend of the legendary hostess Bricktop, a red-haired American black woman whose real name was Ada Beatrice Queen Victoria Louise Virginia Smith. She went to France in 1924, and her club, Chez Bricktop in Rue Pigalle, was frequented by the Prince of Wales, Ernest Hemingway and John Steinbeck, among others. Porter wrote 'Miss Otis Regrets' for Bricktop and for his friend Monty Woolley, who sang it in a film.

Porter's first hit came in 1929 with 'I'm in Love Again', written in 1924. His shows began with *Paris* in 1928, with 'Let's Do It' (saucy lyrics were later added by Noël Coward). *Fifty Million Frenchmen* (1929) included 'You Do Something to Me' and *Wake Up and Dream* (1929) yielded 'What is This Thing Called Love?' He returned to the USA in the early 1930s. A horse fell on him in 1937, shattering both his legs; the sophisticated world-traveller was a semi-invalid for the rest of his life, and constantly underwent surgery in attempts to save his legs. His right leg was amputated in 1958, after which he became even more reclusive, but his work was complete by then.

Some of his songs were suggested by events or by others' remarks, such as 'It's De-lovely' (a sunrise in Rio), or written for vocalists of limited range, such as 'Miss Otis Regrets', and 'Night and Day' (for Fred Astaire). 'Don't Fence Me In' was written as a send-up, but became the best Hollywood cowboy song of all, thanks to his lyrics.

Kern was the godfather of the modern musical show; Berlin wrote both tunes and lyrics; Gershwin was a great composer whose life was tragically short. Porter's tunes alone would have put him in this company, but the literary sophistication of his lyrics, worn lightly, made him a Rodgers and Hart all by himself. There are differences: Hart was unlucky in love, and his lyrics are often bitter-sweet, while Porter's words can fairly be said to represent the essence of the 1930s. Yet no one has surpassed Porter in making great songs of popular speech. A great many songs today are based on clichés, but Porter could write 'Don't Fence Me In', 'Night and Day', 'I Get a Kick Out of You', 'Just One of Those Things', 'I've Got You Under My Skin', 'In the Still of the Night' and many more, and over fifty years later the clichés may as well have been invented by the songwriter himself, so completely do they belong to him. Here is one of the best examples in all music of a tune and the vernacular combining, complete with an introduction and internal rhymes in the stanzas:

> My story is much too sad to be told,
> But practically everything leaves me totally cold.
> The only exception I know is the case
>   When I'm out on a quiet spree,
>   Fighting vainly the old ennui,
>   And I suddenly turn and see
> Your fabulous face.
>
>   I get no kick from champagne;
>   Mere alcohol doesn't thrill me at all.
>   So tell me why should it be true
>   That I get a kick out of you.
>
>   Some get a kick from cocaine;
>   I'm sure that if I took even one sniff,
>   That would bore me terrifically stiff,
>   But I get a kick out of you.
>
> I get a kick every time I see you
>   Standing there before me,
> I get a kick though it's clear to me
>   You obviously don't adore me.
>
>   I get no kick in a plane.
>   Flying too high with some guy in the sky

> Is my idea of nothing to do,
> Yet I get a kick out of you.

Among Porter's shows and songs are *The New Yorkers* (1930), including 'Love for Sale', whose sympathetically adult lyrics were often banned from the airwaves, and *The Gay Divorce* (1932), including 'Night and Day'; it was filmed as *The Gay Divorcée* in 1934. *Anything Goes* (1934) contained the title song, 'I Get a Kick Out of You', 'All Through the Night' and 'You're the Top', and is one of the richest scores of the decade and the most typical 1930s musical. The show was being rehearsed with a libretto by Guy Bolton and P. G. Wodehouse, but the plot, about a shipwreck, had to be abandoned when a cruise liner caught fire off the New Jersey coast, killing 125 people. Bolton and Wodehouse were not available, so the producer introduced director Howard Lindsay and press agent Russel Crouse, whose new book for the show was the first from one of Broadway's most successful writing partnerships. Porter's recording of 'You're the Top', accompanying himself on the piano, was a top ten hit; two lines in the song had to be changed ('I shouldn't care for those nights in the air / That the fair Mrs Lindbergh goes through') when the Lindbergh baby was kidnapped and murdered.

Jubilee (1935) offered 'Just One of Those Things' and 'Begin the Beguine', and the film *Born to Dance* (1936) 'Easy to Love' and 'I Get a Kick Out of You'; 'In the Still of the Night' came from *Rosalie* (1937). *Leave It to Me* (1938) was the show in which Sophie Tucker played the wife of the ambassador to the Soviet Union, and sang 'Most Gentlemen Don't Like Love (They just like to kick it around)'. The score also included the dramatic 'Get Out of Town', but the show was stolen by Mary Martin, making her Broadway début. She sang 'My Heart Belongs to Daddy' while sitting on a trunk at a Siberian railway station, slowly doffing her garments while rhyming 'Daddy' with 'caddie' and 'finnan haddie'. Alec Wilder thinks that the quality of Porter's work declined because of his agonizing physical condition, and certainly the later songs are not on the whole so fine, but perhaps only compared with the best of Porter. His last show was *Silk Stockings* in 1955.

Other Porter film projects were *Broadway Melody of 1940*, which contained 'I Concentrate On You' and reintroduced 'Begin the Beguine' after Artie Shaw's legendary hit record. *Something to Shout About* in 1943 had 'You'd Be So Nice to Come Home To'. *High Society* (1956) had a cast of such glittering stars as Frank Sinatra, Louis Armstrong, Bing Crosby and Grace Kelly, but the quality of the songs had definitely deteriorated: 'Well, Did You Evah!' was resuscitated from the 1939 show *Du Barry Was a Lady* (which also offered 'Do I Love You?' and was filmed in 1943); 'Now You Has Jazz' was simply silly, and the syrupy Crosby and Kelly duet 'True Love' made a Porter song a pop hit just as Elvis Presley was turning the world upside down. The film *Les Girls* (1957) was a disappointment. *Night and Day* (1946), a film biography of Porter starring Cary Grant, was so bad that Porter roared with laughter at it.

Anyone who has recognized the names of these songs will recognize them as being among the greatest of the century. Any younger readers whose musical experience has been too anaemic should get to know them. They have never been far away, but today's songs are so thin, and popular music has developed into such a rich repertory, that most of them are revived again and again. Mick Hucknall of the British pop group Simply Red sings Porter's 'Ev'ry Time We Say Goodbye', while the Irish cabaret artist Mary Coughlan has revived 'The Laziest Girl in Town'. The songs of that era will keep coming back: the great lyricists grew up before television and even before radio, so their speech had not been debased by advertising jingles and third-rate entertainment.

The songwriters who as a team were the equal of Cole Porter were composer Richard Rodgers and lyricist Lorenz Hart. Rodgers wrote his first song at the age of eleven, and saw Kern's *Very Good Eddie* at fourteen; he later said, 'Life began for me at 2.30', curtain time for Saturday matinées. In 1918 the punctual, well-groomed Rodgers met the bohemian Hart, who was adapting and translating German and Viennese operettas for the Shubert brothers; his adaptation of Ferenc Molnar's novel and play *Liliom* was a success, but Hart, on salary, received little credit. Rodgers and Hart's first hit came when 'Manhattan' was put into *The Garrick Gaieties* in 1925, along with 'Mountain Greenery'. They were signed up by a publisher and with five shows running in 1926 were suddenly each making

$1,000 a week. Rodgers used unusual chords, and would write a thirty-two-bar verse with a sixteen-bar chorus instead of the other way round; it was hard to get Hart to work, but then he quickly wrote love songs with wit.

Some of the songs from the shows of 1926 to 1930 were 'The Blue Room', 'My Heart Stood Still', 'You Took Advantage of Me', 'With a Song in My Heart', 'Ten Cents a Dance' and 'Dancing on the Ceiling'. *Jumbo* (1935) was produced by showman Billy Rose in the Hippodrome, a big old venue that was near the end of its life and had begun by sheltering circuses; the show had so many animals in it that Actor's Equity classed it as a circus. It also had Paul Whiteman's band, Jimmy Durante and three classic songs: 'Little Girl Blue', 'The Most Beautiful Girl in the World' and 'My Romance'. *Jumbo* cost so much to put on that it lost half its investment; the 1962 film (Doris Day's last musical) was also a disaster.

On Your Toes (1936) gave us 'There's a Small Hotel'; *Babes in Arms* (1937) had 'Where or When', 'The Lady Is a Tramp', 'My Funny Valentine' and 'I Wish I Were In Love Again', one of the best-known Hart lyrics:

> When love congeals
> It soon reveals
> The faint aroma of performing seals
> The double-crossing of a pair of heels
> I wish I were in love again.

A lesser songwriter might not have bothered with the fourth line, which adds to the wit and suspends the whole verse in mid-air, allowing the last line a bit more punch when it comes.

Pal Joey (1940) included 'I Could Write a Book' and 'Bewitched, Bothered and Bewildered'; the film version in 1957, with Frank Sinatra, added 'The Lady Is a Tramp'. Rodgers and Hart's film work in the early 1930s was less successful, except for *Love Me Tonight* (1932), with Maurice Chevalier, which contained 'Mimi' and 'Isn't It Romantic?' This was one of the first truly innovative musical films, directed by Rouben Mamoulian; in the opening sequence 'Isn't It Romantic?' was so tied to the action on screen that Hart had to rewrite the lyrics for the song's publication. (The song also became the title song of another film in 1948.) 'Blue Moon' never made it into a play or a film, but still became a classic.

Hart was small of stature, an alcoholic and unlucky in love; he died of pneumonia a few weeks after attending the première of Rodgers and Hammerstein's *Oklahoma!* in 1943. Like Hart, Oscar Hammerstein II had attended Columbia University before turning to the theatre; he wrote and acted in Columbia varsity shows and began as a stage manager for his impresario grandfather (hence 'II'; his father William managed one of Oscar I's theatres). He had written with Friml, Romberg, Youmans, Gershwin, Harbach, Herbert Stothart, Arthur Schwartz and Harold Arlen. Unlike Hart, he was always asleep by midnight, but had to work hard on his lyrics; like Hart, he achieved apparent spontaneity in his words, and was floundering in the early 1940s.

Rodgers and Hart's are the greater songs; Hart was one of the finest of all lyricists writing in English in the twentieth century, while Hammerstein was basically an operetta lover with a sentimental streak. But Rodgers and Hammerstein's shows marked an advance on Kern in musical theatre. For *Oklahoma!* the book as well as the lyrics were written by Hammerstein (based on the play *Green Grow the Lilacs* by Lynn Riggs), and the songs propelled the action rather than distracting the audience from a soon to be forgotten plot: with 'Oh, What a Beautiful Morning', 'People Will Say We're In Love' and 'Surrey With the Fringe On Top', it was one of the biggest Broadway hits of all time. *Carousel* (1945, ironically based on *Liliom*) included 'If I Loved You' and 'You'll Never Walk Alone'. *South Pacific* (1949) was, in my opinion, easily Rodgers and Hammerstein's best show, and another smash to match *Oklahoma!* Based on stories by James A. Michener, it offered 'Some Enchanted Evening', 'Bali Ha'i', 'Younger Than Springtime' and 'I'm In Love With a Wonderful Guy'. *The King and I* (1951, based on *Anna and the King of Siam*, by Margaret Landon) contained 'Hello Young Lovers', which has a particularly fine introduction, and 'I Have Dreamed'. In total there were over 6,300 performances of these four shows in their original productions and all were filmed. (Yul Brynner was successful for the rest of his life as the King of Siam.)

Leslie Stuart's *Florodora* was the first show to be recorded by its original cast (1900), but *Oklahoma!* was the first to be a modern hit; it was in the top five on the first *Billboard* album chart in March 1945. *South Pacific* had one of Robert Russell Bennett's most incisive orchestrations; its original cast album, which was available on all three speeds, entered the *Billboard* album chart in May 1949 and stayed there for over 400 weeks, making it one of the biggest hits of all time. Neither the 1958 film soundtrack nor a 1986 London recording, with the opera singers Kiri Te Kanawa and José Carreras, can begin to compete with it.

Rodgers and Hammerstein also wrote for the film *State Fair* in 1945 (including 'It Might As Well Be Spring'), formed a production company that mounted Berlin's *Annie Get Your Gun*, and also wrote the shows *Allegro* in 1947 ('The Gentleman Is a Dope'), *Me and Juliet* in 1953, *Pipe Dream* in 1955 and *Flower Drum Song* in 1958 ('I Enjoy Being a Girl'). Rodgers used a tune from his television music *Victory at Sea* for 'No Other Love' (in *Me and Juliet*); the song was a hit for Perry Como. Hammerstein adapted Bizet's *Carmen* as *Carmen Jones* in 1943, and it was filmed in 1954.

Some of their later shows were not as well received as the early ones, though *Me and Juliet*, for example, ran for a year and turned a profit. Critics usually blamed their disappointment on Hammerstein's plots. The sentimentality of their work together, as well as Hammerstein's affinity for operetta, reached an apotheosis with *The Sound of Music* in 1959, which became one of the most successful musical films of all time in 1965. Hammerstein died of cancer, and Rodgers began to lose his touch in a modern era. He wrote his own lyrics for *No Strings* in 1962, a hit because of a good story about interracial love, but thereafter his career declined. He had outlived his greatest partners and the golden age of Broadway.

Alec Wilder's book *American Popular Song* is recommended to readers interested in pursuing this subject. He wrote some fine songs himself, such as 'While We're Young', 'I'll Be Around', 'It's So Peaceful in the Country', 'Who Can I Turn To'. He makes a superb case for his favourite, Harold Arlen, as an example of 'this "don't-worry-about-the-mud-on-your-shoes" attitude'. Arlen wrote 'I Gotta Right to Sing the Blues', 'I've Got the World on a String', 'It's Only a Paper Moon', 'Blues in the Night', 'That Old Black Magic', 'One for My Baby' and many more, some of the best with lyrics by Johnny Mercer, a master of demotic speech.

While Broadway was providing some of the century's greatest songs, there were exciting things happening in the rest of the country. We must now examine the rest of the immensely rich popular music scene of the 1920s and 1930s, of which the American musical show was only the most glittering ingredient.

7

The Jazz Age, the Great Depression and New Markets: Race and Hillbilly Music

A San Francisco bandleader, Art Hickman, and his pianist-arranger Ferde Grofé are generally given credit for inventing the type of dance band which dominated popular music for half a century. Around the time of the First World War they were among the first to write separate music for the reed and brass sections, combining the higher and lower instruments in each section into choirs, but for dancing rather than listening, as in John Philip Sousa's concert band. Hickman seems to have been the first to hire three saxophones, enabling him to write richer harmonies. He also wrote songs, among them 'Rose Room', published in 1917. It is surely no coincidence that 'Rose Room' is the sort of tune that lends itself to an interesting arrangement, and was recorded by Benny Goodman's sextet nearly twenty-five years later; or that Duke Ellington's 'In a Mellotone' (1940) is a countermelody to it.

Hickman suffered from ill health and died relatively young in 1930, but by then bands all over the USA were playing his kind of music: black and white, hot and 'sweet' (or 'strict tempo', as it is called in Britain). Paul Whiteman's was by far the most successful. Whiteman was a good businessman and a great talent scout; we shall come back to him during the Big Band Era. He was called the 'King of Jazz' because Johann Strauss II had been the 'Waltz King' and Sousa had been the 'March King', and because publicists have tiny minds; Whiteman never took it seriously. But any sort of lively dance music was heard as 'jazz' by the public. The less strict moral atmosphere of the 1920s, in which young women went out dancing with their young men friends without supervision (and smoked cigarettes, and bobbed their hair!) carried the same association: hence the 'jazz age'.

The bands outside the biggest cities, indeed almost any bands outside New York, came to be called territory bands. Among the excellent black groups were Troy Floyd's eleven-piece band at the Plaza Hotel in San Antonio, Texas, with such sidemen as Herschel Evans (later with Count Basie); Alphonso Trent led a band in Dallas which included violinist Stuff Smith, trumpeter Harry Edison (later with Basie) and reedmen James Jeter and Hayes Pillars (who later co-led a popular dance band in St Louis for a decade). The white Coon–Sanders Orchestra, also known as the Kansas City Night Hawks owing to their late-night broadcasts, was led by drummer Carleton Coon and pianist-arranger Joe Sanders, who was nicknamed the Old Lefthander from his days as a baseball pitcher. Both were also singers and composers. In the earliest days of radio the Night Hawks was one of the bands that sold more records as a result of the novelty of broadcasting. The band's national fame ended when Coon died suddenly because of complications following an abscessed tooth; but Sanders remained a popular leader in the Chicago area (where my parents were among the young people who would travel 60 or 70 miles to dance to his music).

Another white band was the California Ramblers, who made an uncountable number of recordings between 1921 and 1937 with constantly changing personnel and under many different names. Trumpeters Henry 'Hot Lips' Levine (later on the NBC staff) and Red Nichols, Tommy and Jimmy Dorsey, bass saxophonist Adrian Rollini and, as vocalists, songwriter Sammy Fain and early country star Vernon Dalhart may be heard on some of these recordings.

Somewhat smaller bands were Roy Johnson and his Happy Pals, which included Jack Teagarden at one time, as did Peck's Bad Boys in Texas (led by the pianist Peck Kelley), and the Blue Devils, led by bassist Walter Page, which melded into the larger band of Bennie Moten. Paul Howard's Quality Serenaders, on the West Coast, included Lionel Hampton and Lawrence Brown, the great trombonist who later spent decades in Duke Ellington's band. Typical of the territory bands was that of the Midwesterner Slatz Randall, who worked and recorded in Minneapolis for a decade after 1929, making a dozen jazz-influenced pop records, such as the slightly saucy 'Bessie Couldn't Help It'; the latter was recorded by Hoagy Carmichael, Louis Armstrong and many others, but Randall's is the most fun. The Benson Orchestra of Chicago was led by Edgar A. Benson, and included Frankie Trumbauer. Erskine Tate's Vendome Orchestra, a Chicago institution, employed many famous jazzmen over the years. It recorded with Freddy Keppard in 1923 and Louis Armstrong three years later, and Tate remained one of Chicago's leading music teachers throughout the 1950s and 1960s.

Among the most successful and prolifically recorded territory bands was Bennie Moten's black band, whose classic 'South' was an acoustic hit in 1925; both the electrical remake in 1929 and its reissue in 1944 were hits. As in the ragtime era, there were a great many musicians and hundreds of bands whose contribution is now lost. Most of the bands never recorded; some remained local in more or less steady hotel or restaurant jobs, while others toured. The musical ferment was intense.

Youngsters often started out in dime-a-dance halls, where the band played one chorus of each tune: that was your 10-cent dance. In the Red Mill on North Main Street in Los Angeles, where trumpeter Buck Clayton played in the late 1920s, the band played only half the chorus of a tune on Saturday nights, speeding up the dance hall's take, much as jukeboxes were speeded up a few years later. Such bands played stock arrangements, provided by the publishers of the tunes. One of the best arrangers was Archie Bleyer, who became better known decades later through his studio and television work and as a label boss. Stock arrangements were usually not very challenging, but Clayton, who was still a teenager in the late 1920s and later became a fine arranger himself, wrote in his autobiography: 'One of my biggest troubles with the stock arrangements that we were playing were the famous Archie Bleyer arrangements ... I could see then that I had a hell of a lot to learn. "Business in F" and "Business in Q" were two particular stocks that used to hang me every night.'

The people who danced to all these bands became the equivalent of the New Orleans 'second line' as popular music changed. Dance band music was already well established by 1920, and was the biggest single category in popular music for decades after the adoption of electrical recording in 1925, for several reasons. The dancing in Broadway shows, and later in films, was incomparably better than it had been in earlier times. The girls in the back row of the chorus had studied ballet, and were better dancers than the star performers of the nineteenth century. American popular music was now a national rather than a regional affair; not only were records sold for dancing at home, but dance music was broadcast live on the radio every evening. Radio was conservative during what came to be called prime time, but later in the evening remote broadcasts from ballrooms caused the folks at home to roll up the rugs.

There was a tremendous upsurge in the popularity of ballroom dancing itself, fuelled by the success on Broadway of Vernon and Irene Castle. Vernon Blythe, an English magician, met Irene Foote in an American show in 1911; their performance in *Watch Your Step* in 1914 made them world-famous. They hired black bandleader James Reese Europe to provide their music, started a chain of dancing schools and invented the ubiquitous foxtrot (which anybody could do), as well as the turkey trot, the bunny-hug, the Castle rock and many more, and were also behind the tango craze which swept the country. Vernon joined a British flying squad in France during the First World War; he taught flying in the USA and was killed in an accident in 1918. A film of their lives made in 1939 starred (who else?) Fred Astaire and Ginger Rogers.

The scores of popular dance bands included that of Vincent Lopez, who made the first live band broadcast on radio in 1921; Wayne King, a new 'Waltz King', whose broadcasts from a Chicago ballroom were sponsored by a cosmetics company, and whose music appealed to an ageing audience (which used more and more cosmetics); and Fred Waring, who forsook mainstream 'hot' dance music and played sweeter and stricter music as time went on, subsiding into a glee club style. Live broadcasts brought fans to the ballrooms, but Waring was suspicious of recording, thinking that it must be bad for live music: he had big hits on Victor until early 1933, and then did not record at all for a decade. A radio show that paid Waring $12,500 a week became a target for pirates, who recorded Waring off the radio and sold the recordings to other stations; in 1936 Waring won one of the first lawsuits against bootleg records. Ted Lewis was a popular entertainer and second-rate clarinettist whose catch-phrase was 'Is everybody happy?'; his show band often included hot soloists on recordings, such as Fats Waller. Isham Jones made a renowned recording of 'Stardust', the third most often recorded song of the century (after 'Silent Night' and 'St Louis Blues'), establishing it as a romantic ballad; previous recordings had been at a bouncy mid-tempo, which is what Hoagy Carmichael intended.

We have met Carmichael before as a close friend of Beider-becke; he was among America's best-loved songwriters. One of his first tunes was called 'Freewheeling'; Bix changed it to 'Riverboat Shuffle', and it became a jazz classic. 'Stardust' had fifteen hit recordings from 1930 to 1943, and several more in later years. Carmichael appeared as himself in a few films, playing piano and singing and acting in his inimitable laconic drawl. He was also a recording artist, and in 1957 made a delightful album of his own songs, backed by all-star jazzmen.

Bix played on some of Carmichael's recordings, playing a fine solo on 'Riverboat', and on the high-spirited novelty 'Barnacle Bill the Sailor' (written with Carson Robison, a maverick who became known for his activities in country music). 'Barnacle Bill' is famous for one of Joe Venuti's pranks: the trio in the vocal refrain consisted of Carmichael, Robison and Venuti, who could not resist singing, 'Barnacle Bill the shithead!'

Carmichael was from Bloomington, Indiana, and many of his songs served to match his laid-back Midwestern personality. One of the most quintessentially American composers, he and his career were inseparable from the jazz age. He wrote words and music for 'Rockin' Chair', 'Memphis in June' and 'New Orleans', but he usually worked with lyricists: Mitchell Parish wrote the words of 'Stardust' and 'One Morning in May', Stuart Gorrell 'Georgia on My Mind', Sidney Arodin '(Up a) Lazy River', Ned Washington 'The Nearness of You', Paul Francis Webster 'Lamplighter's Serenade' and Johnny Mercer 'Lazybones', 'Skylark' and 'In the Cool, Cool, Cool of the Evening' (the last of which won an Oscar in 1951).

After the Swing Era began in 1935, the music was more jazz-oriented, but most of the public just wanted to dance, and the sheer number of bands was astonishing. Composer-arrangers Will Hudson and Eddie DeLange together led a well-known outfit in the late 1930s; among their vocalists was Georgia Gibbs. Horace Heidt's sidemen included Frank DeVol on reeds (later a studio arranger and conductor), Frankie Carle on piano (who later led his own sweet band) and Alvino Rey on electric guitar, which was unusual at the time. (Rey also formed his own band, taking DeVol and the King Sisters vocal quartet with him.) Lobo, a trained dog, took part in Heidt's act, and a later gimmick was giving away money on the radio, until that was outlawed as a lottery; he then held regional talent contests on local radio and early television.

Sammy Kaye and Kay Kyser were among the most successful leaders. ('Swing and Sway with Sammy Kaye' was changed by another bandleader to 'Swing and Sweat with Charlie Barnet'.) Kaye also invented an element of participation in that members of the audience were invited to lead the band, which survived well into the television era. Kyser's gimmick was the College of Musical Knowledge, a sort of quiz. Both bands used the corny device of singing the song title at the beginning of the arrangement. Neither was taken seriously by jazz-oriented critics, but both served up superbly reliable dance music, choosing the best tunes, playing them at the most appropriate tempos and pacing their sets extremely well. They had scores of hit records: Kyser's novelty 'Woody Woodpecker' drove the country crazy in 1948.

Guy Lombardo formed his Royal Canadians in the early 1920s in Canada, and it first recorded in 1924. Lombardo was a violinist turned front man (and later became a well-known speedboat racer); his brothers Lebert played trumpet, Victor baritone saxophone, while Carmen led the reed section and vocal trio, sang solo and wrote some fine songs, including 'Coquette', 'Boo Hoo' (covered by Count Basie and Jimmy Rushing, albeit with some reluctance), 'A Sailboat in the Moonlight and You' (covered by Billie Holiday) and 'Sweethearts on Parade' (of which Armstrong made a beautiful recording in 1930). A sister, Rose Marie Lombardo, was a vocalist; later the band's very popular singer was Kenny Gardner. The band featured a muted trumpet section and quavering reeds and played in strict tempo, and was regarded as a joke by jazz fans, who perhaps were not listening closely enough: the band often seemed to float over the beat, and was a hip 1920s dance band that never changed. The inclusion of some of its early recordings in Brian Rust's *Jazz Records 1897–1942* is evidence that it once played hot. Its music was good enough to make it the third-biggest act on records of the entire period 1890–1954, after Bing Crosby and Paul Whiteman, as well as Armstrong's favourite.

Paul Whiteman may not have been the 'King of Jazz', but he was the king of show business. Bandmaster of a fifty-seven-piece outfit in the US Navy during the First World War, he formed his first group in 1919, adopting Hickman's style as well as Grofé as pianist and arranger. Whiteman's bands were twice as big as those of his competitors; he presented a kind of 'symphonic jazz' which was pretentious even then. But as a dance band it was a harbinger of the Swing Era to come and has long been underrated. Whiteman's vocalists at various times included Morton Downey and Mildred Bailey. Downey was one of the first band singers; some thought Whiteman was mad to hire a singer, but as usual he was merely ahead of the field.

Grofé's arrangements for Whiteman, which initially jazzed the classics, attracted a Victor recording contract. The first disc was a 12-inch 78 of 'Avalon' (the tune taken from a Puccini opera) backed with 'Dance of the Hours' (by Ponchielli). The first hit was the two-sided 'Whispering' / 'The Japanese Sandman' in 1920; each side reached number one and the record sold over two million copies. 'Wang Wang Blues' was another hit, initially released under trumpeter Henry Busse's name. Busse was a German immigrant who later led his own band; 'Hot Lips', recorded with Whiteman in 1922, became his nickname and his theme, and his solo on 'When Day is Done' started a vogue for 'sweet jazz'.

Like Glenn Miller twenty years later, Whiteman saw off a previous era in popular music while summing it up and giving the public a little bit of everything: he recorded 'Last Night on the Back Porch' with a barber-shop quartet, led by Len Murray, in 1923; he not only jazzed the classics, but commissioned new music from George Gershwin, black composer William Grant Still and others, and his orchestra often worked as a pit band on Broadway. His number one hit 'Three O'Clock in the Morning' in 1923 sold 3.5 million copies of the song and led to a contract with Leo Feist as staff writer: this was a euphemism for song plugger and a form of bribe, giving Whiteman access to many of the best pop songs of the day. Whiteman made one of the first musical talking films, *King of Jazz*, in 1930, which contains perhaps ten minutes of worthwhile music. But he helped educate the public to listen to jazz-oriented music as well as dance to it.

Whiteman's vocal trio, the Rhythm Boys, comprised Al Rinker (Mildred Bailey's brother), Harry Barris and Bing Crosby. They had started out in vaudeville, and were lucky to land a spot with Whiteman when they were still very young. Crosby's first solo hit with Whiteman was 'Muddy Water' in 1927, and he recorded two songs from *Show Boat* the next year: 'Ol' Man River' and 'Make Believe' were among his early successes.

The Rhythm Boys left Whiteman in 1930 to work with Gus Arnheim's band at the Coconut Grove in Los Angeles. 'Them There Eyes', with the trio, was a hit that year, and Crosby's first solo hit with Arnheim was 'I Surrender, Dear' (co-written by Barris), which so impressed a CBS executive that Crosby was offered a radio show of his own. Harry Lillis Crosby, nicknamed after a cartoon character with big ears, became the top recording artist of the entire first half of the century, and by a very wide margin; he sold hundreds of millions of records (with over 350 hit titles) and starred in more than fifty films. His fame and worldwide popularity were such that during the Second World War German soldiers called him 'Der Bingle'.

Gus Arnheim wrote 'Sweet and Lovely', a beautiful song and a number one hit in 1931; he employed Woody Herman, who later made a memorable recording of it. Lombardo, Crosby and several others also had hits with 'Sweet and Lovely', and Herman's tenor saxophonist Flip Phillips made a beautiful version in 1944.

At the Coconut Grove Crosby always had a bunch of friends in his dressing room, a card game under way and a radio, so they could listen to Arnheim's two-hour broadcasts. Crosby would dash upstairs to do his bit, and on one occasion ended by saying to a nationwide audience, 'Deal me in, boys; I'll be right down.' He loved cronies, cards, alcohol and women, but, under the influence of his mother and given the example of his unsuccessful father, he realized that he was going to make big money and could not be sure how long the success was going to last: he became a very wealthy businessman, while the success lasted all his life.

Rudy Vallee was one of the biggest stars of the 1920s, and also one of the most generous people in the business. The quintessential collegiate singer of the acoustic era, he crooned through a megaphone, and he later said that as soon as he heard Crosby, he knew his style had been superseded. (He also wrote, in an introduction to Louis Armstrong's autobiography *Swing That Music* (1936), that Crosby and all the other pop singers of the day could not have helped being influenced by Armstrong's singing.) Vallee played drums and reeds, then began singing through a megaphone of his own design, just as his hit records were played through a horn (fifteen of them in 1929 alone, when most record players were still acoustic). He was one of the first to understand the commercial importance of broadcasting, and was famous for his greeting, 'Heigh-ho, everybody!' He later became a well-known comic actor, generally playing stuffed-shirt types in films, and in 1961 starred on Broadway in *How to Succeed in Business Without Really Trying*.

Crosby acknowledged his debt to Pops. By 1930 Armstrong was recording the best pop songs of the day and showing everyone how they could be interpreted with loving care by a superior stylist – in short, what good songs they were. He brought good songs to jazz and vice versa, determining the direction of jazz and pop for decades; his 'Stardust' was no less influential than Isham Jones's record.

Crosby had worked in the same band as Bix and many other first-rate jazzmen; his personal accompanist was the great guitarist Eddie Lang. Crosby's voice was a pleasant baritone – it sounded, Crosby said, like someone hollering down a rain barrel – a voice that everybody could identify with. His earliest records sound dated now, more because of the arrangements than his singing; he seems to be less at ease than at his peak in the 1940s, but he is indubitably *there*, and you can understand every word. Along with Armstrong, he was one of the first to appreciate the importance of the microphone: he sang easily, intimately and without strain, phrasing almost conversationally, as though singing personally to each listener. From jazz, perhaps, Crosby had learned the value of direct communication.

Although never a jazz singer, together with Armstrong he virtually invented modern pop singing.

Crosby recorded for Brunswick until 1934, then followed Jack Kapp to the new Decca label, where he stayed for twenty years, despite attempts to lure him elsewhere. He recorded duets with Armstrong, Jolson, Bob Hope, Mel Tormé, Jane Wyman, Connee Boswell, Peggy Lee, Judy Garland, his first wife, Dixie Lee, his son Gary and others. He was backed on records by Victor Young's orchestra, the Les Paul Trio and the bands of Waring, Lombardo, Eddie Condon, Louis Jordan, Xavier Cugat, Jimmy Dorsey, his brother Bob Crosby and many more. More than twenty of his hits, including 'Don't Fence Me In', were performed with the Andrews Sisters. He had the pick of the best songs of his era, many of which were written by Irving Berlin, but he also ranged back and forth through the history of popular song, from Brahms's 'Lullaby' through 'Mary's a Grand Old Name' (1906) and 'MacNamara's Band' (1917) to 'Swinging on a Star', by Jimmy Van Heusen and Johnny Burke, from the film *Going My Way*; both Crosby and the song won Oscars in 1944. (Young Andy was one of the Williams Brothers backing him on the record, and the song was included in children's music books.) Crosby also recorded several of the best country songs of the 1940s.

His only rival as a male pop singer in the early years was Russ Colombo, who also sang with Arnheim's band; he was credited as co-author of 'Prisoner of Love', and sang Arnheim's 'Sweet and Lovely'. Colombo died in an accident with a desk ornament, a duelling pistol that turned out to be loaded.

A popular female singer in the late 1920s was Helen Kane, the 'boop-boop-a-doop' girl, whose tunes included her theme, 'I Wanna be Loved by You', and the slightly suggestive 'Is There Anything Wrong in That?' Her little-girl voice inspired Betty Boop, the cartoon character. Kane sued the creators of Betty, but it was established that 'booping' had earlier been practised by a black singer, Baby Esther. Kane's flapper persona was soon *passé*, but her tiny voice was revived by Wee Bonnie Baker on her 1939 hit, and Kane herself was dubbed by Debbie Reynolds in a 1950 film, *Three Little Words*. (Betty Boop's sensational curves ran foul of the censors after about a hundred cartoons, but she did a cameo in *Who Framed Roger Rabbit?* in 1988.)

Many fine female singers were admired by jazzmen. Mildred Bailey was married to vibraphonist Red Norvo; in the 1930s they led a band together and were known as Mr and Mrs Swing. Connee Boswell, who was born in New Orleans, had a successful career as leader and arranger of a vocal trio with her sisters before going solo. A victim of polio, she worked in a wheelchair; she said she learned breath control by listening to Caruso records.

Ethel Waters was well known as a vocalist before Louis Armstrong. The English writer Charles Fox has described her as the first important jazz singer, because of the way she told a story; she began by singing popular blues, and could transform a pop song more subtly than Bessie Smith, displaying, as Fox says, 'a remarkably expressive voice, a keen understanding of how language should come across in song, and a rhythmic flexibility very rare at that time'. She became the biggest black star on Broadway after Bert Williams. *As Thousands Cheer* (1933) at Irving Berlin's Music Box had a book by Moss Hart and was a barbed political satire, full of laughs; Waters sang 'Supper Time' (an anti-lynching song), 'Harlem on My Mind' and the sizzling 'Heat Wave'. (Marilyn Miller and Clifton Webb sang 'Easter Parade' in *As Thousands Cheer*, stepping out of a sepia photograph, as from a rotogravure newspaper section.)

Vocal groups, popular in the acoustic era, now sold records with more modern harmony. The Boswell Sisters paved the way for the Andrews Sisters, three girls from Minneapolis whose success began with 'Bei mir bist du schön' in 1938 and whose close harmony is still redolent of nostalgia for millions. (Bette Midler revived their 'Boogie Woogie Bugle Boy' over thirty years later.) They too recorded with many other Decca artists, among them Lombardo, Les Paul, Danny Kaye and Carmen Miranda, as well as Crosby. Patti Andrews had solo hits, Patti and Maxene starred in *Over There* on Broadway in 1974 and Maxene released a new album in 1985. The King Sisters had an unusually rich harmonic style, being a quartet: Alyce, Donna, Louise and Yvonne Driggs sang with Horace Heidt, then with Alvino Rey (Louise's husband), and had a television series in the 1960s.

Male vocal groups included the Mills Brothers and the Ink Spots, both black, and enormously successful. The Ink Spots were a quartet; the voice of its lead singer, Bill Kenny, on 'If I Didn't Care' (1939) and 'To Each His Own' (1946) is unforgettable. Even more popular were the Mills Brothers, Herbert, Harry, Donald and John, the last of whom accompanied the group on his guitar. (When John died in 1935, he was replaced by their father.) They had hits from 1931 ('Tiger Rag') until the end of the 1960s; 'Paper Doll' (1943) sold over six million copies.

An influential genre was the torch song; nearly all the hit records in this style occur after 1926, because it requires an intimacy that was impossible without the microphone. Broadway stars Ruth Etting, Libby Holman, Fanny Brice and Helen Morgan were famous for songs of regretful, passionate love; in some cases their personal lives reflected their stage personae. These four had over eighty hit records, but Etting was by far the most prolific. She was picked out of a chorus line in 1922 by her manager and first husband, mobster Moe 'the Gimp' Snyder, and was best known for 'Love Me or Leave Me' and 'Ten Cents a Dance' (which she sang in Rodgers and Hart's show *Simple Simon* in 1930). Moe shot her piano player, but he recovered, and married her; in spite of all the drama in her life, she had a long and happy retirement. She was played by Doris Day in the film biography *Love Me or Leave Me* (1955), and Jimmy Cagney was Moe.

Fanny Brice was also married to a mobster, gambler Nicky Arnstein; her most famous song was 'My Man', a French import which she sang for Ziegfeld in 1920 and in a film in 1929. She also did comedy and dialect songs, and was the popular brat Baby Snooks on the radio in the late 1940s. Barbra Streisand played Brice in *Funny Girl* on Broadway in 1964 and in the film in 1968. Libby Holman was well known for sultry renditions of 'Moanin' Low' (by Ralph Rainger and Howard Dietz) and 'Body and Soul' (in the show *Three's a Crowd*, 1930). She married tobacco heir Zachary Smith Reynolds; when he was murdered a year later, she was accused but cleared, though her career never recovered. Helen Morgan sang in the Kern shows *Showboat* and *Sweet Adeline*; *The Helen Morgan Story* was made for TV in the 1950s with Polly Bergen, who made fine albums of torch songs for CBS, but the 1957 cinema version unaccountably replaced Bergen with an actress whose singing voice had to be dubbed.

In the Great Depression the record business almost disappeared, because music could be heard free on the radio, but popular music, along with the cinema, became an important avenue of escapism. Curiously, the calamity of the Depression inspired only one memorable song, 'Brother, Can You Spare a Dime?', by Jay Gorney and Yip Harburg. 'Hallelujah, I'm a Bum' is sometimes quoted as a Depression song; actually there were two songs of that title: Harry Kirby McClintock based his on the hymn 'Revive Us Again', while Rodgers and Hart wrote theirs for a film of the same name. But neither was really a Depression song. Hart wrote: 'Why work away for wealth / When you can travel for your health?' This philosophy had little appeal in 1933.

But even the Depression could not alter the fact that new markets had been discovered. Tin Pan Alley and Broadway were oriented towards New York, while many Americans had their own indigenous musics which meant much to them. The great country music producer Art Satherley, born in England, loved American rural, or folk, music, and regarded all of it as country music, whether white or black; but according to the institutionalized racism of the era, it had to be divided into 'race' and 'hillbilly' music.

Cornettist, songwriter, bandleader and publisher William Christopher Handy had become a powerful figure in the music business, having discovered or written such imperishable songs as 'St Louis Blues', 'Beale Street Blues', 'Yellow Dog Blues', 'Memphis Blues' and 'Loveless Love' (also known as 'Careless Love'). 'St Louis Blues', which has a habanera 'Spanish tinge' in the middle section, is one of the biggest hits of the century and was first recorded in 1916. 'Memphis Blues' was originally a campaign song for Mr Edward H. Crump, a Memphis political leader. Handy's songs were not really blues, according to a strict musical definition which has lost some ground in recent years. Blues was a folk music that had evolved among ex-slaves in the nineteenth century from their work songs. Although the blues was and is an important element in jazz, jazz was never a folk music, while blues relied on unsophisticated but subtle and direct communication.

The classic blues is a twelve-bar verse, three lines of four bars each; the lyric consists of couplets, with the first line repeated once. (Leonard Bernstein, in one of his recorded lectures, used Shakespeare couplets as blues.) Each line of text takes about two and a half bars; the rest of each four-bar segment is improvised fill, sometimes vocal, but usually provided by the singer's own guitar or piano. The blues goes against European musical practice, and was therefore frowned upon by educated people both black and white; it uniquely combined major and minor modes. 'Blue notes', which cannot be played on the piano, are now thought to have stemmed more or less directly from African music. Classic blues lyrics came from a storehouse of images, words and phrases, including the argot that American blacks had used to express themselves safely since the earliest days of slavery. The verses and the musical accompaniment are like two voices: the accompaniment is a commentary on the story being told, and the result is a polyrhythmic, almost poly-emotional music. The blues is not a vehicle for self-pity, contrary to the commonplace orthodoxy, but a passionate, intensely rhythmic way of keeping the spirit *up*, by commenting on problems of life and love with lyrics full of irony and earthy imagery: defeating the enemy by confronting him. Blues is, above all, a music of great human bravery.

The commercial market for blues, like that for jazz, was discovered by the record business in time to capture many classic performers. Perry Bradford, an early entrepreneur in black music, placed two of his songs with Fred Hagar, music director of Okeh Records; 'That Thing Called Love' and 'You Can't Keep a Good Man Down', both published by the Pace and Handy Music Company, were recorded by Mamie Smith. To this day we cannot be sure whether the backing group was black or white. The record sold well enough to call for another recording session, this time with a black group dubbed the Jazz Hounds. Bradford's 'Crazy Blues' (not a real blues, but a pop song) was recorded in August 1920. To everyone's surprise it was a sensation, and yet another genre of black music began to enrich the mainstream of American music. Obviously the discovery was waiting to happen; as early as 1920 Jerome Kern wrote songs with 'blues' in the title. More importantly, over five thousand genuine blues records were made before the Second World War.

Among the female blues singers were Trixie Smith (quickly signed by Harry Pace, who left W. C. Handy to form Black Swan, the first black-owned record label, for which Fletcher Henderson handled the musical side), Clara Smith, Alberta Hunter, Lucille Hegamin, Victoria Spivey, Edith Wilson and Sippie Wallace, most of whom were all-round performers who included blues numbers in their acts. The two most authentic were undoubtedly Gertrude 'Ma' Rainey and her protégée Bessie Smith, called the Mother and the Empress of the Blues respectively. (None of the Smiths was related.)

Ma Rainey and Bessie Smith seemed larger than life, having powerful voices, powerful appetites and a reluctance to take any nonsense from anybody. Ma was perhaps the purer blues singer; her biggest hit was 'See See Rider' in 1925, with Louis Armstrong and Henderson. But of all the blues singers Bessie Smith was the one who had most influence on jazz musicians. Like Ma Rainey, she had developed a method of singing each song around centre tones, perhaps in order to project her voice more easily to the back of a room; but she would also choose to sing a song in an unusual key, and her artistry in bending and stretching notes with her beautiful, powerful contralto to accommodate her own interpretation was unsurpassed: she could make a trite pop song into a blues masterpiece. Her biggest hit was her first, 'Downhearted Blues', in 1923, written by Alberta Hunter and Lovie Austin; others were 'Empty Bed Blues' in 1928 (it covered two sides of a 78, which at that time was very unusual) and 'After You've Gone', two W. C. Handy songs.

To accept the obvious orthodoxy that the music of Jelly Roll Morton, King Oliver and Bessie Smith was regarded as old-fashioned by 1930 is to ignore what might have been. What would have happened to American music if the phonograph had captured the cornet playing of Frank Johnson in 1845, or if James P. Johnson had been commissioned to write for Paul Whiteman's concert in 1924 instead of George Gershwin? Who knows how many records Morton, Oliver and Smith might have sold if the bottom had not dropped out of the record business between 1929 and 1932? As it was, Bessie earned as much as $3,000 a recording session, and in 1929 appeared in a short film, *St Louis Blues*, with the Hall Johnson Choir and a band led by James P. Johnson. But she had her last national hit the same year, 'Nobody Knows You when You're Down and Out', with Clarence Williams on piano. After 1931 there was no recording session until her last, in 1933, for which she was paid $50 for each of four sides, and her sales did not even justify that. She spent the rest of her life touring, and died of horrific injuries following a car crash, not knowing that she would influence singers who were not yet born.

The new market for race music led to a scramble to record black artists in the 1920s, not that many of them were 'signed up' in the modern sense: their records are still selling, but few of them received any royalties. Blind Lemon Jefferson, a street singer and guitarist who recorded prolifically, is thought to have been the first to record the slide guitar style (in 1926), in which the guitar is fretted with a knife-blade, steel tube, bottleneck (hence 'bottleneck' style) or some other such tool; this became an important voice in the blues. Jefferson was only in his thirties when he froze to death in a Chicago snow storm. Guitarist and vocalist Big Bill Broonzy was an early urban blues artist, so active in the Chicago area, both as soloist and sideman, that he was one of the most widely recorded and best-selling black artists of the era. Broonzy again was more than a blues singer; when asked if he sang folksongs, he replied that he had never heard a horse sing them.

The alcoholic Leroy Carr, in Indianapolis, Indiana, accompanied himself on the piano, which was unusual for a male blues singer. His smoother, more urban style, along with such songs as 'How Long Blues' and 'In the Evening when the Sun Goes Down', was to be of formative influence on the next generation. He made his classic records with Scrapper Blackwell, a guitarist who also sang and played piano. Another piano-playing bluesman was Memphis Slim (Peter Chatman), who wrote 'Alberta' (a Broonzy speciality), 'The Comeback' and 'Every Day (I Have the Blues)', made famous in 1955 by Count Basie and Joe Williams.

A genre of blues piano playing began in the lumber camps of the South: the barrelhouse piano style was so called because the room with the piano usually had a bar consisting of a barrel of whisky resting on two planks. These pianists taught themselves to play at the level required in such places; the pianism was less sophisticated than that of the ragtime-based stride pianists of the East Coast. They played a rolling rhythm in the left hand (eight notes to the bar) so that they could reach for a drink or a sandwich with the right hand.

As their music reached places like Chicago it came to be called boogie-woogie, and it was a fad in the 1940s during the Swing Era.

The blues was already becoming urbanized, for the First World War had stimulated black emigration to northern cities. But up until the next war the greatest male blues singers were still to be found in rural areas, where they were often recorded on portable disc-cutting equipment. It is significant that nearly all of them accompanied themselves on the guitar. The black woman was not a threat to white male supremacy; she often worked indoors, and if she became a singer, she was accompanied by a pianist. The black male was not a threat either, if he could be kept itinerant, preferably illiterate and utterly poor, so he had to carry his music around with him. The history of the blues provides more evidence of the fractured family lives of black Americans, the result of which is that today black children are still far more likely than white ones to come from a broken home.

The more delicate and lyrical Piedmont blues tradition of the South-east was represented by musicians like Blind Boy Fuller, Pink Anderson and Floyd Council (the last two of whom had a rock group named after them) and harmonica player Sonny Terry and Brownie McGhee. Terry and McGhee were taken up by white liberals as a popular concert act, whereupon they lost their edge.

Like Blind Lemon Jefferson, Lightnin' Hopkins, Texas Alexander and Mance Lipscomb all came from Texas. Lipscomb did not record at all until 1961, when he was discovered by Chris Strachwitz of Arhoolie Records; another all-rounder, he played excellent ragtime, pop songs and children's songs on his guitar. Mississippi John Hurt, who herded cows in Avalon, Mississippi, was another versatile artist. After being discovered by Tommy Rockwell, he recorded in Memphis and New York in 1928, but was then washed away by the Depression; he was rediscovered by Tom Hoskins in 1963, his sly charm and unique guitar playing completely intact.

The purest, most powerful – indeed, harrowing – blues of all came from the Mississippi delta. Eddie 'Son' House, Nehemiah 'Skip' James and Bukka White lived long enough to be rediscovered; Charley Patton, Robert Johnson, Tommy Johnson, Ishman Bracey, Peetie Wheatstraw and many others survive only on old recordings.

(Bracey had left the blues to become a clergyman.) Wheatstraw was known as 'the Devil's son-in-law'. Charley Patton regarded himself as an entertainer, and played an exceptionally interesting ragtime-based guitar; he was related to the Chatmon family of well-known Mississippi blues artists.

Booker T. Washington 'Bukka' White recorded for Victor in 1930, worked as a boxer and a baseball player and then made two sides for Vocalion in 1937: 'Pinebluff, Arkansas' and 'Shake 'Em On Down', the latter a blues classic which had many variants. He was sentenced to Parchman State Farm in Mississippi for assault, where he was recorded by John Lomax for the Library of Congress in 1939. After his release he made twelve sides in 1940 with Washboard Sam (Robert Brown) for Okeh and Vocalion, including 'Parchman Farm Blues', 'Where Can I Change My Clothes?' and 'District Attorney Blues'. The controlled passion of his rough-edged voice and his rhythmically inexorable guitar created some of the most beautiful and powerfully emotional music in the genre. The end of the classic blues era was already near; but White was rediscovered in 1963 by Ed Denson and guitarist John Fahey with much of his power still intact.

As these musicians were more or less self-taught, they invented their own ways of playing what they wanted, and each of the best was inspiring in his own way. Skip James's intensely lyrical style was said to have influenced Robert Johnson; he made twenty-six sides for Paramount in 1931, for which he was paid $40. Son House also served time at Parchman State Farm; he made eight or nine sides for Paramount in 1930 and test pressings for ARC (who decided on Patton instead), and recorded for the Library of Congress in 1941–2. Both House and James were rediscovered in time to perform at folk festivals and to make more recordings; both had tunes covered by rock groups.

Tommy Johnson's classic 'Cool Drink of Water Blues' begins with the famous line 'I asked her for water / She gave me gasoline', and his 'Canned Heat Blues' gave the white blues band of the 1960s its name. ('Canned heat' was used in cooking stoves; the best-known brand name was Sterno. It could be dissolved and used as a poisonous beverage by alcoholics.) Bracey was something of a Johnson sidekick; he played at almost exactly the same recording dates, and recorded a water and gasoline lyric the day after Tommy did. Johnson made few recordings, but through his unique guitar playing he was one of the most influential of all, along with Robert Johnson (to whom he was not related).

Tommy's brother Ledell, who taught him some guitar, said that Tommy had acquired his final polish by selling his soul to the devil. Son House said the same thing about Robert Johnson, who was not at first thought to be a particularly good player, but disappeared for a while, and then turned up much improved. In the hands of the greatest masters, the blues guitar sang with intensity, and Robert Johnson was a complete master. 'Hellhound on My Trail' and 'Me and the Devil Blues' are perhaps his most apposite titles. In a San Antonio hotel room in 1936 and in the back room of a Dallas office building in 1937 he made a total of forty-one sides for ARC labels (including alternative takes). Only 'Terraplane Blues' was anything like a hit in the restricted race market of the time, but 'I Believe I'll Dust My Broom' was adapted by Elmore James and became a post-war anthem of electric blues, while 'Terraplane', 'Love in Vain', 'Stop Breakin' Down' and 'Crossroads' were covered by rock groups in the 1960s. (The crossroads was where you went at midnight to do a deal with the devil.) Johnson's death was violent and said to involve a woman; his acolyte Johnny Shines had heard that 'it was something to do with the black arts'. It is now suggested that Robert Johnson was a far more 'sophisticated' performer than was hitherto thought, which makes his legacy all the more interesting. Meticulous research on his life has not been published yet because his killer is still alive.

John Hammond tried to find Johnson for his 1938 'From Spirituals to Swing' concert, but for once Hammond was too late. Hammond was the legendary producer of generations of great artists: coming from a wealthy family, he was financially independent enough to be able to work freelance during the Depression. He recorded Fletcher Henderson; he produced Billie Holiday's first recording session and Bessie Smith's last, both in 1933; he was an early champion of Benny Goodman, Count Basie, Charlie Christian and many other jazz greats; later he was director of popular music at Vanguard (1950s), which resulted in excellent jazz and folk albums, and helped to discover Bob

Dylan and Bruce Springsteen. The concerts he produced in 1938–9 represented a turning point in American popular culture.

The concert on 23 December 1938 at Carnegie Hall began with boogie-woogie pianists Pete Johnson, Albert Ammons and Meade 'Lux' Lewis, imported from the Midwest (where Ammons and Lewis had made a living washing cars and driving taxis in Chicago). This touched off the fad for boogie-woogie mentioned earlier, and inspired the young German immigrant Alfred Lion to form his Blue Note label. Big Bill Broonzy sang about having a dream in which he had a chat with President Roosevelt. Sister Rosetta Tharpe had hardly sung anywhere other than in church, but demonstrated the connection between the music of the black churches and the passion of the blues; she soon became a leading attraction with the Lucky Millinder band in Harlem. Ruby Walker Smith sang the blues (she was thought to be Bessie's niece, but Hammond said not). Other performers included Sidney Bechet, Tommy Ladnier and James P. Johnson, and the concert ended with the full Basie band; it was well received by the critics, and sophisticated fans found out where their favourite music had come from. Hammond was a man of strong views, some of them strange: he wrote in his autobiography that he thought Duke Ellington had compromised his music for success in a world dominated by whites; but he also admitted that his opinion of Ellington's music might tell the reader as much about John Hammond as about Ellington. In any case, few people have done as much for American music.

John Lomax, who began collecting songs as a child, later published such books as *Cowboy Songs and Other Frontier Ballads* (1910). He worked as a banker, but when jobs for bankers grew scarce during the Depression, he became a full-time folklorist: with the help of his son Alan, he made thousands of 78s using portable recording equipment provided by the Library of Congress. He recorded Leadbelly and Bukka White, among many others, and Alan made the Jelly Roll Morton sessions mentioned earlier. In Stovall, Mississippi, in 1941–2, McKinley Morganfield recorded for the Library of Congress; he soon went to Chicago, where he became the most important of post-war bluesmen, Muddy Waters.

There were other entrepreneurs, and other musics were being

discovered. The blues, a black country music, did not depend upon a slick formula, a New York publisher or a big vaudeville name to perform it. It came unbidden out of the hearts of its practitioners, as did white country music, which also began to enter the mainstream of popular music in the acoustic era; both would revitalize jaded pop scenes in decades to come. How the music business regarded country music has been summed up by Nolan Porterfield in his biography of Jimmie Rodgers (1979): 'a sort of backward, ugly, show-biz step-child that refused to go to school and learn from its betters but could not be locked up in the back room'.

Old-time fiddlers Eck Robertson and Henry Gilliand had recorded for Victor in New York in 1922, but the record was not then released. The country market was discovered by Ralph Sylvester Peer. After working for his father, who sold sewing machines, Columbia phonographs and records, he worked for Columbia, then for Fred Hagar at Okeh. Early in 1923 he recorded harmonica player Henry Whittier, but thought nothing of it. He was sent to Atlanta in June, where furniture dealer Polk Brockman wanted to record Fiddlin' John Carson: 'The Little Old Log Cabin in the Lane' backed with 'The Old Hen Cackled and the Rooster's Going to Crow' did not even get an Okeh release number, but when the first pressing sold out, Peer paid more attention, and became the most important talent scout in a new industry, again and again in the right place at the right time. (Before it became a fiddle tune, 'The Little Old Log Cabin in the Lane' was a parlour song, written by Will Shakespeare Hays in 1871; opera star Alma Gluck had recorded it for Victor.)

Peer discovered Ernest Van 'Pop' Stoneman, whose epic 'The Titanic' was one of the first big country hits in 1925 (and whose family are still folk and country artists today); and the same year he recorded a string band called Al Hopkins and the Hill Billies. They were the first country artists to make Washington, DC, their home base, broadcasting from there; they were also among the first to record in New York, the first to make a short film (for Warner Brothers), the first to play for a president (Coolidge) and the first to use a piano and a Hawaiian guitar. Hopkins told Peer he could call them anything he wanted, since they were 'nothing but a bunch of hillbillies anyway'. Peer liked that name, but the band was not sure until Pop Stoneman approved it.

In the second quarter of the eighteenth century, poorer British settlers had begun moving into the western parts of the colonies. They could not compete with plantation-owners, who had plenty of cheap black slave labour, and they wanted more freedom. They were escaping taxation on their farm produce by a Tory government in London which, unaware of the enormous potential of its most valuable colonies, persistently tried to placate English merchants. A hundred years earlier the Ulster rebels who had been cleared from land in northern Ireland were replaced by hard-working Scottish lowland people who were loyal to James I (who was James VI of Scotland). A good number of them were weavers, and produced cloth that competed with that of English factories, so eventually they too were driven off their land. Many of them went to Penn's Woods – Pennsylvania – where in 1750 the Cumberland Gap to the Appalachian Mountains was discovered; this barrier to the West encompassed the smaller Cumberland, Blue Ridge and Allegheny mountain ranges. As Pennsylvania began to fill up, the Cumberland Gap represented a gateway to cheap land in West Virginia and Kentucky (much of it purchased from Cherokee Indians by Daniel Boone and his business partners). Scots, Irish and runaway slaves (both black and white) poured into the mountains and beyond, bringing with them fiddles, lutes and other instruments, and their songs, ballads and attitudes, many traceable to Elizabethan England – and probably a few copies of John Playford's *Dancing Master*. It was their music that Peer discovered.

String bands consisted of fiddles, guitars, a string bass and often a banjo and/or a mandolin (the most recent addition to the lute family). The music, which had been spreading across the USA for generations, was variously described by record companies and catalogues as old-time music, mountain music, 'familiar tunes' and so on, until Peer's 'hillbilly' stuck.

The most successful string band was Gid Tanner and his Skillet Lickers, who began recording in 1926. James Gideon Tanner was a champion fiddler; George Riley Puckett, blind from childhood, was a vocalist and one of the most influential guitarists; Frank Walker, then an A & R man at Columbia, put them together with fiddler Clayton 'Pappy' McMichen and others to form the group. Puckett's baritone sold the recordings, and he also recorded as a soloist. McMichen was influenced by jazz and resented being called a hillbilly, while Tanner was strictly old-time. Perhaps because of the tension caused by these various strands, their music was hotter and more influential than the others. Comedy recordings were made, beginning with 'A Corn Likker Still in Georgia'; 'Turkey in the Straw' and 'John Henry' were hits in 1926–7. A hillbilly-style pop song, 'Down Yonder', had been published in 1921 and interpolated into the Broadway show *Tip-top*. Popular recordings of it included one by a barber-shop quartet; when the Skillet Lickers recorded it in 1934, it became one of the biggest country hits of the decade.

Another important string band was the North Carolina Ramblers, led by Charlie Poole, a banjo picker who had developed a unique three-fingered style as a result of a boyhood injury to his right hand. Their 'Don't Let Your Deal Go Down' (1925) sold 100,000 copies and remained a country standard.

There were also black string bands, which played much the same kind of music, but rarely recorded. A great many guitar pickers, fiddlers and singers had jammed with blacks. Mandolin player Bill Monroe, guitarist Sam McGee and banjo player Dock Boggs, three of the best in the business, are among those who admitted their debt to black music, while Ma Rainey often had requests for 'Heart Made of Stone', an Appalachian lament. Blues singer Yank Rachell, born in 1910 in Tennessee, also played guitar, harmonica and violin; when he was eight years old, he traded a pig for a mandolin, which added a unique rural flavour to his recording sessions, among them one with the original Sonny Boy Williamson on Bluebird (1938), and to Rachell's own more recent albums, such as *Mandolin Blues* (acoustic) and *Chicago Style* (electric) on Delmark. Brownie McGhee remembered 'jookin'', or country quilting parties, and Bill Broonzy recalled 'two-way' picnics, at which blacks and whites swapped songs. Black guitar player Leslie Riddles accompanied A. P. Carter on song-collecting trips, and had a direct effect on Maybelle Carter's famous guitar style. Jimmie Tarlton, who performed in a well-known South Carolina duo with Tom Darby, said that he picked up bottleneck guitar from a black musician when he was ten years old, which would have been many years before Blind Lemon Jefferson recorded in that style. The great black Swing Era composer Edgar Sampson plays a violin solo on a recording of 'Hot-tempered Blues', by Charlie Johnson's Paradise Ten, the house band at Smalls' Paradise in Harlem in 1928: loaded with double stops, it could have been played by Gid Tanner. Johnson's competition at the Cotton Club was Duke Ellington, who in 1936 recorded 'Lazy Man's Shuffle' (by 'Rex Stewart and his 52nd Street Stompers'). It includes Brick Fleagle (or possibly Ceele Burke) on what sounds like a Hawaiian guitar, which soon became country music's steel guitar. We will never know to what extent the colour bar in broadcasting and in the marketing of records prevented more fusions of black and white musics, but the degree of two-way influence has always been remarkable.

After Ralph Peer left Okeh, he offered to record for Victor in exchange for the song copyrights. He recorded Ishman Bracey and Tommy Johnson in Memphis in 1928, but before that, he went to Bristol, Tennessee, in 1927, because it seemed like a good location, near the Tennessee–Virginia border. There he recorded Stoneman and others, and advertised for players in local newspapers. In August he recorded a vocal and instrumental trio, the Carter Family, and a railway worker named Jimmie Rodgers: having recorded the first string band, he now found the rest of country music.

Jimmie Rodgers, also known as the Singing Brakeman and the Blue Yodeller, pulled together many strands to form the basis of mainstream country music, and became its first legend, recording 110 sides in less than five years, the last just two days before he died of tuberculosis. He had learned his music from hoboes and railway workers, black and white; he combined yodelling with the twelve-bar blues; the first of his thirteen 'blue yodels', 'T for Texas', sold a million copies and has been covered many times. Some of the blue yodels were simply numbered; others also had titles, such as 'Blue Yodel No. 4 (California Blues)'. When 'Blue Yodel No. 9' was recorded in Hollywood in 1930, Louis Armstrong was among the sidemen; Louis plays beautifully, but with unusual caution, as though he was not sure what was going to happen next: Rodgers's time was quirky. His nasal tenor voice and Mississippi drawl, and his transparent informality and good humour, brought sympathy to hoboes and hillbillies everywhere. As Nolan Porterfield put it, Rodgers 'couldn't read a note, keep time, play the "right" chords or write lyrics that fit. All he could do was reach the hearts of millions of people around the world, and lift them up. They listened, and understood.'

Rodgers often recorded solo, but also with what amounted to a dixieland band, and he was one of the first to use a Hawaiian guitar. The guitar had been introduced to Hawaii by Spanish and Portuguese cowboys in the mid nineteenth century; the Hawaiians began playing it horizontally, in the lap, with the strings raised, and in the slide style, without frets. They invented 'slack' tuning (called *ki ho alu*), or open-chord tuning. Joseph Kekeku was the first to fret the Hawaiian guitar with a comb instead of his fingers; King Bennie Nawahi played jazz and blues as well as hulas; Hawaiian guitar became a fad in vaudeville, and was even occasionally inserted into a Broadway show. Rodgers recorded with a Hollywood group called Lani McIntire's Harmony Hawaiians, and with Joe Kaipo, a genuine Hawaiian guitarist (who claimed that his father was mayor of Honolulu). When the Hawaiian guitar was later electrified, it became the steel guitar as we have known it in country music ever since.

In May 1928 Rodgers's fourth record was released ('Blue Yodel No. 2' and 'Brakeman's Blues') and by midsummer his royalties were averaging more than $1,000 a month, at that time a fortune for a peripatetic railway worker. Rodgers helped Victor's profits to return almost to where they had been before radio had bitten deeply into the record business, and Peer was making so much money that he had to start new corporations to put it in.

A song called 'The One Rose (That's Left in My Heart)', written by McIntire, was Rodgers's closest brush with pop fame. Peer did not issue it within the agreed year, so McIntire placed the song elsewhere; Bing Crosby and bandleaders Larry Clinton and Art Kassel all had national hits with it in 1937, while Rodgers's version, released several years after his death, looked like a cover. Among his other backing musicians were Pappy McMichen, who had left Tanner and was leading the first of several groups he called the Georgia Wildcats; he co-wrote 'Peach Pickin' Time Down in Georgia'.

Rodgers's most important collaborator was his sister-in-law, Elsie McWilliams, who could read and write music and play the piano. Rodgers would worry a tune until it sounded as he wanted it to, 'wrong' chords and all; Elsie could help him polish it. The songs she had a hand in were the most completely composed, and set the style of his career: for example, 'Never No Mo' Blues', 'You and Me and My Old Guitar' and 'Daddy and Home'. They wrote 'Everybody Does It in Hawaii', on the recording of which Joe Kaipo played the Hawaiian guitar in 1929. It may have been Peer, seeking more royalties for his artist as well as for his own publishing company, who was behind King Oliver's instrumental version the next year, with Roy Smeck on Hawaiian-style guitar. Rodgers's repertory included sentimental songs ('My Old Pal', 'My Little Lady'), songs about tragedy and death ('T B Blues', 'Hobo Bill's Last Ride') and hard times ('Waitin' for a Train' and many of the blue yodels), and they displayed bravado and *double entendre* ('Pistol Packin' Papa', 'Mean Mama Blues'). 'Muleskinner Blues', 'In the Jailhouse Now' and others have been covered many times; 'Miss the Mississippi and You' was a country hit in 1981.

Rodgers was a happy-go-lucky man who enjoyed his stardom. He counted among his friends crooner Gene Austin, whose record of 'My Blue Heaven' was among the biggest hits of the 1920s (and was not in fact topped until Crosby's 'White Christmas'). Rodgers considered Austin a rival: although his live gigs were mostly in the South and often in tent shows, he thought of himself as an all-round entertainer. He probably sold about twelve million records during his lifetime, which was phenomenal for the Depression. (In later years many a country boy remembered being sent to the general store for 'a pound of butter, a slab of bacon and the latest Jimmie Rodgers record'.) Gene Autry, Ernest Tubb and Hank Snow were just three of the giants in country music who began by imitating Rodgers, and nobody knows how many boys born in the 1930s were named after him.

Equally important was the other discovery Peer made in Bristol, Tennessee: the Carter Family. A. P. (Alvin Pleasant) Carter sang bass or baritone harmony in an improvisatory way, coming in wherever he felt like it; he played some fiddle and collected mountain ballads. His wife, Sara, sang lead and Maybelle (Sara's cousin, who was married to A. P.'s brother Ezra) sang harmony. Both women played autoharp and guitar; Sara's autoharp became a component of the traditional style, while Maybelle played melody on the guitar's bass strings and harmony on the treble – the influential 'Carter style' – and she also played blues licks and occasionally even steel guitar. Their songs, many of ancient lineage, are still sung by folk groups today: 'Wabash Cannon Ball' was a hit for Roy Acuff (and 'I'm Thinking Tonight of My Blue Eyes' was adapted for his 'Great Speckled Bird'); 'I Never Will Marry' was later recorded by the Weavers, 'Wildwood Flower' by Joan Baez, 'Jimmy Brown the Newsboy' by Flatt and Scruggs and 'Hello Stranger' by Emmylou Harris. 'Keep on the Sunny Side', a 1906 pop song, became their theme. 'Worried Man Blues', 'Will the Circle be Unbroken?' and many more became standards as Carter Family songs.

Peer preferred the sound of Sara's voice, while the beautiful harmony of the two women was more in evidence on their recordings for Decca and ARC labels after 1935 and Columbia in 1940; in 1941 the trio returned to Victor and brought their total to as many as three hundred sides. After 1938 the Carters broadcast on Mexican radio, as Rodgers had done earlier. (When broadcasting frequencies were assigned by international agreement, the Mexicans were left out, and so did as they pleased; one of their 100,000-watt transmitters was heard in Canada and Hawaii. Furthermore, Peer had musical interests in Mexico as early as 1930.)

A. P. and Sara were divorced, but continued to work together until 1943; by then their children Joe and Jannette were performing, as well as Maybelle's daughters Anita, June and Helen. After 1943 Maybelle and her daughters formed a group and in 1948 joined the *Grand Ole Opry*. Maybelle became the much loved First Lady of Country Music. She and Ezra had faith in Johnny Cash, whom they helped through a troubled time, and June became his second wife. Maybelle gave Chet Atkins one of his first jobs, influenced the piano style of Floyd Cramer (who later played on Elvis Presley's 'Heartbreak Hotel') and taught her granddaughter Carlene Carter to play guitar (June's daughter by her first husband, Carl Smith). Anita had solo hits until 1971.

Another Carter family began recording in 1936. D. P. 'Dad' Carter met his wife Carrie in singing school; having nine children, Carter formed a group to help make ends meet. He sang baritone, Ernest 'Jim' Carter bass, Rose soprano and Anna alto. They began broadcasting in Lubbock, Texas, as the Carter Quartet, and within a year had moved to KBAP in Forth Worth, one of the most powerful stations in Texas. They took the name of the Chuck Wagon Gang, a western band which had left the station, and sang gospel songs on the radio five days a week for fifteen years. Dad played mandolin on a few of their earliest recordings; thereafter Jim's acoustic guitar was their only accompaniment until 1954, when personnel changes began and a discreet electric guitar was played by Anna's husband. They recorded over four hundred sides; their recording of 'Church in the Wildwood', made in 1936, four years after that of the more famous Carter Family, is even more beautiful. No one knows how many records the Chuck Wagon Gang sold: country gospel music was not important to the compilers of charts, but poor people bought records by all these artists, and those of the Chuck Wagon Gang sold by the carload at revival meetings.

The broadcasting of country music began early. The first of the long-lasting radio shows was the *Chicago Barn Dance* in 1924, which soon became the *National Barn Dance*, on WLS, whose call letters stood for 'World's Largest Store': the station was owned by Sears and Roebuck, whose mail order catalogue was kept next to the bible by many rural families. The show's most famous stars over the years included Gene Autry, Bob Atcher, Red Foley, Lulu Belle and Scotty, Rex Allen, comics Homer and Jethro and bandleader Pee Wee King. The programme transferred to WGN in 1960 (after WLS had become the Midwest's biggest pop station), where it continued until 1970. Its original announcer was George D. Hay, voted most popular announcer by *Radio Digest* magazine.

Hay went to a new station, WSM in Nashville, Tennessee, in 1925. A broadcast in November featuring 85-year-old fiddler Uncle Jimmy Thompson was so successful that the WSM *Barn Dance* began in December with Hay (soon dubbed 'the solemn old judge', though he was just thirty) as MC. In 1927 the show was preceded by a classical concert whose programme included a train composition; conductor Walter Damrosch was patronizing about 'realism' in music on a programme which consisted mainly of grand opera: Hay came on the air promising the 'realest realism' on the 'Grand Ole Opry', and from that time the renamed show opened with a train tune, 'Pan-American Blues', played on the harmonica by Deford Bailey.

For years Hay would allow only string bands, with no drums or horns. The house band was Dr Humphrey Bate and his Possum Hunters. Bate, a physician, played Sousa marches along with country music, and enjoyed classical music as well; he had learned some of his songs as a boy from an ex-slave, and he accepted his hillbilly image with reluctance. (His daughter, Alcyone Bate, still played piano on the programme fifty years later.) Other *Opry* stars included banjo player and comic Uncle Dave Macon, who had turned professional when a pompous local farmer asked him to play at a party: he demanded $15 and to his surprise the farmer agreed. Kirk and Sam McGee played in Macon's Fruit Jar Drinkers; Sam was one of the best guitarists ever to pick up the instrument, and among the first to play breaks and runs in the black style. The McGee brothers had learned their music from black railway workers who hung around the family's general store in Tennessee. But the only black to appear on the *Opry* for years was Deford Bailey, who was the *Opry*'s mascot, and knew it.

Singer and mandolin player Bill Monroe and his guitarist brother Charlie worked with their brother Birch (on fiddle) from 1929 to 1934, then as a duo until 1938. After they split up, Charlie led his successful Kentucky Pardners, and Bill took his Blue Grass Boys to the *Opry* in 1939. His classic line-up in the mid-1940s included Chubby Wise on fiddle, Howard Watts (better known as Cedric Rainwater) on bass, Lester Flatt on guitar and Earl Scruggs playing a five-string banjo in the three-fingered Appalachian style; Flatt and Scruggs left to form their own band in 1948. Bill Monroe is one of the best mandolin players of all time. His string band music came to be called bluegrass; while it was quickly regarded as old-fashioned, it was rediscovered by a new generation and became a staple of folk festivals, as well as a permanent ingredient of country music.

WWHA's *Jamboree* (Wheeling, West Virginia) and the *National Barn Dance* moved on to a national radio network in 1933, the *Opry* in

1939. The *Opry* had a live audience which outgrew the WSM studios, and in 1943 it took over the local Ryman Auditorium, a country music mecca. There were many regional shows; the *Louisiana Hayride* on KWKH Shreveport began in 1948 and became a stepping-stone to the *Opry*.

Among the early country stars had been Vernon Dalhart, who sold millions of records on thirty labels under many pseudonyms; 'The Prisoner's Song' (1925) was one of the biggest hits of all time. But he was a light opera singer whose country material comprised mournful story songs; his work perhaps lacked the sincerity which is the essence of country music.

Ralph Peer had not only discovered the real stuff, but he also saw the value of copyrights and urged his artists to come up with original material. He saw too that it would be foolish to cheat them, and shared the royalties from the beginning. (But Russell Sanjek writes that it was Victor, protective of its reputation for paying its artists better than any other label, who required Peer to pay them $25 a side, as well as a royalty.) Peer was a good businessman. He formed Southern Music and sold it to Victor, the idea being that Victor would pass song copyrights his way in return, but all he got, apart from country music, was scraps (some of them rather fine, such as Hoagy Carmichael's 'Lazy Bones' and Don Redman's 'Cherry'). Victor employees, in particular A&R man Eli Oberstein, sent copyrights elsewhere because they were jealous.

Peer had recruited Oberstein from Okeh and installed him at Victor to keep an eye on his interests, but they became enemies; Oberstein was underpaid by Victor, whose largesse did not extend to staff members, and Peer was making so much money he had to try to hide it from them. Having taken over Victor, RCA then acquired an interest in RKO Pictures in 1932, and RCA boss David Sarnoff realized that he was likely to get into anti-trust trouble, since Victor owned song copyrights and RKO licensed them for film soundtracks, so he sold Southern Music back to Peer, which also resolved the squabbling. Peer also became an expert on international copyright law.

Arthur Edward Satherley, born in Bristol, England, went to the USA in 1913 and worked in a factory in Wisconsin that made cabinets for Edison's phonographs. After working as a promoter for Ma Rainey's and Blind Lemon Jefferson's recordings on Paramount, he became a producer at ARC. Unlike Peer, he loved the music he recorded and promoted; although he regarded both white and black rural musics as equally valuable, he ended up recording mostly whites. Before he retired in 1952 he had helped the careers of Lefty Frizzell, Carl Smith, Marty Robbins and many others. During the classic era he recorded the Chuck Wagon Gang, Gene Autry, Bob Wills, Roy Acuff and Molly O'Day (Acuff's female equivalent, who left music for religion in the late 1940s, but not before influencing people like Wilma Lee Cooper and Kitty Wells). O'Day was the first to record Hank Williams's religious songs, such as 'When God Comes and Gathers His Jewels'.

Singer and bandleader Roy Claxton Acuff, Satherley's favourite, became the grand old man of country music with a traditional style that never changed. He grew up on a tenant farm in the Smoky Mountains; he attended a New York Yankees summer camp, but sunstroke put an end to his athletic hopes. He first broadcast in 1933, first recorded in 1936 and first appeared on the *Opry* in 1937. He played the fiddle, though not often enough, for he lacked confidence. His band, the Smoky Mountain Boys, included string bass, five-string banjo, rhythm guitar, mandolin, accordion and harmonica, but its distinctive sound was contributed by the dobro.

The National Musical Instrument Company in California marketed a guitar with a metal body and three vibrating plates of metal behind the strings for mechanical amplification. Three of the Dopyera brothers, John (who had begun as a violin maker), Ed and Rudy, left National and formed their own company, which built an instrument with only one larger plate: this sounded less tinny and created a larger sound. They may have changed the spelling of their name at that stage, for it is often written as 'Dopera'. They began competing with National in the mid-1920s, and in 1934 the two companies merged.

The National guitar continued to be used by many bluesmen, but it was the dobro that began to help define the sound of country music. 'Dobro' stood for Dopyera brothers, but it is also a Slavic word meaning 'good'; the company's slogan was 'Dobro means good in any language'. Roy Acuff's first dobro player was James Clell Summey (who was later, with Pee Wee King, among the first to play steel guitar on the *Opry*, and still later famous as the comedian Cousin Jody); from 1938 it was Beecher 'Pete' Kirby (who also played banjo and sang high harmony, and later became the comedian Bashful Brother Oswald). Acuff and his band captured the 'high lonesome' sound of mountain music, to which the dobro contributed a passionate yet mellow weight.

With his transparent sincerity (he sometimes wept at his own performance) Acuff became the *Opry*'s greatest star and established the vocalist at the centre of country music. Two of his biggest hits came from his first recording session. 'Wabash Cannon Ball' is a train song, but in the American 'Big Rock Candy Mountain' tradition: the train will take the hobo to the promised land. 'The Great Speckled Bird' is based on Jeremiah 12:9, and is still sung in southern churches. With Fred Rose he formed the Acuff–Rose publishing company in Nashville in 1943, and became wealthy; his other hits included 'Freight Train Blues', 'Fireball Mail', 'Pins and Needles', 'Wreck on the Highway', 'Low and Lonely' and 'Night Train to Memphis'. He continued to be successful throughout the 1940s, and in the late 1950s he and Rose formed the Hickory label.

Both country music and blues were used to sell products on the radio, especially flour, for many Americans still baked their own bread and biscuits. The black harmonica player Aleck Ford (also known as Rice Miller, and who later borrowed the name of Chicago legend Sonny Boy Williamson) was heard along with others on *King Biscuit Time* in the early 1940s. Ten years before that, fiddler Bob Wills was selling on the radio; with his Texas Playboys, he was the father of the dominant genre in the South-west, western swing.

The fiddle, the instrument of frontier America, was played everywhere, by blacks and whites. Eileen Southern, in her book *The Music of Black Americans*, notes that eighteenth-century advertising of slaves for sale or runaway slaves often pointed out that they were musicians, usually fiddlers: 'RUN AWAY ... a Negro Man named Derby, about 25 years of age, a slim black fellow, and plays on the Fiddle with his Left Hand, which he took with him' (*Virginia Gazette*, 1772). The fiddle remained a favourite instrument of early black jazzmen in New

Orleans, but became less common in later jazz, despite the success of Stuff Smith and his Onyx Club Boys, Eddie South (Chicago's 'Dark Angel' of the violin), Ray Nance (with Duke Ellington) and a few others. This was probably due to its lack of volume in the context of a jazz band, but the fiddle has held its own in country music to this day.

James Robert Wills came from a poor white family of Texas farmers, most of whom seem to have been fiddlers. He picked cotton as a boy alongside blacks, hearing the blues played on whatever instruments were available, and grew up without any prejudices against any kind of music. He recorded duets with guitarist Herman Arnspiger in 1929, but they were not released. He won a fiddle contest in 1930 and was already the best-known fiddler in Texas when he led a quartet on the radio called the Aladdin Laddies, for the Aladdin Mantle Lamp Company. In 1931 he went to work for Wilbert Lee 'Pappy' O'Daniel, president of the Burrus Mills and Elevator Company, on Fort Worth's KFJZ.

O'Daniel did not like their music until he realized how popular they were, whereupon he bought them a car, appeared on their show and helped himself to songwriting credits. Vocalist Milton Brown sang on some Victor records as the Light Crust Doughboys. They worked in the mill during the day, but O'Daniel tried to keep them from playing at dances in the evenings, where they made more money. Brown left and formed his Musical Brownies, which were successful until he was killed in a car crash in 1936; Wills hired Tommy Duncan to replace him, and the group played at dances occasionally, but Wills mostly knuckled under to O'Daniel until he was fired for drinking, whereupon half the band left with him.

O'Daniel sued the band for advertising themselves as 'Formerly the Light Crust Doughboys', his object being to destroy them, but the Texas Supreme Court threw the case out; he tried to get the band fired from their radio spot in Tulsa. He left Burrus Mills in 1935. (The band maintained he was fired for falsifying expenses, having paid the band very little and put the rest in his pocket.) O'Daniel started making his own Hillbilly flour and formed a band called the Hillbilly Boys; in spite of his crankiness, his folksy image and his promises to help poor people later got him elected governor of

Texas; in a special election in 1941 he beat Lyndon Johnson to the US Senate, being the bigger crook.

Wills called his new band the Texas Playboys. They broadcast from Waco, then went to KVOO in Tulsa, where Bob or his brother Johnnie Lee Wills broadcast for General Mills five days a week for twenty-three years. (The new Light Crust Doughboys in Fort Worth, with changing line-ups, broadcast well into the television era.) Wills bought prime mid-day radio time and sold it to a sponsor himself; he talked a miller into making Play Boy flour and collected a royalty on every barrel. In 1935 the band was playing to packed dance halls and private parties six nights a week, and began recording. Among its members were Duncan (vocals), Al Stricklin (piano), William E. 'Smokey' Dacus (drums), Arnspiger and C. G. 'Sleepy' Johnson (guitars), Jesse Ashlock (second fiddle) and Leon McAuliffe (steel guitar). McAuliffe had been poached from the new Doughboys; his 'Steel Guitar Rag', recorded with Wills in 1936, was influential, as was his own 'Panhandle Rag' of 1949.

The Texas Playboys played jazz, blues, rags and stomps as well as ballads and sentimental songs. Satherley, a traditionalist, did not know what to make of them at first. He told Wills that he did not want any horns, but Wills said that he would have horns or Bob Wills would not make any recordings. Wills's patented holler ('Ah-haaa!') erupted whenever the band was playing particularly hot; he would shout, 'Take it away, Leon!', just as he did at dances. Satherley got used to it all.

Duncan was a good country crooner; on the marvellous informal Tiffany transcriptions he sometimes chuckles at Wills muttering in his ear while he sings. Wills sang on tunes like 'Corrine, Corrina' and added banter to McAuliffe's vocal on 'That's What I Like About the South'. The rhythm section played in a relentless two-beat style, which dancers in the South-west liked. Charles R. Townsend's biography of Wills, *San Antonio Rose*, is full of anecdotes backed up by scholarship: a farmer who had hired Wills to play for a dance would push all the furniture to one side and roll up the rugs, as friends and neighbours arrived from miles around. The band was the most popular in a five-state area, and soon broke attendance records; Wills was generous, always paying his men well above scale.

As a bandleader Wills had one of the most valuable skills of all: watching his audience and calling just the right mixture of tunes. Once he almost got it wrong. At a dance at the University of Oklahoma, about which he had doubts to begin with, he was determined to concentrate on his big-band material, because he thought that was what the kids would want. They didn't seem to respond much at first, but then the president of the student union approached the bandstand to ask Wills politely if he had brought his fiddle, and in the end the usual good time was had by all.

Wills and his men did not regard their music as country music, and sometimes got down off the bandstand to remonstrate with ringsiders on this point. McAuliffe said years later that they gleaned none of their inspiration from other country artists, but listened to Glenn Miller, Benny Goodman and Bob Crosby. (The two-beat dixieland feel of Crosby's band was perhaps closest to the style of the Texas Playboys.) They were not prejudiced against hillbilly tunes, however, and recorded Jimmie Rodgers songs and numerous others that keep turning up: 'Sittin' on Top of the World' (sung by Wills) bears more than a passing resemblance to the tune of that name recorded twenty years later by Howlin' Wolf (though the composer credits are different).

Many regarded the band as a jazz band. Benny Strickler had played trumpet with Joe Venuti and turned down an offer from Artie Shaw to join Wills. Wills hired him on sight and then asked what instrument he played, saying later, 'I could tell by looking at him he was a good musician.' Clarinettist Woody Wood had played with Red Nichols; Alex Brashear had played trumpet with Jack Teagarden; Tubby Lewis's fine hot trumpet was heard on Wills's big-band number 'Big Beaver'. There is no doubt that Wills's music was a fusion which deserved wider acclaim; today it is stranger than it should be to hear the trombone playing the syrupy waltz 'Mexicali Rose', with Wills's fiddle playing harmony.

Wills wrote a great many songs, including 'My Shoes Keep Walking Back to You', a huge hit for Ray Price in 1957, but one of his tunes became an American classic, better known than all the rest put together. Wills had recorded an instrumental version of 'San Antonio Rose' in 1938 which did well; Venuti was among those who admired the tune and thought that more might be made of it. Irving Berlin's company offered to publish it if words were added, so Wills and a couple of others cobbled together some good lyrics. But the publishers altered the song, making it more orthodox and clearly not understanding what they were doing. Wills insisted that they publish the original version, which they now called 'New San Antonio Rose', and Wills recorded it with Duncan singing, at the same session as 'Big Beaver' in 1940; the eighteen-piece band was larger than Miller or Goodman had used on their biggest hits. In 1944 during the musicians' union strike against the record companies, just as *Billboard* began printing its first country music chart, 'New San Antonio Rose' became the first of eighteen consecutive top five hits for Wills. But before that, in 1941, Bing Crosby's recording of the song sold a million copies. (It was backed with Floyd Tillman's 'It Makes No Difference Now', another country classic; both sides used brother Bob Crosby's band, the one the Wills crew most admired.)

Among other western swing bandleaders were Hank Penny, who took up the style in Atlanta, was also recorded by Satherley and was described by one writer in the 1980s as 'the original Outlaw'; and Spade Cooley, who spent many years in prison for murdering his wife. In the 1950s Hank Thompson and Buck Owens kept the flame burning with fairly large bands. Asleep at the Wheel, formed in the 1960s and led by Ray Benson, released one of its best albums in 1988, *Western Standard Time*.

Bob Wills had made western films from 1940 to 1942 with several of his sidemen, combining music and horses. He may not have considered himself a hillbilly, but for a time he could not resist the lure of Hollywood, which brings us to the era of country and western music.

Satherley had also recorded Gene Autry, who had begun by imitating Jimmie Rodgers. By the mid-1930s Autry's records were selling well, including 'That Silver-haired Daddy of Mine' (co-written and first recorded as a duet with Jimmy Long). Gene Autry guitars were advertised in mail-order catalogues; 'The Death of Mother Jones', a labour-movement song, was available on seven labels in various catalogues from the ARC conglomerate (the Sears label was called Conqueror). Then came Hollywood.

The cowboy movie had been a staple of the silent screen, but had fallen on hard times with the invention of talkies; meanwhile, many films had to be made to fill the second half of the double features (hence 'B' pictures). Ken Maynard was the first 'singing cowboy', in 1930; then in 1934 producer Nat Levine hired Autry, who was no actor, to make films appealing to the people who bought his records. (The owner of Republic Pictures, and Levine's boss, was the head of ARC, Herbert Yates.) Autry's first effort was a cowboy-cum-sci-fi serial in twelve parts called *The Phantom Empire*. He sang 'Silver-haired Daddy' in eight episodes, and went on to make over a hundred films for the Republic and Monogram studios; his comic associates were Smiley Burnette, then Pat Buttram. Champion, Autry's horse, became famous, and his visit to Dublin in 1939 allegedly brought a million people into the streets. Autry's songs became more western-flavoured – for example 'South of the Border' and '(I've Got Spurs That) Jingle Jangle Jingle' – and country artists began to wear phoney cowboy clothes that became more and more vulgar (famously provided by Nudies of Hollywood). The cowboy pictures had interesting aspects, including a broad populist appeal; the bad guys (with the black hats) were frequently lawyers or bankers with pencil moustaches. The kids who flocked to the cinema, black and white, were infected with country music. Otis Blackwell, who later wrote some of Elvis Presley's biggest hits, remembered his own reaction as a child: 'Hot Dog! Now we got us a singin' cowboy!'

Jimmy Wakely and Johnny Bond were among those who went to Hollywood as members of Autry's entourage, and the West Coast country music scene grew in strength. Other singing cowboys were Rex Allen, Tex Ritter and Roy Rogers, who became King of the Cowboys while Autry was flying in Burma during the Second World War.

Rogers, born Leonard Slye, grew up on a farm; his father made guitars and mandolins. As Dick Weston he formed the Pioneer Trio, which appeared in Autry's sci-fi serial, then changed its name to the Sons of the Pioneers. He stayed in the Pioneers until he became a star: he made over ninety films with his palomino horse Trigger, the first being *Under Western Skies* (1938); among the films was a fairly realistic portrayal of the Pony Express. His wife, Dale Evans, who had sung with dance bands, joined Rogers in *The Cowboy and the Señorita* in 1944. Both Rogers and Autry became staples on Saturday morning television in the 1950s; both invested wisely and became very rich.

The Sons of the Pioneers had a successful career of their own. The classic line-up included original members Tim Spencer and Bob Nolan, Lloyd Perryman, who replaced Rogers, and Hugh Farr and Karl Farr, who had worked as cowboys. (When Spencer had left briefly in 1937, he was replaced by Pat Brady, who became Rogers's comic sidekick in his films.) Their close harmony was gentler and sweeter than that of the bluegrass groups; they appeared in *Rhythm on the Range* in 1936 with Bing Crosby, and in many other films. (*Rhythm on the Range* contained Johnny Mercer's 'I'm an Old Cowhand'.) Rogers and the Sons of the Pioneers were the first to perform Cole Porter's 'Don't Fence Me In', apparently both in a film of that name and in *Hollywood Canteen* in 1944, where the reprise was sung by the Andrews Sisters. (The studio recording by Crosby and the Andrews Sisters was a number one hit that year.) In Walt Disney's cartoon compilation *Melody Time* (1948) the Pioneers sang 'Pecos Bill' with Rogers, a hit on the other side of 'Blue Shadows on the Trail'. Nolan and Spencer were fine songwriters, and together they wrote 'Blue Prairie'. Nolan's 'Tumbling Tumbleweeds' was a hit for Autry, the Pioneers and Crosby, and 'Cool Water' was a hit for the Pioneers (1941) and Vaughn Monroe (1949). Spencer wrote 'The Timber Trail', 'Cowboy Camp Meetin'', 'The Everlasting Hills of Oklahoma' and 'Careless Kisses' (a hit for Eddy Howard in 1948). There were no fewer than six hit recordings of Spencer's 'Roomful of Roses' in 1949, and it was revived by Mickey Gilley in 1974.

By the late 1940s the blues and hillbilly genres discovered in the mid-1920s had grown up, and the lines around the edges of all genres were becoming blurred; the Second World War effectively broke in half the history of the century's popular music. For the story of the dominant pre-war and wartime style, we have to go back to the 1920s, when the Big Band Era began.

8

Big Band Jazz

'The world's most glamorous atmosphere. Why, it is just like the Arabian Nights!' said Duke Ellington, the first time he saw Harlem.

There was music in every neighbourhood, just as in New Orleans; even the poorest family had a 'moth-box' (a piano – you could buy one for $100 on a time-payment plan), and keyboard ticklers were employed in every tavern. The East Coast stride piano style was based on ragtime, with complete freedom in the right hand, and the left paying harmonic tribute as it strode along, tenths in the bass being common when a strong beat was wanted. But the great artists of classic stride could also play the melody in the bass, while improvising beautiful ornamentation with the right hand: the artist was a Chopin or a Liszt, and the rediscovery of the tradition of the recitalist as improviser was complete.

Charles Luckyeth 'Luckey' Roberts was drawn to Harlem by 1910, along with many other talented and ambitious blacks. In 1913 he published 'Junk Man Rag' and 'Pork and Beans'; he saw more than a dozen of his musical comedies produced, and part of one of his tunes, 'Ripples on the Nile', was slowed down and became Glenn Miller's 'Moonlight Cocktail' in 1942. Roberts fronted a Harlem club for many years, and was a society bandleader; a favourite of President Roosevelt and the Duke of Windsor, he advised the Duke on his collection of hot records. He was an extraordinary pianist who played the instrument like an orchestra; sadly he recorded very little.

Willie 'the Lion' Smith was born William Henry Joseph Bonaparte Bertholoff Smith, and had an outsized personality to match his name. Like the ragtime 'perfessers' who preceded him, he was a dapper dresser; he would stride into a club growling a warning: 'The Lion is here.' Like Jelly Roll Morton, he was fond of bragging and could back up everything he said. His compositions include 'Contrary Motion', 'Rippling Waters', 'Echo of Spring', 'Portrait of the Duke' and 'The Stuff is Here (and It's Mellow)' (the latter, written with Clarence Williams and Walter Bishop, was recorded by Cleo Brown, who sang and played piano on Chicago radio and recorded for Decca in the 1930s). Like Roberts, Smith played distinctive harmonies and arabesques, and had a pop song recorded by Glenn Miller, 'Sweeter than the Sweetest'. One explanation of his nickname put it down to his bravery during the First World War, but he said that James P. called him 'the Lion' because of his spunk. 'The Lion named him The Brute. Later we gave Fats Waller the name Filthy. The three of us, The Lion, The Brute and Filthy, and a guy called Lippy used to run all over town playing piano.'

Jelly Roll Morton is thought to have visited New York as early as 1911. It is delicious to speculate that his New Orleans freedom might have had an influence like that of Louis Armstrong more than a decade later, but, on the contrary, it is said that Morton's ego took a beating from the skills of the New York pianists. The best piano players on the East Coast sooner or later went to New York; Luckey Roberts was from Philadelphia, Eubie Blake from Baltimore and James P. Johnson from New Jersey. Earlier New York ticklers, such as the legendary John 'Jack the Bear' Wilson (fl. 1900, and another subject of an Ellington portrait), are lost to history; so too are Raymond 'Lippy' Boyette and his contemporaries Stephen Henderson (known as 'the Beetle'), Corky Williams (whose speciality was playing and singing salacious material, such as 'The Boy in the Boat', which became Waller's 'Squeeze Me'). Willie Gant and Cliff Jackson, however, became recording artists and bandleaders.

The 1920s was the era of the rent party: for an entrance fee which helped pay the rent, food, drink and dancing were available, as well as first-class piano playing. Such parties were later celebrated in Waller's hit 'The Joint is Jumping'. Lippy was said to be able to ring anybody's doorbell in the middle of the night, saying, 'It's Lippy, and I've got James P. with me', and gain immediate entrance.

James Price Johnson was the undisputed king of the stride piano style, with his walking bass and his incredible right hand: his 'Carolina Shout' was the number all the others had to be able to play. He was taught by Roberts, and in turn taught Fats Waller. His numerous other tunes include 'Snowy Morning', 'Keep off the Grass' and 'Charleston' (from the show *Runnin' Wild*), which became the biggest dance fad of the Jazz Age. With Waller he was one of the composers of the show *Keep Shufflin'*. ('Charleston' and a great many other piano classics, such as Morton's 'King Porter', were originally created for cotillions, dances which were unofficial contests for showing off and more or less direct descendants of cakewalk exhibitions.)

Johnson's ambitions as a 'serious' composer were as doomed as Joplin's. Some of his music was performed, but the white musical establishment of the time would not reply to his letters. Fragments of his symphonies and other music are still studied by scholars, among them the *Negro Rhapsody*, or *Yamekraw*, inspired by the Negroes who spoke the Gullah dialect from the south-east coastal area Gershwin visited when writing *Porgy and Bess*.

The Lion and the Brute recorded much more than Luckey Roberts; the Lion played on Mamie Smith's 'Crazy Blues' in 1920, and on hit records in a trio with organist Milt Herth and drummer-vocalist O'Neill Spencer in 1938. But Filthy outdid them all: Fats Waller became one of America's best-loved entertainers.

Waller flashed through popular music like a shooting star, but another Harlem piano player became a bandleader, and so had more direct influence. Nothing like as good a pianist as the others, Fletcher Henderson, nicknamed Smack, nevertheless became one of the most important innovators. Born into a middle-class family in Georgia, he played piano from the age of six. He went to New York to do post-graduate work in chemistry, but there were not many jobs for black chemists; he played for Pace–Handy Music and became recording director for Harry Pace's Black Swan label; he accompanied blues singers and led a band on tour with Ethel Waters (who advised him to listen to James P. Johnson's piano rolls). He was elected leader of a band that was resident at the Club Alabam in 1923 and moved to the Roseland Ballroom in 1924. It included Coleman Hawkins and arranger Don Redman on reeds, trumpeter Joe Smith and renowned trombonist Charlie Green (known as Big Green or Long Boy). The band played pop tunes, novelties and pseudo-blues at first, but jazz was in the air. Although Louis Armstrong stayed only a year, his effect was incalculable; New Orleans clarinettist Buster Bailey played intermittently in the band.

Ross Gorman, Paul Whiteman's former clarinettist, led a pit band for *Earl Carroll's Vanities of 1925*, and recorded one of the tunes from the revue with a sixteen-piece band. 'Rhythm of the Day' was prophetic, a simple tune with interesting chord changes in an uncluttered arrangement that gave solo space to Red Nichols and Miff Mole. Despite a dixielandish ride-out, it was a remarkably forward-sounding hint of what was to come.

After Armstrong, Henderson's band was further influenced by the white band of Jean Goldkette. Born in France, Goldkette went to the USA in 1911. He could have been a concert pianist, but formed a dance band in 1924 and hired such arrangers as Russ Morgan and Bill Challis, and sidemen Bix Beiderbecke, Tommy and Jimmy Dorsey, Frankie Trumbauer, Eddie Lang and Joe Venuti; he took over Detroit's Graystone Ballroom when it could not meet his payroll. His band was smaller and more flexible than Paul Whiteman's, and soon became famous. Long after a meeting in October 1926 at the Roseland Ballroom, cornettist Rex Stewart, who was with Henderson at the time, wrote about 'this Johnny-come-lately white band from out in the sticks . . . We simply could not compete . . . Their arrangements were too imaginative and their rhythm too strong . . . Jean Goldkette's orchestra was, without question, the greatest in the world.'

The arrangements that Stewart admired were those of Bill Challis, who came from the same coal-mining country as the Dorsey brothers, where there was a strong brass band tradition, as there still is today in the coal-mining parts of Britain. Challis was virtually self-taught, and first worked for a local bandleader called Guy Hall (who wrote 'Johnson Rag', a typically simple and attractive Swing Era riff). Challis's arrangements are full of witty little surprises that still delight today, nearly seventy years later. But Eddie King, A & R man at Victor, did not like the arrangements and would not let the Goldkette band record them. The band was expensive to operate and it was a struggle to get enough bookings; on top of everything else, violinist and arranger Eddy Sheasby, a volatile drunk, disappeared one day, taking all the band's scores with him, including Challis's. So despite having hit records, Goldkette disbanded in 1927 to concentrate on management, but not before his band had cut the Henderson outfit. Challis had already been hired by Paul Whiteman; Beiderbecke and Trumbauer joined a new band led by Adrian Rollini that played the sort of music they liked. But that band went broke, and they too ended up with Whiteman; thus the legend grew that a band that played pure jazz could not make money.

The Casa Loma band, originally one of Goldkette's groups, was formed around 1929. Saxophonist Glen Gray was elected leader when the band became a corporation; other key members were guitarist-arranger Gene Gifford, clarinettist Clarence Hutchinrider and trumpeter Sonny Dunham. It recorded prolifically and was very popular. Some writers have ignored this band, perhaps because it was white and because it played sweet – ballads such as 'For You' and 'It's the Talk of the Town' were sung by Kenny Sargent. But such recordings as 'I Got Rhythm' and Gifford's 'Casa Loma Stomp' (both 1933) prove that the band could play as hot as any. Gifford was an influential arranger, and in its twenty-year history the band included plenty of first-rate sidemen; its early popularity on college campuses whetted the nation's appetite for swing.

The conservatory-trained Don Redman could play any reed instrument, and wrote virtually all Henderson's arrangements until 1927. He refined the Hickman–Grofé concept of the dance band, no doubt under the influence of Challis, dividing brass and reed sections and having saxophones doubling clarinets and trombones playing against trumpets. He played voices against each other in call-and-response patterns; he wrote music for sections as though they were improvising in unison, while leaving space for hot soloists, behind whom sections often played riffs. While the white music business could not accommodate the real stuff, Redman continued to develop big-band jazz, as Henderson's men began to swing.

This was an even more impressive achievement than it sounds. Armstrong had changed the rhythmic nature of jazz, effectively breaking up each bar into smaller pieces in order to put rhythmic emphasis wherever he wished. This not only left behind the collectively improvised counterpoint, but brought about a new counterpoint between the soloist and the rhythm section. Instead of a 2/4 beat, as in New Orleans jazz and ragtime piano, there was now a 4/4 beat, though it was some years before the change was completely reflected in rhythm-section playing. The stride pianists had also been working in this direction, setting the bass free from the 2/4 of ragtime piano. Redman's scores (or 'charts') had to incorporate these rhythmic advances so that entire sections could play in unison.

Coleman Hawkins (also known as Hawk or Bean) began playing louder, with a stiff reed, to be heard over the band. He rescued the tenor saxophone from its role as a tubby comedian, abolishing the slap-tongue technique, and finally, inspired by the young pianist Art Tatum, began to improvise on the tune's chord structure: he single-handedly established the tenor saxophone as a primary instrument in jazz.

By the late 1920s Fletcher Henderson's band was known to musicians and in Harlem to be the hottest in the land. To list some of the players who passed through is to list the best: trumpeters Tommy Ladnier, Bobby Stark, Henry 'Red' Allen, Joe Smith and Charles Melvin 'Cootie' Williams, cornettist Rex Stewart, trombonists Benny Morton, Jimmy Harrison, Claude Jones, J. C. Higginbotham and Dicky Wells and drummer Kaiser Marshall. In 1927 Waller sold Henderson tunes, probably including 'Whiteman Stomp', 'St Louis Stomp' and 'Variety Stomp'; he allegedly asked for a bag of hamburgers as payment, but Henderson insisted on paying him $10 a tune. He played on one Henderson recording session, including a solo on 'Whiteman Stomp'.

Despite the lack of firm leadership and money (tracks labelled as by 'The Dixie Stompers' seem to have been recorded acoustically, or at least on inferior equipment, as late as 1927), musicians stayed because the music was so good: 'St Louis Shuffle', 'The Stampede', 'Tozo', 'Henderson Stomp', 'Hop Off' and scores more represent a treasure-house of jazz, to say nothing of earlier (mostly acoustic) recordings with Louis Armstrong. To point out just one nugget: on 'The Stampede' (1926) Joe Smith plays a lovely solo, pretty and perfectly constructed; after a bridge, Rex Stewart comes up and pushes the beat with his ferocity, tearing the notes off the page with a terminal vibrato at the end of each phrase: they are two first-class jazzmen, each doing it differently.

Redman left Henderson in 1927, having been hired by Goldkette as music director of a black Detroit band, McKinney's Cotton Pickers. It was fronted by former circus drummer William McKinney, and became the best of the territory bands as Redman refined his skills. When McKinney went out front to stay, he was replaced on drums by Cuba Austin. The band's discographies were long confused, because Goldkette paid Redman to rehearse some of his white bands as well, and because business in Detroit was so good that the band was not allowed to go to New York in 1929 to record, whereupon Redman recorded there with a group of Henderson's sidemen. To complicate matters still further, a Redman Chocolate Dandies date in 1928 was essentially played by the Cotton Pickers.

Under Redman the Cotton Pickers became a more modern jazz-oriented dance band, performing in a smoother but still swinging style. He added a fourth man to the reed section, making possible harmonies in that section so that to modern ears, the Cotton Pickers' records have dated less than those of most of the bands of the late 1920s. The band's number one hit (and its theme) was 'If I Could Be With You One Hour Tonight', with a vocal by reedman George 'Fathead' Thomas and an alto solo by Benny Carter; another big hit was 'Milenberg Joys', credited to Walter Melrose, Jelly Roll Morton and Leon Roppolo, whose clarinet solo from the New Orleans Rhythm Kings' recording (which included Morton) was transcribed and harmonized in Redman's arrangement.

Redman recorded his own pretty tune, 'Cherry', twice in 1928, once with the Cotton Pickers (sung by Jean Napier), and once with a pick-up group including the Dorseys and Jack Teagarden (no vocal). (The Cotton Pickers recorded for Victor, which is how 'Cherry' landed in Ralph Peer's portfolio.) Redman recorded in Chicago with Louis Armstrong's Savoy Ballroom Five, a date that included two of his own tunes. At his Chocolate Dandies date in 1928 he made one of the first recordings of Hoagy Carmichael's 'Stardust', a bouncy, medium uptempo version with a fine guitar solo by Lonnie Johnson. (Johnson recorded as a soloist with Louis Armstrong and Duke Ellington and in duets with Eddie Lang. He also made a great many blues records and had an R&B hit, 'Confused', in 1950; when criticized in later years for not playing a purer style, he complained about fans 'trying to shove a crutch under my ass'.)

At the 1929 recording session at which he used members of Henderson's band, Redman sang in his own slyly intimate, half-conversational and charming style on 'Miss Hannah', 'The Way I Feel Today' (delicately accompanied by Waller), 'Wherever There's a Will, Baby' (which has a fine Hawkins solo) and his own 'Gee Baby, Ain't I Good to You?'

In 1931, armed with management and recording contracts, Redman took over the Collegians; led by Horace Henderson, Fletcher's brother, the band had included Benny Carter and Rex Stewart in its day. Horace was at least as talented as his more famous brother, but made only a few recordings under his own name; Redman kept him on as pianist and arranger for a couple of years, after which he worked with Fletcher. Of about 120 arrangements recorded by Fletcher from March 1931 until 1939, many are uncredited, while others are by Edgar Sampson, Russ Morgan, Will Hudson or Dick Vance; but of those for which information is available in discographies, Fletcher and Horace apparently did about the same number – 28 or 30 – and Horace was the composer of tunes that are often credited to Fletcher.

Redman's first recordings in 1931 were credited to 'Harlan Lattimore and his Connie's Inn Orchestra'; Lattimore was a pleasant pop singer whose straight vocals were sometimes contrasted with Redman's patter and comedy, as on 'I Heard'. In 1932 the fourteen-piece band included Langston Curl (from the Cotton Pickers), Shirley Clay, Sidney De Paris and later Harold 'Shorty' Baker on trumpets; Claude Jones, Benny Morton and Quentin Jackson on trombones; Ed Inge in the reed section and always Bob Ysaguirre on tuba, then string bass, and Manzie Johnson on drums; Horace Henderson was pianist and arranger until he was replaced in 1933 by Don Kirkpatrick. Redman first recorded his theme, 'Chant of the Weed', in 1931; the modern-sounding arrangement proves that there is no such thing as a wrong note, using all the notes in a whole-tone scale. Redman recorded it again in 1940, and still later arranged it for a Duke Ellington album.

Redman was the first black bandleader to have his own radio show. He was an excellent teacher, and his arrangements were well known among musicians for their difficult passages, for example the reed chorus in 'Tea for Two' (which pitted Lattimore's straight vocal against the furiously swinging band) and trombone chorus in 'I Got Rhythm'. 'Nagasaki' was also a brilliant piece of swing, but Redman's band never played so fast for speed's sake that it sounded uncomfortable. He invented the 'swing choir', in which the band chanted a hip paraphrase of the words to a song while a soloist played the melody, as on 'Exactly Like You' and 'Sunny Side of the Street' (1937). The device was copied by others, for example by Tommy Dorsey on 'Marie', one of the biggest hits of the whole era (which Dorsey had got from the obscure Sunset Royals).

Redman recorded for Brunswick, then ARC labels, and by the time he transferred to Bluebird and Victor in 1938 it was a smoother swing band. 'Sweet Leilani' used the swing choir device, 'I Got Ya' had a Redman vocal ('Youse is in mine power!') and 'Rip Van Winkle', a hip rewrite of the legend, was sung by Bootsie Garrison.

Tired of the grind and not achieving the fame he deserved, Redman disbanded the group in 1940; he fronted Jay McShann's band in 1942, and in 1946 took a band to Europe (including saxophonist Don Byas), which was credited with introducing post-war jazz there. Among his freelance work was the lovely 'Just an Old Manuscript' for Count Basie in 1949. His recordings and broadcasts were an inspiration to young Canadians Gil Evans and Robert Farnon; he showed Farnon how to lay out a score, and Farnon became one of the most influential arrangers in the business. In 1951 he became music director for Pearl Bailey, who had a hit with 'Takes Two to Tango' in 1952. In 1954 he played a policeman in Harold Arlen's show *House of Flowers*; in 1957 he made two albums of big-band sides, some with Hawkins. He was a delightful man, whose personality is evident on the recordings and in the few short films he made, as well as an important innovator of popular music.

In 1928 Fletcher Henderson had suffered head injuries in a car crash; he had always been lackadaisical, and now became even less willing to take care of business. The band broke up in 1929, after a date to play a show produced by Vincent Youmans. Originally called *Horse Shoes*, *Great Day!* was modelled on *Show Boat*, and required a black band; Duke Ellington had turned the job down. When Youmans's white conductor began firing Henderson's men one at a time and he did nothing about it, that was the last straw for many of them. But Henderson formed another band, with Hawkins, Harrison and sometimes Morton, and the parade of talent continued: this is when Red Allen, Claude Jones, J. C. Higginbotham and others joined. He lost the Roseland Ballroom booking to the more responsible Claude Hopkins. The band's business was as unreliable as ever, but money meant little: racial equality was not on offer, and one could live very well on a musician's salary during the Depression.

Henderson recorded for Victor in 1932 (including vocals with Harlan Lattimore). He lost a gig at the Cotton Club to Irving Mills's Blue Rhythm Band and a European tour to Cab Calloway. At a Victor recording session in 1934 three of the four arrangements were by Russ Morgan or Will Hudson; Morgan was recording director at ARC, and Henderson may have hoped to curry favour, but it didn't work. Coleman Hawkins gave up and left for Europe, succeeded by Chu Berry, Lester Young and then Ben Webster: thus Henderson managed to employ, however briefly, all four of the greatest tenor saxophonists in pre-war jazz. And it was in 1934 that Henderson, in spite of everything, hit his own stride. His band was never the same after Redman left, for it lost the consistency that had made it a legend; having let alto saxophonist and arranger Benny Carter go, and possibly also feeling the heat of competition from his brother Horace, he took on more of the arranging himself. He further refined the style that Redman had developed to make a smoother music that was specifically for dancing, but still jazz-oriented, and allowed plenty of space for soloists. 'Sugar Foot Stomp' (from Oliver's 'Dipper Mouth Blues') and Jelly Roll Morton's 'King Porter Stomp', which had been Henderson staples for years, continued to be polished. Henderson began recording for the new Decca label, which was signing up all the best black bands, and 'Down South Camp Meeting', 'Wrappin' It Up' and Horace's 'Big John Special' (a tribute to John Reda, the boss at Big John's in Harlem, a favourite hang-out for musicians) were added to the store. His band broke up again and he made no recordings at all in 1935, but that was the year that lightning struck. He sold these charts to Benny Goodman, who had hits with all of them, and it was Fletcher Henderson's 1934 style that touched off the Big Band, or Swing Era.

Henderson formed a new band and made more good recordings: as Dicky Wells later wrote, 'You just had to play the notes and the arrangement was swinging.' Waller's 'Stealin' Apples', Horace's arrangement of Edgar Sampson's 'Blue Lou', 'Christopher Columbus' (a hit, based on riffs by Chu Berry and others) and Louis Prima's 'Sing, Sing, Sing (with a Swing)' were all recorded in 1936, and were also recorded by Goodman. Henderson continued to write for Goodman, for whom he arranged Youmans's 'Sometimes I'm Happy' and 'I Want to be Happy' and Berlin's 'Blue Skies'. He joined Goodman's sextet as pianist in 1939 and in 1941 formed another band with Goodman's help, but that was almost his last spark as a leader. He led a band at the Club DeLisa in Chicago in 1947, where Sonny Blount (whose real name was Sun Ra) was influenced; he led a sextet in 1950, but later that year had a stroke and never played again. The album *Tribute to Fletcher Henderson* (1957) was a joyous, swinging alumni success, unlike most all-star performances. It captured the joy in the music that Henderson played for a decade before the music business co-opted what came to be called swing, and white bands made most of the money.

It is a truism, to which I wholeheartedly subscribe, that the black bands played the best music during the Swing Era. Once jazz and the big dance band had come together in the late 1920s both black and white bands were charting the course; but the white-dominated music business could not tolerate pure jazz except in the 'race music' category, so it was the black bands and their sidemen who continued to provide the innovation.

One of the most commercially successful of all the black leaders was vocalist Cab Calloway, the exuberant, scat-singing, zoot-suited 'Highness of Hi-de-ho'. He attended law school, but left to pursue a career as a musician and toured with his sister's band. Blanche Calloway was a star in the late 1920s; a fine singer who hired good musicians, she was soon eclipsed by Cab's fame and passed over by booking agents who wanted him. Ironically, others traded on the name after Cab became famous – their brother Elmer did not play or

sing, but fronted a band for a promoter, and there was Jean and/or
Ruth Calloway, who was not even related – while Blanche went
bankrupt.

Cab fronted a band called the Missourians, then in 1929 appeared
in *Connie's Hot Chocolates* and led the Alabamians at Harlem's Savoy
Ballroom. After returning to the Missourians, he changed its name to
Cab Calloway and his Orchestra and followed Duke Ellington into
the Cotton Club, where he became famous, as Ellington had, through
live broadcasts. (On their first hit recording, 'St Louis Blues', Calloway's men were billed as the Jungle Band.) The band made several
films, and signed with Victor in 1933. The pianist was Benny Payne,
who later accompanied Billy Daniels and recorded duets with Fats
Waller; other members were such stars as tenor saxophonists Ben
Webster and Chu Berry, trumpeter Shad Collins, bass player Milt
Hinton (who has probably played on more recordings than anyone
else alive) and Dizzy Gillespie (1939–41).

Cab's act was full of physical energy, and his long black hair flew;
he made 'hi-de-ho' a national catch-phrase. He was an underrated
ballad singer, as 'You are the One in My Heart' shows. He had a top
ten hit in 1942 with 'Blues in the Night', and the band of the early
1940s was his best. It played arrangements by Buster Harding, who
later wrote for Count Basie's 1947 band, and it also had tremendous
esprit de corps. As one of the highest-earning leaders for nearly two
decades, he could and did pay his men well. Furthermore, he gave
them credit, saying to George T. Simon, 'I'm up front there doing
my act, but it's the guys themselves who are making this band what
it is.' The early 1940s band would have made more recordings but for
the musicians' union strike, of which more later; but this was the
band that was seen and heard in the film *Stormy Weather* (1943), and
the one admired by musicians. Its rhythm section played slightly
behind the beat in a way that left no doubt that there was plenty of
power in reserve.

When the Big Band Era was over, Calloway led a sextet (1948),
and occasionally formed a bigger band for tours and special engagements. His personality was already permanently established in
American popular culture, but he never stopped making new fans:

among his albums in the microgroove era were *The Hi-de-ho Man* (RCA, 1958), recorded with an excellent big band including Hinton, trumpeter Joe Wilder, trombonist Urbie Green and drummer J. C. Heard. He appeared in the film biography of W. C. Handy, *St Louis Blues*, in 1958, and starred as Horace Vandergelder opposite Pearl Bailey in an all-black version of *Hello, Dolly!* in New York in 1967. (His daughter Chris played Minnie Fay.) He published an autobiography, *Of Minnie the Moocher and Me*, in 1976. He sang 'Minnie' in the film *The Blues Brothers* (1980) and appeared in the show *Bubbling Brown Sugar* and was portrayed by Larry Marshall in the film *The Cotton Club* (1984), which featured 'Minnie', 'Lady with the Fan' and 'Jitterbug', all Calloway compositions. He made a television film *The Cotton Club Comes to the Ritz* (broadcast in the UK in 1985), in which he sang 'Blues in the Night'. His revue *Cotton Club Revisited* toured North America that year with Chris, who has had a recording career of her own. Calloway's influence has been incalculable, reaching up to new jive-jump bands in the 1980s and such pop stars as Joe Jackson.

Chick Webb was a hunch-backed drummer whose band clobbered Goodman's in a famous battle a few months before Webb's death; twenty thousand people were allegedly turned away from the Savoy Ballroom that night. Krupa, then the most famous drummer, said that he had never been beaten by anybody stronger, but Webb was killed by tuberculosis of the spine just as recording engineers were learning how to record him. Webb's arranger, Edgar Sampson, who also played violin and reeds, wrote some of the biggest hits of the era: 'Stompin' at the Savoy', 'Don't Be That Way', 'Blue Minor', 'If Dreams Come True', 'Blue Lou' and 'Lullaby in Rhythm'. Webb also discovered Ella Fitzgerald when she was only sixteen and adopted her (she was an orphan); 'A-tisket, A-tasket', with Ella and Louis Jordan on tenor saxophone, was a big hit in 1938.

The Mills Blue Rhythm Band, a black band run by white music publisher Irving Mills, made many fine recordings with sidemen such as Red Allen and J. C. Higginbotham. It was taken over by its frontman Lucky Millinder, who went bankrupt in 1939 but formed a new band in 1940 which became one of the most popular in Harlem.

Millinder employed early modern jazzmen, among them Freddie
Webster and Dizzy Gillespie (trumpets), Lucky Thompson and Lockjaw Davis (reeds) and Sir Charles Thompson and Bill Doggett
(piano). Vocalists were Sister Rosetta Tharpe, who also played electric
guitar ('Shout, Sister Shout!' / 'I Want a Tall, Skinny Papa', 1942), and
Wynonie Harris ('Who Threw the Whiskey in the Well?', 1945).
Millinder's band shrank as the Big Band Era came to an end and in
the early 1950s was effectively a jump band on the King label (which
also recorded rhythm and blues hits with Harris). A good anthology
of Millinder's work would illustrate the change from big-band jazz to
rhythm and blues that took place in those years.

Trumpeter Erskine Hawkins joined a band at Alabama State
Teachers College in 1935, came to New York the next year as its
leader and from 1936 to 1948 had hits on Bluebird and Victor. His
first, 'Until the Real Thing Comes Along', featured vocalist Billy
Daniels (who later became famous for his delivery of 'That Old Black
Magic'). The band's biggest hits were 'Tuxedo Junction', its own
composition, on which the fine muted trumpet of Dud Bascomb may
be heard, the bluesy 'After Hours', with its composer Avery Parrish
on piano, and 'Tippin' In', also a bluesy instrumental.

Pianist Claude Hopkins led a band that accompanied Josephine
Baker in Europe in the 1920s. By the early 1930s, when it played at
Roseland for three years, it was a very popular band noted for its use
of cup mutes and soft rhythm. Hits included 'Margie' (1934), with
falsetto singer Orlando Robertson. Among its various sidemen were
lead trumpeter Russell 'Pops' Smith (from Fletcher Henderson's
band, where his brother Joe was a star), the superb New Orleans
clarinettist Edmond Hall and trumpeter Jabbo Smith. Hopkins
continued to play fine piano into the 1970s.

Jimmie Lunceford formed a school dance band with Jimmy Crawford on drums; they soon picked up alto saxophonist Willie Smith
from Fisk University, where Lunceford had studied. After a few
years it became a well-drilled show band that was enormously popular
with white and black dancers alike. Other members were vocalist-
trombonist Trummy Young and tenor saxophonist Joe Thomas (not
to be confused with trumpeter Joe Thomas, who played in Henderson's and many other bands). Lunceford's biggest hit was 'Rhythm is

Our Business' in 1935. The vocal groups included Young, Smith, Thomas, trumpeter and arranger Sy Oliver and trumpeter Eddie Tompkins, but the whole band could sing like a glee club. They would imitate Paul Whiteman and Guy Lombardo; Tompkins would copy Louis Armstrong; the trumpet section would throw its horns in the air and catch them in unison. Some other bands looked down on Lunceford's 'trained monkeys', but they could play as well as they could clown. Will Hudson's 'Jazznocracy' and 'White Heat' were popular, if regarded as second-rate by Crawford. In Sy Oliver's arrangements, for example 'Ain't She Sweet' and 'Cheatin' on Me' (with vocal trio) and 'Well, All Right Then' (in which the whole band sings) a vocal trio and a rhythm section are in 2/4 while the rest of the band is in 4/4. They are irresistible, and prove that a 2/4 beat does not have to be lumpy. Oliver and Young were responsible for 'T'ain't What You Do (It's the Way That You Do It)', a Swing Era anthem; trombonist and guitarist Eddie Durham also wrote arrangements for Lunceford. At the time there were several hit versions of Will Hudson's 'Organ Grinder's Swing', an irritating pop song, but Oliver's arrangement for Lunceford was an outstanding piece of orchestral writing, full of contrasts and instrumental timbres.

Despite 'For Dancers Only' and 'Blues in the Night', the band's popularity in ballrooms was not well illustrated by its recordings. The grinding life of one-night performances began to take its toll, and Lunceford died suddenly. (Trummy Young always believed that he was poisoned by a bigoted restaurant manager after insisting that the band be fed.)

The Savoy Sultans, led by reedman Al Cooper, was the house band at the famous ballroom; although it was only an octet, visiting bands were not immune from a thrashing. Drummer Razz Mitchell used a riveted Chinese sizzle cymbal; Rudy Williams was a fine alto saxophonist; Sam Massenberg played trumpet; bass player Grachan Moncur II was the father of modern trombonist Grachan Moncur III. The band's name was carried on in the late 1940s by drummer Panama Francis, who had worked with Millinder opposite the Sultans; in 1976 he formed another band under the venerable name, and it has made some delightful albums.

Earl 'Fatha' Hines, one of the best pianists in jazz, was a prominent bandleader from 1928 until 1947. He had developed a 'trumpet' style, playing an octave higher in the right hand so as to be heard over an ensemble; in the late 1920s his left-hand style was more advanced than that of the great New York stride pianists. He made himself famous before 1930, playing and recording first with Louis Armstrong and then at Chicago's Apex Club with the unusual small band of clarinettist Jimmie Noone (1928), which had two reed players but no brass; his solo recordings in 1928–9 include eight for QRS (Quality Reigns Supreme, the piano-roll company, which also made gramophone records).

In 1928 Hines led a ten-piece group which grew to a full 'big band' while broadcasting from Chicago Grand Terrace Ballroom in the 1930s. His contract with the ballroom made him a prisoner of gangsters, and, as he put it, 'I couldn't afford to buy stars, so I had to find them.' He hired excellent men, among them trumpeters Shirley Clay, Freddie Webster and Walter Fuller, Trummy Young (before he joined Lunceford) and saxophonist-arranger Albert 'Budd' Johnson. Popular vocalist Herb Jeffries joined him in 1934 (and was later with Duke Ellington). Hines bought arrangements from Horace Henderson, Jimmy Mundy, Eddie Durham, multi-instrumentalist Edgar 'Puddinghead' Battle and Johnson. Budd Johnson wrote for many bands – notably those of Hines, Billy Eckstine, Dizzy Gillespie, Woody Herman and Boyd Raeburn – at the time in the 1940s when they employed most of the best young players, both black and white, of what would become bop, and then 'modern jazz'. Johnson's contribution to music is enormous. After disbanding his orchestra, possibly to get away from Chicago's gangsters, Hines formed another on the West Coast in 1940. In that decade, given his need to recruit youngsters, his band was inevitably an incubator for new stars: Gillespie, Charlie Parker, Wardell Gray, trombonist Bennie Green and vocalists Billy Eckstine and Sarah Vaughan.

In 1947 he gave up, along with many other leaders, and worked with Louis Armstrong's All Stars for a couple of years; he was gradually reduced to playing dixieland in West Coast clubs, but came to the fore again after performing at the Little Theatre in New York in 1963. Thereafter he toured the world, both with small groups (often including Johnson) and as a soloist. He made a great many albums in his last two decades (about twenty of them solo), every one of which is a monument to the sheer joy of music-making: again and again, as on 'Tea for Two' (produced in London in 1965 by Alan Bates) and 'C-jam Blues' (from a three-disc collection of Ellington songs made from 1971 to 1975), he walks a tightrope without falling off, the wit and beauty in the music always triumphing over technique for its own sake.

Hines's big band was regarded as a territory band in the mid-1930s, as was Benny Moten's; it played a style then called western swing by New York musicians, who admired it. Kansas City was a hothouse of jazz and blues which exploded at the height of the Swing Era. Corrupt local Democratic party boss Tom Pendergast ran the town until 1938, when he was indicted for tax fraud, and neither Prohibition nor its repeal, nor indeed the Depression, made much difference in Kansas City: the town was wide open and twenty or thirty clubs were doing business (while Pendergast went to bed at nine). Musicians did not get paid much, but they played all night. The Kansas City style that emerged was a blues-based, riffing style, at once looser and tighter than mainstream swing.

Bennie Moten's group, based in Kansas City, was the most prolifically recorded of all the territory bands – it made about a hundred sides for Victor between 1923 and 1932. When Moten died (having his tonsils out), pianist Bill Basie took over remnants of it. Basie, from New Jersey, had toured with vaudeville acts, at the instigation of Fats Waller. Having been stranded in Kansas City, he joined bass player Walter Page's Blue Devils, which also included trumpeter Oran 'Hot Lips' Page, arranger and alto saxophonist Henry 'Buster' Smith and jazz and blues vocalist Jimmy Rushing. Basie joined Moten on piano, so that Moten (also a pianist) had more time for administration; he was featured on Moten's 'Prince of Wails' in 1932.

In 1936 Basie was leading a nine-piece group at the Reno Club in Kansas City; record producer John Hammond heard a broadcast on a car radio in Chicago, and told booking agent Willard Alexander about it. Basie hired more men and went to Chicago, but had signed a bad recording contract with Decca. Meanwhile, in October Hammond took a Basie group into a small studio in Chicago and recorded one of the most astonishing sessions of that decade, or any other.

The quintet – Basie, Page, drummer Jo Jones, tenor saxophonist Lester Young and trumpeter Carl 'Tatti' Smith – was billed as Jones–Smith Incorporated. They recorded 'Shoe-shine Boy' and 'Lady Be Good'; Rushing was added on 'Evenin'' and 'Boogie Woogie'. It was Young's first recording session, and he never played better in his life.

Lester Young began performing in his family's band. Inspired by the pretty sound and thoughtful craftsmanship of Frankie Trumbauer on C-melody saxophone, Young's style was lyrical and linear; he said that in a ballad he liked to keep the words of the song in mind. He had a unique tone without much vibrato, and played at the high end of the instrument's range, sometimes sounding almost like an alto instead of a tenor. His swing was incomparable, and he became one of the most influential musicians of the century.

In fact, the white Chicagoan Bud Freeman had already presented a lighter alternative to the big-toned, chromatic Coleman Hawkins style of tenor saxophone which was then dominant. But during the Swing Era Freeman led his own smaller groups or was a sideman in such bands as Tommy Dorsey's or Benny Goodman's, which were commercially oriented, however strong the jazz content. Lester Young came to fame in Basie's band, which made less money than those of Dorsey or Goodman, but was a much better place for a genius like Young to make his mark. It is true that Young was a greater musician than Freeman; nevertheless, in popular music it has also been true, at least since 1935, that the further you are from the mainstream, the more likely you are to be allowed to develop your full potential. In 1941–2 Young led a renowned band on the West Coast with his drummer brother, Lee, but it never recorded. (Lee Young played in film studios and with Nat 'King' Cole, among others; from the early 1960s he worked for Vee Jay, Motown and other record labels.)

Lester Young was a gentle, humorous, private man; he spoke an argot of his own, some phrases of which entered the language (such as 'I've got eyes', signifying approval); it was he who gave everybody nicknames, including Sweets for trumpeter Harry Edison, and Lady Day for Billie Holiday. An unlikely soldier, born in Mississippi, Young was frightened of racism; after he was drafted the Army put him in a stockade in Georgia, which didn't do him any good. When he came out he found that half the tenor players sounded like Lester Young, but the orthodox canard that he was no longer himself is not true: he knew what he was doing on his horn until the end.

Walter Page was called Big Four. 'He started that "Strolling" or "Walking" bass, going way up and then coming right on down. He did it on four strings, but other bass players couldn't get that high so they started making a five-string bass,' said Edison. Jo Jones was the best and fastest drummer of the Swing Era, but also the smoothest. He was not necessarily the first to keep time on the top cymbal, but did so with such finesse and consummate swing that he permanently altered the course of jazz, partly by setting the rest of the drum kit free to be used as a musical instrument rather than a device for constant timekeeping, as Krupa was doing at the time.

Buster Smith, an important influence on Young and on Charlie Parker, did not want to leave Kansas City (and was still performing in Dallas, Texas, in 1988). Hot Lips Page had been lured away by Joe Glaser, who hoped to make another Louis Armstrong of him; he led a good band from 1938 to 1940 and sang on Artie Shaw's hit version of 'Blues in the Night'. So Basie had not only to add men to make his octet a big band, but also to replace some of them, as well as putting up with John Hammond's meddling. When his band reached New York, it did not make an immediate impact; some of the men did not read music well, and they had trouble playing in tune because they were too poor to buy good instruments. (Don Kirkpatrick wrote arrangements for the band; tenor saxophonist Herschel Evans would tear up his part if it had too many sharps and flats in it.) But they began recording for Decca in early 1937 and soon blew open New York's Famous Door, a long, narrow room which must hardly have been able to contain the band's sound.

The playing of pianist Earl Hines and Basie's rhythm section has been said to 'swing like a (well-oiled) machine', but machines do not swing; the phenomenon is in fact indescribable. No one had ever heard anything like the classic Basie band, which soon included rhythm guitarist Freddie Green. (Young trombonist Dennis Wilson said of Green, nearly fifty years later, 'It's as though they said in the Bible, "Let there be Time", and Freddie started playing.') This was a rhythm section that played music as it swung, Green strumming chords and Page always walking in the direction of the tune.

Buck Clayton played lovely and distinctive open and muted trumpet for decades. Herschel Evans played fine tenor in the style of Hawkins; Basie encouraged an opposition with Young that was like 'Ham 'n' Eggs', as one of the band's instrumentals was called. At his peak Dicky Wells's trombone playing was second only to Teagarden's, reminding us of Whitney Balliet's description of jazz as 'the sound of surprise'. (He made some of his best recordings in Paris with Django Reinhardt in 1937 before joining Basie.) Jack Washington played baritone saxophone, Earle Warren alto; among the trumpeters were Edison, Ed Lewis and Shad Collins; at one point the trombones included Benny Morton as well as Wells and Dan Minor.

The life of guitarist, trombonist and arranger Eddie Durham, one of the most productive in popular music, was celebrated by New York's WKCR radio with a marathon sixty-nine-hour broadcast on his 79th birthday, comprising interviews, lectures and music. He wrote for Lunceford, then Basie; Wells said, 'Basie and Ed would lock up in a room with a little jug, and Basie would play the ideas, Ed would voice them.' It was probably Durham and Buster Smith who created 'One O'Clock Jump', a head arrangement first called 'Blue Balls': a player would think of a good riff and start riding it; other members of the section would play along; somebody in another section would create a piece of harmony, or an opposing or answering riff, and a new tune was born. 'One O'Clock Jump' was one of the era's biggest hits. Durham wrote or co-wrote 'Out the Window', 'Time Out', 'John's Idea' (for Hammond) and 'Swinging the Blues'; 'Topsy' (with Edgar Battle) was revived in 1957 for a pop hit by drummer Cozy Cole; 'Good Morning Blues' and 'Sent For You Yesterday and Here You Come Today' were written with Basie and Rushing. (He wrote the 1941 hit 'I Don't Want to Set the World on Fire' for Bon Bon, a black sweet pop singer with the white dance band of Russian-born violinist Jan Savitt.) Durham was music director of the International Sweethearts of Rhythm, a very good all-girl band that was formed in an orphanage and ran away; he later worked for R & B singer Wynonie Harris, and was still working in the 1980s. An early master of the electric guitar, he may be heard on an enchanting Lester Young small-group date for Commodore in 1938 (as the Kansas City Six); Young plays lovely clarinet as well as tenor, along with Clayton, Green, Page and Jones.

'Basie never did play much with his left hand, so Freddie [Green] substituted for it,' said Clayton. Basie led the band from the keyboard with an economy that became famous, saying more with one note than others did with several. The band's Decca recordings, other than those named above, included 'Jumpin' at the Woodside' (written by Basie) and 'Texas Shuffle' and 'Doggin' Around' (by Evans); 'Blue and Sentimental' featured Evans, while 'Roseland Shuffle', 'Honeysuckle Rose', 'Every Tub' and 'Cherokee' (a two-sided 78) and many others featured Young. Rushing sang 'Pennies from Heaven', and the wonderful Helen Humes 'Dark Rapture', 'Blame It on My Last Affair' and 'My Heart Belongs to Daddy'. Billie Holiday sang with the band in 1937, but could not record with it for contractual reasons (one of the great missed opportunities of the era); 'They Can't Take That Away From Me' is a famous broadcast aircheck. Among Basie's recordings for CBS labels from 1939 to 1946 are 'Taxi War Dance', 'Lester Leaps In', 'Dickie's Dream' (written by Young for Wells) and 'Ham 'n' Eggs'. He also played with the Benny Goodman Sextet in 1940 and on many other small-group recording sessions.

Basie recorded for Victor from 1947 to 1950, as the Swing Era was winding down. He had a number one novelty hit in 1947, the most popular of several versions of 'Open the Door, Richard' (with a 'vocal' by Edison), so untypical it is never included in compilation albums; today it is strange to hear Jones's smooth high-hat on what is basically a piece of R&B jive. The band's original stars were mostly gone (though Green stayed until the end); the trumpets included Edison, and such fine players as Clark Terry, Joe Newman and Emmett Berry, and the reed section Buddy Tate, Paul Gonsalves and Lucky Thompson. The excellent fare is well represented by such songs as 'Cheek to Cheek', Redman's 'Just an Old Manuscript' and a lovely, affectionate updating of Moten's 'South'.

Basie was the most famous but far from the only graduate of Kansas City. Harlan Leonard and his Kansas City Skyrockets was a twelve-piece band, many of whose members had split from Moten in

1931; Leonard had led Moten's reed section. Thamon Hayes played trombone, Ed Lewis trumpet and Jesse Stone piano. The band was initially successful, and in 1934 went to Chicago, where it was run out of town by James Petrillo's musicians' union. Hayes quit in disgust to run a music store in Kansas City, but Leonard re-formed the band as Harlan Leonard and his Rockets, briefly employed Charlie Parker (who could not turn up on time) and made sixteen sides for Bluebird in 1940, playing arrangements by Stone, Durham, Buster Smith, Tadd Dameron and Rozelle Claxton. Tenor saxophonist Henry Bridges had received an offer from Benny Goodman when he was drafted, and Fred Beckett was an advanced trombonist who died of tuberculosis contracted in the army.

Reedman Andy Kirk took over Terrence Holder's Dark Clouds of Joy in Dallas in 1929 and settled in Kansas City. Pianist-arranger Mary Lou Williams joined in 1931, and with popular singer Pha Terrell the band had big hits from 1936 to 1938, among them 'Until the Real Thing Comes Along'. Kirk carried on until 1948. Williams was a great talent whose compositions included 'Walkin' and Swingin'' for Kirk, 'Roll 'Em' for Benny Goodman and 'Trumpet No End' for Duke Ellington. Her friendships with Thelonious Monk and others made her a guru for the bop movement, and late in life she bravely played in a duo with the avant-gardist Cecil Taylor.

Pianist and band leader Jay 'Hootie' McShann in later years became a vocalist as well. Charlie Parker, trumpeter Buddy Anderson, bass player Gene Ramey and drummer Gus Johnson were members of his Kansas City band; his singers were Walter Brown (with whom he wrote 'Confessin' the Blues', which became a standard) and Al Hibbler ('Get Me on Your Mind'). Ramey and Johnson worked with Basie in 1952–3 and again with McShann in the 1970s. McShann, who was still playing fine piano, was the subject of a film, *Hootie's Blues*, in 1978, and recorded occasionally in the 1980s. Pianist and singer Julia Lee, another Kansas City artist, worked with Walter Page and Jay McShann, but mostly as a soloist. A daughter of Missouri, she performed at an inaugural party for Harry Truman. She was best known for songs of a risqué nature (for example 'King Size Papa' and 'I Didn't Like It the First Time'), though they do not show her talent to best advantage.

McShann's recordings have always been of special interest to jazz fans because of Parker. Kansas City bands made a contribution to American music that can stand by itself, but their rhythmic freedom and blues feeling, together with outstanding soloists like Lester Young and Parker, had a direct effect on modern jazz and hence are still influential today.

Benny Carter is one of the grandfathers of popular music. As an alto saxophonist, he was one of the most influential, but he also recorded on trumpet, trombone, tenor saxophone, clarinet and piano. He played with Webb, Henderson, the Cotton Pickers, Ellington and others, and by the age of twenty-one was already a well-known composer-arranger. His trademark of writing reed choruses along the chords of a tune perhaps represents the essence of this kind of music. The most famous of many Carter tunes is 'When Lights are Low'. In the late 1930s he was a staff arranger at the BBC, and led a ten-piece band in Europe which contained musicians of nine nationalities, among them two Englishmen.

Having often led his own bands in the 1940s, Carter then spent twenty-five years in film studios, where he wrote film and television scores and helped to desegregate the film industry; there were two albums written for Count Basie in 1960–61, and his own *Further Definitions* (1961), in which four saxophones together with a rhythm section provide more rich beauty than many a bigger group. This famous album re-created Carter recordings made in Europe in 1937, and was itself re-created on a CD in 1988 and at the Chicago Jazz Festival in 1989. He was still writing and playing in 1993. Listening to Benny Carter's beautiful music, one wonders again why this sort of music, so central to our popular culture, is today rarely heard on the radio.

Of all the bands that entertained crowds during the Swing Era, Duke Ellington's was one of the few that had already become well known in the late 1920s, and the only one that carried on with its leader's musical identity intact into the 1970s.

Ellington's father was a butler at the White House, and a blueprint maker for the US Navy. Duke acquired his nickname as a teenager from his elegant dress and demeanour; his parents and his middle-class upbringing gave him confidence and a knowledge of his own worth which never left him. But he was black, and made his living playing jazz, and was among the first great black musicians to become weary of the term. He was not the first to say, 'There are only two kinds of music: good and bad', though from him the aphorism had a special poignance. He was a pianist, bandleader, arranger and composer, but essentially unclassifiable, because he was all of these things at once; one of the greatest American musicians of the century, he ruled a band of unruly geniuses until he died.

He had a piano teacher called Miss Clinkscales, but was largely self-taught. A talented artist, he had won an NAACP poster-design contest and left high school to start a sign-painting business, but found that piano playing drew the girls. He performed locally, attracting more work than he could handle himself. He went to New York in March 1923 and did not find work, but returned in September with a band called the Washingtonians, led by Elmer Snowden and including trumpeter Arthur Whetsol, saxophonist Otto 'Toby' Hardwicke and drummer Sonny Greer. Vocalist Ada Smith (later famous as Bricktop) recommended them for a job at Barron's Exclusive Club, their first important engagement; then they played for four years at the Hollywood Inn (renamed the Kentucky Club after a fire).

Elmer Snowden was an indefatigable musical businessman. He made countless delightful recordings under various names (the Jungle Town Stompers, the Musical Stevedores, etc.) and at one point got into trouble with the musicians' union because he was running so many bands. Ellington became leader of the Washingtonians when Snowden left in 1925 (possibly because Greer didn't want to be leader). At the beginning of this period it was just another dance band; at the end it was Ellington's, playing his music. Whetsol left to study medicine and was replaced by Bubber Miley; Fred Guy played banjo; Charlie Irvis, who played a growling trombone, was replaced by Joe 'Tricky Sam' Nanton, and they were joined for a brief period by the profoundly influential Sidney Bechet. Duke wrote music for the revue *Chocolate Kiddies*, which toured Europe with Sam Wooding, but it is not clear whether Ellington's music was used. Ellington's band went to the Cotton Club when King Oliver turned down the job because it did not pay enough, performing there from December 1927 until February 1931, except during a few short tours. The band made a short film, *Black and Tan Fantasy*, in 1929 in New York, and became famous through broadcasts from the Cotton Club.

Sam Wooding, a success in Europe who toured as far as Russia, had also turned down the Cotton Club job because he thought that $1,100 a week was an insulting offer. He soon returned to Europe, where (he told journalist Chip Deffaa in 1985) audiences liked a hot black band better than they liked Paul Whiteman's style. Wooding's men were proud of the fact that they could double on bassoons, oboes, French horns and so forth; and anyway, as Rae Harrison, the beautiful vocalist who became Mrs Wooding, said to Deffaa, 'Why would they want to go back to Harlem, where they've been all their lives?' But Ellington had nowhere better to go, and probably appreciated the importance of the radio wire. Among the men Wooding valued most highly in his band was reedman Garvin Bushell, who said many years later that if they had understood the impact that radio was having, they would have *paid* $1,100 a week to play at the Cotton Club.

Charlie Johnson, a pianist from Philadelphia, went to Harlem after working in Atlantic City; he was a surrogate father for Wooding, and helped him to focus on music. He led his Paradise Ten at Smalls' Paradise for more than a decade, and was another leader who smarted because of Ellington's radio success. Johnson's band made lovely records for Victor in the late 1920s, such as 'Hot Tempered Blues', 'You Ain't the One' and 'Boy in the Boat', and his band did not get a chance to play live on the radio. But lightning occasionally strikes in the right place: Ellington wrote and arranged music for the Cotton Club's floor shows, and began to create a unique body of composition; when Wooding returned from Europe for good during the Depression, there were no recording contracts to be had, while Ellington was already justly famous.

Many of the Harlem clubs became legendary. Smalls' Paradise admitted blacks, if they could afford it; waiters danced the Charleston while balancing trays, and owner Ed Smalls encouraged the band to park their cars in front on quiet nights to make the place look busy. Connie's Inn, owned by George and Connie Immerman, was where Fats Waller began as a delivery boy (with bottles of bootleg alcohol hidden about his already large person) and where Waller's shows

Keep Shufflin' and *Hot Chocolates* were later first produced. But the most famous spot was the Cotton Club, built in 1918 at the corner of Lenox and 142nd Street, which had a theatre on the ground floor and a dance hall upstairs. Boxer Jack Johnson changed it into the Club Deluxe, then bootlegger Owney Madden turned it into the Cotton Club, an outlet for his beer that offered entertainment for white downtowners. The cream of society went there, including Mayor Jimmy Walker and Lady Mountbatten (who dubbed it 'The Aristocrat of Harlem'). It moved downtown to Broadway and 48th in 1936, but by then the Harlem Renaissance was over, having been based on a shaky foundation of white patronage fuelled by Prohibition, which ended in 1933.

During the Cotton Club's heyday much of the music for its revues was written by Jimmy McHugh and Dorothy Fields (daughter of vaudeville comedian Lew Fields), then by Harold Arlen and Ted Koehler. McHugh had written 'When My Sugar Walks Down the Street' with Gene Austin, who had a big hit with it in 1925; publisher Irving Mills was also credited as co-author. McHugh and Fields wrote songs for shows and revues, such as 'Diga Diga Doo', 'Bandana Babies', 'Harlem River Quiver', 'Doin' the New Low-down', 'Harlemania', 'Doin' the Frog', 'Hot Feet', 'I Must Have That Man', 'Exactly Like You', 'I Can't Give You Anything But Love' and 'On the Sunny Side of the Street' (though the last two tunes may have been bought from Fats Waller). Many of these were recorded by Ellington, and some by Don Redman as well. In Ellington's arrangement of 'Diga Diga Doo' clarinets whistle through the trees like banshees, while his introduction to 'Bandana Babies' features Wellman Braud's bass prominently and has a vocal by Irving Mills and Ozie Ware. McHugh and Fields went to Hollywood and wrote 'Don't Blame Me', 'I'm in the Mood for Love' and others for films. (Both worked with many others; Fields's important partnership with Cy Coleman in the 1960s yielded the show *Sweet Charity*.)

Harold Arlen was mentioned earlier as Alec Wilder's favourite songwriter, and a distinctively American one. He fell in love with jazz, and played piano in cafés at the age of fifteen; he published songs in 1928 (his 'Album of My Dreams' was recorded by Rudy Vallee), but did not intend to write for a living. While working as a rehearsal pianist for Vincent Youmans, he invented an introductory vamp and was advised by Will Marion Cook to publish it before somebody stole it: it became his first big hit, 'Get Happy', with words by Koehler.

Arlen and Koehler were hired to write for the Cotton Club when McHugh and Fields were busy on Broadway: from 1931 to 1934 they wrote 'Between the Devil and the Deep Blue Sea', 'Kickin' the Gong Around' (a drug song, which was recorded by Louis Armstrong, among others) and 'Minnie the Moocher's Wedding Day' (all of which were recorded by Cab Calloway), 'Stormy Weather' (always associated with Ethel Waters, but also an instrumental hit for Ellington in 1933 and a sensation for Ivie Anderson with him in England that year), 'As Long As I Live' (introduced by Lena Horne at the age of sixteen), 'I Gotta Right to Sing the Blues' (recorded memorably by Jack Teagarden), 'It's Only a Paper Moon' and 'Let's Fall In Love'. Arlen's career was a long one: with Yip Harburg he wrote the songs for the film *The Wizard of Oz* in 1939, and 'The Man That Got Away' in 1954 (from *A Star is Born*), for Judy Garland. His Broadway shows included *Bloomer Girl* (1944, with Harburg), *St Louis Woman* (1946, an all-black show, with Johnny Mercer), *House of Flowers* (1954, with Truman Capote) and *Jamaica* (1957, with Harburg).

Ellington's band could play as hot as any other black outfit, but he was thus influenced by first-class show music almost from the beginning. His natural talent for tone colours contributed a sensual beauty to his music that was and is unique. His first recordings had been made in November 1924; in the Cotton Club period recordings were issued on many labels and under many names: the Washingtonians, the Ten Black Berries, the Jungle Band, the Harlem Footwarmers, the Whoopee Makers, Duke Ellington and his Orchestra or his Cotton Club Orchestra and so on. All the early records have ended up in the vaults of MCA, CBS or Victor, and all are fascinating: almost from the beginning he had the confidence to break the rules, to do as he wished just to see what it would sound like.

The New Orleans bass player Wellman Braud, who had played with Oliver, first recorded with Ellington in October 1927, and shortly after recruited his home-town friend, clarinettist Barney Bigard. Bigard later wrote that at first he found some of the chords he heard behind him strange, but soon realized that Ellington knew exactly what he was doing. Legend has it that European critics, especially Constant Lambert in the UK, were the first to compare Ellington's tone colours to those of Delius and Debussy; in fact (as James Lincoln Collier has pointed out), Robert Donaldson Darrell, later a distinguished classical critic, was the first to do so in *Disques*, an American magazine, in June 1932. Darrell had reviewed 'East St Louis Toodle-oo' in the *Phonograph Monthly Review* in June 1927, and 'Black and Tan Fantasy' in July, not knowing it was the same band under another name. Between November 1926 and April 1930 'East St Louis Toodle-oo' was recorded eight times on six labels (not counting alternative takes) as the young composer experimented.

Other classics of the era included 'Birmingham Breakdown', 'Jubilee Stomp' and 'Flaming Youth'; such titles as 'Jungle Blues', 'Jungle Nights in Harlem' and 'Jungle Jamboree' reveal the flavour of the club, where the musicians were black and the patrons white. Nanton and Miley used a growling 'yow-yow' instrumental device (in Miley's case inspired by King Oliver), which later had to be learned by Miley's replacements, Cootie Williams and then Ray Nance. Nanton stayed with Ellington from 1926 until his death; Miley was an unreliable alcoholic, but his influence from 1924 to 1929 was profound: the main ideas for 'East St Louis', 'Black and Tan Fantasy', among others, were Miley's, and Ellington later wrote that 'that was when we decided to forget about the sweet stuff'.

'Rockin' in Rhythm' (1930) became the band's theme (replacing 'East St Louis'); years later they still played 'The Moòche', 'Black Beauty' (for Florence Mills, the first of many portraits) and 'Creole Love Call'. Adelaide Hall had improvised a wordless obbligato off-stage during a performance of 'Creole Love Call' while standing near an open mike; she was overheard by Ellington, who then included her in a 1927 recording. In Europe Hall had worked in the show *Chocolate Kiddies*, 'with Josephine Baker at one end of the line and me at the other'. Hall was famous for her rendition of 'I Can't Give You Anything But Love'. She went back and forth to Europe before settling in England, where she had a radio show with bandleader Joe

Loss and was seen and heard in Alexander Korda's film *The Thief of Bagdad* (1940). She was still working (and receiving excellent reviews) at the end of the 1980s.

On Ellington's recording of 'Jungle Nights in Harlem' in 1930 the reed section consisted of Barney Bigard, Harry Carney and Johnny Hodges, though it seemed to be much bigger; the Victor recording, with the acoustic bass prominent, sounds astonishingly up to date today. In 'Mood Indigo' (1930) the classic tune is blended by Nanton, Bigard and Whetsol, showing the formidable skill of the arranger. Ellington had begun writing for specific players, and was an infallible judge of what each could do. In 1930 the band included Whetsol, Cootie Williams and Freddy Jenkins (trumpets), Nanton (trombone) and Juan Tizol (valve trombone), Hodges, Carney and Bigard (reeds), Guy (banjo, later guitar), Wellman Braud (bass) and Greer (drums). All were virtuosos, and most of them played intermittently with the band for decades.

If we had to name a sound that was the most important element of all in the band, it would have to be that of Harry Carney. When he joined (with his mother's permission) at the age of seventeen, he played clarinet and alto saxophone, but he soon changed to baritone, and remained the anchor of the band in more ways than one for nearly half a century. He was perhaps Ellington's closest friend; in later years they often drove together from gig to gig in Carney's Cadillac. Carney did for the baritone saxophone what Coleman Hawkins did for the tenor. His modesty and gentleness of spirit were always evident; at his appearance in a master class at the University of Wisconsin in 1973 he looked as though he still could not believe his good fortune in receiving so much affection from the public.

Johnny Hodges (also known as Rabbit or Jeep) had taken lessons from Sidney Bechet; he occasionally played soprano saxophone until 1940, but his main instrument was the alto. He joined Ellington in 1928 and stayed for life, except for the years 1951–5 when he led a successful smaller band of his own. He was the most widely admired alto saxophonist until Charlie Parker, and even after that, nobody could play a ballad like Hodges (Parker called him the Lily Pons of the instrument, and meant it as a compliment), and his hot playing in the Cotton Club period already revealed an unmistakable voice. He put on a veneer of gruffness, but, according to Bigard, was actually shy, and quite a prankster if you got to know him.

Irving Mills managed Ellington's band and published the music, sometimes writing lyrics and often taking credit as co-composer; some recordings were even issued under the name Mills' Ten Black Berries. Mills and his older brother Jack, who had been a song plugger for Waterson, Berlin and Snyder, had formed Mills Music in 1919. Irving, the 'outside' man, bought songs from people at recording sessions for 'three for a dollar' labels which they supervised. Their house group was the Hotsy Totsy Boys: Irving Mills, Mills Music's manager Jimmy McHugh, Sammy Fain (later a very famous songwriter) and Gene Austin. Later the Hotsy Totsy Gang, Goody's Goodtimers and other recording groups included Dick McPartland and the Dorsey brothers, and sometimes Irving (using pseudonyms) sang; we have seen that the black Mills Blue Rhythm Band became the Lucky Millinder band. The purpose of all this was to plug the songs.

Irving's most valuable discovery was Ellington. He helped the band get the job at the Cotton Club and landed the first good recording dates, as well as work in the film *Check and Double Check* with the enormously popular radio comedy stars Amos'n'Andy (1930). He also arranged the band's first trip to Europe in 1933. After leaving the Cotton Club (where it was replaced by Cab Calloway), the band was provided by Mills with Pullman cars when it travelled: unlike many black bands on the road, Ellington's and later Calloway's never worried about where to sleep.

Ellington understood better than most leaders the importance of recording, and of recorded balance. To this day Ellington's early records sound better than those of most of the others; he knew what he was doing in the studio. The band was first called Duke Ellington and his Famous Orchestra at a session for Brunswick in early 1931, when 'Creole Rhapsody' was recorded on a two-sided 10-inch 78; it was recorded again in June for Victor on a two-sided 12-inch record, Ellington's first attempts to exceed the limitations of the medium. In February 1932 trombonist Lawrence Brown and singer Ivie Anderson made their first recordings with the band, among them 'It Don't Mean a Thing if It Ain't Got That Swing', which helped to name the era.

The band recorded medleys on long-playing records for Victor the same month. In this early attempt to achieve longer playing time the relatively primitive 78 was simply slowed to 33⅓ rpm; it failed because the technology of the time was inadequate. But for some reason two microphones were used to cut different masters of the same take: these were combined to make very good stereo recordings more than fifty years later, on the album *Reflections in Ellington* (issued on the Everymans label in the USA in 1985). Hardwicke came back in 1932, after working for Bricktop in Paris; Darrell tried to interview Ellington that year, hoping to write a book about him, but he was already evasive about himself and his work. It was as well that he was on his guard; serious critics would take him almost too seriously.

The orthodoxy that the years from 1940 to 1942 represent Ellington's greatest period is difficult to refute, but there is a large number of masterly miniatures from every decade. The best big-band pieces were tone poems – integrated compositions for a group of specific virtuosos – and no one did this better than Ellington. His recordings in the 1930s included uptempo showpieces such as 'Stompy Jones', 'Jive Stomp', 'Merry-go-round', 'Showboat Shuffle' (with a paddle-wheel effect in the brass section), and also smoochy ballads and mood tunes: 'Prelude to a Kiss', 'Sophisticated Lady', '(There is) No Greater Love', 'Caravan' (written by Tizól), 'Azure' and 'The Gal From Joe's'.

'Solitude' (1934) had a solo by Carney, 'Clarinet Lament' (1936) featured Bigard, and on the other side was 'Echoes of Harlem', featuring Cootie Williams, 'Caravan' in 1937 was followed later in the year by 'Dusk on the Desert', also with Tizol's name on it, which has Ellington's percussion contribution, using a cardboard box. There were many, many more. To describe just one of these treasures: 'In a Jam' contains the simplest of brass riffs, a string of outstanding solos, a muted Nanton delicately traced by Bigard's clarinet, a dialogue between Hodges and Williams, an early guest appearance by Ben Webster and a ride-out by Rex Stewart.

Ivie Anderson, one of the best female singers of the era, with excellent diction and a warm vocal colour, joined Ellington in 1931.

Her numerous sides, many of them hits, include 'Truckin'', 'I'm Satisfied', 'Isn't Love the Strangest Thing?', 'There's a Lull in My Life' and 'If You Were in My Place (What Would You Do?)'. She sang 'All God's Chillun Got Rhythm' with the band in a Marx brothers film, and they recorded it twice.

'Diminuendo in Blue' and 'Crescendo in Blue', recorded on a two-sided 78 in 1937, was a composition that the band could not then play properly, especially with respect to intonation, according to Gunther Schuller in his *The Swing Era* (1989). It had been preceded by 'Reminiscin' in Tempo' in 1935, written on tour after Ellington's mother died. Schuller's essay on this is exemplary. Spread over four sides, the piece is still only about thirteen minutes long, a composition specifically for Ellington's musicians, but without much improvisation or even swing. In its skilful integration of its themes and episodes, Ellington probably never exceeded it. It is true that some of his more ambitious later 'extended' compositions are unsuccessful, or, to put it another way, that the best ones are literally suites, or strings of miniatures. But he did what he did so beautifully that it is impossible to complain that he did not have the formal training necessary to write symphonies and operas. As it was, while he was making the hit parade, he was also transcending it.

His treatments of others' tunes include a lovely 1933 version of the 1905 chestnut 'In the Shade of the Old Apple Tree', with a muted solo by Jenkins, and 'Rose of the Rio Grande' (1938), which featured Lawrence Brown and Ivie Anderson. (Brown had to play that solo for many years.) Ellington's own 'Pussy Willow' became a staple and 'I'm Checkin' Out Goombye' is the only recorded example of the jive repartee that Anderson and Greer developed in the live act; 'The Sergeant was Shy' and 'Tooting through the Roof' were all made in 1939. In the 1930s Ellington had recorded mostly for Brunswick, but the 1938–9 sides often appeared on Columbia; at his last session there in early 1940 he recorded remakes of 'Stormy Weather', 'Solitude' and 'Mood Indigo', with Anderson vocals, and a new instrumental, 'Sophisticated Lady'.

Irving Mills and Jack Kapp must have been equally energetic entrepreneurs, unwilling to take advice. Russell Sanjek reports that in 1935 Mills offered to take over the recording of all dance music for

Decca, and lectured Kapp and his staff on his expertise, where-upon Kapp directed that no talent connected with Mills was to be used. Mills's opinion of himself was justified, however, for in the mid-1930s he was the only contractor of recording artists in the business. In early 1937 he launched the 75-cent Master label and the 35-cent Variety label, distributed by Yates's ARC, and was successful for a while; among Ellington's hits were a remake of 'Caravan' with 'Azure' on the other side. But Mills failed to form an overseas affiliation, and soon turned back to selling his product to ARC labels.

Meanwhile, Wellman Braud had left Ellington, and from 1936 to 1938 the band had two bass players. In late 1939 Ellington discovered Jimmy Blanton playing a three-stringed instrument in a St Louis hotel, and advanced him the money for a four-stringed model. In the short time before he died of tuberculosis, Blanton revolutionized bass playing, not just with his unique time, but playing melody and harmony as well. Bigard had doubled on tenor saxophone, and Ellington had no star tenor player until Ben Webster became a full-time member. Arranger, composer and pianist Billy Strayhorn became more than Ellington's collaborator: in later years they worked to-gether so closely that sometimes they could not remember who had written what (or so they said).

In 1939 the agreement with Mills was severed. Ellington had done well out of it, charging a great many living expenses to Mills which would otherwise have come out of his own pocket. As James Lincoln Collier has pointed out, Ellington was not the type to be much interested in saving anything, but only in living well. There was pressure from the black press, where Adam Clayton Powell accused Ellington of being a 'musical sharecropper', but it is hard to believe, as Collier does, that Ellington, always his own man, would have let this affect him very much. But Mills was always busy trying to build an empire, and still selling Ellington's recordings to what were now CBS labels, and Ellington decided to move to RCA Victor.

Ellington's first session for Victor since 1934 was recorded in March 1940, and it was immediately obvious that a new page in Ellington's book had been turned; the quality of the music reached a new peak. 'Ko-Ko', from Ellington's uncompleted score for a stage work, came to be a jazz classic; its unforgettable opening bars were underpinned by an urgently mysterious one-note motif from Carney's baritone. 'Jack the Bear' was notable for Blanton's amazing ability to make the whole band sound like it was dancing on tip-toe; the furiously swinging 'Cotton Tail' included a controlled explosion from Webster. 'Harlem Air Shaft' had more ideas in it than most bandleaders had in a year, as did 'Sepia Panorama'. Strayhorn's 'Take the "A" Train' became the band's theme. Non-Ellington hits with pop songs were 'You, You Darlin'' and 'Flamingo' (vocals by Herb Jeffries) and 'At a Dixie Roadside Diner' (with Anderson). The hit 'I Got It Bad and That Ain't Good', sung by Anderson, came from Ellington's Los Angeles revue *Jump for Joy* which was ahead of its time. (Not even Los Angeles could take 'I've Got a Passport from Georgia (and I'm going to the USA)', and it was removed.)

There are too many great records to list here, but a few are 'Bojangles (a Portrait of Bill Robinson)' 'A Portrait of Bert Williams', 'Me and You' (with Anderson), 'In a Mellotone', 'C-jam Blues', the erotic 'Warm Valley' and the lovely 'Across the Track Blues' and four duets by Ellington and Blanton. Strayhorn wrote 'The Flaming Sword', 'After All', 'Chelsea Bridge', 'Raincheck' and 'Johnny Come Lately', as well as transmuting the 1927 pop song 'Chloe' into Ellingtonia, with an elegant Nanton 'jungle' introduction. Tizol wrote 'Bakiff' and the instant classic 'Perdido', a riff which summed up jazz composition for a whole generation. Ellington may have been having problems with royalties or income taxes at this time; at any rate, his son Mercer, who was already credited with 'Things Ain't What They Used To Be', was now listed as composer of 'Jumpin' Punkins', 'John Hardy's Wife' and the tragic 'Blue Serge'. The band was recorded live on 7 November 1940 at the Crystal Ballroom in Fargo, North Dakota, where fans took disc-cutting equipment to a dance: the result includes a Webster essay on 'Star Dust', never recorded commercially; perhaps it was suggested by Coleman Hawkins's 'Body and Soul' of the previous year.

Cootie Williams had left in 1940 to join Benny Goodman, with Ellington's blessing: Goodman could pay more, and Williams disliked the lackadaisical attitudes of Ellington's men and preferred playing with Goodman's Sextet. He later described this period as the happiest of his life, but the music business was shocked: bandleader Raymond Scott wrote 'When Cootie Left the Duke'. Williams's multi-talented replacement was Ray Nance, who also played violin (as on 'C-jam Blues') and sang delightful novelty vocals. Late in 1941 Alvin 'Junior' Raglin replaced Blanton, who was dying.

Small groups from the band had begun to record as early as 1930, soon under the nominal leadership of Barney Bigard (and his Jazzopators), Cootie Williams (and his Rug Cutters), Rex Stewart (and his Fifty-second Street Stompers) and Johnny Hodges (and his Orchestra); Ellington was usually at the piano, though Strayhorn began playing on some tracks in 1939. Rex Stewart also recorded in Paris in 1939, with his Feetwarmers: Bigard, Billy Taylor on bass and Django Reinhardt on guitar; on later issues of these tracks the group was called Rex Stewart's Big Four. Among Stewart's Ellingtonians, which recorded in 1940, were several non-Ellingtonians, for example Billy Kyle or Jimmy Jones on piano; the records were issued in a limited edition for a private jazz record club (but reissued on Fantasy's OJC label in 1985). Cootie Williams's Gotham Stompers, which recorded in New York in 1937, included Bigard, Hodges, Taylor and Carney, with such non-Ellingtonians as Tommy Fulford on piano and Chick Webb on drums. Rex Stewart and his Big Eight and Billy Taylor and his Big Eight also recorded for Keynote in 1944, and Hodges and Carney did some particularly tasty moonlighting.

Wherever any of these people played during this era they brought a flavour of Ellingtonia with them; but the cream of the Ellington small-group sessions took place in 1940–41 for Victor. Bigard, Stewart and Hodges each recorded eight tracks, as, for example, 'Johnny Hodges and Orchestra (an Ellington Unit)'. Williams, Nance, Brown, Webster and Tizol played on various recordings; common to all were Ellington (or Strayhorn), Carney, Blanton and Greer. The men were all at the peak of their powers; they had no axes to grind, no reputations to make, no trails to blaze. They played music of a quality which cannot be surpassed, because it is unique. Bigard wrote 'Ready Eddy' for his boss, whose '"C" Blues' soon became 'C-jam Blues'; 'Charlie the Chulo' was a perfect uptempo showcase for Bigard's enormous skill. From the Stewart session, 'Subtle Slough' later became 'Just Squeeze Me (But Don't Tease Me)', with words by Lee Gaines. Stewart growled like a fey lion on the charming 'Menelik (the Lion of Judah)' and Carney played a few bars of alto saxophone on 'My Sunday Gal'; 'Poor Bubber' was a salute to Miley, and 'Mobile Bay' to Cootie Williams. But if I had to choose, perhaps the most beautiful of all these recordings are those featuring Hodges: 'Things Ain't What They Used To Be' was that unforgettable tune's début; 'That's the Blues, Old Man' was the first appearance of a riff that became, a decade later, the climax of the R&B classic 'Night Train'; 'Passion Flower' was an early example of the way Strayhorn's lyricism and Hodges's unique ballad style – erotic, but always elegant, almost understated – complemented each other. On 'Squaty Roo' (another of Hodges's nicknames) the flawless, pulsating time of the performance almost sums up (if anything could) the contribution Blanton made to all these tracks, and indeed to the whole era. In the early days Sonny Greer had been as much showman as timekeeper; he never played better than he did with Blanton.

Billboard began printing its 'Harlem Hit Parade', the first black chart, in 1942. The following were number one: 'Never No Lament' (with a new title, 'Don't Get Around Much Any More', and soon to have words); 'Concerto for Cootie', a three-minute concerto for Williams, which had become 'Do Nothin' Till You Hear From Me'; 'Sentimental Lady', with 'A Slip of the Lip (Might Sink a Ship)' on the other side (a wartime novelty with a hip vocal by Nance: 'It's so bodacious / To be loquacious'); and the dramatic, driving 'Main Stem'. During the recording ban of 1943–4 earlier recordings reached the charts, including 'Going out the Back Way', from Hodges's 1941 date.

Ivie Anderson had to stop singing with the band because of the asthma that eventually caused her early death. She was replaced by Joya Sherrill, a better than average pop singer whose Ellington tracks would make a fine album by themselves: after the ban 'I'm Beginning to See the Light' (with lyrics by Don George) was followed by 'I Didn't Know About You', the non-Ellington '(All of a Sudden) My Heart Sings' (with a simple but spell-binding Strayhorn arrangement), 'Everything But You', 'Tell Ya What I'm Gonna Do' and 'Come To Baby, Do'. The Victor output up to 1946 included vocals by Ray Nance and Al Hibbler (who replaced Jeffries) and a series of remakes (for example, 'Black Beauty' and 'Caravan'). On a remake of 'It Don't Mean a Thing' Sherrill, Kay Davis and Marie Ellington (no relation) introduced the tune as a round.

There was always much beauty and joy, but the burst of creativity that had marked the early years of the decade seemed to be over. Barney Bigard, who left the band in mid-1942, said later to British journalist Max Jones: 'after the original band began to break up, Duke's orchestra was never the same. Never. Cootie Williams left, other people left, and later Tricky Sam took sick and died . . . he had to get different people and change the music.' This is certainly true as far as it goes, but for the genuine Ellington fan, the band always sounded unique: if he wrote specifically for his own musicians, of course he wrote differently as the band changed. Yet it never sounded like anyone's music but his.

At his first Carnegie Hall concert early in 1943 Ellington introduced his fifty-minute composition *Black, Brown and Beige: Tone Parallel to the American Negro*. Excerpts were recorded by Victor; the complete concert was issued on Prestige after decades, and the piece has had several more recordings by other hands. The lovely 'Carnegie Blues' (recorded in 1945) and the beautiful hymn 'Come Sunday' were taken from it. The Carnegie Hall concert was an annual event for several years: Ellington's new works included *Blutopia* (1944); the twelve-minute *New World a-Comin'* (inspired by a Roi Ottley novel) and *The Perfume Suite* (both 1945). ('Dancers in Love', a delightful duet for piano and bass, was also the subject of a George Pal 'Puppetoon' semi-animated short film.) *Deep South Suite* (1946) comprised four parts: the first was 'Magnolias Just Dripping with Molasses' and the last the train anthem 'Happy-go-lucky Local'. The latter's big tune was the same riff heard earlier from Hodges's small group, later used without credit by Jimmy Forrest as 'Night Train'.

Ellington's musical show *Beggar's Holiday* in 1946 was an updating of the *Beggar's Opera* (in which Macheath is recast as a gangster) with lyrics by John Latouche. (Latouche also wrote the Vernon Duke show *Cabin in the Sky* in 1940 – the Ellington band appeared in the film version in 1943 – and the George Moore opera *Ballad of Baby Doe* in 1956.) *Beggar's Holiday* ran for just fourteen weeks. In his exhaustive *American Musical Theatre* Gerald Bordman says it failed because 'Latouche's sting and Ellington's intimacy [were] lost in the cavernous auditorium of the large, inconvenient Broadway theatre'. But its producer, John Houseman, had another explanation. On arriving at the scene, he wrote many years later, he found that Latouche

had been working on several other projects during the summer. He had written a number of lyrics but only the roughest draft of our first act and almost nothing of the second. Ellington, teeming with tunes and mood pieces, still had not faced the necessity of writing a musical score ... [The producers on the spot] were not only inexperienced and inefficient – they were desperately short of money. Finally, owing to the Duke's enormous list of future commitments, we had no leeway at all but must start rehearsals within four weeks or not at all.

Houseman and Nicholas Ray tried to put the production together during the day, and at night worked on the script. The racially mixed cast was chosen for acting ability; as a result, Broadway star Alfred Drake fell in love with a black police chief's daughter in 1947. Libby Holman and Zero Mostel were also in the cast. (The sets, by Oliver Smith, were used a few years later almost without change for Leonard Bernstein's *West Side Story*.) During rehearsals, whenever they needed a bit of music, Strayhorn

would run up to the Duke's apartment and fish out of a drawer, crammed with unperformed music, whatever tune seemed to fit the scene. Some were wonderful, and with Latouche's lyrics, remained for years in the repertory of Lena Horne and other well-known singers. But this did not make up for the absence of a score and a book.

Since it was constantly running out of money, the production had to pay for the sets at the last minute and have them built with thirty hours of 'golden time'. (Expensive overtime is the common lot of those putting on a show that has been inadequately prepared and financed.) The dress rehearsal could not be completed and the last twenty minutes of the opening night in New Haven (under the title *Twilight Alley*) had to be improvised. The show was still a mess when it got to New York; Broadway genius George Abbott was hired to replace Houseman, but it did not help, and Houseman blamed himself, for agreeing to go into rehearsal with a show that was not ready. Houseman described Ellington as 'one of the world's great spellbinders', but if *Beggar's Holiday* was typical of his working methods, in that it relied too much on spellbinding, this would go some way to explain his shortcomings as a composer in larger forms.

The band's immediate post-war period, when there were six trumpets, and Oscar Pettiford on bass, was one of the most poorly documented. But more and more material comes to light: a wealth of broadcasts was made in 1945–6 for the US Treasury to sell bonds; another transcription series (1946–7) includes Strayhorn's works for Hodges's sensuous alto saxophone, 'Violet Blue' and 'A Flower is a Lovesome Thing' (later entitled 'Passion'), as well as Ellington's 'Sono' (a feature for Carney) and a version of 'Happy-go-lucky Local'.

Webster, Hardwicke, Stewart and Tizol had left, and Nanton had died in 1946. There were some hard years ahead for the Ellington ensemble, though Duke was finally recognized as the great American artist he was. Meanwhile, the rest of the Swing Era represents a highwater mark in the quality of popular music.

9

The Swing Era Begins

From 1935 until after the Second World War a jazz-oriented style was at the centre of popular music for the first time (and the last, so far), as opposed to merely giving it backbone. The white bands made the most money, but they had taken up the music because they loved it; they were fully aware of the debt they owed to the black innovators and they made plenty of their own contributions, resulting in popular music whose quality will be rediscovered as long as people play records.

A few white bands had been playing jazz-flavoured music and doing good business for some years, among them the Casa Loma. Roger Wolfe Kahn was the son of a millionaire; his band, which was resident at the Biltmore Hotel in New York, included such sidemen as Miff Mole, Jack Teagarden, Artie Shaw and others, but Kahn later turned to a sweet style. Chicago drummer Ben Pollack followed on from Goldkette and Kahn, employing Benny Goodman, arranger-trombonist Glenn Miller, Harry James and Teagarden, who was recruited by arranger Gil Rodin. Pollack's band was highly rated, but its recordings do not reflect its best work, because Pollack always had his eye on what he thought was the main chance; after struggling for years he sidetracked himself at exactly the time the Swing Era was about to happen. Promoting a vocalist who later became his wife, he neglected the band, which left him and hired Bob Crosby (Bing's brother) as frontman.

A big band might have three trumpets, two trombones, three or four reeds, and four rhythm instruments (piano, guitar, bass and drums): from twelve to sixteen or eighteen players, as well as singers. Henderson and Redman used banjo and brass bass (tuba) at first, but the increasing pressure of the tendency to play in 4/4 rather than 2/4 in rhythm sections accelerated the change to guitar and string bass. Gunther Schuller thinks this process may have been impeded because the tuba was easier to record than a string bass; 4/4 would have been twice as much work for a tuba player, and probably impossible at a quick tempo. But leaders who were arrangers, or who bought good arrangements, were innovating in a search for new voicings. Duke Ellington was the first to feature the string bass on recordings in the late 1920s (probably by shoving it closer to the microphone), yet more evidence of his expertise as a recording artist. When the Goldkette band went east in the mid-1920s it had two trumpets and Bix on cornet; other bands had been getting by with two trumpets, but added another to be up to date. Ellington's and Redman's bands first had three trombones in the early 1930s; Ellington had two bass players in the late 1930s, six trumpets in 1946, and always insisted that all his reed players double on clarinet.

As we have already seen, the arrangers were of the greatest importance, and we will meet many more of them in the following pages. Judging from the recorded evidence, it is easy to jump to the conclusion that it was largely the black jazzmen and arrangers who knew that allowing the music to swing was the same thing as allowing it to breathe (a lesson often forgotten in today's pop music). The recordings from the late 1920s and early 1930s by many prominent white leaders, such as Ted Weems, Irving Aaronson and Gus Arnheim, now sound excessively busy and relentlessly cute. And it is true that the (largely white) music business had concluded that 'hot' music would not sell, and that imaginative arrangers ran into trouble with producers and A & R men. Yet this conclusion must be treated with some caution. The white arrangers Gene Gifford, Gil Rodin, Deane Kincaide and Bill Challis were gifted indeed, and when Don Redman enlarged the reed section of McKinney's Cotton Pickers, he probably did it so that he could write a richer sound like that being made by the Whiteman band. One of the best of all, bandleader, composer and reedman Benny Carter, said to Gene Lees, 'Bill Challis was my *idol.*'

Challis had been influenced by Bix Beiderbecke, whose inventive phrasing, beautiful tone and advanced harmonic thinking were followed by first Goldkette and then Whiteman's band. Bix and

Trumbauer's classic 'Singin' the Blues' had been a Challis chart, as
was Whiteman's little masterpiece 'San', which was recorded in 1928
by a smallish group of ten men, including Bix, Trumbauer, Jimmy
Dorsey and Challis on piano. Whiteman's 'symphonic jazz' may or
may not have been ponderous, but the dance band charts were
excellent. Violinist Matty Malneck, pianist Tom Satterfield and others
wrote good arrangements for Whiteman, but Challis's still astonish
with their freshness.

Challis's arrangement of Rodgers and Hart's 'The Blue Room' was
played by a big radio band, perhaps that of Nat Shilkret around 1930,
and recorded by a smaller group in 1986 on the album *Bill Challis's
The Goldkette Project* (on the Circle label). It illustrates Challis's witty
originality: after the introduction (itself unusually fine for the period),
the reed section states the tune, with a rhythmic break of four notes
by the brass section after sixteen bars, and again at the end. The first
break consists of four notes, in two identical units of two notes each.
A less imaginative arranger might simply have repeated this pattern
at the end of the second phrase, but instead Challis wrote a group of
four descending notes. The effect can still raise a chuckle sixty years
later.

In 1929 *Melody Maker* in Britain devoted eleven pages to an
analysis of Challis's arrangement of 'Sweet Sue', composed the year
before by Victor Young and Will Harris, but the paper attributed it
wrongly to Ferde Grofé (as 'Singin' the Blues' was long attributed to
Fud Livingston). Maceo Pinkard's 'Sugar' and Willard Robison's
''Tain't So, Honey, 'Tain't So', both recorded by Whiteman in
1928, were Challis's arrangements, the first done originally for Goldkette, then expanded for twenty-four men (including four violins).
Both are miles ahead of most of the popular music of the period, and
are full of fascinating chords which still sound adventurous today,
yet exactly right. The Whiteman band's excellent playing of these
charts and the fine recording produced by Victor make it clear why
Whiteman and Challis continued to influence other musicians for
many years.

The section leaders in the bands were important. They rehearsed
attack and phrasing, and often helped to bring along good players
who were not good readers: thus Hymie Shertzer and Art Rollini

taught Vido Musso, the tenor saxophone star in the classic Benny Goodman band. (Musso said it was not the notes that bothered him but the 'resters'. Henderson's wife had helped with the music copying, and her writing could be difficult to decipher.) In the Count Basie band, Lester Young was a much better reader than Herschel Evans. Section leaders such as George Dorman 'Scoops' Carry (with Earl Hines, 1940–47), Langston Curl (with Don Redman, 1927–37) and Hilton Jefferson (who played with Claude Hopkins, Chick Webb, Henderson, Carter and Ellington) were admired by musicians, if less well known to the public. They were often not soloists, though they could hold their own when necessary; Wendell Culley, who played the famous solo on 'Li'l Darlin'' in 1957, was Basie's lead trumpet for years.

It was clarinettist Benny Goodman who was in the right place at the right time, and became the King of Swing. Born in a Chicago slum to an immigrant family, he studied music at Hull House, a charitable institution; he first performed in public at the age of twelve, and was playing good jazz while still in short trousers. He played other reed instruments as well as clarinet, and even trumpet on records in the 1920s; after leaving Pollack in 1929, he became one of the busiest freelance musicians in the business. Often working with John Hammond, he played on Bessie Smith's last recording session and led the studio band on Billie Holiday's first session, both in 1933.

Goodman's successful recordings include Holiday's 'Riffin' the Scotch', 'Ol' Pappy' (with Mildred Bailey and Coleman Hawkins) and 'I Ain't Lazy, I'm Just Dreamin'' (with Teagarden); 'Moon Glow', by a nine-piece group with Teddy Wilson on piano, appeared more than two years before the famous Goodman Quartet version; Waller and Razaf's 'Ain't-cha Glad?', backed with 'I Gotta Right to Sing the Blues' (by Arlen and Koehler), which had vocals and trombone by Jack Teagarden, was a two-sided hit at the lowest point of the Depression, when Goodman had not recorded as a leader for two years. He had played on scores of recordings backing singers, and with the Hotsy Totsy Band (Irving Mills's ongoing project, and one of the many names used by the Pollack gang as freelances), among many others. But there was not much money in records in those days, and anyway Goodman's name on records by studio pick-up groups was not satisfactory.

He formed his own band for an appearance at Billy Rose's Music Hall. Benny Goodman and his (Music Hall) Orchestra, as it was billed at first, did five successful recording sessions for Columbia, the last two in early 1935. He changed to Victor in April, and had hits with 'Japanese Sandman', from his first Victor session, and, at the end of the year, Henderson's arrangements of 'Sometimes I'm Happy' and 'King Porter' back to back, the latter with a famous trumpet solo by Bunny Berigan. Notwithstanding the importance of Henderson's arrangements, historians have also pointed out the contribution of Spud Murphy, who probably wrote as much for Goodman as Henderson did. Murphy played with Ross Gorman in 1928, and also wrote for the Casa Loma band; his 'Get Happy', for Goodman, is especially well remembered for the way in which it turns the jolly tune into a prototypical romp for swing band.

Goodman's band appeared on the *Let's Dance* radio show from late 1934 until May 1935, a three-hour dance programme shared with Xavier Cugat and the sweet band of Kel Murray. The show's radio theme was 'Let's Dance', based on 'Invitation to the Dance', by Carl Maria von Weber, though Goodman used Gordon Jenkins's 'Good-bye' as both opening and closing theme on tour. The programme was broadcast live and was received on the West Coast during prime time, earlier than it was heard in the east. When it embarked on a nationwide tour in May 1935, the band did not do very good business at first; at the Elitch Gardens in Denver, according to pianist Jess Stacy, 'everybody was across town listening to Kay Kyser'. But when the band reached California in August, they found an audience of eager young dancers. It is clear in retrospect that the Swing Era had been waiting to happen, but it was Goodman and his band that touched it off. His ten hits in 1934 doubled to twenty in 1935, and he credited his success to the fact that there were a large number of dancers who were not being well served.

In November 1935 an octet from the band made four sides in Chicago as Gene Krupa and his Chicagoans. Goodman's brother Harry was replaced on bass by the sixteen-year-old Israel Crosby (who later played for a decade with Ahmad Jamal's trio, then George

Shearing); 'Blues of Israel' is particularly fine. In February of the next year they did it again, as Gene Krupa's Swing Band, this time with Roy Eldridge replacing Nate Kazebier on trumpet, Chu Berry replacing Dick Clark on tenor and singer Helen Ward (on two tracks) instead of trombonist Joe Harris. The appeal of Ward is not obvious in retrospect, but she was very popular; to her credit she disliked 'Goody Goody', and was surprised when it became one of the full band's biggest hits in 1936.

Harry Goodman was a merely competent bass player, and Krupa's drumming was very much in the Chicago mould, with dixielandish accents. It always comes as a shock all these years later to hear the lumpy 2/4 beat on 'Down South Camp Meeting', from August 1936. (Stacy said years later, 'you can't ask all drummers to keep good time'.) The band was precise, and the reed section sounded pretty; but it was often no more than pretty, and on some of the records moos monotonously behind vocalists, the way the pedal steel guitar is often used in country music today. Despite having four reeds (as well as Goodman himself), the section had nothing like the character of that of Whiteman's band, not to mention many a black band. Perhaps the formal training of the white musicians prevented them from contributing more in terms of individual tone production, but the smoothness was probably what Goodman wanted.

Arguments still arise among critics and musicians about whether Goodman had a good enough ear to imagine a richer sound or, later, to play more modern jazz, but he was too good a musician not to be able to play anything he wanted. The truth is that he was a strange man, haunted by the poverty of his childhood; having accomplished what he had, he saw little need to change the formula, especially since his audience was getting older when the Swing Era was over, and simply did not wish for a more modern sound. The sidemen and arrangers who wanted to play more modern music were younger than Goodman, and he may have been jealous. In later life he let slip a belief that he had to have his men angry with him in order to be an effective bandleader, which would go some way towards explaining his infamous rudeness; and it may be postulated that tension is necessary in any performance art. He was also torn between popular and classical music, and adopted a different embouchure to play the latter; playing modern jazz would have exacerbated this physical confusion. On top of all that, from the time of his greatest success he was nearly always in pain from a back problem.

Certainly it was the precision and the reliability of his band (perhaps ensured by his hard discipline) that made it a success, as well as its swing, which is more evident on airchecks than on the studio recordings. He led the reed section on alto saxophone on 'Riffin' at the Ritz', one of the band's better studio tracks. The 1936 version of 'Bugle Call Rag' is hard to resist: at the beginning, when the band is stating the riff, one thinks of how many times one has heard it, but in less than three minutes the string of hot solos has worked its magic again. 'He Ain't Got Rhythm' has an irresistible guest vocal by Jimmy Rushing, and 'I Want to be Happy' has just the right chirpy tempo. In the end, one feels that white pop should always be this good. In any case, in 1935 Henderson made no records, Count Basie was still unknown, and the recordings and broadcasts of black bands were simply not promoted and marketed as the white ones were. Good as it was, Whiteman's classic band had broken up in 1930, being too big for the Depression era, and Pollack was busy courting his future wife. So it was Goodman's band that suddenly defined the centre of the era's pop music.

In mid-1935 the first recording session of the Benny Goodman Trio, with Krupa and Teddy Wilson, yielded 'Body and Soul' and 'After You've Gone' back to back; Lionel Hampton was added in August 1936, and the quartet's first recording was 'Moon Glow'. Edgar Sampson's arrangement of 'Stompin' at the Savoy', written for Chick Webb, was a hit for the band in 1936 and even more popular for the quartet in 1937. Goodman got away with a mixed-race group by presenting it during the band's intermission, like a vaudeville act; Stacy was the band's regular pianist. But the excellent chamber music of the trio and quartet, together with the intelligent, witty and swinging interplay between Goodman, Wilson and Hampton, was commercially successful, proving that the public was willing to listen to good music during the Swing Era.

There were several hit recordings of 'Christopher Columbus' in 1936, including those of Goodman and Henderson, and the smaller groups of Andy Kirk, Teddy Wilson and Fats Waller (with Andy

Razaf's words and Waller's saucy interjections: 'Since the crew was makin' merry . . . Merry got up and went home!'). Among Goodman's hits in 1937 were 'Goodnight, My Love' and 'This Year's Kisses', both with black singers, Ella Fitzgerald and Jimmy Rushing respectively. Goodman's rudeness to Helen Ward had resulted in Martha Tilton's taking over as vocalist, and her successes included 'I Let a Song Go out of My Heart' and 'And the Angels Sing', the latter with trumpeter Ziggy Elman's famous 'Hebrew dance party' gimmick: originally an instrumental written by Elman called 'Fralich in Swing', recorded by Elman with members of Goodman's band, the hit had words by Johnny Mercer.

Many bands were playing 'Sing, Sing, Sing (With a Swing)', a tune by trumpeter and bandleader Louis Prima. In 1936 the Goodman band began to interpolate its arrangement (by yet another black arranger, Jimmy Mundy, who had written for Earl Hines) with 'Christopher Columbus', and the new arrangement was recorded in 1937; more than 8.5 minutes long, it was issued on two-sided 12-inch and (edited) 10-inch 78s. It became a symbol of the Swing Era, but the studio recording has lost much of its charm today, despite good playing by the band and solos by Goodman, Harry James and Musso; the long passages of Krupa's tom-toms no longer appeal.

Goodman had played at a jazz concert at the Congress Hotel in Chicago on a Sunday afternoon, and in any ballroom there could be as many people listening as dancing. The first jazz concert at Carnegie Hall was dreamed up by the agency who were promoting the *Camel Caravan*, Goodman's radio programme, sponsored by the cigarette company. According to Irving Kolodin, when Goodman was asked how long an intermission he wanted, he replied, 'I dunno. How much does Toscanini have?'

The band that played at the concert included Hymie Shertzer (alto saxophone), George Koenig, Irving 'Babe' Russin and Art Rollini (tenor saxophones), Harry James, Ziggy Elman and Gordon Griffin (trumpets), Vernon Brown and Red Ballard (trombones), Allan Reuss (guitar), Stacy (piano), Harry Goodman (bass) and Krupa (drums); Wilson and Hampton played in the quartet. James, Krupa, Wilson and Hampton all soon left to lead their own bands, bringing to an end the most famous Goodman line-up. The concert was a celebration of the arrival of jazz as the nation's most popular music, and afterwards many of the men headed for Harlem, where Basie and Webb were battling at the Savoy. The concert offered a jam session and a set-piece billed as 'Twenty Years of Jazz', both with guests, neither of which was particularly successful. There were two Tilton vocals, selections by the trio and the quartet, three Henderson arrangements, Sampson's 'Don't Be That Way', Basie's 'One O'Clock Jump', Mundy's 'Swingtime in the Rockies' and 'Life Goes to a Party', credited to Goodman and James and suggested by a *Life* magazine photo spread on the Goodman phenomenon. The event was recorded on acetates, using a single microphone; an album was released in 1950 and was a surprise hit after the Swing Era was over.

'Sing, Sing, Sing' at Carnegie Hall was not only much better than the studio version, but contained the best item of the concert: an unscheduled piano solo by Stacy, which in 1950 turned out to be just as beautiful as everyone remembered it. In an interview with Whitney Balliet many years later (from which I have quoted above), Stacy said that Goodman usually hogged the solo space, and that he did not know why he had got the green light, unless Goodman had liked what he had been doing behind Goodman's solo. Stacy's solo was built on the tune's A-minor chord, and shows the influence of Edward MacDowell and Claude Debussy; it provided a marvellous balance for the bombastic arrangement which inspired it. It now makes us marvel at how many beautiful solos by uncounted musicians were never recorded at all: it is a high point of the whole era.

It became even more clear in 1952 that the classic Goodman band played better live than in the studio. A two-LP set of airchecks clumsily called *1937/38 Jazz Concert Number Two*, one of the first issues of its kind and a number one album in *Billboard*, demonstrated that the band got as big a kick out of the dancers as the dancers got out of the band. It was the New Orleans 'second line' effect again.

Goodman moved to the revived Columbia label in 1939 and continued to produce a steady stream of hits for another decade. Dave Tough, without doubt the best white drummer of the era, replaced Krupa and was a great improvement. Vocalist Helen Forrest wrote in her autobiography that Goodman was the rudest man she had ever met, and Stacy (a modest man) was still amused decades later that Goodman had fired the estimable Jimmy Rowles in order to re-hire Stacy in 1942. Goodman fired people for undiscernible reasons, as if he needed to remind everybody who was boss.

But he was a great talent scout. It was the young pianist Mel Powell (today a classical composer in the school of Milton Babbitt and Elliott Carter) who arranged 'String of Pearls' and 'Jersey Bounce' for a two-sided hit in 1942, as well as 'Mission to Moscow' in 1943. Eddie Sauter, who had worked for Red Norvo and Charlie Barnet, wrote 'Superman', 'Benny Rides Again', 'Clarinet à la King' and others, which were popular with jazz fans, musicians and critics, but less so with the public (though Sauter's arrangement of 'Intermezzo', a film theme, was a hit in 1941). Sauter's arrangements are regarded by many as a peak in the Goodman discography, yet Goodman often watered them down and seemed to be reluctant to play them or record them. He openly admired Mel Powell and treated him as an equal, partly because Powell would not have taken any nonsense from him, but Powell's better arrangements too were not welcomed without reluctance. And Goodman was not necessarily wrong from his point of view: some of the younger musicians in Goodman's pick-up bands in later years learned to admire Henderson's arrangements when they had been drilled to play them properly. The problem of art versus commerce is endemic in popular music, and it was Goodman's formula that kept the band working.

Henderson continued to arrange for Goodman in the 1940s, and Don Kirkpatrick arranged 'Idaho', with a vocal by Dick Haymes; other vocals were 'Darn That Dream' (Mildred Bailey), 'There'll be Some Changes Made' (Louise Tobin), 'Somebody Else is Taking My Place' (Peggy Lee) and 'Taking a Chance on Love' (Forrest). Goodman also deserved the credit he always got for hiring black musicians. The Benny Goodman Sextet recordings from 1939 to 1941 are probably the best he ever made, with Charlie Christian on electric guitar, Cootie Williams on trumpet and guests such as Count Basie; titles include 'Breakfast Feud', 'Benny's Bugle', 'Shivers', 'On the Alamo' and 'AC-DC Current'. The band's (and the sextet's) tenor saxophone soloist in 1940–41 was the excellent Georgie Auld, who later led his own bands (and played on the soundtrack of Martin Scorsese's period film *New York, New York* in 1977). On one sextet rehearsal

session, unreleased for decades, Lester Young was present, together
with Christian, Basie and Basie's rhythm section, an all-black group
except for Goodman. With tape recording still a few years in the
future, Columbia was recording everything on transcription discs,
which years later yielded the warm-up sessions 'Blues in B' and
'Waitin' for Benny', both with Christian. Mundy was credited (with
Goodman and Christian) on 'Good Enough to Keep', whose title
was changed to 'Air Mail Special'. The band's drummers during the
Columbia period included Nick Fatool as well as Dave Tough.

Goodman himself sang on 'Gotta be This or That' (1945) and 'Oh,
Baby' (on two sides of a 12-inch 78 in 1946). He moved to Capitol
in 1947; 'Moon-faced, Starry-eyed' had a vocal by Johnny Mercer,
'On a Slow Boat to China' had Al Hendrickson and 'It Isn't Fair'
pianist and singer Buddy Greco, later a solo cabaret star.

On Capitol Goodman tried to play more modern music. In 1948 he
hired Stan Hasselgard, an excellent young Swedish clarinet player –
the only time he ever featured another clarinettist – but Hasselgard
was killed in a car crash the same year. He also hired Wardell Gray, a
superb tenor saxophonist who won much acclaim before he was
murdered in Las Vegas, probably in a drug deal that went wrong. In
1949 Goodman employed Arturo O'Farrill, a young arranger from
Cuba. (It was Goodman who nicknamed him Chico; he seemed to
make a habit of not remembering people's names.) But Goodman did
not like bop and soon gave up any willingness to play it. In 1950 he
returned to Columbia, and a sextet version of the Louis Prima tune
'Oh, Babe!' was a hit, with Teddy Wilson, Terry Gibbs on
vibraphone and a vocal duet by Nancy Reed and Jimmy Ricks (of
the doo-wop group the Ravens).

In 1953 Goodman re-formed his classic band for an expensive tour
with Louis Armstrong's All Stars that turned into a famous disaster.
He managed to insult Armstrong at the beginning; then he was
appalled at the vaudeville aspects of Louis's act, in which the overweight Velma Middleton did the splits, a contradiction of everything
Goodman stood for. His insecurities caught up with him and he had
a nervous breakdown. The glory years were over and he knew it; he
retired to become an elder statesman of popular music, still adored by

his fans, playing his classic hits over and over again. In *The Benny Goodman Story* (1955) the otherwise lovable Steve Allen played Goodman; he was not an actor, and was lumbered with the usual awful Hollywood film biography script. Goodman played at the Brussels World's Fair in 1958 and in the Soviet Union in 1962, and offended everyone connected with both tours. (The Russian one is recalled in a hilarious series of articles by bass player Bill Crow, published in lyricist and journalist Gene Lees's *Jazzletter* in 1986.) The original quartet re-formed to make the album *Together Again!* on RCA, a critical and popular success, in 1964. Goodman's niche in music is secure; at the time of writing more than eighty albums and compilations of his old airchecks are listed in the USA Schwann catalogue.

Other white jazz-oriented bandleaders were waiting in the wings in the mid-1930s, with some acclaim already under their belts. The Dorsey Brothers Orchestra had hit records every year from 1928 to 1935 except one; the band included trumpeter Manny Klein (born in 1908), who was later one of the most sought-after studio musicians in the business. The Dorseys split acrimoniously, but both became very popular leaders. Artie Shaw, like Goodman an excellent and busy freelance clarinettist, was soon almost as well known, and Charlie Barnet was also an experienced leader when he hit the charts in 1936. Isham Jones's band became a cooperative in 1937, and leader Woody Herman took it on to greater things. Many white sidemen led their own bands, of whom the best known were Harry James, Gene Krupa and Bunny Berigan.

There were also a great many sweet bands, which were not all completely corny. Jan Savitt's was rather good, and the leader could play a fiddle which was both sweet and swinging. The band of society pianist Eddy Duchin got up a creditable bounce on 'Old Man Mose', sung by Patricia Norman, which was one of the biggest Duchin hits (partly because when she sang the word 'bucket' in the reprise, some listeners thought she had substituted an 'f' for a 'b'). Pianist Frankie Carle wrote 'Sunrise Serenade' and used it as a theme, but the huge hit recordings of it were by the Casa Loma band and Glenn Miller. Another Carle success was 'Oh! What It Seemed To Be', which he also wrote; his vocalist was his daughter, Marjorie Hughes.

He was too good a keyboard player to be offensively rococo; today's marvellous pianist, leader and composer Joanne Brackeen admits that she started by copying Carle off her parents' records.

One of the best of the sweet bands was that of saxophonist Hal Kemp, who was killed in a car crash in 1940. The arrangements were by John Scott Trotter. The band's singer, Robert 'Skinnay' Ennis, had a breathy, half-whispered vocal style on 'When I'm with You' and 'This Year's Kisses', and was later famous for 'Got a Date with an Angel'. Reedman Saxie Dowell did novelty vocals, and later had a charming radio DJ show in Chicago. Ennis later led his own band, playing arrangements by Claude Thornhill and Gil Evans.

Harry James was a superb trumpet player, who began playing at the age of nine in his father's circus band, and was evidently one of the best-liked men in the business. His post-Goodman success was slow in coming, but he finally did well and continued to draw large audiences in places like Las Vegas until he died. His dance band music was not particularly jazz-oriented, though his first hit was a cover of 'One O'Clock Jump' (reissued in 1943 during a recording ban as 'Two O'Clock Jump'), and 'Strictly Instrumental' (written by Edgar Battle, among others) was an attractive chart from the Lunceford book. James's band was good enough in 1950 to be raided by Duke Ellington, and he later employed Buddy Rich on drums. His theme was 'Ciribiribin', in 3/4 time (published in Italy in 1898), and another hit was the trumpet virtuoso's 'Flight of the Bumble Bee'; his 'Sleepy Lagoon' was adapted from the 'valse serenade' of English composer Eric Coates.

Most of James's big hits were vocals. He hired the very young Frank Sinatra, who was soon stolen by Tommy Dorsey, and then Dick Haymes, a good singer in the same mould; Helen Ward and Helen Forrest recorded with James, and Kitty Kallen joined him around 1944. Forrest's hits were 'I Don't Want to Walk Without You' and 'I've Heard That Song Before'; James was listed as a co-writer on Duke Ellington's 'I'm Beginning to See the Light', which, sung by Kallen, was a number one hit in the white chart in 1945.

Gene Krupa's success as a bandleader was also slow at first, but was then enhanced by the great black trumpeter Roy Eldridge (thus linking two generations of jazzmen) and the young vocalist Anita

O'Day, first of a new generation of hip white jazz singers. 'Let Me Off Uptown' was their duet; Eldridge sang on 'Knock Me a Kiss'. Tenor saxophonist Charlie Ventura was another of Krupa's stars. Krupa became a better drummer as time went on, having already raised the profile of the timekeeper to that of pop star. He served some time in jail on a charge of possessing marijuana, but was widely believed to have been framed: a devout Catholic, he refused to pay off crooked policemen. He led small groups well into the 1960s.

The big band fronted by Bob Crosby, the famous crooner's brother, was an unusual one. After leaving Ben Pollack, arranger and reedman Gil Rodin organized the band as a cooperative; it hired Crosby, who was not a bad singer and got better. The band included Deane Kincaide (reedman and arranger), Yank Lawson (trumpet), Eddie Miller (tenor saxophone – he had a lovely, light tone like that of Bud Freeman and Lester Young), Matty Matlock (clarinet and arranger), Bob Haggart (bass), Nappy Lamare (guitar) and Ray Bauduc (drums). Among those who passed through were pianists Bob Zurke, Joe Sullivan and Jess Stacy, clarinettist Irving Fazola and trumpeters Muggsy Spanier and Billy Butterfield. Many of the band's founder members were from New Orleans; they played an unusual big-band dixieland style, and the Bob Cats octet played the real stuff. The band's hits included the vocals 'In a Little Gypsy Tea Room' (1935, with Frank Tennille, father of Toni Tennille, of the 1970s duo Captain and Tennille), 'Whispers in the Dark' (1937, with Kay Weber) and 'Day In, Day Out' (1939, with Helen Ward). On 'Big Noise from Winnetka', a famous novelty duo by Haggart and Bauduc, Haggart whistles through his teeth while Bauduc uses his sticks on the bass's strings. One of the band's best-known records was the 12-inch 78 'South Rampart Street Parade' / 'Dogtown Blues', written by Lawson and Haggart, who formed the Lawson–Haggart Jazz Band in the early 1950s. (It became the World's Greatest Jazz Band after appearing at the annual Colorado Jazz Party and continued making albums well into the 1970s, when there were also frequent Crosby reunions.)

The band of Mal Hallett, a New England violinist and leader, was admired by many others. His earlier groups employed Krupa, Jack Teagarden, Frankie Carle, tenor saxophonist Toots Mondello (later with Goodman) and Jack Jenney, a first-class trombonist and also a legendary prankster. Jenney's own big band of 1938–40 failed, but he played the trombone solo on the famous Artie Shaw hit version of 'Stardust'.

Bunny Berigan was probably the greatest white trumpet player of the whole era; he may be heard on Goodman and Tommy Dorsey records, and led his own bands. He also played on two RCA Victor All-star sessions. A hit version of 'Honeysuckle Rose', backed with 'Blues' (1937), was played by a quintet: Berigan, Tommy Dorsey, Fats Waller, Dick McDonough (guitar) and George Wettling (drums). 'Blue Lou' and 'The Blues' (1939) were by a big band. Berigan's unforgettable hit was 'I Can't Get Started', which he recorded twice. Artie Shaw plays clarinet on the earlier version; the more famous one, with Berigan's vocal and lengthy introduction, was issued on both 12-inch and (edited) 10-inch 78s. In retrospect, the 1938–40 band suffers from having recorded too many second-rate pop songs, while Berigan, an alcoholic, was eventually unable to play his own famous solos. Louis Armstrong is said to have refused to record 'I Can't Get Started', saying, 'That's Bunny's tune.'

Jimmy Dorsey led a band similar to that of Harry James in that it was a good mainstream dance band. He had been a superb alto player on many fine jazz records; when Tommy walked out in 1935, most of the members of the Dorsey Brothers Orchestra stayed with Jimmy, who became one of Jack Kapp's greatest successes on Decca. The band's very good and extremely popular vocalists were Bob Eberly and Helen O'Connell; Kitty Kallen sang with it in the early 1940s before she joined Harry James. Sidemen included Ray McKinley on drums, 'Tootie' Camarata on trumpet, Freddie Slack on piano and Herbie Haymer on tenor saxophone. But, as with James, his biggest hits almost all featured the singers: 'The Breeze and I' (from the Spanish song 'Andalucia' by Ernesto Lecuona), 'Maria Elena' (a Mexican song), 'Blue Champagne', 'High on a Windy Hill', 'I Hear a Rhapsody' and many others were by Eberly; 'Green Eyes' (from Cuba), 'Amapola' (a Spanish song) and 'Tangerine' (from the film *The Fleet's In*) were all duets by Eberly and O'Connell. The band's last big hit was 'Besame Mucho' (from Mexico), a duet by Eberly and Kallen. Like most leaders on Decca, Dorsey also recorded with Bing Crosby and the Andrews Sisters. He is rated as the seventeenth best-selling recording artist up to 1954, but brother Tommy was number four.

Tommy Dorsey was a volatile businessman, as well as a fine musician. He took over Joe Haymes's band in 1935 and won enormous acclaim, despite a high turnover in personnel. Like Goodman, he was not an easy man to work for, but at the time it seemed as though his band could do more things better than most others. He was a first-rate trombonist, though he knew he was outclassed by the likes of Teagarden. His strength lay in his beautiful legato playing on ballads, as on his theme 'I'm Getting Sentimental Over You' (which had already been recorded twice, and was a hit for the brothers' band in 1934). At the RCA Victor All-star date in 1939 Dorsey had to be coaxed to play 'The Blues' with Teagarden present; the enchanting solution was a Dorsey legato statement of the theme surrounded by Teagarden's obbligato.

Tommy's was a great dance band: on a two-CD collection of all of Frank Sinatra's recordings with the 1940 band, it is astonishing to hear how the band could swing at very slow tempos. Among the musicians passing through were Berigan, Bud Freeman and Skeets Herfurt on reeds and Dave Tough and Buddy Rich on drums; in 1938–9 the trumpet section had George 'Pee Wee' Erwin, Yank Lawson and Lee Castle, all of them fine players. The first big hits included 'The Music Goes Round and Round', with Edythe Wright, an inane novelty from 52nd Street that swept the USA. The very pleasant and easy-phrasing Jack Leonard, one of several boy singers, has since been underrated, followed as he was by Frank Sinatra.

On tour Dorsey played opposite a cooperative band called the Sunset Royals, who were fronted by various people, including trombonist Moran 'Doc' Wheeler (who later became an MC at the Apollo Theatre and an R&B-gospel DJ in New York City). Cat Anderson, who later became Duke Ellington's high-note specialist, joined in 1938. The band did one recording session in 1941 as Doc Wheeler and his Sunset Orchestra; but before that, in a theatre in Philadelphia, according to an item in *Metronome* magazine, the band had given Tommy Dorsey a going-over. Dorsey acquired his arrangement of Irving Berlin's 'Marie' from the Royals, and made it one of the biggest and best hits of the Swing Era, early in 1937: Leonard sings a strong straight line while the band chants a paraphrase of the lyrics, the most successful application of Don Redman's swing choir idea, and it has a superb trumpet solo by Berigan. It continued to sell for years, and reached the charts several times. On the other side was Dorsey's arrangement of 'Song of India', borrowed from Rimsky-Korsakov, also featuring Berigan.

Arranger Larry Clinton contributed 'The Dipsy Doodle' in 1937; he also wrote 'Satan Takes a Holiday', and soon led his own popular band. 'Boogie Woogie', Dorsey's most famous instrumental, was based on Pinetop Smith's piano solo of 1928. Dorsey's vocal group was the Pied Pipers, which had begun as an octet and slimmed to a quartet when hired by Dorsey; it contained the excellent Jo Stafford (who later married Paul Weston, one of Dorsey's arrangers). She sang solo on 'Manhattan Serenade' in 1942 and 'You Took My Love' the next year. Sinatra's hits with Dorsey began in 1940 with 'Polka Dots and Moonbeams' (by Johnny Burke and Jimmy Van Heusen, who became specialists at writing for Sinatra); other Sinatra hits, such as 'I'll Never Smile Again' and 'There are Such Things', all had him backed by the Pied Pipers.

From Lunceford Dorsey hired arranger Sy Oliver, whose hits included 'Yes, Indeed!' (vocal duet by Stafford and Oliver), 'Well, Git It!' (featuring Ziggy Elman), 'On the Sunny Side of the Street' (a hip swing choir style vocal by the Sentimentalists, successors of the Pied Pipers) and 'Opus No. 1', a typical Swing Era riff. By the time of the last two, in 1945, the Dorsey band had incorporated strings, an expensive and unnecessary development; the Swing Era had begun to ripen.

Artie Shaw, like Goodman, was a first-rate clarinettist and a busy freelance when he formed his own band in 1936, with vocalist Helen Forrest, arranger Jerry Gray and Tony Pastor and Georgie Auld on tenor saxophones; George Wettling and then Buddy Rich played drums. Shaw was an intelligent man who hated the music business and left it several times; in 1954 (to Goodman's horror) he put his horn down and never touched it again. Of over fifty big hits up to 1946, the most famous was a sleeper. Pastor was also a novelty vocalist who later led his own band; he sang on a joky Shaw version of 'Indian Love Call' in 1938. But disc jockeys turned the record over to discover Gray's arrangement of Cole Porter's 'Begin the Beguine', later voted the third-favourite record of all time by the jockeys in a *Billboard* poll. From the same session, Shaw's composition 'Back Bay Shuffle' was another success, and Billie Holiday recorded her only track with the band, 'Any Old Time'; Shaw's self-composed theme 'Nightmare', from the next session, was another hit.

Shaw shocked the business by walking away at the height of this first success in late 1939, only to return from a holiday in Mexico and form a new band with another outstanding hit: 'Frenesi', a Mexican song, was arranged by William Grant Still for flute, oboe, French horn and strings, as well as the fifteen-piece conventional band. It was even bigger than 'Beguine' and another top D J favourite. Another hit by Shaw's second band was his own somewhat pretentious 'Concerto for Clarinet', issued on two sides of a 12-inch 78. Several bands, including those of Goodman, Tommy Dorsey and Glenn Miller, had huge hits with 'Star Dust' during this period, but Shaw's became the D Js' all-time favourite record (complete with slushy strings). Lena Horne made two sides with the band in 1941; vocalists Forrest, Kallen and Georgia Gibbs also worked with it.

Many of the white swing bands followed Goodman's lead in having small groups within them, such as Tommy Dorsey's Clambake Seven. Shaw's Gramercy Five was among the most interesting. The original cast made eight sides in 1940, with Billy Butterfield on trumpet, Johnny Guarnieri on harpsichord, Al Hendrickson on electric guitar, Jud DeNaut on bass and Nick Fatool on drums. 'Summit Ridge Drive' was a top ten hit. In 1945 six more bop-flavoured sides were made, with Roy Eldridge on trumpet, Dodo Marmarosa on piano, Barney Kessel on guitar, Morris Rayman and Lou Fromm on bass and drums. Shaw's ambitions for his music exceeded his ability; he was not the composer-arranger he wanted to be, and his irascibility got in his way. He later became a novelist and a theatrical producer, among other things; his autobiography *The Trouble with Cinderella* was almost a good book, but contained too much self-pity. He fronted big bands a couple of times in later years, but did not play.

Charlie Barnet came from a wealthy family and in 1929 was leading a combo on cruise liners at the age of sixteen; he led several bands before forming an excellent jazz-oriented outfit. He was a good soloist on all the saxophones, specializing on tenor at first, but later on alto and soprano, because, he said, there were too many better tenor players around. He also occasionally sang, especially in the early years. 'The most enjoyable, in terms of *fun* fun, plus one of the greatest bands I ever worked with was Charlie Barnet,' said Buddy DeFranco (quoted by Ira Gitler in *Swing to Bop*). When interviewing a musician, the story goes, Barnet would ask him if he drank. If he replied in the negative, he was either lying or was the kind of man who never took a drink; in either case, he didn't get the job. Barnet enjoyed life, and so did the people who worked for him.

Of all the white bandleaders of the Swing Era, it was Barnet who most openly admired the black bands, and whose talent and leadership paid them the finest tribute: many of Barnet's recordings are still among the most delightful of the era. He covered several Ellington compositions, notably 'The Gal from Joe's' and 'Rockin' in Rhythm'; 'Charleston Alley' was arranged by Horace Henderson; 'Southern Fried' was co-written by Harlan Leonard; 'Jump Session' was recorded by several bands, including Don Redman's, and 'Flyin' Home' was the famous Lionel Hampton screamer.

But the band (chiefly Barnet, under the pseudonym Dale Bennett) also produced fine originals. Among the best from 1939 to 1941 were 'The Duke's Idea' / 'The Count's Idea'; a month later 'The Wrong Idea', in which the band imitated the sweet bands of the time, was backed by 'The Right Idea', one of the best. 'Leapin' at the Lincoln' was a head arrangement on Gershwin's 'Lady Be Good'; 'Afternoon of a Moax' was also called 'Shake, Rattle 'n Roll' ('moax' was a southern term for a square); 'Wild Mab of the Fish Pond' was for guitarist Bus Etri, whose nickname was Wild Mab: one night after a hotel gig some of his colleagues put him in the hotel's fountain. (Barnet's nickname later became Mad Mab. Etri and trumpeter Lloyd Hundling were killed in a car crash in 1941, a personal blow to Barnet, who could not bear to hire another guitarist for months.) Ray Noble's 'Cherokee' was arranged by trumpeter Billy May; it was Barnet's biggest hit and became his theme, which is no doubt partly why the tune (with its wide-open chords, like 'I Got Rhythm') became a favourite vehicle for modern jazzmen.

The band contained no world-famous soloists during its classic period, but always good sidemen, such as May and Bobby Burnet on trumpets, and reedman-arranger Lloyd 'Skippy' Martin, who also played clarinet (for instance on 'Leapin' at the Lincoln'). The Barnet band represented a peak in the quality of mainstream popular music that has not been exceeded, demonstrating for all time that a high average level of musicianship was more important than stars. All these arrangements were extremely well played, and never fail to swing. Again and again there are felicitous touches on the recordings, for example the tasty Ellingtonian harmony of the trumpets at the end of 'Rockin' in Rhythm'. In Barnet's saxophone solo after the false ending on 'Leapin' at the Lincoln' he starts so high that he sounds like Martin coming back on clarinet, then drops several octaves in four or five notes. Or *is* it Martin coming back on clarinet? – it is done so seamlessly that it is impossible to tell. The swinging out-chorus written by May quotes Gershwin.

When playing 'Cherokee' in concert, the band improvised at some length; a sort of part two was recorded as 'Redskin Rhumba' (and there was also 'Comanche War Dance'). 'Pompton Turnpike' was written by Dick Rogers and trombonist-bandleader Will Osborne. Barnet led the band on soprano saxophone on this blues-flavoured instrumental; it celebrated Route 23 in New Jersey, the Newark–Pompton Turnpike, where the Meadowbrook was located, one of the most popular dance halls of the era. As with the other bands, many of Barnet's hits were by the vocalists. Mary Ann McCall sang 'Between 18th and 19th on Chestnut Street' (also by Rogers and Osborne) and 'Six Lessons from Madame La Zonga' (but was a better singer later, with Woody Herman). 'I Hear a Rhapsody' was sung by Bob Carroll.

'Blue Juice' may have been named after the band's bus; 'The Bar is Now Open' was another Horace Henderson tune. In October 1939 when the Palomar Ballroom in Los Angeles burned to the ground, the band lost almost everything, but Barnet's priorities were always in the right place: according to George T. Simon his comment was, 'Hell, it's better than being in Poland, with bombs dropping on your head.' Count Basie and Benny Carter lent arrangements, and one of the first new Barnet charts was called 'Are We Burnt Up?' Over the years Barnet employed more black artists than any other white leader, and without any fanfare, or even thinking about it. The only question was, 'How well does the guy play?' He simply did not bother to perform in places where there was going to be difficulty with an integrated band. As early as 1936 he hired trumpeter Frankie Newton and bass player John Kirby; among those who passed through were Benny Carter, Rex Stewart, Charlie Shavers, Trummy Young, Roy Eldridge, Clark Terry and Willie Smith, and vocalists Bunny Briggs (who later sang Ellington's *Sacred Music*) and the wonderful Lena Horne. Her lovely version of 'You're My Thrill' in 1941 featured Barnet on soprano saxophone. In 1965 she wrote: 'as far as color was concerned, it just never came up . . . I just felt safe with him.'

Barnet moved from Bluebird to Decca in 1943, and as the Second World War no doubt disrupted his line-up, the number of Barnet hits declined; but 'Skyliner' in 1945 became one of his most famous instrumentals (another 'Dale Bennett' chart), and 'Cement Mixer (Put-ti, Put-ti)' was one of several hit versions of Slim Gaillard's novelty. He later made innovative records for Capitol, using arrangers such as Johnny Richards, Neal Hefti, Kai Winding, Gil Fuller and Tiny Kahn. His autobiography *Those Swinging Years* (1984, written with Stanley Dance) is full of candour and enjoyable anecdotes, and provides trenchant commentary on the reasons for the withering of the Big Band Era.

Trombonist Wilber Schwichtenberg had played with Red Nichols and Ray Noble; he changed his name to Will Bradley when he formed a band in 1940 (co-led by drummer Ray McKinley, who had worked for the Dorsey brothers). One of its first recordings was 'Beat Me Daddy, Eight to the Bar', a two-sided hit at the height of the boogie-woogie fad, soon followed by 'Down the Road a Piece', a trio record, both with Freddie Slack on piano. Later came 'Scrub Me Mama, with A Boogie Beat', and more. It was a good, slick band; the hits included 'Celery Stalks at Midnight', yet another Swing Era riff; a copy of that record was memorably smashed by morons in the film *The Blackboard Jungle* (1955).

Given the quality of Barnet's music, and the stiff competition from the likes of Goodman and Dorsey, the phenomenon of trombonist-arranger Glenn Miller needs some explaining. Miller was far and away the most successful leader of the entire era. His time at the top was short, because he died in the English Channel on his way to entertain troops in newly liberated France, but he still managed to become the seventh best-selling recording artist of the whole period 1892–1954: with more than seventy top ten hits between July 1939 and September 1943, his success will probably never be equalled. Yet he was a tense individual who dealt in formulas, and seemed to avoid allowing his band to swing. (Tenor saxophonist Al Klink said years later, 'We were too scared to swing.') Miller did not acquire a first-rate rhythm section until he led an Army Air Force band. Many years later Billy May, who left Barnet to join Miller because the money was better, told George T. Simon, 'The only man I ever knew him to be envious of was Kay Kyser, because he was the only bandleader making more money than Glenn was.' After the war May joked in a letter to Klink: 'Adolph Hitler is alive and playing Fender bass with Glenn Miller in Argentina.'

Born in Iowa (like Bix), Miller was not a great soloist, and some say he would have given up all his success to be a top-class jazzman. He appeared to have difficulty in expressing himself emotionally, and his employees often did not know whether he liked their work or not. Yet (like Goodman) he was capable of unexpected kindness, and he kept an eye on the ticket prices at the ballrooms and theatres, refusing to allow his young fans to be ripped off. When Barnet fronted Miller's band while Miller was ill, he would have done it for nothing, but Miller insisted on paying him generously. (When Barnet did a similar favour for Goodman, the latter gave him a cigarette lighter with an engraved inscription that had been altered; somebody else had given Goodman the lighter, and furthermore, said Barnet, it didn't work.)

Miller played trombone and wrote arrangements for Ben Pollack (1924–8) and Red Nichols (1929–30). The Charleston Chasers, a Columbia pick-up group, was basically Red Nichols's outfit from 1925 to 1929; for its last recording session in 1931 an eleven-piece band was directed by Benny Goodman, including Miller, Gene

Krupa and Charlie and Jack Teagarden, and Miller wrote some special lyrics for one of Teagarden's several recordings of 'Basin Street Blues'. Goodman and Miller also played together in the pit bands for Gershwin shows. Miller added business management to his tasks while working with Smith Ballew (1932–4). Ballew, a handsome pop singer, led a successful band, employing a good deal of first-rate talent, and had several big hits on various ARC labels from 1929 to 1931; on recordings his band was often the Pollack gang, moonlighting again. (Ballew later went to Hollywood, and the rumour persists that Ballew's voice was dubbed when a studio tried to make a singing cowboy out of John Wayne.) In 1934–5 Miller worked for the Dorsey Brothers Orchestra, where his accomplishments included writing and singing some amusing novelty lyrics on 'Annie's Cousin Fanny'.

The excellent British songwriter and bandleader Ray Noble, whose records sold well in the USA, decided to move there. The musicians' union would not allow him to use his own band, so he brought vocalist Al Bowlly and one or two others, and hired Miller to assemble an American band. Noble had big hits in America every year between 1931 and 1949, except for a couple of years during the war; Miller helped him from 1935 to 1937, when Miller formed his own first band.

Noble's lovely recording of his own song, 'The Very Thought of You', was an international hit in 1934 and featured Bowlly. (Born in what is now Maputo in Mozambique of Greek and Lebanese parents, Bowlly soon returned to London, where he was killed, not by the famous German bomb that hit the Café De Paris in March 1941, killing West Indian bandleader Ken 'Snakehips' Johnson along with many others, but by another bomb a few weeks later.) Noble's HMV discs made in England were admired by producers and recording engineers in the USA for their excellent sound. The secret turned out to be that the band was recorded in a sizeable room at some distance from the microphone, rather than in the typically cramped studios of US companies, some of which were left over from the acoustic era.

Miller had a hit with 'Solo Hop' in 1935, using some of Noble's men. His own first band went broke, but late in 1938 he was recording for Bluebird with a new band, using his pretty 'sound' (a clarinet lead over the reed section) and the familiar 'oo-wah' of the muted brass. He was a huge hit at the Glen Island Casino in New Rochelle, New York, a popular ballroom where leaders played for less money because of the room's radio wire. Miller's long-time associate Chummy MacGregor was not a very good pianist; Herman 'Trigger' Alpert was a good bass player, but the various occupants of the band's drum chair never added up to much. Klink was an excellent saxophonist, but Miller's favourite (and the band's star) was Gordon 'Tex' Beneke, a vocalist whose distinctive Texas drawl was invaluable on many of the hits. Beneke was not as good a saxophonist as Klink, yet Miller featured him instead. Miller was the sort of businessman who thought that talent ran in families: Ray Eberle was nothing like as good a singer as his brother Bob Eberly, while Marion Hutton (younger sister of singer and film star Betty Hutton, the 'blonde bombshell') often had trouble singing in tune. The band's vocal group was the Modernaires. On the band's broadcasts Miller's medley theme was 'something old, something new, something borrowed, something blue'.

Miller's first big hit was his theme, 'Moonlight Serenade', originally called 'Now I Lay Me Down to Weep', a simple, saccharine tune played at a dirge-like tempo, and loaded with the clarinet lead. The uptempo numbers were often absurdly clunky records: 'Runnin' Wild' was first played by Art Hickman (and was sung by Marilyn Monroe in the film *Some Like It Hot* in 1959); Miller's 'Anvil Chorus' was a two-sided 78 based on the tune from Verdi's *Il Trovatore*: both were stinkers. Another 1939 hit was 'Little Brown Jug', a pleasant arrangement (by Bill Finegan) given a lumpy recorded performance. (It is moved to 1944 in the 1954 film biography, because the poverty of the script needed to make a gimmick of it.) A great many of the Miller hits are unremarkable renditions of popular songs of the day, such as 'Wishing Will Make It So', 'Stairway to the Stars', 'Fools Rush In' and the inevitable 'Star Dust'.

So why the enormous success? Why was one of the great peaks in popular music dominated by Glenn Miller? Why do millions of people still love his music, and why are more compilations of his recordings available today than almost anyone else's?

To begin with, despite the importance of the phenomenon of swing in music, it does not matter at all to many people, and in 1939 its lesson had definitely not been mastered by all the musicians. To put it another way, a lot of people still clapped on one and three, and things are not much different fifty years later. Barnet was certain, on the basis of personal experience, that most people cannot tell good playing from bad, let alone what swing is. Also, Miller had decided not to compete directly with Goodman, Dorsey or Barnet, but to build an essentially sweet dance band that could also be defined as a 'swing band', so that he topped polls in both categories. There was an integrity to the sweetness, and the band was superbly reliable. Miller was a stickler for dynamics in performance, for example ('Observe the markings!' he would remind the musicians), so that the kids always got the sound they expected, and many of them bought a new Miller record, whatever it was. The arrangements too were reliable, often predictable but sometimes outstanding. And, finally, the choice of material was nothing less than brilliant from a commercial point of view. Miller's achievement was to sum up popular music, as Whiteman had done earlier: each sounded to his contemporaries as if he were at the centre of it. 'Little Brown Jug' was a very old and familiar tune, and 'American Patrol', while it seems like a wartime novelty now, was in fact a march first published in 1885, and was probably vaguely familiar to Miller's audience. (The hit recording is considerably less disappointing than that of 'Little Brown Jug'.) 'Moon Love' was adapted from Tchaikovsky's Fifth Symphony. In 'Yes, My Darling Daughter', adapted by Jack Lawrence from a Ukrainian folksong, Hutton asks the leading questions and the band chants the title's answer. 'Ida (Sweet as Apple Cider)' had already been made famous by Eddie Cantor, among others, and sounded like a quintessentially American song. (In Britain cider is an alcoholic drink, but in the USA it is just apple juice.) Billy May wrote an arrangement of 'Ida' that set Beneke's vocal against that of the band, but Miller would not use it: the swing choir was not part of his formula.

There were film songs ('Over the Rainbow', 'When You Wish Upon a Star'), radio themes ('You and I', a number one hit, was the *Maxwell House Coffee-time* theme, written by Meredith Willson) and sweet Latin songs ('Adios', 'Perfidia', 'Say "Si Si"'); many tunes were forever associated with Miller because of the sweet innocence of their lyrics, for example 'Elmer's Tune' and 'Moonlight Cocktail' (written by stride pianist Luckey Roberts). Several other bands and recording artists with undoubted musical skills, from Guy Lombardo and Lawrence Welk to James Last and Barry Manilow, have been excoriated by critics for their perceived shortcomings, but to know your market as well as Miller did is an impressive accomplishment.

As in most of the other white bands, riffs were borrowed from black ones, such as Erskine Hawkins's 'Tuxedo Junction' (which is not a bad record, and a head arrangement, very different from Hawkins's own), and one of the biggest hits of the century, 'In the Mood'. A riff is a repeated rhythmic figure that suggests interesting harmonic ideas to the soloists. Among the most charming riffs are the simplest, such as Leonard and Barnet's 'Southern Fried', mentioned above. Most of the Swing Era tunes celebrating dance halls and hotel ballrooms are little more than riffs: 'Stomping at the Savoy', 'Jumping at the Woodside', 'Riffing at the Ritz' and so forth.

'In the Mood' had appeared on several earlier recordings, such as Wingy Manone's 'Tar Paper Stomp' (1930) and Horace Henderson's arrangement 'Hot and Anxious', which was recorded by Fletcher Henderson and Don Redman (at very different tempos: Henderson's is slower, Redman's hotter). The venerable British journalist C. H. Rolph was certain that he heard the riff played by a cinema orchestra before 1920. Edgar Hayes was a black pianist and bandleader whose saxophonist Joe Garland wrote an entire arrangement consisting of nothing but the riff, naming it 'In the Mood'; it appeared in 1938 on the other side of Hayes's record of 'Star Dust' (which would have made the black chart, had there been one at the time). Barnet turned it down, but Miller recorded it within a few months. If you are going to exercise a riff for most of the length of a 78 rpm side, you have to make it swing; otherwise a riff like 'In the Mood', which carries repetition to an extreme, soon becomes irritating. Among the differences between the two recordings was the fact that Hayes's drummer was the young Kenny Clarke. Despite Clyde Hurley's trumpet solo, and the famous 'chase' sequence between Klink and Beneke on tenor, Miller's version sounds like a bright-eyed and energetic imitation of swing. There are much better Miller recordings that are rarely heard – 'Sliphorn Jive', written by Eddie Durham, comes to mind – but you can hardly buy a Miller compilation without 'In the Mood' on it.

It is too bad that Miller's records are not better ones, yet a few of them hold up as well as almost any from the period. 'Chattanooga Choo Choo' and '(I've Got a Gal in) Kalamazoo' were both written by Mack Gordon and Harry Warren for the Miller films *Orchestra Wives* and *Sun Valley Serenade*. Miller saw to it that the story line incorporated the band, rather than a mere appearance by it, making them better than average films of their kind. 'Choo Choo' was the first record to be formally certified a million-seller, serving notice to the business that the Depression was over at last; RCA invented the gold record gimmick for Miller. 'Don't Sit under the Apple Tree (with Anybody Else but Me)', written in 1942 by Lew Brown, Charlie Tobias and Sam H. Stept, is the sort of song which seems always to have existed until somebody plucked it out of the air, almost a good pop song of the nineteenth century. These three continued selling for years; all were jolly arrangements, well played and with a full complement of vocalists, and all were about travel and parting, the admixture of trains and place names helping to cheer up the nation during a world war: they were good pop records, and they still are.

On the other side of 'Moonlight Serenade' was Frankie Carle's 'Sunrise Serenade', also a slow, smoochy instrumental and a top ten hit, but a much better tune, a pretty arrangement and taken at a slightly faster tempo. 'Song of the Volga Boatmen' (cleverly arranged by Finegan) and 'String of Pearls' (Jerry Gray) are unique. All three of these very different sides are among Miller's best recordings; the tempos are just right and the rhythm section plays slightly behind the beat, rather than on top of it. 'String of Pearls' included solos by Beneke, Klink and Ernie Caceres, and a cornet solo by Bobby Hackett. (Critics were irritated that Miller hired the great cornettist to play guitar, but he admired Hackett, and hired him on guitar initially because he was having lip trouble at the time.)

Miller joined the United States Army Air Force as a captain and rose to major. When he was sent to England to entertain troops, the BBC wanted him to play everything at the same volume, to make it easier to broadcast, so he broadcast on the Armed Services Network instead. Robert Farnon led a Canadian band, and George Melachrino a British one. There are those who say that Farnon's was the best, but Miller had finally put together a good rhythm section: Alpert on bass, Ray McKinley on drums and Mel Powell on piano. Miller's contribution to morale was enormous, and he insisted on putting on extra shows wherever the crush was too great to allow everyone in. From the early days he had ensured that broadcasts were recorded; the USAAF band issued no recordings at the time, but Miller broadcasts have been endlessly recycled ever since. When he was lost on his way to France, flying in terrible winter weather in a small plane with no de-icing equipment, he was forty years old. His was one of the most successful sounds in the history of pop.

Klink said, 'Miller should have lived and the music should have died.' Miller ghost bands have continued touring, with the co-operation of the estate; they were seen on UK television on the fortieth anniversary of D-Day. The best of these in musical terms was Tex Beneke and the Glenn Miller Orchestra led by Beneke until 1947, when he fell out with the estate, perhaps because he did not want to stick to the Miller formula for ever. (The estate got even by seeing to it that he was not even mentioned in the film biography of 1954.)

One of Beneke's most interesting sides was 'Lavender Coffin', about the last wishes of a gambler, which he sang accompanied by a vocal group; the arrangement was a clever one, its laid-back jive and hand-claps on the beat reminiscent of 'Volga Boatman'. Interestingly, it was a cover of a rhythm and blues tune, written by Shirley Albert, which was a top ten hit in the black chart by Boston saxophonist Paul 'Fat Man' Robinson in 1949; other recordings of it were made by Lionel Hampton and Joe Thomas, the former vocalist and reedman with Lunceford. Cover versions of rhythm and blues songs would soon become more numerous; new independent labels and other changes in the business were making sure that popular music was mutating by 1949, whether the Miller estate liked it or not.

10

Small-group Jazz, the Jukebox and the New Independent Labels

You can still start arguments by postulating that big-band jazz was not jazz at all. This is nonsense, but the small groups of the Swing Era made a very special contribution, providing more room for hot solos and using simpler arrangements, often made up on the bandstand or in the studio. The greater freedom available to small groups allowed a different kind of innovation, the hallmark of jazz since its beginning. In the small-group recordings of the Swing Era may be heard the seeds of the music of the future, both in the rhythm and blues and the modern jazz directions.

In the mid-1930s several factors combined to create the new jukebox industry, which had an incalculable effect on popular music.

Edison's phonograph had been fitted with a coin slot and four listening tubes by Louis Glass and placed in a saloon in San Francisco in 1889. In 1891 the Louisiana Phonograph Company claimed that one of its machines, costing about $200, had grossed $1,000 in two months. In 1906 the Gabel Automatic Entertainer was the first machine to play a series of gramophone discs, using a spring-loaded hand-wound motor and a 40-inch acoustic horn. There were huge, heavy, brilliantly engineered non-electric machines that played several cylinders in rotation; one handle wound the motor and changed the cylinder and the needle. But the phonograph parlour was replaced by player pianos.

Despite the fact that there had never been any adequate protection for the authors and composers of songs, and that in practice such protection could only be acquired through their publishers, Theodore Roosevelt (the 'trust buster') was outraged that the Music Publishers

Association (MPA) and Aeolian had agreed a royalty of 10 per cent on piano rolls. A revised Copyright Act for popular music in 1909 required a royalty of 2 cents and compulsory licensing of all reproductions, whether piano rolls or sound recordings, and for all publishers, not just those in the MPA. This was said to be the first time in history that the government intervened directly between supplier and user of a product.

Aeolian's Aeriola player piano had been introduced in 1895; in 1898 Wurlitzer built the first coin-operated player piano. By 1910 these had overtaken nickel-in-the-slot record players. In 1916 the 'word-roll' added the words to the songs, printed on the margin of the roll: the words were not covered by the 1909 act, a good excuse to set royalties on such rolls much higher than 2 cents.

The best player pianos, such as the Ampico, reproduced music more or less accurately, and recordings were made by great pianists such as Rachmaninov and Busoni. But the vast majority of piano rolls and players were mechanical in the extreme, and no expression of any kind was available. George Gershwin and a good number of others first heard popular music on the pianola in the corner candy store; many a jazz pianist began by slowing down the piano roll and placing fingers on the keys as they were mechanically depressed. Between 1895 and the early 1920s over two million player pianos were sold; in 1921, of 341,652 pianos of all types, nearly two-thirds were player pianos. But the business failed during the Depression, and by then the radio and electric recording were beginning to have their effect. (In the 1990s the Yamaha Disklavier is operated by 'a full library of pre-recorded discs . . . from classical to contemporary'. So you can still buy a piano that plays itself if you want to.)

In 1927 several firms built electrically operated record-playing machines; it was obvious that simply playing the records in rotation was not good enough, and selection mechanisms were developed. The Automatic Music Instrument Company (AMI) marketed the first electrically amplified, multi-selection device.

Homer Capehart worked for a company that made various coin-operated machines; he bought the rights to a record changer called the Simplex, and was fired for doing so. He formed his own company and made a splash at the Chicago Radio Show in 1928, attracting almost as much attention as the first public demonstration of television. The Capehart was not the first integrally designed automatic-changer for the home; Victor had marketed an Orthophonic acoustic player with an electrically operated changer, but it had problems. For one thing, discs in those days were not of uniform size, and did not always have lead-in grooves and a final groove spiral for tripping the mechanism. Capehart was fired again, this time from his own company, but a few years later the Capehart became the most impressive machine on the market. Its elaborate record changer played both sides of a stack of intermixed 10-inch and 12-inch records, and the machine had good sound for the period; it was slowly improved. Coleman Hawkins owned one in the late 1940s that cost $1,000, but most Americans never saw one. The price put it out of reach.

Meanwhile, Capehart took his Simplex to Wurlitzer, whose sales of pipe organs and player pianos were falling, and became the company's vice-president and sales manager. The Simplex played only one side of each record, but was robust and reliable. Prohibition had been repealed, so a great many new taverns opened up, and most of them wanted mechanical music. In 1933 there were about 25,000 jukeboxes in operation in the USA, of which only 266 were Wurlitzer's; in 1935 there were 100,000, and in 1936 Wurlitzer alone shipped nearly 45,000 machines. It remained the leader of the industry for more than a decade.

The term 'jukebox' did not become common until the mid-1930s. It probably comes from the Gullah 'juke' or 'joog', meaning 'disorderly' or 'wicked' and perhaps ultimately from the Wolof 'dzug', to live wickedly. The *Oxford English Dictionary* quotes a scholarly American source from 1941: to 'jouk' was to dance; to 'go joukin'' was to go pub-crawling. The term 'juke joint' was certainly current; blues singer Walter Roland recorded 'Jookit Jookit' for Vocalion in 1933. (A character in Tennessee Williams's *Orpheus Descending* of 1958 says 'I'd like to go out jooking with you tonight.')

Wurlitzer's Model 24 was the first to offer twenty-four selections instead of twelve or sixteen. Capehart sold the machines to independent jukebox operators, rather than directly to the taverns and restaurant owners, thus ensuring that the machines were regularly serviced and the records changed. He built up such an effective distribution system that by the time he left Wurlitzer his own Packard company could not compete with it. (After the Second World War he left the business, serving three terms in the US Senate from Indiana.)

Canadian-born David Rockola had a perfect name for the jukebox industry; his pinball-machine business went broke in 1930, but he bought the patents of the old Gabel company and, with the help of his creditors, Rock-Ola competed with Seeburg (formed in 1907 as a piano company by a Swedish immigrant) for second place in the USA jukebox business behind Wurlitzer. In 1948 Seeburg's engineer M. W. Kenney developed the first machine to offer a hundred selections – it held fifty 78s, of which either side could be selected – and the Selectomatic mechanism became nearly ubiquitous. Of all these, only Rock-Ola was still making jukeboxes in the early 1980s. Seeburg had got into anti-trust trouble, and when Wurlitzer left the jukebox business in 1974, the company destroyed all its files and spare parts. Most of the principals are now dead, so the definitive history of the industry will probably never be written.

Jukebox cabinets became an extravaganza of light and moulded plastic in the late 1930s. Wurlitzer's Model 24 had been the first to use illuminated plastics in its design; after wartime shutdown designer Paul Fuller produced the most famous jukebox of all, the Model 1015, of which Wurlitzer shipped over 56,000. Nils Miller at Seeburg was another influential designer. Paradoxically, these masterpieces of kitsch are rare and valuable today because they were too well built to wear out; Wurlitzer accepted trade-ins of any make, and then destroyed them.

Early in the Depression the record companies were not slow to understand the importance of the jukebox business. In many parts of the country hillbillies and blacks were more likely to hear their own recording artists on a jukebox than on the radio; people who could not afford to buy a radio could sip a beer and listen to music played by other people's coins in the jukebox. The jukebox used up so many records that it rescued the record industry from the Depression, and retail sales began to improve as people liked the records they heard on jukeboxes, at a time when recorded music on the radio was not yet omnipresent. Small-group jazz was ideal: small-group recordings were cheaper to make than big-band ones, especially if the musicians were black.

Coleman Hawkins and Henry 'Red' Allen co-led three sessions in 1933 that resulted in ten lovely sides aimed at this market. Allen's first recordings in 1929 were credited to Henry Allen, Jr, and his Orchestra, because his father was a prominent New Orleans bandleader. The trumpeter worked for Fletcher Henderson and many other leaders, and was unfairly but widely regarded as an Armstrong imitator for many years; in fact, he was always his own man, and in the mid-1950s, on reunion sessions with Hawkins, sounded as much like Miles Davis as he did like Armstrong. He was also a vocalist of great charm, and the ten 1933 sides capture an era that is gone for ever. Made quickly and cheaply for budget labels like Perfect and Banner, and with whichever sidemen they could pick up (such as Russell Procope, Dicky Wells, Benny Morton and Horace Henderson on some tracks), the recordings are mostly of Tin Pan Alley songs that white artists had turned down.

The most successful small group of all, both on the jukeboxes and in the charts, was led by the pianist who was nicknamed Filthy by his friends in Harlem. Thomas Wright 'Fats' Waller played the piano by ear as a child, slowing down a piano roll to learn 'Carolina Shout'. He then enlisted James P. Johnson as his teacher, who also became something of a substitute father. Waller's father was a lay preacher who could not control his wayward son; they did not get along, and Fats probably never got over the loss of his mother when he was a teenager. He developed an enormous appetite for food, drink, women and song that he could never restrain, and an outsized talent to match.

As a teenager playing the organ in a Harlem cinema he gave some lessons to a boy from Red Bank named William Basie. Later he studied formally himself, knowing that he had to discipline his talent. He made piano rolls, and his first (acoustic) gramophone sides were piano solos, 'Muscle Shoals Blues' and 'Birmingham Blues' (1922). He also accompanied blues singers such as Caroline Johnson ('Ain't Got Nobody to Grind My Coffee'), Alberta Hunter ('You Can't Do What My Last Man Did') and Sara Martin. Having written 'Squeeze

Me' with Clarence Williams, he accompanied Clarence and Sara in duets ('Squabbling Blues', 'I'm Certainly Gonna See About That').

He worked in Chicago in 1925, jamming with Louis Armstrong and Earl Hines, and playing solo piano at a hotel; he told a story about being kidnapped to play at a birthday party for Al Capone, who stuffed hundred-dollar bills in his pocket. In November 1926 he began recording for Ralph Peer on the pipe organ in a disused church in Camden, New Jersey; Handy's 'St Louis Blues' and Waller's own 'Lenox Avenue Stomp' were good enough to get him invited back. Early in 1927 he recorded a series of improvisations with titles like 'Soothin' Syrup Stomp' and 'Sloppy Water Blues'; counting alternative takes, there were fifteen tracks. Let loose with feet as well as hands on what he called the instrument of his heart, he was already a giant talent; the sheer beauty and obvious joy in music-making on the unusual instrument is unlike anything else ever recorded. In May he recorded 'Sugar', a Tin Pan Alley hit that has had many recordings, Handy's 'Beale Street Blues' and 'I'm Goin' to See My Ma', credited on record labels to one C. Todd: all three were recorded both as organ solos and on organ with vocals by Alberta Hunter. 'I'm Goin' to See My Ma (and try to find my pa)' is a sort of happy tear-jerker: you can see Alberta there on the railway platform, at the height of the Jazz Age and just before the Great Depression, perhaps with a cardboard suitcase tied up with clothes-line, happy to be going home, the place where they have to let you in.

Further sessions in 1927 yielded more organ solos, notably a beautiful 'I Ain't Got Nobody', as well as a few piano solos and some organ sides with a combo. In 1928 Waller played 'Beale Street Blues' on the organ at Carnegie Hall (with Handy's blessing), and played piano with an orchestra in a performance of James P. Johnson's *Yamekraw*. (Johnson was not allowed the night off from conducting *Keep Shufflin'*.)

In 1929 came Fats Waller and his Buddies. In *We Called It Music* Eddie Condon tells the story of being detailed to get Fats to the recording session in New York on the first day of March. Condon got him out of bed, fortified with liquid ham'n'eggs and into a taxi, where he wrote the quintet numbers 'The Minor Drag' and 'Harlem Fuss', the titles of which were reversed on the record: 'Harlem Fuss' is a slow drag, while 'The Minor Drag' is a romp. At the same session he recorded piano solos 'Numb Fumblin'' and 'Handful of Keys'. Among other solo piano recordings is 'Ain't Misbehavin'', which he had written for *Hot Chocolates* that year; Waller's recording, and those by Louis Armstrong, bandleader Leo Reisman, Gene Austin, Ruth Etting and Bill Robinson with Irving Mills, were all hits. Another solo was 'Valentine Stomp', a tribute to Hazel Valentine, who ran a Harlem good-time house called the Daisy Chain where Fats liked to hang out. (It was later also celebrated in Count Basie's 'Swingin' at the Daisy Chain'.)

At the end of the year there were more Buddies sessions, this time with a bigger band, including Condon, Red Allen and Jack Teagarden, and singers. 'Looking Good But Feelin' Bad' and 'I Need Someone Like You', both Waller songs, are sung by a male quartet, while 'Ridin' But Walkin'' and 'Won't You Get Up Off It, Please?' were instrumentals and 'When I'm Alone' (not a Waller song) had a pop vocal by one Orlando Robinson. Still another session the same month, by 'Jimmie Johnson and his Orchestra', featured two songs by J. C. (Jimmie) Johnson (another pianist, who probably used his initials so as not to be confused with James P.): 'You've Got to be Modernistic' and 'You Don't Understand' were sung by a male trio (the latter a sweet ballad also recorded by Bessie Smith). In the band were King Oliver, Dave Nelson and both James P. and Waller on pianos.

In the same year crooner Gene Austin bailed Waller out of jail. According to Maurice Waller, the judge was angry because Waller persistently fell behind with his alimony payments, and Waller was let off because Austin told the judge that Waller was needed at a recording session that afternoon, and that if he was not there, it would put several men out of work. So Waller went along to the session, where he and Austin (himself a southerner) were dismayed to find that the other musicians would not play with 'Austin's nigger', who had to be put at the other end of the studio behind a screen, and with a separate microphone. The song recorded was Waller's 'Your Fate is in My Hands', with words by Billy Rose.

The record dates dried up as the Depression began to bite. There were two piano duets with Bennie Payne on Victor in 1930, and two pianos solos on Columbia in 1931, on which he sang, accompanied by himself, his own songs 'I'm Crazy 'Bout My Baby (and My Baby's Crazy 'Bout Me)' (words by Alex Hill) and 'Draggin' My Poor Heart Around', revealing a charming high baritone. The Lion claimed credit for getting Fats to sing, but his writing partner Andy Razaf said that when they went the rounds of publishers hawking their songs, Fats's singing would sell them better than his own. (Andreamen-entania Paul Razafinkeriefo was descended from the royal family of Madagascar.)

Tunes poured out of Waller, but he was profligate in more ways than one, and often sold songs outright when he needed money; the suspicion persists that he sold famous tunes to Jimmy McHugh. Publishers frequently paid an advance to acquire a song, but would then forget to pay royalties; Waller and Razaf got their own back by selling the same lead sheet to several different publishers, sometimes all in the same building on the same day. They wrote scores of songs that were never even published, but their best known, apart from 'Ain't Misbehavin'', include: '(What Did I Do to be So) Black and Blue', an affecting song that takes a swipe at racism, also used in *Hot Chocolates* and superbly recorded by Louis Armstrong; 'Honeysuckle Rose', from the same year (1929), which seems to have been a variation on 'Tea for Two' (he interpolated them on a piano solo in 1937); 'Blue, Turning Grey Over You', 'Keepin' Out of Mischief Now' and 'Ain't-cha Glad?' Razaf wrote words for tunes by many other composers.

Waller also wrote 'I've Got a Feeling I'm Falling' with Rose, and recorded it with the Rhythmakers and vocalist Billy Banks (who had a talent for happy scat and recorded under a great many names with a different line-up each time). Waller recorded with Don Redman's studio groups, Red McKenzie and Ted Lewis; a recording with one of Jack Teagarden's studio bands is notable for the repartee between Teagarden and Waller on 'You Rascal You' and 'That's What I Like About You'. He played the organ for a popular late-night radio programme in Cincinnati (and in the morning the cleaner had to remove several empty gin bottles).

In 1934, as the new jukebox industry was beginning to take off and the record business struggled out of the Depression, Victor invited him back, to record with a combo as Fats Waller and his Rhythm, and jukebox as well as jazz history was made. The group included guitarist Al Casey (a teenager when Waller hired him), Gene 'Honey Bear' Sedric on reeds (one of Sam Wooding's favourite players in his European band), Bill Coleman and then Herman Autrey on trumpet, Charles Turner or (later) Cedric Wallace on bass and Slick Jones, Yank Porter or Harry Dial on drums. They were an instant success.

The songs from Broadway shows that we now regard as standards were not often pop hits at the time, but for the first few years Waller's hits came from some of the era's best Tin Pan Alley hacks. Among Waller's 1934 sessions were James P. Johnson's charming 'A Porter's Love Song to a Chambermaid' (words by Razaf) and 'I Wish I Were Twins', by Edgar DeLange (of Hudson and DeLange), with words by Frank Loesser, one of the great lyricists; 'Two Sleepy People', written by Loesser and Hoagy Carmichael, was a number one hit for Waller in 1938. Loesser wrote dummy tunes for his own lyrics until his own 'Praise the Lord and Pass the Ammunition' was a huge wartime hit; from then on he wrote both words and music, creating such songs as 'Baby It's Cold Outside' and 'On a Slow Boat to China'. His masterpiece, the show *Guys and Dolls* (1950), which included 'If I Were a Bell', was followed by *The Most Happy Fella* (1956) and *How To Succeed in Business Without Really Trying* (1961).

Also from 1934 came Waller and Razaf's 'How Can You Face Me', together with the pop songs 'Then I'll Be Tired of You', 'Don't Let It Bother You', 'Sweetie Pie' and 'Believe It, Beloved'. Like Billie Holiday, Waller recorded tunes that were new at the time; nobody knew whether they would be hits or not, and some survived only because he recorded them, such as 'Dream Man (Let Me Dream Some More)' and 'Do Me a Favor (Marry Me)'. Among the writers were J. C. Johnson, who wrote 'Believe It, Beloved', as well as Bessie Smith's 'Empty Bed Blues' and 'Dusky Stevedore' (recorded by Frankie Trumbauer with Bix and many others). Mack Gordon wrote 'Don't Let It Bother You' (suitable for the recovery period: 'Take it on the chin / Give a little grin / Everything will be okay!'). Arthur Schwartz and Yip Harburg wrote 'Then I'll Be Tired of You'; Schwartz wrote 'Got a Bran' New Suit' and many more with lyricist Howard Dietz. Dietz also wrote with Kern, Gershwin, Vernon Duke and Sammy Fain; Harburg wrote 'April in Paris' with Vernon Duke and, with Harold Arlen, 'It's Only a Paper Moon', 'Happiness is Just a Thing Called Joe' and the songs for *The Wizard of Oz*.

Nobody did more than Fats Waller, except Louis Armstrong himself, to bring jazz to popular music. If he liked a song, he could do it more or less straight, but he often kidded a song unmercifully, improvising his own additions to the lyrics as well as vocal ejaculations during instrumental breaks and bridges. Often he would blurt out (sometimes salacious) tag-lines at the end, such as 'No, Lady, we can't haul your ashes for twenty-five cents. That'd be bad business.' 'I'm Gonna Sit Right Down and Write Myself a Letter', a sweet love song by Fred Ahlert and Joe Young, was played straight. 'Truckin'' was written for a Cotton Club revue by Rube Bloom and Ted Koehler; it became a dance fad (a sequel was 'Let's Get Drunk and Truck', by Tampa Red in 1936). 'All My Life' was a pretty ballad by Sidney Mitchell and Sammy Stept that had several hit recordings, including one by Teddy Wilson with Ella Fitzgerald. 'A Little Bit Independent' was by Edgar Leslie and Joe Burke. As is often true of the pop charts, the best records were not usually the biggest hits, but the Waller number one 'It's a Sin to Tell a Lie' (by Billy Mayhew) is an exception: an uptempo romp, it suited the full Waller treatment: 'Get on out there and tell your lie,' he demands of Sedric before his clarinet solo, and ends with one of his favourite tags, 'What'd I say?!'

Waller was his own worst enemy, so profligate that he was always in need of money. The jukebox operators naturally preferred to buy cheaper records, and in 1939 Victor transferred Waller to its cheaper Bluebird label, the better to compete with Kapp's Decca label for the mechanical business. For whatever reason, towards the end of his career some of the songs were so bad that not even he could save them: 'Little Curly Hair in a High Chair', 'My Mommie Sent Me to the Store', 'Abercrombie Had a Zombie'. But the jazz content was nearly always present, and there are an extraordinary number of gems: definitive versions of delightful songs like 'Lulu's Back in Town' (by Al Dubin and Harry Warren), 'Rosetta' (by Earl Hines, on which Fats plays celesta), 'I Believe in Miracles' (organ), 'What's the Reason I'm Not Pleasin' You?', 'There'll be Some Changes Made', 'I Used to Love You (But It's All Over Now)', 'I'll Dance at Your Wedding' (with the tag 'Go on, get married again') and 'The Curse of an Aching Heart' ('Bump, bump, bump, bump! That's the curse back at ya!'). The mixture of jazz, jive and beauty is unique. 'Your Feet's Too Big', a charming non-love song with the tag 'One never knows, do one?', was a hit in 1939, followed by 'Your Socks Don't Match' and 'Hold Tight (I Want Some Sea Food, Mama)'. (Few knew that the last celebrated cunnilingus.)

The canard is heard that Waller's sidemen were somehow second-rate; certainly his group did not survive the loss of one of the most ebullient musical personalities of the century, but again and again on the recordings his men played exquisitely apposite solos. Waller himself is still admired, for example by Cecil Taylor 'for the depth of his notes'. There were more piano solos, among them 'Clothes Line Ballet', 'Alligator Crawl', 'African Ripples', Duke Ellington's 'Ring Dem Bells' and 'Carolina Shout'.

Waller visited Europe twice; in London in 1938 he recorded pipe organ solos and with such sidemen as trombonist George Chisholm and drummer Edmundo Ros (later the leader of a popular Latin-American band). On a 1939 trip he recorded again on pipe organ and also the *London Suite*, a set of six impressions borrowing themes here and there from some of his other tunes. In Paris he played the organ at the Cathedral of Notre-Dame, an experience at the 'God box' that he regarded as one of the great honours of his life.

He led a big band on one tour. He also recorded with a protégée, pianist and vocalist Una Mae Carlisle, who sang straight to Waller's clowning on 'I Can't Give You Anything But Love' (1939). He made recordings both solo and with his combo for Muzak (the recordings were unreleased for years) and on V-discs for the armed services, including 'The Reefer Song' ('I dreamed about a reefer five feet long . . .'). At his own Carnegie Hall concert in January 1942 he was almost too drunk to play the second half. In December of 1943 his body gave up the struggle, and he died of pneumonia on a train between engagements. He was only thirty-nine.

Following Victor's jukebox success with Waller's records, John Hammond talked Brunswick into a series of small-group sides led by pianist Teddy Wilson, who acted as a contractor, hiring whichever musicians happened to be in town for each date. Wilson, who was from a middle-class background, left college to become a full-time musician; his first recordings as a soloist in 1934 were rejected by Columbia, who did not appreciate his understated elegance, a stylistic influence for generations. From July 1935 to 1942, however, he made nearly three hundred sides for Brunswick, many featuring vocalists such as Ella Fitzgerald, Lena Horne and, above all, Billie Holiday. None of the participants received any royalties, but the records were so popular that the following year Brunswick began recording Holiday under her own name. From late 1937 Wilson was often replaced on Holiday's records by Claude Thornhill, Eddie Heywood and others, but her sessions did not stray far from Wilson's original conception.

Billie Holiday was born Elinore Harris in Philadelphia; neither her mother nor her maternal grandmother had been married, so the surname had passed down on the female side for three generations. Her father, Clarence Holiday, played guitar with Fletcher Henderson and Don Redman. She had a turbulent early life, in many ways the opposite of that of the urbane, well-educated Wilson, but, like him, she had an innate dignity that never left her, and she was a very great jazz musician. When she was young, her voice was pretty and sweet, but it already had the unique vocal colour that was all that remained when she died; if the essence of singing popular songs is to interpret them, she was one of the greatest pop singers who ever lived. She was certainly the essence of languor, always singing behind the beat; she brought high spirits, a laid-back sexiness or deep sadness to her work, depending on the song, but always showed a yearning wistfulness.

Her first recordings were sides with a Benny Goodman studio group in 1933. When she sang on Wilson's first session, she was just twenty, and he was twenty-two: 'Miss Brown to You' and 'What a Little Moonlight Can Do' became classics. Holiday's soul-mate was Lester Young. It is said that they were never lovers, but his solos with her vocals on tracks like 'A Sailboat in the Moonlight', 'On the Sentimental Side', 'Back in Your Own Back Yard' and 'When a Woman Loves a Man' (all 1937) were the musical equivalent of making love. He named her Lady Day, and called her mother the Duchess; she named him Prez, thinking that along with a Duke, an Earl, a Count and a King of Swing there ought to be a President.

Holiday recorded for Milt Gabler's Commodore label, and then for Decca, which backed her with strings: like many jazz artists of that era, she hankered after legitimacy, in the belief that string arrangements bestowed a cachet. In the 1950s she recorded for Verve and CBS (strings conducted by Ray Ellis), and toured Europe; her excellent accompanists included Bobby Tucker, Jimmy Rowles and Mal Waldron. Her career went slowly downhill; she was famous for being a heroin addict, but it was alcohol that killed her, in 1959. Even her later performances were extraordinarily moving. On a famous Timex TV jazz programme in 1957 she sang her own 'Fine and Mellow', and Young was there too; they had not long to live, and little to say to each other, except through their music.

There are too many masterpieces among Wilson's sides to describe them all, but among the highlights is a Chicago session of May 1936, which featured the bass player Israel Crosby, still a teenager, notably on the dramatic 'Blues in C Sharp Minor'; 'Warmin' Up' is a high-spirited tribute to the small-group jazz style just before modern jazz began to evolve. An unusual West Coast date in September 1937, with Wilson, Red Norvo on xylophone, John Simmons on bass and Harry James on trumpet, yielded intimate treatments of Waller's 'Honeysuckle Rose' and 'Ain't Misbehavin''. 'Just a Mood', which stretched to two sides of a 10-inch 78, was an unusually beautiful original.

The success of Wilson's contractor method of making records may have inspired Victor to hire Lionel Hampton to do the same thing in 1937. In his youth Hampton played snare drum in a drum and bugle corps and became a newsboy in Chicago so he could beat the drum in a band sponsored by the *Chicago Defender*. Somewhere along the way he also became familiar with the marimba, and soon hit the road as a drummer; he first recorded in 1929 with Paul Johnson's Quality Serenaders. As a member of Les Hite's band when it backed Louis Armstrong in a Los Angeles club Hampton played Louis's solo from 'Song of the Islands' on orchestral bells, and when the band backed Louis on his recording of 'Memories of You',

Hampton was encouraged to become the first jazzman to record playing the vibraphone. Gladys, his ambitious soon-to-be wife, prompted him to concentrate on it. A few years later he was leading a band at the Paradise Club, and among the musicians sitting in were Benny Goodman, Gene Krupa and Wilson. The Goodman quartet first recorded in August 1936, and both Wilson and Hampton became famous.

Hampton was more of a showman than Wilson, and moved from chair to chair on various sides. Most of his nearly a hundred small-group items were instrumental, except where he himself sang, as on the charming 'I'm Confessin' (That I Love You)' (the original issue of which was backed with 'Drum Stomp', based on 'Crazy Rhythm', with Hamp on drums) and 'On the Sunny Side of the Street'. One of his best-known records, the latter featured Johnny Hodges, and was backed with an uptempo romp on Vincent Youmans's 'I Know That You Know'. From the same date as 'Drum Stomp' came 'Piano Stomp' (based on 'Shine'), and Hampton also played piano on 'Twelfth Street Rag' (1939) at what seemed like an incredibly fast tempo, yet it was not too fast for his fleet two-fingered style. He played the right-hand piano part on 'Wizzin' the Wizz' while Clyde Hart played the left-hand part, and drums on 'Big Jam in the Wigwam' while Cozy Cole concentrated on the tom-toms.

Among the musicians at a session in September 1939 were Benny Carter, Coleman Hawkins, Chu Berry and Ben Webster, as well as the young Dizzy Gillespie, and Charlie Christian in the rhythm section; that date included 'Hot Mallets' and Carter's 'When Lights are Low'. The parade of sidemen used on the Wilson and Hampton records names most of the stars of the bands of Ellington, Basie, Calloway and Goodman. Pianist Jess Stacy was an asset at the first few Hampton sessions, and Hampton used no fewer than eleven of the best drummers of the era, not counting himself. The rhythm section on 'Jack the Bellboy' and 'Central Avenue Breakdown', made in Hollywood in 1940, was the Nat Cole Trio. 'Bellboy' has at least three hands on the keyboard.

As Stanley Dance pointed out in his notes for an RCA set of the complete Hampton sessions, one of the joys of the recordings is the chance to hear musicians who were not recorded often enough.

Dance singles out pianist Marlowe Morris, who was influenced by Art Tatum. Hampton's showmanship was always evident, and as his series wore on, along with all the beautiful jazz there was much joyful jive, with some forward-sounding harmonies and more than a hint of the West Coast rhythm and blues that would soon be under way. Listen, for example, to '(Latch on to Some) Dough-rey-mi', written by Southern, Cole and Hampton, and sung by the 'Hampton Rhythm Boys'. The interaction of Cole's piano and Hampton's vibraphone on this track occasionally predicts the sound of the George Shearing Quintet, which would be enormously popular a decade later. Another interesting thing about the whole series is the guitar players, from the quiet competence of Goodman's sideman Allen Reuss to Danny Barker, Charlie Christian, Al Casey, Freddie Green, Ernest Ashley, Teddy Bunn, Irving Ashby and Cole's Oscar Moore, several of whom played electric instruments.

The Nat Cole Trio used an uncommon instrumentation: piano, guitar and bass. The drummer didn't show up for their first gig, and they decided they didn't need one. Cole later became one of the most popular vocalists in the world, and deservedly so, but the trio's records did well on the jukeboxes, and it is too easily forgotten that his modern-sounding Hines-inspired keyboard was very influential, on such different musicians as Oscar Peterson and Bill Evans.

Hampton formed a big band which began recording for Decca in late 1941, and led it well into the 1950s. It was a crowd-pleaser – critics often ridiculed its theatrical aspect – but among its stars was young tenor saxophonist Illinois Jacquet. (Critics overlooked his skill as a ballad player for years because it didn't fit their thesis of Jacquet as a honker; he began recording as a leader in 1945, and in 1988 led a big band at jazz festivals.) Hampton was still a sure bet in the late 1980s if you wanted to have a good time; his ability to swing and to inspire younger musicians has had an incalculable effect.

An unusual and successful sextet was that of bass player John Kirby, the 'biggest little band in the land'. The group began to come together as 52nd Street in New York became a meeting place for jazz fans. On their first hit record (as the Claude Thornhill Orchestra in 1937) they backed Maxine Sullivan singing 'Loch Lomond'; that band included Thornhill (piano and arranger), Frankie Newton (trumpet), Pete Brown (alto saxophone), Babe Russin (tenor saxophone), Buster Bailey (clarinet), Kirby (double bass) and O'Neill Spencer (drums). They were Buster Bailey and his Rhythm Busters with slightly different personnel, then John Kirby and his Onyx Club Boys with the classic line-up, and later John Kirby and his Orchestra: Kirby, Spencer, Bailey, Charlie Shavers (trumpet), Russell Procope (alto saxophone) and Billy Kyle (piano). Shavers's composition 'Undecided' was a hit in 1939; Shavers was almost as highly regarded as Roy Eldridge then, and also wrote 'Pastel Blue'; most of the Kirby group's arrangements were his.

Kirby and Sullivan were married, and the band became one of the most successful black groups in the country, performing at high-class hotel dates and on a radio show called *Flow Gently Sweet Rhythm*, on which Sullivan sang folksongs such as 'If I Had a Ribbon Bow' and 'Molly Malone' (recorded under her name for a different label). The group also appeared on *Duffy's Tavern* and the *Chamber Music Society of Lower Basin Street*, a popular pseudo-jazz radio spot directed by NBC staffer Henry 'Hot Lips' Levine; it featured Dinah Shore, and had guests like Sidney Bechet and Jelly Roll Morton. All this was extraordinary exposure for a black band, and a tribute to its musical qualities. It was a quiet chamber group (Shavers usually played with a mute) and the arrangements, though tricky and highly stylized, were studded with lively solos. Its similarity to Wilson's stemmed from its elegance and the presence of Billy Kyle, who worked with Louis Armstrong's All Stars from 1953. Anybody who played with that group in its later years was taken for granted, but Kyle had already been an influential and underrated stylist for many years by then. His technique was the equal of Wilson's, but he had a brighter and more rhythmic side, perhaps influenced by Earl Hines. As J. R. Taylor put it in a sleeve-note for the Smithsonian Institution: 'Kyle's rising tremolo lunge behind Bailey [in 'Sweet Georgia Brown'] is probably unique in jazz accompaniment before Cecil Taylor.'

Kirby and Sullivan were divorced, the war wrecked the band's line-up and the post-war world was not interested: the group's big success lasted only a couple of years, and its style had no sequel. This was partly for the same reason that such excellent musicians as

Shavers, Billy Butterfield, Roy Eldridge, Rex Stewart and Red Allen were, in general, not as highly rewarded as they should have been. After the war there was an absurd critical division into 'dixieland' and 'modern' camps, so that the great mainstream graduates of the Swing Era got lost in the shuffle, a loss which record companies and broadcasters did nothing to prevent.

Procope, of course, subsequently played for twenty-eight years with Duke Ellington; Shavers played in the interracial studio band of Raymond Scott (later music director on the radio and television chart show *Your Hit Parade*, whose vocalist, Dorothy Collins, he married). Scott's arrangements, for example, 'In an Eighteenth Century Dining Room' and 'Dinner Music for a Pack of Hungry Cannibals', were slick and intricate, like Kirby's, but had little jazz content. Shavers remained popular among those with long memories. On a tour in England in 1969, according to Digby Fairweather, he was playing brilliantly, and was delighted to find electrical sockets in hotel bathrooms marked 'For Shavers Only'. He said, 'Wait till Eldridge sees this!'

52nd Street, New York, became a place where the amount of good music to be heard was almost unbelievable. One of the first big acts on the Street, just as Prohibition was repealed in 1933, was scat singer Leo Watson and his Five Spirits of Rhythm, a group which used a suitcase as a drum and played with whisk brooms and three tipples (novelty guitars that sounded like ukuleles). Brass players Joe Riley and Eddie Farley used a novelty tune in their act on the Street; 'The Music Goes Round and Round (and It Comes Out Here)' suddenly became a huge fluke hit, and the Riley–Farley Orchestra had one of the money-making versions. Violinist Stuff Smith and his Onyx Club Boys, with Jonah Jones on trumpet and Cozy Cole on drums, made a name on the Street in 1936 with 'I'se a Muggin'' and 'You'se a Viper' (with a vocal by Jones). The Kirby Sextet too started on the Street. By the early 1940s Art Tatum, Billie Holiday, Coleman Hawkins, Fats Waller and many more might virtually all be heard playing on the Street at once. The Street was mostly a venue for small groups, but Count Basie's band first made it big there in 1937 at the Famous Door (whose name derived from an old door it had which was covered with autographs). Other clubs, mostly in what were called 'English basements' under brownstone houses, included the Hickory House, the Yacht Club, Kelly's Stable and the Three Deuces. The Street was so successful that musicians starting a club where they could meet were soon pushed out of their own place by the tourists and fans. Today the brownstones have been replaced by steel and glass buildings occupied by banks.

Independent labels were being formed for the specific purpose of recording small-group jazz; the first one in the USA was Commodore. Milt Gabler began selling records in his father's radio shop in New York in 1926; the Commodore Music Shop became a hang-out for fans and musicians, and the records soon replaced the radio parts. Gabler was responsible for several firsts: his was probably the first record shop to have browsing bins arranged by artist, and he was the first to reissue classic discs. He began by custom-ordering pressings of out-of-print records, because he knew he could sell three hundred copies of, say, 'Pinetop's Boogie Woogie', even if it took a couple of years. But in the case of that title Vocalion decided that if Gabler wanted to buy so many copies of it, they would press a few extra and sell them to his competitors. So Gabler formed the first record club, the United Hot Clubs of America. He also hired jazz clubs on Sunday afternoons offering free jam sessions to music fans. (When other clubs copied Gabler, they charged admission, but still did not pay the musicians.)

The world's first specialized jazz record label was Swing in France, which began because not enough jazz records were available there. The first release in 1937 was the legendary Benny Carter session. 'Honeysuckle Rose' and 'Crazy Rhythm' were played by a line-up that Carter has re-created several times: himself and Alix Combelle on alto saxophones and Coleman Hawkins and André Ekyan on tenor; the rhythm section included Django Reinhardt on guitar, Stéphane Grappelly on piano, Eugène D'Hellemes on bass and Tommy Benford on drums. In January 1938 Gabler's first recording session was with Eddie Condon and his Windy City Seven: Pee Wee Russell, Bud Freeman, Bobby Hackett, drummer George Wettling, bassist Artie Bernstein and Jess Stacy (whose hands were still sore the day after Benny Goodman's Carnegie Hall concert). The hornmen were all among the finest musicians of their generation, but still underrated by the general public because they were not recorded often enough or properly promoted by the music industry, interested then as now primarily in a fast buck. Gabler was also the first to list the complete personnel on the record label.

In April 1939 Columbia lent Billie Holiday to Commodore because they did not want to issue 'Strange Fruit', a song by poet Lewis Allen about lynching, which Billie had made up her mind to record. An early protest recording, its tragic power is undiminished today. The backing band, with which Billie was appearing at Café Society, was led by trumpeter Frankie Newton, who had left the Kirby Sextet just as it went on to its great success (he and Kirby were rivals for the affection of Maxine Sullivan). Café Society, a club started by a shoe salesman named Barney Josephson, with some help and advice from John Hammond and others, was a place which practised discrimination only in favour of good music, and was popular for a decade. One of the other sides made that day was 'Fine and Mellow', which Gabler titled and helped to write; it was intended to be similar to 'Billie's Blues', which Holiday had recorded in 1936 at her first session as a leader. When Decca Records rang to inquire about the new song, Gabler knew that it must be getting jukebox plays, and he quickly registered its composition in Holiday's name before any covers were made.

From 1941 Gabler also worked for Decca; but he kept Commodore going into the 1950s. The complete Commodore reissue programme embarked upon by Mosaic Records of Stamford, Connecticut, in 1988, which fills dozens of LPs in three massive sets, is full of priceless material, the peak of which (for me, anyway) is the previously mentioned Kansas City Six session of September 1938, with Lester Young playing gorgeous clarinet (on a metal instrument), Buck Clayton on trumpet, Eddie Durham on electric guitar and Basie's rhythm section of Freddie Green, Walter Page and Jo Jones. Not to mention fourteen solos by Willie 'the Lion' Smith, Coleman Hawkins sides, clarinet quartet recordings by Edmond Hall and Pee Wee Russell, and too much more to list here.

When Harry Lim emigrated to the USA from Batavia (now Djakarta) in Indonesia in 1939, he was already a jazz fan. He began producing jam sessions and from 1943 produced records for Eric

Bernay's Keynote, until then a left-wing folk label which had recorded the Almanac Singers. One of the first jazz dates at Keynote was also the first solo session by Dinah Washington, a unique and still influential vocalist who had been discovered and re-named by Lionel Hampton. (Her real name was Ruth Lee Jones.) Leonard Feather produced the date and wrote most of the material; 'Salty Papa' and 'Evil Gal Blues' were hits in the black chart. The group from Hampton's band included Texas tenor saxophonist Arnett Cobb (making his recording début) and pianist Milt Buckner (later more famous as an organist, who had invented the 'locked hands' chordal keyboard style that was soon done to death by a generation of keyboard players). Hampton came along to help out, playing drums on one of the four sides recorded and piano on another. The best-known (and best-selling) Lim productions were those by Lester Young at a session of four tunes, made the day before the Dinah Washington date, in a quartet with Johnny Guarnieri, Slam Stewart and Sid Catlett. It was bettered only by four more tracks three months later, this time 12-inch 78s by a quintet with Basie and his rhythm section. The one track of which an alternative take was not made is 'Lester Leaps In' – it was perfect in one take.

In less than four years Lim made well over three hundred sides. His main aim was to indulge himself (though it earned him everlasting gratitude from jazz fans) by recording people who did not get many chances to record, such as trumpeter Joe Thomas, Chicago guitarist George Barnes, Milt Hinton, Willie Smith, Babe Russin, Manny Klein, tenor saxophonist Herbie Haymer and several members of the Woody Herman herd, including trombonist Bill Harris and bass player Chubby Jackson; also Red Norvo, trumpeters Jonah Jones and Roy Eldridge, Gene Sedric, Red Rodney . . . and too many more to list.

Of the several fine Coleman Hawkins dates, the most fascinating is the one with the Sax Ensemble of May 1944, at which 12-inch 78s were made. The group comprised Catlett (drums), Guarnieri (piano), Al Lucas (double bass), Tab Smith (alto saxophone and arranger – he had worked for Basie and Millinder, among others), Hawkins and Don Byas (tenor saxophones) and Harry Carney (baritone saxophone). The septet sounds like a much larger group, thanks to Smith's arrangements and the sound of four great reedmen playing together. To pick out just one track: 'On the Sunny Side of the Street' begins with a Smith solo (very different from that of Johnny Hodges on the classic recording of the same tune made by Lionel Hampton several years earlier) and ends with a dazzling Smith cadenza, which is several seconds longer on the second take and perfectly realized.

Keynote went out with a bang: two trio sessions by the young pianist Lennie Tristano, the last produced by Feather. Tristano's advanced harmonic ideas were enormously influential, but he concentrated on teaching rather than performing, and recorded all too little; the Keynote sessions yielded tracks that were not released for decades. Lim lost control (to Mercury Records) of recordings he had made using much of his own money; he later worked at the Liberty Music Shop (which, like Commodore, had its own label for a while) and, in its heyday from 1956 to 1973, for Sam Goody's record shop, where he was renowned as the world's most knowledgeable record-shop assistant. In 1972 he formed the Famous Door label and was one of those responsible for discovering Scott Hamilton, today's enormously popular Swing Era style tenor saxophonist.

Other independent jazz labels of the period included HRS (Hot Record Society), Solo Art (which recorded, among others, Chicago's Jimmy Yancey, one of the most distinctive of boogie-woogie piano players, with the accent on the blues rather than the boogie), Bob Thiele's Signature label and, the most famous of all, Blue Note. Thiele worked as an announcer on jazz radio shows in 1936, was a bandleader, editor and publisher of *Jazz Magazine*, and formed Signature in 1939, when he was still a teenager. He was among the first to record pianist Erroll Garner, and made small-group dates by Coleman Hawkins, Lester Young, Lockjaw Davis and Julian Dash. Some of the Hawkins and Young sides were 12-inch masters; it was typical of these small labels to attempt to give the artists room to blow, even though 12-inch records were less commercially viable. It was a Signature recording of Davis's 'Lockjaw' that gave him his nickname. Dash had played with Erskine Hawkins, and his tracks for Signature, with Kyle on piano, are fascinating examples of what was intended to get on Harlem jukeboxes in 1950; the smoochy 'My Silent Love' is drenched in echo.

Thiele also recorded four sessions in 1944–5 by Flip Phillips, tenor saxophone star of Woody Herman's band, with other Hermanites in the backing groups. Three sessions with Anita O'Day in 1947–8 paid a dividend: the novelty 'Hi Ho Trailus Boot Whip', arranged by Sy Oliver, was a pop hit.

Blue Note, the best-known of these labels, was formed by German immigrant Alfred Lion in 1939 to record the boogie-woogie pianos of Meade 'Lux' Lewis and Albert Ammons. The Port of Harlem Jazzmen included Ammons, then Lewis, Frankie Newton and, on some tracks, Sidney Bechet, whose 'Summertime' was an instant classic. Lion was joined by his fellow Berliner and childhood friend, Frank Wolff. In 1941 they recorded Edmond Hall's quartet: Hall, Lewis (celesta – they recorded him on harpsichord the same year), Israel Crosby (bass) and Charlie Christian (acoustic guitar). Its 'Profoundly Blue' was a classic. Blue Note too made 12-inch sides. They often recorded at night, which was far more convenient for the musicians, and provided food and drink for them. The unusual attention to the artists' welfare and the distinctive label artwork (overseen by Wolff) heralded the beginning of an illustrious chapter in the record business. The label specialized in 'swingtets' led by tenor saxophonists John Hardee and Ike Quebec, whose 'Blue Harlem' (1944) was another jukebox hit. Quebec joined the staff, and it was due partly to his influence that Blue Note was the first to record Thelonious Monk as a leader, in 1947.

But that is getting ahead of our story. Blue Note was only one of the mostly independent labels documenting the changes in popular music in the 1940s, a decade that needs close attention.

11

The 1940s: War and Other Calamities

The war years are remembered both in Britain and in the USA as an egalitarian time. In Britain food rationing and fairer distribution brought about the best diet some of the population had ever seen, and illnesses such as rickets, caused by poor nutrition, began to disappear. In the USA country boy and city slicker alike served in the armed forces; dance bands and black artists like Fats Waller and Art Tatum made V-discs for the GIs' jukeboxes; and all were exposed to each other's cultures *en masse* for the first time.

The combination of world war and music business shenanigans caused profound changes in music itself. The history of the music business is studded with instances of panic, doomsaying and dramatic events, and the participants themselves – be they music publisher, president of the American Society of Composers, Authors and Publishers (ASCAP) or a lawyer working for BMI – were often outsized personalities. In the late 1920s, for example, it was thought that Tin Pan Alley was moving to Hollywood, and that if the film producers took over completely, it would be the end of ASCAP. The constant buying and selling of music publishing houses was often due to jockeying for power in the industry, which began to worry about how charges would be made for television music years before most people had ever seen a television set. Solutions usually failed to foresee new problems, and some of the disputes directly affected the nature of the music. The decade of the 1940s, while dominated by the war, provided two cases in which self-interested organizations forced changes which had totally unexpected results and were not welcomed by those whose interests were supposedly being served: the ASCAP strike against broadcasters and the musicians' union strikes against the record companies.

ASCAP was the first and is still the largest of the American performing rights societies, which collect and distribute royalties to members from the use of their music. In 1915 ASCAP won a lawsuit against a restaurant in New York City in which Victor Herbert's music was played by a small orchestra. The decision of the United States Supreme Court was that, whether or not use of the music helped the restaurant to make a profit, 'the purpose of employing [the music] is profit, and that is enough'. This allowed ASCAP to insist on licensing fees from vaudeville managers, record companies and then broadcasters. ASCAP grew from 182 members in 1914 to more than 33,000 by the early 1980s. It is affiliated with societies in 40 other countries and runs such annual awards as the Nathan Burkan Memorial Competition for law students' essays on copyright law (started in 1938, in honour of a man who began as Witmark's lawyer) and the ASCAP–Deems Taylor Awards for writing on music (started in 1968).

For years, ASCAP was seen as just another self-serving attempt to create a monopoly in an industry that was full of them. The Board of Music Trade had been formed in 1855 to fix sheet music prices and to fight music teachers, who were middlemen, selling music to their pupils. The National Association of Music Teachers was formed in 1857. Later there were the Music Publishers Protective Association (MPPA), the Vaudeville Managers Protective Association and so on. At one point in the early history of ASCAP the MPPA collected but did not distribute millions of dollars in royalties, cash that ASCAP was supposed to pay to its members in order to justify itself. These organizations constantly squabbled with one another, especially as changes occurred in the music business; publishers joined and left them according to where they saw their best interests.

ASCAP was inevitably dominated by publishers. At one point the classification scheme according to annual turnover included an AAA category of only one publisher, E. B. Harms, who therefore raked off the fattest payments. Songwriters were not even allowed to join unless they had had several hits, and they relied on their publishers to share out the money fairly, which often did not happen. In 1932 ASCAP's operating expenses soaked up 32 cents of every dollar taken in. Its public image was so poor that it considered hiring a public relations firm, but instead it made a deal agreeing low rates with radio stations owned by newspapers, in order to be treated more kindly by those papers.

ASCAP's first agreement with the National Association of Broadcasters (NAB) was made in 1932. During the Depression sheet music sales and record sales decreased and vaudeville was dying; by then it was obvious that radio was the most important source of commercial entertainment in America, while a move to amend copyright law to free music from licence fees had been defeated in Congress. By the 1932 agreement ASCAP was entitled to fees of 3 per cent of 'time sales' (advertising income) rising to 5 per cent in 1935, with a smaller fixed fee for 'sustaining' (non-profit) programmes. Many broadcasters regarded the 1932 agreement as a sell-out, and network affiliates wanted networks to be responsible for the fees for network programmes. There was always plenty of ferment among publishers. Warner had acquired several important publishing houses and held out for a larger slice of the ASCAP pie: for the first half of 1935 the public did not hear any music on the radio by Romberg, Herbert, Gershwin and Rodgers or from Warner's many musical films; more ominously, the public did not appear to notice.

Warner tried to buy the Mutual Broadcasting System, but was rejected in 1936. Broadcasters and others had looked in vain for sources of non-ASCAP music. Schemes to compete with radio, using a signal riding piggy-back on the electricity supply, had been proposed as early as 1922. Muzak was formed in 1934, but the Society of European Stage Authors and Composers (SESAC) won a court case against a hotel in 1936 which helped to thwart Muzak's plans, and in 1938 Muzak finally failed to receive permission from the Federal Communications Commission to compete with the networks.

With cable television ubiquitous today in the USA, it would seem that this ruling has been undone, but meanwhile Muzak turned to supplying special music services for offices and factories, which became ubiquitous even sooner. This has profoundly cheapened and degraded music; no matter whether such services are operated by Muzak or one of its competitors, no matter what the quality of any individual service, the force-feeding of music is ultimately bad for it. In the 1930s Muzak had an agreement with ASCAP, but also relied upon Associated Music Publishers (AMP), which was made up of about 150 small US publishers and some European ones and effectively a holding company for non-ASCAP music. (Muzak's transcribed-music library service used an AMP label.)

In October 1939 Sydney Kaye, a member of CBS's law firm, proposed that broadcasters set up their own licensing agency, relying on SESAC, AMP and other sources, and luring some established composers away from ASCAP with promises of fairer treatment: they would be allowed to retain all non-broadcasting rights, such as publishing and stage performance. Broadcast Music Incorporated (BMI), was chartered, using funds pledged by broadcasters in expectation of an ASCAP strike against them. Many broadcasters saw BMI as yet another monopoly, but it was clear that they were not going to get away with paying nothing, and they soon fell into line. Furthermore, ASCAP was over-confident and insensitive: in two states where laws instigated by broadcasters prohibited ASCAP from interstate commerce, ASCAP offered a per-piece agreement to broadcasters, rather than a licence fee; broadcasters in other states had wanted this for years, and angrily signed with BMI. When its new demand was presented, just before the deadline of 1 April 1940 for the start of BMI's operations, ASCAP did not bother to invite the NAB's agent, Neville Miller, and the meeting ended with harsh words between CBS executives and Oscar Hammerstein II. The new demand was for 3 per cent of income for smaller stations, rising to 7.5 per cent for regional and national chains, as well as sustaining fees. ASCAP's strike against the broadcasters began at the end of 1940.

Kaye's vision of the future of radio was as great as that of Sarnoff and Paley; he already knew the power of it. In 1938 only 368 tunes received more than 47 per cent of the airplay; by September 1940 BMI was providing 14 printed popular songs a week. In 1939, it was later revealed, 13 ASCAP publishers had dominated *Your Hit Parade*, the nation's top chart showcase, collecting 60 per cent of the money paid to ASCAP's 165 members. It was clear that radio helped make hits and could dictate its own terms, and also that the terms being offered were fair. BMI signed M. M. Cole of Chicago, a leading publisher of hillbilly songs; E. B. Marks moved to BMI and Ralph Peer formed a BMI company; new firms such as Acuff–Rose joined BMI. The eccentric and musically conservative tobacco magnate who was behind *Your Hit Parade* would probably have preferred to go back to ASCAP's music of the 1910 era, but reluctantly agreed to broadcast only songs available to radio. During the strike no composition published by a member of ASCAP could be broadcast, except on independent stations that broadcast little live music anyway. In 1940 ASCAP members had sold about 300,000 pieces of sheet music a week, but this dropped to 120,000 a month.

A great deal of music that was out of copyright was performed, from Stephen Foster's songs to 'Tchaikovsky's Piano Concerto in B Flat', an extremely successful classical rip-off by Freddy Martin that was number one for eight weeks that year, with ASCAP making not a penny. The Russian folksong 'Song of the Volga Boatmen' was a big hit for Glenn Miller in early 1941, followed by 'Perfidia', a Latin tune published by Ralph Peer. Peer had scooped up Mexican and South American music, but ASCAP had refused to handle the new companies in which Peer had holdings because they were privately owned for profit (as though ASCAP members were not interested in money). ASCAP now went south of the border, in search of music with which to head off BMI, only to find that Peer had already got the best. 'The Peanut Vendor' had come from a Cuban revue, and was a success in the USA in 1930; it later became part of Peer International, and in 1941 the reissue of Louis Armstrong's delightful 1931 version was another hit. Bandleaders and composers were not fools; Charlie Barnet's 'Redskin Rhumba', for example, recorded in October 1940, was registered with a BMI company, so that it could be played on the radio, and was a hit the same year. It was at this time that Bing Crosby had hits with 'Brahms' Lullaby' and with Floyd Tillman's 'It Makes No Difference Now', a country hit published by Peer. The awful truth began to dawn: the world could get along without ASCAP music.

Various suits had been pending in federal courts against nearly all the principals, and the courts had to arbitrate, bringing order into the marketplace. The networks' creeping monopoly in the increasingly profitable industry was dealt with: General Electric and Westinghouse had disposed of their stock in RCA in 1931, and NBC stations were handed to Sarnoff (while in 1932–3 stations reluctantly began to allow prices to be mentioned in advertising). RCA/NBC had to sell off the Blue Network, which became the American Broadcasting Company. The networks were requested to divest themselves of their booking agencies; CBS's Columbia Concerts Corporation, for classical music, in which Paley still had an interest, was sold to Arthur Judson, while its pop talent agency was sold to the Chicago-based Music Corporation of America. Payment for music at source was required of the networks, removing a headache for the affiliates; all music users were offered the choice of a blanket licence, per-use fees or per-programme fees. ASCAP was barred from exclusive rights to members' work, freeing them for direct licensing, and the self-perpetuating board of directors was abolished by giving members a right to vote for it. Discrimination among similar types of user was banned.

BMI's contract of April 1941 charged a flat fee of 1.5 per cent of income to the networks, while the pressure on ASCAP was mounting: publishing houses were losing money, and Hollywood music was being kept in the can. Walt Disney, for example, anxious to get the songs from *Dumbo* on the air, instructed Irving Berlin Inc. to license them either through BMI or without charge, otherwise Disney would start his own BMI company. In July 1941 ASCAP offered the networks a licence fee of 2.75 per cent of income, considerably less than the 5 per cent they had been collecting. Many smaller broadcasters were opposed to any settlement with ASCAP, but the networks and ASCAP knew that lack of a settlement would lead to the collapse of ASCAP, chaos and anti-trust suits against the networks, so the deal was made.

Broadcasting was booming, and there was plenty of money for all. ASCAP, divested of its internal squabbling and corruption, became more prosperous than ever, and more or less respectable at last. But the formation of BMI had results reaching far beyond competition in the field. BMI's future was not at all secure at first. It soon offered advances to songwriters on getting a song recorded, and doubled the royalty rate from 1 penny per performance to 2 but it also raised the rate paid to publishers to 4 cents, naïvely expecting publishers to share the pay-out fairly with writers. Meanwhile ASCAP's distribution system had been revised and was now fairer to writers, so mainstream songwriters continued to join ASCAP – except for authors of black and hillbilly music, who could now receive advances and royalties from BMI that they had never had from ASCAP. Furthermore, after the war government restrictions on new radio stations were lifted, and by 1950 there were 1,517 independent stations compared with 627 network affiliates; half of the independents served single-station local markets, and courted them with more country music and rhythm and blues than the networks did. The outcome of all this was that BMI members were publishing a good deal of black and hillbilly music, and BMI unwittingly fed and watered the seedbed from which rock'n'roll would grow.

Only two years after BMI was formed *Billboard* began printing the first black chart (the 'Harlem Hit Parade'), and two years later, in 1944, it printed the first country chart ('Most Played Juke Box Folk Records'). Minority musics were becoming more profitable, and the major record labels, having cut back recording of minority musics during the Depression, now fell behind in serving these newly lucrative markets. Dozens of now legendary rhythm and blues labels were soon formed, all of this signalling the beginning of the end of the domination of New York and Tin Pan Alley. In retrospect, the rise of rhythm and blues, crossover hits, rockabilly and so forth was inevitable.

None of this is to be regretted now; those of us who grew up after 1940 would hardly wish to trade the delicious shock of Amos Milburn's 'Let Me Go Home, Whiskey', or Carl Perkins's 'Blue Suede Shoes', for ASCAP's continuing restriction of the music market to the products of Tin Pan Alley. Given the pop charts of the early 1950s, many listeners were bound to notice that more interesting things were happening elsewhere, and again we find apparently unconnected events combining.

BMI affiliated with overseas societies, and from 1944 included the

American Composer Alliance: Roy Harris, Walter Piston, Elliott Carter, Charles Ives and others became BMI composers. BMI has sponsored awards to student composers since 1951; its Musical Theatre Workshop (begun in 1959) and more recent Alternative Chorus Workshop have their best works presented annually to audiences of agents, publishers, producers and record company executives. BMI has long since become respectable, and in any case the competition of minority musics by itself could not have brought Tin Pan Alley and the Swing Era crashing down. There were many other factors, but among the most foolish were the musicians' union strikes.

James Caesar Petrillo was a pianist and bandleader in Chicago; his girl vocalist at one point was Frances Octavia Smith, later known as Dale Evans. Petrillo was already active in the Chicago local of the musicians' union in 1934 when it kicked the Kansas City band led by Harlan Leonard and Thamon Hayes out of town, whereupon Hayes, disgusted, quit the road, and Leonard had to start again. Petrillo, a combative little man who is said to have refused to shake hands for fear of germs, ranted against 'canned music' at the 1937 convention of the American Federation of Musicians (AFM), and was elected leader of the national AFM in 1940.

Record labels bore the legend 'unlicensed for public broadcasting', which was widely ignored. A suit had been brought by RCA, and Supreme Court Judge Learned Hand ruled in 1940 that copyright was not infringed by the playing of a record on the radio. The decision was wrong and unfair, and a contradiction of the decision which had legitimized ASCAP in 1915, but Petrillo and the record companies were also shortsighted: broadcasting helped to sell records. It seems incredible now that the rivalry between records and radio had lasted for more than a decade, when the two industries were so important to each other, but it must be remembered that Martin Block's *Make Believe Ballroom*, the first noteworthy DJ format, only got started at WNEW in New York City in 1935. On the other hand, Milt Gabler was in no doubt about the value of radio: as a record retailer and at Block's suggestion, he was happy to sell the station not only Commodore records but also all the new releases from the other labels. In every industry it is often the people who do the business who make the best decisions, and in the music business, until more recent times anyway, they were often people who liked music. It is the power-brokers at the top who most often get it wrong.

Petrillo commissioned bandleader Ben Selvin, who was already experienced in both recording and radio and had been a Muzak executive, to determine whether recordings were putting musicians out of live work. Selvin reported to an AFM convention in 1941 that record labels paid millions of dollars annually to musicians, and that union action was not the answer to problems caused by the mechanization of music. He received a standing ovation, but while the membership, and especially the bandleaders, agreed with Selvin, Petrillo demanded that record companies refuse to allow records to be played on the radio and jukeboxes, though they had already tried that. Then, on 1 August 1942, he ordered musicians to stop recording.

This had several effects. Studio time was booked solid in the weeks leading up to the strike, as artists tried to get their work recorded before the drought began; this should have been evidence enough that the strike was a mistake, but too often unions forget that their members are likely to know which side of the bread is buttered. It is impossible to know to what extent minority musics were given another boost; presumably there were blacks and hillbillies who did not belong to the union and did as they pleased during the strike. Old recordings were reissued: Dorsey, Miller and Ellington all had hits with sides recorded as early as 1938, some of them entering the charts for the second time. Frank Sinatra's 'All or Nothing at All', made with Harry James in 1939 and unnoticed at the time, reached number one in June 1943, while Bing Crosby's 'Sweet and Lovely', a hit in 1931, was again in the charts in 1944. But worst of all from the point of view of jazz and big-band fans, to say nothing of musicians, the era of the pop singer began.

The vocalists with the bands, such as Sinatra, Dick Haymes and Perry Como, and Kitty Kallen, Rosemary Clooney, Peggy Lee, Kay Starr, Georgia Gibbs, Margaret Whiting and Jo Stafford, had been becoming popular anyway, and they began their rise to domination in the post-war years. They were more logical heart-throbs for fans who bought records. In theory, anybody could sing, while it took many years to learn how to play a saxophone or a trumpet to professional standard. The words to the songs were important to the fans, who had been brought up on a steady diet of romantic love in songs and films, and were only too willing to imagine singing to each other. This theory of the 'singer as amateur' was carried to absurdity by the musicians' union, which did not allow vocalists to join.

Singers recorded a cappella during the strike: Haymes had eight hits backed by the Song Spinners, and Sinatra had seven with the Bobby Tucker Singers, with no instrumentalists at all. (The Song Spinners had a number one wartime hit of their own: 'Comin' in on a Wing and a Prayer'.) In mid-1943 Bing Crosby's recordings of two songs from *Oklahoma!* with Trudy Erwin and the Sportsmen Glee Club were highly successful, while the biggest hit of the decade was the Mills Brothers' 'Paper Doll', which had no backing group. At a time when the demand for union musicians was greater than ever before because so many of them were being drafted, Petrillo helped the record business to discover that it could manage without them: singers were cheaper to record (later with studio musicians on salary) than name bands. Booking agents got the same message, as for various reasons big-band venues were already closing during the war.

The record labels eventually had to cave in: Decca signed with the union in September 1943, Capitol a month later, RCA and Columbia in November 1944. The War Labor Board had instructed Petrillo to lift his recording ban; Edward Wallerstein at Columbia wrote a bitter letter to Judge Vinson of the Office of Economic Stabilization, which ended:

The economic pressures on us are such that we can wait no longer and must now either sign or go out of business. Since no action has been taken by the government, we have today entered into an agreement with Mr Petrillo's union which will include provision for payments by us directly to the Union, the principle which we have resisted for more than 27 months, which we contested before government bureaus for sixteen months and which, although successful in our contests, we are finally accepting because of the government's unwillingness or incapacity to enforce its orders.

Just in case he had not done enough damage, when disc jockeys were becoming ubiquitous and the record business was booming, Petrillo called a second recording ban in 1948, by which time many bands had folded. The result of the strikes was not more money for the musicians making the records, who had lost income through not being able to record during the strikes, but a tax on records which swelled the union's coffers; some of it was used to pay for free concerts. The best musicians thus subsidized the rest, and, according to a War Labor Board report, two-thirds of the union's rank and file did not depend on music for a full-time living anyway.

Petrillo was almost as well known in his day as John L. Lewis, the beetle-browed leader of the USA miners' union. To be absolutely fair, he had to get something right occasionally: Charlie Barnet wrote that when a Las Vegas club-owner wanted him to play in a car park, Petrillo wired him: 'Special scale for bands playing in a parking lot: leader $50,000.00, sidemen $1,500.00.' 'We never played in the parking lot,' recalled Barnet. In Chicago Petrillo had made the first agreement with a radio station and kept the peace between musicians and hotels and theatres. Nevertheless, Petrillo's Chicago local was violent and segregated – the city had been a centre of recording of black music until a strike in the mid-1930s priced it out of the market for a decade – and the damage Petrillo ultimately did to the big bands was immense. Bass player Red Callender is scathing about the musicians' union in his autobiography *Unfinished Dream* (1985): it was not the national union that integrated white and black locals, but musicians themselves, who also had to sue the union to get their money out of Petrillo's trust funds.

In the meantime, bands that had been going through an interesting formative evolution had not visited the recording studios, and much documentation of the music was lost, except for a few broadcast airchecks. Furthermore, during this period the public heard very little of the new music, which might have prepared listeners for the changes to come, changes which were out of the hands of the puny power-brokers.

The Second World War was the end of an era for all sorts of political, social and economic reasons, and the Big Band Era may have been coming to a close anyway. Bandleader Alvino Rey is one of those who reflected years later that the bands had neglected the dancers, who had made Goodman such a big success in 1935, by concentrating on flag-wavers and slow smoochers (with heart-throb vocalists) and offering little in between. Artie Shaw, Tommy Dorsey, Gene Krupa, Harry James and others hired string sections, a move which led nowhere in musical terms (partly because there were few arrangers who knew what to do with violins). But the immediate effects on music of the war were obvious. For one thing, country music became a big business.

In 1945 two soldiers in Europe wrote to Bob Wills to say that upon clearing out some 'Jerries' during house-to-house fighting, they had found some old records, one of which was Wills's 'San Antonio Rose'. (A quarter of a century later Apollo 12 astronauts broadcast the song to countless millions around the world, in an impromptu version from outer space.) The band of the early 1940s had been Wills's best, and the Tiffany Music transcriptions (220 selections made for radio stations in 1945–7) are probably the best Wills collection; he continued having hits until 1950, but with smaller and smaller groups. Decca made a new recording of 'San Antonio Rose' for jukeboxes in 1955, but it was not a patch on the original. Spade Cooley's big band filled California dance halls during the war, and he had a huge hit with 'Shame on You' in 1945 (vocal by Tex Williams). But the days of the big band were numbered.

Wills broke up his band in late 1942, when he was drafted into the US Army at the age of almost thirty-eight, not knowing that nothing would ever be the same again. After being discharged in July 1943 he formed the biggest band he ever had – twenty-two musicians and two vocalists – but it did not record, and lasted for only six months. Times had changed: musicians were in short supply, the Depression was over at last and money was more important than loyalty. It was the same story for all the other leaders.

Country music had always been essentially a small-group music. In the late 1940s the singing cowboy Roy Rogers seemed more typical of country music than he was, with such tunes as 'Chickashay Gal' and 'Blue Shadows on the Trail'. His films, with Republic's sunset-like colour process, are still redolent of nostalgia for millions of middle-aged men, especially the ones made with the Sons of the Pioneers. But more authentic country was also booming. Capitol

Records, formed in Hollywood in 1942, was successful with Tex Ritter, and hired West Coast country DJ, bandleader and radio show host Cliffie Stone to build its country list; he signed Tex Williams, Jimmy Wakely, Tennessee Ernie Ford and Merle Travis; Williams's 'Smoke! Smoke! Smoke That Cigarette' (1947) was said to be the label's first million-seller. In 1949 the name of the *Billboard* country chart was changed from 'Folk Music' to 'Country and Western', after long agitation from those who disliked the 'hillbilly' appellation, especially in the West Coast scene that Hollywood had helped to create. Bing Crosby's hits with country songs encouraged more to break through to the pop chart in the form of 'covers', and in a survey immediately after the war Roy Acuff beat Frank Sinatra as the GI's favourite singer. Canadian-born Hank Snow, after many years of trying, achieved lasting stardom in 1950 with 'I'm Movin' On'.

But country music, though it was becoming big business, was kept in a commercial ghetto. The dominant Swing Era style had been a jazz-oriented one, and jazz itself, in a most dramatic development, moved away from mainstream public popularity to become 'modern jazz'.

In 1939, as politicians in Europe prepared to conduct their diplomacy by other means, Coleman Hawkins returned to the USA and formed an octet. In October he recorded 'Body and Soul', and reclaimed his title as the boss of the tenor saxophone. This technically interesting song was written by Johnny Green, an arranger, conductor and composer of film scores; he wrote few songs, but they are of very high quality, and include 'Out of Nowhere' and 'I Cover the Waterfront', also popular among jazz musicians. 'Body and Soul' was described by Alec Wilder as not only innovatory but strange, having 'one of the widest ranges and one of the most complex releases and verses'. It is another example of a high-class work of art that was accepted by the public without a murmur. Virtually a solo with rhythm section, Hawkins's recording was good for romantic dancing and a big hit, but it is also an enduring jazz milestone. His harmonic commentary on the song becomes a lovely series of arpeggios; his controlled passion from the urgency of getting it all in imparts a forward motion, as does the way he divided the beat into unequal parts. Most jazz musicians did this, but Hawk imbued it with further urgency by 'swallowing' the second part of the beat until it almost disappeared.

Hawkins was apparently influenced by the pianist Art Tatum, whose technical wizardry was unique. Born virtually blind, Tatum began to perform as a teenager, accompanied Adelaide Hall and made his first recordings in 1932. He made commercially-oriented records exclusively for Decca well into the 1940s; in 1934 he formed a trio with Slam Stewart on bass and Tiny Grimes (later replaced by Everett Barksdale) on guitar. Incredibly, he was not recorded at all for two years in the late 1940s, but later made solo and small-group albums for Norman Granz. His quartet album with Ben Webster, Red Callender and drummer Bill Douglass, made weeks before he died of uraemia, is one of the most beautiful ever made, though the sets with Buddy DeFranco, Roy Eldridge and Benny Carter are equally valuable.

Tatum acknowledged his debt to Fats Waller, but it was Waller who announced in a club with Tatum present, 'Ladies and gentlemen, I play piano, but tonight, God is in the house.' Tatum was not a composer (except in the sense that every great jazz musician is a composer); he embroidered standards. Using rich rhythmic and harmonic improvisation, he would paint himself into a corner, then miraculously escape, forcing his ideas to work after all. This was over the heads of some listeners, who complained that he played too many notes – which is one reason why his trio recordings were more commercialized than his solos would have been. After-hours recordings made on portable equipment by jazz buff Jerry Newman in 1940–41 show him in a relaxed mood, playing around the dud keys on a battered piano and quoting anything he liked while he did it.

Among Tatum's fans were Rachmaninov and Vladimir Horowitz; Oscar Peterson has a photograph of himself with Horowitz and Tatum. Contrary to popular belief, Tatum was probably not a primary influence on Peterson, though they were friends. Peterson was afraid to play in front of him, but one night, playing in a club, he heard Tatum's voice from the audience: 'Lighten up, Oscar Peterson.' It is doubtful if Tatum could have been a primary influence on anybody, since he would be impossible to copy or imitate, but his complete freedom to do as he pleased, and his insistence on doing so, was of the greatest importance.

The small-group sessions described in the last chapter document some of the changes in music, and a clue can also be heard in the soundtrack of the 1943 film *Stormy Weather*, mentioned earlier. This all-black musical was almost the only one of its kind; the stars, who included Fats Waller, Lena Horne, Bill 'Bojangles' Robinson and Cab Calloway's band, played successful and glamorous characters as well as the downtrodden, albeit restricted to roles as entertainers. In the scene in which Bojangles dances to the music of a combo, although the men are dressed in rags and it takes place on a riverboat, the music is anything but backward-looking: the rhythm section is dominated by bassist Mitt Hinton, who plays the most ecstatically solid accompaniment, and the oompah two-beat style of New Orleans is abolished by the supreme court of music.

The unique harmonic richness of Duke Ellington's music must have been an influence on younger musicians. The success of Ellington's sensational bass player Jimmy Blanton in making the instrument an equal voice in the band was paralleled by that of young drummers like Kenny Clarke and Max Roach (who replaced Clarke in Hawkins's combo in 1943). Clarke became famous for 'dropping bombs' – putting bass drum accents wherever the music seemed to demand them – later explaining (not altogether convincingly) that his foot got tired. This further liberated the drum kit from timekeeping, and the bass player, who had to take over some of that role, often played on the beat instead of slightly behind it as during the Swing Era, again injecting more urgency and forward motion into the music.

Another new voice was that of the guitarist Charlie Christian, who was born in Texas and played in Oklahoma as a teenager. He brought a blues feeling to a new solo instrument, the electric guitar. He was not the first to play it, but the first to invent a vocabulary for it, using the sustained notes of equal value possible with amplification. His swing and his ear for harmony were impeccable, though his lines were full of rhythmic figures which might have become monotonous. But he did not live long enough to develop further, dying young, like Blanton, of tuberculosis. He has been an influence on every jazz guitarist since.

Minton's Playhouse was a Harlem club run by Henry Minton, a former saxophonist; in 1941 he hired manager Teddy Hill, another saxophonist, who had fronted an excellent band in 1936–7. Monday night was Celebrity Night, and not only visiting celebrities but young turks jammed there, playing free or for tips, and the local musicians' unions often turned a blind eye. Clarke, Christian, a strange young pianist called Thelonious Monk and a confident young trumpeter, John Birks 'Dizzy' Gillespie, were among the regulars at Minton's. But Monk and Clarke were the only ones who *worked* there; the others were hanging out. When Gillespie was working on 52nd Street with Benny Carter, Monroe's Uptown House was more convenient after hours; the musicians did not make any money there either, but both Minton and Clark Monroe made plenty of food available.

Milt Hinton lived across the street from Minton's. He described how 'so many kids from downtown, kids that couldn't blow, would come in and they would interrupt'.

So Diz told me on the roof one night at the Cotton Club, 'Now look, when we go down to the jam session, we're gonna say we're gonna play 'I Got Rhythm', but we're gonna use these changes. Instead of using the B-flat and the D-flat, we're gonna use B-flat, D-flat, G-flat or F and we change.' We would do these things on the roof and then we'd go down to Minton's, and all these kids would be up there. 'What're y'all gonna play?' We'd say, 'I Got Rhythm', and we'd start out with this new set of changes ... and eventually they would put their horns away, and we could go on and blow in peace and get our little exercise.

This accelerated what they were doing, according to Gillespie: 'playing, seriously, creating a new dialogue among ourselves, blending our ideas into a new style of music. You only have so many notes, and what makes a style is how you get from one note to the next.'

Another important double bass player was Oscar Pettiford, who had come from the Midwest; he played melody bass like Jimmy Blanton, but he had been influenced by Charlie Christian, a guitarist. At Minton's, Monk and Dizzy would be showing each other things on the keyboard, exploring chords and inventing a new way of

playing. Unfortunately, there are no commercial recordings documenting the crucial period 1943–4 because of the musicians' union strikes.

Gillespie was greatly inspired by the extremely fluent Roy Eldridge,
whom he had replaced in Hill's band in 1937. Gillespie wrote: 'Roy
used to come by Minton's. "Look, you're supposed to be the greatest
trumpet player in the world," Monk used to tell him, "but that's the
best." And he'd point at me . . . Monk'll tell you the truth, whatever
he thinks about it. He's not diplomatic at all.'

As a member of Cab Calloway's band (1939–41) Gillespie had
written tunes like 'Pickin' the Cabbage'; he was already nicknamed
Dizzy. His facility on the trumpet was similar to that of Tatum at the
keyboard: he could do anything, and he was ready to do it. He
worked with Benny Carter, Charlie Barnet and Earl Hines; he also
began writing big-band arrangements, and he had become friends
with Charlie Parker.

Parker, an alto saxophonist, had been a heroin addict since he was
a teenager in Kansas City and was unreliable, which is why he was
not recorded on Keynote by Harry Lim, who admired him. Lim's
operation was based on efficient use of studio time, and Parker might
not show up; he had been fired by Harlan Leonard and went in and
out of Jay McShann's band. In 1978 James Lincoln Collier, in his
mostly useful history of jazz *The Making of Jazz* (1978), speculated
that the reason Parker died young, while Gillespie lived twice as
long, was that Parker had less character. This is ridiculous. Gillespie
and Parker were both black, both the same age, both from poor
families and both brilliant musicians, but Gillespie's stern, loving
father was around until he was ten years old, while Parker was
spoiled by his mother, and his father, like many other African-Americans, had to be a travelling man, for practical purposes no father at
all. The importance of the presence of both parents in the family has
been too well established to be thrown away so easily.

As for Gillespie, he had not acquired his nickname for nothing. He
was fired from Calloway's band for throwing a spitball, and had been
guilty of too many pranks to be believed when he professed his
innocence (though it seems to have been Jonah Jones who was
guilty); afterwards he nicked Calloway with the knife he carried at
the time. A good marriage no doubt helped Gillespie to survive, and

what made this possible, again, was his earlier experience of a stable family life.

Parker tried to play in Kansas City clubs as a teenager, but was not ready. Having been treated with derision, he went away and practised until he could modulate from any key to any other key, perhaps, it has been suggested, because he did not know that he did not need to know that much to play in a band. He was nicknamed Bird after Yardbird, meaning chicken, one of his favourite foods. (Dizzy called him Yard.) On his first visit to New York in 1939 he washed dishes in a club while Art Tatum was playing out front; soon after, while playing 'Cherokee' at a gig, he began to improvise on the higher intervals of the chords, instead of the lower. This required new harmonic resolutions, and was in effect a new tune: he was playing the music he had already heard in his head.

Parker recorded with McShann's band in 1940–41. He played tenor in the Earl Hines band, which also included Gillespie and Billy Eckstine, for decades one of America's favourite vocalists. Eckstine left to form his own band, with Parker, Gillespie and Sarah Vaughan. Again, there were no studio sets by these epochal outfits, but recordings made in a hotel room in 1943 captured Parker on tenor and Gillespie and Eckstine on trumpets, just as the new music was being born.

Dan Morgenstern, in his notes for the complete Commodore recordings, describes one of the recording sessions as 'prototypical mature swing at its finest hour – just before bebop would change things forever'. He is referring to a 1944 date led by drummer Big Sid Catlett, with John Simmons on bass, Ben Webster on tenor saxophone and the interesting Marlowe Morris on piano; any of these men could have played with anybody at the time. Morgenstern is, of course, quite correct; all the same, the changes were already in the air (even at Commodore, which recorded a good deal of what most people thought was dixieland, though it was essentially the Chicago style of the Austin High School Gang). It is easy to make too much of a distinction between 'modern jazz' and the Swing Era, as though we still have a hangover of the awful and ridiculous war of words that went on at the time between the 'mouldy figs' (those who thought that the original New Orleans style, and its Chicago offshoot, were the only true jazz) and the beboppers. The evolution was under way.

The Benny Goodman Sextet sides of 1939–40 (with Christian) already show a tightness and a forward energy, and Georgie Auld on tenor saxophone an insouciance, which was a portent. The Flip Phillips sessions recorded in 1944–5 by Bob Thiele, using white sidemen from Woody Herman's band, were an example of music which is already modern, in comparison with any similar session of only a few years earlier, in the smoothness of the rhythm section, the stylishness of the riffs and other essential features. But it is true that it was in 1943–4 that the most dramatic turning point seems to have been reached, by the young black musicians who were ready to take things another step further – at precisely the time when the music was not being recorded.

The new music came to be called bop, short for bebop or rebop, onomatopoeic in origin from the music itself. The musicians used altered chords and wider intervals, and insisted on choosing a wider range of notes, a process that had been going on in classical music for centuries. Syncopation seemed to disappear altogether in the new, smoother rhythm section, but there were new accents within bars and even between notes, together with phrases of unusual lengths, so that even the rhythmic nature of jazz changed: an intense and technically brilliant music was created, full of pride, sardonic wit and fierce joy. The scene was accompanied by attitudes and language incomprehensible to outsiders; some of this had been pioneered by Lester Young, an influence in more ways than one, but the zany wit of Gillespie was also important.

Tempos were often furiously fast or very slow, but even when the tempo was slow the soloist might play fast, using what sounded to the swing fan like machine-gun runs of semiquavers. At the time the big bands were playing fewer tunes for dancers, and bop was not for dancers either. (Gillespie protested that he could dance to bop, and we do not doubt it, but most people did not.)

All the independent record labels of the early years of the industry – Paramount, Gennett, Okeh and Black Swan, for instance – had long since disappeared or been swallowed up. The 1940s was the second era (and not the last) in which independent labels were formed to serve an industry whose largest companies were geared towards serving the majority. It is remarkable that so many record labels were formed during the war.

Capitol, the first big label to be located on the West Coast, was formed in 1942 by record retailer Glenn Wallach and songwriters Buddy DeSylva and Johnny Mercer. That year it had a hit with 'Cow Cow Boogie', by Freddie Slack and his band and with a vocal by Ella Mae Morse. (Pianist and vocalist Cow Cow Davenport eventually got some money for his tune.) Capitol quickly became the most innovative company in the industry. The sound of the recordings made in Hollywood in 1945 by Coleman Hawkins, for example, was outstanding for the period; Capitol was the first to record everything on tape, the first to give free records to disc jockeys (not an unmixed blessing, in retrospect) and later the first to issue records at all three speeds.

Even more impressive was the number of labels formed expressly to serve the black community. Apollo was formed in the same year as Capitol in Harlem by Ike and Bess Berman to record black gospel music, and soon diversified into jazz and rhythm and blues. (John Chilton, however, writes that Apollo was formed by Teddy Gottlieb and Hi Siegel from their Rainbow Music Store.) Savoy was formed in Newark, New Jersey, by Herman Lubinsky, another record retailer. National was formed by A. B. Green in Manhattan in 1944, and its A&R director was Herb Abramson (soon to be a co-founder of Atlantic). Syd Nathan left the department store business to form King in Cincinnati in 1945. DeLuxe was formed around 1944 in Linden, New Jersey, by Jules Braun and his brothers; Fred Mendelsohn formed Regent in 1947, Deluxe was sold to King and the Brauns and Mendelsohn formed Regal in 1949. (Mendelsohn formed Herald in 1952, and ended up succeeding Lubinsky at Savoy.) On the West Coast, Specialty was formed in 1944 by Art Rupe, Black and White in 1945 by Paul and Lillian Reiner, Modern by Jules and Saul Bihari (soon to include subsidiaries Kent, Crown and Flair). At about the same time Leo, Edward and Ida Mesner formed Philo, which changed its name to Aladdin in 1946. In 1946–7 Phil and Leonard Chess formed Aristocrat in Chicago, and it became Chess in 1949–50.

Mercury had been formed in Chicago in 1945–6, and ten years later it had the first rhythm and blues hit to reach number one on the national pop chart: 'The Great Pretender' by the Platters. Don Robey formed Peacock in Houston, Texas, in 1949, which was perhaps the first black-owned label since Black Swan, and more 'indie' labels followed in the early 1950s. But another remarkable thing about the independent labels listed in the last paragraph is that they were all formed by Jews, who in those days did not find it easy to make their way in mainstream business in the USA. (It was in 1947 that Laura Z. Hobson's best-selling novel about genteel American anti-semitism, *Gentleman's Agreement*, was filmed; unfortunately it was a dull movie.) The Jews who formed the classic indies in the 1940s lived and worked in black neighbourhoods, and knew and understood the music better than anyone at a larger company could (with the possible exception of Jack Kapp at Decca, who recorded much minority music). If they had not taken the risks and done the work, the Lester Youngs on Aladdin and other priceless jazz, to say nothing of scores of wonderful rhythm and blues hits, would not exist. And these independents were the first to record bop.

Hawkins encouraged the boppers, employing them on recordings. Jazz historians have decided that the first bop recordings were made at a Hawkins session in February 1944 for Apollo, by a twelve-piece group which included Max Roach on drums, Oscar Pettiford on bass and Dizzy Gillespie in the trumpet section, as well as Don Byas in the reeds. (One of the most interesting transitional figures, who was at home in any decade's style, Byas spent his later life in Europe.) At a quartet date on another label in October Hawkins used Thelonious Monk; it was Monk's first recording session. A year later, on Savoy, Parker made his first recordings as a leader, with Miles Davis and Gillespie on trumpet (Gillespie played piano on some tracks), Roach on drums and Curley Russell on bass. The cats were well and truly out of the bag.

Cab Calloway called it 'Chinese music'. Boppers often flattened the fifth note of a chord, inventing short routes between keys; Eddie Condon said, 'We don't flatten our fifths, we drink 'em.' But Stravinsky had used flattened fifths in 1910, and Earl Hines, Bubber Miley and others in the 1920s. Bop was very obviously a black music, and the USA was not ready for black pride just yet. There were white boppers in black combos, for example trumpeter Red Rodney and pianists Al Haig, George Wallington and Joe Albany; but pressure on leaders to practise Crow Jim (the reverse of American racism, dubbed 'Jim Crow' from the early minstrel act) soon sent them into obscurity. (Some made comebacks as bop became repertory music in the 1970s.) It is said that bop left jazz in a shambles, but that is nonsense: the jazz content of pop music was decreasing anyway, and bop was not a revolution, but a further flowering of an art form already decades old, leading towards the emancipation of black music from ballrooms and taverns by making demands on the listeners. Bop was a natural musical evolution, though there must also have been a feeling on the part of the young players that they were taking their music back.

Bop was great fun for anyone prepared to listen, and the records are still selling today. The music business, however, mishandled it. The sudden success of Benny Goodman, then Tommy Dorsey and the others had come as a surprise to the industry in the mid-1930s, but those leaders were already insiders and good businessmen. The boppers were musicians (mostly black) who needed the patronage of the American music business, from the major labels to the disc jockeys, and they did not get it. The major label that recorded the most bop was young and feisty Capitol (run by musicians). Gillespie formed the Dee-Gee label in 1951 and went broke, but the recordings he made hold up better than most of the pop music of the period. The music business (including broadcasters) co-opts and tries to control (or ignore) whatever it does not understand, as it did with rock'n'roll ten years later.

The first frenetic flowering of bop was temporary; the 'hot modern' music soon began to cool off, leading to several styles – modern jazz, cool jazz, hard bop and so on – as the classic New Orleans style had immediately begun to evolve two generations earlier. In the meantime black popular music already had two tributaries. If bop can be seen as the art music of the black American audience of, say, 1949, in that year the name for its pop music was officially changed: Jerry Wexler, then a reporter at *Billboard*, convinced them to change the name of the 'Race Records' charts to 'Rhythm and Blues'.

For the black audience there was so much new music to listen to that the ferment crossed over to some extent. Some of Lionel

Hampton's big-band hits, with their strong backbeat, were not far removed from the R&B hits of later years, and in 1946 'Hey! Ba-ba-re-bop' parleyed its bop-derived nonsense lyrics to the number one spot on the black chart for sixteen weeks. Helen Humes (whose beautiful ballad with Basie a half-dozen years before had been 'Blame It On My Last Affair') had a big hit in 1945 with 'Be Baba Leba' on the new Philo label, backed by a Bill Doggett octet, and followed up in 1950 with the salacious 'Million Dollar Secret', which was recorded live with drummer Roy Milton's band in August. In November of that year she was backed in her live act by another jump band led by Dexter Gordon. A jump band was a small group that combined the beat and the drive of the big jazz band with the repetitious chorus associated with the blues, in effect making something new out of the Swing Era's predilection for riffs. Herb Morand was the trumpeter and manager of the Harlem Hamfats, one of the first jump bands, which began recording in Chicago in 1936; a 'hamfat' was a musician newly arrived from the South who used fat to grease the valves in his horn, and such a group purposely retained the flavour of the South in their sound.

Far more successful than the Hamfats was Louis Jordan, who had worked in Chick Webb's band, occasionally singing as well as playing alto saxophone. In 1938 he formed his Tympany Five (actually larger than a quintet); his showmanship brought him to the fore, and he had nearly fifty top ten hits in the black charts in less than ten years, about twenty of which crossed over to the heretofore lily-white pop chart. 'Caldonia' was covered by Woody Herman in 1945 (and his 'Inflation Blues' by B. B. King in 1983); his version of Jack McVea's novelty 'Open the Door, Richard' (1947) was one of the most popular. His skill as a leader and his innovatory vocal style not only made wonderful good-time music, but also may be seen in retrospect as an early example of a new black consciousness. The attitudes expressed in his vocals on many titles, such as 'That Chick's Too Young To Fry', 'Jack, You're Dead', 'I Know What You're Puttin' Down' and 'Ain't Nobody Here But Us Chickens', were redolent of a southern heritage, as well as of the rich humour and *joie de vivre* of the increasingly large urban black population.

Joe Liggins was a pianist, vocalist and bandleader whose goal was to create a big-band sound with a smaller combo; his own 'The Honeydripper' was number one for eighteen weeks in the black chart in 1945, and was followed by a string of hits up to 1951; his younger brother, guitarist Jimmy, was also in the charts from 1948. Lucky Millinder's band shrank until by the early 1950s it was essentially a jump band. Drummer and pianist Tiny Bradshaw had formed his own band in 1934, and finally had chart success from 1950 to 1953; among Bradshaw's tenor saxophones were Red Prysock and Sil Austin. The saxophone was the most important sound in the jump band era, and has retained an important role in R & B and rock'n'roll to this day.

Guitarist, vocalist and composer of novelty hits Slim Gaillard wrote 'Flat Foot Floogie', which was a hit in 1938 for Slim and Slam, Gaillard's duo with bass player Slam Stewart; several cover versions were also hits, notably that of Benny Goodman. Gaillard was a success in clubs on the West Coast during and after the war, and claimed years later that one of his fans had been film star Ronald Reagan; having invented a hip 'vout oreenie' language, he compiled a dictionary of it. In 1945 he recorded 'Floogie' again in Hollywood, with a small group including Charlie Parker, Dizzy Gillespie and tenor saxophonist Jack McVea. One of the other tracks was a bit of laid-back jive called 'Slim's Jam': the men come in one at a time; Gillespie is in a hurry to get to another session; Parker borrows a reed from McVea, who knocks on the door as he enters, saying, 'Open the door, Richard!'

This was a reference to a comedy routine by Dusty Fletcher, one of the biggest stars in black variety: the comic arrives home late and somewhat the worse for wear and finds himself without a key; he cannot raise Richard, his flatmate, to open the door, because Richard is busy doing something he is loath to interrupt. McVea subsequently composed a riff and turned 'Open the Door, Richard!' into a jump band set-piece which swept the USA in seven hit versions in 1947, among them those of Basie, Jordan, Fletcher and McVea. The novelty became so obsessive that a radio station in New York finally banned the tune, as well as the D Js' Richard jokes.

Most of the small-group sessions recorded in the 1940s seem to have been saxophone-led, and the music is extraordinarily rich: there was a spectrum from pure jazz at one end to good-time exhibitionism at the other. The 'swingtets' from Blue Note, led by Ike Quebec and John Hardee, were beautiful recordings aimed at jukeboxes, as were Bob Thiele's Signature discs.

Earl Bostic played alto saxophone; his compositions for big bands include Gene Krupa's 1941 hit 'Let Me Off Uptown' and he then had his own success in the late 1940s and early 1950s. Bostic had recorded some superb solos as a sideman at Commodore in 1945. He was also highly regarded as a technician and, in fact, had the reputation of sacrificing tone for technique. (Art Blakey later remarked that if John Coltrane had worked for Bostic, he must have learned a great deal: 'Nobody knew more about the saxophone than Bostic . . . and that includes Bird.') Bostic was among the first to employ Coltrane, as well as Benny Golson and Stanley Turrentine, and later wrote albums for Ella Fitzgerald and others.

Big Jay McNeely was the foremost practitioner of the acrobatic, honking R & B saxophone; his biggest hit was 'Deacon's Hop' in 1949, but he remained a legend in clubs well into the 1980s. Illinois Jacquet began with Lionel Hampton's big band, but recorded with his 'Black Velvet' combo for RCA; his main success was 'Port of Rico' on Mercury in 1952 (with Count Basie on organ). Arnett Cobb was another Texas tenor saxophonist whose ability to please a crowd obscured his excellent ballad playing. Johnny Hodges, who never honked, left Duke Ellington in 1951 and for five years led his own smaller group. His was certainly a jazz-oriented band, but his 'Castle Rock' was a hit in 1951, a good year for alto saxophones: Bostic's 'Flamingo' and Tab Smith's 'Because of You' were also hits. Jimmy Forrest was an underrated tenor saxophonist whose jump combo had a great success in 1952 with 'Night Train', actually an Ellington riff, which then became required learning for every embryo high-school rock band in the country.

The valedictory hit of the jump band era came in 1956, in time to let a whole new generation in on the secret: Bill Doggett's 'Honky Tonk' was number one for thirteen weeks in the black chart, and stuck at number two (for three weeks) on the national pop chart. Doggett, born in 1916, had played piano in many a big band when he formed a combo in 1952 and recorded this two-part instrumental with Clifford Scott on tenor and Billy Butler on guitar. Its inexorable rocking lope made it one of the biggest hits the King label ever had.

Electric guitars and pure blues became increasingly stronger in the commercial market. Composer, bass player, guitarist, vocalist and ex-boxer Willie Dixon formed the Five Breezes and recorded for Bluebird in 1940, then with the Four Jumps of Jive on Mercury and the Big Three Trio on Columbia. He did not have a hit of his own until 1955, but meanwhile became Leonard Chess's right-hand man in the studio, as Chicago developed a blues scene of extraordinary power, headed by Muddy Waters, who brought the country blues to town. Muddy's first hit in the black chart was '(I Feel Like) Going Home' in 1948 on Aristocrat. John Lee 'Sonny Boy' Williamson, born in Tennessee, paved the way for a whole generation of Chicago blues harmonica players and had a high entry in the black chart with 'Shake the Boogie' in 1947, the year before he was murdered. Guitarist and harmonica player Aleck Ford (also known as Rice Miller) had already worked as Sonny Boy Williamson in the early 1940s on the radio; now he adopted the name permanently, and, apart from having hits of his own, played on Elmore James's 'Dust My Broom' (on the tiny Mississippi Trumpet label) in 1952, which represents another direct link from the delta to the south side of Chicago. Chester Burnette acquired the apt stage name of Howlin' Wolf; his hits in the black chart began in 1951 with 'Moanin' at Midnight'. Riley 'Blues Boy' King recorded for Nashville's Bullet label in 1949; his 'Three O'Clock Blues' was enormously popular in 1951.

Vocal groups were coming up and inventing a whole new tradition of unaccompanied doo-wop, named after the 'doo-wah' vocal device commonly used in backing harmony. As their grandfathers had sung in barber-shops, so the young groups in the post-war years sang on street corners to get the girls; they rehearsed in hallways and alleys where they liked the echo, and they made uncounted numbers of obscure records on obscure labels. There were bird groups (the Crows, Penguins, Flamingoes) and car groups (the Cadillacs, the Lincolns, the Coup De Villes, the V-eights); there were Velvetones in New York and Chicago, the Vibranairs in Baltimore and the Vibranaires in Asbury Park. The Ravens reached the black chart in 1948 with 'Write Me a Letter' on National, the Robins in 1950 with 'If It's So, Baby' and the Dominoes, with Billy Ward and Clyde McPhatter, in 1951 with 'Sixty-minute Man', which was number one in the black chart for fourteen weeks. Italian-Americans also loved the tradition, and vocal groups both black and white became ubiquitous.

All this was in addition to solo singing, which ranged from beautiful barroom crooning to shouting Kansas City blues: Ray Charles was in Seattle imitating Nat Cole in the late 1940s; Kansas City's singing bartender Big Joe Turner had his first hit, 'My Gal's a Jockey', on National in 1946; pianist and vocalist Amos Milburn's long run of big R&B hits began in 1948. Pianist, singer and songwriter Ivory Joe Hunter had his first hit in 1945 with Johnny Moore's Three Blazers. He was later backed on records by members of Duke Ellington's band, and his singing of his songs, for example, 'I Almost Lost My Mind' and 'Since I Met You Baby', achieved such crossover success that he was welcomed on the *Grand Ole Opry* before he died in 1974. Guitarist Johnny Moore's trio had years of popularity from 1946, with vocalist Charles Brown, who sang as a soloist on 'Get Yourself Another Fool' on Aladdin in 1949 (and toured as far as Scotland in 1990). Roy Brown's 'Good Rockin' Tonight' appeared in 1948 on Deluxe, and Ruth Brown's 'So Long' in 1949 on Atlantic. Black pop retained its emphasis on honest entertainment and could always be danced to, but white pop was flying around in smaller and smaller circles until it almost disappeared.

During and after the war much good music was still being played by big bands, among the best being that of clarinettist and vocalist Woody Herman, who started in show business at the age of six. He formed a band in 1933, but it failed. He worked for Gus Arnheim and then Isham Jones; when Jones retired, the band became a cooperative and each member owned shares. 'The Band That Played the Blues' had an integrity of its own from 1937 on the Decca label. 'At the Woodchopper's Ball' was a hit, 'Blues in the Night' was sung by Herman and the band's theme, 'Blue Flame', was named after a locker-room prank involving the lighting of naturally produced methane gas with a match.

As the original members left the band, a process accelerated by conscription, Herman bought their shares until he owned it. During the musicians' strike 'Woodchopper's Ball' was reissued and was again successful. Decca was one of the first major labels to settle with the musicians' union, but of twenty-four Herman titles recorded in 1944, only four were released. Meanwhile, the band that began recording for Columbia was entirely transformed. Bass player Chubby Jackson and pianist-arranger Ralph Burns had joined in 1943 (both from Charlie Barnet), and Jackson helped recruit most of the rest. Guitarist Billy Bauer had replaced the last remaining member of the old band; other key members were drummer Dave Tough (soon replaced by stand-in Buddy Rich, then Don Lamond), trumpeter-arranger Neal Hefti, tenor saxophonist Flip Phillips, trumpeter Pete Candoli and trombonist Bill Harris. Vocalist Frances Wayne's hits with the band included 'Saturday Night is the Loneliest Night of the Week' (on Decca), 'Happiness is Just a Thing Called Joe' and 'Gee, It's Good to Hold You' (Columbia); Herman sang on the frenetic 'Caldonia'. But it was on the instrumentals that this band romped, stomped, swung and screamed, without ever going over the top: 'Apple Honey', 'Northwest Passage', 'The Good Earth', 'Your Father's Mustache', 'Blowin' Up a Storm', 'Sidewalks of Cuba' and the more relaxed 'Goosey Gander' represented a new generation of young white jazz musicians who had done all their homework and knew how to share the joy with the listener. Burns's 'Bijou (Rhumba à la Jazz)' featured Harris, who wrote the beautiful 'Everywhere' (arranged by Hefti). Margie Hyams played vibraphone, but was replaced by Red Norvo, precipitating a new, modern edition of the Woodchoppers, the band within a band: the nonet – which included Herman on alto as well as clarinet, Jimmy Rowles on piano and the bright new trumpet star Sonny Berman – recorded 'Steps', 'Igor', 'Four Men on a Horse' and similar unique soundscapes. As early as mid-1944 Candoli's sixteen-year-old brother Conte played in the band during his summer holidays from high school. The band gave a famous concert at Carnegie Hall in 1946.

Pianist Claude Thornhill had arranged and recorded 'Loch Lomond' with vocalist Maxine Sullivan in 1937; Thornhill's theme was his own composition, the impressionistic 'Snowfall'. Among the musicians he hired were trumpeter Conrad Gozzo (later one of the most sought-after studio musicians), Irving Fazola and Lee Konitz on reeds and trumpeter Red Rodney, a young bopper who also recorded with Charlie Parker. In the 1940s Thornhill's innovative arrangements (many by the young Gil Evans) caught the ears of musicians and they were influential for decades. The quirky 'Portrait of a Guinea Farm' (1941) had a six-strong reed section; a choir of clarinets played a tune that could have been a Russian dance by Rimsky-Korsakov. The band's hits in the late 1940s included 'A Sunday Kind of Love', a good pop song with a vocal by Fran Warren, who in 1947 also recorded a sung version of 'Early Autumn' (written the year before by Ralph Burns as one of the four parts of 'Summer Sequence' for Woody Herman). In the same year the band recorded Parker's 'Thrivin' on a Riff', 'Donna Lee', 'Yardbird Suite' and 'Robbins' Nest' (a tribute to a DJ which became a sort of jazz classic, written by Sir Charles Thompson and Illinois Jacquet), as well as experimenting with such fare as 'La Paloma' (a Spanish song first published in the USA in 1877) and 'Warsaw Concerto' (an effective British film theme by Richard Addinsell), and such standard dance band material as 'Polka Dots and Moonbeams'. By this time Thornhill was using two French horns, a tuba and occasionally a bass clarinet, and also a crooning vocal group called the Snowflakes. Much post-war jazz, especially of the 'cool school', was influenced by Thornhill's willingness to experiment with textures and harmonies, all the while running what appeared to be a successful sweet band.

Pianist, arranger and composer Stan Kenton made his début with his own band in 1941. He presented, successively, three of the era's best girl singers in Anita O'Day ('And Her Tears Flowed Like Wine', 1944), June Christy ('Tampico', 1945) and, in the early 1950s, Chris Connor; his sidemen in 1944 included Stan Getz and in the late 1940s Kai Winding (trombone), Vido Musso (tenor saxophone), Art Pepper and Bud Shank (alto saxophones), Maynard Ferguson and Shorty Rogers (trumpets) and Shelly Manne (drums), and in the early 1950s Lee Konitz (alto saxophone): most of the best white musicians in West Coast jazz. Apart from twenty or so pop hits, such instrumental tracks as 'Eager Beaver' and a frenetic 'Peanut Vendor' were highly rated. Kenton later turned to pretentious original music beloved of high-school bandmasters, and was prone to utter futile disparaging remarks about country music ('a national disgrace') and the Beatles ('children's music'). In the 1940s his music was seen both as good pop and as good jazz, and indeed, a complete set on four Mosaic CDs of the arrangements of Bill Holman and Bill Russo (1950–63) reveals much beauty and fine playing, an admonishment to those of us who may have given up on Kenton too easily. But he insisted that his music be given parity with European classical music, which led to Kenton's most infamous album: Wagner played by a huge jazz orchestra. Self-conscious art and commerce do not mix well; Kenton was a good bandleader and talent scout, but not himself a particularly inspired composer, arranger or pianist.

Saxophonist Boyd Raeburn led a sweet band when he left college, but in New York in 1944 built a band full of young boppers; he could not record during the strike and henceforth recorded only for tiny labels. He became renowned for hiring such talented musicians as Sonny Berman, Al Cohn, Oscar Pettiford, pianist Dodo Marmarosa and clarinettist Buddy DeFranco. Dizzy Gillespie, Budd Johnson and Tadd Dameron all wrote for the band.

And there were up-to-date black big bands trying to play bop, though it is questionable whether a big band can play bop at all, just as Luis Russell could not play in the New Orleans style with a largish band twenty years earlier. Nevertheless, Billy Eckstine had one of the biggest, deepest and smoothest voices of all time, and with Budd Johnson had encouraged Earl Hines to hire progressive young musicians; in 1944 he and Johnson formed a band which until 1947 employed trumpeters Gillespie, Miles Davis, Fats Navarro and Kenny Dorham; Parker, Gene Ammons, Dexter Gordon and Lucky Thompson on reeds; and Art Blakey on drums. It played arrangements by Dameron, Johnson and Eckstine and vocalists Sarah Vaughan and Lena Horne. The band made few recordings, and its only hits were vocals by Eckstine, who sensibly made a career as a solo singer; his lovely work for MGM includes duets with Vaughan.

Dizzy Gillespie, a composer as well as the most influential trumpeter after Armstrong, an engaging vocalist and a great showman, led exciting big bands between 1946 and 1949, recording for

Musicraft, RCA and Capitol. If the line-up of sidemen was not quite as stellar as that of the earlier Eckstine band, it was more than adequate; among the reedmen alone at various times were Budd Johnson, Cecil Payne, Jimmy Heath, John Coltrane, James Moody and Paul Gonsalves. The arrangements by Johnson, John Lewis, Tadd Dameron, Gil Fuller, George Russell and others were influential as well as interesting. Cuban-born conga drummer and vocalist Chano Pozo, according to Gillespie, could play in one rhythm, sing in another and dance in a third, all at the same time. When they both worked for Cab Calloway, Gillespie had shared lodgings with Cuban trumpeter Mario Bauza (later Machito's music director), who introduced him to Latin music; Afro-Cuban jazz has been an enduring element to this day. Machito (Frank Raul Grillo) led one of the most popular Latin bands, whose music was often jazz-flavoured, and recorded with Parker, among others. Pozo was something of a roughneck, and was shot to death in a Harlem bar, but he wrote 'Tin Tin Deo' with Fuller and 'Manteca' and 'Cubana Be, Cubana Bop' with Gillespie and Russell, and played on Gillespie's recordings of the last two. In spite of everything, however, the band was not a great commercial success. And anyway, the big bands were about to disappear from mainstream popular music.

As a result of the wartime rationing of fuel, tyres and batteries, and the conversion of car factories to war production, it was increasingly hard for the dancers to get to the ballrooms and dance halls where the bands played. Furthermore, many young people had other things on their minds, such as letters from the local draft board. A stiff wartime entertainment tax made life more difficult for ballroom operators and booking agents, and it was not lifted until well into the 1950s, long after most of the clubs and dance halls had closed. All of these problems were obviously experienced in Britain as well.

Despite the popularity of the bands, and the image we all have of Glenn Miller playing for large numbers of service men and women, the primary purpose of going to war was not to entertain: there was not that much work for musicians on the military bases, where many of the dancers had gone. Even making recordings was difficult during the war (when Petrillo was not trying to prevent it) because of a shortage of the main ingredients of 78s. (Capitol signed a young and not very good bandleader because his father owned a warehouse full of shellac.) The labels also bought old records and ground them up to make new ones; quality fell as virgin shellac was mixed with the recycled material. After the war the decline of the Big Band Era was hastened by social, economic and demographic factors.

Films made in the late 1980s, such as *Who Framed Roger Rabbit?* and *Good Morning, Babylon,* featured the famous Los Angeles 'red car'; in the beautiful Californian climate a great deal of dancing took place in outdoor pavilions, and before the war young people used one of the best public transport systems in the world to get there; they could take a trolley-car clear across Los Angeles for 5 cents. The red cars (the Southern Pacific Railroad) and the yellow cars (a smaller system, the Los Angeles Railway Company) together operated over 1,000 miles of track. A great many towns had similar networks knitting together suburbs and amusement parks, a good number of which had dance pavilions. They in turn gave employment to many a local musician, as well as to touring name bands.

In 1936 National City Lines had been created by a cartel including Standard Oil, Phillips Petroleum, Goodyear Tire and Rubber and General Motors, for the purpose of buying up streetcar lines and making bus routes out of them. Those who thought this should be prevented by introducing subsidies for public transport were labelled 'Reds' by newspapers like the *Los Angeles Times,* whose reactionary owner, Harry Chandler, sat on the board of directors of Standard of California and had interests in road construction. An affiliate of National City Lines began taking the red cars out of service and tearing up the track, and after the war most of the damage had been done: few young people in the late 1940s could afford to buy cars, so the decline of public transport was another nail in the coffin of live music. Today Los Angeles has one of the world's few twenty-four-hour traffic jams, and is thinking about how to get rid of the internal combustion engine.

The country filled up with ex-soldiers who set about starting families at the time of the rise of television. It was easier to stay at home and watch TV than it was to go out, and the end of the ballrooms also saw the decline of the cinema. This was the beginning of the 'baby boom': an interesting corollary is that the preceding generation of teenaged girls was relatively small; readers of a certain age will remember that the difficulty of obtaining a babysitter was a stock joke in television sitcoms of the 1950s.

Add to all these problems the fact that after the war it was simply uneconomic to run a big band. Before the war Bob Wills could make good money playing at dance halls full of people who had paid only 75 cents to get in; but afterwards the cost of keeping a band together was much higher, while the takings were lower, since there were fewer dance halls and fewer dancers. In January 1947 the big bands of Woody Herman, Harry James, Benny Goodman, Les Brown, Tommy Dorsey, Benny Carter and Jack Teagarden, as well as the all-girl band of glamorous Ina Ray Hutton, folded. Some of these re-formed from time to time, especially Herman's, but that month was seen by the music business as terminal.

From 1939 clarinettist and arranger Les Brown had led a popular band, which had two number one hits: 'Sentimental Journey' in 1945, with a vocal by Doris Day, and 'I've Got My Love to Keep Me Warm', which was recorded in 1946; during Petrillo's second strike against the record companies it reached the top of the charts at the end of 1948. Everybody knew it was the last number one instrumental of the Swing Era. It had been a heady time, when popular music was good and good music was popular, but it was over.

12

The Early 1950s: Frustration and Confusion

After the Second World War the twentieth century seemed to be the American century. The only nation to come out of the war healthier than when it went in was the USA; the Marshall Plan helped rebuild Europe, while at home the Depression was over, and a great many ex-soldiers were taking advantage of the GI Bill to acquire further education, an opportunity that had mostly been denied their parents. During the war the income of the average white family had doubled, but the income of the average black family had tripled; industry was working flat out to supply consumers (a new buzz-word) with everything they wanted, and the perfect society seemed to be just around the corner. Could we not invent anything we needed?

There were unseen difficulties ahead, but the biggest problem facing the record business as the decade turned appeared to be technological confusion. The invention of microgroove records started the battle of the speeds, which meant dislocation in the industry and headaches for retailers. Mainstream popular music itself in the post-war years became anodyne, as though the hole at the centre of it previously occupied by the big bands could be filled only with marshmallow.

The phenomenon of what is still called light music in Britain and soon came to be called mood music by many, was an interesting one; it briefly had a new life thanks largely to the long-playing record. A good number of recordings of 'light classical' music and orchestral arrangements of popular material had always been used for what was later called easy listening. Victor's director of light music, Nathaniel Shilkret, had over fifty hit records from 1924 to 1932, and during the

1930s and 1940s Al Goodman and André Kostelanetz were tremendously popular on radio and on records that stayed in print for years, accumulating comfortable sales. Violinist and bandleader Leo Reisman not only accompanied Fred Astaire (and composer Harold Arlen singing his own 'Stormy Weather'), but had over seventy hits between 1925 and 1940. Arthur Fiedler became conductor of the Boston Pops in 1930, and stayed until he died in 1979. In 1943 studio conductor David Rose had a hit with 'Holiday for Strings'; in 1949 ace studio conductor Lennie Hayton was successful with Richard Rodgers's ballet 'Slaughter on Tenth Avenue'.

In the early 1950s the studio bandleaders and A&R men, some of them veterans of the Swing Era, were arrangers, composers and conductors: for example, Gordon Jenkins at Decca, Hugo Winterhalter and German-born Henri Rene at RCA, Percy Faith, Paul Weston and Mitch Miller at Columbia, Les Baxter at Capitol and Richard Hayman and David Carroll at Mercury. Trumpet player turned conductor Monty Kelly had a hit in 1953 with 'Tropicana'. The composers of such instrumental pieces were journeymen who turned their hands to many things; 'Tropicana' and 'Life in New York' were written by Bernie Wayne, who also wrote 'Vanessa' (an instrumental hit for Winterhalter), 'Laughing on the Outside (Crying on the Inside)', which had popular recordings in 1946 and 1953, and 'Blue Velvet', a hit for Tony Bennett in 1951 and a much bigger success for Bobby Vinton a dozen years later. Leroy Anderson was a choir director and organist who also played bass in symphony orchestras, and began arranging for the Boston Pops in 1935; his own record of 'Syncopated Clock' was a hit in 1951, and his 'Blue Tango' was in the charts for thirty-eight weeks that year. Most of these people backed vocalists on countless hit recordings, for example, Kostelanetz on Perry Como's number one 'Prisoner of Love' (1946).

Some of the arranger-conductor hits had vocals, sung by studio soloists or a chorus, but the 'popular instrumental' briefly became a genre of its own. Les Baxter was an all-rounder who later wrote scores for some of Roger Corman's horror films; his 'April in Portugal' was a hit in 1953, while Richard Hayman's 'Ruby', on which he played harmonica, reached number three that year; the tune was the theme from the film *Ruby Gentry*. Mitch Miller turned out jolly novelties like 'Oriental Polka', which usually did not reach the charts. The soundtrack title theme from the Italian film *Anna* was a hit in 1953, sung by Silvana Mangano, while Weston made an attractive dance band arrangement of it. Percy Faith was among the most successful in this class, recording over eighty profitable albums and two big hit singles: 'Delicado' (1952), a Brazilian pop song, was played by Stan Freeman on an amplified harpsichord; 'Song from "Moulin Rouge" (Where is Your Heart)' (1953), a film theme, was sung by Felicia Sanders in a brilliant arrangement. (Faith's jolly version of Hugo Alfven's 'Swedish Rhapsody', which was on the other side, also charted.)

The hits of the few dance bands that were still around, mostly playing at college proms, fell into the popular instrumental category. Pianist and arranger Ralph Flanagan was encouraged by booking agents to form a band on the Glenn Miller model; he was successful in 1952 with 'Hot Toddy' on RCA. Trumpeter Ray Anthony on Capitol had an attractive recording of 'Dancing in the Dark' and trumpeter Ralph Marterie reached high in the chart with Ellington's 'Caravan' on Mercury in 1953. 'Skokiaan' was a South African novelty named after a Zulu drink; the Bulawayo Sweet Rhythm Boys had their own hit (on London), while Anthony, Marterie and Johnny Hodges all made recordings of it. Trombonist Buddy Morrow (whose real name was Moe Zudekoff) had played with such bands as Artie Shaw's and Tommy Dorsey's; in 1952 he had a big-band hit with a cover of Jimmy Forrest's 'Night Train', but it did not appear in the *Billboard* chart (probably because by that time everybody was embarrassed, knowing that the riff properly belonged to Ellington). There was not enough work to keep a large number of dance bands in business, yet the remarkable thing about all these records was the playing of the rhythm sections, which was infinitely better than that of the average white rhythm section of earlier decades. Marterie's 'Caravan', though it was inferior to Ellington's recordings of his own tune, was a jumping disc: it introduced a new generation to the name of Ellington, and (like Marterie's pop hit 'Pretend' of the same year) it featured an electric guitar, still unusual at the time.

Most of this music, however, does not hold up very well. The wordless chorus (a common gimmick) on Baxter's 'April in

Portugal' has been known to induce nausea. In any case, the 'popular instrumental', and light music in general, was soon subsumed in Muzak, the name of the largest purveyor of wired music which became a generic term for the slush that came at you out of the walls and ceilings of airports, supermarkets and waiting rooms. Most of this superfluous and gratuitous music was third-rate; it helped to kill off, or at least drive underground, the American market for light music, because it devalued music in general (yet if you asked for it to be turned off, you heard, 'Whatsamatter? Don't you like music?'). There was less wallpaper music in Britain, which is partly why light music still has a considerable audience there. English essayist and novelist J. B. Priestley wrote:

Austere musicians dismiss this flimsy tinkling too easily; so-called light music has its own values, not really belonging to music at all . . . it acts as a series of vials, often charmingly shaped and coloured, for the distillations of memory. The first few bars of it remove the stopper; we find ourselves reliving, not remembering but magically reliving, some exact moments of our past.

That it came to be called mood music was largely due to the Englishman George Melachrino, whose series of such albums as *Music for Dining*, *Music for Reading*, *Music for Daydreaming* led to ribald suggestions for the next title. (In fact, one of them was called *Music for Two People Alone*.) Melachrino's handling of a chamber-sized string orchestra was adventurous compared with the sound cranked out by the Italian-born violinist Annunzio Paolo Mantovani. In the late 1930s Mantovani led the potted-palm sort of hotel combo, and parleyed it into what sounded like thousands of fiddles; he had over fifty hit albums from 1953, helped by UK Decca's excellent sound.

There is nothing intrinsically wrong with an arrangement of a good tune for a full-sized orchestra; the Canadian-born Percy Faith, the former Tommy Dorsey arranger Paul Weston and another Canadian, Robert Farnon, who had played trumpet in Faith's Canadian radio orchestra, were very good at it, and were at their best on albums.

Farnon has worked in England since the Second World War. His albums were used by teachers of arranging as examples of how this sort of thing should be done, and he has probably carried out more film and studio work than anyone else in the business. Weston's album *Caribbean Cruise* was wonderfully tasteful, for listening or dancing to, and his albums *Mood for Twelve* and *Solo Mood* featured solos by jazzmen such as guitarist George Van Eps. (Bobby Hackett played lovely solos on mood music albums conducted by comedian Jackie Gleason.) Weston's earlier albums on Capitol, some of them remade later in stereo, included such elegant innovations that you did not notice them: if he wanted to use violins along with brass and reeds, instead of amplifying the violins he would have everyone else playing softly, or with mutes. This sounded better than most people's efforts in that mode.

Faith had played piano in silent cinemas and might have been a concert pianist, but his hands were injured in a fire. In the USA after 1940 he continued in radio work, apparently recording for Eli Oberstein's Varsity label in the mid-1940s and for RCA in 1949, before moving to Columbia in 1950. His best work dates from the early 1950s, and on albums, which will probably never be reissued (not by Sony, anyway) because they are not stereo. The voicings in his arrangements were unique and immediately recognizable; his use of woodwind was particularly distinctive. He had a predilection for Latin rhythms, perhaps, he once said, because he came from a cold climate; albums such as *Carnival Rhythms* must have used most of the best Latin percussionists in New York. *American Waltzes, Continental Music* and *Romantic Music* belong to an era when what was thought to be sophistication could still carry an aura of innocence. And as for the rhythm sections, I would still like to know the name of Faith's studio bass player, who was always nicely behind the beat on the ballads.

Faith's series of 78s for RCA had included 'Deep Purple', Charles Trenet's 'Beyond the Sea' and the title track of one of the first RCA 12-inch pop LPs, *Soft Lights and Sweet Music*. The cover photograph was a close-up of a woman in evening dress, wearing a veil and with her eyes closed, and a man – dancing? embracing? dreaming? In 1977 when the ten tracks were reissued by Pickwick, the garish and instantly dated cover photograph pictured a fireplace and a bimbo with a skimpy dress and come-hither lipstick. A good deal had changed in less than thirty years.

Faith started the fad for instrumental albums of music from Broadway shows with *Kismet* in 1954. The tunes had been taken from the works of the Russian composer Alexander Borodin, and lent themselves to Faith's concert treatment. That the trend later became hackneyed (with umpteen versions of *My Fair Lady* and *The Sound of Music*) was not Faith's fault. He also wrote film scores that were invariably better than the films, notably *The Oscar* (1966), which yielded a good pop song, 'Maybe September'. In 1960 he had a third number one single, and received a Grammy for the syrupy 'Theme from a Summer Place', slop which limped along with a slow kling-kling-kling piano. Ironically, this was a cliché from rock'n'roll, which by then had helped Muzak relegate light music in America to the status of a bad joke. (That piano style was called claw music by studio musicians, who hated it; it was sent up unmercifully by Stan Freberg on one of his comedy records.)

Somewhere along the way Faith moved to the West Coast, and the sound of his albums was coarsened; they were recorded too close to the microphone to make them more 'hi-fi'. (R. D. Darrell complained about this in a review of Faith's album of songs from *Subways are for Sleeping*, a Jule Stein show that opened in late 1961 and lost money.) Faith later recorded an album of Beatles songs, and another called *Black Magic Woman*; even these reached the chart, for the remaining customers for string orchestras were grateful for small favours.

Easy listening on long-playing records, however appealing some of them were, could not represent the best of a nation's popular culture anyway, and the music business would have been in a state of disarray even without the 'battle of the speeds'. For a generation the centre of popular music had been the big jazz-oriented dance band, and suddenly it was gone.

Country music was seemingly always about to make a break-through. The prudish dominance of the *Grand Ole Opry* was worn away, and adult themes were approached. Floyd Tillman's 'Slippin' Around' was a number one pop hit in 1949, in a duet by ·Jimmy Wakely and Margaret Whiting, showing that the pop chart could handle adultery without the world coming to an end; but Tillman's own version was confined to the country chart. Webb Pierce's 'There Stands the Glass' and Kitty Wells's 'It Wasn't God Who Made Honky Tonk Angels', which treated alcoholism and sexism as something more than jokes, were just around the corner.

The honky-tonk style was considered disreputable, especially on the *Grand Ole Opry*, but it could not long be avoided; its greatest practitioner and one of the all-time great artists in American popular music was Hank Williams. He was born in utter poverty and suffered pain all his life, perhaps from an undiagnosed case of spina bifida, and was killed by the effects of alcohol and pills at the age of twenty-nine. Country music has often ignored fashion and the delicate feelings of the bourgeoisie in order to portray the real world; the fact is that a great many Americans lived from pay-cheque to pay-cheque, and spent much time drowning their sorrows or trying to enjoy themselves in the sort of taverns ('blood buckets') where Williams had served his apprenticeship. He knew these people's hopes, dreams and fears, and wrote their songs for them; he was among the greatest of folk poets.

In 1946 Williams took his religious songs to Fred Rose in Nashville, who recorded and leased them to a Sterling label. Louis B. Mayer, head of MGM film studios, had intended to start a record company around 1940, but the musicians' strike and the war intervened; a Lion label was briefly formed to exploit new songs, but after the war MGM's parent company, Leow's, hired Frank Walker to run a new MGM label. Walker had helped keep Columbia Records afloat in the mid-1920s by signing Bessie Smith; now Rose brought him Hank Williams. He had a few hits in the country chart in 1947–8, but his recording of 'Lovesick Blues' (ironically a song older than he was) was a number one country hit for sixteen weeks in 1949. Although he was already an alcoholic, known to be unreliable and represented a style the country establishment did not like, he nevertheless had to be invited to the *Opry*, where he was a sensation. He had less than four years to live.

Fred Rose was a pop music veteran who had briefly played piano with Paul Whiteman and written or co-written such tunes as 'Deep Henderson' (recorded by both King Oliver and the Coon–Sanders Night Hawks) and others for Sophie Tucker, then Gene Autry ('Be Honest With Me', which was nominated for an Oscar in 1941) and

Roy Acuff. Thus he got into country music by accident, and formed
Acuff–Rose in 1942. Williams was never known to read anything but
comic books and the country charts in the trade papers; he sometimes
bought lyrics from others, and always had a pocketful of scraps of
paper on which he jotted down ideas. Rose helped him to polish his
songs, and could probably have grabbed credit for them, yet his
name appears on only a few.

Williams's songs reached the pop chart in cover versions by Frankie
Laine, Tony Bennett, Guy Mitchell, Jo Stafford and Rosemary
Clooney, among others; they were big hits, mostly on Columbia,
where Mitch Miller knew a good song when he heard one. But
Williams himself never made the pop charts, despite thirty-six top
tens in the country chart in nine years, several of them after his death.
One of his early teachers had been a black street singer called Tee-
Tot (Rufe Payne); he was also influenced by Roy Acuff, and main-
stream America was not ready for a deep southern accent.

He may have been too dangerous in the era of *The Man in the Gray
Flannel Suit*. His recordings and, more especially, his legendary live
performances had an insouciant swagger, almost an improvisatory
quality, and a natural sexuality which presaged that of Elvis Presley.
He insisted on using his excellent stage band, the Drifting Cowboys,
on his recordings, and always gave them plenty of solo space; there
were no drums, and none was needed. His own recording of 'Hey,
Good Lookin'' for example, is much better than the pop duet by
Laine and Stafford, which is too frenetically jolly. Williams sets a
tempo which is just right, jaunty but not expecting too much: there
may be grief tomorrow, but we can have a good time tonight if we
want to. 'I Won't Be Home No More' shows how a lover's complaint
became a swinging piece of bravado:

> You're just in time to be too late.
> I tried to, but I couldn't wait,
> and now I've got another date,
> so I won't be home no more.
>> I stood around a month or two,
>> And waited for your call,
>> Now I'm too busy pitchin' woo,
>> So come around next Fall.

There are more verses, in which none of the perfectly simple phrases is repeated: 'You're just in time to change your tune / Go tell your troubles to the moon' is a new way to rhyme those time-honoured Tin Pan Alley words. Fiddler Jerry Rivers and steel guitarist Don Helms seem to float over the beat, while Williams sings each group of four syllables as though they were triplets, his carelessness matching that of the spurned lover: 'Be on your way / That's all she wrote' may have more than one meaning. There is a 'Well, I'll be damned' feeling about the whole thing.

Williams also recorded quasi-religious or philosophical monologues under the name of Luke the Drifter, and recorded a few duets with his troublesome first wife, Audrey, who thought she could sing. Compilations of Williams's tracks have often selected poor songs, among them the maudlin 'My Son Calls Another Man Daddy', and not enough of the country blues:

> I went to the doctor / he took one look,
> Said 'The trouble with you / ain't in my book.
> I tell ya what it is, but / it ain' good news:
> You got an awful bad case / o' them low down blues.'

The set of the complete singles issued in 1991 still does not include 'Low Down Blues' (which was probably a demo tape with backing later dubbed), but it is an astonishing set and a cornerstone of post-war popular music. The average level of quality of both songs and performances puts Williams on a plateau where only a handful belong; his ability to communicate directly to his listener places his work beyond any consolation of genre, and has influenced generations of songwriters and vocalists. But we were not supposed to have the low-down blues in America in the early 1950s; most Americans who had enjoyed some of his songs as recorded by mainstream pop artists never heard his hillbilly accent (neither the first nor the last example of classism in the business). Nevertheless, country music provided a great many hit records and songs in the post-war years that are still selling and still being covered. As we have seen, Jimmie Rodgers and Roy Acuff had made the male vocalist the biggest star in country music, and Hank Williams was the greatest of all, but there were many more.

Ernest Tubb was nicknamed the Texas Troubadour; he was

inspired by Rodgers and encouraged by his widow, who gave him one of Jimmie's guitars. His first hit was with his own 'Walking the Floor Over You' in 1942, and when the *Billboard* country chart began in 1944, he filled it with mostly top ten hits all the way through the 1950s, and continued to appear in the chart several times a year in the next decade. He was also famous for Ernest Tubb's Record Shop in Nashville, and for a late-night radio show on WSM, where a talented newcomer might get a boost. Webb Pierce, from Louisiana, brought the honky-tonk style to Nashville for good when he joined the *Opry* in 1955. His three successive number one country hits in 1952 began with 'Back Street Affair', another classic song about adultery (called 'cheatin' songs' in the trade). Pierce had a strong voice, piercing yet rough-edged, and used the steel guitar so effectively that he did more to establish it than almost anybody else.

After attending Princeton and other universities, Texan Hank Thompson formed the Brazos Valley Boys, which had hits from 1948. His somewhat larger band helped keep the feeling of western swing alive with country hits throughout the 1950s, including 'The Wild Side of Life' (1952). Lefty Frizzell (from 1950), Carl Smith (from 1951) and Ray Price (from 1952) were among those with great songs that entered the national consciousness; not even people who hated country music could avoid hearing the biggest hits accidentally, on a jukebox or while cruising the dial on the radio.

Brother acts were also important. The male duet tradition was probably established by the Blue Sky Boys as much as anyone. Bill and Earl Bolick, from South Carolina, used the 'high lonesome' harmony of bluegrass music and traditional instruments; they left music in 1951 partly because they would not add an electric guitar to their act. The Delmore Brothers, Alton and Rabon, from Alabama, recorded for twenty years from 1931, and had a direct effect on the rockabillies of the 1950s with their black-influenced ragtime-like style; Alton is said to have written over a thousand songs, many still in the repertory of country artists today. The Louvin Brothers, actually Charlie and Ira Loudermilk, from North Carolina, began recording in 1949; their 'I Don't Believe You've Met My Baby' (1956) is an example of the portrayal of emotional pain that country music dealt with honestly and, contrary to the belief of those who do not understand country music, with pathos but without sentimentality. Johnnie and Jack were from Tennessee, but were not brothers: Johnny Wright married Kitty Wells in 1938, and Jack Anglin was killed in a car crash in 1963 (on his way to a memorial service for Patsy Cline). Their hits began in 1951 with one of their most successful, 'Poison Love'.

Women were not big stars in country music, despite the influence of Molly O'Day and Rose Maddox (of the Maddox Brothers and Sister Rose from 1947 to 1959, later a soloist). Then Kitty Wells came along. Born Muriel Ellen Deason in Nashville, her stage name was chosen by her husband. She recorded for RCA from 1949, and in 1952, almost apologetically, with a deep country vibrato and a southern accent you could cut with a knife, she established the role of women in country music, talking back to Hank Thompson:

> As I sit here tonight, the juke box playing
> The tune about the wild side of life,
> As I listen to the words you are singing,
> It brings memories of when I was a trusting wife.
>
> It wasn't God who made honky tonk angels,
> As you said in the words to your song.
> Too many times married men think they're still single.
> That has caused many a good girl to go wrong.
>
> It's a shame that all the blame is on us women.
> It's not true that only you men feel the same.
> From the start 'most every heart that's been broken
> Was because there was a man to blame.

And that is the whole song, written by one J. D. Miller. The record is less than two and a half minutes long. With a simple, memorable tune and three very plain verses (albeit with internal rhymes in the last), and years before the advent of fashionable feminism, Wells did not find it necessary to feel sorry for all those heartbroken men crying in their beer. And the next year she gently sassed Webb Pierce, with 'Paying For That Back Street Affair'. She is still the Queen of Country Music, having paved the way for such no-nonsense stars as Loretta Lynn and Tammy Wynette. And she did not rely on answer songs by any means: 'Makin' Believe' in 1955 was one of her own heartachers.

The decade was a golden age for country. While the hits of the white pop singers in the early 1950s were slick and studio-bound, it is significant that many of the country stars recorded with their own backing groups, just as the vocalists of the Swing Era had done; like them, they knew who their audience was, because they saw the faces around the bandstand night after night. Decca and Columbia reported that nearly half their sales of singles were rooted in country music, yet still restricted to a ghetto. Eddy Arnold had nearly seventy top ten hits in the *Billboard* country chart in ten years after 1945, but only two of them were allowed in the pop chart. Pee Wee King's 'Slow Poke' (1952) was one of the few country records (as opposed to covers) to be allowed to cross over. The songs and their attitudes proved far more influential than they were thought to be at the time.

In 1947 the Liberian government commissioned *Liberian Suite* from Duke Ellington; including Al Hibbler's vocal on 'I Like the Sunrise' and five instrumental dances, it was one of the first pieces recorded under Ellington's new contract with Columbia Records. *The Tattooed Bride* (1948), thought by some to be among the best of his longer works, and *Harlem* (1950), commissioned by the NBC Symphony Orchestra, were both later recorded, along with such singles as 'Brown Penny', 'Stomp, Look and Listen', 'Boogie Bop Blues' and many other Ducal delights.

Also in 1947, Woody Herman re-formed his band. The Second Herd, as it came to be called, played arrangements by Ralph Burns, Neal Hefti, Al Cohn, Jimmy Giuffre, Shorty Rogers and John LaPorta, and was as musically exciting as the first. In its first year it recorded a fourth part of Burns's 'Summer Sequence', more than a year after the first three parts; 'Keen and Peachy' was a collaboration by Rogers and Burns. The band's most famous recording was 'Four Brothers', written by Giuffre. Its spirited pastel harmony was played by a reed section of Herbie Steward on alto, Stan Getz and Zoot Sims on tenors and Serge Chaloff on baritone. It was the sound of modern jazz, played by young white musicians thoroughly familiar with the harmonic freedom of bop, and that reed section was the only one as famous among jazz fans as Ellington's.

Count Basie disbanded in 1950, led a small group with Wardell Gray and clarinettist Buddy DeFranco, but started all over again in 1952: having been invited to record for Norman Granz, he led a big band for the rest of his life. But neither Ellington, Herman nor Basie had any hits in the national pop chart in 1950. So what were the number one hits of that year?

The record business was booming in the late 1940s; all Petrillo achieved with his second strike was the establishment of a trustee to oversee the payment of record royalties. In 1947 the US industry exceeded its peak of twenty-five years earlier. But the industry, then as now, was dominated by conservative people; the frenetic recording that took place before the 1948 strike resulted in a backlog of material that the public did not particularly want.

The National Association of Disk Jockeys had been created in 1947 by a press agent, partly in order to plug a film, *Something in the Wind*, about a radio station. The disc jockey, however, was now an important figure. Capitol was the first label to send free records to DJs; the others soon fell into line, and it was understood that the DJ of the period had better judgement than the record labels about what the public wanted. Hence the black jump band of Louis Jordan began doing better on the radio and in the charts, and independent labels got a fairer share of the action. Frankie Laine, already a cabaret veteran of some years, finally struck it big on Chicago's new and energetic Mercury label, with 'That's My Desire'. The DJs were credited with putting an end to weekly radio shows by Bing Crosby, Frank Sinatra and Dinah Shore: why should fans tune in to a weekly show when they could hear their favourites just by leaving the radio on? To get a picture of the trend, here first are the number one *Billboard* hits of 1940:

Artie Shaw	'Frenesi'	RCA Victor
Bing Crosby	'Only Forever'	Decca
Tommy Dorsey, Frank Sinatra		
and the Pied Pipers	'I'll Never Smile Again'	RCA Victor
Glenn Miller	'The Woodpecker Song'	Bluebird (RCA)
Glenn Miller	'Tuxedo Junction'	Bluebird (RCA)
Glenn Miller	'In the Mood'	Bluebird (RCA)

| Frankie Masters | 'Scatter-brain' | Vocalion (Decca) |
| Shep Fields | 'South of the Border' | Bluebird (RCA) |

There are no black artists, no country songs, and only two labels are represented. Shep Fields and Frankie Masters were leaders of sweet bands, now forgotten. 'The Woodpecker Song' was an Italian song with new English words, sung by Marion Hutton (not the same as 'The Woody Woodpecker Song', from the cartoon character, which was later a huge novelty hit). 'Only Forever' was a romantic pop song with a weak middle eight, and was revived by Count Basie and Joe Williams in the mid-1950s. Of these eight titles, four are pop classics (all on RCA) and have been continuously available ever since. Compare the *Billboard* 1940 list with that of 1947:

Vaughn Monroe	'Ballerina'	RCA Victor
Francis Craig	'Near You'	Bullet
Tex Williams	'Smoke! Smoke! Smoke That Cigarette'	Capitol
The Harmonicats	'Peg o' My Heart'	Vitacoustic
Perry Como	'Chi-baba, Chi-baba (My Bambino Go to Sleep)'	RCA Victor
Art Lund	'Mam'selle'	MGM
Ted Weems	'Heartaches'	RCA Victor
Freddy Martin	'Managua, Nicaragua'	RCA Victor
Count Basie	'Open the Door, Richard!'	RCA Victor
Nat Cole Trio	'(I Love You) for Sentimental Reasons'	Capitol
Sammy Kaye	'The Old Lamp-lighter'	RCA Victor

When the figures were in, 1947 was overall a landmark year, but not so hot for the major labels. There are more number one hits, reflecting more releases, a shorter average time at the top and the DJs' ability to tickle the public's fancy with something new. 'Near You', co-written and recorded in Nashville by hotel bandleader Francis Craig, was the biggest hit of the year; another top one was 'Peg o' My Heart', a 1913 song and the first release on Vitacoustic (the harmonica group soon changed to Mercury). Another number one was on the new independent, MGM. Neither Columbia nor

Decca had any number ones. Capitol had two, one of which was a country novelty and the other by Nat Cole, the first black artist to achieve wide fame; only his title on this list might be granted 'pop classic' status. Notice that the low-priced labels, Bluebird and Vocalion, are gone: there was no margin in cheaper records. RCA again had six number ones, but two were flukes: Basie's novelty made it for one week only, and 'Heartaches', by Ted Weems, with Elmo Tanner whistling, was a reissue from 1931. Altogether there are seven male vocals, not counting the jive on the Basie record, including Billy Williams (with Kaye) and Stuart Wade (with Martin), but the other five vocalists are stars, not band singers.

The major labels were troubled by these changes, and they reacted by spending too much money on too many releases, chasing hits without knowing what they were doing. Eli Oberstein had been fired from RCA in 1938, but reinstated in 1945; now he was made a scapegoat and bounced again. In the mid-1930s, when he was doing a good job at Victor, Oberstein had been paid about $6,000 a year; in 1947 Mannie Sachs was poached from Columbia to take over pop recording at RCA at a salary somewhere between $50,000 and $75,000 a year. Sachs said that he consulted his ten-year-old niece when deciding which songs to record; this was thought to be a joke at the time, but in retrospect it is not funny.

Here are the *Billboard* number one hits from 1950:

Patti Page	'Tennessee Waltz'	Mercury
Phil Harris	'The Thing'	RCA Victor
Sammy Kaye	'Harbor Lights'	RCA Victor
Gordon Jenkins and the Weavers	'Goodnight Irene'	Decca
Nat Cole	'Mona Lisa'	Capitol
Anton Karas	'Third Man Theme'	London
Eileen Barton	'If I Knew You Were Comin' I'd've Baked a Cake'	National
Teresa Brewer	'Music! Music! Music!'	London
Red Foley	'Chattanoogie Shoe Shine Boy'	Decca
Ames Brothers	'Rag Mop'	Coral (Decca)
Andrews Sisters	'I Can Dream, Can't I'	Decca

The 1950 list is even more various, a complete jumble. Nat Cole is now no longer leading the trio. There are two titles that were perceived as country or 'folk' and another that should have been. Seven labels are represented. There is only one dance band, and few of the other hits could be danced to. The Phil Harris record illustrates a remarkable (and ominous) trend: many of the hits of the new decade would fall into *Billboard*'s 'novelty' category.

Harris was a good entertainer who deserved his success; among his hits in the 1940s had been 'The Preacher and the Bear' and 'Woodman, Spare That Tree', both revived from the acoustic era. Anton Karas wrote the music and played the zither in the soundtrack of the famous Carol Reed film. 'Rag Mop', also regarded as a novelty, had a strong beat and nonsense words; later it was speculated that 'Rag Mop' had been the first rock'n'roll record, which was not far wrong: hit versions of it included one by its co-author, Johnnie Lee Wills, on Bullet. 'Rag Mop' was a country stomp, no different from 'Osage Stomp', recorded by Bob Wills in 1935, with Johnnie Lee on banjo. The big hit version of 'Rag Mop' was less appropriate: the Ames Brothers were a smooth vocal group.

'Tennessee Waltz' is a good country song, written by Redd Stewart and Pee Wee King in 1948 and a hit in the country chart that year. Page's record was at number one for thirteen weeks and sold six million copies. It provides an early example of multi-tracking, and that gimmick, associated in the public mind with new technology, may have helped establish the 45 rpm format, though the 78 sounded exactly the same. (Mercury had been one of the first to market 45s.) Red Foley began on the WLS *National Barn Dance* in 1930; from the first *Billboard* country chart in 1944 until 1956 he had over fifty top ten hits, 'Chattanoogie Shoe Shine Boy' being another country stomp, and Foley's biggest crossover hit. But the most interesting hit of 1950, and also the biggest, was a sleeper. An urban folk scene had created itself, apparently, with no commercial possibilities at all; then along came 'Goodnight Irene', by the Weavers.

This scene had been nurtured by the American liberal left for many years. Josh White was a black folk and blues singer and guitarist; as a child he was the eyes for street singers such as Blind Blake and Blind Lemon Jefferson, but his literacy and ambition took him to the smart

Café Society Downtown in New York, whereupon he was dismissed by purists. He was also well known for his left-wing politics. Huddie Ledbetter, better known as Leadbelly, was less lucky. He was jailed twice for murder, but was discovered by John and Alan Lomax and sang his way out of jail for the second time in 1934. He worked for the Lomaxes and made his way to New York, where he was taken up by café society in an early example of radical chic, but he was less able to take advantage of it than Josh White. The modern era of folk music in the USA began with the meeting in New York of Leadbelly's country folk-blues, the itinerant dust-bowl troubadour Woody Guthrie and the incipient urban folk of Pete Seeger.

Guthrie was born in Oklahoma and became a legend in his own time. Entirely self-taught, he roamed the country, having seen his father go bankrupt, his sister killed in a coal-oil stove explosion and his mother committed to a mental institution. He worked briefly with his cousin Jack Guthrie, who had country hits on Capitol ('Oklahoma Hills' was number one while Jack was serving in the South Pacific in 1945). Woody's songs include 'This Land Is Your Land' (written as a riposte to Irving Berlin's 'God Bless America'), 'Pastures of Plenty', 'This Train Is Bound for Glory', 'Roll On, Columbia', 'So Long, It's Been Good to Know Ya' and nearly a thousand more. A true folk artist, he would put new words to an old tune as necessary, and was opposed to copyright restrictions on any songs, including his own.

Guthrie's guitar bore the legend 'This machine kills fascists.' His politics were unreservedly left and he wrote for communist newspapers, yet in the far-off days of 1940 he was hired to write songs for the Bonneville Power Administration, a little populism being allowed in the Roosevelt years. He joined the US Merchant Marine and survived torpedo attacks with another folk singer, Cisco Houston; from the mid-1950s Guthrie was seriously ill with Huntington's chorea, an inherited disease of the nervous system.

Pete Seeger's father was musicologist Charles Louis Seeger, who told him that a folksong in a book is like a photograph of a bird in flight; his stepmother was composer Ruth Crawford Seeger, whose string quartet (1931) is an American masterpiece, and who was later an editor of songbooks. His half-sister and half-brother are Peggy and Mike Seeger, also prominent folk musicians; Peggy married the British singer and songwriter Ewan MacColl. Pete tried journalism and painting before he realized he could not really do anything but play the banjo; he designed his own five-string instrument, wrote a manual on how to play it and became a sort of Johnny Appleseed of music. He was described as America's tuning fork.

Seeger had admired a mimeographed collection of Guthrie's songs, and when they met, they formed the Almanac Singers in 1940, with playwright Lee Hays, actor Millard Lampell and others. The group was managed for a while by the William Morris Agency; during the time of the Popular Front it was not a sin to sing union songs, but the FBI took an interest anyway. They sang at radical meetings, sometimes narrowly escaping violence. Seeger came from a privileged background, but saw injustice all around him and had only one way to fight it. He was a member of the Communist Party, and sang for them because they were idealists, the hardest-working and most honest people in sight at a time when the world seemed to be going crazy. His politics were naïve, but his admiration was for the rank and file, not the party bosses, who suddenly did not want anti-fascist songs during the Hitler–Stalin pact.

Seeger's ancestors had fought for American freedom in the eighteenth century, and he was not the only premature anti-fascist in 1940. (The phrase 'premature anti-fascist', by the way, was actually invented by the anti-communist brigade.) The FBI went to RCA and asked them what the Almanac label was (actually Keynote recordings): RCA told the FBI to read *Variety* and *Billboard*. The Almanac era ended when Seeger went into the US Army and Guthrie went to sea.

In 1948 Seeger formed the Weavers, a quartet with voice student Ronnie Gilbert, reedy tenor Fred Hellerman and Hays, who could sing a sepulchral bass and had a nice line of gentle comedy. When they began an engagement at the Village Vanguard, poet Carl Sandburg saw them and was quoted in the papers: 'When I hear America singing, the Weavers are there.' Gordon Jenkins decided to record them at Decca, against the wishes of Dave Kapp. Their first recording was 'Tzena Tzena Tzena', a 1941 Palestinian (then Israeli) song sung in Hebrew; this attracted some interest, so they did it again in

English, this time with Jenkins's orchestral arrangement. 'Tzena' reached number two in the pop chart; DJs turned it over to find Leadbelly's 'Goodnight Irene' on the other side, which quickly became number one. The two-sided hit sold two million copies and inspired an answer song: 'Say Goodnight to the Guy, Irene'.

'Tzena' was great fun, while Jenkins's arrangement for 'Irene' began with a solo violin, like front-porch music. The Weavers were a welcome new sound in 1950, and had no competition. Was it folk? Country music? It didn't matter; it was American, straight off the prairie. Their close harmony was redolent of the Sons of the Pioneers, for kids who liked cowboy movies. 'Goodnight Irene' was a song that deserved its success, though it came too late for Leadbelly to enjoy it. They had a few more hits, but then somebody remembered they were lefties. They vanished from the airwaves, and the Decca contract ran out. Hays later said, 'First we took a sabbatical. Then we took a mondical and a tuesdical.'

A New Year's Eve concert at Carnegie Hall was recorded by Vanguard at the end of 1955, and the group sold albums on that label. Also in 1955, Seeger refused to answer questions from Congress that should have been unconstitutional to begin with; he was indicted for contempt and when the case was finally rejected in 1962, the court went out of its way to insult him. The informer Harvey Matusow had testified that three of the Weavers were party members (one had 'quit'), but later admitted that he had made it all up, and was sentenced to five years' imprisonment for perjury. Meanwhile the drunks and crooks on the House Un-American Activities Committee (one of whom was misappropriating taxpayers' money while chasing communists) had stored up trouble for their own country: a generation of kids that had loved the Weavers was not best pleased when it discovered, many years later, why they had suddenly disappeared.

What else was popular in 1950? 'Music! Music! Music!' was the first of Teresa Brewer's many successes. You either hate her squeaky but accurate voice or love it, but she was an irrepressible entertainer; some of her later hits were produced by Bob Thiele, who became her husband. The song is nothing but a jingle (written by Stephan Weiss and Bernie Baum), the middle eight of which is borrowed from a

Hungarian dance; the lyrics reminded us that a nickelodeon was also a jukebox ('Put another nickel in / In the nickelodeon . . .').

'If I Knew You Were Comin' I'd've Baked a Cake', written by Bob Merrill, is another jingle, like 'Rinso White! Rinso White!', which was a soap advertisement meant to sound like a bird-call; there were also 'Be Happy, Go Lucky!' and 'Brush Your Teeth with Colgate!' Radio had been abandoned to jingles, and the pop records of the early 1950s were made to fit between them. Wage and price controls had been abolished in 1946 in the USA; this was certainly preferable to the maintenance of rationing which went on for years in Britain, but it resulted in post-war inflation. Record prices went up; if you didn't have much money to buy records, and a new record player for the plastic discs, you had to get most of your music from the radio. And if you listened to the radio, the centre of popular music in the USA seemed to be slick studio productions that were indistinguishable from the jingles, and were themselves increasingly strident.

The orthodox view is that sales of albums finally became more important than singles in the late 1960s; in fact, much spurious orthodoxy was later dictated by demographics, or by who was buying the greatest number of records. It is evident in retrospect that the new technology of the long-playing record had an effect on the pop chart and on radio broadcasting right from the beginning. The most interesting music was being made for albums, but album tracks were as rare on post-war radio as live music. Things were better for those who lived in big cities with numerous radio stations, but only the most powerful AM stations could be clearly received 70 miles from, say, Chicago, which made them the most profitable stations – that is, the ones with the most jingles. In 1950 the few FM stations were all in big cities, and FM was difficult to receive at any distance. For a large number of listeners America was a musical wasteland: radio had succeeded in creating the illusion that popular music was boring.

It was the era of the white pop singer, who no longer travelled with a band playing one-nighters around the country, but worked mostly in studios of one kind or another, or in high-priced big-city clubs, so that most people never saw the stars in person. It must be said that many of them were fine musicians, whose roots lay in the Swing Era; without doubt the greatest of them was Frank Sinatra.

Sinatra was hired in 1939 by Harry James, who had just formed his own band; his very first notice (in *Metronome*) commended his 'easy phrasing'. After only a few months Sinatra was hired away by Tommy Dorsey, and became a bobby-socks idol well before his solo career began. When he appeared at the Paramount theatre with Benny Goodman, the band played after the film, and Goodman said simply, 'And now, Frank Sinatra.' Goodman had experienced his own stardom, but was astonished by a wall of screaming; he blurted out, 'What the fuck is *that*?' Some of the girls were paid to scream (as perhaps their grandmothers had been paid to swoon for Paderewski in the 1880s), but even more screamed for nothing, and modern pop hysteria was born.

Sinatra had improved on Bing Crosby. His baritone was even more personable and certainly more vulnerable, and, like a jazz singer, he made each song his own by phrasing it as he felt the words, often across the bar lines. Crosby had been a boyfriend; Sinatra clearly wanted to be a lover. Musicians and critics knew that he was a very good singer, yet by 1952 his career was in decline. The pop music business had fallen on hard times; the golden age of songwriting seemed to be over, and anyway the radio wanted only jingles; the boss was now the studio A&R man rather than a bandleader who confronted a live audience nearly every day. What in the world was 'The Dum-dot Song', which Sinatra recorded in 1947? Should Sinatra have been covering 'Goodnight Irene' and 'Chattanoogie Shoe Shine Boy' in 1950? The idea was not to present the vocalist at his best, but to share in the success of somebody else's hit. Sinatra was also singing the top spot on radio's *Your Hit Parade*, which required him to imitate Woody Woodpecker for weeks on end in 1948.

Often a compulsively generous man, Sinatra has helped a great many people anonymously over the years, and has been willing to give praise where it is due. In *Ebony* magazine he described Billie Holiday as a profound influence; he said he learned about phrasing and breath control from Dorsey, and he even commended his rivals, including Tony Bennett, and said that Vic Damone had 'the best pipes in the business'. In 1945 he had recorded with the Charioteers, a black gospel group, and conducted an instrumental album of music by Alec Wilder; he admired the music, and hoped that his name would help to sell it. The same year he made a short film and a record called 'The House I Live In', pleas for racial tolerance. But he had a quick temper, a thin skin and a tempestuous private life, inevitably conducted in public. He divorced Nancy in 1950 (after eleven years) and married Ava Gardner in 1951. 'I'm a Fool to Want You', made that year, was honest and heartfelt pop singing at its best (but it was backed with 'Mama Will Bark', a novelty duet with Dagmar, an 'actress' famous for her mammary measurement).

Sinatra had been one of the biggest stars in show business for a decade, and the knives were sharpening. His television and radio appearances were flops, and he was not being offered good film parts. On top of everything else, his publicity agent and close friend George Evans died suddenly in 1950, at the age of forty-eight, and Mannie Sachs, another close friend, left Columbia to go to RCA, and Sinatra's booking agency dropped him. It did not occur to the tabloid mentality of the newspaper columnists and fanzines that the pain in Sinatra's private life might in the end make him an even better interpreter of good songs.

In 1953 he landed the part of Maggio in *From Here to Eternity*, for which he won an Oscar; he also signed a new contract with Capitol Records, which required Sinatra to pay for all his own arrangements. His first Capitol recording session was with his long-time arranger Axel Stordahl, but the next was with Nelson Riddle. 'I've Got the World on a String' from that session was a good song from 1932, by Ted Koehler and Harold Arlen, and in the summer of 1953 Sinatra's recording of it seemed to inaugurate a new era in pop: as the record came over the air on the radio, the singer was clearly a man who really *did* have the world on a string, in spite of everything.

The lush, string-laden sound of Stordahl and the rustle of spring provided by large numbers of woodwinds had lent themselves to many fine Sinatra records; when he left Columbia, Sinatra owed the label money, but before long his hits of the 1940s, still selling, were paying him royalties. In any case, the sound had been traded for the architecture of Riddle, who knew that a song tells a story, and that the arrangement has to lead up to it, with a beginning, a middle and an end. His unique touches, such as using a bass clarinet or a bass trombone as a springboard for a rhythmic phrase, made Riddle the most sought-after arranger of this kind of music, and his work in this area has dated less than almost anyone else's. Sinatra worked with Riddle on *In the Wee Small Hours*, one of the first concept albums, but also recorded with Gordon Jenkins and Billy May, and later Sy Oliver and Quincy Jones. He made recordings for grown-ups, who bought albums, and his status as the best male interpreter of America's best songs was never again in doubt. Of nineteen Capitol albums from 1954 to 1962, most reached the top five on the *Billboard* album chart; he then started his own Reprise label, and had several hit albums a year throughout the 1960s.

Nat Cole formed his King Cole Trio in 1937. He later became one of the most popular vocalists of the century, and easily the most successful black entertainer of the post-war decades. Much as the public loved his voice, and still loves it, his singing has been underrated by critics; he swings without anybody noticing. But he was even more influential as a pianist, and at first was reluctant to sing. In mid-1944 his own composition, 'Straighten Up and Fly Right', was a top ten hit, and his third number one (without the trio) was 'Mona Lisa', an Oscar-winning film song and also one of the most typical of a new era, in that it was very romantic but not very easy to dance to. Cole's phrasing and the unique beauty of his voice kept him in the charts until he died of lung cancer in 1965, and his albums are still selling.

Tony Bennett had landed a Columbia contract; 'Boulevard of Broken Dreams' revived a good song from 1933, by Al Dubin and Harry Warren, and the record was highly rated by critics, but no hit. At what would have been his last recording session he was backed by Percy Faith on 'Because of You' (from 1940, by Arthur Hammerstein and Dudley Wilkinson), which was number one for ten weeks in 1951; then he did it again the same year with Hank Williams's 'Cold, Cold Heart'. Bennett too was a singer's singer, highly rated by songwriters, musicians and critics alike, and soon sold albums.

Perry Como sang with Ted Weems from 1936 to 1942, then signed with RCA as a soloist, and his total number of hits up to 1955 was second only to Bing Crosby's. His hits included some junk, such as 'N'yot N'yow (the Pussycat Song)' and 'Hoop-de-doo' (between 1947 and that vintage year of 1950), but his transparent sincerity and his respect for a song lent him a winning way with a ballad. He was probably underrated by critics: being laid back is a sneaky way of swinging. One of his hits was 'Don't Let the Stars Get in Your Eyes' (1954), a country song that crossed over; the arrangement worked hard while Como made it sound easy. He was immensely popular on television for decades; Val Doonican copied his style in the UK.

Eddie Fisher, a strong boyish tenor, was the teenagers' heart-throb in the early 1950s. His romance and marriage to Debbie Reynolds did his career no harm, but leaving her later for Elizabeth Taylor did. His RCA recordings, backed by Hugo Winterhalter, were good studio productions and were better than some of the jingles on the radio, but Fisher was nothing like the musician Sinatra or Bennett was. Frankie Laine was regarded as an emotional 'belter' in the context of the early 1950s rather than a crooner; his first hit, 'That's My Desire' (1947), was well deserved, reviving a good song from 1931, but his belting was often deployed on novelties that quickly dated, such as 'Mule Train', 'Cry of the Wild Goose' and 'Jezebel'. Johnnie Ray had a huge hit with 'Cry' backed with his own 'The Little White Cloud That Cried'; he too was an emotional performer and a heart-throb. Guy Mitchell's first hit was 'My Heart Cries for You' (1950), which had been turned down by Sinatra; it was adapted from an eighteenth-century French song by Percy Faith. Mitch Miller, however, backed Mitchell on his hits, including 'The Roving Kind', 'Sparrow in the Tree Top', 'My Truly, Truly Fair' and 'Pittsburgh Pennsylvania', all of which show Miller's distinctive instrumental jolliness (whooping French horns). Nobody was better than Miller at competing with radio jingles.

Who do we regard today as the best male pop singers of the era? The way the singles compare with the albums in the *Billboard* charts provides a clue. Between 1950 and 1955 inclusive, Sinatra had seven hit singles (coming out of a bad period), Nat Cole twenty-one, Tony Bennett eleven, Perry Como twenty-five, Eddie Fisher thirty, Frankie

Laine twenty, Johnnie Ray ten and Guy Mitchell nine. Let us look at best-selling albums: by 1985 Sinatra had sixty-nine hit albums and Nat Cole thirty (not counting albums by the trio, and bearing in mind that he died in the mid-1960s). Tony Bennett had twenty-four hit albums, Perry Como thirty (not counting his perennial Christmas entries), Eddie Fisher nine, Frankie Laine six, Johnnie Ray two and Guy Mitchell none. Sinatra and Bennett were still making albums in the 1980s, and a point to note about albums is that they stayed in print longer and were reissued, like 78s in the old days.

As a measure of artistry, even in the heyday of the pop singer, the singles chart had ceased to matter as an indicator of quality as soon as grown-ups could buy albums.

If anything, there were even more girl singers making hits in the early 1950s, but a direct comparison with the males is difficult. To begin with, the list of hits for each female artist is shorter on average, suggesting that they received less promotion from their record companies and/or less attention from the D Js; or perhaps they simply made fewer records. On the whole, the women were more diffident about success, or less able to chase it for personal reasons: Jo Stafford, Rosemary Clooney and Joni James each retired from the music scene, for various reasons, while Peggy Lee seems to have left it and come back as she pleased. As in the case of the males, however, most had made their start during the Big Band Era.

One of the best, and best loved, was Jo Stafford, a founder member of the Pied Pipers, a vocal octet which became a quartet when it joined Tommy Dorsey in 1940. The group left Dorsey in 1942 and Stafford began a solo career in 1944, having sung lead and solo with Dorsey often enough to become known as 'GI Jo', a favourite of the soldiers fighting overseas. She had a faultless ear (almost perfect pitch), and in many ways was a quintessentially American singer: apart from her warm, distinctive tonal colour (incredibly, some critics called her 'cold'), she had a folksinger's vibrato.

Taking into account jukebox plays, radio plays and other listings, she had about seventy-five hits. Most of these were on Capitol in the 1940s; in 1950 she went with Paul Weston to Columbia, where she had several of the biggest hits of the era: 'You Belong to Me' was written by Redd Stewart, Pee Wee King and Chilton Price; 'Make Love to Me!' was based on 'Tin Roof Blues', an old jazz standard. With a good beat but without stylistic flourishes, Stafford invariably suggested swing in her music. Her last hit singles were in 1956–7. Tired of the grind, she had stopped appearing in public, and then entered a long and happy California retirement.

With Weston, by then her husband, she created Jonathan and Darlene Edwards, a comedy duo in which she sang slightly off pitch (harder than it sounds). Jonathan and Darlene achieved separate identities of their own. Jonathan claimed that he played stride piano better than Fats Waller, to which Darlene replied 'Actually, 5/4 gives you an extra stride.' The jokes convulsed musicians: drummer Jack Sperling had to be replaced on a session because he could not stop laughing.

Peggy Lee joined Benny Goodman when she was twenty-one. The first hit typical of her style was 'Why Don't You Do Right?' (1943). She left Goodman, married guitarist Dave Barbour and retired, but she could not stay away. She and Barbour wrote 'Mañana (is Soon Enough for Me)', a huge hit on Capitol in 1948. (The song has been accused in retrospect of belittling Hispanics, but this is nonsense: white America in those years could have used the advice to slow down and enjoy life; people who make such charges are themselves patronizing.) Lee went to Decca, and her material improved: her first big success there, in 1952, was something that Capitol had not wanted to record, Gordon Jenkins's arrangement of Rodgers and Hart's 'Lover'; the surrealistically, almost frenetically, swirling orchestra was a perfect setting for Lee's deceptively laconic interpretation. In the mid-1950s she went back to Capitol as an album-seller: her first hit album on that label, *The Man I Love* in 1957, was conducted by Sinatra. Her top ten cover of Little Willie John's 'Fever' (1958) was disappointing only for those who loved the R&B original. 'Is That All There Is' (1969) was more suitable: written by Jerry Leiber and Mike Stoller, by then famous for rock'n'roll songs, it was an example of the less well-known side of their talent, and a vehicle for her combination of resignation and sly humour.

Rosemary Clooney had begun in a duo with her sister Betty and the Tony Pastor band in the 1940s, then signed with Columbia, where her first smash hit was 'Come on-a My House' in 1951. A greater contrast to Peggy Lee could not be imagined: in lines like 'I'm gonna give-a you a pomegranate!' the sexuality was joyously raucous. The recording was perhaps the first to feature Stan Freeman's amplified harpsichord (used the next year on Percy Faith's instrumental 'Delicado' and on two more Clooney records, 'Botch-a-me', from an Italian film, and 'Too Old to Cut the Mustard', a duet with Marlene Dietrich). 'Come on-a My House' had been written by playwright William Saroyan and his cousin Ross Bagdasarian in 1939 and used in an off-Broadway play in 1950; its Armenian flavour was probably taken for an Italian one by most Americans at the time. (Bagdasarian later became David Seville, creator of the Chipmunks in the late 1950s.)

Joni James started out as Joan Babbo, a dancer from Chicago; she had more than a dozen hits on MGM (1952–4) with orchestral backing by Lew Douglas. 'Why Don't You Believe Me?', 'Have You Heard?' and 'Is It Any Wonder?' were all questions suited to her wistful little-girl style. The most ambitious was 'Almost Always', which had a sort of soft rhumba beat. All four of these titles had co-writers in common; it looks, in retrospect, like a clever put-up job, and the hits still reek of nostalgia for anyone who went to junior high school sock hops in those years.

Ella Mae Morse sang with Jimmy Dorsey in 1939, and had a big hit on Capitol with pianist Freddie Slack's band in 1942, 'Cow Cow Boogie'; under her own name her hits in the following decade included 'The Blacksmith Blues' (1952), which required somebody in Nelson Riddle's band to play an anvil. Georgia Gibbs had a number one on Mercury in 1952 with 'Kiss of Fire', another tango adaptation ('El choclo'); she had a second chart career a few years later. Kay Starr had been a superior big-band singer, but her hit singles were multi-tracked material, such as 'Bonaparte's Retreat' (1950) and 'Wheel of Fortune' (1952); she came back on RCA in 1955 with 'Rock and Roll Waltz', an unlovely combination of 3/4 time and kling-kling-kling piano which was number one for six weeks.

Stan Kenton's female singers, Anita O'Day, June Christy and Chris Connor, were much too good for the singles charts. Jeri Southern was a pianist and singer in an intimate cabaret style, which is to say too good an interpreter for the hit parade. (She was more popular in Britain, which did not even have charts then.) On the whole the female singers were badly mishandled by the music business of the period. Kay Starr did some attractive album work, and her 1953 duet with herself on 'Side By Side' was a treat, but 'Wheel of Fortune' was not much of a song, and was over so fast it could hardly be called an arrangement (another excellent example of something designed to fit between two jingles). Ella Mae Morse probably had more talent than we knew at the time: Capitol's A & R man Voyle Gilmore had her singing junk like 'Seventeen' and 'Razzle Dazzle', while Dave Cavanaugh was braver, with 'Greyhound' and 'Jump Back Honey'. Her version of 'Smack Dab in the Middle', however, a song which became something of a jazz standard in other hands, had a lame white-bread vocal-group backing. The white R & B of which she may have been capable never really got out of the studio.

The nadir of the whole business was plumbed in 1953. Displaying attractive vocal colour, a professional attitude and not much in the way of style, Patti Page (Clara Ann Fowler, from Oklahoma) had over eighty chart hits in the twenty years following 1948, with everything from country songs to show tunes: 'Tennessee Waltz' was a record breaker, 'I Went to Your Wedding' was another big hit and in 1953 'The Doggie in the Window' was number one in the USA for eight weeks. It would be unfair to call this a nursery rhyme; it was childish rather than childlike. Nobody knows how many music fans stopped listening to the radio after hearing 'Doggie in the Window' too many times. And who wrote 'Doggie in the Window'? Bob Merrill, the same fellow who wrote 'If I Knew You Were Comin' I'd've Baked a Cake'.

The chart album history for the women singers is similar to that of the men. The best stylists, O'Day, Christy, Connor and Lee, have been selling albums to the *cognoscenti* for decades; Stafford and Weston have leased or purchased their material from CBS so they could reissue it on their own Corinthian label, since the fans are still out there; Southern's work has been mostly out of print for years. Clooney made admirable albums, including duets with Bing Crosby; after resolving problems in her personal life, she came back to record for Concord Jazz in the 1980s, her tasteful singing of standards backed by good jazzmen. In a touring Christmas show in December 1990, with her vocalist daughter-in-law, many children and the Minnesota Orchestra (formerly the Minneapolis Symphony), Clooney had more stage presence than everyone else in the room put together. Doris Day, one of the biggest cinema box office successes of the century, had talent that shone through the dross, but her advice was poor; some of the records and most of the films have dated badly. Georgia Gibbs, Patti Page, Joni James and others, for all their successful singles, never did anything much in the grown-up market.

There were occasional pearls among the muck. The experienced Kitty Kallen had a lovely number one (for nine weeks) in 1954 with 'Little Things Mean a Lot', and Dean Martin, who had the virtue of not taking himself too seriously, did some charming work: 'Money Burns a Hole in My Pocket' was an unpretentious film song, on the other side of which was 'Sway' (a Mexican song called 'Quien Sera'); both did well in 1954. And his 'Memories are Made of This' the next year, with gentle, appropriate vocal backing by Terry Gilkyson's Easy Riders, was a more appealing than usual number one (for six weeks). None of these recordings was overproduced. Martin had more hit singles during the following decade, but eventually seemed to parody himself.

In the early 1950s the major labels sometimes shipped 100,000 copies of a new record by an unknown artist on a 100 per cent return basis, hoping for lightning to strike. This was later described by a Capitol executive as 'throwing a lot of shit at the wall to see if anything sticks'. They put their big stars on television, but these were just radio shows with pictures, and did not necessarily help to sell records. Sachs at RCA offered his big stars very expensive contracts, luring Dinah Shore back from Columbia in 1950; she was a success with a television variety show, but no longer a big pop star.

Before leaving one of the most dismal periods in the history of popular music, one more phenomenon deserves mention. Lester Polfus, the 'Wizard of Waukesha', was born in that suburb of Milwaukee in 1916 and changed his name to Les Paul. Inspired by Gene Autry, he taught himself to be one of the best guitar players that ever lived, having begun as a teenager on the radio. He could and did play everything from country music to jazz, and probably did not see much difference, concentrating as he did on musicianship. He made himself an electric guitar as early as 1929, by fixing a ceramic record-player cartridge under the strings in order to play through the amplifier and speaker. Later it took him a dozen years to convince Gibson to market his solid-body guitar, whereupon in the dozen years after 1954 the 'Les Paul model' became one of the most famous instruments ever made.

He recorded with Art Tatum around 1944, and was the best guitarist Tatum ever played with. On Decca he accompanied Bing Crosby and the Andrews Sisters with his own trio. In 1949 he married country singer Colleen Summer, who changed her name to Mary Ford; meanwhile, he had been one of the first to experiment with tape recording and multi-tracking: his solo hits on Capitol included 'Brazil' (1948), on which he played six parts. His hits in a duo with Ford began in 1950, and they had an average of four or five a year for most of the decade. After hearing Anita O'Day singing 'Vaya Con Dios' on the radio, they recorded it as a B side and persuaded D Js to turn the record over: 'Vaya Con Dios' was number one for eleven weeks. A song by Larry Russell, Inez James and Buddy Pepper, the title literally means 'Go with God' (more idiomatically, 'May God be with you'). Les Paul and Mary Ford's Mexican-flavoured waltz treatment at just the right tempo was a hit for so long that you grew tired of it, but it holds up better today than almost anything else of the period.

In any case, the applecart was about to be kicked over. In the same year as 'Doggie in the Window' and 'Vaya Con Dios', a truck driver made a custom recording in Memphis for his mother. Before discussing Elvis, we will examine the other things that were going on in the early 1950s. For it was as true then as it is now that there was a large amount of good music being made.

13

Music for Grown-ups

From the early 1950s the popular music business was fragmented in a new way. Rhythm and blues, country music and modern jazz were never in the minority so far as musical values were concerned; they were large and profitable markets, and with more lasting worth than hit pop singles. Yet the hits appeared to most people to represent the centre of the business, which was dislocated. At a time when technology and increasing prosperity should have made things easier, it became more difficult for the so-called minority musics to recruit new fans, and for hard-core fans to find something to listen to.

Of course, the music business as a whole continued to think of ways of cheating itself. Neal Hefti recorded a successful arrangement called 'Coral Reef' (on the Coral label) in 1951 which sold about 400,000 copies (though Hefti's publicity described it as a million-seller). Hefti later said:

You heard it all over. Disc jockeys used it for themes . . . Billy May was asking for it; Ralph Flanagan asked for it, Ralph Marterie: some of the bands that were sprouting up in those days, they wanted it. And we all thought, 'If you play "Coral Reef", I'll play, whatever.' And we could, sort of, maybe, between the four of us, instigate some interest in bands.

But the publisher, Jack Bregman, would not print it, not even an onion skin (a kind of cheap lead-sheet for information purposes only). Hefti had to print his own onion skin so that he could pass out copies, and after that he started keeping his own copyrights.

Then the union decided it did not like touring bands, after decades in which bands had toured the country and only fifteen years after Benny Goodman had touched off the Swing Era itself on a tour. Local 802 (the New York City branch of the AFM) made a rule that only local bands could play at the Paramount, which touring big bands had made into a shrine. And when D Js wanted to interview Hefti, he could be fined $500 by the union if he did it on a station that did not employ any musicians. 'And so the jockeys would get very salty and say, "Well, my God, Patti Page was here last week, and she couldn't have been nicer." So when I added all this up, I wasn't making any money, got two little kids, I decided to forget about it, very frankly.' And of course Patti Page did not have to belong to the AFM. So another good band bit the dust, and the music industry thus shot off the fragmented parts of itself.

One of the most evident genres throughout the 1950s was the first instance of revivalism, which several decades later has innumerable forms. In 1939 Muggsy Spanier's Ragtime Band had made sixteen sides which represented a tribute to the music that these Chicagoans had grown up with and loved. The New Orleans and Chicago styles had never really gone away, but there had been a quietly simmering attitude during the Swing Era that the only true jazz was the earliest kind, and in 1939 a self-conscious revival got under way, almost unnoticed at the time. In San Francisco Lu Watters began a residency at the Dawn Club with his Yerba Buena Jazz Band, the line-up of which was identical to that of the King Oliver band of 1923: two cornets (Watters and Bob Scobey), trombone (Turk Murphy), piano (Wally Rose), clarinet, drums, tuba (which the acoustic Oliver recordings did not allow) and banjo and vocalist (Clancy Hayes). Revivalism simmered for a while, then exploded into a vicious war of words among jazz fans and journalists at the advent of bop, which gave the traditionalists apoplexy. The word 'ragtime' had finally been dropped, and the music of the revival, along with the remnants of Chicago style, began to be called dixieland jazz, and the word 'jazz' began to lose its usefulness.

Spanier, trumpeter Wild Bill Davison and others recorded for Commodore in the mid-1940s in New York, where they worked in clubs like Nick's and Jimmy Ryan's; Eddie Condon was a spark-plug to the end of his days. Their music, unfairly or not, came to be heard as dixieland by the American public; they had been struggling to make a living in music all their lives, and were slowly relegated to the sidelines. Any recording with clarinettist Pee Wee Russell had at least that to recommend it; he recorded four titles at a quartet date for Commodore which are priceless, and towards the end of his life had opportunities to work in less tradition-bound surroundings.

Some of the dixie was dire. The Firehouse Five Plus Two were a group of amateurs led by trombonist Ward Kimball, who worked during the day at the Disney studios; they started recording in 1949, and their music was never intended to be anything but a jolly noise. The Dukes of Dixieland also began playing in 1949. A second-rate band formed by the New Orleans Assunto family, it achieved its greatest fame by making some of the first stereo recordings in excellent sound in the late 1950s. Trombonist Wilbur De Paris and his brother Sidney also recorded for Commodore, and later for Atlantic; Wilbur was the leader, and his imagination was stuck in the 1920s; the band had a certain following mainly because of Sidney, who did not say much but was a fine trumpet player.

There was nothing defensive at all about the albums made by Paul Wesley 'Doc' Evans, a cornet player from Minnesota, who was extremely well recorded on the Audiophile label; they are pretty, affectionate and cherishable. They often included pianist John 'Knocky' Parker, who had begun in western swing. The Rampart Street Paraders, Hollywood studio musicians, made albums for Columbia: clarinettist Matty Matlock, trumpeter Clyde Hurley and tenor saxophonist Eddie Miller, all of whom had once played for Ben Pollack. Their albums were loose and lovely: they were playing for anyone who wanted to listen, and had no axe to grind, but although the music was essentially Chicago style, it was heard as dixieland – hence Rampart Street Paraders, a name which helped to sell the albums.

Cornettist Bobby Hackett was a musicians' musician. Neither he nor Jack Teagarden was recorded often enough, but they made an album together for Capitol called *Coast Concert!* in the mid-1950s which was absolute magic; as if to thumb their noses at those who would pigeon-hole good music, they used banjo and tuba on one track, guitar and string bass on the next. Drummer Nick Fatool, who had worked with Shaw and Goodman, played with both the Rampart Street Paraders and Hackett and Teagarden. Don Ewell, a swinging pianist who loved to play Jelly Roll Morton and Fats Waller tunes, made a delightful two-piano album with Willie 'the Lion' Smith. Joe

Sullivan and Ralph Sutton were fine traditional pianists, Sutton two-fisted and Sullivan more of a composer. Trumpeter Al Hirt and clarinettist Pete Fountain were very good white New Orleans musicians who did well in the marketplace. Hirt in particular was a fine technician, but he stuck to the safe route of entertaining tourists, and is said to have presented young Wynton Marsalis with his first trumpet.

Watters's band broke up in the early 1950s, and Turk Murphy led a revival band for the rest of his life. He always used banjo and brass bass, but was not out to score any points: privately also admiring more modern music, he played the music he loved best well enough to make many fans happy. Bob Scobey changed from cornet to trumpet, and his Frisco Band entertained crowds in the 1950s with a sort of 'let's pretend, turn of the century, good old days' saloon music. The genial but powerful baritone of Clancy Hayes was ideal on tunes like 'Silver Dollar' (1950, Clarke Van Ness and Jack Palmer), 'Ace in the Hole' (not the Cole Porter song, but another item by James Dempsey and George Mitchell), Irving Berlin's revived 'I Want to Go Back to Michigan' and a very good version of Ma Rainey's 'See See Rider'. (Hayes was also a songwriter, and his 'Huggin' and Chalkin'' was a number one hit by Hoagy Carmichael in 1946.)

Back in the mainstream music business, Woody Herman made a long series of live recordings in various locations in 1948, which were issued years later on 'nostalgia' labels. It was more than a year before Herman's Second Herd recorded again in the studio, and for a new label, Capitol; a year after that, the personnel had almost completely changed. Not only was the band business a rocky one, but the Second Herd was full of drug addicts, which disgusted Herman and was too much trouble. Baritone saxophonist Serge Chaloff was a superb musician, but wrecked his health on heroin; he was also a proselytizer, and set up shop behind a curtain in the back of the band's bus to sell drugs to the others.

Herman continued leading big bands almost until the end of his life. He was a great talent scout, hiring many a fine young musician, and a natural editor; he would touch up an arrangement while the band tried it out until it was just right. Some of the men in the

Second Herd thought he was old-fashioned, but when he played a solo on a Gerry Mulligan arrangement, Mulligan said that Herman's solo was the only one that had anything to do with the music. Somewhere along the way a manager disappeared with money that had been withheld from the band's salaries to pay income taxes; Herman was left holding the bill and never caught up. He was a forgiving man, generous in spirit and loved by everyone who knew him. He died owing the government a large amount of money, which, as someone said, was either a tragedy or a masterpiece of forward planning.

At the other end of the absurd controversy over what was jazz and what was not was Thelonious Monk. By the late 1940s, after much furious activity, there were often clichés in bop, but never in Monk's music: it displayed only daring, boldness and the unexpected. Monk has long been described as a great composer, yet all he did was write beautifully organized and truly original themes. His idiosyncratic rhythm and harmony have meant that very few musicians have been able to improvise on them properly. Monk's keyboard style was technically unorthodox, and some said he could not play very well, but, as Paul Bacon wrote in a record review in 1948, 'his style and approach cost him 50 per cent of his technique. He relies so much on absolute musical reflex that Horowitz's technique might get in the way.' Monk was sitting with several other men in a car in which drugs were discovered; he was arrested and (like Billie Holiday) lost his cabaret card, so that he could not play in clubs in New York. He remained almost unknown to the general public.

In 1948 Miles Davis had put together an unusual nine-piece band, which contained a French horn and a tuba. It gave one performance and recorded for Capitol; the studio tracks have been almost continuously in print on an album called *Birth of the Cool*. The style required a high degree of musicianship, and was highly arranged by Mulligan, Gil Evans, John Lewis and Johnny Carisi; the sound was an outgrowth of Evans's and Mulligan's work for the Claude Thornhill band, and set the tone for what came to be called cool jazz. Many of the players and arrangers in Herman's Second Herd were leading lights in what became West Coast jazz, often considered much the same thing. The Gerry Mulligan Quartet, with handsome young Chet Baker on trumpet and, unusually, with no piano, began recording in California in 1952. When Mulligan received a ninety-day jail sentence for a drug-related offence and Baker went off on his own, his quartet had the excellent Russ Freeman on piano, and Baker began to sing, in a little-boy voice with minimal vibrato – cool, like his trumpet playing. The girls liked it (the ones who listened to jazz) but the critics did not.

West Coast jazz, largely a media invention which had the important side-effect of ignoring its black participants, had plenty of fans at the time, but jazz critics (most of whom are really only commentators) had doubts about it, because it was not pretentious or dramatic; what it was about was beauty. Perhaps there was something in the Californian climate that contributed to the laid-back quality of much of the music. It swung and it was often lovely, but the frenetic quality of bop was largely gone, which may be why the white brand was more popular with the public: they did not have to listen as hard. Yet Baker's playing and singing on 'My Buddy' (1922, Gus Kahn and Walter Donaldson), for example, has just as much integrity now as it did then; his notes were always chosen in the service of beauty. Mulligan has constantly been a spark-plug (the Eddie Condon of modern jazz), ready to jam at any time, and writing many a fine tune. Freeman retired from the road, but years later provided an interesting comment:

three or four times in my life, while playing, I have suddenly become disembodied – in the sense that I seem to be . . . watching myself play . . . you're just creating music and it's like pouring water out of a pitcher . . . That's what you're after, that high. There are a lot of layers, though, that go with it. It's a zig-zag existence and it's one of the reasons I stopped . . . It became very painful to go through those periods where you get on a bandstand and you try something and it's not happening.

Freeman's retirement was our loss for, as Mulligan told him, he was a composer: such well-known Baker tunes as 'Bea's Flat', 'Fan Tan' and 'Summer Sketch' were his. Jazz groups did not make much money recording for small labels and had no hope of jukebox hits;

they had to make a living on the road, just as the big bands had a generation earlier. This was no doubt good for the music, but it was a hard life, and by this time the heroin plague had hit jazz.

Black and white musicians on both coasts were playing contemporary music which was beautiful, important and is still selling. Yet they were treated like dirt by the music business. Coleman Hawkins had had a middle-class upbringing, or at least a secure one, by American black standards; when he was still a teenager, touring with Mamie Smith in 1922, a theatre manager absconded with box office receipts and for the first time in his life he was hungry. He later had a reputation for being fussy about money, no doubt because he never forgot that early lesson. The risks were there for everybody touring in vaudeville and in music, in every decade. But the risks were always worse for blacks, and as bad as ever in the early 1950s for those who were playing some of the best music.

It is difficult to say to what extent the heroin plague was the result of organized crime's finding a new source of income and a new supply of victims in Harlem. Charlie Parker had become addicted to heroin as a teenager in Kansas City, and some people (such as trumpeter Red Rodney) were imitating their idol, though he did everything possible to warn them off it: 'Any musician who says he is playing better on tea, the needle, or when he is juiced, is a plain, straight liar.' Parker did a remarkable job of keeping his own habit under control for a long time, but in his later years even he was affected by his own dissipation. Gerry Mulligan and Miles Davis had enough sense not to become involved at the time; Parker took heroin in front of Mulligan on one occasion: 'And he did it in the most horrendous way possible, with blood all over the place – it was just dreadful. So he made his point . . .' Yet both Davis and Mulligan later became addicted.

It was Parker who said to Davis, 'You better watch out. There's a little white cat out on the West Coast who's gonna eat you up.' Freeman claims that in the early 1950s almost all the jazz musicians were addicted, which would mean, among other things, that most of them managed to kick the habit; he also says that Baker became an addict after most others had given it up. In San Francisco in 1968 five drug addicts beat up Baker so badly that he had to have his mouth rebuilt, and did not play for two years. But Baker never gave up drugs.

Contrary to popular belief, Baker was not at first influenced by Miles Davis. Yet it is more than a coincidence that they both made a speciality of 'My Funny Valentine', emphasizing the minor-key aspects of the tune and making it into a 'feel sorry for yourself' anthem. They contributed to the invention of a new intimate and lyrical trumpet style, different from the shouting brass instrument that it often was (though the intimate side was part of the art of Roy Eldridge, Harry Edison, Gillespie and many others, to say nothing of Oliver, Bix and Rex Stewart, who all played cornet). Joe Goldberg has mentioned the 'feminine principle' of 'Attis–Adonis' adumbrated by literary critic Edmund Wilson when writing about his friend F. Scott Fitzgerald, an alcoholic who died relatively young: 'the fair youth, untimely slain, who is ritually bewailed by women, then resuscitates ... when his legend has become full-fledged and beyond his own power to shatter it'. Only 'such a poet', not necessarily effeminate, but capable of 'a kind of feminine ventriloquism', can 'represent life's renewal'. Baker, like Bix, was supposed to die young, and for some fans he did. Drugs cost him time, money, favour in the music business and ultimately his life, when he fell out of a hotel-room window in Amsterdam in 1988; but he had played beautifully most of the time.

The death in 1947 of Woody Herman's trumpeter Sonny Berman was one of the first drug-related deaths. (In Berman's case we again meet the Jewish influence in jazz: fans have even been advised to listen to a good cantor, and then listen once more to his recorded solos.) Vocalist David Allyn sang with Jack Teagarden, becoming moderately famous (and highly regarded among musicians) while still a teenager; his introduction to drugs came through morphine, which he took after being wounded during the war, and later it wrecked his career. The trombonist Earl Swope was an athlete; in every town he went to he would find the local gym and work out. But then he became addicted. Pianist Joe Albany suffered from poor health for many years; trumpeter Fats Navarro died of tuberculosis, but his heroin addiction could not have done him any good. (Navarro had replaced Gillespie in Eckstine's band, recorded once with Benny

Goodman and had pieces written for him by Tadd Dameron, an important arranger. Navarro's playing was sculptural, perfectly under control yet magnificently impetuous.) Chaloff, Dameron, Ike Quebec and John Coltrane were all at one time narcotics addicts who later died of cancer: no one knows how much drugs predispose the victim to an early death. Parker, Billie Holiday and pianist Sonny Clarke are among those who damaged their health by attempting to wean themselves off drugs with alcohol.

It was not as if the life was not dangerous enough. Another great unfinished career was that of Navarro's disciple, Clifford Brown (known as Brownie), a clean-living man who was already becoming much better known than most jazz musicians when, like Frank Teschemacher, Bessie Smith, Chu Berry and many others, he was killed in a car crash. The excellent pianist and composer Richie Powell, Bud's younger brother, and Powell's wife were killed in the same crash that took Brownie; Doug Watkins, one of the finest bass players of the post-war decades, also died in a crash, and his contribution is now almost forgotten. An excellent black pianist who died in 1984 had contracted Aids from a needle. Why have so many chosen to add to the dangers of the road?

Red Rodney was one of those in the Herman band who did not succumb to the allure of drugs, but later, with Parker, 'standing next to that giant every day, I probably said to myself, "I wonder if I jumped over . . ."'

The issue of the effect of drugs on music has not often been discussed. Ira Gitler bravely approached it in his *Jazz Masters of the '40s* (1966), then in his oral history collection *Swing to Bop* (1985). In the earlier book he wrote: 'In spite (or because?) of [heroin] a great music was made.' Some critics questioned that, but he confesses in the later book that he would take out the question mark. The music would not have been what it was without everything that went into it; and it was hard enough being different. There is a story about a bunch of musicians on the road who got lost, driving around in Shaker Heights, the affluent Cleveland suburb, in the middle of the night. They gawked at the big moonlit houses of the relatively rich, until somebody said, 'Yeah, but what do they know? What do they know about Charlie Parker, about Dizzy Gillespie?' And everybody laughed. In fact, some of the residents of Shaker Heights must have had their stashes of Parker records, but drugs were part of what enabled musicians to say, 'We know; they don't.'

If it is dangerous to 'operate heavy machinery' under the influence of an intoxicating substance, then it is not possible to be a better musician, from a mechanical standpoint, while stoned. Music depends above all on execution, the ability to play. But a professional musician's muscles are highly trained, and the conception, the ideas, are also important. Drugs seemed to facilitate concentration, to the extent that they shut out noise and worries and allowed the musician to get on with the work. Mulligan said that for years he could write for eighteen hours at a stretch.

Gitler quoted Red Rodney: 'I think that a lot of the *good* things in the music were because of drug use. The tempos where guys really played on them . . . The tunes with the great changes in it . . . When a guy is loaded and at peace, he . . . could tune out the honking of the world. And, "Hey man, I just figured this out," and we'd try it that night, and it was great.' Charlie Rouse: 'When you're improvising, when you're playing jazz, you play what you hear. So the rhythm or whatever is behind you, you hear something, and you go ahead and make it. And you may do it when you wouldn't do it sober.' Dexter Gordon: 'I think it can arouse you; it makes you concentrate very well.' But Gordon goes on to define the concentration more specifically: 'It really activates the mind to secure money and to find connections . . . and play your games, do your little movements and all that shit.' And avoid getting arrested. David Allyn: 'You're also blocking a lot of other things out, too, like real feelings. You're numb. A goddam wall.' Rodney: 'a lot of sad things happened from the drugs, and showed in the music . . . Hostility, pettiness, a lot of us became thieves, even though we didn't want to . . . being ashamed that people we liked knew we were hooked.'

Mulligan revealed that he had avoided having relationships with women who wanted to get married; marriage at his age would have been a mistake, but he was avoiding stability: 'I think I managed to not be an adult in just about every imaginable area.' Art Pepper said that he started on drugs because he was lonely. His first wife stopped travelling with him on the road, and he felt horribly guilty if he had anything to do with another woman, and in the morality of the early 1950s he could not deal with that. And some people just have personalities that are prone to addiction.

Many musicians were surprisingly rigid in their attitudes: Herman's men, for example, thought he was corny, which angered Mulligan; it was all right to play like Bird on alto, but not on tenor; Ellington's band was trite, Basie's was the one. White musicians thought they could fight the Crow Jim attitude by aping the habits of black addicts. For blacks, being stoned, especially in such an illegal, exotic and dangerous way, helped in coping with racism, allowing the metaphorical genuflection to white society to be made with some other part of the mind, so that the profound insult could be ignored and only the music mattered.

In any case, and despite everything, contemporary jazz recordings were being made during the 1950s which forty years later are selling much better than Patti Page. Commodore, Keynote and Blue Note were followed by other new labels in the post-war years. Recordings were now made on master tape and released on long-playing records, and more records were being sold to a grown-up audience. On the West Coast, Ross Russell had formed Dial in 1946, Lester Koenig formed Good Time Jazz to record the revivalists and between 1949 and 1952 Koenig started Contemporary, Saul Zaentz formed Fantasy and Richard Bock formed Pacific Jazz. In the east Bob Weinstock started Prestige in 1949, while Orrin Keepnews and Bill Grauer formed Riverside in 1953. Keepnews later formed Milestone and Landmark.

Norman Granz, who worked as a film editor, began producing jazz concerts at the Los Angeles Philharmonic Auditorium in 1944. (The first concert was a benefit for twenty-one Chicanos who were arrested during the 'Zoot Suit Riots', convicted of murder and sent to San Quentin.) When he took Jazz at the Philharmonic (JATP) on tour, he refused to accept an engagement unless the audience was integrated, and it became an institution. He recorded the concerts from the beginning, leasing the first volume (which helped to make a jazz standard of 'How High the Moon') to Moses Asch. This was a hit (but meanwhile Asch went broke, and later formed the Folkways label). In 1947 Granz formed Clef, which was distributed by Mercury, then Norgran, and Verve in 1956. He made more jazz available in public and on record than any other individual. He sold Verve to MGM in 1961, but retained some of his masters and stayed on for a while as an adviser; then he started all over again in the 1970s with Pablo. Today almost all these legendary independent jazz labels belong to the Fantasy group in Berkeley, California, making it easily the most valuable vault of American music still owned by Americans.

A West Coast pianist and composer, Dave Brubeck (who had studied with Darius Milhaud), began recording for Fantasy, first with larger groups, then in a quartet featuring the alto saxophone of Paul Desmond. The quartet was well received on college campuses, Brubeck said, because he had played for free in high schools, and when those kids later went to college, Brubeck was the only jazz musician they had heard of. Brubeck signed with Columbia in 1954, and the quartet had far more commercial success than any other jazz group of the era. From 1956 the tasteful Joe Morello played drums.

It is hard to fault Brubeck's success. A version of 'Stardust' on Fantasy wonderfully explores the spirit of the tune, and a 1954 Columbia album called *Jazz: Red Hot and Cool*, recorded live at a club in New York and designed as part of a cosmetics promotion, had a horrible title and cover, but good music, in particular the wistful original 'Audrey'. Brubeck's tunes 'In Your Own Sweet Way' and 'The Duke' were not to be sneered at. Yet for some his music was cerebral at the expense of emotional content. The tremendous popularity of the gimmicky *Time Out*, a number two album in 1960 on which each track has a different time signature, at a time when Charles Mingus was hitting his stride on the same label but had nothing like Brubeck's sales, raises the irrefutable point that a great many black artists deserved the kind of acclaim that Brubeck had. But that was not his fault; he maintained a higher profile for jazz than it would have had otherwise, the way Paul Whiteman had done thirty years earlier, and many a fan must have gone on to stronger stuff. Besides, one could always listen to Desmond, whose playing was never other than beautiful, and often witty with it. (His memoirs, to be called 'How Many of You are There in the Quartet?', remained unfinished.)

The white cool jazz West Coast phenomenon was neither as

revolutionary as its fans thought nor as reactionary as its critics claimed. Parker and Gillespie had come to California bringing the latest thing, but there was not a large audience for it; yet as soon as Ross Russell had formed his Dial label he began recording Charlie Parker, who thus made some of his best recordings on the West Coast. Jimmy Giuffre's 'Four Brothers' was recorded by Woody Herman's band in 1947 for Columbia, at the same session as the fourth part of Ralph Burns's 'Summer Sequence', which was recorded again at the end of the following year for Capitol as 'Early Autumn'. The sound of both the 'Four Brothers' reed section and Stan Getz's solo on 'Early Autumn' (recorded in Los Angeles) were very influential; but equally influential were the New York recordings of the Miles Davis 'Birth of the Cool' sessions (with Mulligan's 'Godchild' and 'Jeru') and of the arrangements of Tadd Dameron. The Davis nonet sessions were a commercial failure at the time – the name 'Birth of the Cool' was applied to them in retrospect; they were arrangements, with seamlessly interwoven solos. Dameron had failed music at school, but was later described as 'the Romanticist of the whole movement'; tracks on Blue Note long marketed as Fats Navarro's were actually Dameron's, and such tunes as his 'Good Bait' and 'Our Delight' became jazz standards.

The West Coast cool jazz movement focused on arrangements for combos, performed by first-class white jazzmen who played lovely solos on them. Howard Rumsey, a pianist, drummer and bass player who had been a founder member of Stan Kenton's band in 1942, began presenting live music at a club called the Lighthouse in Hermosa Beach, California, in 1949. In 1951 he formed the Lighthouse All Stars, who recorded for Contemporary (with a Lighthouse logo at first), and the famous Sunday sessions started: the house band, augmented with various guests, played from two in the afternoon until two the next morning. Musicians and fans remembered the hard work and the great music for the rest of their lives; the music would sometimes begin for people in their bathing-suits who had wandered in off the street, and who would still be there twelve hours later. It was here that many of the West Coast luminaries jammed and formed their friendships and recording groups. Drummer Shelly Manne seemed to play on nearly all the recordings. Shelly

Manne and his Friends, a trio, had Leroy Vinnegar on bass and talented Hollywood wunderkind André Previn on piano. The trio's second album for Contemporary was a jazz treatment of the songs from *My Fair Lady* in 1956; being reasonably successful, it started a fad for such albums (though it did not make the lower reaches of the pop album chart until Previn did it again under his own name, for Columbia in 1964). Reedmen Jimmy Giuffre, Art Pepper, Lennie Niehaus, Bob Cooper, Bob Morgan, Bud Shank, Bill Perkins, Buddy Collette and Frank Morgan, trombonist Frank Rosolino, pianist and arranger Marty Paich and trumpeters Maynard Ferguson and Shorty Rogers, among many others, played at the Lighthouse and made albums in each other's groups and as leaders; visitors included Max Roach, Wardell Gray, Conte Candoli, Miles Davis and pianist Hampton Hawes. Most of the regulars were veterans of Kenton's line-ups, especially his Innovations in Modern Music Orchestra of 1950, but Kenton himself became less and less influential as his ideas became more grandiose.

Composer Giuffre led combos; his fetching, rhythmic tone poem 'The Train and the River' was filmed for television's *The Sound of Jazz* in 1957 and at the Newport Jazz Festival the following year (as *Jazz on a Summer's Day*, released 1960). Paich became a studio arranger, best known for albums with singer Mel Tormé. Canadian-born Maynard Ferguson was a high-note specialist and a brass technician who has led bands almost continuously, and at the time of writing seems to have come through a phase of playing jazz-rock fusion.

One of the most successful and prolific of these men was Shorty Rogers, who came from the East Coast. He was a professional musician at the age of eighteen; after military service he joined Woody Herman's band, and stayed behind when it left Hollywood in 1946. He was playing in baritone saxophonist Butch Stone's band when Herman formed the 'Four Brothers' band in 1947, wiping out Stone's band by hiring most of its members. By this time Rogers had matured as a soloist and a composer; he wrote or co-wrote 'Keen and Peachy', 'Lemon Drop', 'Keeper of the Flame' and others for Herman, and scored part of a Charlie Parker solo for the reed section on a Herman track called 'I've Got News For You'. He left Herman in late

1948 to join Kenton, and did his best to help the Innovations band swing. (It was a losing battle: there were forty musicians, including strings.) In 1951 Rogers led his first recording session with an octet: Pepper, Giuffre, Manne, John Graas (French horn), Gene Englund (tuba), Don Bagley (bass) and Hawes (piano). A series of 10-inch and 12-inch LPs on Capitol, Pacific Jazz, Atlantic and RCA followed, on which the groups ranged from a quintet and octet to a big band.

The first track recorded, Rogers's 'Popo', is a memorably rhythmic riff; Art Pepper's alto on 'Over the Rainbow' was recorded at the same date. The music was not particularly 'cool', containing plenty of high-spirited soloing, and (at the first session especially) spontaneous vocal sounds of encouragement from various sidemen. At the time the music sounded distinctly hot, yet boppish; for 'modern jazz', it had a considerable success. A quintet date in 1955 included 'Martians Go Home', which is nearly eight minutes long: a low-key Rogers composition, it features muted trumpet and Giuffre playing cha-lumeau (low-register) clarinet throughout; the excellent young Pete Jolly plays piano and Curtis Counce bass. There was plenty of solo space for everyone (especially Giuffre) and duet passages for the two horns; the whole thing is delicately punctuated by Manne, who at one point tuned his snare upwards while playing a soft roll (presumably with one hand). It was the nearest thing to a hit for a jazz record, and must have sold quite a few copies as an Atlantic 45 EP. Among the big-band tracks were a tribute to Basie album and four tunes written by Leith Stevens for the Marlon Brando film *The Wild One* (not the soundtrack recordings, which were played by an octet and released on Decca). In a repeat on 'Infinity Promenade' Ferguson plays a trumpet part an octave higher than the first time round, which was a pleasant shock at the time, but soon became a cliché.

Not all of the music was equally successful. From the first session, Giuffre's 'Four Mothers' is a riff that quickly becomes irritating and is repeated too often: unison riffs were one of the things that many people did not like about modern jazz. The pastel harmonies could become a kind of hip mood music, if played at similar tempos and without any hot solos, as reedman Dave Pell proved: he formed an octet out of the Les Brown band in 1955 and was frank about playing mortgage-paying music.

Rogers's experience as a composer and arranger soon earned him a good living in the studios. Indeed, nearly all these people recorded prolifically on film soundtracks. Bob Cooper played all the reeds, including cor anglais and oboe; he married Kenton's singer June Christy and was also busy in the studios. Bill Perkins was an engineer for World Pacific (as Pacific Jazz was called after it was sold to Liberty Records) and later in the studios. Years later Lennie Niehaus often worked with director Clint Eastwood; Niehaus and Bud Shank did their best work in the early 1950s, and then decided to make a living instead. Shank played on albums with Brazilian guitarist Laurindo Almeida in 1954, the first influence of bossa nova on the US scene; his later pop-song album *Michelle*, with Chet Baker on flugelhorn, made the *Billboard* chart.

Art Pepper played on many fine albums and always had as many fans as any jazzman, but he paid for his drug addiction with frequent arrests, and only survived as long as he did by spending several years of his life in the restrictive routine of the Synanon Foundation. His autobiography *Straight Life*, written with his wife Laurie and published in 1979, is a harrowing book. His best-known album is *Art Pepper Meets the Rhythm Section*, made in 1957 for Contemporary: he was strung out at the time and had not played for weeks, but it was a successful session. (The 'Rhythm Section' was that of the Miles Davis Quintet.)

The tragedy of West Coast jazz was that it was dominated by white musicians to the extent that those excellent black musicians who stayed there were almost ignored. The jazz scene in California was never big, perhaps because the climate keeps people outdoors rather than in clubs and concert halls. Even so, people who were never jazz fans heard of Brubeck, Chet Baker and Gerry Mulligan, maybe even Shorty Rogers. Tenor saxophonist Teddy Edwards went to the West Coast from Mississippi as a young man and made a series of albums on Pacific Jazz, Contemporary and Prestige, but the albums are underrated and most people have never heard of him.

Eric Dolphy and Charles Mingus were two West Coast musicians of great influence who went east to make their reputations; Dexter Gordon went to Europe. There were other black musicians on the West Coast who never achieved the reputations they deserved. Alto saxophonist Sonny Criss was born in Tennessee, and spent some of the 1960s in Europe; he recorded for Imperial in the 1950s (with West Coast drummer Lawrence Marable) and on Prestige in the 1960s. Curtis Amy, who was born in 1929 in Houston, played tenor, soprano and flute; he went to Los Angeles in 1955 and recorded for Pacific Jazz, and later played on pop and rock albums.

Born in Los Angeles, the son of a doctor, Dexter Gordon was one of the first modernists on tenor saxophone. When Coleman Hawkins listed his favourite tenor saxophonists, he included Gordon, a teenager at the time, who was playing in Lionel Hampton's band. He also played with Louis Armstrong, and in the renowned Billy Eckstine band in 1945, then recorded for Dial: in 1947 'The Chase' (with Wardell Gray) and 'The Duel' (with Teddy Edwards), both two-sided 10-inch 78s, were among Dial's best-sellers. An eighteen-minute live version of 'The Hunt' with Gray was recorded the same year by Ralph Bass at the Elks Club in Los Angeles. Gordon recorded for several labels, such as Blue Note, but lived in Europe from 1962 until 1976, and only occasionally visited the USA; he made many albums in Paris and Copenhagen, with associates such as Kenny Drew and Spanish-born Tete Montoliu on piano. Having been addicted to various substances all his life, his health was poor in later years, but he left a great many recordings of his unique tone and endless ideas: while listening, one feels, at least until the record is over, that it will never be necessary to listen to another tenor, so strong, delightful and deceptively laconic is his musical personality. Producer Michael Cuscuna lured him back to the USA for recording dates in his later career. He was nominated for an Academy Award for his portrayal of a character based on Bud Powell in the film *Round Midnight* (1986, directed by Bertrand Tavernier); like many another American actor, he was effectively playing himself.

Howard McGhee, from Tulsa, Oklahoma, became one of the most highly regarded bop trumpeters and worked for Hampton, Andy Kirk, Charlie Barnet and Georgie Auld. He was a member of Coleman Hawkins's small group when it recorded its famous Hollywood sessions in 1945, and made his first recording as a leader that year on Modern, with Mingus on bass. A 1946 Dial date became McGhee's when Charlie Parker was too messed up to play. McGhee recorded in Copenhagen in 1979 with Teddy Edwards.

Hampton Hawes was based all his life in Los Angeles; good-looking enough to be a movie star, he was an excellent modern keyboard player of the Bud Powell school. He was also a drug addict. His most famous recordings are on Contemporary: three trio sets made in 1955 and the *All Night Session* (1956), with Jim Hall (guitar), Red Mitchell (bass) and Bruz Freeman (drums), three more albums of bop classics and standards laid down with unflagging joyous energy, the sixteen selections issued with no editing of any kind. He also made a trio album with Mingus and Dannie Richmond in 1957. He was sentenced to ten years in prison in 1958 for possession of narcotics (as opposed to Mulligan's ninety days a few years earlier – did it make a difference that Mulligan was white?), but was released in 1964 after he wrote a personal letter to President Kennedy (after which everybody else in the jail was writing to Washington).

Carl Perkins, from Indianapolis, became an unusual and influential keyboard stylist. He too was a drug addict; his left hand was deformed by polio, which perhaps led to his adopting a more bluesy style than Hawes, for example. He played with R & B bands; as a leader he made trio tracks for Savoy (1949), DooTone (1956) and Pacific Jazz (1957, with guitar and bass, but no drums). He worked as a sideman with Harold Land and Art Pepper, among others. Perkins was a founder member of the Max Roach and Clifford Brown Quintet, but did not stay with it long; he is best known for his membership of the Curtis Counce Quintet. His tune 'Grooveyard', recorded with Land in 1958, became something of a standard.

Bass player and leader Curtis Counce was originally from Kansas City. After working for a few months with Shorty Rogers, he formed a quintet which recorded four albums (1956–8), all with Frank Butler on drums (once described by Jo Jones as the best drummer in the world) and Harold Land on tenor. Three albums on Contemporary had Carl Perkins on piano: his introduction and accompaniment of Jack Sheldon on 'I Can't Get Started' display bluesy harmonic ideas, which are other-worldly yet exactly right. On the last album (for DooTone) Elmo Hope replaced Perkins. The trumpet players were Jack Sheldon and Rolf Erickson (both white) and Gerald Wilson.

Wilson has rarely performed as a soloist, but has repeatedly (and against the odds) formed big bands on the West Coast, for which he writes and in which all the best musicians want to play. Sheldon (born in 1931 in Florida) has also been a singer, actor and comedian. Erickson (born in 1927 in Sweden) has been a highly regarded modernist since moving to the USA in 1947, was frequently heard at the Lighthouse and played in many of the remaining big bands, such as those of Goodman, Herman and Ellington.

Tenor saxophonist Harold Land said many years later, 'We were making progress in Los Angeles, even if nobody was aware of it. There wasn't much money, but we were having a lot of beautiful musical moments.' This survey of West Coast jazz may as well end with a remarkable Land album: if the best post-war jazz required unison playing of searing and exciting precision by musicians who could also tear the notes off the page in their solos, and furious swinging on original compositions of great quality, then *The Fox* should have been continuously in print and achieving considerable sales over the years. But it was extremely well recorded in 1959 in Los Angeles for the obscure Hifijazz label, and disappeared for a decade until it was reissued by Contemporary. It had Butler on drums, Elmo Hope on piano, Herbie Lewis on bass and the mysterious Dupree Bolton on trumpet. Bolton played on *The Fox* and on Curtis Amy's *Katanga!* in 1963 (the title track of which he wrote) and on almost nothing else; he was a trumpeter who should have entered the polls of history with Navarro and Brownie. Elmo Hope was an excellent player from New York, a childhood friend of Bud Powell; his *Elmo Hope Trio* was also made for Hifijazz and later reissued on Contemporary. He made other albums for Blue Note, Prestige, Riverside and other labels, but never achieved the fame he deserved.

One of the few groups that made it back and forth across the USA, and among the best jazz bands of all time for its integration of intelligence and musical powers, was the Max Roach Quintet. Roach was one of the finest drummers in the new music, destined to be one of those who demonstrated that the best jazz drummers are percussionists and all-round musicians, not just time-keepers. He grew up in New York, but in 1953 he worked for six months in the Lighthouse All Stars, proof enough that this was a straight-ahead blowing outfit rather than a laid-back bunch of beach boys. Promoter Gene Norman offered Roach a concert tour if he would form a band, and Roach offered Clifford Brown a job as co-leader. Brown had been out of action for a year after a car crash in 1950, but then recorded with Tadd Dameron. He was recommended by Charlie Parker for a band that Art Blakey was forming, which recorded in 1954, and it was from this group that Roach plucked him.

Tenor saxophonist Sonny Stitt was hired, but shortly after Teddy Edwards took his place. (Stitt changed back to alto after Charlie Parker died, and was probably more at home on that instrument.) Carl Perkins played piano and George Bledsoe bass. One of their early gigs was recorded by Norman. Before their first studio session Edwards was replaced by 25-year-old Harold Land, and bass player George Morrow joined. Land was a close friend of Eric Dolphy; Roach and Brownie had heard about the all-day jamming sessions at young Dolphy's house, dropped by to listen and hired both Land and Morrow. Richie Powell had wanted to be a drummer, but took Roach's advice and changed to piano; when he replaced Perkins, the classic edition of the quintet was in place. Land's big tenor sound was a perfect foil for Brownie's trumpet. Brownie also recorded for Pacific Jazz with a septet of West Coasters and for Emarcy, Mercury's jazz subsidiary, as the Max Roach–Clifford Brown Quintet made its first recordings for Emarcy: he made seven recording dates in less than two weeks in mid-1954, and in September there was another Gene Norman concert recording.

Then the quintet went back east, where it recorded again for Emarcy. In November 1955 Land was called back to Los Angeles because of illness in the family. His place was taken by Sonny Rollins, who was almost the same age, but already a giant. He had been influenced by Stitt, then by Dexter Gordon. He began recording in 1948, and by 1955 his powers were such that, like Coleman Hawkins, he almost never had to repeat himself; each time he played a tune it was as if for the first time, and he was never at a loss for ideas. The band was even stronger, but lasted for less than a year: in

June 1956 Brownie, Powell and Powell's wife skidded off the Pennsylvania Turnpike and were killed.

The Roach–Brown Quintet, and, for that matter, Curtis Counce's group and the Harold Land band that recorded *The Fox*, all with the same instrumentation, were fine examples of what came to be called post-bop or hard bop. Roach–Brown played standards beloved of the boppers, such as 'I'll Remember April' and 'What is This Thing Called Love', and originals like Dameron's 'The Scene is Clean', and Powell's 'Time' (on which he played celesta) and 'Gertrude's Bounce'. (Powell too had been on the way to becoming a major talent.) But the arrangements never depended on riffs or endless unison playing; they were themselves compositions, tone poems, exquisitely well performed by men who breathed together. In reaction perhaps to cool jazz, it was aggressive music with muscular joy, never frenetic for its own sake, and black music had taken a step beyond bop. Roach carried on for a while; Brownie was succeeded by Kenny Dorham, then by talented newcomer Booker Little. But the grief of the jazz world at the loss of Brownie was nearly unbearable.

In 1948–9 the Jazz at the Philharmonic tours included new young stars as well as familiar faces. Ella Fitzgerald, who also became a Granz recording artist, joined in 1949. Granz began recording Oscar Peterson in New York in 1950. He had played on the radio and recorded for RCA in Canada before Granz persuaded him to move south; he became an extremely popular jazz musician because of his powerful swing and outstanding technique. He mostly led trios, first with Ray Brown on bass and guitarist Irving Ashby, then Barney Kessel, then Herb Ellis; in 1958 he replaced the guitar with drummer Ed Thigpen.

Peterson has been controversial, paradoxically because he is not controversial. His two-handed style is muscular and inventive, but not formally innovative, though he has brought a very high degree of formal excellence to his playing: he has been described as the Liszt of jazz piano. His knowledge of music and his technique are so facile that at his best the phrasing and ornamentation become part of the music. Some have said that he does not swing. This foolish canard is based partly on what is perceived as his 'whiteness': his father worked all his life as a railway porter, and his very talented older sister Daisy worked as a domestic; but he did not come from a tenement slum in Harlem. Apparently being black in a white society is not handicap enough; you have to be seen to suffer, which Peterson simply refused to do. He was recorded too much by Granz; so many albums could not all be first-rate. Some of the finest were made at the London House in Chicago with the original trio, but among the best of all, including his only solo albums, were those made for MPS in Germany in the 1960s, when Granz was between labels.

When Count Basie led a small group in 1950, it contained Wardell Gray and clarinettist Buddy DeFranco. In 1953–4 DeFranco toured with an excellent quartet in which Sonny Clark played piano. Granz recorded it, but the clarinet had been considered unfashionable since the end of the Swing Era. Perhaps it was viewed as an instrument of the New Orleans style, while after its domination by Benny Goodman and Artie Shaw during the Swing Era, suddenly there were a great many very fine tenor saxophonists; perhaps the fingering of the clarinet's registers, which are divided into twelve rather than octaves, like the saxophone, make it more difficult to play fluently. At any rate, DeFranco did it, but was underrated then and has been since.

Meanwhile, Basie was invited to record for Granz in 1952, so he re-formed a big band and led it for the rest of his life. The emphasis in the new band was on arrangements rather than soloists; the early Granz albums were called 'dance dates'. But the Kansas City feeling was still there, and as the decade wore on it remained a superb ensemble, worthy of comparison on its own terms with the band of the late 1930s. Arrangers included Neal Hefti ('Sure Thing', 'Two Franks') and the 'two Franks' themselves: Frank Wess wrote 'Basie Goes Wess' and Frank Foster wrote 'Shiny Stockings' and 'Blues Back-stage', among many others. A third reedman-arranger, Ernie Wilkins, wrote 'Blues Done Come Back' and 'Sixteen Men Swinging'. Marshall Royal also played reeds, as did the 'Vice Prez', Paul Quinichette; Joe Newman and Thad Jones played trumpet.

Vocalist Joe Williams joined in 1954. He had served a long Chicago apprenticeship, during which he was discriminated against by black bandleaders for being too dark; he was a star with Basie until 1960 and was then a successful, musically intelligent cabaret artist. He was typed as a blues singer for many years because of the album *Count Basie Swings – Joe Williams Sings* (1955), a pop masterpiece mostly arranged by Foster. At an all-time low point in the history of chart hits matched only by the 1980s, at least Memphis Slim's 'Every Day' was something of a hit in the black chart. (Williams had had a hit with the same song, backed by the King Kolax band, in 1952.) The album also offered Williams's own 'My Baby Upsets Me', songs by Leroy Carr and Percy Mayfield, and Sammy Cahn's pop hit 'Teach Me Tonight', turned by Williams into an imperishable erotic plea.

At the end of the decade Basie recorded for the new Roulette label: in 1957 Neal Hefti wrote *The Atomic Mr Basie*, which included 'Li'l Darlin'', an object lesson in how to swing at a slow tempo, with its famous muted trumpet solo by Wendell Culley. Among Benny Carter's compositions for the band were *Kansas City Suite* and *The Legend* (1960–61), perhaps the band's last masterpieces. Basie continued touring the world and recorded with Frank Sinatra, Tony Bennett, Teresa Brewer, Billy Eckstine and many others. In its later years the band recorded a good deal of junk and sounded like a Las Vegas show band, but Basie remained a legend until the end; he also made small-group sets for Granz's Pablo label.

Duke Ellington's band went through some rough patches. Under contract to Columbia (1947–52) the new decade's line-up varied, and included trumpeters Nance, Harold 'Shorty' Baker, Cat Anderson, Clark Terry and Willie Cook, trombonists Lawrence Brown, Wilbur DeParis, Claude Jones, Quentin 'Butter' Jackson and Tyree Glenn and reedmen Hodges, Carney and, from 1944 to 1949, Al Sears, who had star roles in the Carnegie Hall concerts. Sears remained in the shadow of Ben Webster, but was quite capable of holding his own. Valuable new recruits were Jimmy Hamilton and Russell Procope on reeds, especially clarinets; and Paul Gonsalves joined in 1950, but Johnny Hodges, Lawrence Brown and Sonny Greer all left at once in 1951. Ellington pulled the 'Great James Robbery', taking drummer Louie Bellson, the returning Tizol and ex-Lunceford alto saxophonist Willie Smith from Harry James's band. (James is said to have asked, 'Can I come too?') Guitarist Fred Guy left in 1949 (after which Duke did without a guitar), and the bass players were Oscar Pettiford, Junior Raglin and then Wendell Marshall.

The decline in the quality of Ellington's output is only relative. More personnel changes than at any other time in the band's history must have been dispiriting; times were hard for bands and from the late 1940s the band lost money and was kept going by Ellington's royalties. The patchy output on CBS, though it is essential for any Ellington fan and has a unique flavour of the period, includes over seventy attempts at pop hits: junk like 'Cowboy Rhumba' (with a vocal by Woody Herman), but also 'Brown Penny', 'Maybe I Should Change My Ways' (from *Beggar's Holiday*), Nance's hip vocal on 'You're Just an Old Antidisestablishmentarianismist' (lyric by Don George), 'Stomp, Look and Listen', 'Boogie Bop Blues', 'Lady of the Lavender Mist', 'Fancy Dan', 'Air Conditioned Jungle', 'VIP's Boogie' (featuring Carney), a famous remake of 'Do Nothin' Till You Hear From Me' (by Al Hibbler) and much more, with contributions from Strayhorn, and 'The Hawk Talks', by Bellson.

As with other artists, albums had become more important in Ellington's work than singles. *Masterpieces by Ellington* (1950) was quite a tribute, a 12-inch LP at a time when most pop LPs were 10-inch albums; on it were extended versions of classics, as well as *The Tattooed Bride*; *Ellington Uptown* (1951) included *A Tone Parallel to Harlem*, and became a best-seller at a hi-fi show because of Bellson's 'Skin Deep', but a six-minute version of 'The Mooche' was better, because of Bellson's rolling, inexorable beat and the clarinets: Procope's melody in the low register, Hamilton's obbligato in an echo chamber.

Among the other projects in the late 1940s and early 1950s were recordings on Musicraft (from late 1946, between Victor and Columbia contracts), a short-lived Sunrise label (1947) and Mercer Records, run by Mercer Ellington and Leonard Feather, with backing from Duke and Strayhorn in 1950–51. The recording quality was not high, and they were probably using inferior studios during a time of technological change; in fact, Mercer foundered partly because of the battle of the speeds. The full band did not violate the CBS contract, but various Ellingtonians contributed: for example, Pettiford plays cello on 'Perdido' and Ellington and Strayhorn play piano duets. Willie Smith, Tizol and Bellson (freshly rustled from the James corral) all played on a driving sextet recording of 'Caravan', which may have inspired Ralph Marterie's hit single two years later.

Duke recorded for Capitol from 1953 to 1955, a musically disappointing period, though as usual there was interesting material; some of the recordings unreleased at the time were better than those that were issued. Dave Dexter, Ellington's producer at Capitol, wrote that Ellington badly wanted hit records; 'Satin Doll' and 'Boo-dah' went into the top thirty, but '12th Street Mambo' disappeared without trace. It was a low point: jazz had apparently moved on, but critics should have known better than to count Ellington out, for he had done it all already. As Miles Davis later said: 'all the musicians should get together one certain day and get down on their knees and thank Duke'.

Johnny Hodges had returned by early 1956 and the band made two albums for the new Bethlehem label in Chicago: *Historically Speaking – The Duke* introduced a set of remakes with a laconically witty version of 'East St Louis' (but 'Ko-ko' was a disaster); the other album included covers of 'Laura', 'Summertime' and other standards, together with 'Frustration', a feature for Carney, and a rocking seven-minute 'The Blues'. Then came Newport.

The Newport Jazz Festival had been inaugurated in 1954 by pianist and club-owner George Wein, with the support of the wealthy Lorrilard family. Ellington played there in July 1956 with the same forces as he had used in the Bethlehem studio: Cook, Nance, Terry and Anderson (trumpets); Jackson, John Sanders and Britt Woodman (trombones); Carney, Hodges, Procope, Hamilton and Gonsalves (reeds); Jimmy Woode (bass) and Sam Woodyard (drums). The band came on last, after people had started leaving. Duke grumbled, 'What are we, the animal act, the acrobats?' Ellington and Strayhorn had written a three-part *Newport Jazz Festival Suite*; and Duke had pulled out 'Diminuendo and Crescendo in Blue', the two-part arrangement from twenty years earlier, for which Woodyard set up a rocking beat (egged on by ringside fan Jo Jones). The original point of the piece, its dynamics, was lost at Newport; the band was in the mood to wail, but Stanley Dance has reminded us that what happened next was not a first: at Birdland as early as 1951 Paul Gonsalves had played a bridge between the two parts. At Newport the bridge turned out to be twenty-seven choruses long: the audience was standing and cheering, and there is a famous photograph of a blonde dancing in the aisle. The concert made headlines, the Columbia LP made the *Billboard* pop album chart and Duke made the cover of *Time* magazine. Some Ellingtonians regarded Gonsalves's pyrotechnics as a disgrace, and the original point of the piece – its dynamics – had been completely lost, but a commercial breakthrough had been made (on an album, not a single) and Ellington's status as elder statesman was never again in doubt.

Ellington wrote film scores and made cameo appearances in films, wrote music for a Canadian production of *Timon of Athens* and a show called *My People* on the centenary of the Emancipation Proclamation in 1963 (with sections called 'King Fit the Battle of Alabam', and 'What Colour is Virtue?'). Among the albums, *Such Sweet Thunder* (1957) was good music and the lovely mood set *Ellington Indigos* (1959) was also recorded for Columbia. The enchanting *Queen's Suite* in 1959 was for Elizabeth II: one copy was made for her, and no other copy was issued until after Ellington's death. (It was not played in public until Bob Wilber's re-creation in 1989.)

Suite Thursday, recorded in 1960, is now only available on a CD with Strayhorn's and Ellington's triflings with Grieg and Tchaikovsky, but is a good example of an Ellington suite (nominally based on the book by John Steinbeck). The colours and themes of the four parts hang together beautifully, and the way the band plays it makes a very exciting seventeen minutes or so: young musicians to be should be trying to play this music this well.

Money Jungle (1962), a trio set with Charles Mingus and Max Roach, brought drama and power from each player unlike anything any of them did in other company. *Duke Ellington Meets Coleman Hawkins* and *Duke Ellington and John Coltrane*, gorgeous small-group sets, were recorded in the same year. World tours resulted in *The Far East Suite* (1966), one of Ellington's best, and the *Latin American Suite* (1969). A tribute to Strayhorn, in 1967, . . . *And His Mother Called Him Bill*, consisted entirely of his tunes, including his last, 'Blood Count', which was sent from the hospital where he was dying of cancer.

The band accompanied Ella Fitzgerald on her two-disc sets of Ellington songs, as well as on the two-disc *On the Cote D'Azur*. Among the albums on Frank Sinatra's Reprise label (1962–5) were

Concert in the Virgin Islands and *Afro-bossa*, as well as one with Sinatra. *This One's for Blanton!* (1972) comprises duets with bass player Ray Brown, remakes of the famous 1940 duets for Norman Granz's Pablo label. The *Seventieth Birthday Concert* opened with a riotous version of 'Rockin' in Rhythm', once again the band's theme.

The late triumph *New Orleans Suite* (1970) had five parts interleaved with portraits of Mahalia Jackson, Louis Armstrong (with Cootie Williams), Wellman Braud (with Joe Benjamin on bass) and Sidney Bechet. Ellington had tried to persuade Hodges to polish his soprano saxophone, but he died days before the session, and the tribute to Bechet was made by Gonsalves on tenor. The suite's opening 'Blues for New Orleans' featured Wild Bill Davis on organ, but the organ effect in Jackson's portrait was made by three clarinets, tenor saxophone and flute – a tone-painter's palette unique in popular music.

André Previn, an accomplished and highly rated musician in several genres, often and crossly denies making this remark: 'Stan Kenton can stand in front of a thousand fiddles and a thousand brass and make a dramatic gesture, and every studio arranger can nod his head and say, "Oh yes, that's done like this." But Duke merely lifts his finger, three horns make a sound, and I don't know what it is.' Yet the substance of the remark had been true as early as the Cotton Club period. In 1965 the Advisory Board of the Pulitzer Prize Committee rejected a unanimous recommendation of its music jury that Ellington be awarded a special citation; his best music was behind him, but that is when prizes are often awarded. He received honorary degrees and a medal from Lyndon Johnson, and Richard Nixon played 'Happy Birthday' on the piano for him.

His 'Sacred Concerts', which started in San Francisco in 1965, were important to him but unfortunately they are not very good. Always urbane and witty, Ellington was also a private man, vain and superstitious: *Music is My Mistress* in 1973 was not an autobiography. He sometimes did not write his music down, let alone his life, and did not even leave a will; but he left recordings, which are still being issued, often produced by Mercer and Stanley Dance. James Lincoln Collier's biography of 1987 examined the band and its members as a composing machine, comparing Ellington to a master chef, who 'plans the menus, trains the assistants, supervises them, tastes everything, adjusts the spices . . . and in the end we credit him with the result'.

Ellington came back to the fore in the 1950s and died famous, but meanwhile, in New York, other younger black musicians were finding their way. The decade of the 1950s was not kind to them, yet they too made recordings that we still listen to forty years later.

Thelonious Monk did not record at all in 1949 or 1950, but Blue Note recorded him again in 1952 and 1953, despite the fact that he did not sell. His associates included alto saxophonists Sahib Shihab (a modest man and an underrated musician) and Lou Donaldson, trumpeter Kenny Dorham and tenor saxophonist Lucky Thompson. Prestige took over in late 1952 and Riverside in mid-1955; in 1962, after European tours and several appearances at Newport, he finally signed a major label contract with Columbia, so that there were albums every year from 1952 to 1968. (At Newport in 1963 Pee Wee Russell played on two tracks.) No doubt in 1968, when Clive Davis was in charge at Columbia, Monk did not sell as well as the now forgotten rock band Electric Flag, and there were no recordings at all in the USA during the last dozen years of Monk's life. The rumour persists that Columbia wanted him to record Beatles tunes; if it is not true, it may as well be.

There is no public record of any violence or serious drug problem in Monk's life; indeed, he seems to have been a gentle man. Yet he frightened club-owners and others with his personal act. He wore goofy caps, and he would get up from the piano and do a little dance when the pulse of the music was not quite right, trying to show his musicians what he wanted. Dizzy Gillespie got away with bizarre humour and even made capital out of it, but Monk was a more private man, who probably wanted to be valued more for his music than for his sense of humour. There was never enough work, and while Dizzy the clown became a much loved figure, Monk the mild eccentric was widely ignored.

His solo recording sessions began with a 1954 date on the French Swing label (later on Vogue), and he recorded Ellington tunes for Riverside the next year; there were also *Thelonious Himself* and *Thelonious Monk Alone in San Francisco* on Riverside. He later made *Solo Monk* for Columbia, and decorated the quartet albums with solo tracks. He would play 'Just a Gigolo' or 'Dinah' or 'Lulu's Back in Town', or a ballad like 'I Love You', just because he liked the song, and the accents were entirely his; a note anywhere in a phrase, or in the rhythmic left hand in a bouncy number like 'Dinah', might seem to come late, yet when it arrives, it is exactly on schedule, and the tune becomes a Monk tune.

The trick was to get other people to play his themes properly. One of his most interesting failures is *Monk's Music* (1957), with a septet: trumpeter Ray Copeland (a highly regarded New York bandleader, arranger and lead player who later toured Europe with Monk), Gigi Gryce (alto saxophone), Coleman Hawkins and John Coltrane (tenors), Wilbur Ware (bass) and Art Blakey (drums). An informal yet structured outing on five Monk tunes (Hawk tries to enter in the wrong place at one point), it was not exceeded in its irresistible way until Monk's tours of Europe in the 1960s, which were widely broadcast and recorded. The opener was a statement of 'Abide With Me', less than a minute long and played only by the horns; the simple, homely hymn was written in 1861 by William Henry Monk (no relation as far as we know).

Other tenor saxophonists who worked for Monk over the years included Chicago's Johnny Griffin, who was not very good at playing Monk's music, Sonny Rollins and Coltrane. Monk first recorded with Charlie Rouse in 1959 on the album *5 by Monk by 5* (on which Thad Jones's perceptive trumpet may be heard on two tracks), and Rouse stayed with him through all the Columbia quartet albums. So afraid of Monk were many of the critics and even some of the musicians that it was whispered that Rouse was lucky to have the job, that he was somehow not a very good musician and was stuck with playing Monk's music because Monk could not get anybody else to do it. That all this was balderdash is proved by later Rouse albums, such as the quintets *The Upper Manhattan Jazz Society* (1981) and *Social Call* (1984), with trumpeters Benny Bailey and Red Rodney respectively; the former has Keith Copeland, Ray's son, on drums.

Monk's music will never be easy to play well, but it now represents a set of post-bop anthems which younger musicians have to approach sooner or later whether they like it or not. 'Epistrophy' and ''Round Midnight' were recorded, in 1942 and 1944, by Cootie Williams's

band. The former was brought to Williams by drummer Kenny
Clarke, though he did not play on the recording, which was called
'Fly Right' and was not released at the time; ''Round Midnight' had
Bud Powell on piano in the band's rhythm section. Soprano saxophonist Steve Lacy, who had begun by playing dixieland and then worked
with Cecil Taylor, joined Monk in 1960. He made it his business to
play Monk's tunes almost exclusively for some time, until he had
learned as much from them as he could for the time being, whereupon
he was qualified to become one of the most interesting and widely
recorded avant-gardists of succeeding years.

It has since become more common for younger musicians to tackle
Monk's tunes, as shown by Anthony Braxton's *Six Monk's Composition*
(1987) and Paul Motian's *Monk in Motian* (1988). Braxton, the Chicago
composer and alto saxophonist, usually plays only his own music; his
album is for a quartet, with Mal Waldron on piano, Buell Neidlinger
on bass and Bill Osbourne on drums. Motian is a poet of the drum
kit, and his album is mostly a duet, with Bill Frisell on guitar,
though tenor saxophonist Dewey Redman and pianist Geri Allen are
added on some tracks. Frisell's electric guitar is an acquired taste, for
the notes lack any attack whatever, and sound like they are being
played backwards on a tape recorder. Both albums are brave attempts
by highly qualified people to pay tribute to one of their great and still
underrated inspirations. Young Marcus Roberts tackles a solo, 'Blue
Monk', on *The Truth is Spoken Here* (1988): he sounds rhythmically
unsure here and there, as though he has not decided whether to play
it in the style of Fats Waller or to attempt Monk's unique accents,
but he makes something of his own out of it while paying his dues,
and he knows that Monk's tunes will remain a challenge.

Words have been written for Monk's tunes and recorded by his
friend Carmen McRae (1988). After Monk's death the right to put
words to the tunes was sold to Ben Sidran, but now others are
allowed to write words by giving the songs new titles, so that 'Well,
You Needn't' becomes 'It's Over Now'. Chicagoan Mike Ferro's
words are as sassy as the tune:

> You're bending my ear?
> Well, you needn't.

You're calling me 'Dear'?
Well, you needn't.
You're acting sincere?
Well, you needn't.
It's over now! It's over now!

Monk's sound was recorded for the last time during one of the Giants of Jazz's tours of Europe, when he played with Gillespie, Sonny Stitt, trombonist Kai Winding, bass player Al McKibbon and drummer Art Blakey. Black Lion's Alan Bates recorded twenty-six trio and solo tracks (including alternative takes) in London in 1971 during the tour. (The complete set is available on Mosaic, along with the 1954 Paris set.) On the charming, informal 'Chordially' Monk is just trying out the piano at Chappell Studios. McKibbon and Blakey were old associates, who first recorded with Monk as a team at a Blue Note session in 1953. A good example of the mystery of what swings and what does not, mentioned earlier, occurs on a take of 'Hackensack': after Blakey's drum solo near the end, Monk enters in the wrong place, and stays there, eschewing his usual built-in swing. He was quite capable of doing that on purpose: in Mexico City in 1971 he played 'I Love You' in a bawdy-house piano style, saying afterwards that the audience didn't know what the song was anyway; and at the Black Lion session there had been some badinage about somebody having played some wrong notes on stage.

Another pianist and composer who had even worse luck was Herbie Nichols. In 1944 he wrote the first-ever article about Thelonious Monk. Later he said, 'It seems like you either have to be an Uncle Tom or a drug addict to make it in jazz, and I'm not either one.' He spent most of his professional career playing in dixieland bands. There were five Blue Note record dates in 1955 and a less successful Bethlehem album in 1957, all trio tracks; his 10-inch Blue Note LPs sold even less well than Monk's earlier ones. But his tunes, like Monk's, are unique. On 'Double Exposure', 'Cro-magnon Nights', 'The Gig', 'Shuffle Montgomery', 'Chit Chatting' and many other carefully titled keyboard tone poems on Blue Note he was accompanied by McKibbon or Teddy Kotick on bass and Blakey or Roach on drums. Nichols died of leukaemia in 1963; all his Blue

Note recordings have been collected on a three-CD set issued by Mosaic.

Bud Powell was probably the most influential pianist in early modern jazz; he had incredibly fleet improvisational skills and an equally incredible ear for harmony. The musical universe was as real for Powell as the 'real' universe; he heard music even when there was no keyboard available. An early promoter of Monk's music, he played his tunes very well and recorded them, and was harmonically influenced by Monk. Like other pianists, he regarded Art Tatum as God. Ira Gitler recounts the story of how one night at Birdland in 1950 Powell told Tatum that he had made mistakes when playing a piece by Chopin. 'Tatum saltily responded with, "You're just a right-hand piano player. You've got no left hand. Look, I've got a rhythm section in my left hand." The next night Bud played "Sometimes I'm Happy" entirely with his left hand at a furious tempo and drew Tatum's praise . . . Bud's jubilation knew no bounds that evening.' There is no doubt that, in using his left hand for harmonic punctuation and inspiring less talented imitators, Powell (and bop piano in general) created a gulf for the ordinary listener between the New York stride style and later development. The exploitation of the keyboard, with its tremendous harmonic possibilities, was perhaps the single greatest innovation in modern jazz. Pianist Billy Taylor told Gitler that using a different part of the keyboard in order to get out of the way of the bass player was part of the experimentation which amounted to a sort of 'pre-bop' period from around 1936; Basie may have been an early exponent. Powell's first influence was probably Billy Kyle, but in his right hand he was finally inspired more by a saxophonist, Charlie Parker, than by any other pianist.

Tales of Powell's live gigs are legion: for example, he played twenty or twenty-five choruses of Monk's '52nd Street Theme' at a blistering tempo at the Three Deuces in mid-1947. But his recordings were sporadic and variable in quality; his most important are probably those made for Blue Note in a quintet (1949) and trio (1949, 1951, 1953, 1957 and 1958).

Powell was apparently badly beaten over the head by policemen in Philadelphia in 1945, and during the next decade had five sojourns in mental institutions, where he was given shock treatments which damaged his memory. In 1951–2 he was subjected to eleven months of this, and allowed to play the piano once a week. In 1959 he took up permanent residence in Paris, where he joined drummer Kenny Clarke and bass player Pierre Michelot to make one of history's great rhythm sections; it often backed such visitors as Dexter Gordon, on *Our Man in Paris* (1963). He returned to New York in 1964 for treatment of suspected tuberculosis, and never made it back to Paris. He was the principal inspiration for the character played by Dexter Gordon in the film *Round Midnight*.

The main line in piano jazz stretches from Tatum to Powell, but Erroll Garner has to be in here somewhere. He was the kind of musician like Fats Waller and Louis Armstrong, whose work was widely loved by people who did not know anything or care about jazz itself. Unable to read music, he improvised unique and richly beautiful tone poems at the keyboard, for all the world like a modern black Chopin. The poetry of his early *Overture to Dawn* sessions, privately (and poorly) recorded in 1944, was probably never exceeded even by Garner. His extremely famous trio album *Concert by the Sea* (1955) and several other sets reached the *Billboard* album chart. Among his many compositions was 'Misty', one of the most widely performed tunes of all time.

Dave Brubeck and Lennie Tristano were both white and of approximately the same age, and both are seen as cerebral modernists, but there the resemblance ends: Brubeck has been among the most popular and successful jazzmen of the century, while Tristano purposely remained obscure, and in the end was more influential. Born during a measles epidemic, he was blind by the time he was eleven years old. Woody Herman's bass player Chubby Jackson, who seems to have been a great talent scout, persuaded Tristano to go to New York.

Tristano could allegedly play anything Tatum could play, only faster. (This, of course, would have required skill, but not invention.) He disliked performing in public and did not record very much, and preferred to play his own music. Nevertheless, he became a cult figure among musicians and hard-core modern fans. He made his most important impact as a teacher; his students included bass players Arnold Fishkin and Peter Ind, pianist Sal Mosca, guitarist Billy

Bauer, alto saxophonist Lee Konitz and tenor saxophonists Warne Marsh and Ted Brown.

These reedmen were all born in 1927. Konitz, a well-known and highly regarded musician, is usually lumped with the West Coast cool jazz school; Marsh, for all his hard work and quite a few beautiful records, remained obscure until his death in 1987; and Brown, who has been even more obscure, performed and recorded with the British-born pianist Ronnie Ball in the mid-1950s, and made one album under his own name on Vanguard in 1955. Exactly thirty years later came his quartet album *Ted Brown in Good Company*, followed by the trio set *Free Spirit* in 1987, both for the Dutch Criss Cross label. The latter, on which Hod O'Brien plays piano and Jacques Schols bass, is one of the finest albums of that or any decade. (Konitz, Marsh and Brown may all be heard on Jimmy Giuffre's lovely *Lee Konitz Meets Jimmy Giuffre*, made in 1959 for Verve with five reeds and rhythm, though Marsh and Brown do not play any solos.)

During Capitol's brief flirtation with modern jazz in the late 1940s a Tristano sextet was recorded in New York in 1949; Tristano, guitarist Billy Bauer, Konitz, Marsh, Fishkin and drummer Harold Granowsky. Five of the tracks recorded were quite advanced enough for the period, but then for 'Intuition' and 'Digression' Tristano merely provided a harmonically free piano part and instructed his men to play along as they pleased, with no cues whatsoever, foreshadowing so-called free jazz by many years. Capitol was furious and refused to pay Tristano's session fee until the musicians' union intervened. Tristano, along with Tatum and Ellington, was among the greatest harmonists in jazz; his object seemed to be to retain a link with the past while forging a future, as Bix Beiderbecke had done, by restricting himself to the chord sequences of a small number of old pop songs. Tristano has been compared to Bach in the harmonic and contrapuntal tension he achieved. He insisted that a drummer, for example, play with an unadorned beat, responding instead to Tristano's subtle deviations of pulse. His music is as hard to play as Monk's, if not harder.

Another influential pianist in the music of the 1950s was Horace Silver. Two 10-inch LPs by the Horace Silver Quintet, in which Art Blakey played drums, were combined in the 12-inch *Horace Silver and the Jazz Messengers*; it includes 'Doodlin'' (soon covered by Ray Charles) and 'The Preacher'. It was the music of Silver and Blakey that was first called hard bop; Silver's came to be called funk, a post-bop style with a rhythm and blues feeling. (The word 'funk' originally referred to strong smells – there was a club in New Orleans called the Funky Butt – and meant 'low-down' or 'gutbucket' in music. In recent times it has been misused, and means nothing in today's post-jazz world.)

Blakey had earlier used the name Jazz Messengers for a big-band recording, and retained it. Between them, Art Blakey's Jazz Messengers and Silver's various quintets employed on their albums, mostly on Blue Note, virtually all the best young black musicians to come forward in the ensuing decades, far too many to list here. (I recommend *The Penguin Encyclopedia of Popular Music*: follow the cross-references and use the index.) It was the sound of these albums that defined the Blue Note ethos for countless fans across two decades; among Silver's best-known tunes was 'Señor Blues'. Others built on his foundation: trumpeter Lee Morgan (who was murdered by a jealous girlfriend) wrote 'The Sidewinder', and keyboard player Herbie Hancock wrote 'Maiden Voyage' before turning to more lucrative pop-rock-funk-jazz in the 1970s. Blakey employed everyone from Morgan to Wynton Marsalis, Branford Marsalis, Terence Blanchard and Donald Harrison, four of today's most successful young post-bop revivalists.

At an opposite pole from the funk of the Jazz Messengers was the Modern Jazz Quartet, formed in 1952: John Lewis (pianist and composer), Milt Jackson (vibraphone), Percy Heath (double bass) and Kenny Clarke (drums); when Clarke moved to Paris in 1955, he was replaced by Connie Kay. Having no horns at all and usually dressing in evening wear, the quartet was unique, elegant and very popular. Lewis has also been active in film music and 'third-stream' attempts to blend jazz and 'serious' music, along with Gunther Schuller and others, which, however worthy, never seemed to set the world on fire. Jackson's nickname is Bags: there have been many recordings of 'Bags' Groove', but none more deceptively powerful than the one on *The Modern Jazz Quartet* (1957, Atlantic). That it sneaks up on you to knock your socks off is a result of dynamics as well as the ideas in the solos, for the tempo never changes. All the players have also had their separate careers; Jackson perhaps plays with more evident soul on his many other albums, such as *Bags and Trane*, recorded with John Coltrane. Dynamics is the strong suit of Connie Kay, whose precision and good taste are reminiscent of Brubeck's drummer Joe Morello; Kay played on a great many rhythm and blues hits as the house drummer at Atlantic and, later, on several Van Morrison albums. Percy Heath's family moved from North Carolina to Philadelphia, where his younger brothers, reedman Jimmy and drummer Albert 'Tootie' Heath, were at the centre of a thriving scene that encompassed composer-reedman Benny Golson, whose 'Stablemates' became a jazz standard, and Coltrane.

The countless 'blowing sessions' recorded by the East Coast jazz labels in the 1950s and early 1960s took the place of the jam sessions and cutting contests of earlier times, which were dying out for various reasons: the musicians' union disapproved of 'sitting in', and anyway there were fewer places in which to do it. The blowing sessions were often informal, and little rehearsal time was allowed because of the low-budget nature of the whole operation; they gave the soloists room to stretch and to work out new ideas. Many of them have by now been reissued and recycled several times, so that an Elmo Hope date called *Informal Jazz* (1956, Prestige) became *Two Tenors*, a Coltrane album with Hank Mobley; a Kenny Dorham date became a Coltrane album, Mal Waldron albums became Eric Dolphy albums and so forth. But none of the jazz labels was making much money. One reason most of Herbie Nichols's tracks were not released at the time was that Blue Note was caught between the large number of 10-inch LPs in its catalogue and the new demand by retailers for 12-inch LPs; a large label could shrug off this sort of problem, but it was a major stumbling block for an independent. The frequency of recording dates, however, was a godsend to the musicians, who could often get an advance against the next one when they were short of cash.

Miles Davis came from a middle-class family (his father was a dentist). Having begun playing trumpet at the age of thirteen, he soon proved to be something of a prodigy; he went to New York to study at the Juilliard School, but hung out on 52nd Street instead.

He was later a drug addict for four years, but by 1954 had stopped thanks to his own effort, aided by his pride in himself and his disgust at what he had become. He was outspoken and could be hard to get along with. His ability to give up heroin had banished fear: 'Some people accuse me of being mean and racist because I don't bow and scrape. When they look in my eyes and don't see fear they know it's a draw.'

George Russell, three years older than Davis, had been asked by Charlie Parker to play drums in his group, but was hospitalized because of his weak lungs; he spent the time thinking about music theory, partly inspired by Davis's remark to the effect that he wanted to be able to play a wider choice of notes. Russell's *The Lydian Chromatic Concept of Tonal Organization in Improvisation* was published in 1953. Russell's own record dates between 1956 and 1962 on RCA, Decca and Riverside were not more frequent partly because his music required rehearsal; he was inventing a style in which the ancient modes were combined with chromaticism, so that instead of using a key signature, which limits the musician's choice to the notes in the chords, the tonal centre of the music is its centre of gravity, and the soloist can select a much wider variety of notes. Russell spent the next fifteen years in Scandinavia, because in Europe there were still radio orchestras, and broadcasting took its responsibility to the arts more seriously. Meanwhile, Davis, once free of drugs, began to discover his own centre.

He had always been an individual stylist, and did not attempt to play in the fleet and quicksilvery way of bop trumpet soloists for long; his studio recordings in the early 1950s were few. In early 1953 he recorded for Prestige in a sextet including two reeds: Sonny Rollins, and Charlie Parker, also playing tenor (under the name Charlie Chan, because he was contracted to Granz). In April 1954 there was a sextet session for which Davis had asked tenor saxophonist Lucky Thompson to write some tunes, as Bob Weinstock at Prestige could not afford studio time for workouts; yet in the end the date's importance was indeed worked out in the studio. Thompson has not recorded since the mid-1970s, which is unlucky for his many fans; on this occasion he stayed up all night writing, but to no avail: the tunes did not work. So Davis took over, and discovered his talent for setting moods. 'Blue 'n' Boogie' and 'Walkin'', were his first masterpieces. Of the first, Ian Carr wrote in his biography of Davis:

After an eight-bar horn introduction over offbeats, the theme of 'Walkin'' is played twice. This theme, with its use of flattened fifths, and its stark call-and-response pattern, is highly evocative – a distilled essence of the traditional and the post-bop blues. The atmosphere and sense of drama are heightened by the sonorities of trumpet, trombone [J. J. Johnson] and tenor all in unison, and their beautifully poised timing . . . an elastic, laid-back, lazy feel on a knife-edge of balance. Kenny Clarke's immensely sensitive and subtle use of the high-hat cymbal which he opens and closes to point up the rhythms of the theme, also intensifies the drama.

Thompson, perhaps partly out of the frustration he must have felt, produced some of the best playing of his career. The truth is that Davis had never really been a bopper. At this time he also began using the cup mute, which is restrictive and difficult to play in tune. Davis's forte was (and remained, despite the changing nature of his backing material in later years) the economical, intimate and voice-like choice of notes, which tug at both heart and intellect.

In June he recorded with a quintet that consisted of Rollins and the same rhythm section as in April: Horace Silver, Percy Heath and Clarke. The session included two of Rollins's tunes, 'Oleo' and 'Airegin' ('Nigeria' spelled backwards), which Davis continued to use for some years. It was on 'Oleo' that Davis first recorded with the metallic harmon mute, adapted by having its stem removed, and in effect amplified, played very close to the microphone. Its full, breathy lower register and thin, shrill higher notes could be contrasted with each other, and completed the development of one of the most important sounds of the 1950s. Weinstock had now turned over all his recording to engineer Rudy Van Gelder, in whose studio in New Jersey most of the best East Coast jazz records were made, and made so well that nearly forty years later they still sound fresh as paint.

At the end of 1954 Weinstock arranged an all-star date which included Monk. Davis admired Monk but the great man was too idiosyncratic for a Davis recording session; yet jazz has always required musicians to communicate with each other, and even from this session there emerged some fascinating toing and froing. In March of 1955 Charlie Parker died, and, as Carr points out, the feeling everyone had had that an era was coming to an end was confirmed.

In July 1955 Davis played at the second Newport Jazz Festival, and was offered a Columbia recording contract with an advance. By this time, after some variable recordings, he had assembled a quintet that Weinstock compared with Louis Armstrong's Hot Five of 1925 in its importance. The drummer was Philly Joe Jones, Red Garland played piano and Paul Chambers double bass; Davis wanted Sonny Rollins, who was unavailable, and the others recommended John Coltrane. This group was important in a different way from that of Armstrong: the greatness of the Hot Five had stemmed almost entirely from Louis, whereas the Miles Davis Quintet of 1956 was one of the most seminal in a market that had more talent than it could support. Despite this it was criticized, not so much by the public as by the critics, who always like to tell their favourites what to do: Philly Joe was too loud, Coltrane's solos went on too long and so forth. But Davis knew what he wanted. Of Philly Joe he said, 'He could turn up with one arm and in his BVDs [underwear] as long as he plays what I want.' Coltrane had toured with Johnny Hodges and Earl Bostic, and had been developing for years in blowing sessions; Ira Gitler invented the phrase 'sheets of sound' to describe the way in which Coltrane, in his controlled urgency, tried to play all the notes in a chord at once.

Davis was still under contract to Prestige, but Weinstock knew that he could not afford to hang on to the phenomenon that the Miles Davis Quintet was becoming, so a deal was made: as long as Davis fulfilled his contract, he could sign with Columbia, take the advance and even record for the other label, as long as no records were released until the Prestige contract was fulfilled. The Five albums made for Prestige, *Miles* (late 1955) and *Steamin'*, *Workin'*, *Cookin'* and *Relaxin' with the Miles Davis Quintet* (all 1956), far from representing too much recording activity in too short a time, showed a progressive strengthening of skills.

'Round about Midnight was released in 1958 on Columbia, and Davis began recording with arranger-composer Gil Evans, which resulted in *Miles Ahead, Porgy and Bess, Sketches of Spain* and *Directions*. There was also a Carnegie Hall concert and a television film with Evans and Davis. Evans was the arranger who came closest to creating a viable third stream, but there was not enough money in the music to pursue it until it bore fruit in the form of more commercial success. And that sort of success was not forthcoming: the music was much too good for what American broadcasting had become by then.

Gary McFarland, who died when a prankster slipped liquid methadone into a drink, and Oliver Nelson, whose album *Blues and the Abstract Truth* (1961) on Impulse was a milestone in the genre, were talented individuals who were lost too soon, though Nelson's later albums consistently missed the mark. George Russell had to go to Europe to make a living, and trumpeter and arranger Johnny Carisi had so little work as a recording artist over the years that his name remained all but unknown.

An album by Carisi in 1956 scheduled for an RCA Jazz Workshop series was not issued; alto saxophonist and leader Hal McKusick recorded tracks by Gil Evans and George Russell which made it on to an album in that series; trombonist and arranger Rod Levitt remained obscure despite RCA albums in the mid-1960s. Mike Zwerin arranged the music of Kurt Weill for the Sextet of Orchestra USA and conducted it on RCA in 1966. (Zwerin had played in Davis's group in 1949, but missed out on the recording sessions, and now writes for the *International Herald Tribune*.) Gerry Mulligan worked with big bands and orchestras over the years, but never for any length of time. The problem in modern jazz was the same as that at the end of a big-band era: it was economically impossible to keep a large performing group together, and repertory groups (such as European broadcasting supported, even in eastern Europe) simply did not exist in the USA.

Of all these, Evans was the most successful. He and Carisi had both contributed to the *Birth of the Cool* sessions, and before that to Claude Thornhill's band. Evans issued no work under his own name until *Gil Evans and Ten* was recorded on Prestige in 1957. Then his albums *New Bottle, Old Wine* (1958) and *Great Jazz Standards*

(1959) on World Pacific, together with the albums with Davis during the same period, announced a major 'new' talent and at least the possibility of a new genre.

Davis's *Porgy and Bess* was the most exciting treatment of Gershwin's music since the opera's première; *Sketches of Spain* included Evans's impressionistic arrangement of Rodrigo's *Concierto de Aranjuez* and an excerpt from Manuel de Falla's ballet *El amor brujo*. The sessions for *Sketches of Spain* were lavish and expensive for the time. George Avakian had produced Davis's first orchestral album, *Miles Ahead*, before retiring, but it was producer Teo Macero, a musician himself with a degree from the Juilliard School, who not only understood and worked with the dichotomy of commerce versus art in the record industry, but had the backing of Goddard Lieberson, then the president of Columbia and one of the most civilized people ever to hold such a post. One problem had been to convince the big band that it could play 'sloppy': most of the musicians had experience of jazz, but they had to be convinced that what was required was not the usual precision of a 'legit' session. The album also required months of editing.

Some of Davis's tracks were recorded with a band led by Michel Legrand in 1958, but another Legrand album from the year before, sometimes included in Davis's discographies, was made in Paris with trumpet solos by Fernand Verstraete. Miles had been in Paris in late 1957, though, recording soundtrack music for *L'ascenseur pour l'échafaud*, with Pierre Michelot, Kenny Clarke, Barney Wilen on tenor and René Urtreger on piano. This was episodic, like most soundtrack music, but its ethereal moodiness was a clue to what was coming next.

At the beginning of Davis's first great period, all of his sidemen were drug addicts, but he was never judgemental, saying that when they got tired of the conflict between the habit and the music, they would stop if they could. (Similarly, Duke Ellington's attitude towards his unruly band was that they were grown men and would sooner or later have to look after themselves.) Coltrane had been fired by Johnny Hodges because he was an addict, whereupon he had played in a succession of rhythm and blues bands. He left Davis suddenly in November 1956.

The story persists that when Davis was forming his quintet in 1955, Rollins had made himself scarce so that Coltrane would get the chance; but Rollins was also dealing with a drug problem. In 1956–7 recording sessions and broadcasts occasionally included Rollins instead of Coltrane. Coltrane joined Thelonious Monk at the Five Spot in New York. The association did not last long – it coincided with one of the periods during which Monk did not record much – but Monk taught Coltrane his difficult music and harmony as well, and encouraged him to take long solos, searching until he found what he wanted to play. And it was in 1957 that *Monk's Music* was made, the septet album with Coltrane and Coleman Hawkins. Art Blakey later reported:

Hawk was having trouble reading [the music], so he asked Monk to explain it to both Trane and himself. Monk said to Hawk, 'You're the great Coleman Hawkins, right? You're the guy who invented the tenor saxophone, right?' Hawk agreed. Then Monk said to Trane, 'You're the great John Coltrane, right?' Trane blushed and mumbled . . . Then Monk said to both of them, 'You both play tenor saxophone, right?' They nodded. 'Well, the music is on the horn. Between the two of you, you should be able to find it.'

It was hard to get Monk to say much, while Blakey loved to talk; he may have embroidered this. At any rate, Coltrane had become much better known while playing with Davis, and his membership of Monk's group caused a stir. Ray Copeland recalled the 1957 recording session in which he took part:

We were sitting near the rhythm section while the leader was taking a long piano solo. It was almost time for Coltrane's solo, and as I turned to look at him I noticed that he was nodding out, holding his horn in his lap. Before I could do anything, the leader happened to look up from the piano, saw Trane's condition, and screamed, 'Coltrane . . . *Coltrane!*' What happened next was so amazing I'll never forget it as long as I live. Trane was suddenly on his feet, playing in perfect cadence and following the piano solo as if nothing had happened. He played a pretty good solo, and when he was finished he sat down and went back to nodding out.

Copeland does not name the recording session, but on *Monk's Music*, on 'Well, You Needn't', you can hear Monk, at the end of his solo, shout 'Coltrane . . . *Coltrane*!' while Blakey's drum roll is announcing a new soloist. In J. C. Thomas's biography of Coltrane, *Chasin' the Trane*, he writes that it was in the spring of 1957 that Coltrane overcame his drug addiction; *Monk's Music* was made in June. After a period of not working much Coltrane decided, just as Davis had thought he would, that his habit was getting in the way of his music. He shut himself in a room in his mother's house and fasted for several days, and never touched drugs again. And soon Miles Davis called and said, 'I want you back.'

Milestones in 1958 was a sextet album, on which Cannonball Adderley was added on alto saxophone. (Miles also played on an Adderley album on Blue Note.) Julian Adderley had led a combo with his brother Nat on cornet, but he knew how valuable his experience with Miles was, for Davis was bridging the gap between funk and third-stream music. When Adderley went back to leading, he contributed to the stock of funk in the land, and his single 'Mercy, Mercy, Mercy' (written by pianist Joe Zawinul) almost reached the top ten of the *Billboard* pop chart. One of the things Miles liked about Adderley was that he never touched drugs; yet the big man, whose nickname was originally Cannibal, from his love of food as a teenager, died after a heart attack at the peak of his success.

Davis liked to use words like 'nigger', but in fact he has always hired the people he wanted without regard to race; in the late 1950s he began using pianist Bill Evans. If Oscar Peterson was the Liszt of jazz, Bill Evans was its Chopin: he thought about getting vibrato from the piano, knowing it to be impossible, because that approach to the keyboard somehow helped to give him the results he wanted; and his economy of notes was also to Davis's liking. In 1959 came the album *Kind of Blue*, a tremendous influence on the following decade, made with Coltrane, Adderley, Chambers, drummer Jimmy Cobb and pianist Evans (who was replaced by Wynton Kelly on one track). On *Kind of Blue* Davis broke through to an entirely modal way of playing. There were no standards, but five originals of pure atmosphere, drenched with Davis's plaintive economical sadness, yet intellectually powerful, and pure jazz. Evans was listed as the arranger and all the tunes as Davis's but it is thought that Evans was the author of 'Flamenco Sketches' and 'Blue in Green'.

In 1959 Coltrane had his own breakthrough. He had signed a one-year contract with Atlantic, with an option for another year. In April he recorded a version of his own tune, 'Giant Steps', which did not satisfy him, so the next month he did it again, with Paul Chambers on bass, Tommy Flanagan on piano and Art Taylor on drums, and the Atlantic album *John Coltrane: Giant Steps* was released in 1960. The mature Coltrane, one of the half-dozen most influential jazz musicians of all time, had arrived, riding an uptempo burst of joy, playing plenty of notes, but not one too many.

Meanwhile, Sonny Rollins, who was three years younger than Coltrane but better known, perhaps because he was less introspective and had more confidence, had solved his drug problem, and made a trio album, with Ray Brown on bass and Shelly Manne on drums, on the West Coast in March 1957: *Way Out West* has been a classic ever since. The lead track is Johnny Mercer's 'I'm an Old Cowhand'. (It was said to be Rollins's idea to have himself photographed in the desert for the album cover with cowboy hat and tenor saxophone instead of a six-gun; he later said he was embarrassed by it.) The album was recorded by Roy DuNann at Lester Koenig's Contemporary studio, and they were just as good at it as Rudy Van Gelder: decades later it sounds like it was recorded yesterday, and the CD edition, with four very different alternative takes, is one of the best buys in the jazz market.

Great black music was once again receiving public attention, and the next decade held more surprises. But one more giant remains to be announced in this chapter. Charles Mingus was the volatile master of the string bass, capable of playing it like a guitar; he had physical power as well as that of a composer. He was born on an army base in Arizona; he died in Mexico of a muscular wasting disease, having been in many ways an eternal exile. His ancestry included Swedish, Afro-American, American Indian and probably Scottish blood. Mingus was unaware of racism until a certain age, and it shocked him profoundly, but he turned it like everything else into an ingredient in his music. He heard Ellington on the radio; his stepmother would allow only religious music in the home, but took him to the Holiness

Church, where the 'moaning and riffs . . . between the preacher and the audience' were perhaps his most basic influence.

As a teenager he studied trombone and cello, then was steered towards playing bass in a school band (which also included Dexter Gordon). His excellent pitch and poor teaching meant that he began as a slow reader, but eventually he found better teachers, among them Red Callender, for decades one of the busiest freelance musicians on the West Coast, whom he replaced in Lee Young's band. He played with Louis Armstrong's band in 1943 and performed widely. He recorded with Illinois Jacquet, Dinah Washington and Ivie Anderson, as well as making obscure sides of his own, one of which (in 1946 for the Excelsior label) was the first appearance of a theme called 'Weird Nightmare'. While he was with Lionel Hampton (1947–8), the band made a recording on Decca called 'Mingus Fingers'. He then gave up and worked in a post office until he was hired to play in Red Norvo's trio, along with Tal Farlow on guitar.

A combination of racism and union rules meant that Mingus would have had to be replaced for a television broadcast in 1951, so he left, wanting anyway to move to New York. He joined his idol Ellington in early 1953, but after a short time his temperament caused a violent clash with Juan Tizol, and Ellington said, 'Charles, I've never fired anybody, so you're going to have to leave.'

Mingus and Max Roach formed Debut Records in 1952, and were thus among the first black jazzmen to try to maintain control of their own product. They recorded the first sessions under their own names, with reedmen Teo Macero, Sam Most and John LaPorta, trumpeters Thad Jones and Kenny Dorham and pianist-composer Paul Bley. There was also a Miles Davis session in 1955, with Mingus, vibraphonist Teddy Charles, trombonist Britt Woodman (Mingus's Los Angeles classmate and a future sideman with both Mingus and Ellington) and Coltrane's future drummer Elvin Jones, brother of Thad (and pianist Hank, all from Detroit).

Another Debut project included four trombonists, and resulted in the success of Jay and Kai, the quintet led by trombonists J. J. Johnson, the first bop trombonist, who played difficult runs with such ease that some thought he must have been playing a valve trombone, and Danish-born Kai Winding. Mingus performed on their first two albums, on Savoy and Blue Note in 1954, and in 1955 they began recording for Columbia, achieving a much higher profile than Mingus ever did.

The most famous Debut release was the first: the recording of the Massey Hall concert, made in Toronto in 1953, with Mingus, Roach, Bud Powell, Dizzy Gillespie and Charlie Parker, and an album of trio selections without the horns. The sound was not as bad as we had been led to believe; apparently it was Mingus's ego that prompted him to overdub his bass part later. The set remains one of the most renowned documents in jazz history.

In early 1955 a reunion was arranged at Birdland for Parker, Bud Powell, Mingus, Art Blakey and Kenny Dorham. They were unable to work together. Powell had to be helped from the stand, incapable; Parker stood at the microphone calling 'Bud Powell! Bud Powell!' over and over. Mingus announced, 'Ladies and gentlemen, please don't associate me with any of this. This is not jazz. These are sick people.' Years afterwards he revealed that later that night Thelonious Monk had said to Bird and Bud, 'I told you guys to act crazy, but I didn't tell you to fall in love with the act. You're really crazy now.' Parker had only a week or so to live, but life and music carry on: Miles Davis would form his quintet the same year, and Mingus's apprenticeship was almost over.

Mingus also recorded as a leader for Period and Savoy, sometimes with LaPorta and Macero. Mingus and Roach could not afford to turn down other work; the only artist Debut signed to an exclusive contract was Thad Jones, for a year, and then Mingus used his own artist as 'Oliver King' on Savoy. Debut suffered, like all small labels, from poor distribution and cash-flow problems, despite the faithful Celia, Mingus's first wife, who did most of the work. Items were later leased to Fantasy, including live performances recorded at the Café Bohemia in late December 1955, on which Mingus combined a Kern standard with a Rachmaninov prelude to make 'All the Things You C Sharp'. Debut closed down in 1957.

While running his Jazz Workshop in the early 1950s in New York, Mingus had learned by trial and error how he wanted his own music played. He recalled that he himself had joined the others in complaining when Teddy Charles left a few bars empty for blowing: 'Man, are you crazy? Write it out!' But he soon realized that no combination of writing it down and leaving spaces for blowing would give him the results he wanted. For much of his career he went through sidemen very quickly, because his patented method was too tough for them: he would proceed with no music at all, teaching it to the men a bar at a time on the piano, leaving it up to them to play his music their way. Although Mingus's personality was very different from Duke Ellington's, his working method was similar. Barney Bigard told Max Jones that Ellington would often not even give the music to his men on paper, but play it for them on the piano; and if he left a blank space, you were supposed to play his music your way. Mingus chose people who he knew could play his music, but he was much less of a diplomat, so it was harder work getting it out of them. His music, like Ellington's, did not sound like anyone else's. He also pointed the way towards greater freedom: out of necessity, he wrote mostly for smaller groups than Ellington, he gave his people more freedom and simultaneously demanded it from them. His bass playing was ferocious; he would bend a pitch not only by stopping a string but by pulling it out of true, as T-Bone Walker did on the blues guitar. And he would not hesitate to shout or sing a snatch of blues himself, encouraging another man's solo. He found resources inside himself, and his men had to do the same.

Early in 1956 he recorded his first typical work, the tone poem 'Pithecanthropus Erectus', for Atlantic, with J. R. Monterose on tenor saxophone, Jackie McLean on alto, Mal Waldron on piano and Willie Jones on drums. It depicted the emergence and grandiose follies of early man in less than eleven minutes; the moaning, inexorable passion of it was vintage Mingus. By now he had a set of tricks in his bag, suggested by tunes like 'Minor Intrusion' and 'Thrice upon a Theme'. Two other tracks on *Pithecanthropus* were 'Profile of Jackie' and 'Love Chant', which is almost fifteen minutes long and does not hold up as well as the title track; it is marred by somebody apparently playing a tambourine almost all the way through.

A year later, by the time of his next Atlantic album, he had discovered Dannie Richmond, a budding young saxophonist who changed to drums at Mingus's suggestion, and was his faithful musical colleague until the end. He played music on the drums to

Mingus's satisfaction, as well as keeping time and pushing the beat as required, adding immeasurably to the Mingus magic. The album, *The Clown*, is spoiled by a recitation on the title track: the combination of poetry and jazz was a fad at the time (another example is 'Scenes in the City', recorded for Bethlehem). Words meant a lot to Mingus; his autobiography, *Beneath the Underdog*, which amounted to a trunkful of manuscript, was savagely edited down to a book in 1971. But the combination of music and recitation works only for a live audience, when it works at all: few want to listen to it on a record.

In July there was the Hampton Hawes trio album (Jubilee) and a quintet album for trombonist Jimmy Knepper (Debut). Later that summer came Mingus's first complete success: *Tijuana Moods* is a thirty-five-minute tone poem in five parts, suggested by a visit to the Mexican border town. It was recorded basically by a sextet, including Clarence Shaw on trumpet, Knepper on trombone and Shafi Hadi (Curtis Porter) on alto, but it sounds bigger, thanks to the best recorded sound Mingus had yet received (good stereo in 1957), to the castanets, extra percussion and voices on some tracks and, mainly, to the complete success of the music. Martin Williams wrote for the album's sleeve-note about two aspects of Mingus's work:

The first is the full texture he achieves with a small group with no feeling of contrivance ... Even with one horn in solo, there is a denseness to the performance, a feeling of total movement that is always integrated. The second is the naturalness with which shifts of dominant rhythm and of tempo usually happen without the feeling of a stilted effort at 'effect'. Almost everything comes because it enables the music and the musicians to say something they have to say.

With the variable luck Mingus always had, *Tijuana Moods* was not released for six years.

In the autumn of 1957 Mingus made two albums for Bethlehem, one of which, *East Coasting*, keeps up the momentum; but they did not sell as well as expected. In 1958 he discovered pianist Horace Parlan, alto saxophonist John Handy and tenor saxophonist Booker Ervin; just when he seemed to have got a hot group together as well as his music, he learned that RCA was not going to bring out *Tijuana Moods*, Bethlehem was not going to record him any more and the William Morris Agency was going to drop him; and on top of all that, the long-suffering Celia left him. He tried to find relief for his frustrations at Bellevue, New York's mental hospital; he went there voluntarily, but bureaucrats locked him up. Critic and record producer Nat Hentoff had to help secure his release. Mingus later said that he had got himself locked up on purpose in order to get out of a personal management contract; his contact with people who were genuinely in mental trouble seems to have concentrated his energies.

Early in 1959 a live concert recording was made at the Nonagan Art Gallery, including 'Nostalgia in Times Square', written for the film *Shadows* (directed by John Cassavetes). In February came *Blues and Roots*, an epochal Atlantic album whose highlight was 'Wednesday Night Prayer Meeting'. This tune, which was something of a hit, was played by other bands and issued in two parts on a single. But the album was not released for more than a year, because Atlantic was then still a smallish label. Mingus in the meantime made two masterpieces for Columbia, *Mingus Ah Um* and *Mingus Dynasty*.

The first is recorded by an octet – Hadi, Handy and Ervin (reeds), Parlan (piano) and Knepper and Willie Dennis (trombones), but again it sounds like a much bigger group. Among the Mingus classics were 'Better Git It in Your Soul' and 'Goodbye Pork Pie Hat'; 'Jelly Roll' is a salute to that master, while 'Fables of Faubus' seems just a sardonic tune with a sarcastic title. *Mingus Dynasty* used a slightly larger group, and included 'Gunslinging Bird', of which the full title (in Mingus's afterthought) was 'If Bird came back as a gunslinger there'd be a whole lot of dead copycats'. (The band knew it as 'Gunslinger'.) There were also 'Open Letter to Duke' and Ellington's 'Mood Indigo'.

In May 1960 he recorded an ambitious and interesting album for Mercury, first called *Pre-Bird* and now once more available under that title. Ten musicians play on some tracks and twenty-five on others. 'Weird Nightmare' receives another outing: it is the same tune as 'Pipe Dream' (1946), 'Smooch' (1953, recorded by Miles Davis) and 'Vasserlean' (1960). 'Nightmare' and 'Eclipse' had vocals by Lorraine Cousins; Mingus said he had written the latter for Billie Holiday, but was afraid to give it to her. 'Half-mast Inhibition' was conducted by Gunther Schuller (as the original sleeve-note pointed out, a good

Mingus title: Half-masked inhibition? Half-past intermission?). The smaller group performed 'Prayer for Passive Resistance', another Mingus standard, and such furious interpolations as 'Take the "A" Train' with 'Exactly Like You' and 'Do Nothing Till You Hear From Me' with 'I Let a Song Go Out of My Heart'. *Pre-Bird* was Mingus's first attempt at a summary: some of the material was nearly twenty years old. He felt until the end of his life that what he was doing was all of a piece, but his chaotic way of working, usually caused by his shortage of cash, was exacerbated by his temperament (and vice versa), and was to bring about some disasters in the next decade.

In July a Mingus set was recorded live at a jazz festival at Antibes; Bud Powell, a guest, plays a furious solo on 'I'll Remember April'. The other tunes recorded were played by Mingus, Richmond, Eric Dolphy (alto saxophone and bass clarinet), Booker Ervin (tenor saxophone) and Ted Curson (trumpet). *Tijuana Moods* had no tenor saxophone; *Mingus Ah Um* had no trumpet; now Mingus had moved further into his vision, and missed out the piano. Mingus's studio dates are wonderful, but the driving, passionate personality of the composer came out even better in an informal setting. 'Wednesday Night Prayer Meeting', 'Better Get Hit in Your Soul' and 'Prayer for Passive Resistance' were full of the feeling of the Holiness Church; among the new tunes were 'What Love?' and 'Folk Forms 1': in the latter the musicians talked to each other on their instruments.

Ted Curson later led a band with Bill Barron, a tenor saxophonist from Philadelphia whose sound was like that of Coltrane; according to Curson, he had developed it 'when John Coltrane was still playing alto'. From the late 1960s Curson lived in Europe and was the first foreign musician to receive a grant from the Finnish government. Booker Ervin and Eric Dolphy were outstandingly gifted reedmen; both died because of kidney problems, Dolphy's exacerbated by undiagnosed diabetes.

Ervin and Dolphy complemented each other wonderfully, and were among Mingus's greatest discoveries. Ervin (and trumpeter Booker Little) are often lost in the shuffle when considering jazzmen of this era who died young, because Dolphy's in particular is another of the unfinished careers in music. Dolphy played all the reed instruments, including flute, but mostly alto saxophone, and was one of the first to take up the bass clarinet, played now by David Murray, Chico Freeman and others. He began in a quintet with drummer Chico Hamilton (a Mingus classmate), which unusually contained a cellist, Fred Katz. When he joined Mingus, he was mature and played with a hard-won voice-like tonal purity and a rich harmonic imagination, influenced by bird-calls, marching bands and much else. He went on to make albums of his own and with Mal Waldron on Prestige, and on Blue Note, before his death while on tour in Europe. Dolphy foreshadowed free jazz, yet his playing was not as far 'out' as it sounded; he purposely stuck to chord structures, but sounded as though he did not. He said that the notes he chose were technically acceptable in the orthodox sense, yet he seemed to lurch into another universe and back again, lending his swing sometimes to a wild and wonderful wackiness, particularly at faster tempos. He was a much bigger influence than many a musician with a longer career.

In October Mingus recorded for Archie Bleyer's Candid label, a short-lived subsidiary of Cadence, at Nola Studios in New York, where a successful attempt was made to create an informal club-type atmosphere. The recordings were produced by Nat Hentoff. The first album from these sessions had just Mingus, Richmond, Dolphy and Curson.

One of the quartet's tunes is called 'All the Things You Could be by Now if Sigmund Freud's Wife was Your Mother'. Dolphy and Curson were both soon to leave Mingus; on a more integrated and even more exciting performance of 'Folk Forms No. 1' than the one played at Antibes, they carry on an impassioned conversation while Mingus and Richmond lay out entirely, but they never drop the driving beat for an instant; in 'What Love?', Mingus and Dolphy talk things over. 'Original Faubus Fables' restores the lyrics Columbia would not allow and is dedicated to 'the first, or second or third, all-American heel, Orville Faubus' (governor of Arkansas, who ran a chicken restaurant and whose hobby was waving an axe-handle at black children). The lyrics not only introduce the superior, dramatic rhythm of the tune, but the vocal interjections and the informal setting allow its sardonicism full rein.

The whole set represents one of the high points in post-war jazz. It is driven and dominated by Mingus and his bass with such power and tone that, on the evidence, there is no reason for anyone to play a solid-body electric bass, ever – except that playing bass like Mingus must be much harder work. Another track by the quartet, later issued on another album, was a marvellous version of 'Stormy Weather'. The second Mingus–Candid session featured the short-lived Newport Rebels and Jazz Artists Guild, with elder statesman Roy Eldridge, who said to Mingus, 'I wanted to find out what bag you're in. Now I know you're in the right bag.'

There were more triumphs and tragedies for Mingus, but as the 1960s began jazz seemed to be in good shape: Miles Davis, Mingus and Coltrane were hitting their stride, and Ornette Coleman was upsetting everybody. A few jazz records were selling tens of thousands, at a time when six thousand was a good average sale. But demographic and other changes were about to turn the whole business upside down: millions of kids who had never heard any jazz were about to wreak revenge on a business that had fed them pap ever since they could sit up and listen. The tragedy of rock'n'roll is that it was forced to become more than music.

14

Rock'n'roll; or, Black Music to the Rescue (Again)

Jazz and blues, or black urban music and black country music, were treated as separate, if related, genres in earlier decades; the saying was that the blues was not jazz, but jazz had the blues in it. But that had altered by the 1950s. While jazz effectively became the art music of the urban black (and some whites), the strands of black pop had come together. The blues had come to town, and rhythm and blues was big business.

Historically, black recording artists had often been given Tin Pan Alley tunes that white artists had already turned down. When Red Allen and Coleman Hawkins together led small-group dates in 1933, of eleven titles from three of the sessions, nine were pop songs of the day, only two of which had any currency: 'The Day You Came Along' was recorded by Bing Crosby and 'You're Gonna Lose Your Gal' by the Casa Loma band. All had probably been shoved at the record producer by song pluggers; 'Shadows on the Swanee', 'My Galveston Gal' and the rest have not been heard of since.

Some of the Tin Pan Alley and Broadway songs were so good that jazzmen improvised lovingly on them. 'How High the Moon' became a bop standard, and countless riffs were composed on its chords. As late as 1960 Mingus did something interesting with 'Girl of My Dreams', a waltz from 1927. Plenty of black tunes were big hits for white bands. The success blacks and whites had with each other's tunes and arrangements was not a fair trade-off, but black bands were never going to get the best jobs anyway, and there was money in black tunes that were hits. Joe Garland was no doubt happy to have 'In the Mood' recorded note for note by Glenn Miller.

By the early 1950s, however, everything had changed. Blacks were doing their own thing in a new era, for labels created especially to sell to the black market; and good white songs were becoming scarce. The Berlins, Gershwins and the rest had died or retired, and the classic songs they had written could not be imitated. What with Hitler, atomic bombs and a new Cold War mentality, perhaps something had been lost which made it impossible to accept songs in the style of a more innocent era. In any case, other changes in the music business meant that new, younger composers did not get a chance to build on what Kern's generation had done. The ballads still played by jazzmen were now standards, the airwaves were filled with jingles and the Broadway musical was beginning to disappear.

In the 1949–50 season the new shows included Rodgers and Hammerstein's *The King and I*, Irving Berlin's *Call Me Madam* and Frank Loesser's *Guys and Dolls*. (The latter included 'If I Were a Bell', soon to be played by the Miles Davis Quintet.) But in 1950–51 only nine new productions were offered, the lowest number since well back in the nineteenth century. Some were revivals, like *Pal Joey* from 1940, and two were Yiddish-American shows which in earlier times would not have found room on Broadway. All the new shows of that season lost money, including *Top Banana*, with lyrics by Johnny Mercer (and starring Phil Silvers), and Lerner and Loewe's *Paint Your Wagon*. Musical shows were increasingly expensive to mount, while television and other social changes meant there were smaller audiences on the Great White Way, as Broadway used to be known. The hit shows of the 1950s, such as *The Pajama Game* (1954) and *Damn Yankees* (1955), both by Richard Adler and Jerry Ross, occasionally produced above-average pop songs, for example, 'Hey There' and 'Whatever Lola Wants', but not of the quality of earlier decades. *West Side Story* (music by Leonard Bernstein and lyrics by Stephen Sondheim) and *The Music Man* (Meredith Willson) were both huge hits in 1957, and great in contrast, the one about racial strife in New York, the other, through rose-tinted glasses, about a small town. *Gypsy* (1959) was probably a masterpiece in every respect: it was Ethel Merman's last big role, it effortlessly revived all the 'shtick' of Broadway tradition, and the songs were by Jule Styne and Stephen Sondheim. But among the most interesting events on Broadway in the 1950s were Bernstein's failure *Candide* (1956, lyrics by Lillian Hellman) and the emergence of Sondheim as a major talent.

Broadway shows were not what they used to be and were trying to become something else; no longer would they provide a central strand of America's pop culture. Nowadays the only shows certain to be profitable, indeed to set records for making money, are those of Britain's Andrew Lloyd Webber; even his third marriage in early 1991 got columns of space in British newspapers. Yet Lloyd Webber's music is perfect FM fodder, of no lasting value at all, in my opinion. Stephen Sondheim is acknowledged to be the most important composer for the stage today, even by the same critics who find something wrong with every show. All the same, even his *Into the Woods*, which received better reviews from the British critics than any of his previous works, lasted only five months in London. The musical theatre, once at the centre of popular music, is now well outside it.

It is impossible to say how much was lost on account of the low standards of American broadcasting. Harold Arlen's *House of Flowers* and many another show may simply have been too good to survive at a time when people went to a Broadway show despite the increasing price of the tickets only because their neighbours had seen it. Cabaret singers such as Bobby Short, Mabel Mercer and Blossom Dearie have had a huge repertory of songs that were almost totally unknown to the general public, raising the question of whether that sort of songwriting disappeared or is living in the garden shed on reduced rations. The big bands and the late-night live radio broadcasts that once promoted such songs no longer exist. It is tantalizing to imagine television's having taken over the function of the Broadway musical, but it was not to be. It did not take television long to descend from the live drama of the 1950s to the banality of today's assembly-line mini-series; there is no original music drama on television. Polly Bergen was a good actress as well as a good singer, but there was no place for her to work; similarly, Maureen McGovern has an excellent voice, a musical intelligence and is a first-class modern actress, but the genre in which she would have been a star has disappeared.

Music on television's variety shows was almost exclusively ASCAP music, partly because there were few black faces to be seen, and radio DJ shows reflected this at first. But as the name of the *Billboard* 'race' chart was changed to rhythm and blues in 1949, a revolution was already brewing.

We have seen that Woody Herman had covered Louis Jordan's 'Caldonia' in 1945, that one of the biggest hits of 1950 was an inappropriate version of a country stomp, 'Rag Mop', and that Buddy Morrow covered the jump band hits of Jimmy Forrest. Along the way an historic court case settled the question of whether musical arrangements could be copyrighted, and the answer was that they could not. 'A Little Bird Told Me', a song by Harvey O. Brooks, was recorded by Paula Watson on a Supreme label. Decca copied not only the arrangement but also the vocal style to the last inflection, and had a big hit in 1948 by Evelyn Knight (whose other most successful hit, the same year, was 'Powder Your Face With Sunshine', a Lombardo song). Supreme sued, and lost. The Watson original sold well, but she had only one more minor hit, and there was now nothing to keep anybody from copying another's hit right down to the backbeat.

By 1954 there were at least 4 radio stations in New York aimed at the black market exclusively, and over 250 stations around the country. The number of black DJs had increased from only a few to over 700, and they were joined by a handful of hip whites, such as Art Leboe in Los Angeles, Dewey Phillips in Memphis, Gene Nobles and John Richborough in Nashville, Zenas Sears in Atlanta, Bob Smith (known as Wolfman Jack) in Shreveport, Ken 'the Cat' Elliott in New Orleans and Alan Freed in Cleveland. Several elements were at work: television forced non-network radio to turn to special-ized programming to find an audience, while many sponsors found television too expensive, and could still reach large numbers of black families, who had fewer television sets than whites, and perhaps found it hard to relate to white sitcoms. But even with regard to black pop, the famous DJs were white: they were the ones that had the effect on the white market. And even today the black market is simply not valued in the marketplace.

In 1953 $15 million worth of R & B records were sold, more than the entire record industry's sales of fifteen years earlier. Ruth Brown's contract was so valuable to Atlantic that it was renewed with an advance of $100,000: having been recommended to Atlantic by Duke Ellington, she had twenty-one top ten hits in the black chart from 1949 to 1960, five of which reached number one, and was the only female star under contract at Atlantic until LaVern Baker, whose first hit was in 1955. The Clovers, a vocal quartet and guitarist, also on Atlantic, had fifteen top ten black hits in four years; one of them reportedly sold two million copies (probably 'Fool, Fool, Fool', which was number one for six weeks in 1951).

Most new releases by the major labels never broke even, for they had to sell 40,000 copies to do so in 1953. The independent labels selling R & B, however, had lower costs and their own distribution, and new releases by artists like Amos Milburn on Aladdin and Little Esther (Phillips) on Savoy regularly sold 150,000 copies, and sometimes much more than that. A Texas-born pianist and barroom crooner, Milburn had nineteen top ten black hits (1948–54); his first, 'Chicken Shack Boogie', was number one for five weeks. Esther Mae Jones, also from Texas, was barely fourteen years old when her 'Double Crossing Blues' was number one in the black chart for nine weeks in early 1950. (Her career was interrupted by drug problems but she came back in 1962 as Esther Phillips.)

The major labels formed subsidiaries for R & B – Decca had Coral, and later Brunswick, while Columbia revived Okeh – but the product was too slick, and the independent producers of R & B had the D Js in their employ, while the big companies were making a late start in black radio. In order to do more business they began to cream it off the top, covering R & B hits with white artists.

The Orioles, a seminal black doo-wop quartet (plus a guitarist) from Baltimore, had black hits almost every year from 1948. Their 'Crying in the Chapel' (on Jubilee, 1953) was a number one black hit, but there were cover versions by Ella Fitzgerald, country singers Darrell Glenn and Rex Allen, former Benny Goodman vocalist Art Lund and (the biggest hit, on RCA) June Valli.

White vocal groups were big business in the early 1950s. The Ames Brothers were a quartet, with a sweet, pretty sound, led by Ed, who is still a popular balladeer today. But the other groups all used the same conventional white harmony, and after decades of beautiful black, country and folk vocal groups, most white pop groups of the early 1950s sounded like they were working too hard. The Four Lads were from Toronto; their voices blended well, but like most white vocal groups they sounded overwrought. They began by backing Johnnie Ray on 'Cry' in 1951. (Significantly, it was released on Okeh: Ray had help and encouragement from LaVern Baker and her manager, and his emotional delivery was seen as appealing to black audiences.) Like Ray, the Four Lads then transferred to the parent Columbia label, where their hits included 'Moments to Remember' (1955), a perennial college prom song for decades, 'No, Not Much' (1956), a good pop song by the same writers, Robert Allen and Ray Stillman, and 'Standing on the Corner (Watching All the Girls Go By)', which at least was supposed to be sung by a group. (It came from the Frank Loesser show *Most Happy Fella*.) The Four Lads had hits throughout the 1950s, according to *Billboard*, but I don't remember any of them.

The Four Aces, from Pennsylvania, were worse. Their biggest hit was 'Love is a Many-splendored Thing', a soupy film song in 1955, and the way they belted out the word 'luuuuuve' with their patented slow shuffle beat made you want to cry with boredom. There were also the Four Coins, the Four Esquires and so forth; the sound of the Hilltoppers on Dot was not too obnoxious (and included Billy Vaughan, who became the label's music director and house band-leader). The Four Freshmen and the Hi-lo's were good singers who used adventurous harmonies and arrangements, and sold mostly albums. Few white groups had learned anything from the essential sweetness of the doo-wop tradition.

The Crew-cuts were the worst of all, another quartet from Toronto, where they had all been choirboys. Their first hit on Mercury in 1954 was a white novelty, 'Crazy 'Bout Ya Baby'. Meanwhile, a black Bronx group called the Chords, on the Cat label, had covered Patti Page's hit 'Cross Over the Bridge', basically a country song; the B side was 'Sh-boom', their own rhythm novelty with a fast shuffle beat. D Js turned it over and made it number two in the black chart. The Crew-cuts, however, had already copied it: their 'Sh-boom' was a number one novelty hit for nine weeks in the pop chart, and is still described as the first rock'n'roll record, which it certainly was not. Their next and lesser hit, 'Oop-shoop', was written to cash in on the success of 'Sh-boom'. In 1955 a Los Angeles group, the Penguins, had a number one black hit on DooTone with a pretty doo-wop ballad written by the group's bass, Curtis Williams, called 'Earth Angel (Will You Be Mine)'; the Crew-cuts' version was a national number three. Gene and Eunice had a rhythm hit with 'Ko Ko Mo' in 1955, originally on Combo, soon picked up by Aladdin; there were several white covers, and the Crew-cuts' was beaten in the charts by that of Perry Como.

Georgia Gibbs, who recorded on Mercury, the same label as the Crew-cuts, was born Fredda Gibbons in 1920 and was a band singer of many years' experience, having worked with Hudson and DeLange, Frankie Trumbauer and Artie Shaw. She had a unique vocal colour, always an advantage in a pop singer, and could set up a rocking beat. In short, she was not as offensive as the Crew-cuts, and might have deserved something better than to go down in history as a rip-off artist. She had one of the hit versions of 'If I Knew You Were Comin' I'd've Baked a Cake' in 1950 and a huge hit in 1952 with an Argentine tango retitled 'Kiss of Fire'. (Mike Stoller: 'I frankly believe that a lot of those songs were bullshit and funny at the same time because they were so terrible.') 'Seven Lonely Days' was a good rhythm tune in 1953, a cover of a country hit by Bonnie Lou on King. In 1955 LaVern Baker had a top five black hit on Atlantic with 'Tweedle-dee'; Gibbs's version reached number two in the national pop chart. (There is a story that Baker and Gibbs, both on tour, met in an airport, and Baker asked, 'Did you buy flight insurance on *me*?')

In 1954 Hank Ballard and the Midnighters had an R & B hit called 'Work With Me Annie', which stayed at number one for seven weeks; the composer credit included Ballard, Johnny Otis and Etta James. The hit was slightly suggestive, in that the work assignment in question was meant to be horizontal. It was covered by James, who was only seventeen in February 1955 when her answer version, 'The Wallflower', was a black number one for four weeks, and this became the most flagrant swindle of all: Georgia Gibbs's 'Dance With Me Henry (Wallflower)' was a pop number one for three weeks. The Midnighters had already followed up with 'Annie Had a Baby' and 'Annie's Aunt Fannie', but Mercury passed on those.

The kids who cared about music and who knew that what they

heard on the radio were cover versions were curious about the originals. In fact, stations in the South that catered for blacks were aware that 20 or 30 per cent of their listeners were white youngsters, who had already discovered that black was best, and that most of the covers were very poor compared with the real thing: the Crew-cuts' 'Sh-boom' was an irritating novelty; in the Chords' original the rhythm was the whole point, yet the singing was sweeter. LaVern Baker's 'Tweedle-dee' reached the top fifteen in the pop chart and her 'Jim Dandy' (1956) was a number one black hit and a top twenty pop hit. The white covers of these artists cheated them of greater success, and in any case was a mistake on the part of the major labels.

Despite the success of Nat 'King' Cole, Billy Eckstine, Ella Fitzgerald and a few other black artists in the white market, there was an unthinking knee-jerk racism working in the music business. Eckstine had been the first black man to appear on the cover of *Life* magazine, which dubbed him 'the Sepia Sinatra'. He was seen to some extent as aping the dominant white pop style of the late 1940s, as though blacks should not be singing the best love songs for their own sake, which rankled Eckstine. Black pop's rhythm tunes were clearly gaining in popularity, and were thought to be more acceptable in their sterilized white versions, but the large minority of young white people who were listening to black radio and to the original black hits were ultimately the taste-makers, the most influential segment of music fans, and they were not fooled by any of this. They lost respect for the music business and for business in general, disgusted by the mindless greed for short-term profits, while the music business had no idea what was going on.

By 1955 the Platters, a black vocal quintet from Los Angeles, had already had their own national hits. Buck Ram had worked as an arranger for Mills Music and had managed the Three Suns, a sweet white vocal and instrumental trio who had hits in the 1940s; he then turned to black music. He managed the Penguins and saw their big hit ripped off; he wrote 'Only You' for the Platters, and it was recorded by a quintet for Federal, which did not want to issue it. Having made a personnel change and added the beautiful Zola Taylor, he took a sextet to Mercury and remade 'Only You', which reached the top five, followed by 'The Great Pretender', a national number one for two weeks. The next year 'My Prayer' (a revival of a French and English song recorded by Glenn Miller in 1939) was number one for five weeks. Furthermore, the Platters had staying power; they had hits every year until 1967, including two more number ones in 1958: 'Twilight Time', a lovely song written in 1944 by Ram and the Three Suns, and 'Smoke Gets in Your Eyes'.

Another factor in the burgeoning success of R&B was that the live shows on tour were cheaper to produce than those of big-name white acts. Promoters in the South and the Midwest found that they could get two top R&B acts for the cost of a white one, while the audience for R&B shows was already integrated and sharply increasing. After some years as a classical and record-request DJ, Cleveland's Alan Freed began playing R&B at the suggestion of a sponsor, a record-shop owner who saw the white kids buying the records. In March 1952 a dance at the Cleveland Arena offered Charles Brown, the Dominoes with Clyde McPhatter (one of the most influential of lead vocalists), the Orioles, the Moonglows and the jump bands of Tiny Grimes and Jimmy Forrest. Seventeen thousand fans of Freed's *Rock'n'roll House Party* radio show bought tickets (according to Russell Sanjek). Unfortunately, the Arena held only ten thousand people, and Freed almost went to jail after the resulting mêlée, and before everybody realized that the whole thing had been an accident: the huge ticket sales had been unexpected. Freed later packed dance halls with such shows, and the audiences were never less than one-third white.

Freed was not the first white DJ to play R&B from choice; that may have been Art Leboe in Los Angeles, who made his station the most popular in the Hispanic community. But Freed knew a good thing when he saw it, and borrowed the term 'rock'n'roll' to describe it. To call it rhythm and blues would have been to point out that white people were listening to black music, and few people knew that rockin' and rollin' was a black euphemism for sexual intercourse. In any case, the term was not new: the Boswell Sisters had recorded a film song called 'Rock and Roll' in 1934, and there were many more song titles and lyrics that used the phrase.

It is possible to excuse various music business practices over the years on the grounds that that was the way it was, and it was not up to individual promoters or record industry moguls to try to change things. But there can be only one reason why the Chords, Penguins, Clovers and the rest did not do better in the lily-white pop chart; why Baker's own 'Tweedle-dee' was not as widely played on the air as Gibbs's version; why 'Dance With Me Henry' had to have its lyrics cleaned up. But the white man's racist fear, not only of the black man's supposed sexual prowess but of the power of sex itself, could not keep down the pressure that had built up by the mid-1950s. Black pop records could no longer be confined to 'race', 'sepia', 'ebony' or R & B charts. White pop was boring and black pop was not, and the floodgates soon opened.

Chuck Berry had grown up in St Louis, where he played guitar and led a trio including pianist Johnnie Johnson, whose importance has long been overlooked: Berry's songs and his guitar style were influenced by Johnson's keyboard, which gave them an unusual sound. Berry took a demo tape to Chicago, where Muddy Waters introduced him to Leonard Chess; one of the tunes on the tape was an adaptation of 'Ida Red', a country stomp recorded, for example, by Bob Wills in 1938. Its name was changed to 'Maybellene' and Berry recorded it in May 1955, with Johnson on piano, Willie Dixon on bass and Jasper Thomas on drums; Alan Freed promoted the song and took a co-writing credit; it entered both charts in August, and was number one for eleven weeks in the black chart, reaching the top five in the white. A fast, swinging blues about cars and a girl, it inaugurated a new era. That month, with a few other kids, I was on my way across country (in a 1951 V-8 Ford, in fact) for a week of camping out, the car radio blasting out 'Maybellene' ('Nothin' outrunnin' my V-8 Ford'), and none of our lives was ever the same again. On the other side was 'Wee Wee Hours', a slow, midnight blues with fine piano playing from Johnson, which also changed a few heads. Berry's singing, his guitar and his lyrics still perhaps represent the essence of rock'n'roll. With his songs the genre became fully the music of a younger generation: 'School Day (Ring! Ring! Goes the Bell)' added high school to the list of teenage obsessions, while 'Rock and Roll Music', 'Sweet Little Sixteen' and 'Johnny B. Goode' all became anthems.

His 'Brown-eyed Handsome Man' and 'Too Much Monkey Business' never reached the white chart, nor did Bo Diddley's 'Bo Diddley', 'I'm a Man' or 'Diddley Daddy', but by now more and more kids were checking out the black charts. Diddley was another transplanted Chicagoan; his records (on Checker, a Chess sister label) were weird, mysterious and slightly scary, known for the bags of echo on the guitar and his 'shave-and-a-haircut, six bits' beat. He has been copied by rockers ever since, but only had one top twenty pop hit: 'Say Man' (1959), listed by *Billboard* as a novelty.

The same year Chuck Berry broke through, New Orleans also got into the act. Lew Chudd had been the producer of the *Let's Dance* radio show that helped Benny Goodman to fame in 1935. In 1947 he formed Imperial Records to record top ten hits in Spanish-language covers for that market in the South-west, and used the profits to expand into square-dance records, kiddie records, country music and R & B. Slim Whitman was a country success on Imperial, and his 'Indian Love Call' was a huge hit; he played in London in 1952 and for years was a bigger star in the UK than in the USA.

Chudd's R & B talent scout and producer was a New Orleans trumpeter and bandleader, Dave Bartholomew, who as a freelance produced Lloyd Price's 'Lawdy Miss Clawdy' for Specialty and Shirley and Lee's 'I'm Gone' for Aladdin (both hits in 1952), as well as his own 'Country Boy' (1949, DeLuxe). He recorded other R & B songs in leftover studio time: 'Preachin' and Teachin'' (Ace, 1952), like 'Country Boy', used the excellent session drummer Earl Palmer; 'Who Drank My Beer While I Was in the Rear' that year was on Imperial. But Bartholomew had more success producing others, such as Fats Domino.

Pianist and singer Domino was born in New Orleans; his first language was French. The New Orleans piano style can be traced directly from Jelly Roll Morton through Joseph Louis 'Red' Cayou (born around 1905) and Isadore 'Tuts' Washington (born in 1907, finally recorded in 1983), through Professor Longhair (Roy Byrd), who worked for Bartholomew in 1949, to Fats Domino, Huey Smith, Allen Toussaint and Mac Rebennack (Dr John, the Night Tripper). Professor Longhair's imposition of fast triplets on a syncopated rhumba beat is directly descended from Jelly Roll's 'Spanish tinge'.

Domino was compared to Fats Waller by the bone-headed musical press when he later had a hit with 'What's the Reason I'm Not Pleasin' You'; he was not a stylist of the calibre of Waller or Jelly Roll, but he did what he did extremely well. His warm personality transcended any question of race, and the music had a lilt, as well as a beat, that could only have come from New Orleans. Domino's smoky, laid-back voice, with just a trace of a French accent, together with the songs and Bartholomew's band, made history.

His first recording session yielded 'Hey La Bas', a coming together of strands of New Orleans history, including voodoo and French and Catholic influences. 'The Fat Man', a cleaned-up drug song recorded the same day, was his first R & B hit. His fifth release, 'Every Night About This Time', was a hit the same year; it incorporated the keyboard triplet which became a trademark, and may have been influenced by Little Willie Littlefield as well as Longhair. (Blues pianist Littlefield had a hit with 'It's Midnight' on Modern in 1949.) Domino's R & B hits 'Goin' Home' (1952) and 'Goin' to the River' (1953) were as good as national top thirty hits, they sold so well and got so much airplay, but they were not allowed on the white chart.

Randy Wood operated an appliance repair shop in Nashville in 1946, and dabbled in radio. He bought several thousand remaindered R & B records and sold them over the radio at six for a dollar; with some of the profits he formed Dot Records in 1950. He produced country records, but the demand for R & B was such that he began covering the songs with a squeaky-clean college student named Pat Boone, who was twenty years old when he had his first hit in 1955 with 'Two Hearts', an R & B hit by the Charms. Boone's second hit was a national number one version of Fats Domino's 'Ain't That a Shame' the same year, which helped pull Domino's own record out of the R & B ghetto into the pop top ten.

Domino's seventeenth and eighteenth top ten R & B hits were back to back, 'Bo Weevil' and 'Don't Blame It On Me'. In the first, an irresistibly rocking folksong, the melody is played tremolo by guitarist Ernest McLean, who floats over the backbeat, making the whole thing a timeless country stomp. 'Bo Weevil' reached number thirty-five in the pop charts, while the slick cover with much less style by squeaky Teresa Brewer entered the top twenty. The other side of Domino's record, 'Don't Blame It On Me', was not covered and didn't make the pop chart, but kids discovered it: the playing of Clarence Ford (alto), Herb Hardesty, Buddy Hagans and Lee Allen (tenors), McLean (guitar), Frank Fields (bass) and Cornelius Coleman (drums) sounded so good on jukeboxes after so many years of pap that we couldn't believe our luck.

In the same year, 1956, Domino's 'I'm In Love Again' was a number three national hit. Altogether he had over sixty Hot 100 *Billboard* entries in less than ten years. The New Orleans backbeat was rock solid, yet is like a happy afterthought compared with the noisy banging on today's pop records, and the riffing saxophones and Domino's laid-back style combine to make these some of the best party records of all time.

Also in 1956, and in New Orleans, the totally impossible, irrational and outrageous became reality; the inmates left the asylum, never to be recaptured, with a cry of WOMP-BOMP-A-LOO-MOMP ALOP-BOMP-BOMP! Little Richard was bisexual, he wore make-up, he was a tornado on stage and he passionately shouted dirty songs in a sanctified style, screams and all:

> Long Tall Sally she's
> Built for speed
> She got everything
> That Uncle John needs . . .

In two minutes Richard Wayne Penniman used as much energy as an all-night party.

He came from a large, poor family in Macon, Georgia. He was influenced by Billy Wright, who wore loud clothes, curled his hair and performed a gospel-shouting R & B style, and was encouraged to play piano by Esquerita (who was also known as Eskew Reeder, SQ Reeder, the Magnificent Malucci and so on, and later imitated Richard, recording in New Orleans in the mid-1960s). Little Richard recorded for RCA with Wright's band in 1951 and 1952 after winning a talent contest; D J Zenas Sears helped make the deal and the sides were recorded at WGST in Atlanta: 'Every Hour' was a local hit, but Richard's persona was not yet let loose. He recorded for

Peacock in 1953 in Houston, at the second of the two sessions using
Johnny Otis's band. But he was washing dishes in an Atlanta bus
station when stardom beckoned. He had sent a demonstration tape to
Specialty in Hollywood.

Art Rupe dispatched his assistant, Bumps Blackwell, to New
Orleans to make records; and Cosimo Matassa's J and M Studio was
primitive by today's standards, or even by major-label standards of
the time: Blackwell placed his microphones by trial and error, going
back and forth into the next room to listen to a two-track Ampex
tape recorder on headphones; the bass player was on the other side of
the room and the drummer was outside the door. But both Richard
and Fats Domino made their classic hits at Cosimo's.

The band on Richard's first sessions, like Domino's band, included
New Orleans' best: Melvin Dowden (piano), Justin Adams (guitar),
Lee Allen (tenor saxophone), Alvin 'Red' Tyler (baritone saxophone),
Frank Fields (double bass) and Earl Palmer (drums); Huey Smith was
present part of the time and probably played some piano, and
Richard himself played on 'Tutti Frutti', an outrageous song from
the club scene. Blackwell heard him playing around with it during a
lunch break – the nearby premises had a piano, and Richard could
not resist showing off. Dorothy La Bostrie was asked to clean up the
lyrics: 'Tutti Frutti, good booty / if it don't fit, don't force it / You
can grease it, make it easy' became 'Tutti Frutti, awrootie / I got a
gal, named Sue / She knows just what to do', which at least left
something to the imagination.

'Tutti Frutti' reached number two in the R & B chart and the top
twenty of the pop chart, and – incredibly – Pat Boone's cover went
higher than Little Richard's. (Bible student Boone later claimed he
had not known what the song was about.) This was a bit like June
Allyson having a hit with 'Jazz Me Blues', and it was the end of the
cover era: white kids were by now sorting each other out according
to who bought 'Baboon' and who bought Richard. Later the same
year Richard tried to record 'Long Tall Sally' as fast as possible so
that Boone would not be able to sing it; they both had hits with it,
but this time Richard's record went higher than Boone's, and the rest
of Boone's hits were mostly Hollywood ballads. A new kind of cover
era immediately began: Blackwell and John Marascalco wrote 'Rip It

Up' and 'Ready Teddy', a two-sided hit for Richard; both were covered by Elvis Presley and Bill Haley, but more appropriately and out of admiration for the songs: ripping it off was out, but ripping it up was definitely in.

Some of Richard's records were too frenetic to dance to. The master of 'Keep a Knockin'' was only fifty-seven seconds long, and a single was made of it by means of repetition. Others were better: 'Lucille' is one of the finest, inexorable at exactly the right tempo, while 'Send Me Some Lovin'' and 'Can't Believe You Wanna Leave' are actually slow. One of Richard's biggest contributions was his personality. His live act was like nothing anyone had ever seen. He wore his hair in a huge pompadour with marcelled waves on top; he wore the loudest clothes in the business and cosmetics to match. At the beginning of a set his band never knew what direction he would come from. When producer H. B. Barnum first saw Richard, Barnum was about fourteen years old, and playing saxophone with touring R & B shows:

He'd just burst onto the stage from anywhere, and you wouldn't be able to hear anything but the roar of the audience ... We might vamp that first number for four to five minutes before he even got to the piano. He'd be on the stage, he'd be off the stage, he'd be jumping and yelling, screaming, whipping the audience on ... Then when he finally did hit the piano and just went into di-di-di-di-di-di-di-di, you know, well nobody can do that as fast as Richard. It just took everybody by surprise ... That's the first time I ever saw spotlights and flicker lights used at a concert show. It had all been used in show business, but he brought it into *our* world.

At the end of a set Richard was covered with sweat, and it was not long before girls started throwing their underwear on to the stage.

For the second time New Orleans permanently altered the course of the world's popular music. Huey 'Piano' Smith had a hit in 1957 with 'Rockin' Pneumonia and the Boogie Woogie Flu', and the next year with 'Don't You Just Know It'. He had played piano on Bartholomew's wonderful 'I Hear You Knockin'', an R & B classic by Smiley Lewis which had not made the pop charts in 1955 (but was covered in a dull but successful version on Dot by actress Gale

Storm). Smith's band, the Clowns, included lead singer Bobby Marchan, as well as Red Tyler and Lee Allen. Another seminal figure was pianist and bandleader Paul Gayten, whose R&B hits in 1949–50 included 'I'll Never be Free' (with vocalist Annie Laurie), and who wrote 'For You My Love', on which he backed Larry Darnell for a number one. (The song was also a hit duet by Nat Cole and Nellie Lutcher.) Later he backed Clarence Henry on 'Ain't Got No Home' (1956), which became a pop hit, and took a co-writing credit for the amusing 'Troubles, Troubles' on the reverse side. Gayten's own instrumental jukebox hits, such as 'Nervous Boogie' in 1957, were tossed off during leftover studio time, like some of Bartholomew's. Tenor saxophonist Lee Allen wrote his 1958 hit 'Walkin' with Mr Lee' while working as Gayten's sideman.

But while rhythm and blues was breaking through to the pop charts and washing away the cover merchants, rock'n'roll was also coming from another direction. Among those white kids listening to R&B in the early 1950s were the hillbilly cats who invented rockabilly; in fact, it was at first called 'cat music'.

For decades the excellent playing of a great many instrumentalists in country music had been directly influenced by black music. There was the lingering effect of the country jazz, or western swing, of Bob Wills, and the important folk poems of Hank Williams, with their swaggering beat and their true-to-life concerns. 'Country boogie' had been gaining ground. The Delmore Brothers had recorded 'Hillbilly Boogie' as early as 1945, and then 'Freight Train Boogie', 'Blues Stay Away From Me' and 'Pan American Boogie' were hits. Jack Guthrie, Woody's cousin, had a hit with 'Oakie Boogie' in 1947, and Hawkshaw Hawkins's 'Dog House Boogie' and guitarist Arthur Smith's 'Guitar Boogie' were successful in 1948.

'Guitar Boogie' may have been recorded much earlier, in 1945, on a Super Disc label; an instrumental, it was played by a string band, with a gently amplified guitar and no drums. It continued selling for years. The chart hit, perhaps a new recording, was on MGM, and it was issued on that label in England. It had a 4/4 feeling but with a backbeat. (Compare it with the other side of the British 78, for example, called 'Bebop Rag': despite the title, its two-beat style is corny.) Tennessee Ernie Ford's 'Shotgun Boogie' was a big country hit in 1950; Webb Pierce's band had hit after hit from 1952 with a honky-tonk backbeat. Meanwhile, Bill Haley and his Saddlemen, billed as the Cowboy Jive Band, mixed yodels, polkas and western swing.

Haley was born in Michigan and grew up in Pennsylvania; he began as a yodelling cowboy on radio. His Downhomers first recorded in 1944, and his various groups included the Four Aces of Western Swing. He started covering R & B hits like Jackie Brenston's 1951 'Rocket "88"', which sold fairly well, then 'Rock the Joint', a 1949 hit by Jimmy Preston, which sold even better. The country covers were not selling at all, so he threw caution to the wind: he changed the name of the Saddlemen to Bill Haley and his Comets and recorded his own 'Crazy Man Crazy' for the tiny Essex label (whose most popular star was the mood music conductor Monty Kelly, whose 'Tropicana' was the label's biggest hit). Haley suddenly reached the pop top fifteen in 1953. The tune was just a stomp, like 'Rag Mop', with words that were not up to much, but seemed at the time to borrow from jazz: 'Man, that music's gone, gone!' This already sounded trite then, but Haley's 'jive' slang was as much a part of the act as the relentlessly slapped string bass. The hit was covered on Mercury by dance band leader Ralph Marterie, who, with his bigger name (and vocal by the Smarty-aires), almost caught Haley in the charts with his own tune.

After a couple of similar, lesser hits on Essex, Haley moved to Decca, where he was produced by Milt Gabler. Haley could not read music, according to Gabler, so he had to hum the riffs to him: 'It was like recording a barbershop quartet or the Mills Brothers, you have to woodshed it and learn it by rote. They'd work out the harmony among themselves.' Gabler had recorded not only Louis Jordan, but the jump band of Buddy Johnson, with vocalist Arthur Prysock. Johnson's drummer, and also Lionel Hampton's, had to be kept from playing too loud for the recording technology of the time, Gabler said, but Haley's band was recorded in a disused ballroom, which had a high ceiling, curtains hanging from the balcony and a live wooden floor. This acoustic, together with up-to-date recording equipment, allowed Haley's drummer to play his tinny rim-shot backbeat as loudly as possible, and the steel player to bang his bar on the strings until sparks flew. Gabler put reverb on the master tape and overdubbed Haley's weak voice.

'Rock Around the Clock' was a Tin Pan Alley rhythm novelty, and similar tunes and lyrics had been around for years. It barely made the top twenty-five. But the next hit, still in 1954, reached the top ten. It was a cover of 'Shake, Rattle and Roll', a number one R & B tune by Big Joe Turner, originally a singing bartender from the roaring days of Kansas City. By the mid-1950s Turner was a seasoned blues shouter; after his R & B hit 'Chains of Love' (1951) on a Freedom label, Turner moved to Atlantic and had big hits in the black chart every year until 1958. He was too big, too old, too black and too powerful to become a pop star, but hits like 'Corrine Corrina' and 'Lipstick Powder and Paint' (both 1956) made him a more deserving father of rock'n'roll than most. 'Shake, Rattle and Roll', with its three-chord tune and the lines 'Get out in that kitchen / And rattle those pots and pans!' was an archetypal rock'n'roll song.

Then came the film *The Blackboard Jungle*, released in 1955, starring Glenn Ford and a very young Sidney Poitier. Gabler makes the point that film soundtracks were usually 'pinched' at the top and bottom of the frequency range, to save the ears of the people in the front rows from the noise of the huge speakers and amplifiers used in big cinemas; but *The Blackboard Jungle* soundtrack was processed wide open. It was a realistic film (for the time) about a rough high school ('juvenile delinquency' had been a media theme for years), and its music director was said to be the publisher of 'Rock Around the Clock'. Haley's record dominated the soundtrack and shot to number one more than a year after it was first released, and also reached number three in the R & B chart.

Haley had sixty USA chart hits in seven years, but 'Rock Around the Clock' was his only number one. It might be named by many as the first number one rock'n'roll record, and therein lies part of the music's tragedy. Bill Haley did for rock'n'roll what the Original Dixieland Jazz Band did for jazz in 1917, establishing it in the public mind as a noisy party music, but the ODJB was at least an innovation at the time. Haley was an unlikely pop star, a chubby married man and almost thirty years old when he came to the fore; he was far more popular in the UK, where he had no competition, than in the USA. By all accounts he was a pleasant man, modest and grateful for his success. It is a pity that the music was so bad. It was worse than bad; it was a major environmental hazard. The bass *had* to be slapped all the way through every record, and the drums *had* to be tinny and loud, and nobody showed any understanding of time. The closest to musical excitement the Comets ever came was 'Rudy's Rock', an instrumental in which Rudy Pompilli plays a decent jump band saxophone style; it moves at a faster tempo than the band's usual clock-ticking, so the rhythm section may have had to concentrate on what it was doing. Haley and his group starred in several rock'n'roll films of the period, such as *Rock Around the Clock* in 1956 (the song was endlessly recycled). The films were mostly dreadful, but this particular Freed epic had at least the virtue of integrating the music, featuring the Platters as well as Haley. Haley was soon reduced to a nostalgia act, eclipsed by more talented hillbillies.

Sun Records, in Memphis, Tennessee, would have more influence on popular music in the 1950s than all the major labels put together. Radio engineer Sam Phillips formed the Memphis Recording Service in 1950, and taped a session with jazz pianist Phineas Newborn for RPM/Modern. He soon launched a Phillips label, with local DJ Dewey Phillips (no relation). The idea was to record local black R&B talent, but masters continued to be leased to other labels. B. B. King worked at the local black radio station, and his hits on RPM began appearing in 1951, some of them recorded in the Sun studio.

Guitarist and bandleader Ike Turner was a talent scout for RPM/ Modern, and saw to it that B. B. King remained an RPM artist, but some of the other records were leased to Chess in Chicago. Howlin' Wolf (Chester Burnett) became an R&B legend. He had a double-sided hit, 'Moanin' at Midnight' / 'How Many More Years', in 1951, the same year Turner scored a massive number one under the name of his saxophonist and vocalist: Jackie Brenston and his Delta Cats were Ike Turner's Kings of Rhythm. 'Rocket "88"' is often described as the first rock'n'roll record; it sounds tame today, but its four-wheeled subject-matter beat Chuck Berry by four years.

Rosco Gordon had a top ten hit on RPM, then a number one in 1952 that had been leased to Chess. RPM/Modern decided that they had Gordon under contract and successfully got 'Booted' back from

Chess. Walter Horton, Earl Hooker, Bobby Bland and Joe Hill Louis were other blues artists who recorded for Phillips, but this was almost too much success. Some of them moved to Chicago. James Mattis and Bill Fitzgerald formed the Duke label in Memphis in April 1952 and leased some tracks from Phillips, but sold Duke to Peacock in Houston only a few months later; Duke squabbled with RPM/Modern over Gordon, and in December Lester Bihari, of the entrepreneurial family that had founded RPM/Modern and Flair, came to Memphis to form the Meteor label. With all this activity the obvious thing for Phillips to do was form another label, and the first Sun records were released in March 1952.

Sun limped for a while because Phillips was still leasing masters to others, but in 1953 it made a distribution deal with Nashville's Jim Bulleit, who had sold his Bullet label and now operated Delta and J-B Records; Sam Phillips's brother Judd came in, bringing his promotion experience. The new label's first success was 'Bear Cat', by Rufus Thomas, Jr, an answer song to Big Mama Thornton's 'Hound Dog' on Peacock, using the same melody. (Don Robey's Lion Music sued and won.) 'Feelin' Good' and 'Mystery Train' by Little Junior (Parker) and his Blue Flames were hits, and Billy 'the Kid' Emerson and Little Milton were doing well.

Phillips was also recording country music: the Ripley Cotton Choppers, Earl Peterson ('Michigan's Singing Cowboy' doing 'Boogie Blues'), Doug Poindexter and his Starlite Wranglers, Malcolm Yelvington and his Star Rhythm Boys (who performed a hillbilly version of 'Drinkin' Wine Spodee-o-dee', which had been the first big R & B hit for the Atlantic label in 1949, by Stick McGhee). And there was Hardrock Gunter. Sidney Louie Gunter may have been the first rockabilly; he growled 'We're gonna rock'n'roll' on 'Gonna Dance All Night' on the Bama label in 1950, and recorded for Bullet, Decca, MGM, King and his own labels, but without much luck. A new version of 'Gonna Dance All Night' came out on Sun 201 in 1954, but it was too late: Sun 209 was Elvis Presley's first record.

Phillips knew there was a bread-and-butter country market out there, and he was doing well with R & B, but his secretary, Marion Keisker, remembered his saying that if he could find a white boy who could sing like a black he would make a million dollars: all the musical fusions in the world would not do any good if the talent could not appear on network television or reach the pop chart. When Judd Phillips was peddling the records out of his car in the early days, 'even then it occurred to me that people were really digging the music that was on our R&B records ... But there was so much prejudice and division that they couldn't idolize the artist that was delivering the song.' Marion remembered the truck driver who had come in one day in 1953 to make a record for his mother's birthday, and suggested getting him in to see what he could do.

In July 1954 bass player Bill Black and guitarist Scotty Moore, who had already played on Sun sessions, got together with the nineteen-year-old truck driver in the studio. It was apparent from the beginning that Elvis Presley had no idea who he was or what he wanted to do. An only child, he had been haunted all his life by a twin who had died at birth; his father was a lazy failure and his mother a doting monster. He had certainly heard spirited singing in church and was steeped in country music; B. B. King said he had seen the kid hanging around the black part of town, but in any case Elvis heard black music on the radio. He played with a guitar and had the makings of a good voice; in fact, he had an enormous natural talent, and the flowing juices of any horny nineteen-year-old, but no confidence to go with it. His life was to be the tragedy of a born loser, yet he became a cultural artefact.

They tried ballads, because Elvis basically wanted to be Dean Martin, but none worked. 'Casual Love Affair' was a tune written and given to Phillips by an inmate at the Tennessee state prison, and years later a version of 'Harbor Lights', such as you might hear in any threadbare small-town supper club, was discovered in Sun's vault. Then, as with Little Richard in New Orleans the following year, the magic happened during a break, fooling around with 'That's All Right (Mama)', a blues by Arthur Crudup. There were no drums, but it didn't matter; the bass was slapped, but with style and urgency, and country jive finally became the fusion known as rockabilly. Bill Monroe's 'Blue Moon of Kentucky' was worked over until it too became something new. A white kid could sing the blues, and a bluegrass tune could yield rockabilly heat.

As soon as the record was played on local radio a few days later, orders for seven thousand copies came in. Elvis was interviewed on the radio, and the name of his high school established that he was white. But the legendary success did not happen overnight. Marty Robbins covered 'That's All Right' on Columbia, adding a fiddle, and the Presley record was the nearest thing to a national hit that Phillips had had since Junior Parker's 'Feelin' Good', but the market was confused: pop stations thought the record was so country that it should not be played after 5 a.m., while country stations did not know what to make of it either. Elvis was a flop on the *Grand Ole Opry*, who told him to go back to driving a truck, but found a regular spot on the *Louisiana Hayride*, and played at county fairs and dance halls for anybody who would have him.

Sun persisted in releasing a country song and a black song back to back: the only way to crack the market was to take it head-on. 'I Don't Care if the Sun Don't Shine', written in 1949 by Mack David and recorded by Presley's idol, Dean Martin, became a country boogie, backed with 'Good Rockin' Tonight', a Wynonie Harris R & B hit in 1948. 'You're a Heartbreaker' was a bore, backed with 'Milkcow Blues Boogie', credited to Kokomo Arnold and complete with some badly dated jive; this was Presley's worst record on Sun. With the fourth single the recording quality improved: 'I'm Left, You're Right, She's Gone' was a good country song with a beat, and a kid named Jimmie Lott on drums; 'Baby Let's Play House' on the flip had been an R & B hit in 1955 on Excello, the only hit Arthur Gunter ever had (not Hardrock Gunter, as Albert Goldman reported). This side of the record did not need the drums; the primitive plea was right up Presley's alley and his first national hit, top five in the country chart. The fifth and last Sun release was 'I Forgot to Remember to Forget' backed with Junior Parker's 'Mystery Train'. The former was a number one country hit for five weeks in 1955, and in November Presley's contract and Sun masters were purchased by RCA.

The effect that Presley had on women did not go unnoticed in the music industry. The fact that he looked and dressed like white trash went with his excess of hormones: like Hank Williams a few years earlier, he had only to twitch a leg to make all the females scream. He enjoyed himself on stage; for the first and last time in his life he did as he pleased, and the girls loved it. He was managed at first by Scotty Moore, then by Memphis D J Bob Neal, and they were all snookered by 'Colonel' Tom Parker, who also snookered his business partner at the time, country star Hank Snow. Parker was a carnival huckster who had managed Eddy Arnold for a while, but Arnold probably had too much self-respect to be handled for long by such a man. Phillips offered Presley's contract to Nashville producer Owen Bradley, who turned it down; Columbia's Mitch Miller made an inquiry, but would not pay the price, allegedly $20,000 and going up. Snow had alerted the industry to the new sensation, and RCA executive Steve Sholes was instrumental in the final gamble. Parker secured Presley for RCA for $35,000, of which $5,000 went to Presley for unpaid royalties on the Sun records, and which he spent on a Cadillac. This was a large amount of money for an artist who was still a cult, but Phillips knew he could not promote Presley properly, and had more rockabillies waiting in the wings.

Presley's first RCA recording session, in Nashville in January 1956, yielded covers of Ray Charles's 'I Got a Woman', a big R & B hit a year earlier, and 'Money Honey', by the Drifters with Clyde McPhatter, which had been at number one for eleven weeks in 1953. Presley's young voice sounded strained on country ballads: 'I'm Counting On You' is a decent song by proven hit-writer Don Robertson, but the dreadful 'I Was the One' was chosen as the B side of 'Heartbreak Hotel'.

The sound quality of that first session was not good, and 'Heartbreak Hotel' is the worst of them all. Chet Atkins played rhythm guitar and Floyd Cramer was added on piano, together with an entirely unnecessary vocal trio led by Gordon Stoker, lead singer of the Jordanaires, a gospel quartet. Scotty Moore's guitar sounds exceptionally, irritatingly tinny, Cramer is too prominent and the whole track sounds like it was made underwater in a breadbox. It was a disgraceful recording for 1956, but a good song for Presley. Written by Mae Axton and Tommy Durden, it was inspired by a newspaper account of a suicide note saying, 'I walk a lonely street'. Despite its shortcomings, 'Heartbreak Hotel' reached all three *Billboard* charts in March. It was number one for eight weeks in the pop chart and for seventeen weeks in the country chart, and a number three R & B hit.

Think of it: one of the biggest, most famous hits of all time, recorded in January and in the charts less than forty-five days later. And this was already well into the age of tape recording, overdubbing, reverberation and all the rest. Why does it take months to make a pop record nowadays? Is it that today's record producers are muscle-bound with their technology? If only the studio had been up to the job: one cannot help wondering what these records would sound like if one could go back to the master tapes and tinker with them. (RCA's release of 'I'm Left, You're Right, She's Gone' revealed it as one of the cleanest records Sun ever made, while an English LP reissue in the 1970s was dreadful.)

More recording dates in New York, in late January and early February, were the most successful of Presley's entire career. With better sound and adding only Shorty Long on piano to Scotty, Bill and D. J. Fontana, the eight sides were a permanent statement of what rock'n'roll is supposed to be, and represent the last time that Elvis Presley's inherent talent was let loose in front of a microphone. Presley was hitting the big time, recording in New York rather than in some provincial hole in the wall, and he gave it everything the natural optimism of youth can offer. He and the group pushed the beat on every track, generating tremendous excitement; Fontana seemed the ideally functional rock'n'roll drummer and Scotty's guitar solos became unpretentious templates for the new genre. 'I'm Gonna Sit Right Down and Cry Over You' and 'One-sided Love Affair' were good rhythm tunes; Little Richard's 'Tutti Frutti', Lloyd Price's 'Lawdy Miss Clawdy' and Joe Turner's 'Shake, Rattle and Roll' were already rock'n'roll classics, and Carl Perkins's 'Blue Suede Shoes' was a brand new one; 'So Glad You're Mine' and 'My Baby Left Me' were both by Crudup. Presley was different: his R & B covers, from July 1954 to February 1956, are equal to the originals, and even better in the case of one or two of Crudup's songs. Arthur 'Big Boy' Crudup made nearly eighty sides from 1943 to 1954, almost all for RCA; 'Goin' Back to Georgia' (1952) is particularly fine, but some of them sound as though there should have been another take, while there was not much money for studio time in major-label

R & B. Crudup never received a penny from his Presley covers, by the way, any of which had soon sold more copies than all Crudup's records put together.

But it was already over. In April, back in Nashville, he recorded 'I Want You, I Need You, I Love You', an incredibly dreary rockaballad and his second number one hit (with 'My Baby Left Me' on the flip side, one of the two or three best records he ever made). They couldn't find decent songs for Presley because they were not looking. We were lucky with 'Heartbreak Hotel'; Axton and Durden were experienced songwriters, but even so Presley got a co-writing credit. 'I Want You, I Need You, I Love You' was written by hacks and published by Elvis Presley Music. 'My Baby Left Me' is mysteriously listed as published by Elvis Presley Music, which did not exist when Crudup had his R & B hit in 1946. Parker knew he was sitting on a gold mine, and became an archetype of everything that has gone wrong with pop music in the decades since then. He milked Presley's career in order to live in a Las Vegas hotel, gambling at Presley's expense for the rest of his life; he started by gambling away the music, and Presley let him do it.

In July 1956 'Hound Dog' and 'Don't Be Cruel' were recorded, Presley's back-to-back third and fourth number ones. 'Hound Dog' had been an R & B hit in 1953 for Big Mama Thornton, credited to Jerry Leiber and Mike Stoller, soon experienced writers of pop hits; Johnny Otis claimed to have had something to do with writing 'Hound Dog' as well. Leiber and Stoller achieved their greatest fame writing for Presley ('Jailhouse Rock', 'Loving You', 'Bossa Nova Baby' and others). 'Don't Be Cruel' was by Otis Blackwell, a black New York songwriter who had sold it the previous Christmas Eve with a bag of others for $25 each. Both songs were ruined by the incessant caterwauling of the Jordanaires, who added hand-clapping on 'Hound Dog', which, in the hands of Presley and his managers, ominously became a novelty.

From then on the songs were pop songs, and almost from the beginning Presley seems to have copied the demo records he was given, such as 'Heartbreak Hotel' (sung by Glen Reeves) and 'Don't Be Cruel' (Blackwell). Leiber said, 'If Jeff Barry was the singer on the demo, Elvis would imitate Jeff Barry.' Presley was willing to work hard and would sing all night; but except for low-down dirty country blues, the boy had no style of his own. He could wiggle an audience of girls into a frenzy, but had no idea what to do with a slow blues, which 'Hound Dog' should have been. It is said that during his first Las Vegas gig, which was a flop, he heard a black vocal group doing a frenetic version of 'Hound Dog', which he simply imitated. By the time he copied 'One Night' in 1958, which should have been his type of song, something was missing: it was a tantalizing moment for those of us who hoped for a return to the truth, but perhaps he had already had too many cheeseburgers. 'One Night' by Dave Bartholomew and Pearl King, an R&B hit for Smiley Lewis in 1956, was now published by Elvis Presley Music; the lyrics were cleaned up for Presley, just as lyrics had been cleaned up for Georgia Gibbs a few years earlier.

Blackwell wrote 'All Shook Up' for Presley, who was credited as co-writer on that as well as on 'Don't Be Cruel', and later 'Return to Sender'. Meanwhile, Scotty Moore and Bill Black had left in 1957, because Elvis was making millions and they were still on $100 a week. Doc Pomus and Mort Shuman wrote '(Marie's the Name) His Latest Flame', 'Little Sister', 'A Mess of Blues', 'Suspicion' and others, all published by Presley. Leiber and Stoller and Pomus and Shuman were hardened professionals who at least did not have to give up a writing credit, but if Presley published the song and recorded it, he was paid twice every time a record was sold; and if he got a co-writing credit, he was paid three times, and so was Parker, who had set it all up. Hence the dire quality of most of Presley's later material, and the dire future of pop music. (To be fair, Presley disowned his songwriting credits, admitting he'd never written anything.)

A few of these were fine pop records, especially, for example, the two-sided hit 'Little Sister' / 'His Latest Flame'. Presley's voice matured and became a beautiful one, and he acquired an easiness which the best pop singers had had ever since Bing Crosby. He continued to be influential, in the same way as Crosby had been, but he had abdicated, and was no more the 'King of Rock'n'roll' than Paul Whiteman was the 'King of Jazz': rock'n'roll was supposed to wash away the Crosbys. He became the God of show business because he had been a nobody who had come from nowhere to accomplish the important thing that he did in two or three years, and the illusion that people with talent are Just Like Us was becoming the guiding principle of show business.

He had been controversial at first because he was sexy, 'ruining the morals of our youth' and all that, but he confused everyone, for off-stage he was polite and soft-spoken and worshipped his mother. He ended up singing for blue-rinsed matrons in Las Vegas. Those of us who were interested in a fence-flattening fusion like rock'n'roll had known the worst since Presley's first appearance on Ed Sullivan's show. The Sunday evening vaudeville hour was the biggest thing on the air; in September 1956 came the first Presley appearance on the show, and we all metaphorically flipped a coin when we tuned in. We had listened to the ballads alternating with the rock'n'roll, some of them excruciating, and we knew that Elvis was going to be a movie star, and that he was going to sing the title song from his first film. We held our breaths, and we lost the toss. 'Love Me Tender' turned out to be 'Aura Lee', the Civil War campfire ballad, conveniently out of copyright, with new words; claiming 'words and music by Elvis Presley and Vera Matson', it was published by Elvis Presley Music.

He made over 30 films, each one worse than the last, full of songs like the one about how to do the hula in a sports car. During his lifetime he had 146 Hot 100 hits and 75 chart albums (including most of the wretched film soundtracks), but the good recordings he made after the first 19 months might fill up a compact disc. His number one hits in 1960–61 were 'It's Now or Never', adapted from 'O Sole Mio', 'Are You Lonesome To-night?', a 3/4 time porch-ballad from 1927, and 'Surrender', adapted from 'Come Back to Sorrento'. From 1962 to 1969 he had no number ones at all. His status as an icon carried a once great record label for twenty years; he should have had as much power over pop music as anyone who ever lived, but he blew it. There were no worthwhile interviews with Presley because Tom Parker would have charged a fortune for the privilege. Parker saw to it that Presley paid the maximum in income taxes and never toured overseas, because Parker was an illegal immigrant (from Holland) and didn't want the government snooping around. He was divested of his interests in Presley in 1983, long after it was too late.

Presley's recording of Paul Anka's 'My Way' was a hit after he died; the tragedy was that he had done almost nothing his way.

Carl Perkins, also from a poor family, had formed a band with his brothers to help make ends meet. They played country songs and jump tunes, and Carl started writing his own songs, in the style that did not yet have a name. He picked cotton during the day and his wife took in laundry. When they heard Presley's 'Blue Moon of Kentucky' on the radio, the brothers went to Memphis and camped on Sam Phillips's doorstep; having signed a contract and added drummer W. S. Holland, they made their first recording, 'Movie Magg', a two-beat bit of country fatalism about a boy who is taking his girl out on horseback. He might also want to get up to something else; he knows her father is keeping an eye on her, and that all this might lead to a lifetime of obligations, but he doesn't mind:

> That double-barrel behind the door
> Lordy, waits for me I know,
> So climb up on ol' Becky's back
> And let's ride to the picture show.

The second release was happy rockabilly jive, 'Gone, Gone, Gone', and a month after Presley had left for RCA 'Blue Suede Shoes' was recorded. In February 1956 it was number one on the country jukebox chart for two weeks, after which it was knocked out of the top spot by 'Heartbreak Hotel'. In March Perkins's record reached number two in both the pop and R & B jukebox charts, being kept from the top by Presley, and was number two or three in the 'best seller' charts in all three categories. The song had been suggested by a remark overheard at a dance; but a hillbilly singing about his shoes was widely regarded as a novelty, because middle-class Americans do not know who is in their midst.

A poor man has nothing to look forward to but a lifetime of working for somebody else; this, above all, was what the great majority of southern blacks and whites had in common. On his way out to 'Rip It Up', Little Richard announced:

> Well, it's Saturday night and I just got paid,
> Spend all my money, don't try to save.

Hank Williams, out on the town with his best girl, had told her:

> You clap hands and I'll start bowin',
> We'll do all the law's allowin',
> Tomorrow I'll be right back plowin',
> Settin' the woods on fire!

Carl Perkins allegedly worked in a bakery, as well as picking cotton. In a bakery in the 1950s the hours were long, the pay was low, the work was hard and it was *hot*. In the car factory, on some summer nights, they had to send you home, it was so hot; you could not even light a cigarette, because the sweat ran down the Lucky Strike and soaked it before you could get the match to it. But if you came from a poor family, or if you were poorly educated, and above all if you were black, you were going to sweat in that bakery or on that assembly line from pay-cheque to pay-cheque, since that was what your father did, and his father before him. This sort of fatalism on the part of the people who do most of the work is exactly what the American economy has always depended upon. The hillbilly cat with the new shoes is just going out to rip it up on a Saturday night, and if he has squeezed a few bucks out of his pay-cheque for some fashionable footwear, he will have just that much more fun. He knows that on Monday he is going to pick that cotton, or punch that time-clock, and he knows that the shoes will be worn out in a few months and thrown away. But that does not bother him either; he can't afford to think too far ahead. It is not surprising how many early rock'n'roll songs are about working for a living.

T-Bone Walker sang in 1947, 'The eagle flies on Friday / And Saturday I go out to play.' US military parlance was 'the eagle shits on Friday' (payday). In 'Blue Monday' Fats Domino sang:

> On Monday my head is bad.
> But it's worth it,
> For the times that I've had.

Chuck Berry made us feel guilty every time we bought a buck's worth:

> Workin' in a filling station,
> Too many tasks: wipe the windows,
> Check the tires, check the oil,
> Dollar gas! Ahhhh!
> Too much monkey business!

Carl Perkins's hillbilly goes out to party:

> Well, you can knock me down, step in my face;
> Slander my name all over the place.
> Do any thing that you wanna do,
> But uh, uh, buddy, lay offa my shoes!

The way Presley sang 'Blue Suede Shoes', he was daring you to step on them, so he could try to punch you out. Perkins, by contrast, is almost saying please. He doesn't want any fuss; he is tickled with his new shoes, and all he asks is, please don't step on 'em. But if you step on 'em by mistake, let alone on purpose, you *might* get into trouble. 'Blue Suede Shoes' is what rock'n'roll (or rhythm and blues) is supposed to be: instant folk music for the working class. It sounds as though it has been made up on the spot, rather than calculated to sell a million; and it is also full of joy, because you can dance your feet off to it.

The other side of 'Blue Suede Shoes' was 'Honey Don't', too strange in 1956, too country, and without the novelty aspect of the shoes. 'How come you say you will when you won't' seemed like a powerful, swinging line, but when you played that side at a party, the other kids didn't want to know. In another era, just a few years later, the Beatles covered it.

Johnny Cash was another of Phillips's discoveries. His first recording on Sun and his first country hit was 'Cry! Cry! Cry!', with the Tennessee Two (Luther Perkins on guitar and Marshall Grant on bass). 'I Walk the Line' (1956) was his first country number one and his first pop chart entry. He wrote those two, as well as 'Train of Love' and others. His songs were similar to each other but his words were as simple and memorable as those of Hank Williams and his voice was both yearning and sepulchral; rhythmically the records had that rockabilly inevitability about them. 'Ballad of a Teenage Queen' was overproduced, but 'Guess Things Happen That Way' was better;

both were written by 'Cowboy' Jack Clement, a maverick producer who cut his teeth at Sun. Cash became renowned, but stayed in the country camp; he had sixty-nine hits in the *Billboard* country chart up to 1970, but only forty-five in the pop chart.

The last Sun superstar was Jerry Lee Lewis, whose cousins include country singer Mickey Gilley, television evangelist Jimmy Swaggart and Myra Gale Brown, his third wife, whom he married when she was thirteen, and evidently without quite divorcing his previous wife. Jerry Lee was shy at first, but on tour Perkins and Cash told him to make a fuss, so he began kicking over the piano stool, revealing a compulsive and frenetic pianist and performer. After that he always wanted to close the show, but on another tour, with Chuck Berry, he was forced to open it, so he set fire to the piano as he left the stage, saying, 'I'd like to see any son of a bitch try to follow *that*.'

Lewis's first hit was 'Whole Lot of Shakin' Goin' On' in 1957, closely followed by 'Great Balls of Fire' and 'Breathless', both written by Otis Blackwell. These were big pop and R&B hits, and the first two were number one country hits: they were pretty noisy and not very good to dance to, but exciting novelties. The flip side of the second, a cover of Hank Williams's 'You Win Again', also reached the country top five. His 'pumping piano' was simplistic and dominated by right-hand glissandos, though effective in its context.

In 1958 when he went to England on tour, he took young Myra with him and introduced her to the British tabloid newspapers. The British have some of the worst newspapers in the English-speaking world; they sell millions of copies daily to the kind of people who like to spy on the neighbours from behind the curtains, pretending that the Presleys, Perkinses and Lewises are not the direct descendants of British white trash. Lewis was crucified by the press, the nonsense spread to the USA and Lewis never had another top ten pop hit. He remained a compelling performer, and made a strong comeback in the country charts from 1968, with songs like 'What's Made Milwaukee Famous (Made a Loser out of Me)' and 'She Even Woke Me Up to Say Goodbye'. He was nicknamed the Killer, not necessarily because some of his wives died young; Myra lasted longer than most and wrote a book about it. Like Presley and some of the others,

Lewis was a gun freak, and once shot his bass player. Myra's father was a bass player.

Roy Orbison's recordings for Sun included his 'Ooby Dooby', a minor hit. His soaring voice on 'Only the Lonely' and 'Oh! Pretty Woman' and aching ballads like 'It's Over' were influential in the next decade on another label, Monument. Pianist, singer and songwriter Charlie Rich, a sideman at Sun, became a country star from 1968 on other labels and was known as the Silver Fox. Doug Poindexter, Malcolm Yelvington, Warren Smith, Charlie Feathers and other Sun artists were good rockabillies, but never broke into the national charts. Dorsey and Johnny Burnette were just about the only local rockabillies who never recorded for Sun.

Phillips carried on into the 1960s, but by then his era was over. His credit was always good in the record industry and he could have had a bigger label, but he never wanted to order pressings too far ahead; he became famous without risking too much. 'Until rock'n'roll came along,' he said, talking about genres, 'the worst discrimination in America was in music . . . I just hope I played some part in breaking that segregation down in some way.'

Meanwhile, other labels were scrambling to catch up with what Sun had discovered. Capitol's Gene Vincent and his Blue Caps had a top ten hit with 'Be-bop-a-lula' in 1956, which seemed an archetypal bit of rockabilly. The new West Coast Liberty label discovered Eddie Cochran, whose first hit was 'Sittin' in the Balcony', a sweet tune about going to the cinema with his girlfriend. It was also a hit on an obscure Colonial label for Johnny Dee; this was the song's composer, John D. Loudermilk, a singer-songwriter who later found his own following.

Cochran's next two hits were his own songs. 'Summertime Blues', a top ten hit in 1958, was perfect teen fodder, the story of a kid who can't go out because he has to work late:

> I called my congressman,
> And he said, quote:
> 'I'd like to help ya, Son, but
> You're too young to vote.'

This was followed by 'C'mon Everybody', about a boy who is rolling up the rugs for a party because his parents aren't home. Cochran was a good guitar player and an innovator in the studio who knew exactly what he was doing; and the session drummer on his best records was Earl Palmer. (When rock'n'roll spread through the industry, many of the best session musicians were black, including pianist Ernie Freeman and tenor saxophonist Plas Johnson, who first played Henry Mancini's *Pink Panther* theme.)

At Art Rupe's Specialty label the bread-and-butter acts were black gospel groups. One of the most successful was the Soul Stirrers, who had been around for a while: they had once recorded for Lew Chudd. Their new lead singer, Sam Cooke, had a gorgeous voice and a big following among young female gospel fans. Rupe knew that gospel fans disapproved of their heroes recording secular material, so when he caught Bumps Blackwell recording Cooke on a song called 'You Send Me', he told them to keep the tape in lieu of royalties and get out. Blackwell took the tape to Bob Keene, who put it out on his own Keen label and had one of the biggest hits of the year – number one in both the pop and R&B charts in 1957. The dreary song was a vehicle for Sam's melisma, the gospel-derived technique of wordless improvisation on the melody; his uncanny voice was one of the most beautiful in pop. He was signed by RCA, where he was over-produced; like many black entertainers, Cooke had different acts for black and white audiences.

Johnny Otis, a musical all-rounder, was born in California, where his Greek parents (named Veliotes) ran a grocery store. He grew up in a black neighbourhood and never considered himself anything but black. He helped to invent rhythm and blues; at his shows in the Watts area of Los Angeles Hispanics were among the most enthusiastic fans. On his other label, Del-Fi, Bob Keene recorded Richard Valenzuela, renamed Ritchie Valens, whose 'Donna' was a number two hit in 1958. It was not much of a song, but good for slow dancing, no doubt born out of long experience of playing for teen dances. It was backed by 'La Bamba', a pan-Latin folksong sung in Spanish, with a guitar riff that generated excitement, and became a legend. (Keene later recorded more of what came to be called Tex-Mex groups, including the Bobby Fuller Four, whose 'I Fought the Law' was a hit in 1966.)

Norman Petty was a musician from Clovis, New Mexico, across the border from Texas, where he had a small recording studio. His trio had a couple of minor hits in the mid-1950s (among them Ellington's 'Mood Indigo', with Norman on organ, his wife on piano and a guitarist). He used the money to improve his studio, and began recording local rockabillies. Buddy Knox had written 'Party Doll' as early as 1948, and was leading a trio called the Rhythm Orchids, with Jimmy Bowen on bass. 'Party Doll' was released with Bowen's 'I'm Sticking With You' on Knox's Triple-D label, using a cardboard box as a drum because Petty did not know how to record drums. It aroused national interest and was picked up by Roulette, who separated the tracks and had two million-sellers in 1957. (Bowen later became one of the most successful producers of country music.)

Roulette had been formed in New York in 1956 by George Goldner and Morris Levy. Goldner, who had started out in black doo-wop, had a hit on his Rama label in 1954 with 'Gee', by the Crows. On the Gee label he had an international million-seller, 'Why Do Fools Fall in Love', by Frankie Lymon and the Teenagers. The thirteen-year-old Lymon sang himself into history: bouncy, beautiful and heartfelt, replete with doo-wop trimming and a rocking saxophone solo, the record almost justifies all the sins committed in the teen-love genre since.

In the meantime, back in Clovis, Petty was recording Buddy Holly, from Lubbock, Texas. Holly had signed with Decca Records and recorded in Nashville in early 1956 when he was only nineteen; his group included guitarist Sonny Curtis and drummer Jerry Allison, and among the sides was an early version of 'That'll Be the Day'. In 1957 he formed a new group, the Crickets, and began experimenting with Petty. Together they taught themselves how to do what they wanted to do in the studio, such as recording drums. Roulette turned the records down; Bob Thiele signed them to separate Decca subsidiaries as Holly and as the Crickets. 'That'll Be the Day', early but fully-fledged rock'n'roll, was number one in August 1957; 'Peggy Sue' and 'Oh, Boy!' reached the top ten; 'Early in the Morning', written by Bobby Darin, was not with the Crickets, but had Sam 'the Man' Taylor on tenor saxophone; 'It's So Easy' and 'Every Day' did not enter the chart.

Holly's career was not moving fast enough to suit him; he split from the Crickets and from Petty. His last recordings, in New York, included a Paul Anka song, 'It Doesn't Matter Any More', made with strings. Like Cochran, Holly was an innovator in the studio, though some of his songs amount to little more than cowboy jingles; he had a good voice, but his hiccupping vocal style was an acquired taste. Like many of the others, he was more popular at the time in Britain.

In 1957 a new phenomenon appeared in the record shops: advance orders for a record that nobody had yet heard. Archie Bleyer, author of those remarkable stock arrangements in the late 1920s, became prominent as music director for radio and television personality Arthur Godfrey, and in 1953 formed his own Cadence label, which had high production standards and good technology. He had hits by the Chordettes ('Mr Sandman') and Julius LaRosa from Godfrey's television show, by pianist Roger Williams and singer Andy Williams, and also his own instrumental hits, such as 'Hernando's Hideaway'. Then he signed the Everly Brothers, Don and Phil, whose parents had played and sung on the radio. (Ike Everly had inspired many a guitar player.)

However the excitement over their first Cadence release was generated, it was not misplaced: distributors and jukebox operators were besieged with orders for 'Bye Bye Love', a song by Felice and Boudleaux Bryant, who had been writing country hits since 1949; its rockabilly beat (provided by acoustic guitars and bass, no drums) and the brothers' traditional country harmony was irresistible. The Everlys' first album contained two big hits, but their second, *Songs Our Daddy Taught Us*, was a beautiful compilation of their roots, folksongs and old country songs, including Gene Autry's 'That Silver-haired Daddy of Mine'. They had a total of thirty-eight Hot 100 *Billboard* hits before they split up in 1968.

There were a great many miscellaneous hit records, or one-hit wonders, that gave the quick pleasure of a novelty, yet seemed to be more than that. Cadence had one in 1958 with Link Wray; for the menacing instrumental 'Rumble', holes were poked with a pencil in the speaker fed by the electric guitar's amplifier, giving the music (and the listener) a buzz. (In the 1950s a rumble was a gang fight.)

The fuzz-tone became every electric guitar's accessory, and was done to death in the next twenty years. The slightly uptempo flip, 'The Swag', was also a good instrumental; Wray made a few albums over the years which became cult items.

A Texas DJ, J. P. 'Jape' Richardson, chuckled and nonsensed his way through 'Chantilly Lace' on Mercury as the Big Bopper in 1958. There was Sanford Clark's laid-back rockabilly 'The Fool' in 1956, with Al Casey on guitar (not the same Al Casey who played with Fats Waller). Jim Lowe's 'The Green Door' was a hit the same year. (Was the mysterious door the back entrance to the local hot-spot, or to the musicians' union?) Doo-wop continued to produce lovely records which did not appear in the chart, and a few that did: the Dell-Vikings' 'Come Go with Me' (1957) and 'Get a Job' by the Silhouettes (1958). The latter, which included rhythmic doo-wop nonsense syllables, was about a kid whose parents are nagging him to get a job.

Parents did not like rock'n'roll, of course, whatever it was called. Elvis Presley 78s were given away free at a Texas petrol station, so that customers could smash them. ASCAP did not like it because many of the hits were BMI publications (though 'Rock Around the Clock', the most notorious hit of all, associated with riots in cinemas, was an ASCAP song). When BMI added an annual R&B award to its pop and country awards in 1957, an NBC executive huffily declared that this was bad public relations in view of the anti-R&B attitude in some quarters; the obvious response, that NBC's subsidiary RCA should divest itself of Elvis Presley, was met with silence.

Frank Sinatra had long complained that Mitch Miller at Columbia had forced him to perform sub-standard material, and sent a telegram to a congressional subcommittee investigating the networks in 1956. It turned out that of all the songs Miller had recorded during his sensationally successful period at Columbia, 95 per cent were ASCAP songs. Of the fifty-seven tracks Sinatra had recorded, only five were BMI songs, and two of those were published by Sinatra's own BMI company. Furthermore, it was revealed, the sweet ballad that had done the most for Sinatra's comeback, 'Young at Heart' (on Capitol, 1954), was a BMI song.

Much of the music business hated rock'n'roll, even as it scrambled to take it over and reap the profits. Yet at the time rock'n'roll suddenly seemed to be dead almost as soon as it had been born. In March 1956, while on the road promoting 'Blue Suede Shoes', Carl Perkins was badly injured in a car crash. Little Richard's lifestyle and his sincere religious feelings were in conflict; in 1957, on tour in Australia, he suddenly quit, which cost him a good deal of money in cancelled dates. Presley was selling out, and was drafted in 1958; Jerry Lee Lewis's career had gone on hold; in February 1959 a plane crash took Buddy Holly, Ritchie Valens and the Big Bopper. That year Chuck Berry opened a club in St Louis, and was arrested for taking a fourteen-year-old hatcheck girl (who already had a criminal record for prostitution) across a state line for immoral purposes. In 1960 a car crash in England killed Eddie Cochran and badly injured Gene Vincent, who, already unstable, soon became an alcoholic. It was 1964 before Sam Cooke was murdered; but the great white hopes of rock'n'roll and a couple of the black ones were out of action. Some came back, and of course Elvis and Tom Parker got richer, but one way or another, none of these careers ever recovered its momentum. The music appeared to have been strangled in its cradle, yet it was too late: the rock generation had already been born.

15

The Abdication of a Generation

We have moved in less than half a lifetime from a scene in which live music was still ubiquitous to a time when *Top of the Pops*, the major British television pop show, celebrates not music, but children prancing in funny clothes; while a factory-made tape unreels in the background, they do not even pretend they can play or sing. On the USA's MTV the music no longer competes with the jingles, but has become the advertising. In the later 1950s the confusion and hypocrisy in the music business seemed to grow. This was an illusion – the business had always been stupid and greedy – but new factors causing the illusion were ever increasing amounts of money and runaway technology.

In about 1953 I attended a stage show at a theatre in Chicago. I forget whether the main attraction was Patti Page or Kay Starr, but I was startled to hear not a multi-tracked voice, but just a singer: it had not occurred to me when I was a child that the studio trick I heard on the radio could not then be reproduced on stage. A quarter of a century later, in London, I saw Joan Armatrading in concert at the Hammersmith Odeon, and was impressed that the slightest shimmer of echo on a single cymbal sound could be reproduced accurately, just as it was on the album. Armatrading's songs and her honest delivery of them were a welcome oasis in the popular music of the late 1970s, but she was reproducing her album on stage: impressive technically, but why not just stay at home and listen to the record? Tenor saxophonist Stan Getz told the story of a performance at which the electricity failed, whereupon he rediscovered the pleasure of making entirely acoustic music. Afterwards, a young fan came up to him and gushed about his tone, which was flattering at first, until Getz realized that what had astonished the fan was the sound of the reed instrument, without microphone or amplification. The young fan had never heard it before.

Technology and money have reigned supreme for so long that the manufacture, marketing and distribution of the product has long since become more important than its content, while an uncountable number of tiny record labels around the world who care about music cannot get their records into the shops or on the air. The confusion of values in the music business and the beginning of the complete abandonment of musical considerations are illustrated by the appearances of Elvis Presley on television variety shows in 1956.

In 1984 RCA issued a five-record set called *Elvis 50th Anniversary*, collecting together tracks from the Sun vault (including the infamous, dismal 'Harbor Lights'), live performances from the Mississippi-Alabama State Fair and Dairy Show in September 1956, and informal tracks made while filming a TV show in June 1968. For years these last had been rumoured to be the most exciting recordings Presley had made since early 1956, but they are a terrible let-down. To our purpose, however, are the appearances on the *Dorsey Brothers Stage Show* and the Milton Berle, Steve Allen and Ed Sullivan programmes, between early 1956 and early 1957. Berle's Tuesday night comedy and variety show was the hottest thing on US television in 1948, but it was limping in the ratings by 1956. It was Presley's appearance on Steve Allen's show on a Sunday evening in July that reduced Sullivan's ratings, and led to three Sullivan spots. Tommy and Jimmy Dorsey were two of the best white musicians in popular music. They had each led one of the most popular bands of the Swing Era, and worked together on a film biography in 1947; then Jimmy joined Tommy's band, and their television variety show in 1954 (a summer substitute for the Jackie Gleason show) was so successful that it was given its own spot, and continued until Tommy died in November 1956.

The Dorseys, their sidemen, music directors and arrangers must have been among the most experienced of studio players; they probably considered themselves jazzmen, or at least jazz-oriented musicians. Yet they threw away Elvis Presley. I was there watching, nearly thirty-five years ago; something was wrong, but I was too young to know what it was. In retrospect, it is obvious. I had listened to country music, to rhythm and blues and to Tommy Dorsey; Elvis Presley was exciting, but it was not as if he had come from Mars. These would-be jazzmen, their music directors and arrangers, however, apparently had no idea what was going on. Presley came on and did his thing, just as he did at a great many country fairs, while the band sat on its hands as though none of them had ever heard of the blues.

It doesn't matter whether you regard Elvis Presley plonked in front of the Dorsey band as a weed in a flower-bed or a pearl in a pigsty – it is the deliberate abdication of everyone involved that is interesting. On the six appearances with the Dorseys' band, it plays the same brief, corny fanfare it must have played for every performer, then sits quietly for Presley, and at the end of each song plays a single, blaring brass chord, perhaps to let us know the song has ended. Thirty-three tracks were recorded on the total of twelve television spots, including several of 'Heartbreak Hotel'. (One or two of these are better than the commercial record; they take the tune at a slightly slower tempo and have no piano, and Scotty Moore's guitar is either less tinny or absent.) But the first version, from March 1956, is the only one of these thirty-three opportunities on which television tried to do anything with the new show business sensation.

There is an appropriate introduction from the brass section; the band's drummer starts out playing the backbeat too softly, and thereafter overdoes it; there are brass punctuations at the end of each phrase in the chorus, where Scotty Moore's guitar usually clangs. At the end of the first verse and as the next one begins, the reed section rises with a smooth moan out of the background, sliding downwards in a glissando at the end of the verse to meet the beat, and it sounds like they are trying to do something appropriate with this music. But then in the middle of the simple arrangement there is a trumpet solo, not particularly thoughtful to start with and soon dissolving in confusion, as though the trumpeter suddenly woke up and did not know where he was; after that Presley screws up the beat and the whole thing turns into a shambles. Presley's amateurish guitar strumming is occasionally heard throughout.

This was the same kid who, years later, put on professional shows in Las Vegas, and some of his television tracks are already better than the studio tracks: the showman was there somewhere. Was there no money for a rehearsal for this band, whose co-leaders had already been showbusiness legends for the best part of thirty years? And on the other thirty-two television tracks there is nothing except, towards the end of the sequence, the familiar banality of the Jordanaires. No wonder Presley let Tom Parker tell him what to do; nobody else was doing it.

We know that Jimmie Rodgers and Louis Armstrong made a lovely recording together in 1929. On the Tiffany transcriptions made by Bob Wills's band in 1946, there is nothing bashful or inappropriate about hot solos from Fred Kelso's piano, or from Alex Brashear's muted trumpet, sometimes behind Tommy Duncan's vocals: they fit right in with the fiddle and the electric guitar. T-Bone Walker, the most influential of all guitarists and blues singers, made 144 tracks between 1940 and 1954, and many of them feature felicitous touches of reed writing, and saxophone and trumpet solos. Buddy Morrow's big-band R & B covers in 1952 were full of the right spirit. Why could the Dorseys not do it?

I do not believe that there was nobody in New York in 1956 who knew what was going on. I think they did not *want* to know. If Elvis Presley became the God of show business basically because all the white trash in the country could identify with him, the other side of the coin is that the music industry abandoned the Presleys to the Tom Parkers by pretending that white trash had no business being anything but a fluke, a novelty. The same white liberals who had made a fuss over Leadbelly in café society could not credit a Mississippi redneck singing the blues. New York studio musicians who were spending their working lives playing a jazz-oriented style were good readers of music, but not so good at reading the writing on the wall; and the power-brokers in the music industry were so helpless that they could not even find the wall.

There was a time when the music business, when it had to present a novelty act or cover a country song, would at least go through the motions of pretending that everybody was working in the same industry. But there had been a complete change in the way it all worked since the music publishers gambled on the songs, promising to make this or that their number one plug if so-and-so would record it. By the early 1950s the record labels' artist and repertory executives did the choosing, and by the late 1950s it was the disc jockeys.

Among the industry giants who abdicated at the threat of rock-'n'roll was Mitch Miller, the most successful A & R man in the history of the record business. Miller was only about six years younger than Tommy Dorsey. He began his career as a virtuoso on the oboe and the cor anglais and toured with an orchestra accompanying George Gershwin on piano; it was conducted on various occasions by Joe Reisman or Charles Previn (André's father). He played with the Budapest String Quartet, and with such conductors as Fritz Reiner and Sir Thomas Beecham; he was hand-picked by Leopold Stokowski for recording sessions in 1947, and may be heard on classic versions of Sibelius's 'Swan of Tuonela' and Dvořák's Symphony 'From the New World', which contain two of the most famous cor anglais solos in music. In short, before he became a record company executive, he was an accomplished musician and recording artist.

In the late 1940s he was involved with the Little Golden Records for children; they were unbreakable plastic 78s to begin with and sold millions of copies. He was asked by John Hammond to produce some classical recording sessions for Keynote, which was taken over by Mercury, where Miller helped with the first multi-tracked record-ings, as well as developing the careers of Vic Damone and Frankie Laine, who later followed him to Columbia. He played on and helped to produce the album *Charlie Parker with Strings*. When interviewer Ted Fox asked Miller in 1985 if it had not been a big change moving from classical to pop, Miller replied that he was always surprised when asked that:

I never compartmentalised it in my own mind. And the same rules apply . . . taste, musicianship, get the best out of the artist. Many times the artist doesn't know what his best characteristics are, and you're there to remind them. You can't put in what isn't there, but you can remind them of what they have and they're not using.

Alec Wilder, Goddard Lieberson and Miller had all been classmates at the Eastman School. When Mannie Sachs left Columbia to go to RCA, Lieberson, a composer, Renaissance man and CBS employee since before the war, hired Miller to replace him. Columbia's hit rate shot up by 60 per cent or more, and the label dominated popular music in the USA for the rest of the decade. Miller reported to Jimmy Conkling, who at thirty-five was the youngest major-label chief in the industry until he was succeeded in 1956 by Lieberson. (Conkling had come from Capitol, and went on to Warner Brothers.) They all believed that the label was there to have hits and to make money, but also to preserve the best of popular culture, so that, for example, Columbia recorded Duke Ellington during one of the least commercial periods of that great career.

During the 1950s Miller selected or passed on most of the company's singles output, overseeing more than seventy-five hit singles in the pop charts, of which at least a third reached the top ten – a much higher percentage of hits to releases than any other label could boast. At first, nobody could cover a hit faster than Miller, such as 'Tzena Tzena Tzena', with a chorus, under his own name, and 'Goodnight Irene', with Sinatra (both 1950). But he soon made his own hits for others to chase. Sinatra refused to record the pseudo-folksongs that Miller was bringing in, so he gave them to a singer named Al Cernick, who became Guy Mitchell, and they were all huge hits. It was Miller who first made pop hits out of Hank Williams's songs, and the themes from *Bridge on the River Kwai* and *High Noon*. The lyrics of the latter were rewritten at Miller's insistence.

All A&R men were pestered by songwriters, but Miller had his pick of the songs and got his way because he was so successful, and when he made a deal, he kept his word. It was Miller's idea to change around Percy Faith's arrangement of 'On the Street Where You Live' for Vic Damone, so that it began with the bridge – 'Oh, that towering feeling . . .' – making the record a grabber, and a top five hit.

George Avakian discovered Johnny Mathis, who was young and derivative. His first records flopped, but Miller waited until the right songs came along: 'Wonderful! Wonderful!', 'It's Not for Me to Say', 'Chances Are' and 'The Twelfth of Never' (all 1957) made a star of Mathis. (The second and third of these were written by Stillman and Allen, who had written hits for the Four Lads; the fourth was an adaptation of a folksong.)

During Miller's time countless classic country hits were made, by

Carl Smith, Ray Price, Lefty Frizzell, Marty Robbins and many others. These were honest recordings, not overproduced, though it was Art Satherley and Don Law who were in charge of country music. It was under Miller that more country songs crossed over, such as 'Just Walkin' in the Rain', by Johnnie Ray. In 1956 Miller came as close to rockabilly as he ever did, with 'Singing the Blues', a huge hit which was the best and most popular of Guy Mitchell's career. Robbins had an equally big country hit with that song, whereupon Robbins crossed over with his next, 'A White Sport Coat'. Mahalia Jackson recorded classic gospel music on Columbia from the early 1950s; Miller gave gospel songs to Rosemary Clooney and Johnnie Ray.

Miller had too much power and not enough taste. We do not know how much he had to do with the *Charlie Parker with Strings* album back at Mercury, but arranger Jimmy Carroll's charts were worse than unimaginative; he had no idea what to do with strings. Miller was as responsible as anyone for turning pop music into jingles. He had a penchant for unusual sounds, and it was probably his idea to amplify a harpsichord for Faith's 'Delicado' and for Clooney's biggest hits. One of his bad ideas was putting bagpipes on a recording by Dinah Shore; DJs took the record off and broke it on the air. Some of his material was overproduced: the relentless snare drum on his 'Yellow Rose of Texas' (1955) was a natural target for satirist Stan Freberg, but the snare came back on Johnny Horton's 'Battle of New Orleans' in 1959.

Still, live pop music seemed to be dead by Miller's time and, as jingles went, Miller's jolly records had more personality than most. His own instrumental 'Oriental Polka' was a wacky twittering tune for woodwind doubled by a marimba. Percy Faith's 'Funny Fellow' was a slowish, cock-eyed samba, which had a cheerful, noisy rhythm section and a piccolo carrying the tune, to test the speaker on your 'hi-fi' record player; in the middle of the arrangement the band laid out and the tune was carried by a solo bassoon, and the band's 'funny fellow' made you chuckle. On the other side of the record was 'Amorada', a Latin frenzy, on which Artie Ryerson played an electric guitar solo that most of today's rockers could not even attempt.

None of these reached the chart; perhaps they were too much better than the jingles, but they were what Miller called 'turntable hits': you enjoy it, but you don't go out to buy it. They were all musical fun.

A typical Miller coup was 'Let Me Go, Lover'. The producer of CBS TV's *Studio One*, a top-rated drama showcase, needed a song, so Miller dusted off a temperance plea called 'Let Me Go, Devil', which had flopped on another label, and had new lyrics written. A slow country waltz, the song was just right, because it did not get in the way of the play's action. He used an unknown girl singer, since he did not want a star's distraction either: 21-year-old Joan Weber's record was number one for four weeks at the end of 1955. But Weber never had another hit.

It was no secret that Miller was not crazy about rock'n'roll, but neither did he join in the pulpit crusade against it, declaring that there was no such thing as an 'immoral' music. But he also did not like the way the music business was changing, and was unwilling to do what you had to do in the later 1950s to get your records played on the radio. In those days Columbia kept its hands clean. At first it did not own a music publishing company, so that Miller could not have cut a DJ in on a song if he had wanted to; and the company would not buy radio spots, which should have been perfectly legal, except that CBS was also a radio network, and afraid of an anti-trust suit. Record labels and promotion men have always paid to get records played; part of the problem was that many DJs were not paid much in the way of a salary, but they played Columbia records because they liked them. When the business began to get dirtier and the money got bigger, fewer Columbia singles were heard on the radio. Miller was always working hard, making a hundred decisions a day, flying back and forth between coasts and selling truckloads of product. He was also an opinionated man, whose tough attitude was justified by his track record, and he occasionally stepped on toes; but why should he bribe DJs?

The most important change in the business was demographic. The largest group of young Americans in history would also have more spending money in its pockets than any earlier American generation, and already in the 1950s they were spending it on rock'n'roll records. Soon some of them were even going out on the road and playing the stuff, generating more easy money, and by then it was not just kids who were buying rock'n'roll records. At the first annual Pop Music Disk Jockey Festival in March 1958 Miller complained in a famous speech called 'The Great Abdication':

You carefully built yourselves into the monarchs of radio and abdicated your programming to the corner record shop, to the eight to 14-year-olds, to the preshave crowds that make up 12 per cent of the country's population and zero per cent of its buying power. It must be more than a coincidence that single record buying went into a decline at the very time the number of stations that programme Top 40 climbed to a new high.

But the coincidence was that grown-ups were using their purchasing power to buy LPs, not singles. Two years earlier RCA had released an unprecedented six singles at once by Elvis Presley (they even had sequential catalogue numbers), as well as 'Heartbreak Hotel', making Presley's Sun material and some of his February 1956 classics available nationwide. The singles were selling twelve thousand copies a day, representing two-thirds of RCA's singles sales, and for the first time the company had to use outside pressing facilities. If rock'n'roll fans had zero buying power, who was buying all those records? Presley's first album broke sales records set by Mario Lanza's *The Student Prince* and the soundtrack from *The Glenn Miller Story*.

Nevertheless, the issue concerned not solely Elvis Presley. A lot of pop music was junk and everybody knew it. Miller's main point was that adults had more buying power than their children, the albums they bought moved fewer units but made up 65 per cent of the record industry's volume and a much higher portion of its profits, and the adults were listening to less and less radio. The convention gave Miller its only ovation, but the Storz broadcasting chain, which was sponsoring the convention, banned Columbia records.

Miller didn't care. Power had long since gone to his head. He had talked Lieberson into putting him in charge of albums as well as singles, and one of the first things he did was fire Paul Weston in California, who had been making beautiful albums for grown-ups for a decade. (Weston was immediately snapped up by a television network.) Les and Larry Elgart co-led a polite dance band on Columbia; according to one story, Larry said to drummer Karl Kiffe, 'When the band starts to swing, I want you to play the ride cymbal', and Kiffe replied, 'When the band starts to swing, will you please raise your hand?' Miller suggested that trombonist Ray Conniff should rearrange his old Artie Shaw material to include male and female choruses. These records amounted to superior Muzak, but never mind; grown-ups could dance to them, and they made pots of money. It was Miller's idea to do the first greatest hits album, by Mathis, which cost the company nothing and sold in the millions. A few months after that DJ convention, in July 1958, *Sing Along with Mitch* was the number one album in the USA for eight weeks. Fourteen later male chorus singalong albums, helped by Miller's television show, reached the top ten albums; twenty-two million were sold, and people stopped buying them only because there were so many of them in the shops that they could not remember which ones they already had.

But it was Miller and his generation who had abdicated. He cannot be blamed for not wanting to get his hands dirty, and he must have thought, as many people did, that rock'n'roll and an increasingly cutthroat music business were passing fads. But the singalong albums are of no importance to the history of music. It is interesting to speculate about what would have happened if Miller had put up the $20,000 that Sam Phillips was asking for Presley in 1955; Presley probably would have ended up in Las Vegas anyway, but at least Miller might have been a match for Tom Parker. But Presley went to RCA, as did Leiber and Stoller, in 1958. All the offices at RCA were identical cubicles; Jerry Leiber could not find his. They told Ted Fox:

By the time you filled out a requisition for something, the idea was stale ... We produced seven records in the first four months we were there, and had six Picks of the Week in *Cashbox* ... But they never sold any of those records. Meanwhile we made one record for Atlantic during that period and it was a smash ... The records were being sold by people who sold refrigerators.

Maybe RCA did not want to bribe DJs either, but, on the other hand, post-war RCA never had a hand at the helm as firm as Miller's. That once great label was coasting, and never recovered; and meanwhile broadcasting was going down the drain.

Robert 'Todd' Storz bought a radio station in Omaha, Nebraska, for $60,000 in 1949; in 1953 he added a station in New Orleans. Most radio stations were soon relying on music, news and jingles, and Storz's new Mid-Continent Broadcasting Corporation was no exception. Storz had grown up listening to *Your Hit Parade*, which simply performed the top ten hits live each week. (The music publishers had never liked it, because the constant plugging of hits kept new songs from getting exposure.) Storz was not going to allow DJs or anybody else to deflect him from his purpose of making money; at the same time, neither was he the type to pay DJs enough money to keep them straight: Miller thought that Storz's DJs were among those on the take, whether Storz knew it or not. The twenty-four-hour format of hits Storz invented, varied with a few white covers of R&B or country hit songs, did not require any talent or musical knowledge, and therefore demanded of a DJ only the ability to cut a ribbon at a new supermarket. In 1956 Storz's corporation sold $3.5 million worth of advertising, and his method was being copied by others, including the Plough group, which bought Chicago's WLS and turned it into the most popular station in the Midwest. In 1957 Storz sold the Omaha station to William F. Buckley, America's leading conservative pundit, for $800,000; Buckley, of course, preserved the deadening format. (In America, 'conservative' rhymes with 'easy money'.)

Somewhere along the way Storz and his programme manager were having a beer in a nearby tavern when they noticed that the other patrons kept playing a small number of hit tunes over and over again on the jukebox, and not only that, but the barmaids or waitresses would then use some of their tip money to play the same tunes. The 'hit parade' formula was tightened up still further, and the Top 40 programming format was born. By the late 1950s a Plough station had a playlist of only one hundred records, concentrating on forty of them and playing them so as to vary the tempo to keep listeners from falling asleep. This meant that whatever was already a hit got constant airplay. It meant that novelties, such as David Seville's 'Witch Doctor' and Sheb Wooley's 'Flying Purple People Eater', which sold quickly anyway, oozed up the charts like castor oil through a pig. And it meant that country music was confined even more to its ghetto, that black hits had less chance of getting wider exposure and that jazz, folk music, Sinatra albums, polka bands and all the rest might as well not even exist. Storz and his imitators sold American airwaves for cash, and nobody cared.

The better music is, the more dangerous it seems. Millions of Americans grumbled that the Swing Era was over, but they did nothing to make it possible for big bands to survive in the 1950s, while every country in Europe still has radio big bands today (though how much longer the BBC's will last is a moot point). It is tempting to suggest that Americans are afraid of swing, in the broadest sense of the term. We have seen that for most of the nineteenth century American songs were regarded by the biggest publishers as not worth publishing, while European music was 'good' music. The fact that American publishers did not pay royalties on European music until 1891, so that there was several hundred per cent profit on each piece of sheet music, was, of course, irrelevant.

In 1899 the *Musical Courier* complained, 'A wave of vulgar, filthy and suggestive music has inundated the land. Nothing but ragtime prevails, and the cakewalk with its obscene posturings, its lewd gestures ... our children ... are continually exposed to ... this vulgarising music.' The owner of the magazine also hated Victor Herbert, to the point where Herbert finally sued him for libel, and won. Coincidentally, Witmark, Herbert's publisher and also the biggest publisher of ragtime songs, had long refused to buy advertising in the *Musical Courier*. Naturally there was no connection.

It was black bandleader James Reese Europe's advice to dancer Vernon Castle to make his moves to the backbeat, in the style of black music, which led to the two-step, the foxtrot and the fad for dancing that swept the country before 1920 and was regarded as corrupting the morals of youth. Come to think of it, while in minstrelsy the blacks remained comic darkies, and were therefore not threatening, from ragtime to rock'n'roll it was music with a black element that was found most objectionable. In mid-1956 local members of the White Citizens Council beat up Nat Cole at a concert in Birmingham, Alabama, in front of an all-white audience, because they disliked 'nigger music', at a time when Elvis Presley was selling more records in black neighbourhoods than Cole.

There is no such thing as a dangerous music; Americans just like being paranoid. Speaking of paranoia, many people wondered why Presley's local draft board, made up like all draft boards of solid, respectable citizens, happened to choose him to drive tanks in Germany. And why was the pilot of the chartered plane carrying Holly, who was not qualified to fly on instruments, not informed that only a few thousand yards from the airfield the weather was turning very bad? And when Chuck Berry's first trial had been thrown out as blatantly racist, would the law not have earned more respect, in the case of a violation of the outmoded Mann Act, which was widely regarded as a joke anyway, by dismissing it? But there was another trial, just to make sure that Berry was sent to prison. We did not have to be paranoid; the decision-makers were probably only stupid, but, one way or another, it seemed as if they really were after us.

Since any business can be manipulated, rock'n'roll was soon taken over by banal (but less dangerous) teen-love songs, or by jingles with a pseudo rock'n'roll beat. Typical of early rock acts were Johnny and the Hurricanes, an organ-led trio whose hit 'Red River Rock' was a nervously fast shuffle on 'Red River Valley', a folksong dating from 1896 and itself based on earlier songs. Somehow it was copyrighted in 1959 as a new song (by a BMI company, let us admit), and was followed by rock versions of the bugle call 'Reveille', 'Blue Tail Fly' and others. Then there was 'The Happy Organ', by Dave 'Baby' Cortez, which was number one for seven weeks in 1959. This was the kind of trash that was being played by hopefuls in a great many bars across the USA, while the nation's best white musicians, and some of the black ones, made a living in the studios, their names unknown to the public. No wonder many of them hated rock'n'roll.

Rock'n'roll may have been taken over, but the charts were not. What were some of the other number one hits of the era? In 1958: 'It's Only Make Believe', a country ballad by Conway Twitty; 'Tom Dooley', a slicked-up folksong by the Kingston Trio; 'It's All in the

Game', a ballad by Tommy Edwards, whose Tin Pan Alley words were set to a melody composed in 1912 by General Charles Gates Dawes, later vice-president of the United States (how respectable can you get?); 'Volare', by Domenico Modugno, an Italian cabaret song; 'All I Have to Do is Dream', another country ballad, by the Everly Brothers; 'Twilight Time', from 1944, by the Platters. In 1959: 'Mack the Knife', sung in his new Sinatra style by Bobby Darin; 'The Three Bells', a French folksong sung by the Browns, a country trio; 'The Battle of New Orleans', by Johnny Horton, and 'El Paso', by Marty Robbins, a pair of country story songs; 'Smoke Gets in Your Eyes', by the Platters, from 1933, one of Jerome Kern's greatest songs (which rock writer Dave Marsh thinks was a 'Tin Pan Alley trifle').

All these were number one, along with some Chipmunk novelties and a sprinkling of rock'n'roll. (Presley's 1924 front-porch ballad, 'Are You Lonesome To-night?', doesn't count as rock'n'roll either.) Top 40 radio saw to it that a hit stayed a hit, because it was all you heard, which is why 'Volare' nearly drove us nuts. So what was the music business afraid of? The truth is that America was floundering; the most powerful nation in the history of the world was frightened of that responsibility, because there were no cultural or political values at the top. Hence the paranoia about rock'n'roll, among other things, even as the USA was selling its own popular culture down the river.

'It was general knowledge in the industry in 1955 that payola flourished,' wrote Russell Sanjek, a retired BMI executive. He meant specifically the bribing of DJs to play records, but, of course, bribery had been endemic in the music industry from the beginning, and for that matter can be found in any industry in any country. (The Soviet economy depended on it until not even bribery could keep it going.)

Perhaps payola began with short-changing the creator. In Britain for generations composers depended for their living upon selling music outright and then writing and selling new music; they offered whatever inducements they could to get it performed. When top bananas from Al Jolson to Elvis Presley sang a song in exchange for a co-writing credit, they were demanding payola. The term itself was invented (like much other entertainment terminology) by *Variety*, which in 1938 carried the headline 'Plug Payola Purplexed': maybe that was the case of the two West Coast bandleaders who were listed as co-writers of a song neither of them had yet seen. In 1953 *Time* carried a story about 'cut-ins' (performance shares of a song) and 'hot stoves' (outright bribery).

'Videola' was already a less well-known aspect of the business. Guests on quiz and variety shows were introduced with a drum roll or a simple fanfare, until television producers realized that if they could lock up the copyrights on recognizable pieces of music, they could make a good deal of extra money. It is an irony that the corny and inappropriate fanfare with which Elvis Presley was greeted on the Dorsey Brothers' programme may have been worth a fat weekly sum to whoever owned it. By 1958 $6 million was being paid annually by ASCAP just for theme songs and background music, chosen not by the public but by television producers.

It was no accident that the theme tunes of radio soap operas, usually played in the studio by an organist, used music that was out of copyright: the big tune from Tchaikovsky's Sixth Symphony for *Road of Life*, the old Italian pop song 'Funiculi Funicula' for *Lorenzo Jones* and so on. *The FBI in Peace and War* used the march from Prokofiev's *Love for Three Oranges*. (Whether or not royalties were paid on that, the interesting question here is did J. Edgar Hoover know that the FBI was being promoted by a Soviet composer?)

But radio themes soon disappeared. In 1954 there was panic in the radio industry when advertising investment suddenly fell. Daytime radio drama is still a strong and very special genre in Britain, thanks to the BBC, but it died decades ago in the USA, where the mass audience, having turned to television, used radio only as aural wallpaper while they worked, or in their cars, and minority audiences of any kind did not matter.

Top DJs in big cities earned as much as $35,000 a year, a lot of money in the mid-1950s. Men like Bill Randle in Cleveland and Howard Miller in Chicago had recognizable personalities, but most DJs were staff announcers with a talent for talking about anything that came into their heads, and as long as they didn't stop talking between records, it was assumed that they had some taste in music. They had long been courted by special interests with drinks, meals and complimentary adverts in trade magazines. But in the mid-1950s the stakes went up; radio drama had been heard mainly on the networks, and the sudden death of it made many more poorly paid local DJs available to circling record industry promo sharks. With Top 40 radio, Storz, whether his DJs were on the take or not, had helped create a situation in which they were worth bribing.

Martin Block, who had pioneered the DJ format in 1935, retired in 1960; he was frank, describing the $10 that came with a new record as the equivalent of a head waiter's tip for a good table in a nightclub. Alan Freed never denied accepting gifts, but denied taking them in advance: 'If I've helped somebody, I'll accept a nice gift, but I wouldn't take a dime to plug a record . . . I'd be giving up control of my program.' Besides, it was Freed who had discovered the popularity of R&B among white kids and popularized the term 'rock'n'roll' when it was a daring thing to do and before there was much money in it, and who almost went to jail when early rock concerts turned into mini-riots. Later he bragged that he could name rooms in his house after record companies; he said that Atlantic had paid for his swimming pool, but also that when Atlantic reminded him of the pool because they wanted a favour, he told them that when they sent him some records he liked, he would play them. He was believed when he said that he had never played a record that he didn't like, and the truth seemed to be that payola was not against the law anyway. But Freed's flamboyance and lack of political awareness made him the most prominent victim of the payola 'scandal'.

Howard Miller said he could name people who took money, or paid it, but that it would be unfair to put a few on the rack for a practice that was so widespread. Willie Dixon, a power in Chicago R&B at Chess Records, was open in his autobiography *I Am the Blues* (written with Don Snowden, 1989). It was necessary to give free records to jukebox operators and to distributors; they were supposed to be promotional copies, but everybody knew they were sold. Furthermore:

no disc jockey was going to play your record then without you paying him and that was the truth . . . They would play 'em two weeks, three times a day and that was it unless you came up with more money.

Some of the disc jockeys would play all of one company's records and there wasn't a whole lot of radio stations like there are now.

Joe Smith began as a DJ at Yale. In the 1950s he wanted to play Nat Cole records.

Frankly, I didn't understand Elvis Presley. I had no background to understand Elvis Presley. But I could instantly sense the impact the guy was having, so I figured I'd better play his records. [The decision to play rock'n'roll was made easier as time went on.] The record companies . . . took care of you, you never picked up a tab anywhere. Some guys gave you $100 or $200 a month.

Some years after Freed was ruined, Smith became president of Capitol Records, but he still finds time to write letters. Gene Lees is a former editor of *down beat* and contributed to *Stereo Review* and *High Fidelity* for many years. A successful lyricist, he has published English words to music by bossa nova composers, Charles Aznavour, pianist Bill Evans and others. Since launching his own monthly *Jazzletter* in 1981 he has regularly chastised the music business. Smith wrote to him in January 1989 to say that he had never heard of him: 'Just who are you and what credentials do you possess to wrap up this industry with that kind of rhetoric? . . . When lessons in honesty, ethics and principle are given, I wouldn't be looking to enroll in your class.' Smith had no doubt been careful to pay taxes on the money he took.

In 1959 it was big news that television quiz shows such as *Twenty One*, *The $64,000 Question* and *The $64,000 Challenge* were rigged, often at the request of the sponsors, in order to keep the most popular contestants on week after week. Congressional Representative Oren Harris of Arkansas, chairman of a Special Subcommittee on Legislative Oversight, decided to dig deeper, hoping to find more scandal to keep the subcommittee in the public eye. This was good for votes: the House Un-American Activities Committee, populated by alcoholics and bounders, had kept themselves in office for many years by getting some of the most valuable people in the State Department sacked, and by encouraging blacklists in the entertainment industry. That blacklists themselves were against the law was not important; and as for the name of Harris's subcommittee, if it is not against the law to bribe a DJ, that must be a Legislative Oversight, or a job for the boys.

Burton Lane, president of the American Guild of Authors and Composers, wrote to the chairman of the Federal Communications Commission (FCC), urging it to require owners of broadcasting licences to divest themselves of conflicting business interests, such as music publishing companies. Payola was only a symptom of the disease, wrote Lane, which was 'the involvement of the entire broad-casting industry, networks and local stations, in a deliberate and successful distortion of music programming for their own financial gain'. This was fine as far as it went, but Congress was not going to do much about the state of broadcasting; there was more publicity in going after DJs. And Lane did not mention videola, because that put money in his members' pockets.

After a riot at a concert in Boston in 1958, Freed was indicted on a charge of inciting to destroy public property, which was later dropped. Some stations banned rock'n'roll. Freed moved from the most popular station in New York, the independent WINS, to an ABC affiliate, where he had an evening show, but he was already being eclipsed in the fame stakes: on television Freed had to make do with a local independent station, because ABC-TV already had Dick Clark.

Clark had begun as a newsreader at WFIL in Philadelphia at the age of twenty-three; he replaced Bob Horn (who'd been fired for being convicted of drunken driving) on the station's *Philadelphia Bandstand* in 1956. The show had kids dancing, guest artists miming their records and not much talk. It was broadcast five days a week after school, rather than in more expensive prime time, and teenagers rushed home to watch it. Clark's low-key, squeaky-clean personality helped make it a success. In 1957 it was networked for ninety minutes a day as *American Bandstand*, and by 1959 it was shown on over one hundred affiliates and had twenty million fans, or 60 per cent of the audience. Imitations of the show included Chicago's *Bandstand Matinee*, and the dancing kids on the show themselves became mini-stars.

Clark used local television time, before the network part of the show, to test new records, and once played the wrong version of

'Tequila' for weeks before his studio audience let him know. On network time he nearly always played records that were already hits, but the record companies and distributors pushed him as the most influential DJ in the country. They must have done this hoping for favours, so it was a sort of pre-payola. By 1959 Clark had investments in the music business, of which he divested himself on ABC's advice.

Despite occasional reactions against rock'n'roll, Top 40 continued to grow. National advertisers took over the printing of tip sheets, which were plug sheets for new records, and were displayed in record shops. Record companies stepped up releases to around a hundred a week, so that more records had less chance of being heard, thus raising the stakes still further. On the first day of 1959 the CBS radio network cut back programming again, leaving affiliates with twenty more hours a week to fill with music. The Federal Communications Commission and the Federal Trade Commission both started investigations, but they were not investigating the basic causes of the degradation of American radio broadcasting. Soon Representative Emanuel Celler was gunning for BMI, seeing public unrest about 'dirty songs' as a ticket to a seat in the Senate. It was clear that complainants were often connected with ASCAP, using unease about rock'n'roll as a stick with which to beat BMI; but if it was a conflict of interest that some broadcasters had holdings in BMI, ASCAP itself had brought this about in the first place with its strike against the broadcasters in 1940.

The hearings revealed the usual special pleading and hypocrisy. One witness stated that a record company had paid to have its recording of a Tchaikovsky symphony favoured over another, whereupon it was observed that the committee was interested only in corruption as it applied to 'bad' music. Burton Lane ranted about BMI's influence, but had to admit that ownership of radio stations by such members of his organization as Bing Crosby, Frank Sinatra and Pat Boone might also represent a conflict of interest. ASCAP's general counsel Herman Finkelstein stated that the 'artificial ratings' for BMI songs would be substantially reduced if Congress acted, claiming that ASCAP hits were successful on 'sheer merit'; but he also did not know how top ten tunes were chosen, so he could not be more specific. (*Variety*'s headline was 'Put Up or Shut Up'.) Sydney Kaye of BMI refuted much of this: the percentage of BMI records in broadcaster–DJ charts was lower than that in retail record sales, and the performance rate of BMI music had been lower in 1958 than in 1957. Kaye also brought up the subject of videola, pointing out that a snatch of an old song accompanying the closing of a door in a melodrama brought in just as much money as if an artist sang the whole song on a musical programme; and it was noted that in 1957 more than 42 per cent of all ASCAP's payments came from television networks. Kaye said that if BMI was held in greater esteem by broadcasters than ASCAP, it was because BMI did not habitually vilify them.

Celler proposed a bill which would have prohibited DJs' interviews with recording artists from leading to a playing of the artist's new record, or a 'Salute to ASCAP' on Ed Sullivan's show from involving appearances by member songwriters whose songs would then be used. It would have required radio stations to buy all their records, playing free ones only if it was announced on the air that they were free. This was silly, because of the way the economics of the industry had changed. When so much airtime had to be filled with recorded music, buying new releases would have cost stations thousands of dollars a year, which the smaller ones could not afford, and would have made it even harder for an independent label or a new artist to be heard at all.

Dick Clark and Alan Freed were heard in closed as well as open session. Clark's lawyers testified that he had earned $500,000 in twenty-seven months from music publishing, record pressing and distribution and talent management, but that he had disposed of these interests. Freed said that he had been paid $40,000 a year by WABC-AM, but that he had paid $30,000 of it back to the station in exchange for advertising of his rock'n'roll concerts. Representative John Moss said that Freed was 'one of the few completely truthful men we've had before us'. Three hundred and thirty-five DJs admitted having received $263,245 for being 'consultants' in recent years. The sheer abundance of product had taken the control of hit-making away from song pluggers and publishers and given it to radio; a station or a DJ in a major market might receive one thousand LPs and five thousand singles in a year, which would give rise to payola, because there was no way twenty thousand or so tracks could each get an equal hearing.

The result was an amendment to the Communications Act of 1934 outlawing play-for-pay, but committee lawyer Bernard Schwartz had wanted a more wide-ranging investigation. He wrote in the *New York Post* that improprieties other than those of DJs remained buried in Harris's subcommittee's files: 'Those fully aware of the material involved know we are really deceiving ourselves to believe that the Congressmen carried out anything like the really thorough investigation of the federal agencies that is so urgently needed.' To make sure Schwartz remained an obscure voice, he was fired in early 1959.

In the middle of the unsuccessful war on rock'n'roll came news of the international popularity of it. In the Soviet Union rock'n'roll records were being bootlegged on exposed X-ray film, while other bootlegs on 7-inch 78s made from short-wave broadcasts were being sold by the GUM department store in Moscow. As far as anyone knew, there was no related bribing of DJs in the Soviet Union.

Freed had earlier suffered severe internal injuries in a car crash. He was a heavy drinker; his son said years later that he had never seen him drunk, but Freed was not supposed to drink at all. He was an enthusiastic man who enjoyed life; in refusing throughout his career to play white covers of black hits he had made enemies, and it seemed he could not stay out of trouble. He was fired from WABC in late 1959 for refusing to sign an affidavit to the effect that he had never accepted payola; his combination of honesty and naïvety resulted in twenty-six charges of commercial bribery. He escaped with fines and a suspended jail sentence, but his career was over and his health was failing; he died a broken man in 1965, facing charges of income tax evasion. *Cashbox* wrote that 'he suffered the most . . . for alleged wrongs that had become a way of life for many others', and which for the most part were not against the law when he committed them; but the hypocrites had got their scapegoat.

Both Freed and Clark did their bit to break down racism. Clark's dance party programme integrated a live network show in 1957, allowing black teenaged couples to join the whites without any fanfare, not knowing if they would get away with it. He later said that the first time he talked to a black kid on the air he was frightened to death, but there was not one single complaining letter out of fifteen thousand a week. (To put this in context, it was not until well into the 1960s that Duke Ellington's granddaughter became the first black in a mixed group of professional dancers on television.)

Clark was seen by some as a goody-goody who was let off lightly while Freed was ruined, but Clark was simply better at public relations. He told the hearings that he felt as though he had been convicted of something before he had even testified, and years later was still bitter, describing politicians as pimps. In an interview with *Rolling Stone* in 1989 he observed that the whole thing had been about headlines: congressmen left the hearings early to make the evening television news. One was a drunk who did not even know who Clark was; the most insulting interrogating lawyer would afterwards ask Clark for an autograph and to pose for a snapshot. The government finally sent Clark back to work with a pat on the head, but they had broken into his home and tapped his phone: he was twenty-seven years old and he was shocked. It is worth remembering that those were the Eisenhower years, before assassinations, Vietnam, Watergate; most people still hoped that the government was on the up and up, but Clark learned early that the lawyers in Congress are worse than the rest. According to *Rolling Stone*, he is even more scathing off the record; what he learned from the payola hearings was 'Protect your ass at all times.'

So far as his image is concerned, he also points out that his suit-and-tie style deflected criticism of rock'n'roll, and that most of the people who have been elected to the Rock and Roll Hall of Fame made their television débuts on *American Bandstand*. He had all the wild ones on his programme that parents hated most, such as Little Richard and Jerry Lee Lewis, though not Elvis. (It was a low-budget show, and Tom Parker would not allow his boy to appear for a low fee, while others who demanded big money from Perry Como and Ed Sullivan did *American Bandstand* for scale.) When Hank Ballard didn't turn up to record 'The Twist', Clark gave the job to a former chicken-plucker named Ernest Evans, and Clark's wife changed his name to Chubby Checker. There was also Clark's

Caravan of Stars: an integrated group of big-name entertainers toured the USA, including the Deep South, on a bus for sixty or ninety days.

All Clark did was 'stock the store with what the public wanted', but inevitably, given the association with Philadelphia, where so much cheap pop came from, he was linked with music as poor as anything before or since. About a recording artist such as Fabian, Clark observes that he was a sign of the times; the fans went for his looks, not his singing. The uncomfortable question remains: did Alan Freed play Fabian's records?

One of the first teen-pop stars was Ricky Nelson. Bandleader Ozzie Nelson had married his vocalist, Harriet Hilliard, and, with their sons David and Ricky, their *Ozzie and Harriet* was a top-rated sitcom on radio and then television, and is still typical of American television in its idealization of family life (not necessarily intended as a put-down). The first hit was part of a plot: Elvis Presley was big, and Ricky wanted to impress a girlfriend. 'A Teen-ager's Romance' (on Verve) was pretty lame, but it was a hit, and it is interesting that he covered a Fats Domino hit on the flip side rather than imitating Presley: 'I'm Walkin'' also entered the chart, around Ricky's seventeenth birthday in May 1957. Having plugged his first record on a top-rated national showcase, he was snapped up by Imperial, Domino's label, where he stayed well into the 1960s. He improved as a vocalist; produced by Jimmy Haskell with Ozzie meddling, he achieved several gold records in a row, and they were not bad pop records. The best of his later work falls into the country rock category; his Stone Canyon Band in 1969 used excellent sidemen, such as James Burton. He had many fans when he was killed in a plane crash in 1985.

In July of 1957 Canadian Paul Anka, almost a year older than Nelson, reached number one with 'Diana'. A successful songwriter as well as a vocalist, Anka turned out to have staying power, and had over fifty hits in the *Billboard* chart in the 1970s. He had his own television show in 1973 and was long popular in Las Vegas. His best-known accomplishment is the English lyric he wrote to a French song, 'Comme d'habitude', which became 'My Way' and was sung by Frank Sinatra in 1967. It is hard to argue with success, but 'Diana' was trash, a brash bellowing of a teenage heartache, to say nothing of the banal harshness of the sound of the record. Any girl responding to 'Put Your Head on My Shoulder' (1959) must have used earplugs as a precaution. He had nothing to do with rock'n'roll and everything to do with parting teens from their money.

But much worse was to come. Frankie Avalon, born Francis Avallone in Philadelphia, was more than a year younger than Nelson; he played trumpet as a child on radio and television with Paul Whiteman. He was seventeen when he reached the top ten with 'Dede Dinah' in 1958, and he then had twenty-four hits up to 1962, of which the only one I remember is 'Venus', an inescapable number one for five weeks in 1959. He sounded like a kid who had been inveigled into singing at a high-school dance, having no idea that he was making a fool of himself; in only six years we had come from 'Doggie in the Window' to 'Venus'. It mattered to me, deeply mattered, that he could not sing at all; already a lifelong music fan, the same age as Avalon, I could not figure out where this junk was coming from, and I was ashamed for my generation. Then came Fabian, also from Philadelphia, who was barely fifteen in early 1959, when he had the first of ten hits in two years. These two oafs were the real beginning of what is remembered as the 'teen idol' era.

They were both on the same label, Chancellor, which was formed in 1958 by Peter de Angelis. The promoter was Bob Marcucci, who was consultant to the well-made film *The Idolmaker* (1980), based on the period. The promoter in the film is a frustrated performer and songwriter himself, and makes a star out of a nasty Italian-American kid he knows from local cabaret; the payola is graphically illustrated. The promoter (played well by Ray Sharkey) is betrayed by his star, and sets out to find another good-looking boy (a waiter in the film) who has no experience or discernible talent, but whom he can mould. Most of the music in the film is infinitely better than the Philadelphia hits of 1958 to 1960; written by Jeff Barry and sung by Jessie Frederick (dubbing for actor Paul Land), the cabaret rock gives no idea at all of the awfulness of the stuff of the period. At the end the film asks whether the waiter has any real talent, but we already know the answer. The period was sent up by Stan Freberg, whose character

Clyde Ankle is discovered on his front porch. I quote from memory:

'Hey, kid, ya wanna be a star?'
'Who, me? But I can't sing.'
'Believe me, kid, that don't matter . . .'

The Cameo and Parkway labels were formed by songwriters Karl Mann and Bernie Lowe; they issued recordings by Charlie Gracie, also from Philadelphia, a good guitarist with a rockabilly vocal style who had only three hits, all in 1957, including 'Butterfly'. Bobby Rydell (born Ridarelli, in Philadelphia) had played drums in 1956 in a group with Avalon, but was a much better singer. His forgettable material did not keep him from having thirty chart hits from 1959 to 1965. Parkway was also Chubby Checker's label. Freddy Cannon (born Picariello, in Massachusetts) had a hit on the Swan label in 1959, 'Tallahassee Lassie', which was written by his mother; Dickie Doo and the Don'ts (Philadelphia) also recorded 'Click-clack' and 'Nee Nee Na Na Na Na Nu Nu' on Swan. In case teenagers did not have enough trouble with puppy love and pimples, the death song arrived and became a genre all its own; the Los Angeles Demon label offered Jody Reynolds on 'Endless Sleep', a top five hit.

Not all the hits were totally devoid of merit, and some had interesting aspects. Jimmy Clanton, from Louisiana, recorded 'Just a Dream', a rockaballad, in New Orleans, with a band that included Huey Smith on piano, Earl King on guitar and Lee Allen on tenor saxophone. But his later hits included 'Venus in Blue Jeans', written by Neil Sedaka. Bobby Vee came to fame because he knew the words to Buddy Holly's songs; his newly formed band replaced Holly in Fargo, North Dakota, when Holly did not make the gig. Among Vee's hits were 'Take Good Care of My Baby', 'Run to Him', 'The Night Has a Thousand Eyes' and 'Rubber Ball', the last co-written with Gene Pitney, whose biggest hit was 'It Hurts To Be In Love'. Then there was Mouseketeer Annette Funicello, who recorded for Disney. Avalon and Funicello were still making beach party movies as late as 1965, but nobody will admit to having seen them.

Most of this material either had an irritatingly monotonous shuffle beat or was saccharine, banal and obvious in its sentiment, or both.

As a body of songs it is beneath consideration and has nothing to do with R&B or rock'n'roll. Yet some of it is now regarded as classic early rock in some quarters, principally because no distinction is made between nostalgia and art. Around 1957 composer Virgil Thomson, one of the most highly respected music critics in American history, spoke at New York's Yale Club:

[A] society must have some vulgarity if it is to have vigor and energy. As for Presley . . . he has never missed an engagement, or given a bad show, and that is the mark of a responsible workman. Twenty years ago, Frank Sinatra created a scandal as Presley does today. Frank Sinatra was at the time a first-class artist-workman and so is Presley.

Rock'n'roll was not the problem. The taste-makers of earlier times were musicians (mainly bandleaders), then the DJs, who played records because they liked them. By 1960 they had abdicated, broadcasting had sold its soul and there was a youth market, encouraged to think that people with talent were kids just like them. What we now call pop music (defined as what we hear on the radio, and including a large amount of 'rock') was invented in the late 1950s in an artistic and commercial vacuum. Layers of this lucrative, faddish rubbish have been accumulating for over thirty years.

16

A Last Gasp of Innocence

As the first wave of rock'n'roll performers was devastated by accidents, racist arrests and other disasters, sales of singles seemed to be falling. Paul Ackerman, music editor of *Billboard*, said that at the end of 1959 only 20 per cent of the dollar volume of the record industry was in singles, and 80 per cent in albums. It must be remembered, too, that singles were not loss leaders for albums in those days; most album artists no longer expected to have hit singles. Presley was in the army and Chuck Berry almost absent from the top forty; when the likes of Fabian had seven hits in 1959, adults had probably stopped buying singles altogether.

But the pop revolution was only taking a breather. During this transitional period people emerged who were at least able to impose a personal stamp and in some cases even integrity on their work. The writing and production of Jerry Leiber and Mike Stoller, the hit factory at Motown in Detroit and the songs of the Brill Building era appealed to the first generation of rock'n'roll fans without excessively pandering to it.

Leiber and Stoller were both from the East Coast, but met in Los Angeles as teenagers. They were enchanted by black culture, including jazz and R&B, and began writing songs for R&B acts, having been helped into the industry by Johnny Otis. Their first hit was 'Hard Times', sung by Charles Brown in 1952, and the same year they wrote 'Kansas City' for Little Willie Littlefield. It was Stoller's idea to write a blues with a melody, rather than use the familiar blues changes. They were working with Ralph Bass, who had taken his Federal label to King in 1951. Bass had produced records by Charlie Parker, Charles Mingus and others, but had most success in R&B; he was described by Peter Guralnick as a 'flamboyant, white jive-talking hepcat'. Bass had been responsible for 'Open the Door, Richard' (1947) and several of the biggest R & B hits of 1950 by Little Esther, among others, 'Sixty-minute Man' by the Dominoes (1951) and 'Work With Me Annie' by the Midnighters (1954); later he discovered James Brown, and worked at Chess in Chicago. He changed the title of 'Kansas City' to 'K. C. Lovin'', but revived with its original title in 1959 by Wilbert Harrison on the tiny Fury label it was a number one pop hit and became a rock classic.

Big Mama Thornton's 'Hound Dog' was the first record Leiber and Stoller produced themselves. They took over the session because their work had sometimes been misrepresented, and on this one they knew how they wanted the drums to sound; Otis was supposed to produce it, but they wanted him on drums. They formed their own Spark label and worked with the Robins, who had had an R & B hit on Savoy as early as 1950. Produced by Leiber and Stoller, the Robins had success on the West Coast with 'Framed' and 'Riot in Cell Block Number Nine', helped by Lester Sill, said to be the world's greatest record salesman; in a record shop he would pull some sand out of his pocket, throw it on the floor and do a sand dance to the record. Sill was the promo man for Modern Records, and had introduced Leiber and Stoller to the Bihari brothers at Modern, to the Messners at Aladdin, to Gene Norman, who ran jazz and blues concerts, and to Bass.

Spark did not have national distribution, but 'Smokey Joe's Café' was picked up by Atlantic for their subsidiary Atco label, became an R & B hit in 1955 and crossed over to pop. The Robins' management was not satisfied with the new arrangements, so Leiber and Stoller formed a hand-picked group called the Coasters, whom they later described as a bunch of comedians. They did what they did with no thought of making history, but above all because it was fun. And the original Coasters – lead singer Carl Gardner and bass Bobby Nunn from the Robins, tenor Leon Hughes and baritone Billy Guy – had as much fun as they did.

The first big hit in May 1957 was a two-sided one: 'Young Blood' reached the top ten, but the flip side rose even higher: 'Searchin'' was an unusual Coasters hit, in that it was done quickly at the end of a recording session, just to make four sides. Most of their recordings should have sounded overproduced, but somehow did not: they were meticulously spliced together from many takes to make a fast, aural cartoon strip. (Leiber and Stoller compared them to little radio plays.) They did as much as anything in the period to transcend race. The funniest and biggest hit was 'Yakety Yak' (1958), about nagging parents and a sassy kid. The father is played by Will 'Dub' Jones's deep voice:

> Don't you give me no dirty looks!
> Your father's hip, he knows what cooks!
> Just tell your hoodlum friends outside
> You ain't got time to take a ride!
> YAKETY YAK!
> Don't talk back!

In 'Charlie Brown' a high-school boy shoots craps in the boys' gym, smokes in the auditorium and complains 'Why is everybody always pickin' on me?' 'Along Came Jones' was about a cowboy movie hero coming to the rescue. Leiber and Stoller said to Ted Fox, 'What could be funnier than a bunch of black cats doing a send-up of a bunch of white cowboys? . . . The most fun we ever had . . . was with the Coasters. We'd be falling on the floor – all of us – staggering around the room holding our bellies because we were laughing so hard.'

After writing hits for Presley, Leiber and Stoller were hired by Jerry Wexler at Atlantic as independent producers, the first such arrangement in the record business. The Drifters had had a string of top ten R&B hits with lead singer Clyde McPhatter, who began a solo career in 1955; the story is that the Drifters had gone cold, but after all those hits, maybe they just wanted more of the money. They had some success in 1956-7, then were re-formed by their manager George Treadwell, who owned the name and distributed the cash. New lead singers included Johnny Moore, Bobby Hendricks and bass-baritone Ben E. King (also a songwriter), who sang the lead on 'There Goes My Baby' in 1959.

Leiber and Stoller produced 'There Goes My Baby', which they wrote under the pseudonym Elmo Glick, along with King and Lover Patterson, and Treadwell took some credit as well. (That kind of payola was still not against the law, and never will be.) 'There Goes My Baby' was the first R&B record to have strings: Stoller invented a line on the piano that needed unison violins and cellos. The beat was a Brazilian *baion*, which Leiber and Stoller had been fond of since 'Anna' in 1953, and thereafter influenced pop music for several years; and timpani were played out of tune by an R&B drummer. It was an experimental date since the planned material had not worked out, and the group seemed to be singing in a different key from the backing; Leiber described the result as sounding like a radio bringing in two different stations at once. Wexler thought it was so bad that he threw a tuna fish sandwich at the wall. But Tommy Dowd, Atlantic's brilliant engineer, tinkered with it, and it became the Drifters' first crossover top ten pop hit, and launched the new, better-known Drifters.

King had started with the Moonglows, and joined the Five Crowns in 1957, who became the new Drifters in 1958; he left the Drifters to pursue a solo career because he was being paid practically nothing. Leiber and Stoller helped him with his 'Stand By Me', a pop hit (and a hit again over twenty-five years later, when it was used in a film of the same title). It was during this period that Leiber and Stoller spent some time at RCA, gave Phil Spector work as a favour to Lester Sill and also helped the Brill Building songwriters with their hits. They would demand rewrites as necessary for the sake of the finished product: Doc Pomus rewrote part of 'Save the Last Dance for Me', the Drifters' first number one pop hit, and Carole King part of 'Up on the Roof', her Drifters hit of 1963.

Leiber and Stoller left Atlantic, had hits on United Artists and then decided to do it themselves, but records on their Daisy and Tiger labels disappeared without trace because they were released during the period of John F. Kennedy's assassination. They formed Red Bird Records in 1964 with George Goldner, and delegated much of the production to George 'Shadow' Morton (another legend of the period). They had hit after hit with girl groups, starting with a spectacular number one, 'Chapel of Love' by the Dixie Cups (written by Jeff Barry, Ellie Greenwich and Phil Spector). The black female trio from New Orleans had five hits in two years, the most interesting being the last, 'Iko Iko', which had a simple call-and-response pattern and a percussive backing, like an African children's song. The Shangri-las, two sets of sisters from a high school in Queens, New York, had eleven hits in three years, including the death song 'Leader of the Pack'. This playlet about a biker boyfriend who gets killed (motorcycle noises and a crash are heard on the record) had an answer song, 'Leader of the Laundromat' by the Detergents (on Roulette, in which Goldner no doubt still had an interest).

Leiber and Stoller grew bored with Red Bird and sold it to Goldner for a dollar. They were already bored with Elvis Presley. They admired his voice and his knowledge of R & B and country music, but they had to shut themselves up in a room to write the songs for the film *Jailhouse Rock* in one afternoon, and after that the films got even worse, so that it was no longer any *fun*. In 1962 they wrote 'I'm a Woman' for Peggy Lee, and later 'Is That All There Is?' (inspired by the Thomas Mann novella *Disillusionment*) which was arranged by Randy Newman, then unknown. Johnny Mercer said to Leiber, 'Kid, you finally wrote a good song.' They had started out with profound admiration for writers like Gershwin and Cole Porter, but thought all the standards had been written. While writing songs for Peggy Lee was not as much easy fun as writing jokes for the Coasters, it may have been more gratifying.

Already famous, and having written perhaps fifty pop hits, in the last twenty-five years Leiber and Stoller have applied their theatrical sense and expanded musical vocabulary to new genres. 'Is That All There Is?' and 'Longings for a Simpler Time' were intended for an experimental play in the 1960s; 'Humphrey Bogart', a send-up of cinema idolatry, and 'I Ain't Here', about a black domestic servant working in a white middle-class home, were both meant for another production in the 1970s. 'Tango', about a murder, was 'provoked' by an obituary for actor Ramon Navarro. 'I've Got Them Feelin' Too Good Today Blues', they said, was 'as simple and straightforward a song of joy as Jerry Leiber is capable of writing'. These and others were recorded by pianist William Bolcom and mezzo-soprano Joan Morris for an album called *Other Songs by Leiber and Stoller* (1978). Bolcom and Morris have made albums of the works of Rodgers and Hart, Gershwin, Berlin and others, as well as collections of hit songs from Edwardian vaudeville and the golden age of Tin Pan Alley –

pretty good company for the men who wrote 'Hound Dog', but of course there was not as much money in it. Most of their erstwhile fans probably thought they had retired.

Phil Spector, Neil Diamond, Neil Sedaka, Barry Mann and Cynthia Weil, Gerry Goffin and Carole King and Jeff Barry and Ellie Greenwich were all born between 1939 and 1942, mostly in New York, and all except Spector became songwriters in the neighbourhood of the Brill Building, at 1619 Broadway in Manhattan, which had been part of the heart of Tin Pan Alley (Fats Waller once had an office there) and became the generic name of an era of pop. It began across the street, where Aldon Music was located. Aldon consisted of Al Nevins and Don Kirshner: Nevins was an experienced older man, originally one of the Three Suns, and Kirshner, not much older than the writers he hired, had the key to the youth market of the period. Most of these writers have also made records: Diamond had thirty-six hits in the *Billboard* pop chart (1966–83); Sedaka, who also plays piano, had thirteen top forty hits (1959–63); Carole King made albums of her own songs.

The time when teenagers, especially girls, went to the record shop and bought the latest record by Perry Como, Frankie Laine or Eddie Fisher, whatever it was and whoever had written the song, was over. Record buyers in the early 1960s became aware of the songwriters and producers (though it was not until the 1970s that *Billboard*, always a few years behind, began to include this information on its charts). The Brill Building era was the beginning of a new singer-songwriter genre, in itself a good thing.

Sedaka (with Howard Greenfield, another successful writer) wrote 'Stupid Cupid' for Connie Francis, a 1958 hit whose irritation quotient was exceeded by 'Lipstick on Your Collar' the next year (by Edna Lewis and George Goehring). Francis has to be mentioned here somewhere, for she had over fifty *Billboard* Hot 100 entries in ten years and represented a transition from the period of early 1950s jingle-pop, with a foot in each camp: her hits were either junk like those named above, or revivals of chestnuts like 'Who's Sorry Now' (1923) and 'Among My Souvenirs' (1928). Her backing groups usually sounded like slick aspirants for a Las Vegas cabaret spot.

Sedaka himself was not much of an improvement. He wrote 'Oh!

Carol' about King (who wrote 'Oh! Neil', which flopped), as well as 'Breaking Up Is Hard To Do'. Neil Diamond was a notch above this, writing 'Sunday and Me' for Jay and the Americans, and later 'I'm a Believer' for the Monkees; he had a duet hit with Barbra Streisand in 1978 with 'You Don't Bring Me Flowers'. He wrote songs for a film of *Jonathan Livingston Seagull* (1973), one of the wettest cultural artefacts of the most self-indulgent period in American history, and for his own remake of *The Jazz Singer* (1980) which was widely panned, but both albums sold very well. Sedaka and Diamond are staples now in the MOR market (which means 'Middle of the Road').

Kirshner was a personal friend of Steve Lawrence and Eydie Gormé, who increasingly appealed to the middle-aged audience both as a duo and separately, and who were hip enough to sing a good song no matter where it came from. Hence Barry Mann (with Hank Hunter) wrote 'Footsteps' for Lawrence, Mann and Weil wrote 'Blame It on the Bossa Nova' for Gormé; Goffin and King wrote 'Go Away, Little Girl', a hit for Lawrence which has been revived several times since, and 'I Want to Stay Here', a duet hit. The successes of the Brill Building era ranged from Jeff Barry's death song 'Tell Laura I Love Her' (for Ray Peterson in 1960) to Mann and Weil's 'You've Lost That Lovin' Feelin'' (for the Righteous Brothers, Bill Medley and Bobby Hatfield, the inventors of blue-eyed soul, in 1964) and Barry, Greenwich and Spector's 'River Deep – Mountain High' (for Ike and Tina Turner, in 1966). Ray Peterson's second and last top ten single, 'Corinna, Corinna' (also 1960), was produced by Phil Spector, because Leiber and Stoller were busy, and the Hatfield and Turner tracks were Spector's as well. Those six years represent the rise and fall of Spector, who was the other producer, with Leiber and Stoller, of the girl groups, a genre all by itself.

Spector began in high school in Los Angeles with the Teddy Bears, writing and singing in a trio. 'To Know Him, Is To Love Him', an extremely slow, mournful song suggested by the inscription on his father's tombstone, became a huge pop hit in 1958. He worked with Lester Sill and Lee Hazlewood in Phoenix. Hazlewood was another successful producer of the period who, with session guitarist Al Casey, began experimenting with studio techniques; they were the ones who recorded Sanford Clark's 'The Fool', leasing it to Dot. They formed the Jamie label and developed minimalist guitarist Duane Eddy, who obligingly played melodies (such as they were) on the bass strings while the sound was drenched in echo; the biggest of twenty Eddy hits was 'Rebel Rouser'. The production gimmicks that Hazlewood was developing were useful to Spector when he went east to work with Leiber and Stoller. Among other things, he wrote Ben E. King's hit 'Spanish Harlem' with Leiber, but he walked out on his contract with them, using as an excuse the fact that he had been a minor when he signed it.

Spector then formed the Philles label with Sill, for which Johnny Mathis's manager Helen Noga put up the money. The first release was 'There's No Other (Like My Baby)' by the Crystals, a female vocal quintet from Brooklyn, which reached the top twenty. At the same time Spector had taken an A&R job at Liberty; after learning that Liberty was going to record Gene Pitney's 'He's a Rebel' with Vikki Carr, he beat them into the shops with the Crystals, and the sixth release on Philles reached number one. Of the first twenty Philles numbers, at least fifteen were hits, which would have been an astonishing achievement in any decade; Spector bought out his partners and was a millionaire at the age of twenty-one.

Part of his success was due to his instinct that the day of the girl groups had arrived, and part to his production style. Some of the Crystals' recordings ('He's a Rebel' among them) were not by the Crystals at all; Bob B. Soxx and the Blue Jeans had Darlene Love singing lead, who was also a solo artist and lead singer on some of the Crystals' recordings. The Ronettes were a trio who had worked professionally since junior high school, and sang back-up for Spector. He fell in love with Veronica Bennett, the lead singer, and did his best to make a star out of her. Eight of the Ronettes' records made the Hot 100, but only 'Be My Baby' the top twenty. (He was married to Ronnie from 1966 to 1975.)

Spector overproduced on purpose. 'Uptown', written by Mann and Weil, had an interesting theme: a boy who might be black works downtown in a menial job, but he is nothing there; when he goes uptown, where the real people live, to visit his girlfriend, she makes him feel important. Kirshner didn't like it, but the Crystals took it into the top fifteen; the backing consisted of strings, a strummed mandolin, castanets, flamenco guitar, a feisty bass part and sandpaper blocks. Few noticed that it had no drums. But it was with Barry, Greenwich and Spector's songs 'Da Doo Ron Ron (When He Walked Me Home)' followed by 'Then He Kissed Me' that Spector's 'wall of sound' was perfected. He jammed a studio so full of instruments and musicians that there was nowhere to move; he wanted to record everything in one take, reserving overdubs for repeating sounds, just to make them bigger. He did plenty of that; in those days overdubs created a good deal of tape hiss, but that could be covered up with echo. The result, combined with the songs, made a complete melodrama in less than three minutes. The sound grabbed the listener; it was compelling as it came out of the era's tiny transistor radios, but it was not a good model and has dated badly. The engineer and the producer traditionally tried to make the best recording they could, so that a great many records made over sixty years ago can still sound good today, but Spector's records still sound like they are trying to come out of a tiny, tinny speaker. You feel instant nostalgia for the period if you are the right age, but the music does not breathe, and becomes claustrophobic.

Carole King and Gerry Goffin's 'The Loco-motion' was a hit for Little Eva (Boyd), their babysitter; they were amused by a dance she did while they were playing the piano at home. It hit the charts the day after Eva's seventeenth birthday. Goffin and King were probably the most talented of the Brill Building crowd. Aldon's house label was Dimension, and 'Loco-motion' appeared on that label, as did King and Goffin's 'Chains' by the Cookies (which was soon covered by the Beatles).

One of their best was 'Will You Love Me Tomorrow' (1960) for the Shirelles. A daring song for the time, it addressed a real problem, as opposed to puppy love: the girl wants to give her boyfriend what he wants, but will he still be around after she has lost her 'reputation'? The Shirelles were a black quartet, and almost the only girl group of the era not created by either Leiber and Stoller or Phil Spector (although Leiber and Stoller produced some of their records). Their manager, Florence Greenberg, issued 'I Met Him On a Sunday', which they had written themselves, on her tiny Tiara label; having been picked up by Decca, it was a minor hit in 1958, the beginning of the girl group genre. Greenberg formed the Scepter label and the group had twenty-five more hits, including 'Dedicated to the One I Love' (which was written by Lowman Pauling of the '5' Royales – though Ralph Bass was also credited – and revived a few years later by the Mamas and the Papas) and 'Baby It's You', by Mack David and Burt Bacharach (also covered by the Beatles).

Bacharach soon teamed with Mack's brother, Hal David. They wrote a great many songs for Dionne Warwick, who was also a Scepter artist and had thirty-eight hits on that label, beginning in 1962 with Bacharach and David's 'Don't Make Me Over'. Bacharach and David are often included in the Brill Building set, but they outlived it; some of their songs became cabaret classics and used a wider musical vocabulary than that to which pop was already restricting itself. Many of the records of the era, in fact, written by and aimed exclusively at young people (Goffin and King had married at nineteen and were writing from personal experience), have a sameness and a lack of adventure about them – they often suggest the shuffle beat that seemed to be the arranger's favourite in those years, and in any case the cluttered production tends to preclude any chance of swing. In Spector's production of Darlene Love's '(Today I Met) the Boy I'm Gonna Marry', written by Ellie Greenwich and Tony Powers, and a top forty hit in 1963, a glockenspiel delicately accompanies the vocal; Spector, who had begun his career as a teenager himself (and perhaps remained one), understood the lies that kids allowed themselves to believe. But the songs are sometimes better than the records. Goffin and King went on to write '(You Make Me Feel Like) a Natural Woman' for Aretha Franklin, one of the classics of the soul era, which was already under way.

Mann and Weil's 'You've Lost That Lovin' Feelin'' (1964), recorded by the Righteous Brothers, presaged the soul era. Although Hatfield and Medley were white boys, they had the right feeling; the record was number one for two weeks, and almost reached the top of the black chart as well. Their versions of 'Just Once in My Life', 'Unchained Melody' and 'Ebb Tide', full of soul even in Spector's production, also did well in both charts. They left Spector, saying that they wanted more control over their own work, and never did as well again.

Meanwhile, the experienced Ike Turner had met Annie Mae Bullock, married her in 1958 and developed the Ike and Tina Turner Revue around her. Their black hits began to cross over, and Spector produced them on 'River Deep – Mountain High', which he co-wrote with Barry and Greenwich. Perhaps the song and its title were too obscure for the pop market; perhaps Spector had made many enemies. It was claimed that the record was too black for white radio and too white for black radio. It stalled at number eighty-eight in the pop chart, and Spector, resentful and increasingly reclusive, effectively retired, and has since been only intermittently active.

In the spring of 1963, after sweeping the BMI awards, Nevins and Kirshner sold Aldon Music to Columbia Pictures–Screen Gems, and Kirshner took over Colpix Records. Mini-eras in pop were ending almost as soon as they began, while Kirshner began his descent into complete banality. If it was not true in the late 1950s that the people who were buying rock'n'roll records had zero per cent of the nation's buying power, it was true by the late 1960s that Kirshner and others were selling comic-strip records to pre-teen children by groups that did not even exist. Jeff Barry thought of the songs they were all writing in the early 1960s as 'ear candy'; he took his craftsmanship to Kirshner's Hollywood bubble-gum empire, and wrote 'Sugar, Sugar' for the Archies, who were cartoon characters. In 1969 it was the fastest-selling single in RCA's history.

Barry Mann was disappointed by the fate of 'Only in America', which he had written for the Drifters: 'Only in America, land of opportunity, do they save the seat in the back of the bus just for me.' Jerry Wexler made him rewrite it to the effect that only in America can anybody become president. The Drifters recorded it, but R & B DJs would not play it. It was finally a hit for Jay and the Americans, a white group.

Gerry Goffin thought that 'Go Away Little Girl', originally written for Bobby Vee, 'should have died in the closet . . . I was never happy with the song, but I am happy with the money I received on it.' Early on he asked himself, 'Am I going to have to write this shit until I'm thirty-two?' But by the time he was thirty-two the era was over, and they had all moved on to other things. As with Leiber and Stoller, Goffin's later work included biting lyrics and adult emotions; if America had had anything like the thriving Broadway stage it had once had, some of these people might have continued to be the voices of their generation, as both they and their contemporaries matured. Carole King's style as pianist and vocalist was an acquired taste, but there was no denying the wide popularity of her songs, and the singer-songwriter genre remained important for a decade. In the meantime, other things were happening, in England, in Newport, once again in Memphis and, most immediately, in Detroit.

No one could have predicted that an unskilled car-factory worker one generation removed from the cotton fields would be one of the most successful black businessmen in American history; nor that black music would invent its own brand of pop, immeasurably popular with the white audience, and still loved by it decades later. Berry Gordy left school at the age of sixteen to become a professional boxer, after working out with a Golden Gloves winner named Jackie Wilson, but his light weight kept him from being a contender. He later worked in his father's printing and plastering businesses, and frequented Detroit clubs at night. He had a jazz record shop in 1953 but went broke because Detroiters did not want jazz, but rhythm and blues; so in 1955 Gordy joined a Ford assembly line for $86.40 a week. And he began writing songs.

When Clyde McPhatter left Billy Ward's Dominoes to join the Drifters in 1953, he was replaced by Jackie Wilson. Gordy's old sparring partner became a soloist in 1957 and had hits with three Gordy songs: 'Reet Petite', 'That Is Why (I Love You So)' and 'I'll Be Satisfied'. Gordy was still an inexperienced writer, but Wilson's genuinely warm personality, his crowd-pleasing act and, above all, his big, beautiful and supple voice made him a star. 'Reet Petite' is not much of a song, and the big-band backing on the record has dated, but the joy in Wilson's glorious voice is unforgettable.

Wilson was a hard worker, and after suffering a massive heart attack on stage he remained in a coma for eight years before he died; 'Reet Petite' was reissued for a number one hit in Britain in 1986. As Nelson George points out in his history of the Motown sound, *Where Did Our Love Go?* (1985), the records included elements both lyrical and musical which would later become part of the hallmark Motown sound, for example, the use of the tambourine on the drum beat. George notes that 'the lyric of "That Is Why" is full of specifics about relationships, something Gordy would later preach'.

But as any writer will tell you, having a few hits does not bring in vast amounts of money. With the help of his second wife, Raynoma Liles, who had been a musical child prodigy, Gordy went into production; their Rayber Voices were available for backing. Detroit vocalist Mary Johnson's 'Come to Me' was Berry Gordy's first release, on Tamla 101. It was picked up by the United Artists label in early 1959, and reached the top thirty of the pop chart, and the top ten of the R & B chart; among other Gordy and Johnson records were 'You Got What It Takes' and 'I Love the Way You Love' (1959–60). According to George, however, Gordy's income was $27.70 a week in 1959, taking into account $1,000 for 'Lonely Teardrops', one of Wilson's biggest hits.

Gordy's big hit songs were earning him a fraction of what he earned on a Ford assembly line; that is what the music business is still like, the business that Gene Lees scolds and Joe Smith defends. Billy Davis and Berry's sister Gwen Gordy had started the Anna label, named for another sister, which was distributed by Chess in Chicago; 'Money (That's What I Want)', by Barrett Strong, became their biggest hit, and they kept more of the profits, because the song was co-written by Gordy and the record produced by him as well. The next step was clear: forming Motown.

The first release from Tamla-Motown in mid-1959 was 'Way Over There', by Smokey Robinson and the Miracles; Amos Milburn, Mabel John (sister of R & B Star Little Willie John) and Singing Sammy Ward generated cash with regional hits; in 1960 the Miracles' 'Shop Around' was number one in the R & B chart and two in the pop chart, and the company never looked back, becoming the success story of the new decade: it had 110 singles in the pop top ten between 1961 and 1971. Gordy's accomplishment was to become more successful than Mitch Miller in the previous decade, and there are more areas of comparison than just record sales. Gordy's hand was as firm on the tiller as Miller's had ever been, and on the till; he had learned from his father the importance of hard work and attention to the bottom line. Berry Gordy, Sr, had come from a family of rural entrepreneurs who were too good for Georgia, where clever blacks often came to a violent end. When he first arrived in Detroit in the 1920s, he bought a house which soon had to be condemned, but that was the last time anybody ever cheated him. Diana Ross, Marvin Gaye, Smokey Robinson and Stevie Wonder had a hit in 1979 with 'Pops, We Love You (a Tribute to Father)', on Gordy Sr's ninetieth birthday.

The new record company became a family operation; Pops gave good advice, selected close friends were allowed in the door, and the boss made the rules. None of the Motown hits of the 1960s was certified gold, because not even the Record Industry Association of America was allowed to see the books. No talent manager would have accepted the contractual conditions that Motown artists did; it is true that the staff and the artists were paid salaries even when they were not working, but some of the artists continued being paid a salary when their records were selling in the millions.

Harvey Fuqua had formed the Moonglows in Cleveland in 1951; as vocalist, writer and producer he had been responsible for many a hit when he came to Detroit, bringing young Marvin Gaye with him. Like all small labels, Fuqua's faced the problem of how to pay for more pressings of a hit when the money came in so slowly from the distributors. Fuqua married Gwen Gordy and Gaye married Anna; they all joined the family firm, while another sister worked in the billing department.

A & R director was William 'Mickey' Stevenson, who had earlier failed to get the local black bourgeoisie to invest in a black Motortown record company. He knew that the product had to be polished to be successful, and that jazz musicians were more skilful than bluesmen. Local musicians became Motown staff members and worked for less than scale on the promise (hardly kept) that they would be able to make jazz recordings as well. Barney Ales, vice-president in charge of distribution, was the only white person on the staff. He knew distributors all over the Midwest and how to deal with them; he and Gordy were close friends, and if some of the distributors thought at first that the company was run by whites, that was good for business.

Gordy had met seventeen-year-old Smokey Robinson in 1957 and changed the name of his group from the Matadors to the Miracles. The first recording by Smokey and the Miracles was 'Got a Job' (an answer to the Silhouettes' 1958 hit 'Get a Job'), which Gordy had placed on the End label. Smokey, a bookish boy, had been writing poems and songs for years, and his love songs made him the favourite poet of a whole generation of Americans; the Miracles had nearly fifty Hot 100 pop hits in fifteen years. The Temptations, originally called the Primes, with such sensational co-lead singers as Eddie Kendricks and David Ruffin (whose brother Jimmy also had soul hits), remain perhaps the best-loved male vocal group of their generation, and had over fifty hits between 1964 and 1986. The Supremes, first called the Primettes, came from a Detroit housing project to become the most famous girl group of all: both with and without Diana Ross, they had forty-five hits from 1962 to 1976 (including those with the Four Tops or the Temptations); of seventeen top ten hits between 1964 and 1969, eleven reached number one. The Four Tops were formed in Detroit in 1954 as the Four Aims. Levi Stubbs, Renaldo 'Obie' Benson, Lawrence Payton and Abdul 'Duke' Fakir refused to be typecast, leaving Motown and later returning. Basically a first-class cabaret act, they had forty-four pop hits before 1983 and are still performing today in their original line-up.

Martha Reeves was a secretary at Motown; already an experienced singer, she sang in the backing group on Marvin Gaye's recordings, then formed a trio, Martha and the Vandellas, which had twenty-three hits on the Gordy label in eight years. Their 'Dancing in the Street' was number two in 1964, the year of the riots in America's ghettos; nothing more or less than a joyous pop anthem, it was suspected by American puritans of being an incitement to insurrection. The favourite Motown star of all may be Mary Wells, said to be the first to record on Motown, whose thirteen hits in four years included 'My Guy', written and produced by Smokey Robinson. Unable to take Gordy's patronizing attitude, she left in 1964 and had hits on several other labels. Gladys Knight and the Pips, a family group from Atlanta, first recorded for Brunswick when Gladys was fourteen; by the mid-1980s they had had over forty hits, mostly on Gordy's Soul label, among them their majestic 'I Heard It Through the Grapevine' (1967).

The Jackson Five were a male quintet managed by their father, and began in Gary, Indiana, in 1967, when the youngest, Michael, was only nine. It may have been Gladys Knight who recommended them to Motown, but Gordy gave the credit to Diana Ross. They were one of the biggest acts in show business during the 1970s, and their first four singles in 1969–70 all reached number one. After leaving Motown for Epic in 1976, they had to call themselves the Jacksons, because Gordy had tied up the name. Little Stevie Wonder, born blind in Detroit, signed with Tamla-Motown when he was ten; he played harmonica, sang back-up and was the office prankster, but he was learning all the time. His hits began in 1963 and had totalled over ninety by 1993; he is still with the firm. And there were hits by Junior Walker and the All Stars, the Marvelettes, the Velvelettes, the Contours, the Isley Brothers, Brenda Holloway and others.

Eddie Holland looked like becoming another Sam Cooke; his 'Jamie' was a top ten R&B hit and reached the top thirty in the pop chart in 1962. But he hated performing, and started writing and producing with his brother Brian and Lamont Dozier. The legend 'Holland–Dozier–Holland' appeared under the title on scores of Motown records, including seventeen hits in a row for the Supremes. They fought with Gordy for royalties and left on bad terms; the husband and wife team of (Nickolas) Ashford and (Valerie) Simpson took up some of the slack, writing duet hits for Marvin Gaye and Tammi Terrell, and for Diana Ross when she began her solo career.

The Motown show had soon gone on the road, promoting the records but also generating income which helped make up for late payments from distributors. Strict conditions of behaviour were laid down and an eye was kept on expenses; the acts were taught manners, deportment and stagecraft by Maxine Powell, who ran a Detroit finishing school, and Cholly Atkins, a legendary Broadway choreographer who was teaching nearly every act that appeared at the Apollo: he knew that Motown was a black-owned company and wanted to see it grow.

There were tragedies along the way. Drummer Benny Benjamin

and especially bass player James 'Jamie' Jamerson created some of the most influential pop sounds of the decade, but both had fatal weaknesses for alcohol. Florence Ballard, co-founder and original lead singer of the Supremes, was squeezed out when she resented Gordy's grooming of Diana Ross for greater stardom; her solo career failed and she died of drug abuse. But the greatest tragedy was that of Marvin Gaye.

Stevie Wonder and Gaye were the only Motown artists to get their own way in the Gordy empire. When Wonder turned twenty-one the company owed him a lot of money, and it became apparent how much he had learned over the years: he was the master of increasingly sophisticated studio techniques. (Whether this is a good thing is debatable: in 1988 one of Wonder's concerts had to be postponed when somebody swiped his Synclavier discs containing backing tracks.) He soon dictated his terms to Berry Gordy, who would have been a fool not to accept them.

Gaye had duet hits with Tammi Terrell, among others; a beautiful girl with a wonderful voice, she died of a brain tumour in 1970 in her early twenties. After this shattering blow Gaye wanted to make concept albums, both brooding and personal and also containing social statements: *What's Going On* (1971) reached number six in the *Billboard* album chart (and three of its singles were hits) and *Let's Get It On* (1973) reached number two. But Gaye lacked self-confidence; he was dominated by his father, a fundamentalist clergyman and a transvestite. One of Gaye's wives was Janis Hunter, Slim Gaillard's daughter; Slim recalled Marvin's father coming downstairs in the middle of the night 'wearing a dress, with lipstick on, and carrying one of those little dogs. It was a real strange house to be in.' Marvin's life ended when his father shot him in 1984.

The production on the classic Motown hits is very tight and busy, designed like Phil Spector's to sound good on a car radio or a teenager's radio; yet they are not as claustrophobic. In the days of eight-track rather than twenty-four-track recording, Motown pioneered then difficult recording techniques which were soon widely used, such as 'punching', whereby a vocal or a saxophone solo could be brought up or down or covered by a new take. In the early days the easiest way to do this was to cut the tape, so two tapes were made of everything, for safety. The resulting hits are a goldmine – good songs, good singing and slick production that never loses that R & B feeling in the beat. The connection with Detroit clubs and Detroit housing projects is always evident; the people who made these records could never forget where they came from. It is often hard to tell how good the hits sound when they are remastered; a compact disc available in Europe called *Motown's Greatest Artists: The Most-played Oldies on America's Jukeboxes* has the virtue of beginning with Gladys Knight and the Pips' 'I Heard It Through the Grapevine' (written by Norman Whitfield and Barrett Strong) and ending with Marvin Gaye's even bigger hit on the same tune (later used to sell raisins). But some of the tracks are better in the mono mode, which in turn sounds like an entirely different mix. Some fans say nothing is as good as the original 45 singles.

Gordy moved his empire to Los Angeles in 1971, and his dabbling in films was less than successful. The company grossed $40 million in 1973, but by then the glory years were over. Gordy signed a distribution deal with MCA in 1988, effectively giving up control; but nothing lasts for ever. Stevie Wonder, Diana Ross and Michael Jackson, among the biggest stars in show business, all started out in the Motown stable, and the empire of the one-time Ford worker was the only American pop enterprise that probably did not even notice the British Invasion.

17

The 1960s: A Folk Boom, a British Invasion, the Soul Years and the Legacy of an Era

Like everything else in post-war Britain, popular music was controlled by an ineffective establishment. Rationing of consumer goods went on for many years after the Second World War, as the British desperately tried to be polite to one another rather than allowing the market to do its work. This contributed to a continuing British drabness while the Germans and the Japanese were well on the way to recovery.

Which musics would make money in Britain was decided by this establishment through the BBC; as a result, popular music was a mixture inherited from the British variety tradition of music hall.

Pianist Winifred Atwell, whose cheerful keyboard hits from 1952 included 'Britannia Rag', 'Coronation Rag', 'Let's Have a Party' and 'Let's Have Another Party', was perhaps typical of this. Venezuelan-born drummer Edmundo Ros had recorded on drums with Fats Waller in London in 1938; his Latin dance band, said to be one of Princess Margaret's favourites, had a hit in the USA in 1950 with 'The Wedding Samba'. In 1952 Vera Lynn, the most popular British vocalist during the war, reached number one in the USA with her British top ten hit 'Auf Wiederseh'n'. Arranger-conductor Frank Chacksfield's lush instrumentals 'Limelight' and 'Ebb Tide' were hits in 1953, and David Whitfield's operatic voice reached the USA top ten with 'Cara Mia' in 1954, backed by Mantovani. All of these were on the London label in America, aided by excellent sound, but in general British pop music was not exported; Alma Cogan had her own UK television show, but she is remembered as much for her gowns as for her voice. American stars like Johnnie Ray, Rosemary Clooney, Frankie Laine, Perry Como and the rest were so popular in Britain that it was noteworthy when British vocalist Dickie Valentine sold out the London Palladium.

The big band of trombonist Ted Heath, formed in 1944 and one of the best of the post-war era, at various times boasted such fine musicians as drummer Jack Parnell, trombonist Don Lusher, trumpeter Kenny Baker and tenor saxophonist Ronnie Scott. Valentine was the band's vocalist, and later a solo success: among his biggest hits was a cover of Frankie Avalon's 'Venus'. Heath's band had a few hit singles in the early 1950s, but in general the Big Band Era was over in Britain as it was in the USA.

British jazz fans had a hard time of it, because until 1956 the British musicians' union would not allow American musicians to perform in Britain unless there was a reciprocal opportunity in the USA for British musicians. Visiting American stars might have made news and generated enthusiasm for the music in general; home-grown British jazz musicians did not have much work anyway, and wanted to see their heroes in action and perhaps get a chance to play with them. But when Charlie Parker, Coleman Hawkins and others toured Europe, they could not work in Britain, for the government let the unions call the shots. It was only in instrumental music that this discrimination was practised; as in the USA during the musicians' union strikes, pop singers came and went freely.

As rhythm and blues began to have its influence in the USA, it was not heard on the radio in Britain, and few American blacks toured there at first, except for a small number of bluesmen who were seen as folk artists. The British Isles are rich in folk heritages, but unlike the rural musics of America, British folk forms never became urbanized and commercial. This is part of the reason why American country music has always had as big a following in Britain as the indigenous folk music, if not bigger. While Americans sold their popular culture down the river, Britain stood at the opposite extreme: if there was any hint of payola on the BBC, the artist and the song publisher would be banned for a year. But musical conservatism caused pressure to build up. British kids were fascinated by rock'n'roll, but they had to hear it on Radio Luxembourg or on pirate radio.

In the early 1960s the BBC offered the Home Service (chat, public service and cosiness), the Light Programme (entertainment) and the Third Programme, which was not just classical music, like Radio 3 today: it was the BBC's finest hour, a showcase of all aspects of European high culture, a sort of university of the air. The widest knowledge of American trends was found in seaports such as Liverpool, where merchant seamen often brought home records that were not played on the BBC, or in London, where a few shops had imported records.

Then on Easter Sunday in 1964 Radio Caroline opened up. *Caroline* (named after President Kennedy's daughter by its operator, Ronan O'Rahilly) and her sister ship, *Mi Amigo*, were anchored in the Channel at opposite ends of Britain, and had an audience of twenty-two million on Sunday mornings. 'They took the music that only London hipsters were listening to,' remembered one old fan, 'all those rare, imported records, and put them where spotty little bozos like me could have their minds twisted.'

The Marine Offences Bill of 1967 made advertising on pirate radio illegal, but by then BBC Radio had transformed itself into Radio 1 for pop-rock, 2 mainly for chat and drama, 3 for classical and 4 for news and chat, some drama and very little music. (There are now also thirty-nine local BBC stations in England, which play some music, and then Radio 5, which at this writing is floundering.) Caroline's more popular D Js found work on the BBC; Caroline reopened in 1973 and limped along until 1989, but its work had been done. Meanwhile it is hard for an American who grew up within range of Dick Biondi on Chicago's WLS to imagine how frustrating radio was to a British kid in the early 1960s, and this goes some way towards explaining the hysteria that eventually occurred.

Jazz in Britain was based on the style of the Swing Era until a New Orleans revival began during the Second World War; George Webb's Dixielanders trained trumpeter Humphrey Lyttelton, who later went more modern. In the 1950s the revival was watered down (as in America) to become 'trad', which had a considerable following. Lyttelton's musical integrity, gigs and recordings with visiting Americans such as Buck Clayton and Buddy Tate have ensured his influence; his only hit single, 'Bad Penny Blues' (1956), however, is inane, repetitious and unrepresentative of his work. Knowing how popular trad was in Britain in those years, one is surprised to learn that there were so few hit singles. It remained a cult until around 1960; American-born film director Richard Lester later became famous directing the Beatles, but his first feature was *It's Trad, Dad!* in 1961. The Temperance Seven had a number one hit that year with 'You're Driving Me Crazy' from 1930 (their trombone player was John R. T. Davies, also a transfer engineer who has been responsible for an uncounted number of excellent transfers to modern master tape of old 78s). Trumpeter Kenny Ball and his Jazzmen had fourteen hits from 1961, perhaps because he led one of the worst trad bands; 'Midnight in Moscow', a Russian tune, was also a success in the USA. Trombonist Chris Barber and his Jazz Band had a big transatlantic hit with 'Petite Fleur', written by Sidney Bechet in 1952, a pretty record, mostly a solo by clarinettist Monty Sunshine, who seemed to imitate Bechet's vibrato but actually sounded more like Boyd Senter, an American dance band leader of the 1920s.

Trad never became a force in British pop, but soon gave rise to another genre that did. Anthony Donegan, from Glasgow, changed his name to Lonnie in homage to bluesman Lonnie Johnson; he played guitar or banjo in trad bands, and began appearing on stage between sets playing what came to be called skiffle. The cheap Spanish guitar, the washboard and the bass made out of a tea-chest and a broom-handle created a do-it-yourself movement, causing countless British schoolboys to take up the guitar.

The word 'skiffle' had already been used in the USA to describe music played by those who were too poor to buy musical instruments and used washboards, jugs and so on instead; 'Hometown Skiffle' (on Paramount, 1929), one of the first samplers, included the Hokum Boys and Blind Lemon Jefferson. Like rock'n'roll in the USA, skiffle was a novelty at first, but it is impossible to underestimate its importance. As one British writer put it, 'A strange bedlam was taking over which had nothing to do with anything we had previously known.' This would not be a bad description of the impact of rock'n'roll in the USA. One of the skiffle hits was a portent of things to come: both Donegan and the Vipers Skiffle Group had hits with 'Don't You Rock Me Daddy-o', written by members of the Vipers, some of whom later turned to electric guitars and became the Shadows, the best-known British rock band of the early 1960s.

Another skiffle hit, with an indefinably sweet sound, was 'Freight Train', by the Charles McDevitt Skiffle Group and singer Nancy Whiskey. It reached the UK top five in 1957 on the Oriole label, an independent soon purchased by CBS to form the basis of CBS UK, and also entered the top forty in the USA. The song had been written by Elizabeth Cotton as a child; Libba was a protégée of the Seeger family. But Donegan was the first and most successful skiffler; in early 1956 his 'Rock Island Line' beat Elvis Presley's 'Heartbreak Hotel' to the British charts by several months. The popular British jazz singer Beryl Bryden played washboard on that record.

Skiffle was easy to satirize. 'Rock Island Line' was also a hit in the USA, where it was sent up by Stan Freberg; in the UK Jim Dale recorded 'Piccadilly Line'. The genre plundered the American folk-songs of Woody Guthrie and Leadbelly, some of which had anteced-ents in Britain to begin with. Donegan's over thirty UK hits included 'Lost John', 'Stewball', 'Cumberland Gap' and 'Grand Coolie Dam', but also his own quintessentially British 'My Old Man's a Dustman' (or 'garbageman', as we said in the USA), and the 1924 hit 'Does Your Chewing Gum Lose Its Flavour on the Bedpost Overnight'. Donegan was another beneficiary of Decca/London's excellent sound, which all through the 1950s was a light-year ahead of RCA's. When he recorded the music hall material, he was accused by folk purists of selling out.

'Freight Train' had been introduced to Britain by Peggy Seeger, whose husband, Ewan MacColl, was born James Miller, of Scottish parents, in the English town of Salford, and grew up there at a time when the social attitude of 'us and them' was the only realistic one to take. He learned proletarian songs from his parents, and took the name of an obscure Scottish poet. In those days what is still called the working class in Britain was inclined to try to better itself; MacColl spent much time reading in public libraries, joined the Communist Party and spent the rest of his life making a case for the proletariat. With his first wife, Joan Littlewood, he formed a theatre workshop in London in 1945, and became a highly regarded playwright. He later turned to folk music with Seeger, his third wife; he wrote some fine songs, among them 'Dirty Old Town', based on his memories of Salford, which was covered by Rod Stewart, and 'The First Time Ever I Saw Your Face', a love song for Seeger, which was a number one hit in the USA for Roberta Flack in 1972 and has become a cabaret standard (partly because it was included in Clint Eastwood's film *Play Misty for Me*). Through all his various activities and workshops, including documentaries on radio about the working class and its music, MacColl had become one of the most important British 'folkies'.

MacColl and Seeger were delighted with skiffle. Young people making their own music could be influenced by the songs of their ancestors, and indeed a folk revival seemed to be happening, in the USA as well as in the UK. Alan Lomax, son of the pioneering folklorist John Lomax, lived in Britain during the 1950s, and gave some encouragement. Ramblin' Jack Elliott, a singing cowboy from Brooklyn and Woody Guthrie acolyte, spent most of the 1950s in Europe, especially England, where his guitar playing influenced folk music. And in the 1950s some Americans still followed the peripatetic fortunes of the Weavers.

Children always love folksongs, which are easy to remember, easy to sing and seem to be about things that matter. Such musicians as Pete Seeger, Burl Ives, Oscar Brand, Ed McCurdy and Win Stracke ('Chicago's Minstrel') often worked for and with children. Some of these artists were not taken in by the cranks in the American Communist Party: Ives testified before the House Un-American Activities Committee about the party's attempts to co-opt folk music for its own ends; Canadian-born Brand refused to testify and was not subpoenaed. MacColl was chairman of the Pete Seeger Committee in London in 1961 during the period when Seeger was being persecuted. It is a nasty paradox for those who love both music and freedom that while the USSR devoted resources to researching and preserving its multitude of folk styles before they disappeared, the Library of Congress's archive needed private donations, and Pete Seeger, collecting songs around the world, was blacklisted.

Folkish sounds had occasionally been heard in US pop during the

1950s. Harry Belafonte's cabaret-style calypso was very successful; his 1956 album, which was number one for thirty-one weeks, included 'Banana Boat (Day-o)', of which there were half a dozen hit versions. Since an increasing number of people from the Caribbean were settling in Britain, and especially London, real calypso could be heard there. One of the most attractive US hits of the period was 'Summertime, Summertime', by the Jamies, a quartet led by Tom Janison, who wrote the song; its combination of bounce and almost medieval harmony made the top forty twice. Around 1960 *Continental Café* on Chicago's Channel 9 regularly presented international folk dancers and singers, among them the young Judy Collins.

Folk music goes in and out of fashion; by the late 1980s it was in fashion once again, included in 'roots' music. When folk music is not in fashion, it is always there on obscure labels in specialist shops for those who want it, and those who do not want it are people who have no souls. In October 1990 on a BBC TV programme about MacColl, a year after his death, Peggy Seeger, accompanied by her own autoharp and a discreet background guitar, sang 'Thoughts of Time': it was one of the most frankly and directly beautiful musical moments I have ever seen on television.

The folk act that made the biggest stir in the late 1950s was the Kingston Trio, three Californian boys who deflected the left-wing taint attached in America to folksingers by wearing matching short-sleeved shirts and short haircuts. Their whole act was so slick that purists dismissed them, but their intent was honest enough; their first and biggest hit, in 1958, was a real folk-song, 'Tom Dooley', about a man who was hanged for murder in 1866. When Dave Guard, who wrote 'Scotch and Soda', later a cabaret staple, left the group and formed the Whiskey Hill Singers with Judy Henske, he was replaced by John Stewart, still a highly regarded singer-songwriter today. The Kingston Trio eventually had six alumni, seventeen Hot 100 singles and over thirty albums. They inspired the Brothers Four, the Highwaymen and other such groups, including perhaps the Limeliters: Glen Yarbrough, Lou Gottlieb and Alex Hassilev were good singers with an amusing cabaret act who had only one minor hit single, but ten chart albums in four years from 1961. Clearly there was a market hungry for folk, even if it was urban folk.

In 1959 the Kingston Trio were booked for the first Newport Folk Festival, where they were outclassed by the likes of Pete Seeger, Earl Scruggs, Sonny Terry and Brownie McGhee, John Jacob Niles, Jean Ritchie, Brand and McCurdy. Niles, one of the patriarchs of folk music, presented old songs in a formal style rather than as early hillbilly music. Jean Ritchie was born in a Kentucky family of fourteen. Her parents collected songs, and were visited by English folklorist Cecil Sharpe in 1922, five years before Jean was born; in the 1930s the family was recorded by John and Alan Lomax. Later Jean was on the board of directors of the original Newport Folk Festival.

The sensation at Newport in 1959 and 1960, however, must have been Joan Baez, whose first albums on Vanguard, made in 1960–61, reached high in the *Billboard* chart, and were followed by live concert sets which did even better. Born in 1941, Baez was a revelation for her own generation, playing acoustic guitar and in a silvery soprano singing straight unfussy versions of Child ballads (collected by Francis James Child in the nineteenth century) and similar material, such as the Scottish border song 'Mary Hamilton' and 'House Carpenter' (from the 'daemon lover' genre). 'Wildwood Flower' was a Carter Family song, the melody of which Woody Guthrie had used for his 'Reuben James' (about a disaster at sea). Baez's contemporaries also knew that the compilers of blacklists had had their day: she sang Guthrie's 'Pretty Boy Floyd', and Malvina Reynolds's 'What Have They Done to the Rain?' Thus in popular music the new decade began with chart success for Motown on the one hand, as black pop was coming of age, and folk music which was not preserved in aspic on the other.

After fighting for democracy during the war, Seeger had started People's Songs, Inc., to publish songs, which was taken seriously by the FBI. In May 1947 the United States Army's *Weekly Domestic Intelligence Summary* listed PSI as a communist front. In September its tiny staff was joined by Irwin Silber, a left-wing college kid who was sounder on radical theory than on compassion. When Leadbelly died in 1949 he was on welfare, but Silber complained about Seeger misusing Leadbelly's music when the Weavers had their hit with 'Goodnight Irene' in 1950; Leadbelly's widow was taking in laundry, and no doubt did not misuse the money. The American far left had long been dominated by people like Silber. With the Communist Party marginalized, its membership and its ties with the unions shrinking, Seeger drifted away, hoping that the fundamental democracy implicit in folk music would seep through to the people. This did not prevent him from being victimized by paranoia on both left and right; while he was building a house with his own hands during this period, living through the first winter in New York State without any heat and feeding his family on beans, his former comrades and others kept a rumour going that he had a lavish estate on the Hudson. But his aim was to get America singing, and during the 1950s he flitted from one meeting hall or college campus to another, often coming and going before the local patriots could organize themselves to keep him out. Whatever his views on communism, his musical instinct was correct: when the Weavers sang 'Rock Island Line', the Senate Internal Security Subcommittee investigated them for sedition; when Lonnie Donegan had a hit with the same song a few years later, the only result was a Freberg send-up. The USA had survived the internal communist menace, and also a tendency towards Stalinist show trials.

The songbook *Sing Out!* was edited by Silber from 1951 to 1967. When Seeger visited England in 1961, he was impressed with the number of topical songs being written; he went home and formed *Broadside*. By then the coffee houses of New York City were hothouses of folk-oriented singer-songwriters: Jack Elliott, Phil Ochs, Eric Andersen, David Blue, Dave Van Ronk, Tim Hardin, Eric Von Schmidt and Bob Dylan were soon joined by Tom Paxton, Tom Rush, Arlo Guthrie, John Prine, Steve Goodman, Loudon Wainwright, Canadians Buffy Sainte-Marie, Ian and Sylvia and scores more, many of whom had songs published in *Sing Out!* or *Broadside*. The greatest of all these was Dylan, who was introduced by Joan Baez at the Newport Folk Festival in 1963.

Like almost everyone else of his generation, Dylan had grown up cut off from the pre-war history of popular music, listening to Little Richard and Buddy Holly; maybe he really did play piano with Bobby Vee. He certainly valued Hank Williams and Woody Guthrie; he made his way to New York and joined the folk boom while still a teenager. The only category he could fit into was the category of people who come from nowhere; his home town of Hibbing, Minnesota, had no 'other' side of the tracks. The mainstream music business that had tried to ignore Elvis Presley meant nothing to him at first; he went to the East Coast because that was where Woody Guthrie was.

Some people thought that Dylan had the solution to the banal hypocrisy of the post-war era. He had a relatively small number of fans; of about thirty albums in the twenty-five years from 1962, only two were certified as million-sellers. But crazies picked through his garbage, urban terrorists named themselves after a phrase in a Dylan lyric, college professors lectured on Dylan's words, and they all missed the point. One of Dylan's intellectual predecessors was a radical union leader early in the century, Eugene V. Debs, who told a cheering crowd of railway workers that if they needed him to lead them into the promised land, somebody else would lead them right back out again. Dylan never intended to tell anyone what to think; the only thing he understood was that there is nothing to be understood, that there are no rules and no answers except those that come from within us as individuals. That is what freedom ultimately means; but this was not convenient for a generation who became consumers in the end, like every generation, and wanted their politics off the shelf, like breakfast food.

Dylan was ignored by Folkways, Vanguard and Elektra, the primary folk labels of the early 1960s, but was signed to Columbia by John Hammond. His first album in early 1962 was a straight folk album, described by a Columbia record salesman as a 'piece of shit'. (It should have included 'Talking John Birch Society Blues', but Columbia would not allow it.) The second album, *The Freewheelin' Bob Dylan*, consisted almost entirely of originals: 'Blowin' in the Wind', 'A Hard Rain's a-Gonna Fall' and a few others made him a 'protest singer', though in retrospect were merely pithy observations. Everybody was writing anti-war songs, like Dylan's 'Masters of War', or 'Talkin' World War III Blues'. 'The answer, my friend, is blowin' in the wind,' Dylan wrote, and it still is. He changed nothing, but never said he would.

Dylan did what Cole Porter had done in a very different decade, and for a very different audience. He combined cadences and catch-phrases from everyday speech in such a way that they re-entered the language, but instead of promoting escapism into a world of pent-houses and evening clothes, Dylan offered solace to a generation living on a moral desolation row. We had grown up in an era when many of America's friends were butchers, all breeding chickens which would come home to roost, from Trujillo, Batista and Samoza in our own back yard to generals and potentates in the Middle East and Asia; the threat of nuclear war was becoming tiresome and the Cold War merely good for business. We were tired of it, but could only keep on keepin' on, in spite of the blood on the tracks.

Dylan continued to accompany himself on harmonica and acoustic guitar. His third and fourth albums contained much rich material, and then *Bringing It All Back Home* (1965) included a whole side that seemed to top off Dylan's acoustic era: 'Mr Tambourine Man', 'Gates of Eden', 'It's Alright, Ma (I'm Only Bleeding)' and 'It's All Over Now, Baby Blue' were all masterpieces. But on side one of the album he was backed by an electric rock band. Rock'n'roll came of age with Dylan, just as its element of folk music had been revived.

At a Newport Folk Festival in that period the Paul Butterfield Blues Band was loud and electric, and nobody was bothered, because few in the audience knew anything about the blues anyway. But when Dylan's electric set began, fans as well as the Seegers and the MacColls were outraged, perhaps because they knew that their time was over. Their best songs would live, but their politics had been rendered absurd by history; we may not be able to keep our politicians under control, but we don't have to work on Maggie's farm if we don't want to. Irritated by criticism of his new music, Dylan said, 'Folk music is a bunch of fat people.' Some of the controversy was caused by the endemic problem of electric rock that it is nearly always unnecessarily loud; but for better or worse, among the influences on Dylan were skifflers from Liverpool who spearheaded the British Invasion of 1964.

The Quarrymen, one of countless British schoolboy groups inspired by skiffle and/or rock'n'roll, was formed in Liverpool in 1956 by John Lennon, who named it after his school. Lennon sang and played rhythm guitar; Paul McCartney on rhythm guitar and George

Harrison on lead were added in 1957. In 1958 Lennon's close friend from art school joined; Stuart Sutcliffe could not play at first, but he had money from the sale of a painting which he was willing to spend on a bass guitar. As they evolved from skiffle to rock'n'roll, the group's name changed to Johnny and the Moondogs; for the next incarnation Sutcliffe suggested Beetles, after Buddy Holly's Crickets, and Lennon's predilection for puns finally made them the Beatles. Their first regular drummer was Pete Best, whose broody good looks made him a heart-throb among Liverpool fans.

Like many overnight sensations they served a long apprenticeship, playing in tough seaside clubs in Hamburg, Germany, for prostitutes, drunks and slumming tourists while honing their stagecraft. Like a good number of show business folk, they took amphetamines and other drugs to keep going; the squeaky-clean Beatles of a few years later had little to do with the rough-and-ready English rock'n'roll band that played covers of American hits. They also began writing songs of their own.

In between their Hamburg tours they played hundreds of gigs at the Cavern Club in Liverpool, thereby building up a substantial local following. They had recorded in Germany (produced by bandleader Bert Kaempfert), backing UK pop singer Tony Sheridan on a few tracks which did nothing, but their fans in Liverpool began asking for the imported record. Brian Epstein, manager of the record department of his parents' furniture emporium, was intrigued to learn that they were a local band. He was a middle-class Jewish boy and an unhappy homosexual (at a time when it was still illegal in Britain to be a practising homosexual) and he preferred classical music, but he literally fell in love with the Beatles, and became their manager. The orthodoxy is that Epstein was a poor businessman, but that can only be said with hindsight; nobody predicted the extent of Beatlemania, and, as Lennon put it after Epstein's death from an accidental drug overdose, they never would have made it without him.

Sutcliffe was not a good musician and did not get along with McCartney, who wanted to play bass. He left in 1961 to settle in Hamburg with his German girlfriend, photographer Astrid Kirchherr; he died of a brain tumour, possibly caused by a vicious kick in the head from a hooligan after a 1961 gig in England. Kirchherr had influenced the group's sartorial style, including their haircuts, which though seen as traditional English 'pudding bowl' cuts, were modelled on what upper-class German boys had worn for decades. Kirchherr's photographs represent the beginning of the importance of visual style, which would carry more weight in pop than the music. Her then boyfriend, Klaus Voorman, was also impressed by the group, and became an influential designer of record covers. Epstein forced the boys to sharpen up their act, nagging them about deportment and reliability, and building their image on what Kirchherr had started; then he began trying to get them a recording contract. Decca, among others, turned them down, a mistake that lives in history. Then came an audition with George Martin.

Martin deservedly became one of the most famous producers in history, and was known as the fifth Beatle. He had attended the Guildhall School of Music and worked in the BBC music library before joining Parlophone as an assistant. Parlophone had been an internationally famous record label; in the 1920s it issued records by pianist Claudio Arrau, for example, and was the main British source of jazz records in its Parlophone Rhythm Style series (which included issues of Louis Armstrong's Hot Five). But by the 1960s it had become EMI's repository for material that did not belong anywhere else. Martin produced a Scottish dance band led by Jimmy Shand, and the hit novelty 'Experiments with Mice' (1956) by Johnny Dankworth, in which the British saxophonist led a group playing 'Three Blind Mice' in the styles of Glenn Miller, Stan Kenton and others. Martin made comedy records by Peter Ustinov and Peter Sellers, as well as skiffle hits.

The Beatles recorded 'Love Me Do' at an audition, and Martin, seeing something in their raw energy, advised Epstein that Pete Best was not good enough. Best seemed to be the odd man out anyway, unimpressed as he was by Kirchherr's ideas, so the group recruited Richard Starkey, alias Ringo Starr, from Rory Storm and the Hurricanes, another Liverpool group which had shared the Hamburg gigs. A recording of 'Love Me Do' by the new quartet reached the top twenty of the British charts in October 1962. 'Please Please Me', number two early the next year, was followed by three number ones;

the Beatles could not go anywhere in public without being mobbed, and popular music would never be the same again: rock'n'roll began to change to rock, which was no longer a fad, and in the decade of the 1960s the music business was altered beyond recognition.

Philip Norman, in his *Shout! The True Story of The Beatles* (1981), described what Kirchherr had captured in her photographs as their 'would-be toughness and undisguisable, all-protecting innocence'. For all Lennon's cynicism, a blanket of self-protection that came from his background as an orphan, and for all the high-jinks they had got up to in Hamburg's Reeperbahn, they were still Liverpool lads who could not believe their luck. They were greater than the sum of their parts; Lennon and McCartney wrote the songs, Lennon's acerbity balancing McCartney's tendency to sweetness, and their native cheekiness was a sort of genuine bravado.

The music of the British Invasion represented a climax of a decade of pop jingles. It was British variety influenced by the first wave of rock'n'roll, which was already over in the USA. The Beatles did it better than anyone else, and should have been the end of it, instead of inspiring generations of imitators. As long as the baby boom lasted, there was an inexhaustible supply of children who wanted either to be pop stars or to worship pop stars, so the business accommodated itself to raking in increasing amounts of money, and there was no reason to change anything, except that more accountants were required. Meanwhile, Bing Crosby, American cinema and Broadway songs had invaded and conquered Britain for decades, so now the British reversed the flow for a time.

'Love Me Do' was a sort of bouncy white blues which had the virtue of simplicity, and there was something pleasant about their essentially folkish harmony. 'She Loves You' was unremarkable, its 'Yeah, yeah yeah' chorus typical of the trashiness of pop. 'I Want To Hold Your Hand' was worse: one of the most irritating aspects of pop was the growing tendency not to bother writing a song at all; and the seven notes on the word 'hand' was a good example of the use of a cheap white imitation of melisma to disguise the paucity of the lyrics. This was a warning of the triumph of style over substance that was already taking place in pop, but in the Beatles' case better work was to come. They were tempted to follow Ringo around with pencil and paper because of the way he talked: 'That was a hard day's night,' he said after one gig, which gave them the name of a song and of their first film.

Capitol Records had been sold to EMI in 1955 for £3 million. Joseph Lockwood was criticized for paying so much, but by the end of the decade the label of Frank Sinatra, Nat 'King' Cole, the Kingston Trio and others was said to be worth £85 million. The UK came up with rock'n'roll stars such as Tommy Hicks (renamed Tommy Steele) who were pale imitations of the US product, until they found Cliff Richard, who in thirty years has had only nineteen hit singles in the USA, but a hundred in the UK. (Steele, not so incidentally, became an all-round entertainer in the end, in the music hall rather than the Presley tradition.) *Billboard* published an annual list of the world's best-selling artists based on charts in thirty-four countries, and suddenly in 1963 the top four were Cliff Richard, Elvis Presley, the Shadows (Cliff's backing band) and Frank Ifield, an Australian-born pop singer who specialized in old songs. All except Presley shared the same label (EMI-Columbia), producer (Norrie Paramor), manager and agent. Number seven on the list were the Beatles, also EMI artists, who the following year went to the top. Capitol in the USA passed on all of them, quite understandably; neither Richard nor Ifield became superstars in the USA, while the Ventures, a guitar band from Seattle, were already the homegrown equivalent of the Shadows. And who could have expected four kids from Liverpool to become the biggest act of the decade?

Frank Ifield's 'I Remember You' (a top ten hit by Jimmy Dorsey in 1944) was a top five US hit in 1963 on Vee-Jay, the black-owned Chicago label which also picked up the Beatles. After Motown in Detroit and Duke/Peacock in Houston (which remained strictly R & B and gospel), Vee-Jay was the most important black-owned label in the USA. It had been formed in 1953 by Vivian Carter Bracken and James Bracken, who were joined by Vivian's brother Calvin Carter. Their biggest act was the guitarist and singer Jimmy Reed, who also wrote songs and played a harmonica fixed on a wire bracket around his neck, as street singers had done and as Dylan did later. Reed's blues had a sweetness that took the edge off the usual Chicago passion; he began crossing over to the pop chart in 1957. Soul balladeer Jerry Butler had fourteen Vee-Jay hits between 1960 and 1966, nearly all of which dented the white chart; the Spaniels, the Dells and the El Dorados were vocal groups who crossed over. Frankie Valli was lead singer and Bob Gaudio (formerly of the Royal Teens) keyboard player and tunesmith in the Four Seasons, a white group which had three number ones in the pop chart in 1962 and 1963 on Vee-Jay before moving to Philips. There were many more Vee-Jay hits by Dee Clark, Rosco Gordon, John Lee Hooker and others; Gene Chandler's 'Duke of Earl' was a number one in both the white and black charts in 1962.

Ifield's hit came from left field to make a little money for Vee-Jay in 1963, more than a year after it had been more successful in England. The label had also taken a chance on 'Please Please Me' and 'From Me to You' back to back, the Beatles' second and third UK hits from early 1963, but they made no mark in the USA at first. Vee-Jay lost interest, and 'She Loves You' came out on Swan in the USA; 'Twist and Shout' / 'There's a Place' and 'Love Me Do' / 'P.S. I Love You' were issued in the USA on a Tollie label. But Capitol was prodded into action by their head office in London. As the Beatles flew to New York in January 1964 with an appearance on Ed Sullivan's show lined up, 'I Want To Hold Your Hand' backed with 'I Saw Her Standing There' was screaming up the USA pop chart, narrowly beating the Swan and Vee-Jay singles to the top. Vee-Jay had released the first Beatles album in the USA in July 1963, and it suddenly reached only number two in February 1964, because a Capitol album was already at number one: hip fans sought out the imported Parlophone editions, because they had seven songs on each side instead of six, owing to different methods of calculating song royalties on albums. Adding further to the confusion, two of the Tollie tracks appeared on the first pressing of the Vee-Jay album, and had to be changed in later editions. And this success was the beginning of the end for Vee-Jay.

Having suddenly to buy truckloads of pressings of Beatles records meant that Vee-Jay was short of cash, because distributors sat for up to ninety days on money needed to pay for new pressings. But that was not the whole story; a label that had already achieved so much in a decade should have been in a better position. When Vee-Jay

collapsed in 1965, there were recriminations about financial dishonesty, but the truth was probably more prosaic. Nelson George quotes
an anonymous participant at a Vee-Jay party for a dozen Chicago
DJs that took place in Las Vegas in the early 1960s: they were
asked what they wanted, and they did not want free poker chips; they
wanted women, so the company flew a dozen tall blondes from Oslo
across the North Pole for the weekend, spending a good deal of
money that would have come in handy a couple of years later. Vee-
Jay might have been as big as Motown, but it did not have Berry
Gordy watching the bottom line.

John Fitzgerald Kennedy was murdered in November 1963; in
early 1964 the Beatles helped cheer up the nation. Music lovers had
to withhold judgement until hearing the records: the screaming on
Sullivan's show in February was insane. If you went to the shopping
mall to buy a Beatles album and they were sold out, you could buy
the Dave Clark Five instead; this was another EMI act on which
Capitol had passed, a beat group formed in London to benefit a
football club. All they could do was thump, but they sold records.

Between 1963 and 1965, the height of the British Invasion (so
dubbed by *Billboard*), fifteen EMI acts reached the chart in the
USA, only six of which eventually appeared on Capitol. Capitol
mopped up what was left of Vee-Jay and rode the gravy train for a
few years: Nat Cole, whose Capitol albums are also still selling
decades later, telephoned one day to be greeted by a cheerful 'Capitol
Records, Home of the Beatles!' After the Fab Four broke up in 1970
Capitol found itself with a rack-jobbing distributorship, a mail-order
record club and a bloated staff of hangers-on and their girlfriends, all
losing money. The once great label formed by Johnny Mercer and
his friends was managed no better than Vee-Jay.

Years later Bob Dylan (in Anthony Scaduto's 1971 biography)
remembered driving across country in 1964 with the Beatles all over
the radio dial. 'Their chords were outrageous, just outrageous, and
their harmonies made it all valid. You could only do that with other
musicians . . . I knew they were pointing the direction where music
had to go.' They were certainly pointing the direction in which rock
would go, and gave Dylan the excuse to do it his way.

Another result of British interest in American roots music was a blues boom. Guitarist and vocalist Alexis Korner and banjoist turned harmonica player Cyril Davies had been members of Chris Barber's Jazz Band, which they left in 1961 to form Blues Incorporated. Despite visits from such bluesmen as Big Bill Broonzy, playing the blues was not an economic proposition. Caught between British imitation rock'n'roll and trad jazz, Korner and Davies played once a week or so in any club that would have them, ending up at the Marquee in London's Wardour Street.

Davies left in 1962 to form his own All Stars, taking over Screaming Lord Sutch's Savages, in which Nicky Hopkins played piano. When Davies died of leukaemia, vocalist Long John Baldry stepped in and formed the Hoochie Koochie Men, which included vocalist Rod Stewart. Baldry and Stewart went to Brian Auger's Steampacket, an interesting group that did not succeed; Baldry took over Bluesology, whose keyboard player was Reg Dwight (who later became Elton John). David Sutch was a rocker who never had much commercial success; he imitated Screaming Jay Hawkins and Jack the Ripper on stage, and now stands for Parliament for the Raving Monster Loony Party. Hopkins played piano with most of the rock greats, while Baldry eventually took his big voice to ballads, where he won some acclaim.

The British blues boom was destined to be eclipsed by rock when Mick Jagger and Keith Richards met on a train. They had been close friends when they were small, and they recognized each other and found something new in common: Jagger had been sending away to the USA for Chess albums, and had a bunch of them under his arm. They began to get together for private jams with Dick Taylor, who later formed the Pretty Things, a band which 'resembled nothing so much as *Spitting Image* puppets of the early Rolling Stones', according to English writer Charles Shaar Murray. When Jagger and Richards went to a gig at the Marquee, they heard a guest who sounded like Elmore James on slide guitar: Brian Jones. After adding older men Bill Wyman on bass and Charlie Watts on drums, they began performing.

'Can you imagine a British-composed R & B song? It just wouldn't make it,' said Jagger in 1963, before somebody told him how much money the Beatles were making with their own songs. Jagger was

right; British R & B was and is a contradiction in terms. The first
Stones album included songs by Rufus Thomas, Willie Dixon, Chuck
Berry, Slim Harpo and even Motown artists (Holland–Dozier–
Holland). They had their first UK chart entry in mid-1963; an
American edition of their first album reached number eleven in the
Billboard album chart in 1964, but many Americans could not figure
out why they should listen to white English kids singing Chuck
Berry when they already had Chuck Berry records. Giorgio
Gomelsky, manager of London's Crawdaddy Club, was the first
manager of the Stones; the bluesmen visiting London used to get
together at his home. He recalled, in Dixon's autobiography:

I'll never forget – it was an afternoon about four o'clock in March of
1964 or something. There was Howlin' Wolf, Sonny Boy [Williamson]
and Willie Dixon, the three of them sitting on this sofa . . . Willie was
just singing and tapping on the back of the chair and Sonny Boy would
play the harmonica and they would do new songs . . . These three grand
viziers were sitting on this thing and there's like Jimmy Page, Eric
Clapton and everybody sitting at their feet . . . I remember '300 Pounds
of Joy', 'Little Red Rooster', 'You Shook Me' . . . We'd heard them
really fresh, before anybody had made a record of them.

In fact, a song called 'Little Red Rooster' had been an R & B hit by
someone called Margie Day in 1951, and Wolf had already recorded
it. 'Little Red Rooster' was the first number one UK hit for the
Stones, in November 1964. But songs like that, when performed by
blacks for blacks in Chicago, were celebrations of the joy of sexuality;
sung by spotty ex-schoolboys, they conjured up only sweaty palms.
Whether that is fair or not is beside the point; there are social and
economic as well as rhythmic reasons for this. Songs such as Muddy
Waters's 'Rock Me' are pleas for comfort, for sanctuary in a cruel
world. When they were taken over by the rock generation, they came
to be about the domination of women, leading to the heavy metal
threat to 'nail your ass to the floor'.

   On the one hand, the Stones were one of the few groups who gave
proper credit and paid royalties to the composer. As Jagger put in his
letter to *Melody Maker* in 1964, 'These legendary characters wouldn't
mean a light commercially today if groups were not going round

Britain doing their numbers.' In the early 1960s the US music industry was not admitting Willie Dixon to any Hall of Fame. On the other hand, the Stones were being promoted as opposite numbers to the Beatles: the Mop Tops were cute (however outrageous their behaviour behind closed doors); the Stones were arrested for urinating in public in 1965 and they refused to wave bye-bye with the other stars at the end of a television pop show. The dirtier and more surly the Stones were, the better. The credit 'Nanker Phelge' began to appear on their songs; a 'nankie', said Brian Jones, is a little man who thinks he represents authority; but it is an appropriate rock joke that 'nanker' rhymes with 'wanker', British slang for one whose greatest skill is for the solitary vice.

In any case, once the Stones were convinced they could write songs, 'Stupid Girl' may have been about a female who subscribed to social shibboleths which seemed to be going out of date, whether we liked it or not; 'Mother's Little Helper' was about the drugs house-wives took to get them through the day, while the press screamed about marijuana; 'Sittin' on the Fence' was about bitter-sweet reluc-tance to join a new generation of baby-boomers, helping the economy by tying themselves up in knots with mortgages and a new generation of babies. 'I Can't Get No Satisfaction' was their first number one in the USA in 1965. Jagger couldn't swing, and his execrable accent and phrasing should have been a drawback, but his narcissistic image was useful, and the band could swing. Watts was a jazz drummer who played well behind the beat, Richards and Jones were very good musicians indeed, and the band set Jagger off perfectly. Later, after Jones had left, Jagger seemed to be the nominal leader, but their manager Andrew Loog Oldham recalled years later:

Mick may have thought he was running the show, but Keith was always in charge of the music. When I was remastering one of the tracks for CD I came across something I had not noticed at the time. There was a song where the key was easy for Keith's voice, but had caused Mick trouble and he could hardly sing it.

I said to Keith: 'Did you pick the key for that song?' And he just looked at me and smiled.

In 1964 the Stones paid their respects in Chicago, where they made the EP *4 × 5* at the Chess studios; but they had eschewed the purism of the blues and soon garnered the title 'The World's Greatest Rock and Roll Band', and deserved it. The decade of the 1960s cannot be understood without their albums *Beggar's Banquet* (1968) and *Let It Bleed* (1969); the horrors of assassinations and war in Vietnam told us all too much about our 'Sympathy for the Devil'.

After the Beatles and the Stones, the two most successful British groups were the Who and the Kinks; both remained bigger in the UK but had cult followings in the USA. Pete Townshend's 'My Generation' (for the Who) typified the blatant self-indulgence of the era; their act made a fetish out of smashing their instruments, and they graduated to the grandiose 'rock opera' (*Tommy*). Drummer Keith Moon died in 1978 of an overdose of a drug he was taking to combat his alcoholism, and the survivors later realized they should have quit.

The Kinks' first hit was 'You Really Got Me' (1964), which resembled the Dave Clark Five's thumpers, but Ray Davies went on to create English music of his own. Even more than the Beatles' work, his was in the music hall tradition, and also grieved for a disappearing England. The caustic weariness of his 'Tired of Waiting for You' (1965) was followed by social commentary in 'Dedicated Follower of Fashion' and 'A Well Respected Man', and vignettes such as 'Sunny Afternoon' and 'Waterloo Sunset'. Davies was too bright to turn to drugs like others of the era, and understood the nature of the music business. (He went to the House of Lords to get himself out of a terrible management contract.) His concept albums in the 1970s were among the least grandiose of that genre, and the Kinks outlasted everybody except the Stones.

The British Invasion carried with it harmless pop and measures of fraud. The Small Faces had a fresh sound, and recorded on Andrew Loog Oldham's Immediate label: in 1969 they re-formed as the Faces, from which Rod Stewart emerged to become a generation's favourite Jack the Lad. The first three singles by Gerry and the Pacemakers, another Liverpool group produced by Martin, made history by all being number one UK hits. Billy J. Kramer's success was due to Martin's production and songs lent by the Beatles. Peter and Gordon were a preppy duo; Gordon Waller later imitated Elvis in *Joseph and His Amazing Technicolor Dreamcoat*, and Peter Asher became a prominent record producer. Some groups were successful in the USA because they were British, and remained virtually unknown at home, but the Strangeloves, Myles, Gyles and Nyles, pulled off the best joke: putting on accents and pretending to be British by way of Australia, they had hits in the mid-1960s, but they were actually American music insiders Bob Feldman, Jerry Goldstein and Richard Gottehrer.

The Strangeloves supported the Beach Boys on tour, who were in on the joke. The Beach Boys were an American act whose popularity was unaffected by the British; Brian, Dennis and Carl Wilson and cousins Mike Love and Al Jardine had over fifty hit singles from 1962. They stole some of their tunes from Chuck Berry, but their harmony was different; their clean-cut sound owed much to decades of pop from Glenn Miller's Modernaires to the Four Freshmen and the Hi-lo's. Dennis was full of alcohol when he drowned in 1983, while Brian, the most talented of the group, had addled his brain with drugs; yet what could be more innocent than their concern with surfing, cars and pretty girls? The apparent divorce of their hedonism from its consequences is a paradigm of their Californian lotus-land, and of rock itself.

There are many reasons why the 1960s still look like a golden age compared with the following decades. It had already been several years since the successful use of obviously black material by Elvis Presley, and the explosion of Chuck Berry, Fats Domino and Little Richard into the pop chart; the girl groups were mostly black, and the Motown hit factory's formula clearly appealed equally to black and white fans. Furthermore, the civil rights era was well under way: Americans were making a collective decision that second-class citizenship for a large minority was no longer acceptable, if only because they did not want to see southern police chiefs using dogs and firehoses against black schoolchildren on television. Between 30 November 1963 and 23 January 1965 there was no R&B chart in *Billboard*: for the first time in the history of popular music black and white fans were following the same music to such an extent that separate charts did not seem to be necessary, because rhythm and blues had triumphed in the form of soul music.

Ray Charles had left the Atlantic label for ABC-Paramount, where he made an unprecedented deal for a black entertainer, retaining

ownership of his own recordings. His version of Hoagy Carmichael's lovely 'Georgia on My Mind' was a huge hit in both charts.
He had already had a hit with Hank Snow's 'I'm Movin' On' on
Atlantic in 1959; for ABC he made two albums of country songs,
and his version of Don Gibson's 'I Can't Stop Loving You' was even
bigger than 'Georgia'.

Charles was born in Georgia but soon moved to Florida, where he
went blind as a child. He performed in the mid-1940s in Florida,
playing piano with a white country band, among others, and then
went as far away as he could within the USA, to Seattle, Washington.
There he led a trio in a style similar to that of Nat Cole, and had hits
including 'Baby Let Me Hold Your Hand' in the style of the West
Coast R&B crooner Charles Brown. On his very first recordings,
made at the age of seventeen on a friend's wire recorder in Florida,
although he was using the Nat Cole and Charles Brown trio style, his
honest moaning was that of a seasoned sufferer. (His mother had
recently died and he was extremely poor.) In 1951 he went on the
road with guitarist and vocalist Lowell Fulson, filling the shoes of
Lloyd Glenn, one of the most successful pianists in R&B. Jack
Lauderdale's West Coast Swing Time R&B label was going out of
business, and Atlantic snapped up Ray Charles.

The guitar turned out to be of the greatest importance – indeed it
has been played to death by countless white soundalike 'guitar
heroes' in the last twenty years. Aaron Thibeaux 'T-Bone' Walker
was the prime mover behind rock guitar, sharing the same teacher
and influences as Charlie Christian and doing for the instrument in
R&B what Christian did for it in jazz: he brought his intimate
baritone and his guitar playing to a huge number of tracks, nearly all
of which were blues but usually had a jazz-flavoured backing that
reveals much about the origins of R&B, and which must have been a
big influence on the young Ray Charles. The slide guitar of Elmore
James and his somewhat rougher country blues style derived from
Robert Johnson. The four Kings, B. B., Albert, Earl and Freddie, all
unrelated, all played guitar and had black hits. Riley 'Blues Boy'
King is the first of these in more ways than one, having become one
of the world's best-loved entertainers after decades of working the
chitlin' circuit, without changing himself or his act.

An extremely rich stew of rhythm and blues had been bubbling in the early 1950s. Ray Charles arranged and played piano on Guitar Slim's 'The Things That I Used to Do', a number one black hit for fourteen weeks in early 1954. (He was the best known of several entertainers to use the name Guitar Slim and one of the first to use a long lead on his electric guitar, so he could move around the stage.) Ray Charles then brought to black pop one of its most important ingredients: the music of the black church. In the late 1950s he finally crossed over to the white chart, but by then he was already a national institution; one of Bill Cosby's comedy routines had Columbus sailing to America so he could discover Ray Charles.

At his first Atlantic recording session Charles allegedly wanted to stick to his Brown-style crooning, but the label soon helped him change his mind. Tired of using pick-up musicians, he was now successful enough to form his own band. His first Atlantic hit was 'It Should've Been Me', a ghetto comedy which owed something to Louis Jordan and was the sort of thing which probably influenced Leiber and Stoller's work with the Coasters. In later hits he became completely himself, bringing the passion of religion to the aches and pains of the secular world, and even using the melodies of gospel music: 'Talkin' 'Bout Jesus' became 'Talkin' 'Bout You'; Clara Ward's 'This Little Light of Mine' became 'This Little Girl of Mine'; 'How Jesus Died' became 'Lonely Avenue'; and 'I've Got a Savior' became 'I Got a Woman', his first number one in the black chart, which shortly after was covered by Elvis Presley, who brought rockabilly urgency to it. Charles added a preaching, commentating female trio to his act, the Raelettes (sometimes spelled Raylettes), and there was even a touch of feminism: black women are not famous for taking a lot of nonsense, and the Raelettes carried 'What Kind of Man are You?' by themselves. Later, on Percy Mayfield's 'Hit the Road, Jack', Charles adds a man's patronizing puzzlement to the Raelettes' lead: 'Well, I guess if you say so / I'll have to pack my bags and go / . . . You can't *mean* it!'

Religious blacks were scandalized when one of their stars changed to secular music. Popular as Sam Cooke had been with the Soul Stirrers, he was booed when he turned up at a gospel meeting after having pop hits. Of Ray Charles, Big Bill Broonzy said, 'He's mixing the blues with the spirituals. I know that's wrong . . . He should be singing in a church.' The relationship between the blues and the church was already well known to aficionados, and the gospel recordings of Blind Willie Johnson (1927–30) and Rev. Gary Davis (from 1935) were highly prized. Black gospel music, though a thriving market, was not widely known in the white community; nevertheless, such fine singers as Claude Jeter (with the Swan Silvertones) and Archie Brownlee (with the Five Blind Boys) had a profound indirect influence on popular music.

In the early 1950s Mahalia Jackson, an artist of the stature of Bessie Smith who refused to record secular material, became known throughout the white community. While Ray Charles was still registering only in the black chart, Little Richard's sanctified screaming and Sam Cooke's beautiful gospel melisma reached the white charts. The Staple Singers' gospel recordings for Vee-Jay in the 1950s included 'This Could be the Last Time', later covered by the Rolling Stones, with the lyrics adapted. Charles's first top ten hit in the white chart, and one of his last singles on Atlantic, was 'What'd I Say', which came as a considerable revelation in 1959 because of its driving passion and call-and-response moaning.

His 1961 album with members of the Basie band was called *Genius + Soul = Jazz*. The word 'soul' was already in wide use in black culture: soul food, soul music; one of Charles Mingus's best-known tunes is 'Better Git It in Your Soul'. The addition of the feeling of the church to R&B was immediately called soul. As the soul is the essence of a human being, so soul in music, like swing, is self-expression.

The gift of soul to America at last began to bear fruit during the civil rights era, which unexpectedly, perhaps, seemed to begin with Louis Armstrong. Louis had given up leading big bands after a sensationally successful Town Hall concert in New York in 1947 by a small integrated band including Jack Teagarden, Bobby Hackett, Peanuts Hucko (clarinet), Dick Cary (piano), Bob Haggart (bass) and Sid Catlett (drums). He toured for the rest of his life with his All Stars. In 1955 a European tour was so successful (more so than an East–West summit in Switzerland at the same time) that it made headlines all over the world; an album of live recordings was issued as *Ambassador Satch*, on which Edmond Hall plays clarinet and Trummy Young trombone. The State Department then decided to sponsor tours by one of America's most popular exports.

Louis was never noted for racial controversy; some regarded him as an Uncle Tom, but others knew better: as Billie Holiday put it, 'Pops toms from the heart.' Music transcended race. But in May 1957 the United States Supreme Court struck down the pernicious 'separate but equal' doctrine that had ensured second-rate educational facilities for black children, ruling that the states must end segregation in the schools; on 3 September at Little Rock, Arkansas, the state's National Guard was used to prevent black students from entering Central High School; and on the 18th, in Grand Forks, North Dakota, Armstrong was watching live coverage on television as a howling mob of white trash confronted a handful of frightened black children. A local reporter got the scoop of his life when a furious Armstrong told him that the President had 'no guts', allowing a 'plowboy' like Governor Orville Faubus to run the country, and that 'the way they are treating my people in the South, the government can go to hell'. America's best-loved entertainer had made headlines in spite of himself. Two days later a federal court ordered Faubus to stop using the National Guard to defy the law, and on 23 September Eisenhower sent federal troops to Little Rock to prevent mob rule. After nearly a century of *de facto* second-class citizenship for blacks, the civil rights era was under way.

The Interstate Commerce Commission ordered the desegregation of bus and rail terminals. A new Civil Rights Bill was to be introduced by the Kennedy administration when he was murdered (and one of my co-workers in the car factory muttered, 'It's about time somebody got that nigger-lover'). A few days later the *Billboard* R & B chart was abolished. Up to that date both black and white acts such as Garnet Mimms and the Enchanters, Jackie Wilson, the Chiffons, Mary Wells, Leslie Gore, Jimmy Gilmer and the Fireballs had had hits riding high in both the black and white pop charts. But the Beatles and the rest of the British Invasion dominated the pop chart from early 1964; the *Billboard* R & B chart reappeared a year later, and no Beatles record ever appeared in it, despite their love for black pop. It was not until August 1969, when classic soul had peaked, that the name of the chart was changed to 'Best Selling Soul Singles'.

James Brown was unique, as important a progenitor of soul as Ray Charles. He came from poverty and prison for teenage offences to put together a soul revue made up of elements of gospel, black vaudeville and the influence of R&B pioneers such as Jordan (who thought of himself first and last as an entertainer). Singer, songwriter, producer and bandleader James Brown maintained absolute control over every aspect of his show, riding his band so hard that they would leave him, forcing him to re-form more than once; also the best in the business, they were called the Famous Flames, and later the JBs. He was known as the Godfather of Soul, Mr Dynamite and the Hardest-working Man in Show Business. His first hit, 'Please, Please, Please' (on Federal), was nothing but a passionately incantatory plea: Syd Nathan at King did not understand it, but Ralph Bass talked him into it, and it was a top five in the black chart in 1956. Brown's next hit, 'Try Me' (1958), crossed over to the pop chart.

Again and again Brown was ahead of the label. When King would not record his dance hit '(Do the) Mashed Potatoes', he recorded it in Florida under his drummer's name (Nat Kendricks and the Swans, with vocal shouts by Miami DJ 'King' Coleman), and it was a 1960 hit on both charts. When King didn't think a live album would be worth doing, Brown paid for the recording himself, and had a number two hit in the *Billboard* pop album chart in mid-1963 with *Live at the Apollo*, still regarded as one of the most exciting live albums ever made. In twenty years he had nearly one hundred hits in the pop chart, and well over one hundred in the black. Not only were 'Papa's Got a Brand New Bag' (1965) and 'Say It Loud – I'm Black and Proud' (1968) number one black hits and top tens in the white chart, but their titles entered the language. His hits slowed down when he was eclipsed by mechanical disco music and hip-hop, both of which owed nearly everything to him.

Clyde McPhatter was essentially a soul singer; with the various editions of the Drifters, the voice of Ben E. King and all its other assets, and the perfection of its sound, thanks to engineer Tommy Dowd, and its backbeat, thanks to arranger Jesse Stone, Atlantic might have been the most important soul factory all by itself. When Mercury covered LaVern Baker's 'Tweedle-dee' with Georgia Gibbs, they hired the musicians who had played on the Baker record and they wanted Dowd as well, but he would not take the job. And the importance of Stone cannot be overestimated.

Stone's territory band, the Blues Serenaders, recorded for Okeh in 1927, and 'Starvation Blues' is described thus by Gunther Schuller in his *Early Jazz*:

In fact, in 1927 jazz could as yet offer very little that matched the depth of feeling that Stone's orchestra purveyed ... This expressivity was achieved in terms of (or perhaps despite) written-out arrangements, and very advanced, sophisticated ones at that. For Jesse Stone was a well-trained musician, a composer and arranger.

Stone played piano for George E. Lee (Julia's bandleader brother), and for that band wrote 'Paseo Strut', of which a lovely recording was made in Kansas City in 1929. He wrote arrangements for the Kansas City Skyrockets in 1934, and later for Jimmie Lunceford, Harlan Leonard and Earl Hines. Then he replaced Eddie Durham as music director of the International Sweethearts of Rhythm, a very good all-girl mixed-race band that had run away from an orphanage. (It played for big crowds and appeared in films during the 1940s, but never had a good recording contract.) Stone's compositions included 'Idaho' for one of Roy Rogers's films, a hit for the bands of Alvino Rey and Benny Goodman, and 'Sorghum Switch' for Doc Wheeler, covered for a hit by Jimmy Dorsey (both 1942); retitled 'Cole Slaw', the latter was a hit for saxophonists Frank Culley and Louis Jordan in 1949.

In 1950 Stone experimented at Atlantic, working on Ruth Brown's recordings, and rehearsing and recording the vocal groups. He was not the only arranger at Atlantic, but the most important. When the Chords brought in 'Sh-boom', Stone recorded it for Atlantic's subsidiary Cat, and was thus responsible for one of the first big hits of the rock'n'roll era (albeit in the nasty copycat version by the Crew-cuts). He arranged 'Chains of Love' and 'Shake, Rattle and Roll' (taking composer credit as Charles Calhoun) for Joe Turner and wrote 'Money Honey', the first recording by the Drifters and their first big hit; it was number one in the black chart for eleven weeks in 1953, and later covered by Elvis Presley. Stone was one of those who helped persuade Ray Charles to let his hair down when he came to Atlantic. He took a break in 1954 to be A & R director at Lamp, an East Coast subsidiary of Aladdin which failed, but one of its groups, the Cookies, became Ray Charles's Raelettes.

It was at Atlantic that Stone had an unsung influence on the music of ensuing decades. Atlantic's recordings were more polished than those of other R & B labels, as though they were intended to be hits, rather than just slung into the market to see what happened; yet they also swung, because people like Stone brought the skills and values of decades of black music with them.

As the golden age of soul approached, Atlantic received a massive boost from a historical accident. Satellite Records was formed in 1960 in Memphis, Tennessee, by Jim Stewart and his sister, Estelle Axton, to record local talent. A local white R & B group called the Royal Spades became the house band, and had a national hit with 'Last Night' on Satellite, but shortly after the name of the label was changed to Stax, because there was already a Satellite label on the West Coast. In the band were guitarist Steve Cropper and bass player Donald 'Duck' Dunn; it soon mutated into Booker T. and the MGs (for 'Memphis Group'), which had Booker T. Jones on keyboards and Al Jackson on drums. The Memphis Horns originally included Charles 'Packy' Axton on tenor saxophone, Don Nix on baritone and Wayne Jackson on trumpet. Thus a bunch of country boys, both white and black, working for an amateur record company, laid down their own tracks as well as backing some of the most beautiful black voices of the decade, and together polished one of the great facets of American music at a time when they could not eat together at a local lunch counter.

Fame Studios was started in Muscle Shoals, a town built on reclaimed land across the river from Florence, Alabama, with producers Rick Hall and Billy Sherrill (who was later a leading producer in Nashville country music). Bellboy Arthur Alexander wrote songs and worked with Hall, and Fame leased his hits to Dot: 'Anna (Go to Him)' was a top ten black hit in 1962, and was covered by the Beatles. Otis Redding was the greatest Stax discovery; he died in a plane crash just as he was hitting the big time, but had about thirty hit singles in six years. Stax had made a distribution agreement with

Atlantic, and that label's Jerry Wexler sent Aretha Franklin, Wilson Pickett, Solomon Burke, Don Covay, Ben E. King, Joe Tex and others to Memphis and/or Alabama to record.

With the success of Redding, Jerry Wexler assigned Sam and Dave to Stax; Isaac Hayes and David Porter wrote songs for them. Wexler dispatched Tommy Dowd to Memphis to bring Stax's technology into the modern era, and Stax and Atlantic began copying each other. The Memphis black and white soul fusion, Wexler saw, was something that no money could buy, yet his influence inevitably helped to ruin it, by changing it. There would always have been a danger that Atlantic's polish would be overdone (and in fact the label soon turned to slickly produced white pop), but Memphis had been a return to head arrangements and to a house rhythm section. The amateurish management and racially charged atmosphere was available for classic recording until Stax made the mistake of asking itself how it had done what it did in the first place: personalities intruded and the magic was lost. But not right away.

Wilson Pickett, who was not an easy man to get along with, went to Stax after two flop singles to record with Booker T. and the MGs. This resulted in 'In the Midnight Hour' (co-written with Steve Cropper) and '634–5789' (by Cropper and Eddie Floyd), Pickett's first two black-chart number ones, in 1966. After three sessions at Stax Pickett never came back and neither did Wexler; but Pickett recorded at Fame.

Aretha Franklin was the daughter of the Rev. C. L. Franklin, a famous gospel artist; she sang in his Detroit Baptist church and was contracted to Columbia between 1961 and 1966, when she made worthy recordings which didn't sell, and then changed to Atlantic. She made only one recording session in Muscle Shoals. Alcohol was flowing and hostility broke out between her husband and one of the locals, but 'I Never Loved a Man (the Way I Loved You)' was recorded, and a start made at the flip side, 'Do Right Woman – Do Right Man'; this was a mess that nobody liked, a demonstration tape with Dan Penn's voice on it. The first became a pop top ten and was number one in the black chart for seven weeks in 1967; the second was turned into another soul classic at Atlantic, with Aretha's piano and her sisters singing back-up. Wexler and Hall had quarrelled, so

Wexler hired Oldham and others to come to New York to work on a King Curtis album and, without telling Hall, also used them on the rest of Aretha's first Atlantic album, named after the first hit. It was number three in the *Billboard* album chart, and included her first number one pop hit, which was also number one (for eight weeks) in the black chart: she made Otis Redding's 'Respect' for ever her own. Nobody who listened to the radio at all could be ignorant of soul, once the Queen arrived; but Wexler had soon broken with everybody.

By this time psychedelia and the drug culture were well under way. In New York the Velvet Underground, including vocalist-songwriter Lou Reed, made albums of understated songs about heroin and masochism which recorded the underbelly of urban culture without celebrating it: their feeling of doom was real, not schoolboy self-indulgence. Their influence did not become evident until after they had split up. To some extent it was pressure from the counterculture that stopped Lyndon Johnson from running again in 1968, and it was a victory of sorts when Chicago policemen stupidly rioted outside the Democratic national convention that year, for Mayor Richard J. Daley was several decades out of touch. The Grateful Dead, Jefferson Airplane and others were basically very loud West Coast folk bands. The Beatles and George Martin had produced their music hall masterpiece, *Sgt Pepper's Lonely Hearts Club Band*, and at the end of that year the Rolling Stones, who were hopelessly unsuited to psyche-delia, released *Their Satanic Majesties Request*, a failure, and then went on to do their best work. Jim Morrison ('Death and my cock are the world') and the Doors had seven top ten albums from 1967 to 1971. The Woodstock Festival in August 1969 was a sodden disaster in a muddy field, but felt like the triumph of peace. Black San Francisco DJ and sometime producer Sylvester Stewart, as Sly Stone, put together Sly and the Family Stone, an integrated 'psychedelic soul' outfit, which experimentally pulled together several of the era's strands to make joyous music that made dancing shoes twitch.

Janis Joplin, from Port Arthur, Texas, seemed to have an exciting voice for a white girl because she was willing to throw it away for the sake of a good time tonight, and forget tomorrow. She was an unhappy, insecure girl who took to drugs and alcohol; appearing at a

Stax/Volt Christmas party at the end of 1968, she strolled on after her band had spent fifteen minutes setting up, carrying her bottle of Southern Comfort, and could not understand why people started to leave; they had watched some of the classiest professional acts in the business, including all the Stax stars and Mr James Brown himself, acts that prided themselves on their professionalism and their respect for their audience. They were insulted by Janis Joplin.

The black guitarist Jimi Hendrix had been fired from job after job on the R&B circuit. He was unpunctual, he wore funny clothes that looked like they had been slept in, and indulged in his own funny business on the stand, distracting the audience from the attraction, whether it was a nobody MC like 'Gorgeous' George Odell or a star like Little Richard. Black entertainers who had worked themselves out of poverty by putting on a professional show did not need a weird black hippie like Hendrix to spoil it; he would not have lasted five minutes with James Brown. Nevertheless, let it be said that 'I Don't Know What You've Got (But It's Got Me)', a Don Covay song recorded by Little Richard in 1965 with Hendrix on guitar, is described by Peter Guralnick as 'the Mount Rushmore of Soul'.

In any case, Hendrix was nothing like as confused as Joplin. He knew exactly what he was doing; it was just that his guitar was everything, and the rest didn't matter. He had absorbed the Delta blues, the R&B of the chitlin' circuit and the lessons of soul. He became the complete master of the electric guitar at a time when its technology was still relatively primitive, and he knew his jazz too: when he went to 'swinging' London to set it on its ear, he carried with him his favourite album by Roland Kirk, a blind saxophonist who could play three horns at once. Joplin was a mess, the Beatles were prisoners of their own fame and some of the biggest white pop stars of the era were vain monsters. But Hendrix was the best musician of them all, and the only black to become a superstar on the same level as the rest. He returned to the USA a conquering hero.

The Jimi Hendrix Experience, a trio, included Mitch Mitchell on drums and Noel Redding on bass, both of whom were basically jazz-oriented English musicians. They had hit singles in England and the USA and made hit albums, but Hendrix was hassled by money problems (because of a contract he had signed in New York with a music business shark named Ed Chalpin), by racial politics (certain people thought he should be using black sidemen) and by his own propensity for hedonism. But he was composing unique material, with lyrics as allusive as Dylan's, and there were signs that he was pulling his act together: Hendrix might have made a fusion of black and white musics to be getting on with.

The legendary decade of the 1960s really began only in 1964, when the Beatles swept the USA, or perhaps even later, when the hippie phenomenon was celebrated in *Time* magazine, at about the time Hendrix returned to the USA. By then the psychedelic influence in design (posters, record albums, clothes) seemed ubiquitous, and use of marijuana was becoming common among middle-class youth. And there was the foolish disaster of the war in Vietnam to protest about. Only a bit more than two years had passed between the first Monterey Pop Festival, where the Hendrix Experience made its US début, and Woodstock, which in retrospect was the beginning of the end. But it all seemed to have happened rather suddenly, and it did seem like the counterculture was taking over.

It has become commonplace to speak of the 1960s as being dominated by the narcissism of the baby boom, but the fact that that generation had enough leisure and prosperity to allow introspection was not in itself a bad thing; in fact, it is a necessary (if not sufficient) condition for the creation of art. Furthermore, that generation had to make its own popular culture, including its music, out of the influences that it found available, and unlike previous generations, it had been largely cut off from many of its own cultural roots, yet it was a large enough generation to sustain some artists of integrity. It is clear with hindsight that it was the singer-songwriters, the troubadours, rather than the pop groups and rock bands, who recorded the 1960s with humour and style.

The most important trend in the broader popular music of the last two decades has been that rock'n'roll and its best songwriting have gone back to the prairies and the gin mills whence they came. Country music, with its strings and choirs, was overproduced during the 1960s, and came to be called 'countrypolitan', leading to the reaction described in Jan Reid's book *The Improbable Rise of Redneck Rock* (1974). But this is not so surprising. The folk-rock and country-rock of the fab decade, with elements of the singer-songwriter phenomenon mixed in, soon retired from the charts, but the best rock was always a fusion of several genres.

It was not necessary to pay much attention to pop in the 1960s unless you were a card-carrying member of the counterculture; if any of it was any good, it would be around long enough to seep into the consciousness. We knew from the history of popular music that if we liked something that turned out to be a cover, the original would be worth investigating: many people had discovered black music through white covers in the 1950s, and, similarly, some discovered Bob Dylan through the Byrds and Peter, Paul and Mary. Meanwhile, we danced with each other's wives, for example in a basement joint in Kenosha called Mr Z's. (We were so much older then; we're younger than that now.) We heard numerous touring rock'n'roll bands in the period when the music was coming to be called rock; those of us in backwaters like Kenosha didn't mind that we had never heard of any of the bands, and anyhow some of them were pretty good. One of them was probably the Hawks.

They were a quintet of Canadians, except for the drummer, who was from Arkansas. They were called the Hawks because they had started out backing an Arkansas rockabilly called Ronnie Hawkins. Then they backed blues singer John Hammond, son of Columbia's A & R man, and, in 1966, Dylan, on a controversial tour. After much screaming and cat-calling from outraged folkies, for example at the Albert Hall in London, guitarist Robbie Robertson later said, 'We'd go back to the hotel room, listen to a tape of the show and think, shit, that's not so bad. Why is everybody so upset?' The folkies did not know that rock'n'roll *is* folk music. Maybe they should have danced at Mr Z's with other people's wives.

When the Hawks wanted a new name, they chose the Band, because that was what they had always called the group. They made the famous bootleg 'basement tapes' with Dylan near Woodstock, New York, later released commercially; their own first album, released in 1968, was called *Big Pink*, after the house with the famous basement. They had learned how to do what they did by playing in bars, back rooms and dance halls back and forth across North America, so that shortly after they began making their own albums they were described as the only band that could have warmed up the crowd for Abraham Lincoln. They played 'Long Black Veil', a country hit in 1959 which had been covered by Joan Baez, and which sounds like a copyrighted folksong. They sang Dylan songs and songs co-written with Dylan, such as 'Tears of Rage' and 'This Wheel's on Fire', as well as Robertson's 'The Weight', 'Up on Cripple Creek' and 'The Night They Drove Old Dixie Down' (which was a hit for Baez, who would have done better in the late 1960s if she could have found more good songs). They quit, after sixteen years on the road, so as not to end up parodying themselves. On Thanksgiving Day in 1976 the Band had a party in San Francisco, with an audience and many musical guests, which was recorded and made into the film *The Last Waltz*.

Another good band was Little Feat, whose albums *Dixie Chicken* and *Feats Don't Fail Me Now* carried the same fusion of rock'n'roll, country, blues and folk, and the singing and slide guitar of Lowell George, who was to die of a drug-related heart attack in 1979. Essentially, the Hawks and Little Feat were two of the best and most successful bar bands, of which there were plenty, especially in the South-west, just as in the 1920s, when they were called territory bands. In the 1960s, Doug Sahm (born in San Antonio in 1941) had a few hits with a Tex-Mex flavour as the Sir Douglas Quintet (either muscling in on or sending up the British Invasion); his later career has marked the tip of a valuable sub-genre called swamp rock. In Tulsa, Oklahoma, Rockin' Jimmy and the Brothers of the Night made two albums in the early 1980s and then gave up, because vocalist and songwriter Jimmy Byfield did not want to go on the road: a rocker who actually walked away from fame. But the albums are great fun.

The Byrds, whose pretty harmony came by way of bluegrass, and Gram Parsons, who had various groups, are credited with inventing country rock. Parsons was a member of the Byrds when they recorded their album *Sweetheart of the Rodeo* (1968), which is regarded as a rock classic and a signpost to the fusion, but true rock'n'roll already had a good deal of country in it. Ex-Byrd Chris Hillman and Parsons formed the Flying Burrito Brothers, who were less self-consciously pop: *Burrito Deluxe* (1970) was a better classic in its own quiet way, some tracks using an accordion for a touch of Tex-Mex. Parsons was not yet twenty-seven when he died of the effects of too much drink and drugs in a motel in California, in 1973; meanwhile, Hillman and Parsons had discovered Emmylou Harris, a would-be folksinger who made one terrible album in 1969.

Having found her true musical nature singing harmony with Parsons, she became the Queen of Country Rock and easily one of the most valuable American recording artists of the era. Her proper début album *Pieces of the Sky* (1975) included 'From Boulder to Birmingham', her tribute to Parsons; before long she had formed her aptly named Hot Band, with such good musicians as the British-born guitarist Albert Lee, multi-instrumentalist Ricky Skaggs, soon a country star himself, and James Burton, sometime sideman with Rick Nelson and Presley and one of the best American guitarists of all. Although she seems basically to be a country artist, every Harris album reaches high in the pop chart; she writes songs herself, but has enough taste and good sense to draw her material from wherever she likes – R & B, classic country, even Hollywood – making it all her own. Each track is respectably skilful in production terms, yet the band sounds like a bunch of friends having a good time. Her guest appearance in the film *The Last Waltz*, singing Robertson's 'Evange-line', was one of its high points.

Kitty Wells had staked out territory in the country market that would for ever belong to the women. Patsy Cline, Loretta Lynn, Tammy Wynette and several more have been highly regarded; even if the production of some of their albums had been too smooth in Nashville's countrypolitan era, their professionalism, good songs, down-home values and no-nonsense attitudes defined them as people who could be trusted. There are too many fine songs and songwriters to list here, but Harlan Howard's hits, for example, many for girl singers, include 'Pick Me Up on Your Way Down', 'Heartaches by the Number', 'Too Many Rivers', 'I Fall to Pieces', 'Busted' (for Ray Charles); the total is said to include sixty number ones in a chart where success still meant something besides money. Dolly Parton came from a television and recording partnership with country star Porter Wagoner to be one of the greatest of all. Her own excellent songs, such as 'Coat of Many Colors' and 'Jolene', show a degree of integrity that so many women in music have known how to retain; she branched out into the cinema and the chat-show circuit and now seems to have left songwriting, but not before she reminded us how important good songs are.

Linda Ronstadt, originally in a folk-rock group called the Stone Poneys, came to be widely popular in the 1970s. Her albums, produced by Peter Asher, were too slick, and when she tried to do Frank Sinatra's type of songs, she was utterly unable to phrase them as required. But there was no doubting her lovely voice and her skill with more suitable material. Harris, Parton and Ronstadt made an album called *Trio* in 1987 which in several ways capped all their careers: singing solo and in various combinations, they demonstrated many of the strengths always to be found in American music, especially beauty.

Bonnie Raitt, daughter of John Raitt (Broadway star of *Carousel* in 1945, *The Pajama Game* in 1954 and others), was a good guitarist with a distinctive voice and emotionally mature beyond her years. She performed a selection of material that could have been called white blues or country rock, but added up to what rock'n'roll should always have been. Most of her albums made the pop chart without setting any sales records; in the mid-to-late 1980s a couple of them suffered from the endemic pop problem of overproduction, ridiculously stiff rhythm sections and bad songs. She came back in 1990 with *Nick of Time*, which won four Grammys and single-handedly almost restored some honour to the whole idea of music awards. Guitarist and singer Ry Cooder was a well-known sideman on many record dates, including some with the Rolling Stones. He began making a series of albums celebrating the whole history of American post-war pop, from R & B and rock'n'roll to Tex-Mex and much else; although they are still selling, he was never rewarded in chart terms, and latterly concentrated on atmospheric film music. (But in the 1990s he branched out even further, making duet albums with 'world music' guitarists such as the Indian Vishwa Mohan Bhatt and the West African bluesman Ali Farka Toure, and gathered kudos all over again.)

Singer-songwriters contributed a viable commercial genre for a while, and among the best of the confessionalist type was James Taylor, who came through much self-indulgence and a marriage to Carly Simon, which was destructive to both their careers, to retain a large following. Two confessing narcissists in one household may have been too many, but Simon herself, from the publishing family of Simon and Schuster, was a valuable commentator. Her best-known song was 'You're So Vain', which might have been about any of the world's most visible boyfriends, but was mainly a flash of insight into her own generation. Jackson Browne, despite the critical wise-guy label of 'chilled white whine', has done some good work. Carole King's *Tapestry* in 1971 matched *Sgt Pepper* in the US charts.

Joni Mitchell was a Canadian whose singing, writing, guitar playing, painting and photography were all of a piece. She examined herself and her emotions with the detachment of an artist, and wrote such songs as 'Big Yellow Taxi', 'Both Sides Now' and 'The Circle Game', which were unusual in her generation (but not in her genre) in that they were good enough to be widely covered.

One of the greatest of all was Van Morrison, from Northern Ireland, an unlikely pop star who hates the music business and rarely gives interviews. His father's record collection included Hank Williams and Leadbelly; he began in a pop group called Them, made one solo album in 1967, which he later disowned, then threw the dice. Stranded in New York when his producer Bert Berns died of a heart attack, he signed a solo deal and made *Astral Weeks* in forty-eight hours, embarking on a career that combined the blues, biographical yearning and Celtic mysticism. He became a giant, one of the few troubadours to compare with Bob Dylan.

Many of these people have done their best work. Several of Mitchell's last albums have suffered from the studio-bound production of her husband; some people complain that Van the Man is repeating himself. Some of the chroniclers of their times did not survive: Phil Ochs was a powerful songwriter whose work was tied up with his politics, and killed himself when it was evident that music could not change the world. David Blue died of a heart attack while jogging. Tim Hardin died of drugs, his own haunting version of his folk-blues 'If I Were a Carpenter' showing up any number of polished hit covers. The much loved Jim Croce ('I'll Have to Say I Love You in a Song') was killed in a car crash.

But there are dozens, probably hundreds more still at it: Jack Elliott, Loudon Wainwright, John D. Loudermilk, Tom Paxton (whose other love is baseball), John Prine, Janis Ian, Laura Nyro, John Stewart, Ian Tyson, to name just a few. Mitch Miller made a wisecrack about Nyro, talking about the music of the era: 'Where is Laura Nyro now?' But she had left music for a few years, which was her business, and when she came back, the commercial success of the genre had peaked. Those who were enchanted by her albums still are; her delivery of her songs may have been highly wrought, but they were good enough to be covered by the likes of Ronstadt, Aretha Franklin, Thelma Houston, Frank Sinatra and Barbra Streisand, as well as pop groups.

John Stewart left the Cumberland Three to join the Kingston Trio, unable to turn down such a lucrative offer, but knowing that he could not bring politics to their act; he later worked for Bobby Kennedy, who had a tin ear but understood the importance of music, and (some feel) may have been our greatest political loss in a bloody decade. Ian Tyson was successful with his then wife Sylvia Fricker in the Canadian folk duo in the 1960s, and is now a rancher; both Stewart and Tyson are still writing good songs.

Some of the Byrds stayed in country rock or went back to the neo-bluegrass they started out with: there are all kinds of lovely records on tiny labels by people like Chris Hillman, groups called Old and in the Way and others who never found it necessary to pretend to be progressive. Buffalo Springfield was a pop band, for whom Steven Stills wrote 'For What It's Worth (Stop, Hey, What's That Sound)' after a police riot in Los Angeles; the song was a hit in 1967 and remains a potent artefact. Crosby (from the Byrds), Stills and Young (from Buffalo Springfield) and Nash (from the British group the Hollies) formed a vocal supergroup; they sang pretty, but reunions didn't work. Canadian-born Young carried on; over twenty albums of varying quality have now been in the chart. His earliest ones, with a group of friends called Crazy Horse, are essential, and another in 1990 was a reunion with them; rock critics gave it high marks with obvious feelings of relief.

In England such folk-rock bands as Steeleye Span, Pentangle and Fairport Convention mutated into new groups, or have reunions. The number of good musicians who have passed through them and sing and play together in various combinations is very high: any gig with Ashley Hutchings, Martin Carthy, John Kirkpatrick, Bert Jansch, John Renbourn, Dave Swarbrick or Ralph McTell must be worth attending, while singer, songwriter and guitarist Richard Thompson was described as England's best-kept secret. Among the younger generation of eclectic folk-popsters, the Pogues are always interesting. The Men They Couldn't Hang was a British folk-rock band that has already gone: their label, MCA, released the single the boys wanted to put out, but did not bother to promote it. Why did they sign them in the first place? And since the market is already there, why cannot broadcasters make more room for it at the expense of pre-teen music? The way the business makes its decisions remains a mystery.

There were occasionally new singer-songwriters, of whom one of the best was Joan Armatrading, who released her first solo album in 1975. Her love songs were literate, and had the detachment that is necessary for a useful appraisal of anything, qualities which seem to be lacking in later, younger confessors.

There can be no doubt that today many of the best troubadours and balladeers come from the prairies, a psychological and metaphysical area the geographical centre of which is Texas. Jerry Jeff Walker is a folkie turned country rocker who had a couple of chart entries decades ago and has long been an adopted Texan. His music, like all the music in this genre, is full of smiles; he introduced a live album by saying 'Howdy, buckaroos', both sending up and celebrating himself, his music and his audience. His generous CD selection of his own songs, *Gypsy Songman* (1987), is a joy: no intrusive production, just guitars, fiddles, love songs, story songs and jump tunes.

J. J.'s earlier album tracks include 'Standing at the Big Hotel', and one of his Hot 100 entries was called 'L.A. Freeway'. Among the joys of country rock is that the songs are real songs, worth covering; consequently it is again fun and rewarding to look at the name of the composer under the name of the song on the label: 'Standing at the Big Hotel' is by Butch Hancock, and 'L.A. Freeway' is by Guy Clark.

Hancock's first set, around 1978, was a solo effort called *West Texas Waltzes and Dust Blown Tractor Tunes*, and obviously influenced by Bob Dylan. His words are worth listening to, like Dylan's, but this is shit-kicking music, in the best sense: his family have survived farming in that tough country for decades, and no Hancock needs a major-label deal to make music. He has more energy, more positive directness and more humour in his music than Dylan. *Firewater Seeks Its Own Level* (1981) was recorded live in the Alamo Lounge in Austin, with Butch, a bass, an electric guitar and a fiddle: no drums, no production to speak of (no room behind the bar), just a great deal of fun. A. P. Carter's gospel blues 'There's No Hiding Place Down Here' swings like anything and has hot solos, and the title song is one of Butch's best:

> You got drunk last night
> You say you seen the Devil?
> Don't you know firewater
> Seeks its own level?

The verses are too long to quote here, but they excoriate the self-pity of the loved and lost, with rough humour and sympathy. The song's structure, interestingly, seems to recover and turn on its head those Tin Pan Alley story songs of around 1910, but it is done artlessly, adding the swing and vernacular values that that genre lacked; and the long verses are not one word too long.

Guy Clark's songs have been covered by David Allan Coe (a jailbird whose own 'Would You Lay With Me in a Field of Stone' and 'Take This Job and Shove It' are classics in the genre), as well as by Walker, Skaggs, Johnny Cash, Bobby Bare and others. Some of his songs are the ones against which all others should be measured: like all good songs, they are for people who have to try to live in the real world. 'L.A. Freeway' is for anybody who wonders what he or she is doing stuck in a traffic jam; 'Home Grown Tomatoes' should make you want to go out and plant some seeds; 'Texas 1947' is about the day the steam locomotive was replaced by the diesel-electric: a small, dusty town turns out to watch the silver Streamliner go by, and it doesn't even stop, but nothing will ever be the same again. 'Desperadoes Waiting for a Train' is about a bunch of old men playing dominoes, beer stains on their shirts, waiting for death, one of whom is the singer's father: 'I mean, he's one of the heroes of this country / What's he doin' dressed up like some old man?' If 'Virginia's Reel' and 'New Cut Road' don't make you feel good, if 'Fool in the

Mirror' doesn't make you laugh, you may as well lie down; you must be dead.

There is Willie Nelson, godfather of all the redneck rockers, whose 'Hello Walls' and 'Night Life' became country classics in the 1960s, by Faron Young and Ray Price respectively. His annual outdoor Fourth of July party, held near Austin for eight years during the 1970s, pushed along the movement. He began to become a star after years of doing it his way, and his old labels had to scrabble in their vaults, so that in 1976 he had eight singles in the country chart on three labels. RCA released an album called *Wanted: The Outlaws* that year, with tracks by Nelson, Tompall Glaser, Jesse Colter and Colter's husband, Waylon Jennings (perhaps the original outlaw, who had played bass for Buddy Holly, and just missed going along on Holly's last ride); it was the first country album to sell a million copies. Willie and Waylon made three albums of duets and became the biggest-grossing country act in the USA. In 1983, with Merle Haggard, Nelson recorded Townes Van Zandt's 'Poncho and Lefty', because he knew his friend Townes was a great songwriter who needed the money: it was a number one hit. He has recorded Irving Berlin and Hoagy Carmichael, and he has everybody foxed: my mother bought his records, and she would not have been caught dead listening to country music twenty-five years ago. I saw Willie on PBS a few years ago, and he was not even singing, just picking: there were three guitars, a bass and a fiddle, the same instrumentation as the pre-war Django Reinhardt Quintet of the Hot Club of France, and the music made you feel good in the same way.

Richard Dobson's albums on his own label are showcases for his songs. His *Save the World* in 1982 offered mostly songs about work, including 'The Ballad of Robin Wintersmith', which was covered by Nanci Griffith, who calls it his 'lifestyle justification song'. Based on a true story, it is about a young man who jumps over cars on a motorcycle, and gets killed. Dobson understands why he does it: we each have to do whatever we can do for a living. Terry Allen is a sculptor and an art teacher; his two-disc *Lubbock (On Everything)* is a funny, moving memoir, with much in it to touch the heart of any baby-boomer, such as 'The Pink and Black Song', an affectionate send-up of the late 1950s. Allen thought he had left Lubbock, but producer Lloyd Maines convinced him he did not have to stay away; his *Smoking the Dummy* truly smokes. When it comes to rock, Dobson's backing on *Save the World* and Allen's Panhandle Mystery Band are the best there is. Joe Ely made a reputation in his native Texas, and has since struggled with MCA to make the music he wants to make, but he is pulling it off. A tiny English label has collected together all Ely's covers of Hancock's songs on one LP.

And they keep coming out of the woods: Jimmie Dale Gilmore (erstwhile sidekick of Hancock and Ely – Richard Dobson's first CD was a set of Gilmore's songs in 1993), Lyle Lovett, Darden Smith, Wes McGhee (from Texas by way of London), Steven Fromholz, David Halley (from the Lubbock axis), Robert Earl Keen, Steve Earle (with the accent on rock, but his 'Hillbilly Highway' is as country as they come). They are not all from Texas, they are not all hillbillies and they are not all men: there is Griffith, k. d. lang, K. T. Oslin, Kathy Mattea, Reba McIntyre, the Forester Sisters; from Ireland, Mary Coughlan; from Canada, Mary Margaret O'Hara and the French-Canadian McGarrigle Sisters. Some of them are not so young, because by the time you and I have heard of them they already know a lot of songs and how to put them across. Such is the legacy of the legendary decade: good songs, good friends and good times, if you know where to look. Some of the older songwriters, storytellers and country rockers had chart success once upon a while ago, but most of them have long since retired to their valuable subculture; Jerry Jeff is fond of saying to his audiences that the music business is so awful he is glad he is not part of it, a rueful joke on more than one level. For there is another legacy of the 1960s.

At the end of the decade it had all gone wrong. Stax changed hands, and Jim Stewart found to his surprise that Atlantic owned its classic soul hits. In April 1968 Martin Luther King was murdered in Memphis; the mood in black neighbourhoods all over the USA was immediately hostile, and the staff at Stax could not even go to work. In August 1968, just a year after Otis Redding's joyous party in Atlanta for all his friends at the convention for the National Association of Radio and Television Announcers, the thirteenth annual convention in Miami was haunted by gun-toting scum who wanted something for nothing: an effigy of Wexler was hanged, New Orleans

R & B entrepreneur Marshall Sehorn was pistol-whipped in a toilet and Phil Walden, a champion of black music, was frightened out of it entirely and switched to white rock.

Brian Jones had become a victim of alcohol, drugs and his own lack of confidence; eased out of the Rolling Stones, he drowned in his swimming pool in July 1969. In December the Stones put on a free concert at a disused racetrack in California, and Altamont was a shambles, just a few months after Woodstock: a young black man (stupidly waving a pistol) was kicked and stabbed to death by some hell's angels, who had been hired as security. The Beatles could not stand each other any more and broke up in April of 1970. Hendrix accidentally killed himself with a cocktail of alcohol and drugs in September and Joplin did the same thing in October. (Her version of Kris Kristofferson's lovely 'Me and Bobby McGee', probably the best record she ever made, became her only number one single, indeed her only top forty hit: 'Freedom's just another word / For nothing more to lose'.) Jim Morrison, self-appointed poet of the counterculture and the original monster of narcissism, died from the effects of drugs in July of 1971. Sly Stone, who had as much influence as any of them, slid away in a haze of drugs and unreliability.

Rock'n'roll had seemed to be over in 1960. A decade or so later rock should have been mercifully allowed to retire to the roadhouses of Austin and Lubbock. But by then there was far too much invested in it; the younger generations knew nothing else, and neither did the greedy music business. The pop charts of the last two decades have been dominated by the toys of technology and the sound of money talking.

18

The Heat Death of Pop Music

In 1955, just before Elvis Presley appeared on network television, I was fifteen years old. Five years later, in 1960, there were almost half a million more fifteen-year-olds in the USA than in 1955; between 1960 and 1965 the increase in that age group was well over 700,000, and in another five years it increased by over half a million again. By then the rate of increase in fifteen-year-olds was slowing down, but this already represented a phenomenal rise in the number of young Americans.

All those new citizens needed baby clothes and housing; then more primary schools had to be built, and later more college professors were needed, and all the while there were more cars on the road, still more houses in the suburbs and, finally − the ultimate shrine to western civilization − the shopping mall. America's post-war economy is a progress of the demographic bulge through it. All this economic activity meant more tax money for politicians to spend, but the individuals who comprise that demographic bulge will soon start reaching retirement age, and as they each expect to receive hundreds of dollars a month in Social Security whether they need it or not, the fall in the relative number of people paying the bills may result in economic disaster, and even growing social unrest.

Meanwhile, the American economy has had a free ride for over forty years, and has turned into a simple computer, with only one instruction: make a profit. The car factory in which I worked years ago has been closed and torn down, because it is easier to make a profit selling Japanese or German cars than it is to do the necessary investment and development to keep the domestic industry going. The nation which once thought of itself as the most competitive in the world has forgotten how to do it in less than a lifetime.

Of those thousands of jobs lost in my home town, many were jobs for African-Americans. America may or may not still have a racial problem, but it certainly has something new to the USA: a highly visible and apparently intractable class problem. The reason there is a black urban underclass – or, to put it another way, the reason the black middle class has not grown fast enough – is because there are not enough decent jobs to get people out of the ghettos. The economic machine is not necessarily racist, but it is stupidly blind. If you have money, it will sell you a piece of the action, but there is no money in black neighbourhoods, so they crumble: $50 million could be found to make a flop movie called *Harlem Nights*, but nobody can borrow money to fix up Harlem, and New York City has no money because Washington is a leech that sucks it away. And if you add the white people who are losing hope, the underclass is massive: unlike earlier generations of Americans, today we fear that our children and grandchildren are never going to have it so good; but the white underclass does not tug at the racial conscience, so we do not read much about it in the newspapers.

Nelson George, in *The Death of Rhythm and Blues*, complained that there are no longer any black-owned record shops in black neighbourhoods. The fact is that there are no longer any mom'n'pop record shops in white neighbourhoods either. Thirty years ago in my home town of perhaps 65,000 people, there were three full-service record shops, where you could buy any kind of music you wanted; now there are none. The only decent record shops are in big cities, and the reason is that the record companies and their distributors could no longer be bothered to sell small numbers of records directly to smaller shops, which then had to pay a commission to middlemen for their stock, and went broke.

The effect on the music business of the increasing stupidity of the economic machine does not end there. In 1947 the American record industry finally matched its previous best year (1921); the 1947 sales were matched again in 1955, and four years after that they had doubled. The plastic long-playing record made it possible for shops to stock a greater selection and for people to have larger record collections at home (because LPs took up so much less room than 78s), at the same time as growing prosperity made it possible for people to buy more records. But something has gone wrong. In 1975 John D. Glover of the Cambridge Research Institute said that in 1963 61 per cent of long-playing records did not make a profit; in 1965 an LP broke even at about 7,800 copies, while in 1975 the break-even point for an album was a massive 61,000 copies, and 77 per cent of releases lost money. And that trend has continued.

Just as it is easier to sell Japanese or German cars than to build American ones that people will buy, so it is easier to sell a million copies of one album than to sell 100,000 copies each of ten albums. (That is why all the shopping-mall record shops are the same.) Today the major labels still throw a lot of shit at the wall to see what sticks, but it is much more expensive to operate that way than it was thirty-five years ago. If you guarantee Michael Jackson, Prince, Madonna and whoever millions of dollars for each album, you are taking a very foolish risk.

Today's pop-rock is a paradigm of a society that has no values; it is ubiquitous even though the record companies admit that most of it loses money. Perhaps the problem begins with the fact that nowadays we have less input into our own popular culture. For example, nearly all of it comes to us electronically, whereas years ago we bought tickets: in 1942–3, 80 per cent of the hit songs were from films or Broadway shows; that figure had fallen to 40 per cent by 1950, and has dropped to zero today. Television helped to kill Broadway and musical films, and has not replaced them; on TV we are given endless footage of Californians getting in and out of their cars, but no original music of any kind.

The demographic bulge allowed a marketing style that is now in the process of collapsing. The power of the song pluggers of old passed to the A & R men; when there was a great deal more money involved than ever before, the A & R men were reduced to functionaries, and the power passed again, this time to label bosses who were no longer musicians. The deal-makers have now retained the power for a quarter of a century; the major record companies of today are riding an expensive tiger, and they do not know how to get off.

Suppose for a moment that rock'n'roll had never happened. Suppose American radio had been successful (as the BBC was for a few years) in suppressing it. Suppose nobody had ever paid Tom Parker's price for Elvis Presley, so that he remained a regional phenomenon, and then went back to driving a truck. Suppose that the Beatles had never been signed by George Martin, and remained a short-lived Liverpool cult, and that in 1970 all we heard on the radio was the style of Glenn Miller and Tommy Dorsey, but played absurdly loud by synthesizers. That is what we have got now: rock'n'roll, the urban folk music of the working class, has been around for over forty years (if you count its hillbilly and rhythm and blues antecedents), and it is as inflated and worn out as minstrelsy was a century ago. The economic machine unwittingly created by the counterculture sees to it that pop-rock is aimed at each generation of new customers, yet each year not only is it of less musical value, but the market gets smaller, so it is not selling very well these days. You need not take my word for that. Here is Maurice Oberstein, chairman of Polygram UK, interviewed on television in 1991: 'By and large we have been starved of the hit records turning into hit artists turning into album performance that we can sell. I think as a result we have fewer new artist development [*sic*] . . . We don't have any new artists delivering big new albums.' Oberstein was explaining why Polygram is repackaging Eric Clapton, Jimi Hendrix and the rest on CD, having discovered that the baby-boomers are still the biggest market. Other labels are doing the same thing. And why do CDs cost so much? Jon Webster, managing director of Virgin Records UK, complained to Sean O'Hagen in *The Times* that the record industry's expenses include 'launching a new act. We're in a fashion business. Ninety per cent of what we release loses money; that has to be recouped somewhere.' Every time we buy a record we are subsidizing trash that nobody wants; that has always been the case, but today it is absurdly expensive trash.

The twin problems, fuelling each other, have been overuse of technology and the sound of money shouting. It is hard to deal with them separately, but let us begin with the studio toys. The possibilities of the tape recorder used in the creation of the multi-tracked recordings of Patti Page and Les Paul of the early 1950s, and carried on by Phil Spector and others, were adopted and developed by producers on both sides of the Atlantic, and the monster began to devour the shop.

Joe Meek in England performed miracles in a hole in the wall above a shop in north London; John Leyton's 'Johnny Remember Me' was a UK number one in 1961: Meek had created a pop artefact by twiddling knobs, using compression, echo and overdubbing; he was accused of manufacturing a pop star from a non-singer, which was of course correct. One of Meek's biggest hits was 'Telstar' (1962), an instrumental by the Tornados, his house band. The overdriven sound was the first transatlantic number one, the first USA number one by a UK rock act and is still the only British instrumental to have reached number one in the USA. One of the Tornados described 'Telstar' as 'crap', but kids liked the gimmicky sound, and Meek made major-label producers in the UK look rather sad, because all they could do with their more elaborate studios was imitate each other imitating American pop hits.

Meek became a legend, yet you will find few who will claim that the records are anything but junk: they are quite remarkably bad. His echoing productions of singers who sounded like you or me in the bathtub had an element of sadness in their badness, a hint of doom, as though lamenting their own ignorant boredom. Meek became paranoid about his techniques being copied. As the Beatles and their imitators brought about a new era, in which such producers as George Martin learned to use their equipment to its limits, the likes of Spector and Meek with their claustrophobic production were superseded: Spector retired in 1965, and Meek committed suicide in early 1967, on the anniversary of Buddy Holly's death. They were not the last pop people to take themselves too seriously.

Leiber and Stoller had already been aware that they were making records rather than recording music, but they were smart enough and talented enough to keep that fact in perspective. Suddenly there was so much money in it that the trend became the manufacture of pop artefacts instead of the recording of musical events. The stars would then tour fewer but larger venues to promote the records, rather than making records for fans they had already gained by touring.

The Beatles became so popular that they stopped touring; their work had got so highly polished that there was nothing more to be done with the jingle format. Their hits were witty, slick and catchy little jewels of pop; Maureen McGovern sings some of their love songs along with those of Cole Porter. In the same month as Meek shot himself, 'Penny Lane' and 'Strawberry Fields Forever' came out back to back, surreal (or psychedelic) snapshots respectively of Paul McCartney's and John Lennon's Liverpool childhoods: masterpieces of pop production, they revealed Meek's stuff to be the junk it was. They had been intended for a new album which was taking so long that they were issued as a single; four months later *Sgt Pepper's Lonely Hearts Club Band* was released. It was the number one album in the USA for fifteen weeks and stayed in the UK charts for nearly three years.

As a carefully assembled concept album, *Sgt Pepper* was an expensive production; it was the first Beatles album released in identical editions in both the USA and the UK, and cost $1 more in the USA than most pop albums. In the future a great many rock-pop albums would be expensive productions, taking many months and hundreds of thousands of dollars to produce, and the Beatles were blamed. But they had made eight albums in about four years, including *Sgt Pepper*. In 1989 Kate Bush, Tears for Fears and Blue Nile released new albums which had taken a total of fourteen years to produce: these were reviewed variously as 'drifting piece of atmospheric waffle ... woefully studio-bound extravaganza ... moody sonic ramble ... serves in the end as an example of what an exhausted and exhausting business mainstream pop-rock albums have become'. Today it is the record companies who invest huge amounts of money in grandiosity; let us not blame the Beatles any more than we blame Leiber and Stoller.

In those far-off years *Sgt Pepper* was a complete success on its own terms, the apotheosis of pop. 'When I'm Sixty-four' was nothing more or less than pure music hall, and a better indicator of the Beatles' roots than the rock'n'roll of Chuck Berry or Elvis Presley. McCartney's earlier 'Yesterday' was evidence of the skilful tunesmithing that would make McCartney one of the richest men in the world, and it has been covered hundreds of times. Yet in general the new pop songs of the 1960s would not stand on their own, for the Beatles had accomplished something else. The trade of the professional songwriter began to wither, because each new pop group was required to write its own material. Thousands of tenth-rate songs were published, while the craft of interpretation of good songs fell by the wayside; and the customers had been plugged into their radios and televisions for so long, and had heard so little live music, that they did not know that anything was being destroyed. Music became a throw-away commodity, hence the word 'bubble gum' was used to describe the worst of it. The fans bought records, not music; and the experience was not a musical one, but had become a social one.

Oblivious in their complete economic power and ignorant of other kinds of music, the new generation mistook the smooth efficiency of modern record production for art itself, and the new pop began to be called 'progressive rock'. Pink Floyd, Moody Blues, Genesis, King Crimson, Emerson, Lake and Palmer, Yes and many more groups composed meandering, pretentious and pseudo-philosophical music to get stoned by, which had nothing progressive about it at all, but a touch of doom left over from the Meek influence. The adoption by the Moody Blues of the Mellotron, an early synthesizer, so that they could tour without the big orchestra their ponderous stuff called for, was another sign of things to come. Today's rock critics poke fun at it, but in many cases they are the people who were buying these records when they were a little younger, and they are still looking for something progressive in a music scene that becomes less progressive each year.

The blues were not neglected, however. The legend 'BIRD LIVES' was chalked on walls in New York after Charlie Parker died; but 'CLAPTON IS GOD' was chalked in London when Eric Clapton was barely out of short trousers. A very good young guitarist who wanted to play the blues, he left the successful Yardbirds because they were turning from R & B to pop; he played with John Mayall's Bluesbreakers and then formed Cream, with Jack Bruce on bass and Ginger Baker on drums. The lyrics of Pete Brown were important on their hit singles, but in concert their improvisation was thought to be meaningful because it was very loud (hence the label 'power trio'). It is easy to make fun of progressive rock, but an even greater tragedy was the attempt to force the blues to carry the weight of pop's white-bread narcissism. Cream covered Skip James's 'I'm So Glad' and Robert Johnson's 'Crossroads'; the trio was commercially successful, but soon disbanded, perhaps because Clapton knew perfectly well that their self-indulgence was about as far from Robert Johnson's sort of authority as you could get.

After some vicissitudes, Clapton embarked on a long series of studio albums that continues today. He is still a very good guitar player; he fills the Albert Hall for a series of concerts early each year, and six nights in 1987 became twenty-four in 1991. This is in spite of the fact that he has little more to say than many another good guitar player; the critics have been disappointed in virtually every album since 1970.

Jeff Beck, Robert Fripp and Jimmy Page are three more English musicians who became famous guitar heroes. Beck has never made an album or led a band that has fulfilled the promise he seemed to hold out. Fripp, a technician, came from King Crimson to combine his guitar with electronics, and has become a darling of pop-rock's avant-garde. Jimmy Page was a member of Led Zeppelin, one of the most successful bands of all time.

Like the American West Coast hippie bands, Led Zeppelin were loud folkies, and had their own distinctive sound. They were less pretentious than some of the other progressives, and they were carefully recorded as four individuals: of its kind, the production of their records is still to be admired, and, remastered by Page, is impressive today on CD. Their music had space in it, and they resorted occasionally to acoustic instruments. But their sound was more original than their material, and their best-known anthem, 'Stairway to Heaven', has to be likened to the Moodys' 'Nights in White Satin', in that its primary function today is one of nostalgia. After decades of classic black rhythm and blues and soul music, the riff that imitators have started out with more often than any other is Page's riff from 'Stairway to Heaven'. But Led Zeppelin's worst legacy was not their fault. Their imitators invented heavy metal.

Out of the post-war boredom with Joni James's records and lookalike Levittowns inhabited by GI Bill graduates came the black motorcycle jacket and the image of Marlon Brando in *The Wild One* (1954) who, when asked what he was rebelling against, replied 'Whataya got?' Each generation has thought that it invented sex, iconoclasm and much else, but the larger generation of the 1960s could get away with more; and there was the notion that rock'n'roll was somehow dangerous. Today there are a great many parents who were themselves rock fans. You would think that the notion of dangerous music would have withered, but in the meantime rebellion has become a market: in the middle of the Vietnam War, which was, after all, something worth protesting against, was there not a book called *Revolution for the Hell of It?* So in 1968 a band called Steppenwolf, named after a novel by Hermann Hesse which few had read, had a hit called 'Born To Be Wild', a biker's anthem, which included the words 'heavy metal thunder', taken from a William Burroughs novel.

Heavy metal is the ultimate in phoney rebellion, the logical and boring exaggeration of rock'n'roll as the music to make our parents angry, just as a logical and boring heat death of the universe may be the ultimate result of the original Big Bang. Heavy metal combines blues-based rock with the portentous doom of progressive pop; it is the loudest music of all; it uses the imagery of vaguely Viking mythical heroes, like the trashy children's cartoon 'He-man': the artwork heroes ripple with muscles, while heavy metal's guitar heroes are often skinny weeds. Or the HM bands promote images of devil worship, suicide and even Nazism, showing a paucity of any values at all. Yet heavy metal's largely working-class audience is curiously well behaved; the male fans at the concert-as-ritual are succoured by the phallic symbolism of the guitar hero, the females content to play their supportive roles, and all go back to work on Monday morning feeling as though they have rebelled. The cost of their cheap rebellion is that when they are older, they will find that their hearing has been damaged.

Vanilla Fudge's gimmick in the USA in the 1960s was playing pop covers very slowly, for listeners who were stoned. Deep Purple began as British Fudge imitators; Grand Funk and Mountain carried on in the USA; Britain's Black Sabbath started the sword-and-sorcery nonsense, and Charles Shaar Murray points out that if the Sabs had not been so loud that they took your head off, it would have been obvious that they were not very good. Some of these ponderous giants made so much money that they stopped playing or went into tax exile, hence the New Wave of British Heavy Metal: Def Leppard, Iron Maiden, Whitesnake, Saxon. 'Heavy metal is the basic rock and roll message,' said John Swenson of *Rock World*. 'The least sophisticated kid can get as much out of it as its dedicated followers.' There is no arguing with that.

David Bowie seemed to have more substance than most in the 1970s. He began as David Jones, and wanted terribly to be a star. With his finger on the pulse of the times he changed images, from Ziggy Stardust to Plastic Soul to the dissolution of the Thin White Duke and beyond, mourning lost innocence as he searched for himself, as he knew his generation was searching. His lyrics were allusive and full of the grief of the search. He was intelligent enough to know how perfectly his unbridled ambition and his chameleon act fitted the decade. He ran out of images and faded back into combo rock'n'roll, but with less good songs; in 1993 the latest news was that he had found a new image again.

And there have been groups without number coming and going on both sides of the Atlantic, in a spectrum from bubble gum for the kiddies through ear candy for grown-ups to arty stuff for the critics. As the Beatles grew up, then broke up, the music business was handed a formula on a plate, and used it to rope in each new generation of pre-teen children, while slightly older teenagers were only too happy to become recording artists. Acts which did not exist had hits like 'Yummy Yummy Yummy I've Got Love In My Tummy', vehicles for hack songwriters; as the customers grew older, they were herded into the corral by pop-rock groups who wrote their own material and were more pretentious, but still just looking for a piece of the action, each hoping they did not sound too much like all the others.

Pop-rock acts appeared on the chat shows, such as those hosted by Terry Wogan in the UK, watched mostly by housewives, and Johnny Carson in the USA, unassailable in his polished cynicism. The kids who buy pop records do not watch the chat shows, but the pop group is given the slot because the press agents and the television producers do not know what they are doing. The Wogans and the Carsons do not even talk to the popsters; there may be a musical guest on the sofa, but the guest talks and then sits while Richard Marx, say, does the musical slot. Marx has a slick band, an expensive hairdo, a polished act and no soul; his song is instantly forgettable.

The lead singer of the Del Fuegos sounds like a tired mixture of Mick Jagger, Bob Dylan and Randy Newman. Fairground Attraction's song is not even finished. *Each line* is not finished: the gimmick is that each line runs out of energy, the words trailing off, the rhythm section stumbling. But the rhythm sections often sound amateurish. One of the Cure's videos in early 1991 seemed to portray a bunch of kids noodling, or improvising, in the basement, which is appropriate. In today's entertainment business we can all be stars, because the stars are just like us; and the Cure were made by their videos, not their music.

During the 1970s it was already obvious that the original thrill that was rock'n'roll had become a middle-class marketplace, as many of the heroes of the 1960s become tax exiles and Elvis Presley killed himself with pills. A few teenagers in flared trousers were still furtively getting stoned, but the counterculture was dead. The answer to the problem of the death of rock'n'roll, since the younger generations knew nothing else, was more of it. Rock split into the rock generation's answer to Mantovani on the one hand and punk rock on the other.

Punk was supposed to make rock'n'roll dangerous again, but the danger had been an illusion, and the pathetic fallacy of punk was another. The difference was that the punks bragged about not being able to play or sing, and spat on their audience, and the audience cooperated by spitting back. (If any punk rocker had tried spitting on Jerry Lee Lewis, he would have found out what danger was.) Acts in New York clubs such as Richard Hell and the Voidoids wore torn clothes and safety-pins through their skin, and made a ranting anarchic style of noise. English entrepreneur Malcolm McLaren, working in New York, knew a good thing when he saw it, and never made any bones about *The Great Rock'n'roll Swindle*, as the 1978 film was called. Back in London, McLaren ran a boutique, and recruited the Sex Pistols from among his customers; the most famous and typical of the punks, their music was an indescribable noise of buzz-saw guitar whine and tuneless screaming. Punk became a do-it-yourself era, and entire reference books have been compiled of terrible, amateurish pop singles made in garages with a shelf life of two weeks. Virtually the only band to survive from punk with any reputation is the Clash, and nobody calls their music punk today. David Johansen of the New York Dolls, who later changed his name to Buster Poindexter and invented a cabaret act, said of his earlier career: 'I was basically just doing a rock-oriented or a teen-oriented show – you know, for rebels without a clue.'

In the pop charts punk disappeared into New Wave, followed by the New Romantics. Pop songs by Boy George in the UK, Blondie in the USA and countless more were slick, harmless and slightly cynical, but less portentous. Boy George was frank about dressing up and wearing make-up because it was fun; not much portent there. The songs were forgettable, but by now the pop charts were ignored by serious music fans anyway.

We could always go to the disco. *Discothèque* is French for 'record library'. Already in the 1960s American towns had discos, bars where scantily clad women danced in cages to the jukebox. Workers, white collar and blue, would stop on their way home to sip a beer without blinking, so as not to miss anything: the working-class dancer was often a single mother, with no other way of making a living, but she might get into the spirit of the thing and flash a bit of something naughty. The dancers were also called go-go dancers, because several French clubs and American imitations called themselves 'Whiskey à gogo' (from the French title of the 1949 Ealing comedy *Whiskey Galore*).

In larger cities the gay male subculture picked up on the disco. Banned from the semi-literate suburban family rooms where popular culture is legitimized, a subculture embraces the absurd, which then emerges to become the norm, and suburbia does not even know that it has been sent up; you cannot make fun of a society which has no taste. Young urban blacks also adopted the disco as a place to dress up and show off, playing records being a cheaper way to run a club than hiring live music. And the machinery began to take over completely.

Dr Robert A. Moog had built the first synthesizer in 1964; he combined a PhD in engineering with experience as a composer of jingles. Sly Stone had been the first to use a drum machine, on a 1971 number one US hit, 'Family Affair'. The Family Stone was racially, sexually and stylistically integrated, and played a fusion of pop, soul and rock that was unique; Larry Graham's popping electric bass was one of the most important elements. The drum machine was first used in the family room's electric organ, in case somebody wanted to play a rhumba, a cha-cha or a little bebop. But Sly's followers were mere imitators; the music of the disco came initially from black pop, and Sly's music was a natural source for copycats, as was James Brown's.

Music business insiders had their ears to the ground. Shirley Pixley Goodman was half of Shirley and Lee, whose huge R & B hits included 'Let the Good Times Roll' (1956); her disco hit was produced by Sylvia (Vanderpool) Robinson, who as half of Mickey and Sylvia had the wonderful 'Love is Strange' the same year. Soon 'bpm' numbers (beats per minute) were printed on record labels, to make it easier for the disco DJ to segue from one disc to the next, and the formula of pop-rock pabulum was complete: soon we had everything from Mozart to Beatles tunes set to the mechanical thump. Larry Graham became a crooner, and his bass was replaced in the pop chart by a computer chip.

Thus good party music became godfather to a formula that did more to wreck pop music than any other, because the market for it had more to do with dressing up than with music. And the pop video was coming along, which meant that the stars could make films of themselves having fun, and sell the films at a profit too. Chic was a disco band that could play, including Nile Rodgers, who soon became a producer of plastic music; Giorgio Moroder, with a studio full of toys in Munich, took it all international. In 1977, with the film *Saturday Night Fever*, it became a larger bubble that soon burst, but whose effects are with us still.

In 1979 came this first crash in the pop-rock market. Rock's original customers were growing up and the size of each following generation was shrinking. Disco albums, such as the soundtracks from *Saturday Night Fever*, *Grease* and *Sgt Pepper's Lonely Hearts Club Band* (nothing to do with the Beatles), had been overshipped by the record companies and came back by the truckload. Nevertheless, what is now called dance music is made by computers. A late 1980s manifestation was house, named after a club in Chicago; acid house was another spiral further into computer sampling of other people's music. But the twanging synthesizers and thumping machines all have one thing in common: they do not and cannot swing, so that generations of popsters making music by imitating metronomes do not know what swing is, and often cannot play at all. Once again we have recording engineers who cannot record real drums.

The label 'dance music' implies that previous generations did not dance to music made by humans; but there are amusing aspects. Today's dance hits are made by independent one-off technocrats rather than by pop stars, and are throw-away items, like the good old singles of yore: buy one, enjoy it for a while, then buy another. This confounds the major labels, who need a marketing strategy before they can sell anything. The phenomenon of dance music that sounds like a malfunctioning compact disc player is laden with irony. Since it is all on tape tracks generated by machines, it is a simple matter to remix it, taking the fans' money several times, or to issue several versions until one finally becomes a hit.

Another side of the rise of technology is that in pop-rock the visual record of the act, the video, is more important than ever. Paula Abdul is not a singer but an ex-cheerleader and a choreographer of video dancing. Of her latest album, Tony Parsons wrote in the *Daily Telegraph*: '*Spellbound* is slightly less spontaneous than a pocket calculator . . . Her dance tracks consist of boil-in-the-bag funk and her sexy stuff has fewer erogenous zones than Barbie's boyfriend.' But the fans who buy the records visualize her dancing while they listen. The kids who danced on television's *Bandstand Matinee* thirty-some years ago and the girls who danced in the cage at Freddy's Bar in Kenosha in the next decade are now the stars, and the streets of Los Angeles are full of hopefuls.

The epitome of all this in the 1980s was the success of producers Mike Stock, Matt Aitken and Pete Waterman, who perfected knob-twisting, switch-flipping and button-punching until their bank managers were very happy. They were responsible for thirty or forty hit singles in the UK; they told *Time* magazine that they have 'pretty much a hard and fast rule that no one we work with is over 25': they thus ensure that should they run across anyone with talent, he or she will not have had much time to hone it. Stock–Aitken–Waterman's ménage included Bananarama, three pretty girls; Mel and Kim, two pretty girls; and Kylie Minogue, one pretty girl. I am sure someone called Sonia was not unattractive; Jason Donovan and Rick Astley were pretty boys. None of these people had any discernible talent. Minogue and Donovan were the teenage stars of an Australian soap opera; an Australian commentator put Minogue's appeal down to her 'blinding ordinariness'; a British critic whose job required him to attend her live concert described her as a 'prancing dancing antiseptic swab'. The funniest artefact was Astley's version of 'When I Fall In Love' in 1987. Not only was he covering a classic Nat Cole hit from exactly thirty years earlier, but the producers programmed their computers to imitate Gordon Jenkins's arrangement. The result was so bad it helped the reissued original into the UK charts.

Critics pretended not to take the likes of Stock–Aitken–Waterman seriously, but why not? They were only doing what Joe Meek did, and somebody wrote a whole book about him; in the next century we may be expected to read a book about the technocrats of the 1980s. But actually by this time something is beginning to trouble the critics. They might like to try to ignore the kiddie pop, but anything taking itself seriously is given a good deal of space in the so-called quality newspapers.

In Britain in September 1990 a new Broadcasting Act empowered the government to award three new national radio services to the highest bidders, stipulating only that one should be other than a pop station and one should be for talk. Richard Findlay, managing director of Radio Forth Ltd (one of the hopefuls, to be sure), wrote to *The Times* to complain:

There is a potent and vociferous lobby at work attempting to prove that rock music is not pop music and that ... rock music consortia should be allowed to bid [along with pop consortia]. Needless to say, it is likely that such groups would outbid groups seeking to establish a classical-music station.

In the same issue of *The Times* a letter was printed from Robert Plant and Phil Collins, also complaining:

It is a fact that the majority of records, tapes and compact discs sold in the UK are sold to rock music fans ... Rock music has become an essential part of contemporary culture ... There is, however, no national radio station that caters for the musical tastes of this large percentage of our population. A pop station, based around top 40 singles, does not reflect the depth and quality of a vigorous popular art that supports this multi-million pound industry in which Britain enjoys world leadership.

The pop-rock industry's greatest talent is for begging questions. Are they saying that the people who do not listen to 'rock' are uncultured, or not contemporary? If rock is separate from pop, then let us add up pop, classical, jazz, country and everything else and see if rock still sells the majority of records. Is Michael Jackson rock or pop? How many top forty singles have Plant and Collins sold?

Phil Collins, the drummer with Genesis, has become a big-time rock crooner, helped by the image of the 'nice guy next door'. As Led Zeppelin's vocalist, Plant is one of the giants of the pop-rock of the last twenty-five years. His four solo albums spent a total of forty weeks in the UK charts in the 1980s, three of them making the top ten. Collins had fourteen hit singles in the UK during the 1980s (seven in the top five) and four hit albums (only one of which did not reach number one – it was number two) in the UK album chart for a total of 592 weeks. This is not counting their MOR success in the USA, nor the chart success of Genesis and Led Zeppelin. What are these people moaning about? The truth is that the only distinction between pop and rock is that the popsters are out to be stars and to make money, while the rockers take themselves more seriously and pretend they care less about the loot. Rockists would maintain that their music has progressed since 1956, but there is so little musical difference between rock and pop that many of the artists would be impossible to place in one camp or the other.

As for the words of the songs, we have come from the folk poetry of Hank Williams, Carl Perkins and Bob Dylan to empty posturing; the rockists are no more literate than the popsters. Take U2, an Irish group who began composing their own material because they could not perform anybody else's, and who were suddenly found to be relevant in the wasteland of the late 1980s. In the *Daily Telegraph* film critic Iain Johnstone reviewed their film *Rattle and Hum*, which is so lame it does not bother to tell you which member of U2 is which:

The Edge, I think, says: 'There are people who say you shouldn't mix music and politics but I think that's bullshit.' And we wait, open-mouthed, for him to expand on this sententious theory; but answer comes there none. Accordingly, names like Bishop Tutu and Martin Luther King are taken down from the shelves like proprietary brands and lobbed into their songs, like supermarket shopping thrown into a basket . . . Bono, I think, tells us that he is upset about the Enniskillen bombing [an IRA outrage]. He begins the song, 'I can't believe the news today . . .', but then his well-intentioned sentiments are drowned by the backing. Compared to John Lennon's threnody on the death of Tara Browne – 'I read the news today, oh boy' – there is no comparison.

David Sinclair in *The Times* described the soundtrack album as 'a brilliant patchwork . . . which found the hottest rock'n'roll band in the world on a belated quest to acquire some roots'. The hottest rock'n'roll band in the world is only now looking for some roots, and the track singled out for praise is the one featuring guest B. B. King, and this is in a round-up of the year's best albums.

Bruce Springsteen was basically a folkie whose concerts were incredibly popular because he had working-class sincerity. His song 'The River' is about a young couple in an industrial town who were married too young; their lives are over, and all they can do is sit by the river and watch it go by. This song is about the first half of my life, and it should reduce me to a puddle of self-pity, but it doesn't, because it's not a very good song. His solo acoustic album, *Nebraska*, was a relative failure, but the critics were too embarrassed to point out that stripped-down Springsteen is unfinished: the songs have not got the bumps ironed out of them, the words do not fit the tunes. It was Springsteen who said that 'Chuck [Berry] played in a lot of strange keys, like B-flat and E-flat'. (I always wondered what was so weird about Beethoven's 'Eroica'.) But Springsteen, like Elton John, scooped up fans who had no other home. Charles Shaar Murray notes that Springsteen's concerts were better value than his records: he was, after all, only a white boy playing R & B; in person he acknowledges his debt to the golden oldies, and with a good live band he is at least a showman.

Then there is Prince, who has been described as a toothpick in a purple doily. His obsession with sex is partly the obsession of each new generation and partly narcissism. There is no doubt about the professionalism of his act (he paid his dues in Minneapolis clubs), but there is nothing new in his music. He must be a serious artist, because he never laughs or smiles, never gives interviews and goes everywhere with bodyguards. Sting also never smiles. His hit single 'If You Love Somebody Set Them Free' was a perfect farrago of me-too noise, the almost drowned-out sentiment being today's excuse for a love song: 'I'll have sex with you, but don't expect me to hang around.' George Michael was a big hit in a pop duo called Wham! and made all the money he wanted, then gave interviews about being a serious artist; the name of his latest album was *Listen Without Prejudice*. Madonna is not a singer or a dancer or a songwriter, but a 'performance artist' who knows how to get the media to manipulate themselves. In 1991 she told Robert Sandall of *The Times*: 'My musical career was an accident. I got a record deal in 1982 and just veered off that way. But the more I did it, the less interested I became in being superficial.' I suspect that the pop-rock critics despise her, but it takes somebody like Michael Ignatieff, not a music critic at all, to blow the whistle:

Last week, in an amazing abdication of editorial responsibility, the BBC's usually excellent arts programme, *Omnibus*, allowed [Madonna] to go on ... and on ... about 'her work'. Her work? You mean the bits where she writhes on satin sheets, miming self-abuse, while two Egyptian-style hermaphrodites sporting huge strap-on conical breasts give her a helping hand? Surely some mistake. But no. The usual po-faced 'cultural critics' were rounded up ... The weird thing about modern celebrity is that mediocrity does not give itself away when magnified to planetary dimensions ... When planetary marketing takes over, some smooth intellectual sucker can always be found to tell you it is Culture, with a capital C.

These artists do not give concerts; they put on 'shows'. The stadium act is said to be an important phenomenon – music as spectacle. But if an act has big enough hits, it will sell enough tickets to fill a stadium, and if the show has lasers, smoke machines, costumes and choreography, this will distract from the fact that in most cases there is nothing compelling about the music. The huge audience, waving its arms in the air in unison like a giant beetle on its back, is celebrating itself at a social event.

The rock critics write reviews and articles in the papers which are supposed to make us run out and buy records. With all the records coming out, they wouldn't waste space on stuff they don't like, would they? Here is Simon Reynolds in the *Observer* on Suicide, the 'two-man performance art group': 'brutally simple use of the synthesizer and the drum machine ... critically reviled and ignored ... strict adherence to the fundamental precepts of minimalism and monotony ... too much even for the punk crowd. After recording two excellent albums in the Seventies ...' You can read the whole article over and over, but you keep missing something. Here is Sinclair in *The Times* on a trio with the enchanting name of Rapeman: 'Albini favours a thin, scratchy guitar sound, massively overcranked to deliver squalls of feedback at the drop of a hat ... Solos ... unfold like so much sonic splatter ... Albini's singing [is] a rabidly incoherent, hysterical shriek that brings a number of the songs to the verge of self-destruction.' Yet it displays 'a high degree of individual musicianship ... and the scalpel-sharp sense of purpose to which it is harnessed'. To be fair, the most serious rock acts (which do not include Phil Collins and Robert Plant) are trying to make their comment on the nasty world we live in, but the only vocabulary they have is the same one Elvis Presley used, and it will not do the job, so they trash it, and become part of the problem.

John Peel is a British DJ who made his name presenting bizarre popsters, few of whom became as famous as Peel. In his review of an appearance in London of an American group called Pussy Galore, which plays 'deeply confrontational music', six paragraphs read like an amusing send-up of the pop-rock concert scene and of irritating noise. But then he assures us that, although our initial impression would have been 'of undisciplined uproar and unreasonable aggression',

a more informed listen would have revealed highly structured pieces of some complexity, through which wildly distorted quotes were whipped as though carried in the teeth of some mephitic gale ...

Pussy Galore played a vicious street brawl of a set, leaving the impression that the band pursue a musical scorched-earth policy in the hope that the traditions on which they base their impressive music can never be used again.

If flower power manifestly failed to solve our problems, we can turn to feedback. (Bass player and producer Bill Laswell: 'I never need songs ... The most interesting thing in the last 50 years is noise – the sound of technology.') The frustration of these people is understandable, but it is unclear why anyone should listen to their music.

Closing his review, Peel makes a gratuitous remark (typical of a British critic) about the 'clodhoppery that infests most of American music'. Meanwhile, not only are the clodhoppers and shit-kickers in America making some of the best music, but their fans, far from being rock critics and D Js, are people who have the same old trouble making a living as Carl Perkins had when he worked in a bakery. 'I think a lot of the stuff I'm playing now is crap,' Peel said recently. He is suffering from syndromes that can be overcome with liberal doses of happy music; he ought to try some British clodhoppers, like the Famous Potatoes, an octet of melodeon, accordion, trombone, clarinet, fiddle and rhythm, who first called themselves the Folk Pistols, and who, instead of destroying their roots, play them all. They had made six albums by 1992, but most of them are already out of print, partly because people like Peel make a career of not having a good time.

He could take a cue from Wolfman Jack, one of the great D Js of early rock'n'roll, who played a lovely cameo role in the film *American Graffiti* (1973), which was set in 1962. (It is curious how much nostalgia there is among baby-boomers for the period just before they became a counterculture.) In 1989 the Wolf was working on Nashville Network Radio via satellite, and he told a Florida newspaper that he plays a lot of country music these days. 'It's old-fashioned rock'n'roll, man.'

Mojo Nixon is an American who has coined the terms 'Stingism' and 'Stingology' to describe the phenomenon of the rock person as Serious Artist: 'Sting? *George Michael*? Are these people *kidding*?' Nixon calls himself a punk rocker, but he is using the term in its original meaning of garage music: he is a rock'n'roller who knows that the music is supposed to be *fun*.

Most of today's pop-rock is not fun; it is tired and boring and its energy is forced. But the difficulty in being a pop-rock critic nowadays is relieved occasionally; it's OK to denigrate something that is going to sell millions anyway. Here is Sinclair on Phil Collins's album . . . *But Seriously*: 'Like those Woolworth's paintings of little urchin girls with pearly tears on their cheeks it is of course all superficial tat, airbrushed without guile to mass market perfection.' But you cannot do this too often. Elsewhere Sinclair, reviewing Rick Astley's live act, thinks that he 'demonstrated the timeless ability to carry a good tune, irrespective of style'. Unless it's Nat Cole's style. Robert Sandall seemed to praise a new album in early 1990 by Robert Plant: '*Manic Nirvana* does sound in many respects like the best album Led Zeppelin never made, as, in fact, it was supposed to . . . The interesting point . . . is that Plant hasn't merely set out to recapitulate himself.' And again we've missed something.

The critics on the daily national papers in Britain are paid well for pretending that the fodder of the consumer culture is worth writing about, and it is not easy to write about something that basically is not very interesting. David Cheal in the *Telegraph* reviewed a gig by a band called the Dream Academy. The sound, lights and visual effects were fine, he wrote.

So why was this such a disappointing experience? Some blame could be attributed to lead singer Nick Lairds-Clowes, whose rock-star demeanour seemed at odds with the intimacy of this cosy auditorium. The show was badly paced; often there was an unsettling silence between the end of the applause and the beginning of the next song (though the exceptionally polite audience could be held partly responsible for this).

Then there is the band's dearth of first-class material.

The critic is watching a group which has no stagecraft, doesn't know how to work an audience, doesn't know what kind of room it is in and has made three albums yet cannot fill up a live gig with worthwhile material. It is true that British audiences are sometimes too polite, but why is Cheal so polite?

Attempts at live performance by such non-acts as Minogue, Bananarama and the Pet Shop Boys bring out the best in the critics; they have to depict a disaster as they have seen it, and they enjoy it. These performers have to depend on their backing tapes, and sometimes they don't work. The Pet Shop Boys' tape accidentally included their vocals, so at their live début they stood on stage with nothing to do. In mid-1991 Betty Boo, voted most promising newcomer by the British pop industry a few months earlier, was pretending to sing on stage when she dropped her prop microphone. There are groups called Pop Will Eat Itself, and the Scene That Celebrates Itself. Perhaps the whole point is that it is all meaningless.

Bandleader Bon Jovi treads a careful and cynical path between very loud music that is just melodic enough to be pop and not quite loud enough to be head-banging music. Steve Turner describes the familiar ritual of a pop concert, and concludes: 'Bon Jovi music can only really work for you if you believe the Bon Jovi myth. If you don't believe, you are left with the sound of one man worshipping himself in the mirror of an audience and an audience worshipping itself in the mirror of a man.' Bon Jovi also provides us with an example of the nature of today's record business. His series of theatre concerts on the West Coast in early 1990 was compared with that of Steve Lawrence and Eydie Gormé. Steve and Eydie attracted about the same number of customers and grossed roughly the same amount of money, but Bon Jovi is promoting the new album, whereas Steve and Eydie do not bother making records at all, because they will not be played on the radio or available in the shops.

Then there is Jonathan King, sometime pop star, producer turned self-appointed critic. 'Jump Up and Down and Wave Your Knickers In the Air' was one of his in the early 1970s. More recently, he presented a series of travelogues on television called *Entertainment USA*, each segment of which included a music slot as inappropriate as those on the Johnny Carson show. When he visited New Orleans, we got a pop video featuring a skinny young woman who had nothing to do with New Orleans and whose raucous female Mick Jagger imitation was filmed close-up with a fish-eye lens so that she appeared to fellate a bulbous microphone, itself unnecessary with today's technology. Jonathan King would be of no importance, except that when showing us New Orleans on prime-time television, he could have offered us the R&B dynasty represented by the Neville Brothers, or legendary pianist Tuts Washington, or Ellis Marsalis, pianist father of the talented clan. He could have pulled off a coup by presenting Harry Connick, Jr, then on the brink of stardom. Instead he showed us a pop video, and this brings us to the problem that is even bigger than the technology of pop-rock. The music business has been chasing money for many years; the problem is that the true cost (as economists call it) includes the cost of not doing business some other way. But the deal-makers took over twenty-five years ago.

Clive Davis, a lawyer, became head of CBS's Columbia Records in 1967. That year at the Monterey Pop Festival he was surrounded by West Coast rock groups who already had followings, though many of them had no recording contracts. Discovering an unserved market, Davis signed everybody in sight. After a decade of rock'n'roll the major labels were still undecided about it, but as the rest of the nation was losing its soul to the marketplace, Davis tied Columbia to a phenomenon that corporations did not even understand.

Davis bought Big Brother and the Holding Company (with Janis Joplin) from tiny Mainstream Records; other acts he got for less. He signed Electric Flag and Moby Grape (where are they now?), Blood, Sweat and Tears (successful after one-time rock superstar Al Kooper was replaced by vocalist David Clayton-Thomas) and Chicago (originally Chicago Transit Authority), the last two of which sold records because rock was already becoming easy-listening music. Davis signed baby acts (those without previous contracts) for nothing; if they made money he reaped the credit. Santana, and later Billy Joel and Earth, Wind and Fire, were profitable. John Hammond brought Bruce Springsteen to Columbia, but Bruce took so long to become a superstar that Davis got the credit.

By around 1970 Simon and Garfunkel had split up; Andy Williams and Johnny Cash no longer had television shows and their sales began to drop. Davis had run out of baby acts, so he raided other companies, and Columbia became the house of deals. He grabbed Pink Floyd (from Capitol) and signed Neil Diamond for what seemed like a large amount of money, but everything turned out all right. In 1971 Davis was made president of a reconstituted CBS Records

Group, which included all the labels and their overseas offices. Columbia was doing very little in the black music market; it invested money in what was left of Stax, and lost it. Davis became involved with black record producers Kenny Gamble and Leon Huff and their label, and once again he was lucky: in less than a year Philadelphia International had crossover success with the O'Jays, Harold Melvin and the Blue Notes (including Teddy Pendergrass) and others.

The lush, overproduced sound of Philadelphia International was one of the things that was happening to black pop. Worse than that, however, Gamble and Huff did not like Columbia's promotion and were allowed to handle their own, and they were into payola. Davis had also made a promotion deal with Kal Rudman, a talented tip-sheet operator who took payola: Rudman had a real skill for picking hits, and took money for records he liked (why not?). There was now even more money involved. Davis, full of himself, liked big money, the power and stardom that could be found in an industry where flash counted for more than talent. He charged a bar-mitzvah party to a false account. He hired an assistant, David Wynshaw, who had gangster friends and who cheated Columbia with phoney invoices. One of Wynshaw's friends was caught with a roomful of heroin; Gamble was later fined for payola; it had all begun to stink, and Davis was fired in 1973. Everyone was shocked, because even if Davis had been careless with money, he was one of the most successful record men in sight; but CBS was always a conservative company, and Davis's luck had run out. (Charges were brought against Davis and later dropped, which is common in the record industry when firing somebody. The same thing had happened to Eli Oberstein decades earlier.)

Jann Wenner had also discovered a market when he launched *Rolling Stone* magazine after the 1967 Monterey Pop Festival. *Rolling Stone* became the voice of the counterculture, another example of how middle class it was. Wenner never pretended to be anything but a commercial operation. There were not many bad record reviews, because advertising was important. The connection with Davis lies in the contradiction that while CBS, one of the country's biggest corporations, had pushed rock records by advertising in *Rolling Stone* that it was on the side of the Revolution, it bounced Davis at the first sign of getting its fingers burnt.

The counterculture never knew that it was a middle-class phenomenon, though Davis at Columbia Records in New York wearing Nehru jackets should have been a give-away. As Louis Menand wrote in the *New Republic* in 1991, the American middle class is too insecure to resist a new self-concept when one is offered.

The difficulties begin with the word 'counterculture' itself ... For during those years the counterculture *was* culture ... It had all the attributes of a typical mass culture episode: it was a lifestyle that could be practiced on weekends; it came into fashion when the media discovered it and went out of fashion when the media lost interest; and it was, from the beginning, thoroughly commercialized. Its failure to grasp this last fact about itself is the essence of its sentimentalism.

Bob Dylan knew that nothing had changed. On *Street Legal* (1978), his last album before he turned to religion, he asked:

> Can you tell me where we're headin'?
> Lincoln County Road, or Armageddon?
> Seems like I've been down this way before.
> Is there any truth in that, Señor?

The counterculture, as consumers, became the willing partners of big business. But Clive Davis had done nothing good for Columbia. He brought the label back to the top of the marketplace, but on a much less sound basis. The ever larger amounts of money involved resulted in the major labels being forced to try to buy success, and he helped destroy the tradition that a recording artist should have some kind of following before a contract was offered. What happened to Columbia Records was what was happening to the country: the deal, the quick profit, the clever scam that impressed one's rivals was more important than the product.

Davis's ultimate successor, in 1975, was Walter Yetnikoff, another New York lawyer. He bragged that he was tone-deaf; one of his girlfriends told Frederick Dannen (author of *Hit Men*, 1990) that Yetnikoff could not tell one piece of music from another. Yetnikoff was the boss when the disco boom collapsed in 1979. One of the worst deals he presided over was the acquisition of Paul McCartney. Columbia not only paid $20 million, but gave McCartney the priceless Frank Loesser publishing catalogue, and did not even get in return any of McCartney's backlist. (Much of the profit in a big star comes from steady sales of old hits.) McCartney's next few albums did not do that well; Columbia lost money on McCartney, and will continue losing money as long as Loesser's *Guys and Dolls* keeps making it. Yetnikoff had bought the Loesser property in the first place, and promised the estate that it would be the jewel in the crown of CBS Songs; Mitch Miller's comment was, 'If I were a Columbia stockholder, I would sue for dilution of its assets.'

WEA (Warner–Elektra–Atlantic, including Reprise) is a much better-run company. It was WEA and its predecessor companies who gave Ry Cooder a contract at a time when he had not made a single album of his own, and who have issued albums of integrity by Emmylou Harris and many others. This was possible because WEA was the artist-oriented company that Columbia used to be, with bosses for each label who were allowed to make their own decisions. Yet WEA too got sucked into the table-pounding ego-ridden style of management: Yetnikoff took James Taylor from WEA (just as Taylor was passing his commercial peak); from Columbia WEA took Paul Simon, who wanted to leave anyway, and it was some years before WEA began to get its money back with Simon's *Graceland*. Mo Ostin at WEA renewed Rod Stewart's contract for an absurd $2 million each for ten albums, believing that Stewart's manager was talking to Yetnikoff. Compare the cost of Rod Stewart's contract with the $425,000 for each Neil Diamond album, which seemed so high in 1970. How long could this hyperinflation go on?

After the disco crash of 1979 Columbia came back on the strength of only two albums: Michael Jackson's *Thriller* and Bruce Springsteen's *Born in the USA*. But its erratic performance contributed to a climate in which one of the crown jewels of the record industry was soon sold overseas. The oldest record company in the world had become a liability.

The Network, the system of independent promo men of which Kal Rudman had been one of the midwives, had begun to take over. The major labels farmed out their promotion work so that the payola was kept at arm's length, and a handful of gangster types controlled what records were played on the most important stations in America. In 1985 the US record industry grossed $4.5 billion (maximum) and made pre-tax profits (maximum) of $200 million. That is only about 2.5 per cent return (pre-tax) on an investment, but there is more: they were also spending (minimum) $60 million, or 30 per cent of their pre-tax profits, on promotion, some of which, everybody knew, was kicked back to corporate vice-presidents.

In December 1989 Joseph Isgro, a record promoter and leading member of the Network, was indicted on fifty-one counts of racketeering and conspiracy to defraud and to distribute cocaine. In March 1990 the American press reported with a straight face that Columbia had been revived, thanks to Yetnikoff's appointment of failed 1960s popster Tony Mottola to head the domestic label. Mottola hired three more executives away from Arista, Atlantic and Polygram, which made five high-powered big shots to revive the label, set to have a good year thanks mainly to a bubble-gum act, New Kids on the Block. The label of Bessie Smith, Robert Johnson, most of the best of Fletcher Henderson, Duke Ellington, Billie Holiday, Tony Bennett, Johnny Mathis, *South Pacific* and much else is now over one hundred years old, and wastes so much money that it has to rely on bubble gum to stay afloat. Sony, the new owners, finally dismissed Yetnikoff in early 1991, reportedly with a $25,000,000 handshake.

As Frederick Dannen points out in his book *Hit Men*, if the pioneers of rock'n'roll, such as George Goldner and Morris Levy, were all crooks, at least they did not pay out tens of millions of dollars in bribery. It took New York lawyers to do that. All the promotion money goes to sell singles, which do not even make money nowadays; what the industry is after is a hit single to sell an album, where there is more profit. The Top 40 format is now called CHR, Contemporary Hit Records: it can't be called Top 40 any more because some of the radio stations don't even have forty records on the playlist. And who was the top-selling artist in the pop album charts of 1991, according to *Billboard*? Country singer Garth Brooks, whose label did not even bother to promote his singles in the pop market.

After 1975 sales of pop singles fell by 50 per cent in ten years, both in the USA and in the UK. Twang-thump 'dance music' on 12-inch singles survives, but in early 1993 Sony and EMI in Britain announced that they were going to stop making singles almost entirely. The pop single is as dead as an Edison cylinder, because there are a great many toys to distract kids today, such as computer games, and anyway there are fewer kids to buy records than there were twenty-five years ago.

In the 1950s radio abandoned the adult audience, which had more purchasing power and bought albums rather than singles, which meant more profit for the record companies. You could argue that this was a smart thing to do at the time, because the youth market was increasing, but there is no evidence that broadcasters were studying demographics; and in the 1970s they did it again as the baby boom passed its peak.

In October 1965 the Federal Communications Commission ordered broadcasters to stop duplicating their AM and FM transmissions, and around that time manufacturers of radios were required to include FM as well as AM bands. In the early 1970s FM discovered new prosperity when Tom Donahue, a California DJ, pioneered a policy of playing longer, more interesting album tracks with less talk and no commercial jingles, taking the counterculture away from AM radio. But by the end of the 1970s, as the pop chart was taken over by overproduced AOR (Adult or Album Oriented Rock), electro-pop and bubble gum for all ages, FM broadcasters discovered that they could make money faster by playing CHR on FM: by this time the number of fifteen-year-olds in the country was declining and the number of thirty-year-olds increasing. Once again the broadcasters and their advertisers had abandoned a sizeable percentage of listeners with purchasing power, but this time it was a growing rather than a shrinking group. AM stations were given over to talk and pop music continued to decline in quality.

Not making easy money the way it used to, and having to find the money for the bribery somewhere, the industry now wants a tax on blank tape. *The Times* reported in a subhead: 'Home taping costs European music companies about £10 million a year.' The testifying witness in the text turns out to be the record companies' trade body, the International Federation of Phonogram Producers. It is not the little independent record labels who want the tax. They know perfectly well that people tape each other's records for the same reasons they used to swap them and borrow them, and that more fans for more music will result, if the music is any good.

Meanwhile, Clive Davis landed at Arista, where he was successful with Barry Manilow and Melissa Manchester, not Monterey-type acts, but MOR or AOR (which also means 'All Over the Road'). Davis has been compared to Mitch Miller, who snorts with derision:

A record executive must be a nurturer, in the mold of Conkling and Lieberson, and not take credit that rightfully belongs to his staff ... There's guys in the field who brought the stuff to [Davis], and the rest were all deals ... I could take a list of people who were promoted with four-color posters as the second coming of the Lord who couldn't ad lib a burp after a radish dinner.

Miller thought it was ironic that Manchester and Manilow were his kind of artists, but more typical of the industry was an album by British rocker Roy Hill in 1978. There are demonstration tapes by Roy Hill that sound good enough to release: tough, spare, inexorable urban laments full of sexual and social grief. But the album Davis released was a party record and grossly overproduced by Gus Dudgeon, a flavour of the month in the late 1970s. It went well over budget, sank without a trace and Hill never made another. The way the major labels do business almost guarantees that records will be overproduced. Less and less has been done in-house since the 1960s, since the lawyers don't know anything about records anyway; they call in experts who have had a couple of hits and who behave like children in a toyshop. B. B. King gave one of the best live shows ever seen at the Hammersmith Odeon in October 1977, but his album at the time had twelve dull soundalike songs by two writers nobody had ever heard of: the music business had succeeded in making B. B. King boring.

More recently, the English rocker Graham Parker complained, 'I don't *want* my cymbal to sound like a refrigerator falling on to a pile of glass.' Tom Waits, the Californian chronicler of the seamy side, said, 'If I want a sound, I usually feel better if I've chased it and killed it, skinned it and cooked it.' Steve Earle would sound less rockist if his production was not so claustrophobically amplified and had more space in it. The Forester Sisters, a quartet from Georgia, sang beautifully and their songs were mostly good ones, but their albums had a tad too much sheen. Country rocker T. Graham Brown's act was praised in *Country Music People*, but the magazine was a bit reserved about the albums: sure enough, Brown's touring band had been replaced by bags of studio production, including loud, stiff, unswinging rock drums.

The paucity of good music in the mainstream marketplace and the domination of technology mean that the record producers have become stars. Jazz trumpeter Wynton Marsalis unwittingly provides a good story; he used as a guest on an album the elderly New Orleans guitarist Danny Barker, and was impressed because Barker did not wear headphones in the studio. It is hard to believe that Marsalis does not know that the best records of the century have been made with the headphones on the engineers. Musicians cannot listen to each other sitting in cork-lined cubicles wearing headphones; one hopes that Marsalis's drummer does not need a click track to tell him where the beat is. Bob Dylan comments in the notes to *Biograph*, a retrospective collection, about the simple way he used to make records; he should take a cue from the fact that the reviews of his new albums jabber more about his production than about his songs.

By the time Manilow and Manchester had faded, Davis had discovered Whitney Houston. Somebody had to find this beautiful girl with a beautiful voice from a whole family of beautiful voices: Cissy Houston is her mother; Dee Dee and Dionne Warwick are her cousins; she calls Aretha Franklin Auntie Ree. Knowing from personal experience how precarious employment in the record business can be, Davis signed Houston to a personal contract, so that if he gets fired again, he can take her with him. She has had huge hit albums and singles, and Davis has done it again; but the only memorable song Houston has recorded is 'The Star Spangled Banner'. Her hit material consists of non-songs written in the studio by hacks and producers, and laden with that sterile sheen that makes good wallpaper for the ears. The girl is still young, but nobody knows whether she can sing a good song or not.

In a pub recently I heard a cassette playing which was so typical of today's pop-rock that I asked to see it. It was a compilation called *Soft Metal*, with several pop-rock acts of which the only one I remember is Saxon. What was typical about it was skill combined with empty content. The rock beat had nothing to do with any of the roots of country music, rhythm and blues or rock'n'roll. The songs were sung well enough, for all the tools in the modern pop vocalist's kit had been adequately mastered: the gospel melisma, the country catch in the voice, the blues inflections. All the bits copied from all the musics had been liquidized and squirted into a dozen moulds of utterly uninspired songs, adding up to rock as elevator music. First the deal-makers in fast food took the malt powder out and made the milkshake; then in the music business they took the soul out and made pop-rock.

It is no surprise that when *Billboard* introduced a more accurate method of counting sales in May 1991, using the bar codes on the packaging and including more supermarket racks, country music received a big boost up the album-chart ladder at the expense of pop-rock; country music has been unfairly neglected by the industry for decades. But there is another parallel music industry which still cannot be counted, because the records are not found in the racks at all. A large number of small independent labels put out everything from Cajun swamp rock to avant-garde jazz for knowledgeable hard-core music fans; a small army of them spends a lot of money on their favourite sounds, of which most people remain totally unaware. In this market will be found much of the best music of today. Nowadays a great many records are sold through the post; the music magazines are full of advertisements for this service. Who counts the records that are sold through the post because they cannot be found in the shopping-mall record shops, which are little more than racks? When we read in the papers that jazz, for example, amounts to only 1 or 2 per cent of the market, we know the figures are distorted by the domination of the major labels, and we have their word for it that most of their stuff doesn't sell any more.

And that is almost the end of the history of popular music, because the best of it nowadays remains a secret.

19

Black Music: Everybody's Still Doing It

'Trouble is, he can't play it straight.' So said Charles Mingus about Ornette Coleman. Mingus had been regarded as avant-garde in his own time, and should have known better. In fact, he later assessed the situation more carefully: 'I'm not saying everybody's going to have to play like Coleman. But they're going to have to stop playing like Bird.'

Nearly fifty years after the advent of bop it is now revival music, and some youngsters are playing it without the fire of the generation of the 1940s, so that some of it sounds like wine-bar Muzak. In the 1940s bop was controversial; similarly, thirty years after the advent of free jazz one could wonder what all that fuss was about. Ornette Coleman's earliest tracks are simply and perfectly beautiful, especially to anyone who listens to contemporary classical music, to say nothing of horror-film soundtracks, where Hollywood hacks have used 'weird' sounds since the beginning of talkies.

I have defined popular music as commercial music, but what we used to call jazz has effectively become art music, confusing my definition. You will find records by Anthony Braxton, Bill Dixon and George Russell in the jazz section of the record catalogue, but all three are academics, like most classical composers. There is not much room for art in a music industry dominated by greed, but it is no coincidence that as the mainstream music industry has concentrated on making deals, music that can be described as contemporary has had to find a specialist audience.

It may be argued that the best music has often had a small audience. The court composers of the Renaissance who developed the classical forms which later flourished in Vienna were working for a musically educated aristocracy, which did not admit riff-raff to its music rooms. San Marco in Venice, the church for which Andrea and Giovanni Gabrieli, uncle and nephew, composed their innovative music in the sixteenth and seventeenth centuries, held 420 people comfortably, which was exactly the size of the Venetian government; there is no evidence that anyone else ever heard it. Opera was originally created for an audience that represented a small proportion of the total population of Italy around 1600. And it is fair to point out that some people want to leave the theatre whistling the tunes – or, to put it another way, Schoenberg never wrote a comic opera. (Actually, he did, *Von Heute auf Morgen* in 1928, but Schoenberg was not a funny man.) We will wait a long time for a laugh from Andrew Lloyd Webber, whose music is popular (that is, makes money) but is derivative and second-rate.

Irving Berlin said that popular music is popular because lots of people like it. But Berlin would not sanction much interpretation of his songs, and Jerome Kern's estate did not like Dizzy Gillespie's first recordings with strings (1946), which were not issued for many years (despite some extraordinary trumpet playing), nor the Platters' version of 'Smoke Gets in Your Eyes' (1958) until they realized how much money they would get from a number one hit.

The anti-modernists among us will turn Berlin round and say that some contemporary music is not very popular because not many people like it, but that argument will not wash with me. Grandma Clarke's idea of culture was a cracked 12-inch 78 of Madame Schumann-Heink singing 'Stille Nacht', but that did not stop me from embarking on a lifelong voyage of discovery. We do not know how popular Ornette Coleman, Cecil Taylor, Roscoe Mitchell or Braxton or the others might be, because we do not hear them on the radio, nor can we buy their records in the shopping-mall record outlets. Listeners who allow music to be pigeon-holed for them are effectively shutting their ear-holes. There are many instances of the public's adopting new music more enthusiastically than the critics. ASCAP used to complain with regard to BMI that if you restrict the public's listening, the public will quite happily settle for whatever it gets. This, of course, ignored the monopoly that ASCAP and Tin

Pan Alley had operated for many years, but the statement is true enough as far as it goes. Anthony Braxton has made albums of standards and of Monk's tunes, but you will not find them in the shopping-mall racks any more than you will find his spikier stuff.

It is also fair to add that the music of such avant-garde rock groups as Suicide, Rapeman and Pussy Galore is not meant to be easy-listening music, and is also not heard on the radio. But their thrashing is the sound of desperation, without any leavening of beauty. Most contemporary music still makes its point using acoustic instruments, and the musicians still listen to each other without the help of thousands of watts.

In any case, jazz has not been allowed near the centre of the marketplace for decades. That is partly why several of the best-known young (mostly white) saxophonists of today, although they play the same instruments as Johnny Hodges, Lester Young and Ben Webster played, all sound like they are playing for television commercials. Their carefully neutral tone is like the cooked milk you get for your tea or instant coffee in British restaurants, and the shopping-mall chord changes of their jazz present a big problem. It must be admitted that the modal method offers a cop-out opportunity, like having to use only the white keys on the piano. Some of today's jazz is wrapped in cellophane, like one of those big Easter baskets full of cheap chocolate and fake grass.

In fact, the word 'jazz' does not mean much any more, so the real stuff we now call improvised music, and even that label is not good enough; some modern music is entirely improvised, and some not very much at all. Jesse Stone told Frank Driggs that he wrote out the solos for his Blues Serenaders on 'Starvation Blues' in 1927. And despite all the efforts to create a third-stream music over the years, jazz and classical (contemporary) music have been cuddling together over in the corner while nobody was watching.

As we saw in an earlier chapter, pianist and composer Lennie Tristano was a retiring sort, whose teaching points were adventurous harmony and complex inner rhythms. Among his pupils were saxophonists Lee Konitz, Warne Marsh and Ted Brown, of whom Konitz is the best known. Having studied with Tristano, he was one of the few alto saxophonists who was not overwhelmed by Charlie Parker.

Warne Marsh died in 1987, still in obscurity; he made twenty or so albums, most of them on tiny labels. *All Music* (1977) is probably one of the best: touring with Supersax, a band that played transcriptions of Charlie Parker solos, he made an album in Chicago because Chuck Nessa offered him the chance. His tone was unique, and his approach to tonality and his slightly quirky time (a matter of personal accents) made him a more interesting player than most, for those who cared to listen. Ted Brown recorded with Marsh and British-born pianist Ronnie Ball in the 1950s, but made only one album as a leader, in 1956, and did not make another for twenty-nine years. I found Brown's trio set *Free Spirit* (1987), his second album for the Dutch Criss Cross label, not on the radio, not in the media, not in a record shop, but in a friend's basement. For me it was one of the discoveries of a decade: Jacques Scholes on bass provides a strong walking beat from which the piano and the saxophone can launch themselves; Hod O'Brien's agreeable, swinging piano would alone be worth the price of the album, and Brown's tone is the kind of sound your best friend would make if he or she could play saxophone. The whole thing is so mellow and so beautiful that it is astonishing to realize that Brown had not made any albums for three decades.

These people play standards: *Free Spirit* includes 'Body and Soul', 'Darn That Dream' and 'Lover Come Back to Me'. They play jazz classics, like Lester Young's 'Lester Leaps In' and Charlie Parker's 'Relaxin' at Camarillo', and their own tunes, such as Brown's 'Smog Eyes' and Marsh's sardonically titled 'Background Music', all of which are more or less based on the same chord structures that were used by the composers of the standards. And where else is there to go? If you want something a little more adventurous, there is the bold humour and unique tone of Von Freeman, and the 'metallic cocaine bebop' of Fred Anderson, both black Chicagoans, both available (though you have to try hard to buy good records) and neither particularly hard to take for tender ears. Or you can listen to somebody who has taken a leap and invented his own music, as Louis Armstrong, Coleman Hawkins, Lester Young and Charlie Parker did in the past.

Enter Ornette Coleman, and free jazz. Alto saxophonist and composer Coleman played in a school marching band with reedmen

Prince Lasha and Dewey Redman, and drummer (and trumpeter) Charles Moffett. At sixteen he changed from alto to tenor for a while, inspired by local tenor saxophonist Red Connors. He had never listened to R&B as a boy, but played in R&B bands to make a living, sometimes getting fired because he was trying to find his own way; he settled in Los Angeles, working in day jobs while studying theory. He did not find sympathetic collaborators until he had been playing for a decade. He worked with trumpeter Bobby Bradford, drummer Ed Blackwell and pianist and composer Paul Bley in the mid-1950s, and then he began intensive private sessions with trumpeter Don Cherry, drummer Billy Higgins and bass player Charlie Haden, the group that became the Ornette Coleman Quartet.

After being introduced by bass player Red Mitchell to Lester Koenig, head of the Contemporary label, Coleman made his first album in early 1958, *Something Else!!!*, with a quintet that included Cherry and Higgins. *Tomorrow is the Question!* in early 1959 included Cherry, Shelly Manne and Mitchell. Mitchell then introduced Coleman to third-streamers John Lewis and Gunther Schuller, who helped him get to a summer jazz school at Lenox, Massachusetts, and a gig at the Five Spot in New York in November. He had signed with Atlantic, and made seven albums' worth of tracks between May 1959 and March 1961 (there was still unissued material, and a six-CD set of the complete Atlantic recordings is available in 1994). He played at the Newport and Monterey jazz festivals, and a recording of a Town Hall concert in late 1962 was issued on ESP, but he did not record again in the studio until mid-1965. He was composing and studying trumpet and violin, but he was also disgusted that Dave Brubeck's quartet could get much more money: Coleman demanded similar fees, and did not get any work. He was criticized for this, but he had a right to price his own work, and he has been a good deal more influential than Brubeck ever was.

Coleman's appearance in New York was a great shock, much more sudden than bop had been. During the acoustic era a tin-eared A&R man at Victor would not record Bill Challis's arrangements for Jean Goldkette, and did not like Bix Beiderbecke's 'wrong' notes; in the late 1940s the boppers ran into the same problem, and in 1960 it was Coleman's turn. For a while he was famous, as fame in jazz goes, though controversy does not pay the rent. He played a white plastic alto saxophone, because he liked the sound of it, and Cherry played a pocket trumpet. The instruments looked like toys, which gave the critics something else to complain about (but perhaps led to the Coleman title 'Joy of a Toy'). Some people thought Coleman was a charlatan, but Leonard Bernstein was a fan, while George Russell, who had written a textbook on the use of modes, knew exactly what was happening: 'Ornette seems to depend on the overall tonality of the song as a point of departure for melody ... This approach liberates the improvisor to play his own song, really, without having to meet the deadline of any particular chord.' I do not know what Coleman's theory of 'harmelodics' means, but it doesn't matter; to the ordinary listener the music is aharmonic.

Writing about music is not as secure as working in the car factory, and certainly does not pay as well, but it has one big advantage. There was no music in the car factory, whereas while writing this I am listening to *The Art of Improvisation*, a 1970 compilation of unissued Coleman tracks from a decade earlier. 'The Fifth of Beethoven', for example, with Cherry, Haden and Blackwell, is enormous fun; it is a bright, funny, uptempo piece on which Coleman's alto sound reminds me of Eric Dolphy (who also came out of intensive private jams in Los Angeles). The influence of Charlie Parker is there, and also of Thelonious Monk, in that Coleman is first and last a composer whose time is unique – like Monk's, a matter of phrasing and accents. As I listen, I hear Blackwell's tom-toms in a duet with Coleman, and just as I am chuckling at that, I notice that Haden's driving bass on the other channel is doubling the alto's phrases, and while my attention is away, Blackwell is up to something else. The music has the cry of the blues in it, and we are reminded once again that the blues was never a dead end in the black community in the way that rock has become a blind alley for the white. The best black music always has the blues in it.

It was called free jazz, and some people still call it that, but it is certainly hard to see now why it was controversial, or why it has not made more money for Coleman, especially since some of the shopping-mall Muzak rockers of today are trying feebly to imitate it. It was, of course, not free at all, not as free as those experimental tracks Tristano made in 1949, with Marsh and Konitz. Coleman's Atlantic album of late 1960, *Free Jazz*, was played by a double quartet of Coleman, Cherry, Haden and Blackwell, and Eric Dolphy, Freddie Hubbard, Higgins and the brilliant young bass player Scott La Faro (who was killed in a car crash). The album is generally regarded as a noble failure, though Max Harrison, in his brilliant collection *A Jazz Retrospect* (1976), describes it as a perfectly coherent whole, its shape arising out of its language. In any case, this was not completely free either.

There is completely free music. The British guitarist Derek Bailey is an exponent of it and has written a book about it. But music seems to need a leadership factor, however much the leader may rely upon or allow a supporting cast to do its own thing. This is not to denigrate Bailey or saxophonist Evan Parker or any of the free players; many of them are loaded with talent. They know that improvisation is of enormous importance to music, and always has been; and improvisation is one of the things missing from today's rock and pop; the Grateful Dead have been improvising since the 1960s and still have an enormous following for their live gigs. It is not the public that is afraid of improvisation, but the record companies and the broadcasters. Yet the freest experiments have the smallest audience of all, for the same reasons that spaceships do not carry passengers: the air is too thin and the risk too great.

Ornette Coleman's many projects have included the *Chappaqua Suite* (1965), written for a quartet and a studio band, and *Skies of America* (1972), for the quartet and the London Symphony Orchestra. Coleman's work at the rehearsals and recording sessions earned him a standing ovation from the LSO, but the project must have been a commercial disaster. *Dancing in Your Head* (1973) was for sextet, two guitars and musicians in Joujouka, Morocco. In the late 1970s he formed Prime Time, whose electric sound was influenced by rock. Critics seem to have been disappointed with whatever he has done since the early 1960s; he seems not to be providing the leadership factor he began with. He has not been as influential as he was in those first few years, but then we do not know what he might have done had he been able to do whatever he liked. He set us all on our ears with a new kind of fire and beauty three decades ago, and

Harrison believes that Coleman was the single most revolutionary musician in the history of jazz: while Louis Armstrong and Charlie Parker accelerated development, Coleman opened doors.

Cecil Taylor, who has almost become celebrated, is one of the best-known international performers in this music, and has many recordings under his belt. He first recorded in 1956, with Steve Lacy on soprano and Buell Neidlinger on bass (both of whom were white and had started in dixieland) and Dennis Charles on drums. From his playing of standards, it was already obvious that Taylor was singing in his own language. A fascinating if unsuccessful session for United Artists in 1959 included John Coltrane (and is now marketed under his name); the trumpet player was Kenny Dorham, a fine bop musician who was already aware of Taylor's reputation and did not like it. (Taylor had wanted Ted Curson for the date.) Taylor soon decided to play only his own music, developing his unique keyboard sound into a musical world of tough, dancing beauty.

He and Neidlinger led sessions on Candid in 1960–61, which were not issued in full until a Mosaic box in 1989. In the early 1960s he was involved in a jazz composers' collective in New York that failed. His Blue Note recordings, *Unit Structures* and *Conquistador* (1966), were breakthroughs, his first commercial recordings for five years.

Like all the best musicians, Taylor understood and valued tradition without being bound to it and without showing any self-conscious need to be avant-garde. He has been described as using the piano as '88 tuned drums', yet again and again his sidemen and collaborators, such as Neidlinger, who once shared a flat with him and watched him practise, speak of the importance of singing and dancing in Taylor's music. We are reminded again of Dizzy Gillespie's complaining that he could dance to bop: why couldn't others?

Whitney Balliet compared Ornette Coleman with Cecil Taylor:

Taylor and Ornette Coleman are the nominal heads of the jazz avant-garde, but they are very different. Coleman refuses to record or play in public unless he is paid handsomely. Taylor until recent years often played for pennies – when he was asked to play at all. Coleman's music is accessible, but he is loath to share it; Taylor's music is difficult, and he is delighted to share it ... The American aesthetic landscape is littered with idiosyncratic marvels – Walt Whitman, Charles Ives, D. W. Griffith, Duke Ellington, Jackson Pollock – and Taylor belongs with them.

But so does Coleman. Balliet warns us that Taylor's music is difficult, but he was writing about an audience that had just listened to Oscar Peterson, and walked out in droves on Taylor. It is a weird concert or festival that plans juxtapositions like that. Contemporary improvised music is sometimes loud; so are symphonies, and, like the symphonies, improvised music does not need electronics. It sometimes has everyone playing at once; so did New Orleans jazz. It is often passionate, even angry, but it is equally often about tonal beauty. The screaming avant-garde electric rock group seems to attack its roots; contemporary improvised music celebrates them, but it is tough music for people who know that music is important.

The young Miles Davis had evolved an economic style that did not require him to compete in a front line with the fiery likes of Charlie Parker; his limitations became his starting point. There had always been some danger in bop of using too many notes, which might get in the way of the rhythm; in earlier styles of jazz each note was an essential part of the story, while in bop the overall feeling of the solo and the ensemble made the individual notes less important. Bop was bound to cool off, and Davis had always been a lyricist. Over the years since 1960 the modal style of composition has sometimes produced players who sound like they are taking it easy, but Davis's combination of soul, economy and lyricism and the weight of each note made him a complete master of the style. His effect on the free movement has probably been underrated. His development was always in the direction of a stripped-down music without any unnecessary adornments (showing the influence of Monk), so that he helped to create the new freedom to use structure and harmony as tools in the musician's kit along with melody and rhythm.

By 1965 his quintet included Wayne Shorter on tenor; Ron Carter's acoustic bass and cello had been influential on Prestige albums with Eric Dolphy and pianist-composer Mal Waldron; pianist Herbie Hancock and drummer Tony Williams rounded out one of the most important rhythm sections of the 1960s. They would all go on to become inspirational leaders and producers in their turn. Davis's group still played standards on the bandstand, and was more adventurous in the studio; *Live at the Plugged Nickel* was made in the Chicago club in 1965, but not released in the USA until 1976: Shorter in particular might have been even more influential at the time if this set had been released earlier. Their studio album *Nefertiti* (1967) was the last album Davis made without electric instruments.

Davis's music became more controversial and left some jazz fans behind, but commercially he was the most successful jazz musician since Brubeck. Every album he ever made is still selling, and eight of them made *Billboard*'s list of the top two hundred best-selling albums during the 1960s, four in the top hundred. Yet throughout his career he battled to squeeze out of record companies, booking agents and promoters the money to maintain the lifestyle to which he felt he was entitled. Monk had lost his cabaret card and was unable to work in jazz venues in New York; Mingus struggled through the 1960s; it is clear that very few of the best American musicians of the past thirty years have received sufficient support from the music industry to be able to do whatever they may have liked to do, in terms of writing, recording and touring with larger groups, for example. Mingus especially saw himself as a composer, his work all of a piece, yet his gigantic *Epitaph* was not put together and recorded by a twenty-nine-piece group directed by Gunther Schuller until 1989, a decade after his death. But he had written an appropriate chant for the black community, which adds to the flavour of his *Cumbia and Jazz Fusion* (1977):

> Who said mama's little baby likes shortnin' bread?
> Who said mama's little baby likes shortnin', shortnin' bread?
> That's some lie some *white* man upped an' said!
> Mama's little baby likes *truffles*!
> Mama's little baby likes *caviar*!

As drummer Dannie Richmond joins in, the chant is 'Diamonds! Diamonds in the nose! Diamonds in the toes! Diamonds all *over* mama's little baby!' And 'Schools! So our kids won't be raised to act like no fools!' But America still has not heard the message.

Cannonball Adderley was the only jazz musician to rival Davis as a commercial success, but he was not progressing musically. Without a doubt the single most influential jazz musician of the decade, spawning legions of imitators as Armstrong, Young, Hawkins, Gillespie and Parker had done before him, was John Coltrane, who sought overtly spiritual values through his music – indeed, sought to go beyond music with his horn – and almost single-handedly made it hip to buy jazz records in an era dominated by rock.

In 1950, playing alto in Dizzy Gillespie's big band, Coltrane had been introduced to Islam by Yusef Lateef. He later studied the cabbala and Sufism, the mystical branches of Judaism and Islam respectively. Coltrane had discovered the soprano saxophone in 1959; in 1960 he first played it on a one-off album for Atlantic called *The Avant Garde*, for which he borrowed sidemen from Coleman, and also first recorded Rodgers and Hammerstein's 'My Favorite Things' on Atlantic. His ballad 'Naima' was named after his first wife, and remained one of his own favourite tunes. He had always played long solos, as though unable to get it all in; the ballads and modal tunes began to set a pattern of an almost hypnotic function of music-making. Just before his death he was experimenting with the Varitone electronic device, which would have allowed him to play a duet with himself in octaves.

In 1961 he was the first artist signed to the Impulse label, a new jazz division of ABC-Paramount. *Africa/Brass*, on which he was backed by a large ensemble (including four French horns), offers hints of African rhythms and Indian ragas, as well as 'Greensleeves'. It was produced by Creed Taylor, but Bob Thiele then joined Impulse; Coltrane had found a label that helped make him the highest-paid black jazzman after Davis, and a producer who would let him record as much as he wanted.

His epochal quartet included Jimmy Garrison on bass, Elvin Jones, a furiously polyrhythmic powerhouse of a drummer, and McCoy Tyner on piano, a still underrated player whose function was often to pour oil on turbulent waters. Among the albums in 1962 was *Ballads*. Coltrane's essential modesty came to the fore on the date for *Duke Ellington and John Coltrane* (on various tracks of which Duke and Trane swap sidemen); he had to be assured that one take was good enough. With all his passion and religious intensity, Coltrane was also always a lyricist, and named Stan Getz as one of his favourite saxophonists. In 1963 *John Coltrane with Johnny Hartman* featured a Chicago vocalist with a deep, beautiful voice whose career needed help at the time.

The quartet recorded *A Love Supreme* in 1964, perhaps Coltrane's most famous album and certainly one of his most fully realized: he said that the four-part composition came to him all at once. His albums sold twenty-five to fifty thousand copies, which was very good for jazz, but *A Love Supreme* made it to six figures. As Bob Thiele remarked, you did not hear Coltrane's music on the radio, but he discovered that college students and young musicians were buying it. *Ascension* (June 1965) was more ambitious: a single piece covers an entire album played by eleven instruments (including five reeds: Coltrane, Pharoah Sanders and Archie Shepp on tenors, John Tchicai and Marion Brown on altos). 'Vigil' and 'Welcome' were recorded by the quartet the same day, and in October 'Kulu se Mama' completed an album of that title, a strongly rhythmic African-influenced piece for octet inspired by a poem by Juno Lewis. The five-part *Meditations* was recorded twice: once with the quartet in September 1965, and again by a sextet a few weeks later, adding Sanders and drummer Rashied Ali.

Coltrane's soprano was compared to the sound of Indian and African oboe-like instruments (today all his imitators play soprano, and they mostly all sound the same). He closely questioned Ravi Shankar, the genius of the sitar, about Indian music (and named one of his sons after him). He was inspired by his friend the Nigerian drummer Babatunde Olatunji, whose albums had been released on Columbia, but they never recorded together. He took to using two basses, because the sound reminded him of African water drums. He always valued Elvin Jones (despite Jones's volatile personality and voracious appetites) for his polyrhythmic abilities, but even Jones was not enough; Jones left after Coltrane began using two drummers. Tyner had already left, both because he wanted to pursue his own musical ideas and because Coltrane had added his second wife, Alice, on piano. (After his death she released Coltrane recordings with herself dubbed on harp, which was widely regarded as a questionable move.)

Coltrane was never afraid to use a certain coarseness of tone, or a squeak or an overblown note, yet none of it was ever gratuitous. The hypnotic qualities in some of his music worked perfectly, rather than sounding like hippie repetition celebrating the stoned state, of which there was plenty in that decade. Coltrane's music, sometimes incorporating chanting, and often atonal passages next to tonal ones, was a broad church. Artie Shaw was an admirer. Coltrane had fans who were jazz enthusiasts and others who were hippies, and he also had fans who were essentially religious people, for whom Coltrane's spiritual side was an open book. Shankar liked Coltrane's music, but was also troubled by it, for the passion in the music was troubled passion: Coltrane was a gentle, modest man who put everything he had into his vision of a world conquered by a love which transcended race, religion or nationality. Perhaps he knew that his was an unearthly vision, and that he did not have long to describe it.

After Eric Dolphy died, his parents gave his bass clarinet and his flute to Coltrane, who played them both. *Expression* was made in early 1967, by the quartet plus Sanders, and the music has been reduced to an emotional essence: on 'To Be' Coltrane on flute and Sanders on piccolo accompany each other, and on the rest of the album Coltrane plays tenor. Much of the music is relatively quiet and reflective, yet there is none of the tension-and-release structure normally associated with jazz: the emotional intensity is complete, unrelieved and harrowing. He died of cancer in July of that year. It would be interesting to know how sales of, say, *A Love Supreme* over twenty-five years compare with the total sales of, say, *In-a-gadda-da-vida*, by Iron Butterfly, a piece of hippie junk that was number four not long after Coltrane's death.

There are those who regret that so many tenor saxophonists have sounded like Coltrane since he died, but that is not Coltrane's fault. All the best have had large numbers of imitators. Those influenced by Ornette Coleman do not get many chances to be heard; there have been fewer places for young saxophonists to play in recent decades, and fewer chances for them to hear each other.

Pharoah Sanders formed a band that contained pianist-composer Lonnie Liston Smith and Leon Thomas, a vocalist who had sung with Count Basie and whose bag of tricks in the late 1960s included an evocative yodelling technique learned from central African music. Archie Shepp was a failed guru in that decade, a sort of safe shadow of Albert Ayler. He also recorded for Impulse. His style was described as darkly operatic, but he changed it too often and lost the thread, the theory becoming as important as the music. In 1991 Shepp seemed to have mellowed – among the songs played at a gig in London were Ellington ballads – yet still produced a unique sound on his horn.

Miles Davis turned to electric music in 1969 and sold records to the more stylish rock fans; from *In a Silent Way* and *Bitches Brew* onwards he lost old fans and made new ones. His sidemen from that period, electric pianists Chick Corea and Joe Zawinul, Wayne Shorter, guitarist John McLaughlin and others, formed electric fusion bands, such as Weather Report and Return to Forever. Electric bass player Jaco Pastorius brought considerable artistry to this music, and was destitute when he died in 1987, not yet thirty-six years old, manic depressive and alcoholic; the music seemed to have run out of steam as well. Its most ardent fans would have to admit that the quality of the noodling was variable; other fusions were going on which were not self-consciously forced, and did not need electricity.

All these fusions, forced and unforced, are a clue to the reason why there has been no single influential figure in recent years such as Armstrong, Parker, Coleman or Coltrane. Contemporary music has become an international and collectivist endeavour, and a post-modernist one in that all music is now repertory music. Such a multiplicity of styles is played everywhere that there may never again be domination by a single individual. This is a serious inconvenience to those young artists who need somebody to copy as they start out, and this may be another reason why Coltrane has been so imitated: there has not been anyone so powerful since.

Albert Ayler might have been similarly influential, but he did not live long enough. The tenor saxophonist burst upon the public apparently using the honks and squawks of the early Jazz at the Philharmonic concerts, but had more than that in mind; he was searching even more aggressively than Coleman or Coltrane for spiritual and musical freedom. John Litweiler wrote about two simultaneous solos on 'Green Dolphin Street' on one of Ayler's first albums, a tape made for Danish radio in early 1963:

One solo is inside, in observance of the bland harmonic structure (he pays dogged attention to turnbacks, chorus outline, alarming turns of phrases from free motions to inside tonality), and the other solo is outside by way of his sound (alternately gigantic, braying, slurring, or else whiny and querulous) and his occasional phrasing (fast, arhythmic, spiraling upward like fireworks from which smaller explosions shoot off). There's no doubt that in these performances Ayler's music is in great crisis; 'Summertime' . . . accepts the crisis, balancing the standard setting against his ideas of sound and his drifting sense of tonality to result in a long, tragic masterpiece.

Ayler came from a middle-class background, but knew the cry of the church, and had spent two summers as a young man touring in R&B with Little Walter and his Jukes. Then he seemed to take apart the history of jazz in order to reinvent it. Soon, like Taylor, he began playing only his own music (he made eight recordings of 'Ghosts'). Musicians like drummer Sunny Murray and bass player Henry Grimes were already playing free, but under Ayler's influence they gained in authority. Murray, for example, was not a loud drummer and never used a fancy kit, yet completely liberated percussion by means of delicacy and dynamics. Ayler puzzled or irritated many; Alan Bates recorded him for an appearance on a BBC jazz programme in 1966, but the BBC wiped the tape. He changed direction, changed to alto (losing some weight in his music) and dabbled in Mexican and folk musics, and in 1968 even tried rock on an album called *New Grass*. Some thought he was in decline, distracted by the powerful effect the psychedelic counterculture was having at the time, but Ayler, like Coltrane, was searching for something beyond music. He may have been recovering his sense of purpose in 1970, but his body was found in the East River, his death never explained. His music ultimately included everything, and for all the shortness of his career, he has been more influential than most.

African drummer Olatunji and John Coltrane had begun to form a centre for the creation of African-American music, but it was never fully realized. Musicians began to see that there was not enough room in the American commercial market for everyone, and that they had no choice but to take matters into their own hands. Trumpeter, composer and academic Bill Dixon was behind the 'October Revolution', a series of concerts at New York's Cellar Café in 1964, the same year in which lawyer Bernard Stollman formed ESP Records, an almost underground label that recorded Ayler, Milford Graves and others (as well as the Fugs and other New York City exotica). Dixon was a charter member of the Jazz Composers Guild, with Shepp, Cecil Taylor, Carla Bley, Paul Bley, Mike Mantler, Sun Ra, alto saxophonist John Tchicai, trombonist Roswell Rudd and others; they gave concerts in late 1964. Then Shepp signed a contract with Impulse, foolishly regarded as a sell-out by some of the others, and, according to Valerie Wilmer, bandleader Sun Ra professed himself superstitious: like a sailor, he did not like having a woman on board. The Guild failed, but led to the creation of the Jazz Composer's Orchestra Association (JCOA), formed by Carla Bley and Mantler. The first fruit was a two-disc set of Mantler's thickly textured music for a large orchestra called simply *JCOA* (1968), with such soloists as Taylor, Pharoah Sanders, Don Cherry, Roswell Rudd, guitarist Larry Coryell, tenor saxophonist Gato Barbieri and bass player Steve Swallow. Further albums by Carla Bley, Charlie Haden, soprano saxophonist Steve Lacy and others were released. Carla Bley became the leader of one of the few avant-garde big bands, directly competing with Ra for the audience: in music there is no more place for misogyny than for racism. In 1970 the Jazz and People's Movement interrupted taping of the chat shows of Merv Griffin, Johnny Carson and Dick Cavett (thus hitting all three television networks), and the result of this attention-seeking device was an appearance on Ed Sullivan's show by an all-star band including Roland Kirk.

The Archie Shepp–Bill Dixon Quartet and the New York Contemporary Five, for which Dixon wrote, never had enough work. It was clear that the music had to be taken back to the community from which it came, so that the community could demand support for it. There was always an enthusiastic response to open rehearsals and so forth, especially from young people, but there was never going to be enough commercial sponsorship. Dixon taught art history for a living; a University of the Streets was formed by Puerto Ricans in 1967 and Dixon helped form the Free Conservatory of the University of the Streets the following year, leading an orchestral rehearsal which helped to clinch one of the first federal grants for such a project. Percussionist Milford Graves was also an activist in this field, and among other, similar projects was Graves's Storefront Museum, a warehouse converted into a community project in Queens. In Harlem writer Leroi Jones (who later became Amiri Baraka) had formed the Black Arts group, which presented music in the street. The Jazzmobile was a bandstand on a truck that in 1964 began to take music from neighbourhood to neighbourhood. Encouraged by the Harlem Community Council and originally sponsored by Coca-Cola and Ballentine beer, it took the music to several New York boroughs, often presenting it to black youngsters who had never heard it before. People emerged from their houses out of curiosity and always responded positively.

Despite all this activity, the omens were never good. The artists who recorded for ESP were irritated that it did not result in more income for them, but if the music is not widely heard and the records widely distributed, there is never going to be any money in a record label. When Roland Kirk asked Ed Sullivan in 1970, several years after John Coltrane's death, why he had never had Coltrane on his programme, the most famous presenter of American talent asked, 'Does John Coltrane have any records out?' An important source for recordings of contemporary music, the New Music Distribution Service, originally connected with the JCOA, lasted until 1990 before going under.

The Black Artists Group was formed in St Louis, Strata in Detroit; but easily the most important of the collectives was the Association for the Advancement of Creative Musicians in Chicago.

Chicago has always been a centre of musical activity. In the 1920s the scene of the thriving black culture was virtually next to the Loop (the downtown area defined by the tracks of the elevated trains). The recording of black music in Chicago was hurt by one of Petrillo's early strikes, but nothing can keep Chicago down for long. In the late 1940s and 1950s pianist and composer Andrew Hill, saxophonists Eddie Johnson and Von Freeman, multi-instrumentalist Hal Russell and many others played in Chicago clubs, and bigger names from New York also visited. Pianist Ahmad Jamal formed a trio and became a national figure, and an influence on Miles Davis.

The importance of Captain Walter Dyett cannot be overestimated.

He began on violin, and played banjo and guitar in Erskine Tate's Vendome Theater Orchestra; he conducted an all-black US Army band, and in 1931 became bandmaster at Wendell Phillips High School, the name of which was changed to DuSable High School in 1936. According to Dempsey Travis, Dyett 'could hear a mosquito urinate on a bale of cotton'. He directed five high-school bands and the annual *Hi-jinks* show, which raised money to buy instruments (since the Board of Education would not buy them), as well as an alumni band which played in local clubs, at annual entertainments for Shriners conventions and so forth. He taught Bo Diddley violin. His students over the years included pianists Nat Cole, Dorothy Donegan and John Young, trombonists Bennie Green and Julian Priester, bass players Fred Hopkins and Richard Davis (who said, 'Maybe you weren't afraid of the cops, but you were afraid of Captain Dyett'), drummers Wilbur Campbell and Bruz Freeman, vocalist Dinah Washington, reedmen Gene 'Jug' Ammons (son of boogie-woogie pianist Albert), Eddie Harris, John Gilmore, Clifford Jordan, Johnny Griffin and Von Freeman, and guitarist George Freeman. (The three Freemans are brothers.) Some of them went straight off to work with Lionel Hampton or Count Basie. The names of teachers are usually obscure, but they are of the highest importance, and Captain Dyett was one of the greatest of all.

Sonny Blount, a young pianist and composer from Birmingham, Alabama, worked for Fletcher Henderson at Chicago's Club DeLisa in 1946–7; before long he was reincarnated as a messenger from the planet Venus called Sun Ra, whose influence and example have been priceless. 'Who knows the history of a prophet?' wrote J. B. Figi in a sleeve-note in 1967, for a reissue of Ra's first album:

July 12, 1956. Charlie Parker was but fifteen months dead. John Coltrane was barely beginning to tug ears as a sideman. No-one expected the still-distant messianic coming of Ornette Coleman. The musician usually credited with being the first of the current avant-garde to make his statement, Cecil Taylor, was gingerly putting together his first pieces, and would have to wait two months for his first recording date . . . On that day, [the Transition label] was busy elsewhere, having come to Chicago to summon to a recording studio Sun Ra and his frankly far-out rehearsal band . . . 'Music rushing forth like a fiery law,' Sun Ra promises in a poem, and delivers. The band moves like a big loose threshing machine through a field of heavy, sun-swollen grain. This mystic band of Chicagoans, driven by donkey-engine rhythms, roars, stomps, chugs along full of its own purpose, sounding like a Midwestern riff-jump band and a wig band at one and the same time, solos jumping out of the whole with spontaneity, yet spare and telling.

That first album, *Sun Song*, is now available on CD, and sounds as though it ought to have been a *Billboard* best-seller in 1957. It is impossible now to understand how those donkey-engine rhythms, like Chicago itself chunky and swinging at the same time, could ever have been called 'far out'.

The band left town in 1960 for a gig in Montreal: the club-owner seems to have been expecting a rock band, and the gig was not a success. They drifted to New York, and maintained a worldwide hand-to-mouth existence, staying together because nobody else can do what they do, and because big bands are important. Countless records with little in the way of documentation were issued on their own Saturn label, and finally in the 1980s the market and the listeners' ears began to catch up. Ra's music had soon admitted more abstract sounds, and later electronics, but never any effects for their own sake; the band's Buck Rogers costumes acquired an African flavour. The act included powerful percussion pieces, in which everybody in the band contributed to a multi-rhythmic sound that could make the building jump; musical melodramas with reedmen chasing each other around the stage, always with beautifully clear individual tone and never dropping a beat or a note; and a cappella chants ('Space is the place!') that could make a mob follow them into the nearest teleport chamber. Suddenly they might break into their version of a fifty-year-old arrangement by Henderson, or Ellington or Lunceford. Long before he died in 1992, Ra did not sound so weird any more; and the band's earlier works are being reissued on the Evidence label.

But back in Chicago, Sun Ra's departure had left a hole in the musical scene. Pianist and composer Muhal Richard Abrams formed his Experimental Band to encourage creative collaboration between composers and improvisers: 'Now I can take eight measures and play a concert,' he later said to John Litweiler. After several years of

Abram's inspiring tuition the cooperative became official in May 1965 with the formation of the Association for the Advancement of Creative Musicians (AACM), when thirty or so founders gathered at the home of trumpeter Phil Cohran.

Cohran ran an Afro-arts Ensemble, which included drummer Robert Crowder. Thurman Barker is a percussionist whose career as a composer and recording artist had to fight with steady demand for his skills: he had regular employment at Chicago's Schubert Theater for a dozen years, and only released his own first album, *Voyage*, in 1984. Fred Anderson, a distinctive tenor saxophonist and composer, ran a tavern, practising in the back when business was slow. Anthony Braxton, an extremely bright, witty and serious composer, reedman and leader, has since become one of the leading international concert artists in contemporary music, working as a teacher to pay the bills. Reedman Henry Threadgill, bass player Fred Hopkins and percussionist Steve McCall formed Air, which became well known on the concert circuit and made several fine albums, but never had enough full-time work.

McCall was replaced by Pheeroan akLaff when New Air was formed in 1983, and at about that time Threadgill also began putting together his Sextet (actually a septet, counting the leader); after three albums on the New York label About Time, Threadgill signed to Novus, a subsidiary of RCA/BMG, and the spelling changed to Sextett; they had released three more albums by 1990. Threadgill's tunes were structured tone poems, not at all 'atonal', but also used gospel voicings and collective improvisation. Like all the best music, they were unclassifiable and immediately unique, and the reeds, trumpet, trombone, bass, cello and two percussionists played them with the spirit of neighbourhood street music. In the 1990s Threadgill's new group was Very Very Circus, a septet containing two electric guitars and two tubas.

The purpose of the AACM was to seek employment among themselves instead of waiting for somebody to hire them. They began with concerts and open rehearsals of free jazz, original compositions only, and composers wrote for anyone who wanted to play. Perhaps it was the flavour of Chicago, laid back yet positive, that made it work. The AACM has remained one of the most popular and fertile collectives ever organized, despite the fact that, for example, a series of ten concerts celebrating its twentieth anniversary in 1985 had to be run on a shoestring. The collective itself has never had any money, concentrating as it does on presenting Chicago's music to Chicago's neighbourhoods.

The best-known and most successful progeny of the AACM has been the Art Ensemble of Chicago. The original members, also founder members of the AACM, were bass player Malachi Favors, trumpeter Lester Bowie and reedmen Joseph Jarman and Roscoe Mitchell; Jarman had led an informal group with Barker and others. Iowa-born Chuck Nessa, who worked in the Jazz Record Mart for peanuts in exchange for the opportunity to produce some records, recorded Abrams, Jarman and Mitchell for Delmark, then formed his own eponymous label and recorded the nucleus of what was to become the Art Ensemble.

Three albums made in 1967–8, released under the names of Bowie, Jarman and Mitchell, included trio, quartet and solo items. *Old/Quartet*, with Philip Wilson (who shortly after joined the Paul Butterfield Blues Band in order to make a living), was their basement tapes; a good introduction to their casual brilliance, it reaches out to nourish its roots in the street. Once again Chicago was a world-beater in music, but this time fewer were listening. Born and raised only 65 miles away, I did not hear of the AACM until it had been under way for several years, and this was at a time when there were more radio stations and the record industry was moving four or five times as much product as twenty-five years earlier.

Mitchell's *Congliptuous* was recorded by a quartet of Bowie, Mitchell, Favors and Robert Crowder; the other side of the record contained three solos, for Favor's bass, Mitchell's alto and Bowie's trumpet. After being asked by the journalist Dave Flexenbergstein (of *Jism* magazine), 'Is jazz, as we know it, dead, yet?', Bowie plays a seven-minute solo, built on what sounds like a marching-band fragment, stopping halfway through to ask Flexenbergstein to please remove his hat. Having established himself with his slurs and burnished tone as the Cootie Williams of the avant-garde, he answers at the end, 'Well, that, I guess, that all depends on, uh, how much you *know*.'

Pianist Christopher Gaddy and cellist and bass player Charles Clark

were immensely gifted, and seemingly had brilliant futures; they both
died at the age of twenty-four. They had both played on Jarman's
Delmark album *Song For*; Gaddy died in 1968; Jarman recorded
'Song for Christopher' on his *As if It Were the Seasons*, on which Clark
played; then Clark died in April of 1969 of a brain haemorrhage.
These tragedies may have concentrated the minds of the group:
Mitchell, Jarman, Bowie and Favors left for France (instead of New
York, marking a change in the history and economics of modern
music), became the Art Ensemble of Chicago and, from June, made
about a dozen albums in less than two years, including studio sets,
live concert performances and a soundtrack for the film *Les Stances à
Sophie*, featuring Mrs Bowie, Fontella Bass, one of the best voices in
the black chart in the mid-1960s. ('Rescue Me' had been a number
one, on Checker.)

The soundtrack and the tone poem *People in Sorrow* were recorded
in Boulogne for Pathé and issued in the USA on Nessa. Jean-Luc
Young and Jean Georgakarakos had formed a chain of record shops
in France; they also formed *Actuel*, a trendy paper, and, in 1967, the
Byg label, for which they leased the American Savoy catalogue and
made over sixty albums of new free jazz, much of it by Chicago
artists. They went broke in 1975, mainly because of spending too
much money on one of the biggest festivals Europe ever saw. There
were accusations of carelessness with their properties, and at one
point they dumped carloads of LPs in America, getting into trouble
with the American owners of some of the material. Jean Karakos, as
he is now known, formed Celluloid in 1976 in New York, and
several offshoots, still serving experimental music. Young formed
Charly in Paris in 1974 and moved it to London the next year. Charly
reissues rockabilly, country and R&B and has a delightful catalogue;
its managing director, Joop Visser, started Affinity in 1976 for jazz
reissues, including most of the Byg recordings.

Byg recorded several of the Art Ensemble's classics. *Message from
Our Folks* offered Charlie Parker's 'Dexterity', the percussion feature
'Rock On' and the moving, hypnotic avant-garde revival meeting of
'Old-time Religion', as well as the tone poem 'Brain for the Seine'.
There's a Jackson in Your House was a wacky, swinging statement of
fact: there had been a Jackson in the house for decades, and it was

long past time that Robert Crumb's nervously sweating comic-book Whiteman (no relation to Paul) joined the parade.

By early 1971 they had recruited percussionist Famoudou Don Moye; in 1972 their performance at the Ann Arbor (Michigan) Blues Festival was recorded; that album and a 1973 studio set, both produced by Michael Cuscuna, were released on Atlantic. More albums were issued on Freedom, Prestige and other labels; they ended up on Manfred Eicher's high-class ECM label in the late 1970s, and recorded the mature classics *Nice Guys*, *Full Force* and *Urban Bushmen*.

Nessa was twenty-two years old in the mid-1960s. At first, he said, 'I honestly had no idea what they were doing . . . I had to figure out how this music worked and whether it was bullshit or not . . . The thing that was obvious to me was that they knew what they were doing musically. I was lost but they had such confidence in their presentation that I was drawn to it.'

[Roscoe's] idea was for each to make his own music but to have stuff happening on different levels that meshed into a full sound, where each player would play at a different tempo (say) to create a kaleidoscopic effect . . . On *Old/Quartet* there is a piece where you have really soft drum patterns with brushes, and the bass playing a fast running line, with the saxophone and the trumpet each sounding like they are playing a different kind of music. The overall effect of the tension and release of this music is wonderful, and is really hard to sustain. I think this was the greatest creative music band that I've ever heard. They were incredibly consistent; it takes intensive rehearsal to sustain that kind of music, and keep a flow going in it.

Not long after being interviewed at length in Canada's venerable *Coda* jazz magazine, in 1993 Nessa issued a limited-edition five-CD set of everything in his vaults by these men, one of the releases of the decade. Working most of his life as a record distributor, he has never made a profit from his tiny record label and never will, but the twenty or so albums he made in Chicago over a period of twenty-five years are pearls without price.

The Art Ensemble that went to Paris was not Roscoe's group but a collective, and the music changed; some pieces were more Roscoe's and some Jarman's. Their 'Great Black Music' did not just practise collective improvisation, but swelled and roared with the sheer joy of it. Experiments with bassoon and bass saxophone had generated a desire for an infinite number of textures and timbres; everybody played 'little instruments', an uncountable collection of tuned and untuned percussion and horns from cowbells and woodblocks to whistles, steerhorns, bicycle horns and garbage-can lids. Yet the music is never cluttered, each timbre surprises in exactly the right place and the whole contains the entire history of black music and the black experience. A theatrical element – warpaint, costumes and mime – probably inspired by Jarman, enlivened the act and helped maintain the connection with community roots. Its absence took little away from the recordings, however; the music works without a video.

That the great Chicago tenor saxophonist Von Freeman is not a household name is partly because he preferred to play at the Enterprise Lounge on the South Side rather than chase precarious fame in less friendly environments. He tossed off two albums for Nessa in one day in 1975, and anyone who owns them knows that he belongs up there with Dexter, Rollins and Coltrane. He was no doubt available to the younger generation for moral support; his son Chico Freeman was a member of the AACM in the early 1970s and became a prolific recording artist. Chico is a master of the reeds, including the bass clarinet; his touring groups and albums have employed such musicians as bass players Cecil McBee and drummers Elvin Jones, Jack DeJohnette and Fred Waits. Chico is a composer, but not an innovator, and his music ought to work fine on the radio. You will not hear it on the radio, though, and the last time I talked to him he was selling computers on the side.

Anthony Braxton plays the music of Monk and has made albums of standards; he writes books about his own music, but his books make it look more difficult than it is. His quartet – Mark Dresser on bass, Gerry Hemingway on percussion and Marilyn Crispell on piano – set London on its ear in 1985, but Braxton does not make a living composing and playing. Since the Art Ensemble does not tour as much as it used to, Lester Bowie has been leading a crowd-pleasing brass ensemble. Roscoe Mitchell is, in my opinion, one of today's greatest composers, whether he is warming up his alto saxophone until it says, 'OK, you can play me now', or demonstrating all the timbres of which sixteen brass and woodwind instruments are capable, as in 'L-R-G', with only three musicians, or conducting 'The Maze', for eight percussionists, shot through with light, space and texture. But few have even heard of Roscoe.

How the obscure pianist and composer Joel Futterman survives is anybody's guess. He spent two years with the AACM, and released two or three albums on his own label from 1979. The loss of his frequent collaborator, the great alto saxophonist Jimmy Lyons, to cancer in 1986, was a terrible blow. His original, percussive and tough-minded solo pieces and his trio and quartet work with Jarman, Lyons, bass player Richard Davis and others deserve much wider exposure and are now available on CD (on Ear-Rational and Bellaphon, two more of the world's smaller labels).

Whitney Balliet might describe Futterman's music as difficult. If you want sheer obvious fun from the so-called avant-garde, you could have tried the white Chicagoan Hal Russell and his NRG Ensemble. Born in Detroit, Russell worked in Chicago most of his life, performing with such visiting firemen as Ellington, Miles, Rollins and Coltrane. He played drums at Newport with the free-jazz trio of saxophonist Joe Daley in 1963, began leading his own groups in the early 1970s and only discovered that the reeds were his true love around 1977. He led four younger men in a repertory of a couple of hundred original tunes whose stomping vigour and zany humour had to be heard to be believed. They made their first album in 1982; there were only two personnel changes in over a decade.

On their albums the quintet plays two trumpets, two basses, several reeds, drums, vibraphone, electric guitar, didgeridoos and anything else they fancy. After hearing them at the Moers Festival in June 1990 (their first trip to Europe), Steve Lake wrote in the *Wire*: 'Tales of neglect are the stuff of jazz, but I've rarely encountered a case as extreme as this one . . . Trust me, one of the hottest, hippest, wittiest bands on the globe.' Russell also made a duet album, *Eftsoons*, with reedman Mars Williams, who had been an early member of the NRG and re-joined in the late 1980s, and a solo album (with a lot of overdubbing), *Hal's Bells*. Only five NRG albums were released (on Nessa, Chief, Principally Jazz and ECM). Russell had once issued a cassette called *Don't Wait Too Long or I Could be Dead*; he died in 1992 at the age of sixty-six: the music business had waited too long. Three of the younger men were not even full-time musicians: drummer Steve Hunt works in the family clothing firm, and one of the others restores houses. Such is the best of the music business; but the NRG Ensemble intends to carry on.

This chapter should be several times as long. I have not said anything about Julius Hemphill, Frank Lowe, Charles Tyler, Hamiet Bluiett, John Stevens, Leo Smith, Rory Stuart, Edward Wilkerson, Jr, John Carter, Sunny Murray, David Murray, Ronald Shannon Jackson, Charles Brackeen, Joe Locke, Phil Markowitz, Slava Ganelin, Ran Blake, Paul Bley, Kenny Wheeler or Randy Weston. Youngish people who carry on the traditions and may or may not do something original someday are Jason Rebello, Tommy Smith, Andy Sheppard, Courtney Pine, Marcus Roberts, Roy Hargrove, Christopher Hollyday, Terence Blanchard, Donald Harrison and a bunch of Marsalises. These people are white, black, American, British, Russian. (The Norwegian Jan Garbarek, born in 1947, plays folk styles on the saxophones, and may be one of the most influential musicians in the world today, for better or worse.) They are revivalists and avantgardists. Not enough of them are women, but Joanne Brackeen, Geri Allen and Marilyn Crispell, more or less in that order of 'accessibility', are pianist-composers worth any music lover's time. Bass player Richard Davis plays with post-bop revivalists and then turns in the wittiest, most zinging and precise avant-garde playing (with Futterman, for example) you have ever heard. Meanwhile, so many people are still sounding like John Coltrane, who has been gone over twenty-five years, that Scott Hamilton feels free to play in the fifty-year-old Ben Webster style, and gets better and better at it. Soprano saxophonist and clarinettist Bob Wilber, who studied as a teenager with Sidney Bechet, has recreated Benny Goodman and Duke Ellington sessions, and performed as a guest on an album of Bill Challis's arrangements recorded in 1986. Not only is improvised music alive and well, but revivalism has never been in better hands.

Guitarist George Benson, pianist Herbie Hancock and others have left jazz for high-class pop or for rock fusion, sometimes coming back again. Producer and arranger Quincy Jones seems to have disappeared entirely into slick studio pop. Miles Davis played his spare phrases over disco-flavoured backing tracks in the 1980s; you could hear more Miles by listening to his old recordings. Trumpeter Donald Byrd left for academia and formed a band of students called the Blackbyrds to play what amounted to disco, but at least they were flesh-and-blood musicians instead of computers. We can call it selling out, but they call it paying the rent. Arthur Blythe, a reedman, seems to change styles with every album; as he put it, 'I don't want to make records for posterity. I want to make records for prosperity.' Benson has a family to raise, and points out that when he recorded jazz, most of the record-buying public never heard it.

Yet a former car dealer has built a big catalogue on California's Concord Jazz label, recording mainstream jazz for an audience which has been starved of it for generations, while the major labels waste so much money chasing bubble-gum blockbusters that they cannot afford to bother with the audiences that are there. And yuppies fill their shelves full of immaculately recorded note-spinning 'New Age' dinner party music, the contemporary equivalent of Mantovani's strings. They are probably searching for chamber jazz, but they never learned how to listen. They should buy records by Stan Getz, Paul Bley, Bill Evans, Ted Brown, but the jazz bins in the shopping-mall record shops are full of the new mood music.

Will Ackerman ran a construction company and also played the guitar. When he released *In Search of the Turtle's Navel* in 1976 for a few fans, naming the Wyndham Hill label after his company, he effectively launched New Age, and had sales of $20 million in 1984. The artwork on the New Age records resembles that of ECM, the European label for improvised music formed by Manfred Eicher in 1970. Guitarist John Abercrombie made nine ECM albums between 1974 and 1981, and there are so many albums on that label by several people that some of them inevitably amount to note-spinning. Keith Jarrett spins out his notes across entire albums, moaning along with it, and sells many records, while the British pianist and composer Keith Tippett remains virtually unknown.

Pure New Age, sometimes confused by marketing people and by

magazine critics with jazz, perhaps began with the recordings of John Fahey and Leo Kottke on acoustic guitar in the 1960s. It is sometimes called new acoustic, and indeed often sounds folkish. The *Los Angeles Free Press* wrote of the album *Timeless* (1974) by keyboard player Jan Hammer and drummer Jack DeJohnette: 'You lie back, close your eyes and journey-soft . . .' If we have loud narcissism in pop-rock, New Age is contemplative narcissism. The new mood music is impeccably played and recorded, but my old Percy Faith records have more musical content and less pretence. The acoustic piano album *Pianissimo* (1990, on Private Music) composed and played by Suzanne Ciani is also immaculately recorded, but her piano style on her soundalike tunes sounds to me like Carole King with a muscular spasm.

Many jazz musicians are still noodling. Chick Corea strolls on-stage with so many electronic keyboards around his neck it is a wonder the clatter does not drown out the music, but in 1991 an album was issued in five or six formats, including videodisc. Reedman Steve Coleman and others are playing something called M-base, combining elements of rock with jazz. What I have heard of it sounds rockist to me, but at least it is not background music. Maybe something will come of the various fusions some day; after all, most of Gunther Schuller's third-stream music over the decades has not been recorded and much of it has not even been played. If contemporary musicians sign conventional deals with major labels, tin-eared lawyers and producers try to tell them what to play; perhaps it is just as well that nearly all their best work is on dinky labels that the shops do not stock, many of them live recordings from European festivals such as Moers, Willisau and Zurich.

I began by describing the popular songs of the eighteenth century as strophic – that is, repetitious, so that the audience hears the melodic fragments over and over. It is clear that the most profitable popular music has been repetitious in nature, and that the golden age of American songwriting and the Swing Era itself were accidents of history, perhaps never to be repeated. Popular music since the invention of electrical recording has developed a spectrum that now includes kiddie music at one end and at the other music which is, to quote the title of Wilmer's book, *As Serious as Your Life*. But the word 'serious' in this context does not mean without joy. Our greatest artists do not strike poses for the media; the media do not pay much attention to them anyway. So why is it that everybody's doing it? If you have to ask, you are not listening. As for me, new records by Braxton, Mitchell and the others come out faster than I can afford to buy them, so as a music lover, I am happy.

But what about black pop?

In his book *The Death of Rhythm and Blues* Nelson George points out that forty years ago black communities had their own restaurants, hotels, baseball teams and so forth. Then came improvements in civil rights. The best black players were hired by major-league baseball and the black leagues went out of business, and where are the black owners and managers in the major leagues? Similarly, when blacks could use white restaurants and hotels, their own smaller businesses went broke: thrown into the same economic meat-grinder as the rest of us but with less money in their pockets and fewer jobs, they can now vote, but their neighbourhoods have crumbled. What remained of R & B was prettified, overproduced and burdened with technology, like white pop. Bedroom crooners and often beautiful 'sweet soul' voices were heard, but for the most part, unless you were Lionel Richie, the business did not want to know about black music. And meanwhile music education in the schools disintegrated. American taxpayers will vote against anything that costs money if they get a chance, so forget frills, like libraries. Forget music. The schools in some American states almost closed in the late 1970s because there was not enough money to keep the doors open; at the same time a new generation of black kids were inventing rap.

You can draw a parallel between black music and the American economy as a whole. The tiny middle class are the composers and performers celebrated around the world: Roscoe Mitchell, Leo Smith, Braxton and the rest, relatively poor as they are. The working class is really nowhere: if all an aspiring young black musician wants to do is play in the Hollywood studios or in a symphony orchestra, there are not enough jobs.

And there is the underclass, which could not even afford to go to discos, and had no musical training whatever. But they had turntables and a few records. So they invented their own mixes, by switching

back and forth between two copies of the same record, such as James
Brown's 'Get on the Good Foot', the harder, funkier music that
disco had come from. Using microphones, they chanted over their
music, as in Jamaican dub, in which the DJ chants over an instrumental reggae track (one of the first in the new rap genre was Jamaican-
born Kool Herc of the South Bronx). The inventiveness of the street
dancers was soon called breaking, or break dancing. The amateur
DJs would break into a street-lamp for electricity in the middle of
the afternoon, and by two or three the next morning there would be
hundreds of kids hanging out, watching the dancers, enjoying the
sounds.

The fad was called hip-hop, from a Lovebug Starsky record: 'To
the hip, hop, hippedy-hop.' Then it came to be called rap, itself
originally from black slang, a trendy 1960s word for conversation.
The chanting was supposed to be improvised, and the whole thing
remained a cult for a while, until it crossed over into the commercial
music business. Fifteen years later the fad is still with us.

'Rapper's Delight' by the Sugar Hill Gang (producer Sylvia Vanderpool again, seizing the opportunity as she had done in the early days
of disco) was a freak hit in 1979. 'The Breaks' in 1980 on Mercury
was regarded as a novelty. Afrika Bambaataa and his Soul Sonic
Force were big in 1982; James Brown himself may be heard in a duet
on 'Unity' (1984). Grandmaster Flash (Joseph Sadler) was one of the
first to use 'montage' on records, adding sound effects and making
rhythmic fills by 'scratching' the stylus back and forth in the groove.
(He made a video with director Spike Lee.) Finally, Run DMC, a
trio from Queens, had the genre's first million-selling album in 1986,
Raising Hell. Using a drum machine and scratching on a double-deck
turntable, the trio filled Madison Square Garden and were seen as
controversial, but stronger stuff was on the way.

Many people hate rap. Considered purely as music, it is the
ultimate reduction of pop to absurdity. Charles Shaar Murray claims
that rap was the most exciting thing to happen in pop in the 1980s,
but that's not saying much. There are, however, interesting things to
be said about it, not least that it made its own way with little help
from the mainstream music business. Originally it was improvised,
and may have had some value as street poetry; the rappers prize

words and are more literate in their own way than your average pop star: where words are found there must be a message. But the uncomfortable fact is that rap was born of musical starvation. In the late 1980s the great jazz percussionist and composer Max Roach received a foundation grant, and was widely interviewed in American newspapers. One of the subjects he spoke about was music education. No matter how poor they were, no matter what kinds of backgrounds they came from, Roach's generation, including Charlie Parker and Dizzy Gillespie, had been able to get real musical tuition, on real musical instruments, in the schools. But that had changed. 'If you don't like rap,' Roach pointed out to the American people, 'you're getting what you paid for.'

But each generation has to make its own noise, invent its own genre; and what we paid for, or did not pay for, is rap. 'The Message' (1982), by Grandmaster Flash and the Furious Five, had more meaningful words than most pop songs of that period; it is about the neighbourhood and its 'junkies in the alley / with a baseball bat'. The rap groups did the best they could to communicate with America about the conditions to which they were confined, and to which their brothers and sisters are still confined. The message, however, has already been ignored.

Boo-yah TRIBE are 'Six Bad Brothas' of Samoan extraction from the Carson district of Los Angeles; 'Boo-yah' is derived from the sound of a sawn-off shotgun. Their track 'Once Upon a Drive By' tells of teenagers killing each other from the car window while driving by; 'Rated R' is about how to use the word 'motherfucker' fifty times in one song. NWA ('Niggers with Attitude'), from California, were the first successful rap group to come from outside New York; their album was called *Straight Outta Compton*. They too celebrate the world of drive-by killings and robbery with violence; one of their tracks urges listeners to kill and fuck the police. Public Enemy's second album, *It Takes a Nation of Millions to Hold Us Back*, reached the top twenty in Britain. The group's 'minister of propaganda', Richard Griffin, alias Professor Griff, said in an interview, 'The Jews are evil. And we can prove this.' 2 Live Crew rap about bitches, dicks, cunts and pussies: 'Forget the salad, just eat my meat', 'I can't be pussywhipped by a dick-sucker', and so on.

Of course, this stuff has its defenders among today's college professors and literary critics – drama critic Kenneth Tynan thought that the Beatles' *Sgt Pepper* was a turning point in western civilization – but they miss the point. As David Toop noted in England, 'the concoction appealed to intellectuals, who saw rap as the supreme expression of post-modernism, creative retro, television inspired blip culture and goodness knows what else'. The *New Republic* remarked that the rock critics 'are regularly laughable in their nervous transla-tions of the primal and the obscene into the polysyllabic prettifications of their trade'.

The magazine quoted Jon Pareles on the subject of rap: 'Rappers live by their wit – their ability to rhyme, their speed of articulation – and by their ability to create outsized personas with words.' But not even a *New York Times* critic can justify rap by himself, so Pareles called in Professor Henry Louis Gates, of Duke University, who has become a prominent black critic by embracing the intellectual con-trick of structuralism, or deconstructuralism, or post-structuralism, or whatever it is called this week. What 2 Live Crew do, Professor Gates says, is 'take the white Western culture's worst fear of black men and make a game of it'. But the fear is 2 Live Crew's fear of women in general, and black women in particular. It does not scare me, it disgusts me, and I do not think it is a game.

Gates soon got his own space in *The New York Times* in which he carried on the literary criticism: to understand 2 Live Crew we must become 'literate in the vernacular traditions of African Americans'. We are now so anti-élitist that we invent crackpot critical theory to justify anything as art. The *New Republic* again:

There are mistakes of which only professors are capable, and this is one of them . . . When you promote 'Suck my dick, bitch, and make it puke' into a 'vernacular tradition', you wound your culture. You teach that the culture need aspire to nothing high, because the low *is* the high; and that your culture – in this instance, the culture of Duke Ellington and Ralph Ellison – need look no further than the street . . . The truth about the street, of course, is that it is the scene of the greatest catastrophe to have befallen black America since slavery.

And so we get to the point. Rap is an illustration not just of what pop music has come to, but of what a nation has come to. We have known for years that American black males suffer more strokes and heart attacks than American white males. Murder is the leading cause of death among young black males in Washington, DC; the life expectancy of a male in Harlem is shorter than that of a male in Bangladesh. An American secretary of health has warned that 'the young black American male is a species in danger'. The rappers see Jews only as their local shopkeepers and landlords; nobody has ever taught them that for generations Jews were the best friends blacks had in America, because they knew what it was like to be slaves thousands of years before the first African was taken to the New World. Nobody has ever taught them that Jews as businessmen (and musicians) did more for black music in this century than any other non-black group. Nobody has ever taught them that men and women are supposed to console each other. No doubt some of them have never heard of Duke Ellington, and even more have never heard of Ralph Ellison. Nobody has ever taught them anything because they have no schools to speak of. All they have is the label 'underclass', which means 'garbage'. Naturally they are angry.

NWA's Easy-E sings:

> Do I look like a motherfucking role model?
> To a kid looking up to me
> Life ain't nothing but bitches and money.

The rest of us may appear to behave ourselves, but there is little evidence that we care about anything more than Easy-E does. All the rapper knows is what he sees, and he does not see a society which is interested in any kind of justice, to say nothing of the quality of its music. He may appear to be a creep, an idiot, a moron, but he is more honest than we are: he knows that he has no control over his life, while we pretend that we have control over ours. His anger is what we have paid for, or the result of what we have not paid for; and his warning has been wasted, for rap has been processed by the music industry.

There is already, of course, white rap. Every black genre has been imitated so far, and not even rap could escape. The Beastie Boys were among the first off the mark, three middle-class boys whose parents are music business veterans; four million copies of their first album were sold. Their second received rave reviews in 'quality' newspapers: the one by David Sinclair in *The Times* was headed 'Rude, lewd and shamelessly funny': '*Paul's Boutique* is strewn with foul language and lewd innuendo; it shamelessly glorifies all manner of deviant, violent and criminal behaviour and it unequivocally condones recreational drug-dabbling. It is also very funny . . . Brooklyn's Beastie Boys have recaptured the essence of rock as the perfect adolescent vehicle for the flaunting of outrage.' If some of our children are murdering each other, they are just reviving the whiskered old essence of rock'n'roll, invented by the media in the first place. This is so funny I am holding my sides.

There must also be rap that is completely innocuous, which happens as soon as a genre starts making money. Some thought that Run DMC were funny in the beginning, but, having been knocked from the commercial top of the genre by newer acts, they were unintentionally amusing when they appeared on a British music magazine programme in early 1991, obviously puzzled and uncertain, these big black kids from one of the toughest neighbourhoods on earth. So what were they doing about competition from the likes of Vanilla Ice? They were in England to 'sample' Manchester bands for sounds to use in their act. (That is one way to get out of Queens; the last I heard the police in Manchester still did not carry guns.) Vanilla Ice is, inevitably, white, and has impressive cheekbones; he was described by one critic as 'all mouth and trousers', but his backing tracks are very slick. M. C. Hammer is black; his 'We've Got the Power' was used in 1991 in Britain as psych-up music for people selling time-share schemes.

A few of these youngsters who grew up in the street are making money from hit records, but there are many more still in the street, still angry and still shedding each other's blood. And as rap is legitimized and joins the mainstream, it is clear that it now bears the burden of being a phoney sign of hope. As fast as its obscene cry was mistaken for mere outrageousness, it has become one of the commodities which substitute for social and economic stability, no more useful than any other and less useful than most, because if it is not angry, it has no substance. Lloyd Bradley in *Q* got it right, reviewing

Public Enemy's *Fear of a Black Planet*: 'the music is only a background for the most singleminded attack on the state of modern urban America heard on record'. Evidently that group had not been bought off yet.

Of course, some older musicians must try to make sense of rap. A year or so after his remarks on the state of the music education in America, Max Roach told Chris Parker in England that he was working with the Fab Five, and quoted them:

'The political system in the inner cities has taken out all the cultural enrichment courses, no music, no rhetoric, visuals, dance – so we created something . . . no one gave us anything, it's pure.' So they came up with a way of dealing with this world of sound and rhetoric, which is rhyme and visual, graffiti and dance . . . total theatre. So I became interested from that aspect, but I have to have it explained by them.

Conventional methods of making music have 'just about been used up. So if you don't want to repeat, you have to deal with this world out there that's blessed us with electronics,' says Mr Roach. Thanks, but when all the drummers have been replaced by computers, I will stay indoors and listen to my Max Roach records.

In late 1990 a piece called *Long Tongues: A Saxophone Opera*, by composer and saxophonist Julius Hemphill, was seen at the Apollo Theatre. The interlocutor was once master of ceremonies at a Washington club, and is now a street sweeper. He shows a rap duo through black history since the 1940s: the end of the Swing Era, the beginning of rhythm and blues and bop, later modern jazz and several styles of dancing. In the end the rappers trade licks with a saxophonist. I would rather see Julius Hemphill's opera than watch Michael Jackson's movie again. *Moonwalker* had no story to speak of, but lots of high-tech sci-fi fireworks, to make the children happy, and good dancing. There was a wonderfully designed scene that looked like a black club of the 1940s, and in the background a suggestion of a piano and a saxophonist. Was there a piano in the soundtrack? Any reeds at all? No: just the usual pop-rock, all at the same volume and tempo. Jackson appears to be a sort of superhero in the film; he could have made himself a real hero, by exposing all our children to his rich cultural heritage, but he threw away that opportunity and opted for flash. I wonder how much his multi-talented producer Quincy Jones had to do with it, but I am reminded of James Blood Ulmer, on his album *America – Do You Remember the Love?* 'I belong to the USA / I don't know if I want to stay.'

Having raped black music, today we have world music, in which there are many lovely things. The Cajun music of French-speaking white swamp dwellers in Louisiana, and zydeco, the black variant, are happy and unpretentious folk-dance musics, which may properly belong to folk roots rather than to world music. Klezmer is being rediscovered, a sort of Yiddish dance music that has things in common with jazz, from the Odessa of eighty years ago. The multi-part harmony of a Bulgarian women's choir is already familiar to anyone who has heard Janáček's *Glagolitic Mass*. Africans play music resembling the blues on folk instruments, their time as subtle and beautiful as that of Robert Johnson or Charley Patton. Forty years ago the janitor at my primary school played Japanese 78s for us which he had brought back from there after the war; they sounded infinitely strange and interesting. I do not know whether they represented traditional music or the Japanese pop of the period, but I do know that today the Japanese play the most banal pop-rock in the world, adopting our poverty-stricken values with perfect unselfconsciousness.

The performers of the music of the so-called Third World know that they will not be allowed into our marketplace until they have already been influenced by western pop-rock, and in any case their own pop music has already been so influenced. The songs of Thomas Mapfumo, in modern Zimbabwe, for example, although they still sound like they ought to be played on the thumb piano, are played on the electric guitar, and all at the same tempo. White and black South Africans formed Juluka (which means 'sweat' or 'work') which performed beautiful folkish songs full of poetry and African harmony, but that era is over; and Johnny Clegg has since formed Savuka ('we have awakened'), which is 'dance music', still African-flavoured, but electric and with the usual thumping beat. Raï is the music of the north African Muslim working class; it is already electric, and tacky nightclubs are similar the world over. We have not heard much lately about fado, a sort of Portuguese blues; perhaps the artists refused to be plugged in. Jamaican reggae has already had its superhero, Bob Marley, who was admitted to the pantheon by the sentimentality of the counterculture; but the biggest Jamaican influence is the dub aspect of rap.

We can hope for a liberating influence on our pop music from the Third World, but we will force our trendy values on music from anywhere. Novelist Sousa Jamba, writing for the *Spectator*, hoped 'that the "world music" frenzy will not be ephemeral, like most things in Western culture'. He walked into a London record shop to hear his mother tongue booming at him.

The Kafala Brothers, two Angolan singers . . . made me proud to be an Angolan: the lullabies were the best I ever heard; and the words to the songs were first-class poetry . . . But I fumed when I read the English translation of the songs that came with the cassette. It read like the work of a semi-literate party hack with an edict that he should give a political twist to every line. One song, for instance, concerns a man returning to his village and finding his relatives maimed. No reason for their injuries is given. The song's translation says that the injured are 'victims of the traitors to the nation and the lackeys of apartheid'.

A girl called Yarima from a Stone Age tribe in the Amazon rainforest married an American, and went with him to live in televisionland. 'I did not know what music was. My people have no musical instruments. All is chanting. When I first heard your music I hated it. Then I started snapping my fingers and tapping my toes. Madonna has a good voice and I like the way Michael Jackson moves.' Never mind that the word 'chant' means 'song'; so much for music. We cultists who have money in our pockets can celebrate six centuries of music on records, but our own best musicians and composers live on hand-outs. Our republic has failed; our Caesars have feet of clay; the barbarians are inside the gates. We have seen the enemy; he is in the mirror.

Afterword

What can be done about what most people think of as popular music?

Britain still has better record shops than American towns. Norwich, in the English county of Norfolk, has three or four record shops that are better than any between Chicago and Milwaukee, a distance of around 100 miles; the Norwich City Council area has a population of about 124,000. The tiniest village shop may not have much stock, but the salesperson there will know how to order any record you want (from a middleman, at full price).

The number of recordings available commercially in Britain is much smaller than in the USA, yet the shops have better selections: this is partly because Britain has better broadcasting, by a wide margin, than the USA. Britain's first national commercial radio station is a classical one, because the government awarded the franchise with some care; launched while this book was being written, it is already commercially successful. Margaret Thatcher, however, arranged for commercial television to be sold to the highest bidder before she left office, and was then astonished at the unfair results of the auction: there are signs that Britain is only a decade or two behind the USA in trashing itself.

The real problem began in the USA, and it is not too late for the Federal Communications Commission to wake up. The experience of the last twenty years shows that the USA needs regulation. The deregulation of the Savings and Loans led to the biggest financial disaster in American history; long after the deregulation of the airlines it still cost $700 to fly from Milwaukee to New York and back in December 1990, while some of the oldest airlines in the world have gone bust. Similarly, the playing of non-stop pop videos is nothing but free advertising for the record companies; if the government is going to regulate anything at all, America's MTV channel ought to be seen as violating existing law. If Americans can chop up the world's best telephone service into fifty small bits and require car manufacturers to obtain an overall mileage from their products, they can do anything.

Radio stations relying on recorded music should be required to do their own programming, rather than subscribing to a factory-compiled tape which is identical in every urban area. Mass-produced pap is bad enough in a supermarket; and, for that matter, it is not too late to ban wired music in public places, if music is thought to be of any value: it is an irony typical of our times that although the stuff must make a profit, *nobody would miss it*. A law prohibiting any radio station from playing any track more than once a day (or even better, once a *week*) would still allow any station to play all the hits, but would require somebody somewhere to think about which records to play for the rest of the time. Such rules might result in jobs in radio for people who actually like music.

Needle time could be made more expensive by raising the royalty on the records played after a certain number of hours a day, forcing stations to think about what kind of music they want to pay for; or the additional expense could be avoided by allowing a balance with live music: the practical difficulties broadcasters will foresee would quickly be overcome with the pressure of necessity, putting today's technology to some good use for a change. The need for live entertainment would soon result in a wider variety of it; broadcasters would learn to choose a good polka band over a mediocre teen-pop outfit, and, for that matter, a great many university music departments have excellent ensembles of various kinds. Why should there be relatively more live music in British broadcasting, with fewer stations and a fraction of the population, than there is in America? The performers would have to learn how to play for a live audience, and as listeners discover what live music sounds like, they might demand records that sound like music.

Small specialist and local stations could be exempt from some of this, and if Congress or the FCC will not act, state legislatures could do something. None of these measures would amount to discrimination against any musical genre, but another result would be the redundance of pro-censorship groups, such as the American Parents Music Resource Center, who will accomplish nothing anyway because they attack symptoms instead of problems. Successful pressure on behalf of a wider range of musics would swamp much of the childish dirtiness to which the censors object.

But the Davises and the Yetnikoffs are in charge of American business, and legislatures are full of lawyers who make too many laws and too few examples. Our only hope is that the pop-rock business goes smash, so that we can start all over again. Maybe it is only a matter of time; Michael Jackson's latest album has sold fifteen million copies at the time of writing, and apparently has not made enough money for Sony. Any industry that does business that way will go to the wall sooner or later.

Bibliography

Here is a listing by author or editor of many of the best books I have been using. I have not named editions, since they vary from one country to another, many of my copies are old and some of the books are out of print. There are also entries under the headings Biography, Discography and Reference.

ALLEN, Walter C.
Hendersonia (1973; self-published)
Allen, who died in 1974, was a doyen of the small army of researchers into early jazz. His book about Fletcher Henderson is a history of the band, almost day by day, and includes a complete discography. Hard going for the uninitiated but indispensable for the dedicated fan, it is the fruit of the sort of meticulous scholarship that only a fan could produce.

BALLIET, Whitney
American Musicians: 56 Portraits in Jazz (1986)
American Singers: 27 Portraits in Song (1988)
Barney, Bradley and Max: 16 Portraits in Jazz (1989)
Balliet is jazz correspondent of the *New Yorker*, and these are the latest collections of his journalism. Barney, Bradley and Max ran the most famous clubs in New York.

BIOGRAPHY
Biographies of individual musicians and pop stars are uncountable, but here are some of my favourites. (*See also* ALLEN, CHILTON, LEES, MURRAY, SHAW and WRIGHT.)

Bix: Man and Legend, by Richard M. Sudhalter and Philip R. Evans (1974), was the first great jazz biography, and new ones can still be measured against it: Hoagy Carmichael, Paul Whiteman, Bill Challis and the whole cast are discussed in great detail. Also recommendable are *Mingus* by Brian Priestley (1982), *Miles Davis* by Ian Carr (1982), *Forces in Motion* by Graham Lock (1988; interviews and notes on Anthony Braxton's 1985 tour of England), *Swing, Swing, Swing: The Life and Times of Benny Goodman* by Ross Firestone (1993) and *Wishing on the Moon: The Life and Times of Billie Holiday* by Donald Clarke (1994). There is no definitive book on Duke Ellington, and perhaps cannot be, but a recent one that bodes well for the future is *Ellington: The Early Years* by Mark Tucker; Tucker's *Duke Ellington Reader* and *A Lester Young Reader*, edited by Lewis Porter (1991), are excellent compilations.

Autobiographies are usually 'as told to' books. Some of the best of these are mentioned in the text.

Biographies of pop people tend to be disappointing, such as the several fat books about Bob Dylan, perhaps because the whole point of his work is that we are supposed to be living our own lives, not reading about him. (*See* MURRAY for Jimi Hendrix.) The best books about pop and rock tell us as much about the times as the lives, for example, Jon Savage's *England's Dreaming: Sex Pistols and Punk Rock* and Chris Heath's *Pet Shop Boys, Literally*. Significantly, both these are too long, telling us more than we need to know.

In country music, Nolan Porterfield's *Jimmie Rodgers* (1979) and Charles R. Townsend's *San Antonio Rose: The Life and Music of Bob Wills* (1976) are excellent, and Roger M. Williams's *Sing a Sad Song: The Life of Hank Williams* (1970) is also good; all have discographies.

BORDMAN, Gerald
American Musical Theatre: A Chronicle (1978; rev. 1986)
This describes year by year all the musical shows that opened on the New York stage from 1866 (*The Black Crook*) to 1984–5, with enough style to make the book a time-eater: once you open it, a couple of hours will go by.

Bordman's other books include a biography of Kern (1980); in this connection Andrew Lamb's *Jerome Kern in Edwardian London* also must be mentioned (ISAM monograph no. 22). The Institute for Study in American Music, Conservatory of Music, Brooklyn College of the City University of New York, has published about thirty monographs, all worthwhile (*see* SANJEK), and needs support.

BROVEN, John
Rhythm and Blues in New Orleans (1977)
South to Louisiana: The Music of the Cajun Bayous (1987)
The first of these was originally called *Walking to New Orleans*. The books combine passionate advocacy with good writing and an almost off-hand ability to set everything in its time and place.

CHAPPLE, Steve, and Reebee GAROFALO
Rock'n'roll is Here to Pay (1977)
A useful book about the development of the modern music business, though the last chapter predicts some sort of flower-power utopia.

CHILTON, John
Who's Who of Jazz (1985)
Sidney Bechet: The Wizard of Jazz (1987)
The Song of the Hawk: Life and Recordings of Coleman Hawkins (1990)
English trumpeter and bandleader Chilton is a very good researcher. *Who's Who of Jazz*, first published in 1972, is subtitled 'Storyville to Swing Street'. An A–Z of jazz people born before 1920 who did most of their work in the USA, it is a specialists' lodestar of accuracy.

Biographies of Louis Armstrong (1971, with Max Jones) and Billie Holiday (*Billie's Blues*, 1975, surveying only her musical career from 1933) were trail-blazers; monographs on McKinney's Cotton Pickers (1978) and the Jenkins' Orphanage (*A Jazz Nursery*, 1980) are each one of a kind; *Stomp Off, Let's Go* (1983), about the Bob Crosby band, is fun (though it apparently had no editor and looks like an explosion in a print shop). With his biographies of Bechet, Hawkins and recently Louis Jordan, Chilton reached a new height: the combination of the cantankerous and the lyrical that was Bechet and the very private Hawkins will probably never be better captured, and all the recordings are expertly dealt with.

COOK, Richard, and Brian MORTON
The Penguin Guide to Jazz (1992)
The first print-run of this book was too short, because bookshops refused to order enough copies; sales are brisk, and no wonder. Virtually every jazz artist is found here in A–Z format and nearly all their currently available releases are intelligently commented upon, so that if you are interested in an artist, you can decide which records to take a chance on. The coverage is international, and sensibly ignores the fact that many discs nowadays are imports in various countries. There are almost 1,200 pages and an index for finding side men and women. This book is indispensable.

DANCE, Stanley
The World of Duke Ellington (1970)
The World of Swing (1974)
The World of Earl Hines (1977)
The World of Count Basie (1980)
'As told to . . .'
Night People by Dicky Wells (1971)
Duke Ellington in Person by Mercer Ellington (1978)
Those Swinging Years by Charlie Barnet (1984)
The British-born Stanley Dance, long resident in California, once had a letter printed in a British jazz journal in which he angrily refused to understand why so many jazz records have been bootlegged over the years, despite the way the owners of the masters sat on them, or occasionally issued a few tracks as though they were a dog's dinner. He is an opinionated man and no doubt a 'mouldy fig', but a valuable journalist. Most of the books are oral histories, revealed by Dance's power of observation and editorial skill to be perhaps the most important genre of all. *The World of Swing*, for example, covers over forty musicians and singers, mostly interviewed, from the world-famous to the more obscure but still influential. It is a myth that jazz musicians are inarticulate. Dance lets the feeling of what the music is all about come through the personalities.

DANNEN, Frederick
Hit Men (1990)
The damning book we were all recommending to each other, and well written too. The subtitle, 'Power Brokers and Fast Money inside the Music Business', says it all. The paperback edition is updated.

DEFAA, Chip
Voices of the Jazz Age (1990)
Swing Legacy (1991)
Eight vintage profiles and twenty somewhat later ones. The first contains a good article about Bix, and the interview with Sam Wooding not long before he died is good stuff taken down in the nick of time.

DISCOGRAPHY
A thriving industry. (*See also* ALLEN, COOK and MORTON, HARRISON, KINKLE and WHITBURN.)
RUST, Brian. *Jazz Records 1897–1942* (n.d.). Now published by Storyville Publications (*see* WRIGHT), these two fat volumes are the basis of jazz discography, and have been used for many years by fans, collectors, researchers and authors of sleeve-notes, who sometimes even acknowledge it. Rust's *The Victor Master Book*, vol. 2 (self-published) was a fascinating one-off, listing Victor records made from 1925 to 1936 by master number (with indexes for artists and song titles). There never was a volume 1. A new edition of Rust's two volumes on American dance bands is being prepared.
DIXON, Robert M. W., and John GODRICH. *Blues and Gospel Records 1902–1943* (1982). Another classic from Storyville.
LEADBITTER, Mike, and Neil SLAVEN. *Blues Records 1943 to 1970*, vol. 1. An update of an earlier classic including R&B, published by Paul Pelletier's Record Information Services in 1987. It is touch and go as to whether volume 2 will ever appear; Leadbitter died in 1974 and Pelletier has done his best, but some of the other people involved are evidently not reliable.
BRUYNINCKX, W. A complete jazz discography printed in Belgium, divided into categories of traditional, swing, modern,

progressive, modern big band and vocalists. It comprises a total of thirty-five paperback volumes.

HOUNSOME, Terry. *Rock Record* (1991). Began as the limited edition *Rockmaster* in 1978. This edition (which could be the sixth, depending on how you count them) lists all the albums by 10,000 rock bands and artists, with personnel, labels and numbers of editions in various countries. A new edition has just come out in 1994. His Record Researcher Publications also issues *Single File*, which lists over 100,000 British singles.

FLANAGAN, Bill
Written in my Soul (1987)
Interviews with 'rock' songwriters (including Carl Perkins and Willie Dixon). Elvis Costello: 'I can't actually play any musical instrument properly. I can't read music. And here's the *New York Times* calling me the new George Gershwin ... It was embarrassing to watch these people fall into the trap of their own critical conceits.'

FOX, Ted
Showtime at the Apollo (1985)
In the Groove (1986)
The first covers fifty years of the great Harlem venue, while the second contains interviews with a dozen record producers, from John Hammond and Milt Gabler to Nile Rodgers.

GARFIELD, Simon
Expensive Habits (1986)
Subtitled 'The Dark Side of the Music Business', stories from the British pop industry about how easy it is to get cheated. Of Gilbert O'Sullivan's hit albums in the early 1970s, *Back to Front* was number one and grossed £1,700,000, of which he received only £60,000. He had to go to court to get more royalties and control of his own copyrights.

GELATT, Roland
The Fabulous Phonograph 1877–1977 (rev. 1977)
Still a good survey, updated from the 1955 edition.

GEORGE, Nelson
Where Did Our Love Go? (1985)
The Death of Rhythm and Blues (1988)
The first tells the history of the Motown label. The second study asks how black music can retain its identity in a white-dominated music industry, inevitably touching on the perilous position of black culture in a society whose engine is white-bread economics.

GILBERT, Douglas
Lost Chords (1942; repr. 1970)
'The Diverting Story of American Popular Music', a period survey of songs and business up to the 1930s. The last chapter is titled 'Juke Box, Jazz, Swing, and Boogie-woogie' to make the book look up to date, but says little about any of these, sticking to Tin Pan Alley.

GILLETT, Charlie
The Sound of the City (1970; rev. 1983)
Somewhat breathless 'Rise of Rock and Roll' story by a British DJ and label boss who knows his stuff, written around the records themselves and not neglecting byways such as swamp rock.

GITLER, Ira
Jazz Masters of the '40s (1966)
Swing to Bop (1985)
The first is one of a series, of which the others (*Jazz Masters of the '20s* by Richard Hadlock, *'30s* by Rex Stewart, etc.) are also worthwhile. The more recent book is 'an oral history of the transition in jazz in the 1940s' in the musicians' own words, and priceless.

GOLDBERG, Isaac
Tin Pan Alley (1930)
A period piece on the heyday, with an introduction by Gershwin.

GORDON, Robert
Jazz West Coast: The Los Angeles Jazz Scene of the 1950s (1986)
The largely white cool jazz scene was commercially successful (as post-war jazz went), but suffered from critical snobbery in a sort of

reverse racism. This survey is full of good sense and especially useful now that many of the records are being reissued on CD. *West Coast Jazz* by Ted Gioia (1992) looks pretty good too.

GURALNICK, Peter
Feel Like Going Home: Portraits in Blues and Rock'n'roll (1971)
Lost Highway: Journeys and Arrivals of American Musicians (1979)
Sweet Soul Music: Rhythm and Blues and the Southern Dream of Freedom (1986)
Two volumes of affectionate, well-written portraits, and a definitive history of soul music. His latest book is about Robert Johnson, but will be superseded when controversial research may be published.

HAASE, John Edward (ed.)
Ragtime (1985)
A marvellous survey of every aspect – waltzes, the banjo, women in ragtime, everything you can think of – in nineteen chapters. Contributors include Max Morath and Edward A. Berlin (whose own 1980 book is very good), and there are interviews with Gunther Schuller and Rudi Blesh.

HAMM, Charles
Yesterdays: Popular Song in America (1979)
The best survey I know, it begins in England and sticks to songs, and is well illustrated. Weakest in the last couple of chapters, because the rock era's songs lend themselves less well to serious treatment.

HANNUSCH, Jeff
I Hear You Knockin' (1985)
'The Sound of New Orleans Rhythm and Blues', in the form of profiles of over thirty musicians and producers. The best sort of fan's book, to put alongside Broven.

HARRISON, Max
A Jazz Retrospect (1976; new edn 1991)
A collection of first-class jazz journalism, the kind that never goes out of date. Harrison was one of the first to describe Ellington

accurately as a miniaturist. He also wrote the jazz entry in *The New Grove Dictionary of Music and Musicians*, and he writes about classical music too; a collection of that would also be worth having.

HARRISON, Max with Charles Fox and Eric Thacker
The Essential Jazz Records, vol. 1: *Ragtime to Swing* (1984)
Thematically arranged by decades and styles, it provides commentary on a great many of the most valuable recordings. LP issues are listed, but that does not matter; original recording dates and complete personnel are given, so you can know what you are getting in today's CD editions. The point is that the commentary is illuminating, and so stylish that it can be enjoyed for its own sake; it is even fun to read about music you have already been listening to for years. A neat hardback published by Mansell in Britain, this is the sort of book that will become a legend without selling many copies.

HIRSHEY, Gerry
Nowhere to Run: The Story of Soul Music (1984)
Well written, full of interviews and love of the subject, to go on the shelf next to Guralnick.

HOSKYNS, Barney
Say It One Time for the Brokenhearted (1987)
Subtitled 'The Country Side of Southern Soul', this is an eye-opener of a book, about the influence of country and soul on each other. His list of forty masterpieces of country soul ought to be bootlegged if necessary on CD.

JONES, Max
Talking Jazz (1987)
A valuable collection by one of the best British music journalists, introduced by Jones and intelligently edited, often from interviews over a period of years. His piece on Billie Holiday alone is worth the price.

KINKLE, Roger D.
The Complete Encyclopedia of Popular Music and Jazz 1900–1950 (1974)
Compiled by a dealer and auctioneer in old records, these four fat
hardback volumes have now been out of print for a while. Two
volumes are an A–Z of recording artists (many mainstream people
with no entries in other books) and two are lists and indexes: one
lists musical shows and films, representative hit songs and records
year by year; also listed (by catalogue number, which sounds boring
until you learn how to wallow in it) are all releases on several
important labels from the mid-1920s to the early 1940s. Incredibly
accurate, Kinkle's work was computer typeset in the USA twenty
years ago, and after many years of using it I finally found one
mistake: he got Judy Garland's death date wrong by six months.

LAX, Roger, and Frederick SMITH
The Great Song Thesaurus (1984)
Lists songs with dates and information about each, and is divided
into several sections (British, American, Indexes, etc.). Goes back
much further than Shapiro, but accepts stories as fact, such as that
Mother Goose was an American.

LEES, Gene
Singers and the Song (1987)
Meet Me at Jim and Andy's: Jazz Musicians and Their World (1988)
Oscar Peterson: The Will to Swing (1988)
Inventing Champagne: The Worlds of Lerner and Loewe (1990)
Journalist, editor, lyricist and sometime vocalist, Gene Lees always
writes well, but when he writes about something he loves, magic
happens. The first two of these books collect pieces from his unique
monthly *Jazzletter*, launched ten years ago. His biographies of Peter-
son and Lerner and Loewe are useful, but an 'as told to' book, Henry
Mancini's *Did They Mention the Music?* (1989), is less good; apparently
Mancini is too private a man for an autobiography.

LITWEILER, John
The Freedom Principle: Jazz after 1958 (1985)
A first-class book on the subject by an important Chicago journal-

ist. You know it is good because it sends you straight to the record shelf for a listen. His new book about Ornette Coleman will be worth a look.

LYTTELTON, Humphrey
Best of Jazz: Basin Street to Harlem (1978)
Enter the Giants (1981)
Trumpeter, bandleader and a famous voice on British radio through his jazz record programme, Lyttelton is also a good writer. His article on Basie trombonist Dicky Wells, for example, should send you to the records to hear what he is talking about.

MALONE, Bill C.
Country Music USA (1968; rev. 1985)
Impossible to imagine a better survey of the subject: fat, authoritative, a good read, a good index.

MARSH, Dave
The Heart of Rock and Soul: The 1,001 Greatest Singles Ever Made (1989)
You can argue with Marsh, founder of Detroit's *Creem* magazine in 1969, about his choices, but not about his love of the music. Relive the days when it was fun to buy singles, and be reminded why.

MATTFELD, Julius
Variety Music Cavalcade (1959; rev. 1962)
Subtitled 'Musical-historical Review 1620–1961', this was a terrific idea spoiled by its lack of proper indexes. A list of hit songs for each year is accompanied by contemporary news: with 'Shake, Rattle and Roll' in 1954 came the US Senate's censure of Joe McCarthy, the first news of a link between cigarettes and lung cancer and the coining by *McCall's*, a women's magazine, of the word 'togetherness'; the fiction best-seller, Lloyd Douglas's *The Robe*, was held over from the year before. But the index lists only the songs.

MURRAY, Charles Shaar
Crosstown Traffic: Jimi Hendrix and Post-war Pop (1989)
Shots from the Hip (1991)

Murray is the brightest and most amusing of rock critics. The American Lester Bangs had an enchantingly surreal style, but was a believer in rock myths and did not convince me. You have to love the music to be a critic, and I know some who have gone off it, but Murray (who is British) will never have to give up on it, because he has no illusions about it, or about anything else: he seems to have the sense to find most things funny. His biography of Hendrix is a model of its kind, ranging more widely and intelligently than most rock biographies; his collection of journalism from 1972 to the present will remain valuable. You can *trust* this man (even if he does like rap).

RAMSEY, Frederick, Jr, and Charles Edward SMITH (eds)
Jazzmen (1939; repr. 1985 with introduction by Nat Hentoff)
A collection of fifteen pieces by such authors as Wilder Hobson and Otis Ferguson, two of the earliest American jazz journalists. Hentoff's generation was inspired by it, and it is still recommendable.

READ, Oliver, and Walter L. WELCH
From Tinfoil to Stereo (1959; rev. 1976)
Written by enthusiasts, wordy and even repetitious but 'unput-downable', this classic came from an obscure publisher in Indianapolis. Still the best account of the evolution of sound recording, by the time it was updated and republished copies of the original edition were changing hands for up to $200. Interesting illustrations too, as well as several indexes.

REFERENCE
A–Z books of rock, pop, country music and so on have too many words and not enough entries, rarely an index and usually an unacceptable number of factual errors. *The Penguin Encyclopedia of Popular Music*, edited by Donald Clarke (1989), was the first single-volume reference book to cover all the genres; I name my own work because it is still the best value, with more than three thousand entries (including entries for genres, and listing albums for most artists) and a very good index. Its nearest competition was compiled by rockers who have Buck Clayton playing saxophone instead of trumpet, and have no index at all.

In jazz, however, there are irreplaceable books for specialists. John Chilton's *Who's Who of Jazz* is mentioned above, Leonard Feather's venerable three volumes of *The Encyclopedia of Jazz* (1960, 1966 and 1976) are valuable for the large number of more obscure entries, and a new project is on the way. *Jazz: The Essential Companion*, by Ian Carr, Digby Fairweather and Brian Priestley, is a well-written and useful A–Z. *Blues Who's Who* by Sheldon Harris (1979) is also indispensable. (*See also* KINKLE; for A–Z books of songs, *see* LAX and SMITH, and SHAPIRO.)

REID, Jan
The Improbable Rise of Redneck Rock (1974)
The story of how country music was reborn in Texas when Nashville got too slick while remaining intolerant. Incredible that this book does not have an index.

RUSSELL, Ross
Jazz Style in Kansas City and the Southwest (1971)
A good survey. Russell was the founder of Dial Records, recorded Charlie Parker and was Parker's manager for two years; he also wrote *Bird Lives!* (1973), the first and still the fullest Parker biography, but all the books about him seem to be flawed by bad memories and wishful thinking on the part of the witnesses, as though Parker were a mirror in which people saw what they wanted to see.

SANJEK, Russell
American Popular Music and Its Business (1988)
Sanjek was a BMI executive who spent his retirement completing this massive three-volume work, which began as an ISAM monograph. The volumes are titled 'The Beginning to 1790', '1790 to 1909' and '1900 to 1984', and have nearly 1,500 pages as well as indexes and bibliographies. When I obtained my copies, I stopped everything and wallowed in them for weeks, and still consult them as often as any books on my shelves. Statistics, squabbles, technology and takeovers are all here; since Sanjek's death his son has done an abridged single-volume edition.

SCHULLER, Gunther
Early Jazz: Its Roots and Musical Development (1968)
The Swing Era (1989)
There is not really a recommendable single-volume history of jazz; you need to read several books, of which these should be the first. Recognized as a gem of good sense and scholarship on publication, *Early Jazz* is also immensely readable, and the recent volume is just as good.

SHAPIRO, Harry
Waiting for the Man (1988)
'The Story of Drugs and Popular Music' is more than that, going back to the medicine shows seen in so many old Westerns, which were peddling nothing but dope; it comes up through the Harrison Narcotics Act of 1914 and the problems of Keith Richards and the Allman Brothers Band to the substitute addiction to scientology, giving a list of victims.

SHAPIRO, Nat, and Nat HENTOFF
Hear Me Talkin' to Ya (1955)
One of the first oral histories of jazz, compiled from interviews, letters, magazine articles and so on. A classic and still fascinating.

SHAW, Arnold
52nd St: The Street of Jazz (1971)
Honkers and Shouters: The Golden Years of Rhythm and Blues (*c.* 1974)
The Rockin' 50s (*c.* 1974)
Black Popular Music in America (1986)
The Jazz Age: Popular Music in the 1920s (1987)
Shaw joined Leeds Music (which later became MCA) in 1945; a songwriter, publicist, record producer and college professor, he won ASCAP's Deems Taylor Award a couple of times. He also wrote biographies of Frank Sinatra (1968) and Harry Belafonte, among other things. The first three listed here are the best. *52nd St* was originally called *The Street That Never Slept*, and is good on the clubs and their influence on music. The next two are insider's books, full of vitality, detail (for example, on the origins of the classic R & B

labels) and, especially *Honkers*, valuable interviews with such people as Ralph Bass and Art Rupe. Shaw's later books are surveys and appear hurried; they are cramped and hard to read and have the occasional minor error.

SMITH, Joe
Off the Record (1988)
In this book, record-company executive Joe Smith combines arrogance and ignorance. His book is a disgrace (and from a Warner Communications Company). Not only is there no index, you have to make your own table of contents: over two hundred short interviews are put together in no particular order. The interviews themselves do not look like interviews at all, and many of them are worthless. There are so many that there are nuggets to be found, however, and the book goes on the shelf next to Fox and Flanagan. Smith is like a cook in a bad restaurant, not knowing that the job could just as well be done properly.

SOUTHERN, Eileen
The Music of Black Americans (1971; rev. 1983)
A masterpiece of scholarship by a Harvard professor of music and Afro-American studies, it covers every aspect of black musical achievement in the USA beginning in the early seventeenth century, and provides plenty of social context as well. Indispensable.

SPELLMAN, A. B.
Black Music: Four Lives (1966)
Originally called *Four Lives in the Bebop Business*, a classic on the music of its period in the form of profiles of Cecil Taylor, Ornette Coleman, Herbie Nichols and Jackie McLean. It also paints a depressing picture of what it is like to be a black artist trying to make a living as an original, competing with your own dead predecessors, who themselves struggled all their lives.

TOSCHES, Nick
Country: Living Legends and Dying Metaphors in America's Biggest Music (1977)
Unsung Heroes of Rock'n'roll (1984)

Country gives the lie to the Nashville image of country music as upright and puritanical: not just gossip, but songs, personalities, forgotten roots and the darker side of the history. The second book is useful fun on the most influential popular music of the late 1940s and early 1950s; not all the heroes are entirely unsung, but most people have never heard of Hardrock Gunter or Jesse Stone. His book on Jerry Lee Lewis, *Hellfire*, is useful. His recent book on Dean Martin had bad reviews because, although unauthorized, it apparently puts words into Martin's mouth.

TRAVIS, Dempsey J.
An Autobiography of Black Jazz (1983)
An affectionate memoir of Chicago's musical history, using a great many interviews and illustrations. Travis became a pianist like his father, and at the age of sixteen in the mid-1930s was the youngest bandleader registered with the musicians' union. A good read.

VAN DER MERWE, Peter
Origins of the Popular Style: The Antecedents of Twentieth-century Popular Music (1989)
A scholarly book and a delight, tracing influences around the world and down through a thousand years. European folk music, for example – hence much American country music – probably comes originally from the Middle East, not medieval or Renaissance Europe.

WARD, Ed, Geoffrey STOKES and Ken TUCKER
Rock of Ages: The Rolling Stone History of Rock and Roll (1986)
A readable history by three journalists, one each for the 1950s, 1960s and 1970s. Like most rock books, it assumes that nothing much happened before 1956; it is not true, for instance, that Stephen Foster never received any royalties. But when it gets to the meat, there are insights, such as Stokes on why Bob Dylan did not sell records to blacks: 'Though Dick Gregory might joke about finally getting served at a Woolworth's lunch counter only to find out that the food was lousy, the subversive sentiment underlying the joke would remain buried.'

WHITBURN, Joel
Top Pop Singles 1955–1986
Top Pop Albums 1955–1985
Top R&B Singles 1942–1988
Top Country Singles 1944–1988
Pop Memories 1890–1954
Whitburn's Record Research, Inc., began reprinting the *Billboard* charts in the early 1970s, producing expensive books for DJs and cultists which turned out to have a wider appeal. The latest editions do much more than this, providing blurbs on the artists and much else; they are still expensive but unusually well made for a good deal of use. *Top Pop Singles* has recently been updated and a new edition of *Albums* is coming. There is an annual *Music and Video Yearbook* update; the spiral-bound *Daily No. 1 Hits* tells you what was number one in the USA each day from 1 January 1940.

The most remarkable is *Pop Memories*, which goes far beyond *Billboard*, researching hobbyist columns, sheet music sales, record company lists, radio plays and so on to create charts going right back to the beginning, the only source for the hits of the acoustic era (though I would like to know more about just how the calculations were made). The earliest *Billboard* charts had only fifteen or twenty places, but *Pop Memories* effectively creates a longer list, giving a better view of many artists. By including jukebox sales the book makes it clear that somebody made money from Billie Holiday's recordings of 1935 to 1942, for example, even if she did not.

WILDER, Alec
American Popular Song: The Great Innovators 1900–1950 (1972)
A gentle, loving, intelligent masterpiece: an appreciation of the best songs and composers of our century by a man who was one of them, but too modest to include any of his own. Of perhaps 300,000 songs, Wilder examined about 17,000 and mentions or quotes the music of around 800 of the best. More valuable for those who read music, but there are insights for everybody who loves songs.

WILMER, Val
As Serious as Your Life: The Story of the New Jazz (1977)
A detailed survey, full of interviews, about how hard it is to make
a living at it, it also affirms that the music is an important part of the
community; by a British woman who earned the trust of that
community.

WRIGHT, Laurie
Mr Jelly Lord (1980)
'King' Oliver (1987)
'Fats' in Fact (1992)
Like Walter Allen's *Hendersonia*, these are documentary histories of
the artists' activities with discographies and illustrations. *'King' Oliver*
is an update of an earlier book by Allen and Brian Rust. Wright is
publisher and editor of *Storyville* magazine, and also publishes Tom
Lord's *Clarence Williams* (which documents the activities of one of the
busiest people who ever worked in black music), Rust and Dixon and
Godrich (*see* DISCOGRAPHY).

Index